CMIS and Apache Chemistry in Action

CMIS and Apache Chemistry in Action

FLORIAN MÜLLER
JAY BROWN
JEFF POTTS

MANNING
SHELTER ISLAND

For online information and ordering of this and other Manning books, please visit www.manning.com. The publisher offers discounts on this book when ordered in quantity. For more information, please contact

Special Sales Department
Manning Publications Co.
20 Baldwin Road
PO Box 261
Shelter Island, NY 11964
Email: orders@manning.com

♾ Recognizing the importance of preserving what has been written, it is Manning's policy to have the books we publish printed on acid-free paper, and we exert our best efforts to that end. Recognizing also our responsibility to conserve the resources of our planet, Manning books are printed on paper that is at least 15 percent recycled and processed without the use of elemental chlorine.

Manning Publications Co.
20 Baldwin Road
PO Box 261
Shelter Island, NY 11964

Development editor: Karen G. Miller
Technical proofreader: David Caruana
Copyeditors: Benjamin Berg, Andy Carroll
Proofreader: Katie Tennant
Typesetter: Dottie Marsico
Cover designer: Marija Tudor

ISBN 9781617291159
Printed in the United States of America
1 2 3 4 5 6 7 8 9 10 – MAL – 18 17 16 15 14 13

brief contents

contents

PART 2 HANDS-ON CMIS CLIENT DEVELOPMENT 115

foreword

What would the IT industry be without standards? We wouldn't have compatible databases, communications protocols, print data streams, compression and encryption specifications, or the World Wide Web. It's hard to debate how standards have benefited the IT industry, enabling growth, collaboration in solving problems, interoperability across vendors (reducing vendor lock-in) and, most importantly, a much wider range of choices for companies. Unfortunately these benefits didn't apply to the ECM industry until recently.

I first realized the need for a content management standard in 1992. I was involved in developing an application for a large corporate client that needed to access content stored in a popular repository. We immediately hit a problem—the content repository didn't have public APIs. In order to get access to the APIs, we had to negotiate a long and complex contract with the repository vendor and agree that we wouldn't use those APIs to migrate content out of the repository. This made no sense to me because we were adding significant value to the vendor's software through this new application. Unfortunately, this type of thinking was typical of many content management vendors.

There have been several attempts at creating Enterprise Content Management standards over the last 15 years. The Open Document Management API (ODMA) in the mid-1990s defined an interface between desktop applications and content management systems. In 1996, work began on the Web Distributed Authoring and Versioning (WebDAV) extensions for HTTP. In the early 2000s, many of the key ECM vendors began work on a Java ECM standard called JSR 170. Although the technical contributions to all of these standards were excellent, none of them succeeded as a widely supported content management standard.

There were many reasons these standards didn't achieve widespread success. Lack of interoperability testing led to incompatible implementations, and the lack of commitment by some vendors resulted in limited implementations and few exploiting applications. One of the biggest challenges with JSR 170 was the difficulty in supporting it on top of existing repositories that didn't have a hierarchical data model.

In May 2005, AIIM started a standards group called Interoperable ECM (iECM). This group brought together many vendors and users to discuss the critical need to enable better interoperability across ECM vendors and applications. The iECM meetings were well attended, and it was clear there was still a strong need for a better ECM standard. In 2006, while attending an iECM meeting, I began talking with Cornelia Davis of EMC on jump-starting a new standard. We believed that coming up with an initial draft specification targeting key ECM use cases would reduce the amount of time it would take to produce a final standard. Ethan Gur-esh from Microsoft joined Cornelia and me, and we created the concept of Content Management Interoperability Services (CMIS). Additional people from our companies, including David Choy from EMC and Al Brown from IBM, became key participants. It was exciting to see how three major competitors could work together on solving an industry problem.

As we defined the initial CMIS specification, we knew we had to approach the problem differently than in the past. We had three key objectives in defining CMIS: (1) ensure the standard could easily be supported on a wide range of existing content repositories; (2) agree on the right level of function so the standard was usable for an initial set of key ECM use cases; and (3) define a process to ensure interoperability between vendors.

Once the initial CMIS draft was complete, we invited Alfresco, Oracle, SAP, and OpenText to participate. Momentum around CMIS built, and a lot of technical work was accomplished in a short period of time. We then moved the standard into OASIS, and twenty additional companies began actively participating in the CMIS work. In May 2010, CMIS 1.0 became an official OASIS standard.

I'm often asked if CMIS will become a widely used standard for Enterprise Content Management or if it will suffer the same fate as the previous attempts. There's no way to know for sure, but CMIS is seeing tremendous interest and support and has very powerful supporters, such as Apache Chemistry, that enable companies to get started quickly. We're seeing CMIS projects in large corporations and application vendors that are very promising.

There's little debate that CMIS has the potential to increase the usage of content management systems across all industries and applications, dramatically simplifying and standardizing access to unstructured content. IT projects such as a customer portal that requires access to multiple content sources can be implemented more quickly with fewer dependencies on proprietary client APIs. Small software vendors who want to build cross-vendor industry vertical solutions can now easily do so. As CMIS matures, there will be creative new uses that we haven't yet thought about. It's exciting to watch the growth and evolution of CMIS.

A lot of people were key to creating CMIS, and I want to personally thank Cornelia Davis, Ethan Gur-esh, John Newton, Al Brown, Betsy Fanning, and Paul Fontaine. Without these people, and many others, CMIS would never have become a successful industry standard.

I would also like to thank Jay Brown, Florian Müller, and Jeff Potts for writing this book. *CMIS and Apache Chemistry in Action* is the most complete, authoritative work on CMIS you will find. It contains a wealth of technical insights as well as practical hints and tips. If you want to learn about CMIS, or start building software using CMIS, you will want to read this book.

RICHARD J. HOWARTH
DIRECTOR, ECM SOFTWARE DEVELOPMENT
IBM SOFTWARE GROUP

foreword

Content has never been more important. Content drives transactions, websites, and engagement. Content is the container of information that makes data consumable, usable, and actionable and has become the lifeblood of many businesses and business processes. Financial service, media, government, and high-technology organizations wouldn't exist without electronic documents and other forms of content. Today the Enterprise Content Management industry is worth $5 billion in software alone, according to analyst group IDC. Businesses dealing with the overload of information and the need to keep that information timely and accurate are willing to pay a lot to get content under control.

However, in the three decades since the introduction of content management, the number of content systems has proliferated, with many similar systems sitting side by side. Internal IT organizations and system integrators are frequently reinventing the wheel as the CIO struggles to meet the information needs of the enterprise. Over the last two decades, this has led enterprises large and small to spend over $50 billion on software, hardware, and services to deliver content solutions to end users. Solutions such as invoice capture, contract management, regulatory submissions, and responsive websites, among many, many other solutions, can take months and even years to go into effective production.

If only we could reuse these solutions on our other content systems! If only we could develop solutions without worrying how and where they were going to be deployed. If only applications developers built these solutions as complete solutions that could deploy faster and cheaper. If only we could hire the developers trained to build these solutions.

It says a lot about the content management industry, populated by some of the most competitive firms in enterprise software, that those competitors recognized the customer need for these solutions and to make them affordable. The same competitors recognized that a content management industry built on standards and interoperability could be even bigger with higher value to the customer. That's why these software companies got together to form CMIS as an open and common way of accessing all their systems and to provide a consistent way of developing their applications.

This was no easy feat. Developing standards is a laborious process and takes a lot of persistence. The content management industry had tried several times before, in the previous decade, with little success. In 2008, competitors set their differences aside and decided that growing the market for content was more important than expanding their piece of the pie. Beginning with EMC, IBM, and Microsoft, then adding Alfresco, OpenText, Oracle, and SAP, and finally opening it to the whole world of content through OASIS, these competitors started the collaborative project known as CMIS. Reacting to customer requests to provide for interoperability between diverse systems and a desire to build a stronger ecosystem, these companies wanted to work together to make a bigger market. The pragmatic approach of the committee, led by Chair David Choy and editors Al Brown, Ethan Gur-esh, Ryan McVeigh, and Florian Müller, produced a specification that was implementable on a wide range of systems.

What was even more remarkable was the way that many of those same companies and individuals came together to jointly develop the Apache Chemistry project, an open and standards-based software platform to speed the development of the CMIS standard. Florian Müller, in particular, had the vision to have one common code base that would support multiple communication protocols and could be used either by the vendors providing a CMIS interface or applications using CMIS to access content repositories. Initially, the OpenCMIS group in Apache Chemistry, by sharing the load of developing common software, made sure that everyone won—vendors, developers, and users.

This book illustrates the breadth and possibilities of CMIS, because having open standards and common open source code has dramatically cut the time to implementation for both providers and users of CMIS. With the original vision of CMIS not being tied to any particular programming language or binding, this book develops example applications using many languages and development approaches. It's a testament not just to the ingenuity of the authors, but also to the dedication of the men and women who participated in CMIS and Apache Chemistry.

I've always been a keen optimist about what can be accomplished with CMIS. The timing of the arrival of CMIS and Apache Chemistry couldn't have been better to tackle new applications that are social, mobile, and in the cloud. By considering RESTful interfaces, developers can use modern tools to create these applications and have access to some of the most important information in an enterprise, whether serving an employee, a customer, or a consumer. CMIS also provides an important bridge of new, productive, mobile and social applications to legacy systems of production enterprise systems. Content will be delivered wherever it's needed, whether it's in a social media conversation, presented on a mobile device, captured in a high-throughput scanner, or annotated in a critical process application.

I hope this book not only educates you on how to develop portable content applications, but inspires you to put content to work in new and imaginative ways.

JOHN NEWTON
CHAIRMAN AND CTO, ALFRESCO
CHAIRMAN, AIIM

preface

It was early 2012 (Q1), long past the OASIS approval of CMIS 1.0 as a standard. Due to my work on the OASIS CMIS Technical Committee (TC) since 2008, I had become a sort of hub for CMIS support within IBM, but over the last year this role had begun to snowball. By looking at my inbox each morning, it was quickly becoming clear to me that answering internal and customer CMIS questions could end up being a full-time job if the volume increase continued. I figured this must also be the case for many of my TC colleagues.

It should have been obvious to me before then, but it wasn't. Not until a few customers and other IBMers had asked, "When will there be a book about CMIS?" did I realize the time had come. I needed to talk to Florian about getting a lineup of authors together to approach this subject. One thing I knew for sure is that his participation would be critical. Probably a third of the internal support questions I received about Apache Chemistry had to be deferred to him already. Hands down, nobody knew as much about OpenCMIS as he did, and he was turning out to be a very important library to IBM and our customers.

Florian and I had a few meetings about this, and we decided that it would be nice to have two more authors to help shoulder the load, because this book would have to cover a lot of ground (we were guessing more than 500 pages), and we both had day jobs.

First on our wish list was Jeff Potts. Not only was Jeff the author of cmislib, which eventually became the Python library part of Apache Chemistry, but he was already an experienced technical author. (He had single-handedly written the very successful

Alfresco Developer Guide in 2008.) The combination of CMIS expertise with that level of technical writing prowess meant he was a must for this writing team.

Luckily for us, both Florian and I had worked with Jeff in the past—Florian in his former role at Alfresco, and myself when Jeff and I coauthored a developerWorks article about cmislib in March 2010. Even more fortunate, Jeff agreed to join us. But there were still some gaps to be filled. So far we had IBM, Alfresco, Apache Chemistry, and SAP on board, but that still left us with a conspicuous gap in our lineup: Microsoft...

A month later, we had begun courting publishers and had something tentative going with Manning, but our roster was still not complete. SharePoint is a subject that we didn't want to gloss over, and we still didn't have anyone on board with a SharePoint CMIS background. To make a long story short, through a contact at the TC (Adam Harmetz), we ended up getting one of the engineers who was working on the CMIS implementation for SharePoint 13 (Matt Mooty) to commit to writing the chapter that would eventually cover not only SharePoint but .NET as well.

Of course, we still had a long list of areas we wanted to cover where we were going to need some more outside help. That's where Jens, Jean-Marie, Richard, Gi, Jane, and Dave came in to save us (see the acknowledgments for details and special thanks to these very important contributors).

And now here we are, over a year later. We hope that this book will stand as the authoritative CMIS reference for years to come. This was a primary goal early on, and the reason we've taken on a lot of extra work to cover the new 1.1 spec, even though the ink has barely dried. In fact, as I type this, the public review has just completed and Oasis has made version 1.1 official.

I know its cliché, but I'll say it anyway. This has been more work than we ever thought, going into the project, but now that it's almost done I know we're all glad we did it and we're extremely proud of the end result. We hope that you enjoy it and, more importantly, that it helps you succeed in whatever project you're undertaking with CMIS.

JAY BROWN

acknowledgments

Apart from the efforts of the authors, the success of this book has depended on many other people who have made this possible.

First, thanks go to the OASIS TC, without whom there would be no CMIS in the first place. Writing about the protocol is certainly hard, but writing the protocol in the first place is much harder!

Second, we thank all the individuals who gave us support in the form of content based on their specific areas of expertise, as well as the staff at Manning Publications, who guided and encouraged us every step of the way through the publication process.

We thank the many reviewers of the book who helped us with their feedback through numerous readings of the manuscript during development: Andreas Krieg, Andrei Bautu, Bashar Nabi, Blake Girardot, Dave Brosius, Dirk Jablonski, George Gaines, Gregor Zurowski, John W. Reeder, Jose Rodriguez, Martin Hermes, Musannif Zahir, Nadia Noori, Robert Casazza, Ryan McVeigh, Sebastian Danninger, and Stephen Rice.

Special thanks go to David Caruana who, in his role as technical proofreader, took on the enormous task of going though every page of the book and verifying each of the code examples for all of the subject areas and programming languages.

We are grateful to Richard J. Howarth at IBM and John Newton at Alfresco and AIIM for generously contributing the forewords to the book and for endorsing our work.

We'd also like to acknowledge Jane Doong (Software Engineer, Enterprise Content Management, IBM) for her significant contribution of technical material for chapter 5 ("Query") and her role in helping make sure that the information on CMIS Query that we presented was not only current but complete and authoritative.

We were fortunate enough to have Matt Mooty (Software Development Engineer, Microsoft) at our disposal for the DotCMIS section in chapter 9. And, later in that chapter, Richard McKnight (Principal Technical Consultant, Alfresco) pitched in with the PHP section. We're grateful these guys were able to give their time to the project.

Chapter 10, which covers developing mobile applications with CMIS, wouldn't have been possible without Jean-Marie Pascal (Mobile Engineer, Alfresco), who contributed the Android section, and Gi Lee (Technical Architect, Zia Consulting) who contributed the iOS section. Thanks to you and your respective teams and companies for the great content.

Also, many thanks to Jens Hübel (Software Architect, SAP AG), whose contribution of the OpenCMIS Server (among many other things, including all the content from our JavaScript development appendix) made it possible for us to include our own server with this book.

Thanks to Dave Sanders (Senior Developer, Enterprise Content Management, IBM) who tested and converted all The Blend metadata into FileNet's XML metadata import format. Now readers who want to run the part 2 examples on a test FileNet server can do so just by importing the data we've included with the book.

Thanks to all of you, and to the many others who provided support, both technical and otherwise, and who would be too numerous to list here. We'd also like to thank our families and friends, who showed patience and understanding when we had to stay glued to our laptops for the many nights and weekends it took to complete this project.

about this book

The OASIS CMIS (Content Management Interoperability Services) standard is the lingua franca of Enterprise Content Management (ECM) systems. This book is a comprehensive guide to the CMIS standard and related ECM concepts.

The focus of this book is on hands-on experience with the standard and with the Apache Chemistry libraries and tools. We start with providing the basics for developers, but these early chapters will also be beneficial for nondevelopers who want to understand the standard. As you get deeper into the book, by the end of part 2, you should be able to build an application that connects to any content repository that supports CMIS. We provide practical code examples for Java, Groovy, Python, C#, Objective-C, PHP, and JavaScript. And in the final chapters, we cover expert topics like optimizing your CMIS application and building your own CMIS server.

Audience

This book was written primarily for software developers and architects who design and build content-centric applications. You don't have to be an ECM expert to follow along, but some familiarity with content management systems is assumed. Basic programming skills will be useful for the first part of this book. Parts 2 and 3 require knowledge of a standard programming language like Java or C#, but no previous CMIS expertise or knowledge of the Apache Chemistry libraries are required.

Roadmap

This book is divided into three parts, each with a different target audience with respect to experience level.

Part 1 (chapters 1–5) is for newcomers to ECM and CMIS. The examples in this section are very simple and cover a broad spectrum of CMIS operations at a basic level.

Part 2 (chapters 6–10) is for a more intermediate audience, who at a minimum are comfortable with the CMIS basics covered in part 1 and have a bit more application development background. Part 2 is where you'll build a functioning content-centric application with CMIS. You'll notice a distinct increase in pace when you get into part 2, especially by the time you get to chapter 7.

Part 3 (chapters 11–14), as well as some of the appendix material, is for an advanced audience, with some of the material aimed at lead developers or architects. This part covers low-level details around the CMIS bindings, security, and performance, and also covers how to implement your own CMIS-compliant server.

Code conventions and downloads

All source code in listings or in text is in a `fixed-width font like this` to separate it from ordinary text. Code annotations accompany many of the listings, highlighting important concepts. In some cases, numbered bullets link to explanations that follow the listing.

You can download the source code for all listings from the Manning website, www.manning.com/CMISandApacheChemistryinAction.

Author Online

The purchase of *CMIS and Apache Chemistry in Action* includes free access to a private web forum run by Manning Publications, where you can make comments about the book, ask technical questions, and receive help from the authors and from other users. To access the forum and subscribe to it, point your web browser to www.manning.com/CMISandApacheChemistryinAction. This page provides information on how to get on the forum once you are registered, what kind of help is available, and the rules of conduct on the forum.

Manning's commitment to our readers is to provide a venue where a meaningful dialogue between individual readers and between readers and the authors can take place. It is not a commitment to any specific amount of participation on the part of the authors, whose contribution to the forum remains voluntary (and unpaid). We suggest you try asking the authors some challenging questions lest their interest stray!

The Author Online forum and the archives of previous discussions will be accessible from the publisher's website as long as the book is in print.

about the authors

JAY BROWN

A software developer for over 25 years, Jay has been building ECM products for IBM and FileNet since 1999. These include the design and construction of the Java and .NET APIs for FileNet Content Manager.

Jay started working with CMIS in 2008 when he joined the OASIS TC (Technical Committee) and designed IBM's first CMIS implementation for FileNet, followed by a list of other ECM CMIS projects. He was one of the original contributors for CMIS 1.0 in addition to having authored several of the new CMIS 1.1 specification features.

As the CMIS Evangelist for IBM, he works with other development projects inside and outside of the company, helping teams implement the standard while ensuring interoperability with the ever-growing CMIS ecosystem.

Jay lives in Los Angeles, California, with his wife Cindy.

FLORIAN MÜLLER

Florian has been developing enterprise software since the late 1990s. His focus on document management systems began when he joined OpenText in 2002. A few years later he moved to Alfresco and is now working as an ECM Development Architect at SAP.

In 2008, Florian joined the OASIS CMIS TC (Technical Committee) and became one of the specification editors for CMIS 1.0 and later for CMIS 1.1. A year later he joined the incubator project Apache Chemistry and became the project chair in 2011 when Apache Chemistry turned into an Apache top-level project. He is one of the core developers of the Apache Chemistry subprojects OpenCMIS (Java) and DotCMIS (.NET).

Florian lives near Heidelberg in Germany.

JEFF POTTS

Jeff has been working with unstructured data and document-oriented data stores for most of his 20-year career, starting with Lotus Notes in the early 1990s, then Web Content Management and Document Management platforms like Interwoven and Documentum, until diving into the world of open source full-time in 2006. After 5 years implementing open source software for clients and playing a big part in the Alfresco community, Jeff joined Alfresco as their Chief Community Officer in 2011, where he's responsible for growing the Alfresco community through product evangelism and developer outreach.

Jeff starting working with CMIS in 2008 when he created a proof-of-concept to integrate Drupal and Alfresco via CMIS, which eventually grew into the Drupal CMIS API module. Then, in 2009, he created cmislib, the Python API for CMIS, which later joined Apache Chemistry as the first non-Java contribution to the project. Since then, Jeff has continued to maintain cmislib and to review and comment on the CMIS specification as it continues to evolve.

Jeff lives in Dallas, Texas, with his wife, Christy, and their two children, Justin and Caroline.

about the cover illustration

The figure on the cover of *CMIS and Apache Chemistry in Action* is captioned "Le Gamin de Paris," which means a street urchin in Paris. The illustration is taken from a nineteenth-century edition of Sylvain Maréchal's four-volume compendium of regional dress customs published in France. Each illustration is finely drawn and colored by hand. The rich variety of Maréchal's collection reminds us vividly of how culturally apart the world's towns and regions were just 200 years ago. Isolated from each other, people spoke different dialects and languages. Whether on city streets, in small towns, or in the countryside, it was easy to identify where they lived and what their trade or station in life was just by their dress.

Dress codes have changed since then and the diversity by region and class, so rich at the time, has faded away. It is now hard to tell apart the inhabitants of different continents, let alone different towns or regions. Perhaps we have traded cultural diversity for a more varied personal life—certainly for a more varied and fast-paced technological life.

At a time when it is hard to tell one computer book from another, Manning celebrates the inventiveness and initiative of the computer business with book covers based on the rich diversity of regional life of two centuries ago, brought back to life by Maréchal's pictures.

Part 1

Understanding CMIS

This part of the book is a gentle introduction to the Content Management Interoperability Services (CMIS) standard, as well as the tools and concepts you need to know to work with CMIS-compliant repositories. Chapter 1 shows you how to perform the most basic interactions possible. Chapter 2 covers the basic building blocks of a CMIS repository: folders and documents. As the chapters progress, you'll learn more and more about CMIS concepts, such as versioning (in chapter 3), types (in chapter 4), and queries (in chapter 5). By the end of this part of the book, you'll be ready to write your own CMIS client.

1 Introducing CMIS

This chapter covers

- Presenting the CMIS standard
- Setting up your development environment
- Taking your first CMIS steps using Groovy and the CMIS Workbench
- Understanding possible limitations before using CMIS for your project

This chapter introduces the Content Management Interoperability Services (CMIS) standard. After running through a high-level overview of the standard and learning why it's important, you'll work on a simple hands-on example. By the end of the chapter, you'll have a reference server implementation running on your local machine and you'll know how to use Groovy to work with objects stored in a CMIS server by using a handy tool from Apache Chemistry called *CMIS Workbench.*

1.1 What is CMIS?

We're willing to bet that at some point in your career you've written more than a few applications that used a relational database for data persistence. And we'll further wager that if any of those were written after, say, 1992, you probably weren't too concerned with which relational database your application was using. Sure, you might have a preference, and the company using your application might have a standard database, but unless you were doing something out of the ordinary, it didn't matter much.

This database agnosticism on the part of developers is only possible because of the standardization of SQL. Before that happened, applications were written for a specific relational back end. Switching databases meant porting the code, which, at best, was a costly exercise and, at worst, might be completely impractical. Before standardization, developers had to write applications for a specific database, as shown in figure 1.1.

This notion of writing applications that only work with a particular database seems odd to modern-day developers who are used to tools like ODBC and JDBC that can abstract away the details of a particular database implementation. But that's the way it was. And that's the way it still is for many developers working in the world of content management.

Until recently, developers writing applications that needed to use Enterprise Content Management (ECM) systems for data persistence faced the same challenge as those pre-SQL-standardization folks: Each ECM system had its own API. A software vendor with expertise in accounts payable systems, for example, and a team of .NET developers were locked into a Microsoft-based repository. If a customer came along who loved the vendor's solution but didn't want to run Microsoft, they had a tough choice to make.

That's where CMIS comes in.

CMIS is a vendor-neutral, language-independent specification for working with ECM systems (sometimes called *rich content repositories* or more loosely, *unstructured repositories*). If you're new to the term *repository* (or *repo*, for short), think of it as a place where data—mostly files, in this case—lives, like a file cabinet.

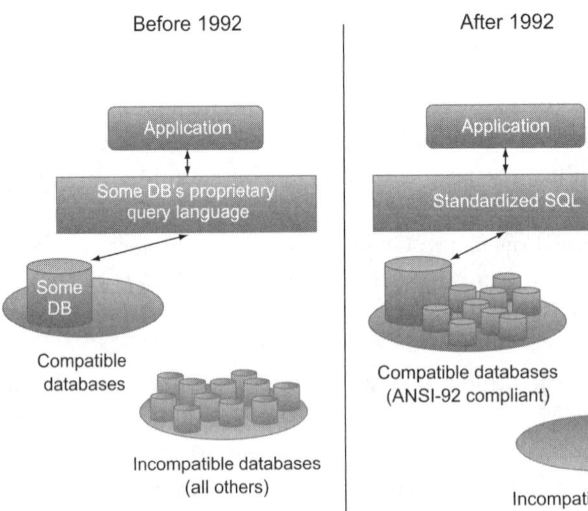

Figure 1.1 Before SQL standardization, developers wrote applications against specific databases.

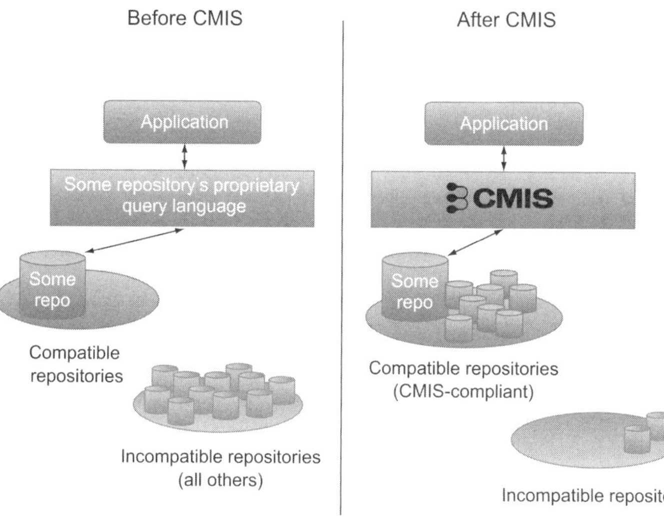

Figure 1.2 CMIS standardizes the way applications work with rich content repositories in much the same way SQL did for relational databases.

With CMIS, developers can create solutions that will work with multiple repositories, as shown in figure 1.2. And customers can have less vendor lock-in and lower switching costs.

The creation of the CMIS specification and its broad adoption is almost as significant and game-changing to the content management industry as SQL standardization and the adoption of that standard was to the relational database world. When enterprises choose repositories that are CMIS-compliant, they reap the following benefits.

Content-centric applications, either custom built or bought off the shelf, are more independent of the underlying repository because they can access repositories in a standard way instead of through proprietary APIs. This reduces development costs and lowers switching costs.

Developers can ramp up quickly because they don't have to learn a new API every time they encounter a new type of repository. Once developers learn CMIS, they know how to perform most of the fundamental operations they'll need for a significant number of industry-leading, CMIS-compliant repositories.

Because CMIS is language-neutral, developers aren't stuck with a particular platform, language, or framework driven by the repository they happen to be using. Instead, developers have the freedom to choose what makes the most sense for their particular set of constraints.

Enterprise applications can be more easily and cheaply integrated with content repositories. Rather than developing expensive, one-off integrations, many enterprise applications have *CMIS connectors* that allow them to store files in any CMIS-compliant repository.

OK, you're convinced. CMIS is kind of a big deal in the Enterprise Content Management world. Let's talk a little bit about how the CMIS specification is defined, look at an example of what you could use CMIS to do, and see a list of places where CMIS exists in the wild.

1.1.1 About the specification

CMIS is a *standard*, and the explanation of the standard is called a *specification*. The CMIS specification describes the data model, services, and bindings (how a specific wire protocol is hooked up to the services) that all CMIS-compliant servers must support. You'll become intimately familiar with the data model, services, and bindings as you work through the rest of this book.

The CMIS specification is maintained using a collaborative, open process managed by the Organization for the Advancement of Structured Information Standards (OASIS). According to its website (www.oasis-open.org), "OASIS is a non-profit consortium that drives the development, convergence, and adoption of open standards for the global information society." Using an organization like OASIS to manage the CMIS specification ensures that anyone who's interested can get involved in the specification, either as an observer or as an active voting member.

The group of people who work on the specification is called the *Technical Committee* or *TC*, for short. What's great is that the CMIS TC isn't made up of only one or two companies or individuals but is composed of more than 100 people from a wide range of backgrounds and industries, including representation from the who's who of content management vendors, large and small.

1.1.2 What does CMIS do?

OK, so CMIS is an open standard for working with content repositories. But what does it do? Well, the standard doesn't do anything. To make it interesting, you need an implementation. More specifically, you need a CMIS-compliant server. When a content repository is CMIS-compliant, that means that it provides a set of standard services for working with the objects in that repository. You'll explore each of those services in the coming chapters, but the set includes things like creating documents and folders, searching for objects using queries, navigating a repository, setting permissions, and creating new versions of documents.

Let's discuss a real-world example. Suppose you work for a company whose content lives in three different repositories: SharePoint, FileNet, and Alfresco. The sales team comes to you and asks for a system that will build PowerPoint presentations on the fly by pulling data from each of these repositories. The PowerPoint presentations need to be based on a template that resides in SharePoint and will include, among other things, images of the last three invoices. The invoice images reside in FileNet. The final PowerPoint file is stored in Alfresco and accessed by the sales team using their tablets. A high-level overview of this application is shown in figure 1.3.

Before CMIS, your system would have to use at least three different APIs to make this happen. With CMIS, your system can use a single API to talk to each of the three repositories, including the mobile application.

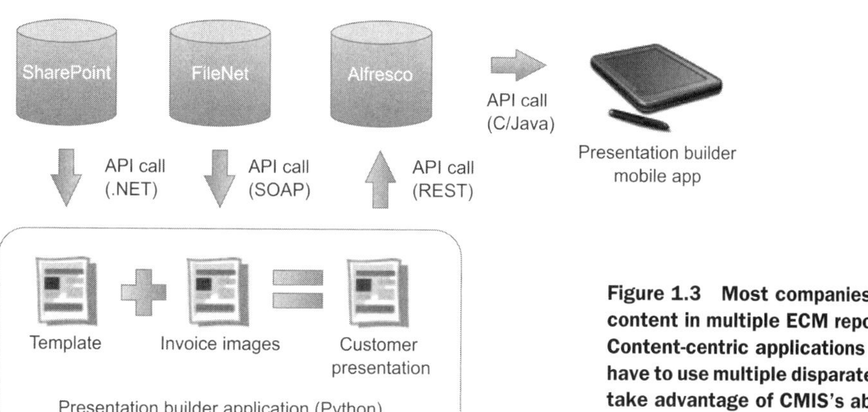

Figure 1.3 Most companies store content in multiple ECM repositories. Content-centric applications either have to use multiple disparate APIs, or take advantage of CMIS's ability to use each repository in a standard way.

Three different ECM systems in the same organization?

You may be wondering how real-world this example is—three ECM systems in the same organization? In fact, it happens quite often. According to AIIM, the Association for Information and Image Management, which is a major ECM industry organization, "72% of larger organizations have three or more ECM, Document Management, or Records Management systems" and "25% have five or more" ("State of the ECM Industry," AIIM, 2011).

How does a company find itself in this situation? It happens for many reasons. Sometimes these systems start out as departmental solutions. In large organizations where there may not be an enterprise-wide ECM strategy, multiple departments may—knowingly or unknowingly—implement different systems because they feel their requirements are unique, they have timelines that don't allow for coordination with other departments, or any number of other reasons.

Similarly, companies often bring in multiple systems because they may fill niche requirements (like digital asset management or records management) and one vendor may be perceived as offering a better fit for those highly specific requirements. But ECM vendors, particularly large ones, often use their niche solution as a foot in the door—it's a common strategy for ECM vendors with "suites" of products to subsequently expand their footprint from their original niche solution to other product offerings.

As each department or niche implementation sees success, the rollouts broaden until what once were small, self-contained solutions may grow to house critical content for entire divisions. Once each ECM system has gotten so big, the business owners are reluctant to consolidate because the risk may not justify the benefit. After all, the business owners are happy—their requirements are being met.

As a result, it's common to walk into a company with many different ECM systems. If this is a problem you deal with, we hope the techniques you learn in this book will save you time, money, and frustration.

1.1.3 Where is CMIS being adopted?

Standards that no one implements aren't useful. So far, CMIS has avoided this fate. Thanks to the early involvement of a number of large ECM vendors in developing the specification, and the specification's language neutrality, CMIS enjoys broad adoption. If you're currently using an ECM repository that's updated to a fairly recent version, it's likely to be CMIS-compliant. Table 1.1 shows a list of common ECM vendors or open source projects and when they started to support CMIS. This list is only a subset of the CMIS-compliant servers available at the time of this writing. The CMIS page on Wikipedia (http://en.wikipedia.org/wiki/Content_Management_Interoperability_Services) contains a more exhaustive list. If you don't see your favorite content server in the list, ask your vendor.

Table 1.1 Selection of ECM vendors, or open source projects, and their support for CMIS

Vendor	Product	Release that first provided CMIS 1.0 support
Alfresco Software	Alfresco	3.3
Alfresco Software	Alfresco Cloud	March 2012
Apache Chemistry	InMemory Repository	0.1
Apache Chemistry	FileShare Repository	0.1
EMC	Documentum	6.7
HP Autonomy Interwoven	Worksite	8.5
IBM	FileNet Content Manager	5.0
IBM	Content Manager	8.4.3
IBM	Content Manager On Demand	9.0
KnowledgeTree	KnowledgeTree	3.7
Magnolia	CMS	4.5
Microsoft	SharePoint Server	2010
Nuxeo	Platform	5.5
OpenText	OpenText ECM	ECM Suite 2010
SAP	SAP NetWeaver Cloud Document Service	July 2012

As the previous table illustrates, a variety of CMIS-compliant servers are available. CMIS gives you a single API that will work across all of these servers.

1.2 Setting up a CMIS test environment

Alright, time to roll up your sleeves and set up a working CMIS development environment that you can take advantage of as you work through the rest of this book.

We'll give you a proper introduction to Apache Chemistry in part 2 of the book. For now, it's important to know that Apache Chemistry is a project at the Apache Software Foundation that groups together a number of CMIS-related subprojects, including client libraries, server frameworks, and development tools. It's the de facto standard reference implementation of the CMIS specification. One of the Apache Chemistry subprojects is called *OpenCMIS*, and it's made up of multiple components. For the rest of this chapter, you'll use two of those components: the OpenCMIS InMemory Repository and the CMIS Workbench.

The OpenCMIS InMemory Repository, as the name suggests, is a CMIS-compliant repository that runs entirely in memory. It's limited in what it can do, but it'll serve our needs quite nicely.

The CMIS Workbench is a Java Swing application that we'll use as a CMIS client to work with objects in the CMIS server. The CMIS Workbench was created using the OpenCMIS API and is typically used by developers who want a view into a CMIS repository that is based purely on the CMIS specification. For example, suppose you're working with Microsoft SharePoint, which has a variety of ways to create, query, update, and delete content that resides within it, and you want to integrate your application with SharePoint using CMIS. You could use the CMIS Workbench to test some queries or inspect the data model. If you want to know if you can do something purely through CMIS, one test is to try to do it through the CMIS Workbench. If the CMIS Workbench can do it, you know you'll be able to do it as part of your integration.

One of the key features of the CMIS Workbench, from both a "developer utility" perspective and a "let's learn about CMIS" perspective, is its interactive Groovy console. The Groovy console is perfect for taking your first steps with CMIS.

When you're finished setting up your environment, it'll look like figure 1.4.

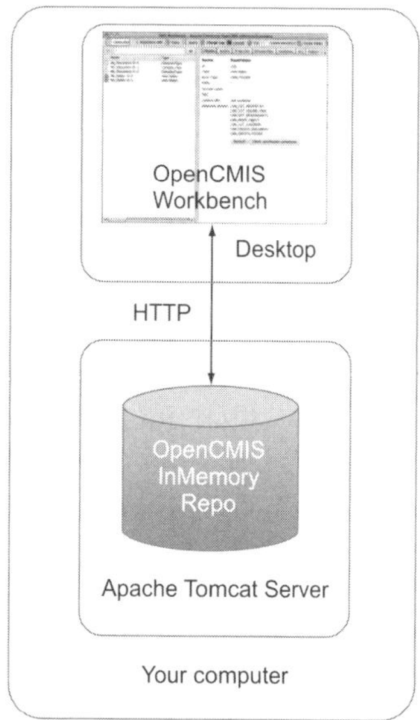

Figure 1.4 Your local CMIS development setup includes two components: the CMIS Workbench and the OpenCMIS InMemory Repository. This is all you'll need for the examples in part 1 of this book.

We've made it easy to set up your local CMIS development environment. Everything you need is in the zip file that accompanies this book (see appendix E for links to resources). Let's unzip the components you'll need for the rest of part 1.

Downloading and building your own CMIS tools

To save you time and make the setup easier, we've taken distributions from the Apache Chemistry project and packaged them together with some sample configuration and data that will be used throughout the book. When you're ready to learn how to download out-of-the-box versions of these components, or you want to know how to build them from source, or you want to get the latest and greatest release of OpenCMIS, refer to appendix A.

1.2.1 Requirements

For the rest of part 1, all you need is the CMIS Workbench and the OpenCMIS InMemory Repository. These components both need a JDK (version 1.6 or higher will do). Other than that, everything you need is in the zip.

Before continuing, find a place to unzip the archive that accompanies this book. We'll call it $BOOK_HOME. Within $BOOK_HOME, create two directories: server and workbench.

1.2.2 Installing the OpenCMIS InMemory Repository web application

Let's install and start up the OpenCMIS InMemory Repository:

1. Change into the $BOOK_HOME/server directory and unzip inmemory-cmis-server-pack.zip into the directory.
2. Run ./run.sh or run.bat, depending on your platform of choice.

This will start up InMemory Repository on your machine, and it will listen for connections on port 8081. If you're already running something on port 8081, edit run.sh (or run.bat) and change the port number. All of the directions in the book will assume the InMemory repository is running on port 8081.

After the server starts up, you should be able to point your browser to http://localhost:8081/inmemory and see something that looks like figure 1.5.

Now you have a working CMIS server running on your machine. The CMIS server has some test data in it, but in order to work with it, you need a CMIS client. In part 1, you'll use a CMIS client that's already been built. It's a Java Swing desktop application called CMIS Workbench. Setting it up is the subject of the next section.

Apache Chemistry OpenCMIS InMemory Repository is up and running!

CMIS Web Services Binding: http://localhost:8081/inmemory/services/RepositoryService?wsdl
CMIS AtomPub Binding: http://localhost:8081/inmemory/atom
CMIS Browser Binding Binding: http://localhost:8081/inmemory/browser

Figure 1.5 Apache Chemistry OpenCMIS InMemory Repository welcome page

1.2.3 Installing the CMIS Workbench

The CMIS Workbench is distributed as a standalone Java Swing application. Everything you need to run it is in the package included with the book. To install it, follow these steps:

1. Open a new window and switch to the $BOOK_HOME/workbench directory.
2. Unzip cmis-workbench.zip into the directory.
3. Run the appropriate batch file for your operating system. For example, on Windows, run `workbench.bat`. On Mac and Unix/Linux systems, run `workbench.sh`.

The Workbench will start up, and you should see an empty login dialog box, like the one in shown in figure 1.6.

Congratulations! You now have everything you need to explore a working CMIS implementation.

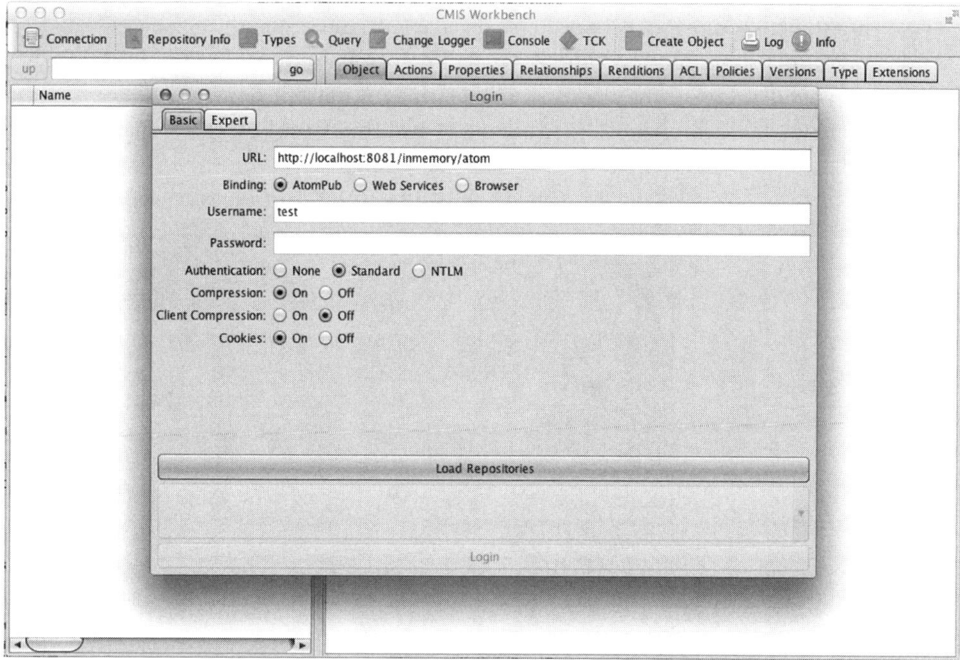

Figure 1.6 An empty CMIS Workbench login dialog box

1.3 Writing your first CMIS code using Groovy

Your OpenCMIS InMemory Repository is running, and so is the first CMIS client you'll be working with, the CMIS Workbench. It's time to get the two to work together.

1.3.1 Connecting to the repository

To talk to the OpenCMIS InMemory Repository, you need to choose a *binding* and you need to know the server's *service URL*, which depends on the binding you choose, as you can see in figure 1.7.

The binding is the method the CMIS client will use to talk to the server. You can also think of it as the protocol it'll use to communicate. In CMIS version 1.0, the two choices for binding are Atom Publishing Protocol (AtomPub) and Web Services. CMIS version 1.1 adds a third binding called the Browser binding. We'll go through the binding details in chapter 11. For now, we'll use the AtomPub binding.

The service URL is the entry point into the server. The CMIS client will learn all it needs to know about the server it's talking to by invoking the service URL and inspecting the response it gets back. The service URL depends on the server you're using, the binding you've chosen, and how the server is deployed. In this case, the server is deployed to a web application under the inmemory context, so the URL will begin with http://localhost:8081/inmemory; and the AtomPub service URL is /atom, so the full service URL is http://localhost:8081/inmemory/atom.

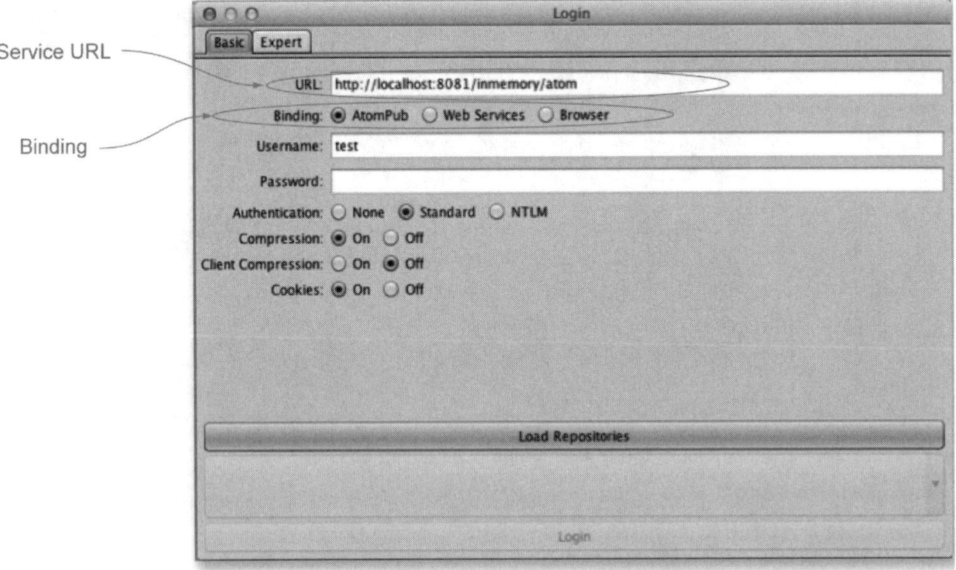

Figure 1.7 To connect to the repository, you must select a binding and specify the service URL.

THE CMIS WORKBENCH CAN CONNECT TO ANY CMIS SERVER We're using the Apache Chemistry InMemory Repository throughout this book because it's freely available, easy to install, and compliant with the CMIS specification. But, as the name implies, it stores all of its data in memory. That would never work for most production scenarios. Real ECM repositories persist their data to a more durable and scalable back end. Typically this is some combination of a relational database and a filesystem. If you have access to an ECM repository like Alfresco, FileNet, SharePoint, or the like, you can use the CMIS Workbench to work with data stored in those repositories. All you need to know is your repository's service URL.

1.3.2 *Try it—browse the repository using the CMIS Workbench*

You now know enough to be able to connect to the server. Follow these steps to use the CMIS Workbench to connect to the server and browse the repository:

1 If the CMIS Workbench isn't running, run it as previously discussed.
2 If the CMIS Workbench isn't displaying the login dialog box, click Connection in the upper-left corner.
3 Specify http://localhost:8081/inmemory/atom as the URL.
4 Take all the other defaults. Click Load Repositories.
5 The InMemory Repository only has one repository. You should see it in the Repositories list. Click Login.

If everything is working correctly, you should see the login dialog box close and the Workbench will display the contents of the repository, as shown in figure 1.8.

Take a few minutes to explore the Workbench. You can't hurt anything. Every time you restart the InMemory Repository, it'll revert to its original state.

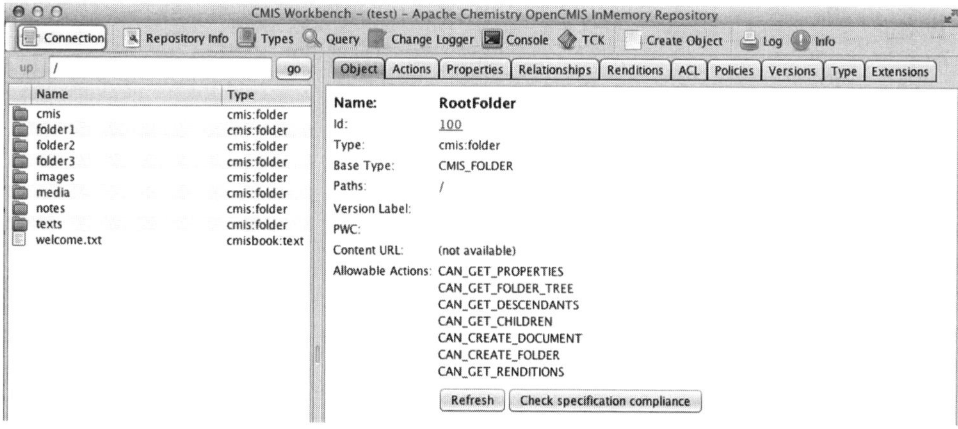

Figure 1.8 Root folder of the OpenCMIS InMemory Repository

Here are a few things to notice as you explore:

- As you click objects in the left-hand pane, the right-hand pane updates to provide details on what's selected.
- The right-hand pane has tabs across the top that group different sets of information about the selected object as well as actions you can take on the selected object.
- The items in the menu bar let you do things like change the connection details, inspect repository information, view the types defined on the server, and open a Groovy console. That's where we're headed next.

1.3.3 Try it—run CMIS code in the CMIS Workbench Groovy console

Groovy is a dynamic language that's easy for Java programmers to learn. It can run anywhere Java can run. It's different from Java in a few respects, such as the fact that semicolons are optional in most cases, closures are supported, and regular expressions are natively supported.

DON'T KNOW GROOVY? NO PROBLEM! Don't worry if you don't know Groovy. We picked it for the examples in part 1 of this book because it's easy to learn, it looks similar to Java, it doesn't require a compiler, and the CMIS Workbench features a Groovy console. You'll probably easily grok what's going on as you work through the examples. But if you want to dive into Groovy, you can learn more from the Groovy home page (http://groovy.codehaus.org/) or from *Groovy in Action, Second Edition* (Manning, 2013).

The best way to get a feel for Groovy is to jump right in, so let's do that. Follow these steps to write a Groovy script that will display the repository's name:

1. From the CMIS Workbench, click Console, and select Main Template in the submenu.
2. A Groovy console window will be displayed with eight or nine lines of prepopulated code. Delete those lines.
3. Add the following two lines of Groovy:

   ```
   def info = session.getRepositoryInfo()
   println "Repository Name: " + info.getName()
   ```

4. Click the Execute Groovy Script button, which is the little document with the green arrow.

Your code should run without a hitch. The output of the program will be displayed in the bottom half of the Groovy console. It should look something like figure 1.9.

Let's look at a few important things:

- You didn't have to import anything.
- You didn't have to retrieve a session. It was handed to you in a variable called `session` that was already defined. The `session` variable represents a connection to the CMIS repository for the user you provided when you launched the

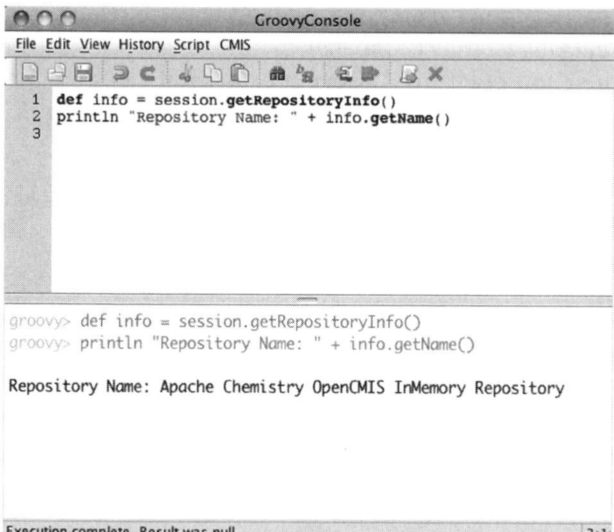

Figure 1.9 Groovy console after running code to retrieve the CMIS server name

Workbench. The object is an instance of `org.apache.chemistry.opencmis.client.runtime.SessionImpl`.

- You could have omitted the "get" and the parenthesis from the no-argument getters. For example, you could have said `session.repositoryInfo` and `info.name`.
- Any time you feel you need some help with the API, you can click CMIS > OpenCMIS Client API Javadoc, and the documentation will open in a browser window.
- When you first click Console in the CMIS Workbench, you'll see a list of Groovy script templates. You the choose - Main Template - and then replace it with your own code. When you have a chance, you might want to take a look at some of the other sample Groovy scripts that are provided.

And that's it. You've written your first CMIS code. We sense some disappointment, though. "I don't feel like I've experienced the true power of CMIS yet," you say. OK, overachiever. Earlier you learned that one of the beauties of CMIS is that, as a developer, once you learn CMIS you should be able to write code that works with any CMIS-compliant repository. You've demonstrated your ability to use the OpenCMIS InMemory Repository. How about an enterprise-grade repository from a completely different vendor?

It so happens that publicly available CMIS servers are waiting for folks like you who are testing client libraries or exploring CMIS. One of them is run by a company called Alfresco Software; its AtomPub service URL is http://cmis.alfresco.com/cmisatom. Unlike the InMemory Repository, you'll need credentials to authenticate with Alfresco. You can use the administrator's account, which is *admin*, and the password is also *admin*. Fair warning: the response time will be significantly slower than what you see with the local InMemory Repository.

SAVE YOUR SCRIPT To save some typing, do a File > Save on your current Groovy script before clicking Connect to specify the Alfresco service URL and credentials. Then, when you open the Groovy console, you can do a File > Open to reopen your script.

Now you know how to install a reference CMIS server and a handy CMIS client. You've had a glimpse of the power of CMIS as you used the same client to talk to two different implementations.

1.4 CMIS considerations

In the next chapter, you'll start to dive into the CMIS specification a little more deeply. But before doing that, let's discuss a few of the limitations of CMIS and how it compares to other content management standards. This will help you decide if CMIS might be right for your next project.

1.4.1 Understanding the limitations of CMIS

Like any industry-wide standard, CMIS has some limitations that may affect your ability to use it for a particular project. Whether or not these limitations affect you depends on your specific requirements.

LIMITED IN SCOPE

Enterprise Content Management systems vary broadly in their capabilities and functionality. Some of the differences are significant, such as whether or not the system has an embedded workflow engine, and others are minor, like whether or not the system supports access control lists (ACLs). The CMIS specification is flexible enough to accommodate differences between implementations: A repository doesn't have to support ACLs and can still be CMIS-compliant, for example. Or one repository might support "unfiled" documents, but another might require that documents always live in a folder.

In cases where the differences between repositories are too significant to be covered by one standard definition of a repository, CMIS omits those areas from its scope. Workflow is one example—you won't see anything about workflow in this book, even though workflow is a relatively common feature of ECM systems.

As a developer, you may be able to meet all of the requirements of your application by staying strictly with pure CMIS API calls. But there may be times when you'll have to supplement what CMIS provides with calls to your ECM system's proprietary APIs.

OBJECT MODEL IS BASED ON DOCUMENTS AND FOLDERS

In the next chapter, you'll see that two prominent domain objects covered by the specification are `cmis:document` and `cmis:folder`. That's because the CMIS specification assumes a general document management use case: you're using CMIS to manage documents (files) organized in a hierarchy of folders.

NO USER OR GROUP MANAGEMENT

A CMIS repository typically uses named user accounts to control who can authenticate with the repository. But the CMIS specification provides nothing that helps you create user accounts or organize users into groups.

Does this mean your application can't assign ACLs to documents and folders? No. It means that if your application needs to create new users or modify groups of users, CMIS isn't going to help you to do that in a standard way. You'll have to use your repository's API or an LDAP directory to manage users and groups, if that's something your repository supports.

NO SUPPORT FOR DEFINING CONTENT TYPES UNTIL CMIS 1.1

You'll learn about content types in chapter 4. For now, realize that content in a CMIS repository belongs to a particular type, like document, folder, image, invoice, or web page. It's quite common for companies to define their own business-specific content types by updating the repository's data dictionary.

The first version of the CMIS specification doesn't provide for creating or updating content types, even if the underlying repository supports this feature natively. This may be a challenge if your application assumes that the types it needs are already configured in the repository's data dictionary. If they don't already exist, you'll have to provide documentation or configuration scripts when you deliver your CMIS application so that the system administrators can update the data dictionary with types to support your application.

Luckily, this is addressed in CMIS 1.1. With CMIS 1.1, your CMIS application can check to see if the required types have been configured, and if not, it can go ahead and create them using code, to avoid the need for manual changes to the data dictionary.

1.4.2 *Comparing CMIS to the Java Content Repository (JCR) API*

If you've worked with content management repositories for a while, you may already be familiar with the Java Content Repository (JCR) API, which is sometimes referred to as Java Specification Request (JSR) 170. What's the difference between CMIS and JCR? Table 1.2 breaks it down.

Table 1.2 Comparing CMIS and JCR

	JCR	CMIS
Standards body	Java Community Process	OASIS
Date first ratified	June 2005	April 2010
Vendor adoption	Limited. Several vendors provide JCR support in their repositories, but Adobe is the primary driver of the specification.	Many big-name ECM vendors actively participate in the specification and reference implementation, including EMC, IBM, Alfresco, SAP, HP Autonomy Interwoven, Oracle, Microsoft, and several others.

Table 1.2 Comparing CMIS and JCR *(continued)*

	JCR	CMIS
Primary language	Java, although work is being done to expand support to PHP.	Language-neutral. Any language that can speak HTTP can work with CMIS.
Reference implementation	Apache Jackrabbit	Apache Chemistry

It's important to note that CMIS and JCR aren't completely mutually exclusive. A given ECM repository might be compliant with both standards, which would mean developers would be free to choose which standard to use when working with that repository. Work has also been completed recently to bridge the two standards. You could, for example, write CMIS-compliant code that talks to a JCR repository.

1.5 Summary

You should now have a good idea of why the CMIS specification is so important to the ECM industry. After seeing some real-world examples of how you can apply CMIS to make your life easier as a content-centric application developer, you've probably already started thinking about some of the advantages of working with CMIS to build your applications:

- Content-centric applications can be more independent of the underlying content repository because they can access repositories in a standard way instead of through proprietary APIs.
- Developers can ramp up quickly because CMIS reduces the need to learn a proprietary API for every repository that's involved in an application.
- Developers have the freedom to choose what platform, language, or framework is the best fit for their particular constraints, without worrying whether or not it's supported by the repository they're working with, because CMIS is language-neutral.
- Expensive one-off integrations don't have to be built—applications can take advantage of standards-based connectors to CMIS-compliant repositories.

Beyond learning the *why* of CMIS, you rolled up your sleeves and put CMIS to *work*. You now have a working CMIS development environment based on freely available components from the Apache Chemistry project. You'll use this setup for the rest of the examples in part 1.

Now that you have a working development environment, it's time to start learning how to navigate a CMIS repository and what kind of objects you'll find in a CMIS repository once you connect to it. We'll start with two of the fundamental building blocks—folders and documents. On to chapter 2.

2 Exploring the CMIS domain model

This chapter covers

- Establishing communications with a CMIS service
- Using the features of a repository
- Navigating the folder hierarchy
- Retrieving a document with its content stream and properties (metadata)

In chapter 1, you received a high-level introduction to CMIS as a specification. Every object that lives in a CMIS repository is an instance of an object type. In this chapter, we'll explore the basic object types that make up the CMIS domain model as well as some of the key concepts that bind them all together into a useful system. Along the way, you'll write some Java/Groovy code (using the Workbench that was introduced in chapter 1) to illustrate key concepts.

Although it's a bit of a cliché, a picture is still worth a thousand words, so we'll start this chapter with an illustration of the object types we'll be talking about. Sometimes a clear image in your mind can help you organize related ideas as they arrive. Figure 2.1 shows the interrelationships between all of the high-level object

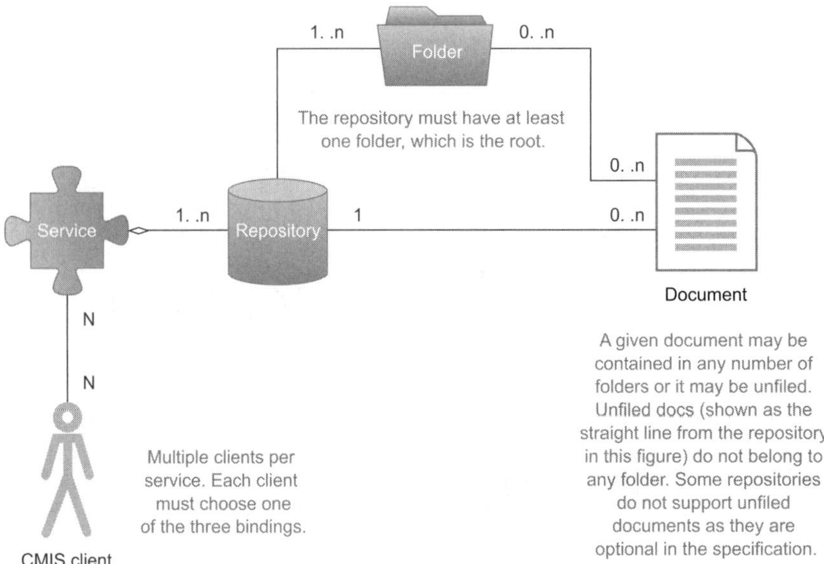
1. .n
Folder
0. .n
The repository must have at least one folder, which is the root.
0. .n
Service
1. .n
Repository
1
0. .n
Document
N
A given document may be contained in any number of folders or it may be unfiled. Unfiled docs (shown as the straight line from the repository in this figure) do not belong to any folder. Some repositories do not support unfiled documents as they are optional in the specification.
N
Multiple clients per service. Each client must choose one of the three bindings.
CMIS client

Figure 2.1 CMIS high-level object types (all of which we'll discuss in this chapter)

types we'll cover in this chapter. Ordered from the highest level and progressing downward (left to right in the figure) are the CMIS service, the binding chosen between the service and the CMIS client, repository, folder, and finally, document. Refer back to this diagram as you move through the sections of this chapter to refresh your understanding of their respective roles.

By the time you've finished this chapter, you'll have a clear picture of what the object types in figure 2.1 are, what they do in the context of a CMIS server, and how they relate to each other. We'll be revisiting this diagram as we move through the individual sections of the chapter to remind you of where you are in the big picture, but try to remember this image as we move on to the service.

2.1 The CMIS service

Of all of the items in figure 2.1, the CMIS service is unique in that it's not a persisted object like all of the other items; rather, it's a running program to service your requests. Think of the CMIS service as an interface to all of the CMIS objects you'll be dealing with (see figure 2.2). If a real-world analogy helps, think of it as a concierge at a hotel. This is probably a hotel somewhere in Europe, though, because this particular CMIS concierge *must* always speak two languages, and in some cases can even speak three. This is because CMIS servers must implement two bindings (three in CMIS 1.1).

This section will familiarize you with the CMIS service and how it's the key to this whole picture.

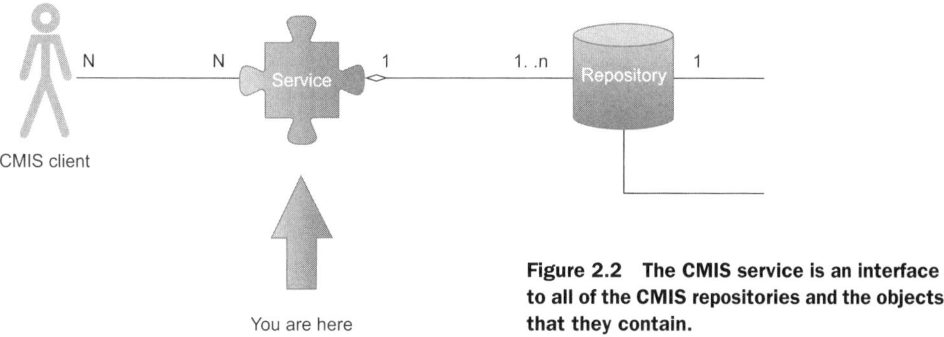

Figure 2.2 The CMIS service is an interface to all of the CMIS repositories and the objects that they contain.

2.1.1 The role of the CMIS service

At the highest level, the CMIS service is responsible for these three functions:

- Allow a client to discover what repositories are present for this particular CMIS service.
- Provide all the details about the capabilities of these repositories.
- For each of the repositories, publish the interfaces for the nine subservices that are exposed for every CMIS repository (see the following note).

THE NINE SUBSERVICES OF CMIS We'll cover all of these subservices in detail in later chapters, but in case you can't wait, here's a quick list:

- *Repository services (discussed in this chapter)*—Example: `getRepositoryInfo`
- *Navigation services*—Example: `getFolderTree`
- *Object services*—Example: `getObject`
- *Multifiling services*—Example: `addObjectToFolder`
- *Discovery services*—Example: `query`
- *Versioning services*—Example: `checkOut`
- *Relationship services*—Example: `getObjectRelationships`
- *Policy services*—Example: `applyPolicy`
- *ACL (access control lists) services*—Example: `applyACL`

Don't worry too much about these nine subservices yet, because from a client perspective they're somewhat arbitrary groupings of the functionality. We'll introduce you to them gradually as we move through the basic exercises in this book. By the time you're done with this chapter, you'll be familiar with the first three in the list. By the time we're done with part 1 of the book, you'll have used most of them.

2.1.2 Bindings: what does a CMIS service look like?

Recall that our concierge *must* speak at least two languages. These two languages are analogous to the two protocol bindings (Web Services and AtomPub) that all CMIS servers *must* speak. If you're a CMIS client, you can speak either of these languages

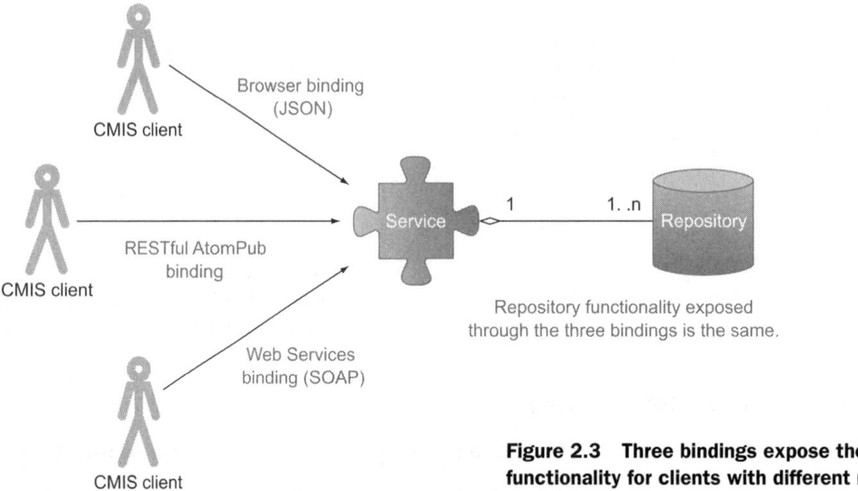

Figure 2.3 Three bindings expose the same functionality for clients with different needs.

(bindings) and always know that the hotel desk will be able to understand you. In a perfect world with lots of unicorns and rainbows, we'd have been able to require only one protocol, and every possible client would be able to speak it. In that same perfect place, our European concierge would only ever have to speak one language. But the reality is that many different types of processes exist on many platforms that need to talk to CMIS, and some protocols are easier for some to manage than others.

In the case of CMIS 1.0, we have the Web Services and the RESTful AtomPub bindings. What about that third language that's sometimes used? Well, CMIS 1.1 adds a new optional binding called the Browser binding. This optional binding or protocol is similar to the AtomPub binding in a lot of ways, except that it's designed to be easy to access from JavaScript in a browser. We'll cover more differences later in the book, but this will suffice until we get to chapter 11, when we'll go into greater detail about the innards of all of the bindings. Figure 2.3 shows multiple clients talking to one CMIS service, each using one of the CMIS 1.1 supported bindings.

Let's get back to the questions we were trying to answer. What does a CMIS service look like? Regardless of the binding, it looks like a simple HTTP URL. In the case of the Web Services binding, this URL is the address of the WSDL (Web Services Description Language) document for the web service. In the case of the AtomPub and Browser bindings, it's the address of the service document (XML or JSON). When a client retrieves these documents, they have the keys they need to start talking to CMIS in earnest.

2.2 Repository—the CMIS database

If you were asked to distill a CMIS repository down to its most simple role, you could safely get away with thinking of it as a database. More specifically, it's a database that knows a lot about the semantics of unstructured content and even more specifically about content management. It's a hierarchical store of content and the metadata

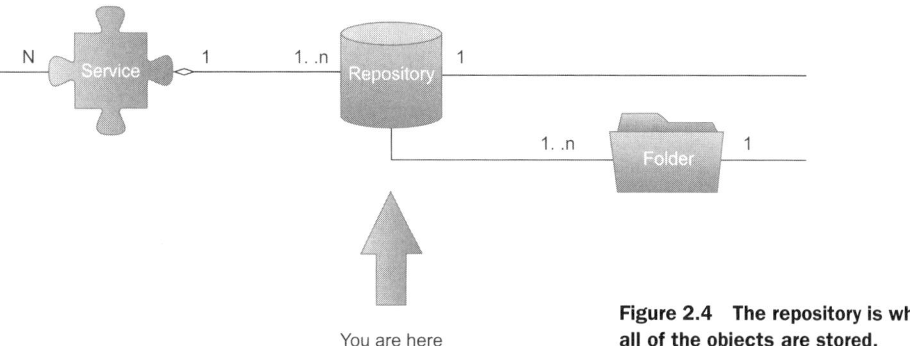

Figure 2.4 The repository is where all of the objects are stored.

describing not only the content itself but its organization and relationships to other content within the same repository.

As you can see in figure 2.4, multiple repositories can optionally be exposed by a given CMIS service. When you connected to the repository in chapter 1, you clicked Load Repositories and then chose the only repository presented—a repository with an ID of A1. Behind the scenes, the server was responding to a `getRepository` call and returning the list of available repositories.

A helpful analogy to use for the repository is that of a disk drive in a typical desktop computer. A server (which would be the CMIS service in this analogy) can host many disk drives, just like a CMIS server can support multiple repositories. Each of these drives may be formatted with different filesystems (different metadata, in CMIS terminology), and each has its own root directory, which may optionally contain other folders and files.

2.2.1 *Repository info and capabilities*

In chapter 1, you connected to the repository and went straight to the root folder for the example. Normally, however, when you first talk to a CMIS service, you may want to know a bit about what its capabilities are so that your client code can expose the menus and commands that match the repository.

> **SPECIFICATION REFERENCE: GETREPOSITORYINFO** For a more formal discussion of `getRepositoryInfo`, check out section 2.2.2.2, `getRepositoryInfo`, in the CMIS 1.0 specification. (See appendix E for references.)

For this exercise, you'll need to go back to the CMIS Workbench session you set up in chapter 1. Once you're connected, look at the buttons across the top of the application (shown in figure 2.5).

You'll see at the top left that the second one is labeled Repository Info. If you click this button, the CMIS Workbench will display the information returned for the CMIS `getRepositoryInfo` call. Figure 2.6 shows this information. The ACL capabilities are omitted here because we'll talk about those in detail in chapter 12.

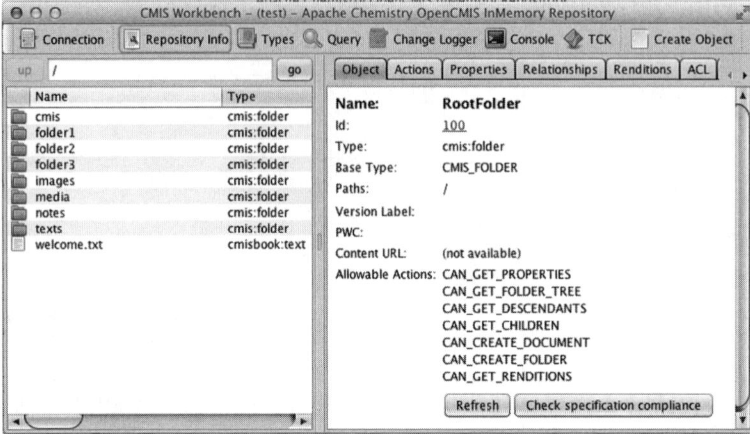

Figure 2.5 Repository Info button in the Workbench

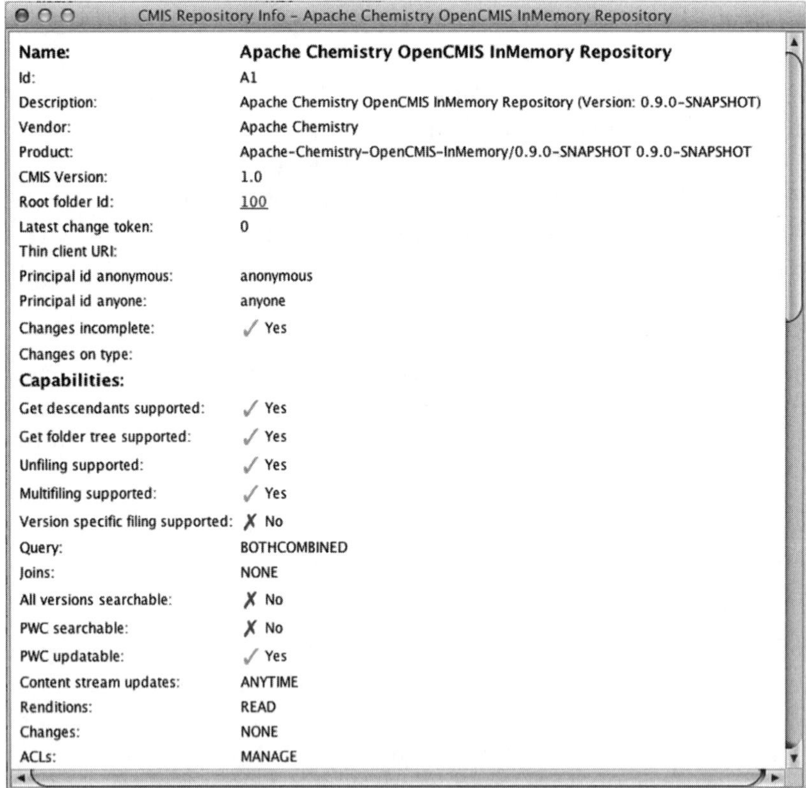

Figure 2.6 CMIS Repository Info display in CMIS Workbench

As you can see in figure 2.6, this call returns a wealth of information, including the following:

- Information about the server vendor
- The supported CMIS version
- The ID of the root folder (very important)
- Details on support for certain navigational operations
- Details on supported filing operations
- Details on supported versioning operations
- Details on supported query functions and advanced query features

We'll discuss all of these items in more detail in later chapters. All you need to know for now is that this response contains everything that a client needs to start talking to a CMIS server.

2.2.2 Capabilities across different repository vendors

As you look over the capabilities that your test InMemory server is reporting, you can start to see how CMIS manages to smoothly communicate with so many different repository implementations. CMIS needs to be able to accommodate repositories that have advanced features while at the same time enabling repositories with minimal features to play. This *optional capabilities* information is the most coarse-grained level of this type of information, and you'll see more of this throughout the specification as we explore further in upcoming chapters.

> **SPEC REFERENCE: OPTIONAL CAPABILITIES** For a detailed list of all of the *optional capabilities*, as well as their definitions, see section 2.1.1.1 of the CMIS 1.0 specification. (See appendix E for references.)

Say you were building a folder-browsing client and you wanted to be able to pull down the entire folder tree hierarchy in one round trip to the server, for efficiency reasons. Your client would then want to check to see if the repository capability `getFolderTree` was supported. If so, it would have the most efficient code path, and if not, it could degrade to iteratively crawling the hierarchy to collect the needed information.

2.2.3 Try it—retrieve the repository info

Let's look at the code you need to get at the repository info. You'll continue to use the CMIS Workbench for this exercise. Your code will list the repository info and the capabilities of the repository you're connected to in the Workbench.

In the code exercise in chapter 1, you used Groovy for the example. A nice thing about the Groovy interpreter is that pure Java syntax is valid as well. To illustrate this, the code in the examples for this chapter will be in Java form. Feel free to use the form you feel more comfortable with, or switch back and forth if you like variety. Keep in mind that the project you'll build in part 2 of the book will be written mainly in Java.

For this exercise, return to the Groovy console window in the CMIS Workbench and then copy this code into your code pane.

Listing 2.1 getRepositoryInfo code example

```
import org.apache.chemistry.opencmis.commons.*
import org.apache.chemistry.opencmis.commons.data.*
import org.apache.chemistry.opencmis.commons.enums.*
import org.apache.chemistry.opencmis.client.api.*

RepositoryInfo info = session.getRepositoryInfo();
println("");
println("Abbreviated repository info:");
println("  Name: " + info.getName());
println("  ID: " + info.getId());
println("  Product name: " + info.getProductName());
println("  Product version: " + info.getProductVersion());
println("  Version supported: " + info.getCmisVersionSupported());

RepositoryCapabilities caps =
  session.getRepositoryInfo().getCapabilities();
println("");
println("Brief capabilities report:");
println("  Query: " + caps.getQueryCapability());
println("  GetDescendants: " + caps.isGetDescendantsSupported());
println("  GetFolderTree: " + caps.isGetFolderTreeSupported());
```

Display some repository info and repository capabilities properties associated with current session

Figure 2.7 shows the output in the Groovy console.

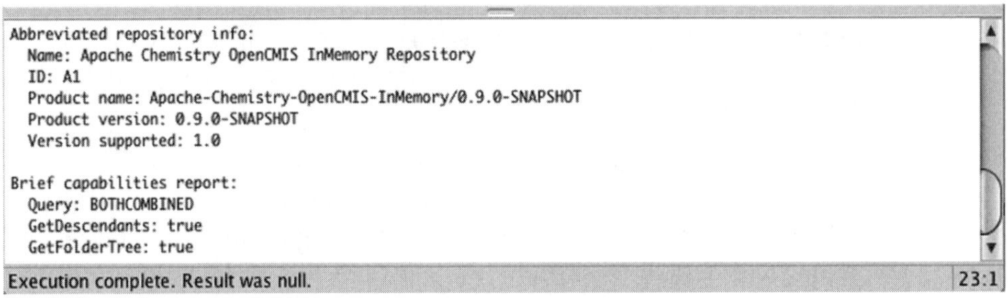

```
Abbreviated repository info:
  Name: Apache Chemistry OpenCMIS InMemory Repository
  ID: A1
  Product name: Apache-Chemistry-OpenCMIS-InMemory/0.9.0-SNAPSHOT
  Product version: 0.9.0-SNAPSHOT
  Version supported: 1.0

Brief capabilities report:
  Query: BOTHCOMBINED
  GetDescendants: true
  GetFolderTree: true
Execution complete. Result was null.                                23:1
```

Figure 2.7 Groovy console output for the getRepositoryInfo code example

As you can see, the OpenCMIS API makes parsing this information trivial. If you were doing this without Chemistry, you'd need to parse the raw XML response into your own structure of values either manually or with a library like JAXB (Java Architecture for XML Binding). For a discussion of what bindings are available and what the XML schema looks like for each, have a look at chapter 11.

2.3 Folders

In this section, we'll cover CMIS folders at the highest level: what they do, what they look like, and how they're related to each other and to documents.

2.3.1 *The role of folders*

Folders in CMIS are much like folders in filesystems that you're already using from day to day. Every CMIS repository must have at least one folder, the *root folder*, as you can see in figure 2.8. When you retrieve the repository info, you'll see there's always a root folder ID present. This is the starting point that clients must always use if they're doing folder navigation.

The important rule to remember with CMIS folders is that every folder must have one, and only one, parent folder. The only exception is the root folder. You can think of the root folder's parent as the repository that hosts it, even though technically CMIS root folders are parentless—that's the only attribute (aside from their place at the top of the folder hierarchy) that makes them unique among all of the other folders. All folders (like their filesystem equivalents) have an associated path, as do all CMIS objects that are contained in folders. (We'll talk more about the path properties of CMIS objects in part 2 of the book.)

Also note that every base CMIS object type has a unique ID defined by the specification. For folders the ID is `cmis:folder`. When you see the name of an object type with the `cmis:` prefix, you'll know that this is an object type that's defined in the CMIS specification's object model. We'll talk a lot more about the base object types when we get to chapter 4.

> **SPEC REFERENCE: FOLDERS** To see the full normative definition of CMIS folders, including all of their attributes, see section 2.1.5 of the CMIS 1.0 specification. (See appendix E for references.)

CMIS Workbench has a simple, built-in folder navigation feature as well. If you recall from your exercises in chapter 1, when you first connect to a repository, you see the folders and documents contained in the root folder displayed in the left-most pane. But it only shows a flat list at one level. If you want to see it presented as a hierarchy, you'll have to move on to the next section, where you'll write some code to display the entire folder hierarchy from your InMemory server.

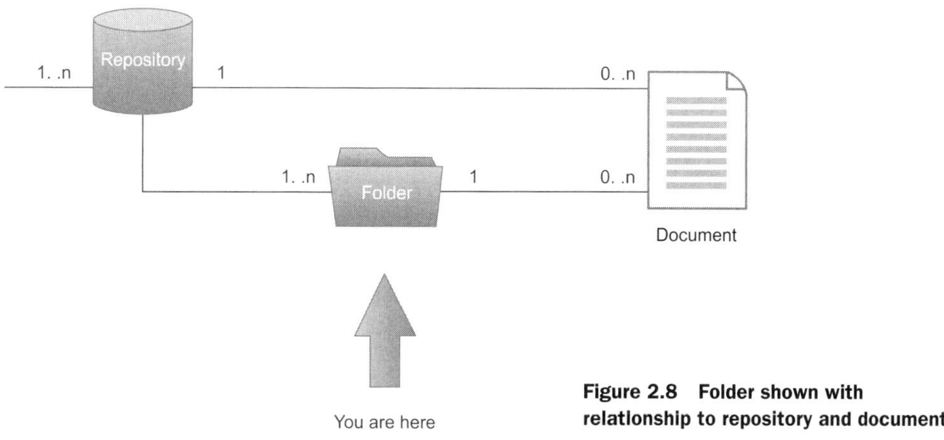

Figure 2.8 Folder shown with relationship to repository and document

2.3.2 *Try it—folder navigation*

For listing 2.2, we'll go back to the CMIS Workbench Groovy console view again. This time you'll use the CMIS folder's `getDescendants` function. After making the call, you'll recursively iterate through the results, dumping them to the console output window using spaces to indent each level you traverse.

Listing 2.2 `getDescendants` code example

```
import org.apache.chemistry.opencmis.commons.*
import org.apache.chemistry.opencmis.commons.data.*
import org.apache.chemistry.opencmis.commons.enums.*
import org.apache.chemistry.opencmis.client.api.*

RepositoryInfo info = session.getRepositoryInfo();
RepositoryCapabilities caps =
  session.getRepositoryInfo().getCapabilities();
Folder rootFolder = session.getRootFolder();

if (!caps.isGetDescendantsSupported()) {
    println("n Warning: getDescendants " +
            "not supported in this repository");
} else {
    println("ngetDescendants " +
            "is supported on this repository.");

    println("nDescendants of " +
      rootFolder.getName() + " : ");
    for (t in rootFolder.getDescendants(-1)) {
        printTree(t , "");
    }
}

private static void printTree(Tree<FileableCmisObject> tree,
       String tab) {
    println(tab + "Descendant "+ tree.getItem().getName());
    for (t in tree.getChildren()) {
        printTree(t, tab + "  ");
    }
}
```

There's only one root per CMIS repository.

The -l tells the method to return an unlimited depth of descendants.

The output for this exercise is shown in figure 2.9.

Note that in addition to the `getDescendants` function you used, CMIS contains a full suite of other navigation-related functions for you to explore. We'll touch on all of these navigation functions in more detail in later chapters, but the full list is as follows:

- `getChildren()`—Gets only the direct containees of a folder
- `getDescendants()`—Gets the containees of a folder and all of their children to a specified depth
- `getFolderTree()`—Gets the set of descendant folder objects contained in the specified folder
- `getFolderParent()`—Gets the parent folder object for the specified folder
- `getObjectParents()`—Gets the parent folder(s) for the specified nonfolder object

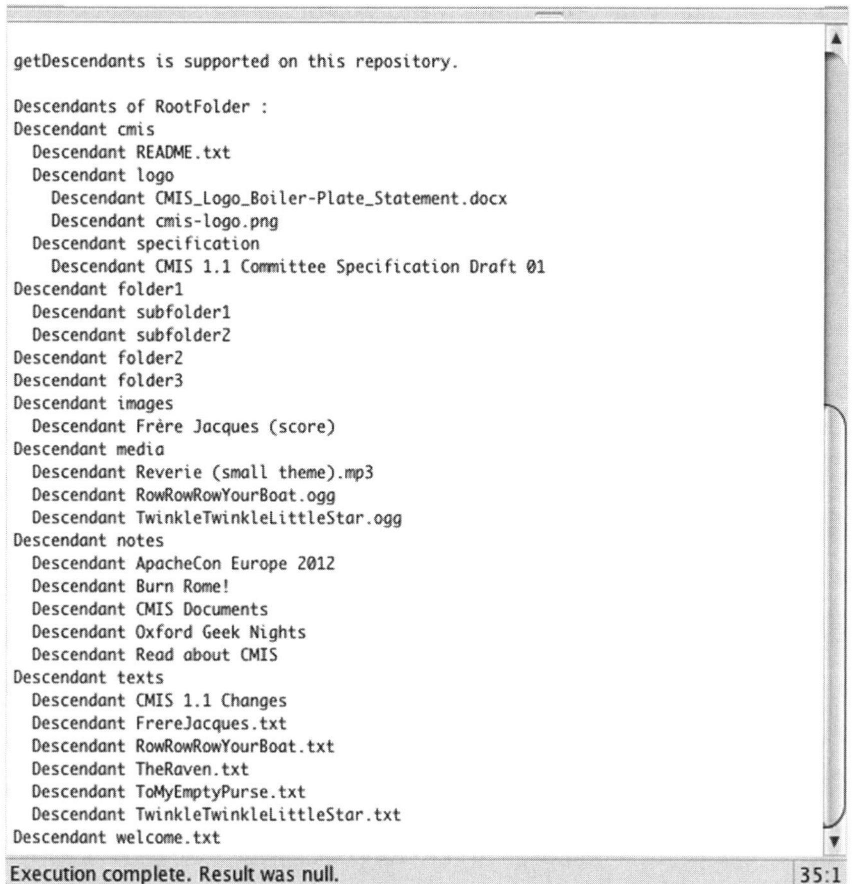

getDescendants is supported on this repository.

Descendants of RootFolder :
Descendant cmis
Descendant README.txt
Descendant logo
Descendant CMIS_Logo_Boiler-Plate_Statement.docx
Descendant cmis-logo.png
Descendant specification
Descendant CMIS 1.1 Committee Specification Draft 01
Descendant folder1
Descendant subfolder1
Descendant subfolder2
Descendant folder2
Descendant folder3
Descendant images
Descendant Frère Jacques (score)
Descendant media
Descendant Reverie (small theme).mp3
Descendant RowRowRowYourBoat.ogg
Descendant TwinkleTwinkleLittleStar.ogg
Descendant notes
Descendant ApacheCon Europe 2012
Descendant Burn Rome!
Descendant CMIS Documents
Descendant Oxford Geek Nights
Descendant Read about CMIS
Descendant texts
Descendant CMIS 1.1 Changes
Descendant FrereJacques.txt
Descendant RowRowRowYourBoat.txt
Descendant TheRaven.txt
Descendant ToMyEmptyPurse.txt
Descendant TwinkleTwinkleLittleStar.txt
Descendant welcome.txt
Execution complete. Result was null.
35:1

Figure 2.9 Groovy console output—dumping the folder and document hierarchy

2.4 Documents

Moving right along in our tour of the domain model, we've arrived at *document*. Figure 2.10 gives you a quick high-level picture of where we are now and how documents fit into the larger picture.

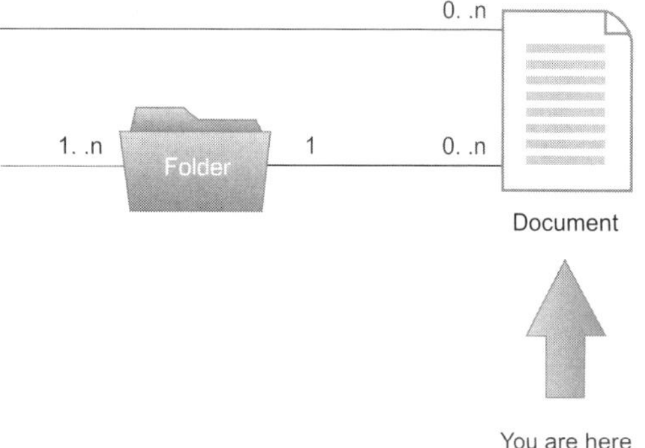

Figure 2.10 Documents can be contained in folders or unfiled children of a repository. Unfiled documents are retrieved from the repository's "unfiled documents" collection.

In CMIS, documents are where the rubber meets the road. Without them, there wouldn't be much point in having a document management system, would there? This section will get you familiar with the CMIS document type at an introductory level.

We'll also introduce the subject of properties, which are present on all of the other CMIS object types, like folders, but are used more extensively on documents. This is why we waited until now to spring them on you. After we've covered the basics, we'll pop back into the CMIS Workbench to write some more code, and then create, file, and retrieve documents and their properties. Here we go!

2.4.1 The role of documents

To properly explain the role of documents, we'll switch to a different perspective. Figure 2.11 shows an object model view that describes the base `cmis:object` common to all of the objects you'll see in CMIS. As an extension to this base type, you see `cmis:document` (which is the CMIS ID for this object type) with its content stream indicated as a contained subobject. Keep in mind that there's a lot more to `cmis:document` than just being an additional content stream. We'll cover all of those details in later chapters, but this is all you need to be aware of for now.

A WORD ABOUT CMIS:OBJECT In this book (as well as in the 1.1 specification), you'll see some mention of `cmis:object` as if there were a base class for all of the five base CMIS object types. Technically speaking, the specification doesn't call out the existence of such a base class. But the CMIS Technical Committee has made an effort to keep a certain key set of properties common to all CMIS objects (see section 2.4.2) so that in object-oriented (OO) language bindings, they could be modeled as if they were from a common parent (object). Whether you choose to think of all of the base objects as sharing these properties, or inheriting them, the end result is the same.

SPEC REFERENCE: CMIS OBJECT MODELS If you'd like to see a much more detailed model type view of all of the CMIS object types, see section 2.1 (Data Model) in the CMIS 1.1 specification. (See appendix E for references).

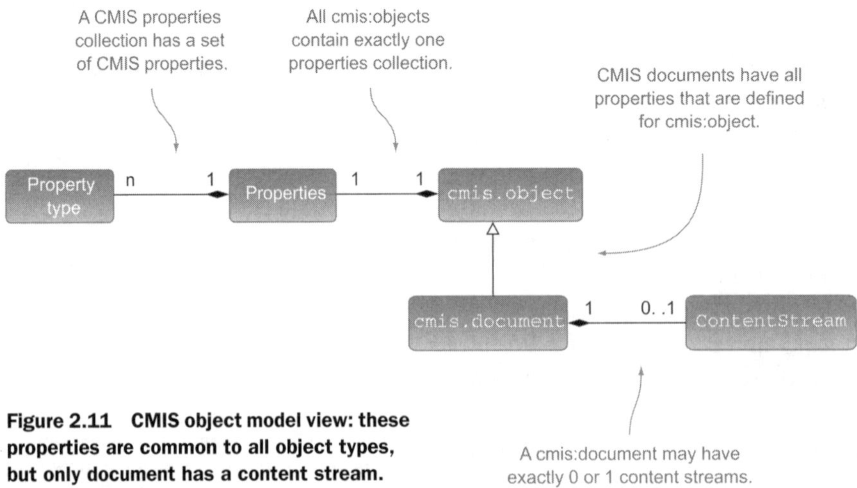

Figure 2.11 CMIS object model view: these properties are common to all object types, but only document has a content stream.

2.4.2 *Properties*

As you can see in figure 2.11, all CMIS objects have properties. We'll get into much more detail about types in chapter 4, but one of the things that distinguishes one object type from another is the specific properties that are defined for that type. But before we can talk about the properties on documents, we first need to take a short diversion and talk about the properties that are common to all CMIS object types.

PROPERTIES COMMON TO ALL CMIS 1.0 OBJECT TYPES

These are the properties that you'll find on all CMIS object types, regardless of their base type. For a given repository, there may be many more custom properties in addition to these:

- `cmis:name` (String)—The name of this object.
- `cmis:objectId` (ID)—The opaque identifier for this object. It's unique among all other objects in this repository.
- `cmis:baseTypeId` (ID)—The opaque identifier for the base type of this object. We'll cover types in chapter 4.
- `cmis:objectTypeId` (ID)—The opaque identifier for this object's type.
- `cmis:createdBy` (String)—The name of the user that created this object in this repository.
- `cmis:creationDate` (DateTime)—The date and time when this object was created.
- `cmis:lastModifiedBy` (String)—The name of the user who last modified this object.
- `cmis:lastModificationDate` (DateTime)—The date and time this object was last modified.
- `cmis:changeToken` (String)—An opaque token used to identify a point in the lifecycle of this object. We'll talk more about these tokens in chapter 8.

Why are these identifiers opaque?

You probably noticed that the identifiers in the list of common object types aren't only identifiers, they're *opaque identifiers*. When something is described as opaque, it means it should be treated as if you can't tell what's in it.

For example, if we showed you an identifier that looked like "jeff-potts-tulsa-1.2," you might try to make some sense of that string. You might assume the identifier is talking about something having to do with a person named "Jeff Potts" who has a relationship to a city named "Tulsa" and that maybe this is version 1.2 of that object. You might even write some code that implements those assumptions. But in CMIS, when you see that something is opaque, you must avoid the temptation to write code that depends on an understanding of how that particular identifier is constructed, because the repository is free to change how it implements opaque identifiers at any time.

PROPERTIES COMMON TO ALL CMIS 1.0 DOCUMENTS

These are all of the properties that are both unique to and present on all CMIS 1.0 documents (remember that all of the properties common to all objects are also common to documents):

- `cmis:isImmutable` (Boolean)—Indicates the CMIS service will throw an exception on an attempt to modify this object.
- `cmis:isLatestVersion` (Boolean)—Indicates whether this object is the latest version of its version series. We'll talk more about versions in chapter 3.
- `cmis:isMajorVersion` (Boolean)—Indicates whether this object is a major version (`true`) or minor (`false`).
- `cmis:isLatestMajorVersion` (Boolean)—Indicates whether this document is the latest major version. The latest major version has special significance in some repositories.
- `cmis:versionLabel` (String)—The string rendering of the document's version information. For example, 1.5 would indicate major version 1 and minor version 5.
- `cmis:versionSeriesId` (ID)—The opaque identifier of this object's version series. We'll look more at version series objects in chapter 3.
- `cmis:isVersionSeriesCheckedOut` (Boolean)—Indicates whether this document is currently in a checked-out state.
- `cmis:versionSeriesCheckedOutBy` (String)—The name of the user that performed the checkout operation on this document.
- `cmis:versionSeriesCheckedOutId` (ID)—An opaque identifier of the Private Working Copy (PWC) for this object's version series. More on PWC objects in chapter 3.
- `cmis:checkinComment` (String)—The comment associated with this version of the document.
- `cmis:contentStreamLength` (Integer)—The length of this document's associated content stream, if one is present.
- `cmis:contentStreamMimeType` (String)—The MIME type of the content stream associated with this document.
- `cmis:contentStreamFileName` (String)—The name of the file stored in this document's content stream, if present.
- `cmis:contentStreamId` (ID)—The opaque identifier of this document's content stream, if present.

You may notice that all of these additional properties deal with versioning and content stream information. In later chapters, when we explore the other types of base CMIS object types, you'll see that they each have their own set of object-type-specific properties.

A FEW MORE BASIC RULES ABOUT PROPERTIES

A CMIS property may hold zero, one, or more typed data value(s), and each property may be single- or multivalued. Single-valued properties contain (drum roll here) a single data value, and multivalued properties contain an ordered list of data values of the same type. The ordering in a multivalued property should be preserved by the repository, but this isn't guaranteed.

Any property (single- or multivalued) can be in a not-set state, but the CMIS specification doesn't support a null property value.

If a multivalued property is set, it must contain a non-empty list of individual values. Each individual value in the list must have a value (that is, it can't be not set), and each of those values must be of the same type, conforming to its multivalued property's type. In other words, a multivalued property is either set or not set in its entirety.

Individual values of multivalued properties must be set to hold a position in the list of values. Empty lists of values are not allowed, nor are sparse lists. For example, you may not have a sparse string list property with values `{"a," "b," null, "c"}`, but a string list with values `{"a," "b," ""}` would be OK, because for strings an empty string is a set value distinct from null.

BASE PROPERTY DATA TYPES

All CMIS properties are typed and must be one of the eight base property data types listed in the specification. Table 2.1 shows these base property types and their corresponding OpenCMIS interface names. All of the OpenCMIS property interfaces are in the `org.apache.chemistry.opencmis.commons.data` package, and all inherit the `org.apache.chemistry.opencmis.client.api.Property` interface.

Table 2.1 Eight base property data types supported by CMIS and OpenCMIS

CMIS property	Java data type	OpenCMIS interface
`string`	`java.lang.String`	`PropertyString`
`boolean`	`java.lang.Boolean`	`PropertyBoolean`
`integer`	`java.math.BigInteger`	`PropertyInteger`
`decimal`	`java.math.BigDecimal`	`PropertyDecimal`
`datetime`	`java.util.Gregorian-Calendar`	`PropertyDateTime`
`id`	`java.lang.String`	`PropertyId`
`html`	`java.lang.String`	`PropertyHtml`
`uri`	`java.lang.String`	`PropertyUri`

RULES TO BE AWARE OF WHEN DEALING WITH HTML, ID, AND URI PROPERTIES

- An `html` property value can be a fragment and need not be valid. For example, the following string isn't completely valid from an HTML standpoint, but it's allowed to be stored in an `html` property: `<html><body>My body is truncated.`
- A `uri` value may or may not be checked by the repository.
- An `id` value doesn't need to be a valid ID in the repository.

CUSTOM PROPERTIES

Although we'll cover this in much more detail in chapter 4, it's worth mentioning that the types we've shown you so far are only the properties that are defined by CMIS for all documents. These properties are common to any ECM system. The flexible thing about ECM systems and about CMIS is that there can be many different types of documents with any number of custom properties defined on them. When we get into part 2 of the book and start building a custom CMIS music management application, we'll define custom properties that are specific to music MIME types. You'll see some of the powerful things you can do with these properties when we talk about Query in chapter 5.

2.4.3 *Try it—list a document's properties*

It's time now to go back to the Groovy console in CMIS Workbench to write some code. This time you'll find the first document object in the root folder and list all of its system properties.

Listing 2.3 List the system (`cmis:xxx`) properties for the first document we find.

```
import org.apache.chemistry.opencmis.commons.*
import org.apache.chemistry.opencmis.commons.data.*
import org.apache.chemistry.opencmis.commons.enums.*
import org.apache.chemistry.opencmis.client.api.*

// obtain the root folder object
Folder rootFolder = session.getRootFolder();
foundCount = 0;

for (t in rootFolder.getChildren()) {
  // until we find an object that is a doc type or subtype
  if (t instanceof Document) {
    println("name:" + t.getName());
    foundCount += 1;
    List<Property<?>> props = t.getProperties();

    // list all of the system properties that is those
    // that begin with the cmis: prefix we listed earlier
    for (p in props) {
      if (p.getId().startsWith("cmis:")) {
        println("   " + p.getDefinition().getId()
            + "=" + p.getValuesAsString());
      }
    }
  }
```

```
    if (foundCount > 0) {
      break;    // we can stop after the first one is found
    }
  }
```

Copy the code from listing 2.3 into your Groovy console and give it a run. Figure 2.12 shows the output from CMIS Workbench when it's connected to the OpenCMIS InMemory Repository with the default sample data loaded. The output from the run is always displayed in the lower window.

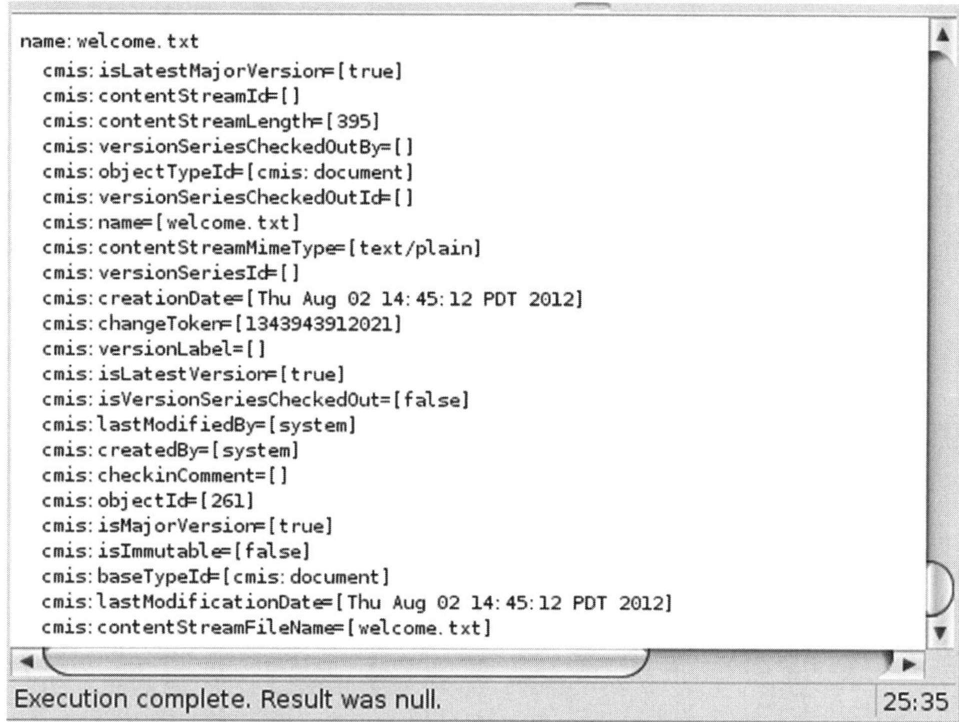

Figure 2.12 Output from default data in the document property exercise

> **USING THE GROOVY CONSOLE IN WORKBENCH** Don't forget that every time you use the session object in the Groovy console, you're sharing the session object from the CMIS Workbench session. If the CMIS Workbench isn't connected to a live server, your session object in the console isn't going to do you much good.

2.4.4 Content streams

Now that we've covered all of the properties of a document, we can finally get to the document itself. As you can see in figure 2.13, there can be either 0 or 1 associated content streams with every CMIS document. This is what's sometimes referred to as

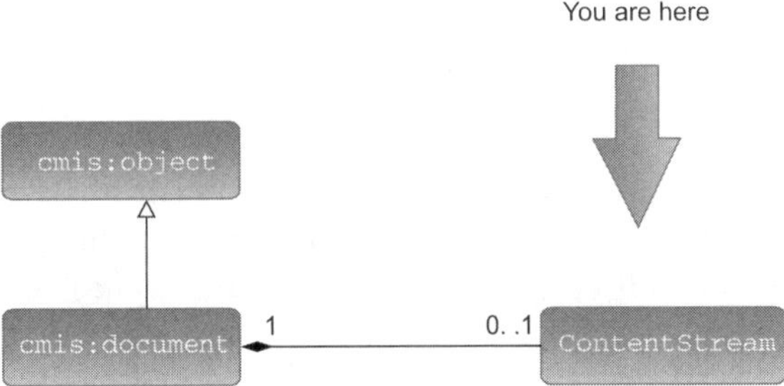

Figure 2.13 A content stream of 0 or 1 per document is accessible via CMIS.

the payload of the document. It might be a binary or text file of any MIME type and of any size, depending on your repository limitations. This is one of a handful of things that make a document special in CMIS and, more generally, special in all ECM systems.

2.4.5 Try it—retrieve a document's content stream

In this exercise, you'll retrieve a text document from your test InMemory server and inspect its contents. Because the InMemory server starts up with some test data, you'll search for the first text document that you find in the root folder, and then retrieve its content stream, as shown in listing 2.4 (the helper method that gets the contents of a stream is taken from the "OpenCMIS Client API Developer's Guide" at http://chemistry.apache.org/java/developing/guide.html). Finally, so you have something to show for all of this, you'll display the first line of the document's stream text to the console.

Listing 2.4 Retrieving a document's content stream and stream properties

```
import org.apache.chemistry.opencmis.commons.*
import org.apache.chemistry.opencmis.commons.data.*
import org.apache.chemistry.opencmis.commons.enums.*
import org.apache.chemistry.opencmis.client.api.*

// obtain the root folder object
Folder rootFolder = session.getRootFolder();
count = 0

// iterate through the children
for (t in rootFolder.getChildren()) {
   if (t.getBaseTypeId().equals(BaseTypeId.CMIS_DOCUMENT)) {
      count +=1;
      println("name:" + t.getName());
      Document d = (Document) t;
      String mimeType = d.getContentStreamMimeType();
      if ((mimeType != null) && (d.getContentStreamLength() > 0)) {
         if (mimeType.startsWith("text")) {
            println("Name of doc:" + d.getName());
            println("FileName:" +
              d.getContentStreamFileName());
            println("Stream length:" +
              d.getContentStreamLength());
```

Filter out only document objects, because folders won't have content streams.

Verify that MIME type is text so you can display it as a string.

Note that the document's name and content stream's filename don't have to be the same.

```
            String fullStream =
              getContentAsString(d.getContentStream());
            println("nFirst line of stream:n->" +
              fullStream.substring(0, fullStream.indexOf("n")));
          }
        }
      }
      if (count > 0) {
         break; // we can stop after the first one is found
      }
   }
   private static String getContentAsString(ContentStream stream)
       throws IOException {
       StringBuilder sb = new StringBuilder();
       Reader reader = new InputStreamReader(stream.getStream(),"UTF-8");

       try {
           final char[] buffer = new char[4 * 1024];
           int b;
           while (true) {
               b = reader.read(buffer, 0, buffer.length);
               if (b > 0) {
                   sb.append(buffer, 0, b);
               } else if (b == -1) {
                   break;
               }
           }
       } finally {
           reader.close();
       }
       return sb.toString();
   }
```

This helper method gets the contents of a stream.

The output of this code is shown in figure 2.14.

```
name:welcome.txt
Name of doc:welcome.txt
FileName:welcome.txt
Stream length:395

First line of stream:
->Welcome to CMIS and Apache Chemistry!
```

Figure 2.14 Output of code for retrieving a document's content stream

2.5 The item object type (version 1.1)

You're probably thinking, "Hey, where did this CMIS item object type come from anyway? I don't remember seeing this in the main diagram." That's because CMIS item (`cmis:item`) is new to CMIS version 1.1, so we decided to leave it until you understood the document basics. It turns out that many CMIS repositories have object types whose instances are fileable, like documents, but that are much less heavyweight. For example, they might not have any content streams associated with them, and they might not be versionable either. Don't worry, we'll talk about versioning in chapter 3.

In CMIS 1.1, we created a brand-new, top-level type named *item* that would be the base type for all objects that have properties but aren't documents. At the most basic level, you can think of an item as a fileable collection of properties or even a complex object type. For example, suppose you want to store some configuration information for your application in the CMIS repository. You might choose to persist the application configuration as a set of key-value pairs that would be defined as properties on an object type that extends `cmis:item`.

> **SPEC REFERENCE: CMIS ITEM** For a detailed list of CMIS item's properties and attributes, see section 2.1.8 of the CMIS 1.1 specification. (See appendix E for references.)

2.6 Summary

In this chapter, you were introduced to the key high-level concepts in a CMIS system: the service, repository, folder (`cmis:folder`), document (`cmis:document`), and item (`cmis:item`), and each one's respective properties. We even sprinkled in a little taste of the bindings. You used the OpenCMIS API to discover a repository's capabilities, browse its folder hierarchy, and retrieve its document's properties and content streams. Along the way, you were given your first peek at the object model for CMIS and you saw how all CMIS object types share a common set of properties. In later chapters, we'll fill out these images you now have in your head with more details. These concepts will be your guideposts as you progress through the rest of part 1. By the time you have completed the next three chapters, you should have a good general understanding of CMIS, enough to dive into part 2 and build a useful (and we hope fun) application.

3 Creating, updating, and deleting objects with CMIS

This chapter covers

- Creating folders
- Creating documents with and without content
- Updating properties on objects
- Checking content into and out of the repository
- Creating versions of documents
- Deleting objects

In the previous two chapters, you've learned how to access a CMIS repository as well as the objects contained within it, but you haven't made any changes to those objects and you haven't created new objects. You'll learn how to do that in this chapter. As in previous chapters, you'll continue using the CMIS Workbench to run Groovy code, but now you'll create, update, version, and delete objects in the repository.

3.1 Creating objects

Traversing the folder structure in the repository and reading documents and their properties is all well and good, but at some point you'll need to create new objects. Let's look at how to create the two objects you know about so far: folders and documents. You'll learn how to create instances of other objects in the CMIS domain model in later chapters.

3.1.1 Requirements for creating an object

At a minimum, a CMIS server will always need two pieces of information from you in order to create a new object: the name of the object and the type of object to create. Do you remember the list of properties common to all CMIS objects that was provided in chapter 2? If so, you may recognize the name and object type from the list:

- `cmis:name` (String)—The name of this object
- `cmis:objectTypeId` (ID)—The opaque identifier for this object's type

Creating a new object is a matter of calling the appropriate method and passing in these two properties with the appropriate values.

3.1.2 Try it—create a folder

Let's create a new folder called *my first folder* in the root of the InMemory Repository. You saw in the previous chapter how to grab an instance of the root folder using `session.getRootFolder`. That returns a folder object. If you look at the Javadoc for the folder interface, you'll see a `createFolder` method. In fact, you'll see two, but here you'll use the one that only needs a properties map.

To create the folder, you first need a handle to the folder that will contain the new folder. Then you set up a properties map with the name and object type ID and pass the properties to the `createFolder` method, as shown in the next listing.

Listing 3.1 Creating a folder with Groovy

```
def rootFolder = session.rootFolder          <— You saw this in chapter 2

// create a map of properties
def props = ['cmis:objectTypeId': 'cmis:folder',
             'cmis:name' : 'my first folder']

def someFolder = rootFolder.createFolder(props)

println("Folder created!")
println("id:" + someFolder.id)
println("name:" + someFolder.name)
```

Annotations: **Set up a map to hold the properties** — **Add object type and name to the map** — **Pass properties to the createFolder method**

After running this code in the Groovy Console, you should be able to flip back over to the CMIS Workbench, refresh the root folder listing by clicking Go, and see your new folder in the list, as shown in figure 3.1.

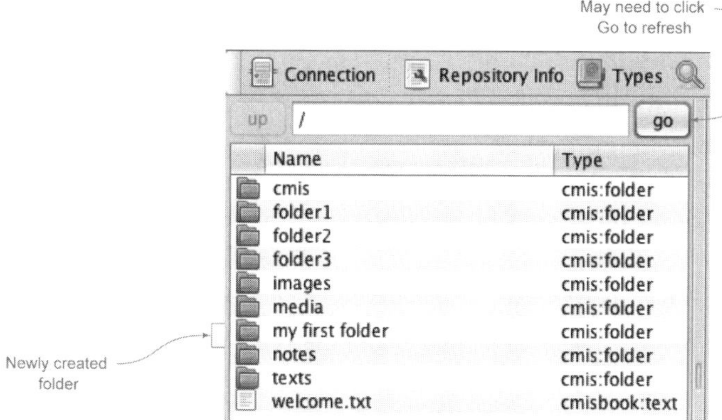

Figure 3.1 The new folder shows up after you run the `createFolder` code in the Groovy console.

3.1.3 *Things to think about when creating folders*

Creating a folder is a straightforward process. Still, we should review a few things you might want to think about. We'll do that in the following sections.

FOLDERS—CREATED CONTEXTUALLY

In the previous example, you saw that the `createFolder` method was called on the `rootFolder` object. Folders are created contextually. In other words, CMIS has to know where to create the new folder.

OBJECT TYPE

In listing 3.1, you saw that `cmis:folder` was used as the object type ID. Many CMIS repositories have types that inherit from `cmis:folder`. These might be out-of-the-box types or even types that you've defined to make the schema match your specific business requirements. Any type that inherits from `cmis:folder` can be specified.

FOLDER NAME

The definition of what constitutes an allowable folder name is server-specific. It's usually nearly identical to what you would expect when creating folders and files in a filesystem.

ARE YOU ALLOWED TO CREATE A FOLDER?

In listing 3.1, you didn't check to see whether or not you were allowed to create a folder in the root folder—you tried to create it and it worked. As you work through the rest of this book you'll come across several actions that may not always be possible due to limitations of the underlying server, permissions, or the state of an object.

You can code defensively by checking to see if you're allowed to do something before you do it. In this case, there's an allowable action called `CAN_CREATE_FOLDER`. If you wanted to, you could make your `createFolder` call conditional on the presence of that allowable action, as follows:

```
if (Action.CAN_CREATE_FOLDER in
    rootFolder.allowableActions.allowableActions) {
    ...set up the properties, create the folder, etc.
}
```

You'll see more examples of allowable actions later on in the book.

3.1.4 Try it—create a document

Creating documents isn't much different from creating folders. You still need the name and object type at a minimum.

In this section, you'll learn how to create documents. First you'll create documents that don't have content, and then you'll create documents using files on your local filesystem.

The simplest example is to create a document that doesn't have content (a file) associated with it. When you do that, it looks like you're creating a folder. The only difference is the object type you're passing in, as shown next.

Listing 3.2 Creating a document that has no content looks much like creating a folder.

```
def someFolder = session.getObjectByPath('/my first folder')

// create a map of properties
def props = ['cmis:objectTypeId': 'cmis:document',
             'cmis:name' : 'my test doc']

def someDoc = someFolder.createDocument(props, null, null)

println("Doc created!")
println("id:" + someDoc.id)
println("name:" + someDoc.name)
```

Create document in folder you created earlier

Specify 'cmis:document' for object type ID

Pass in null as content stream to create a document with no content; second null is the versioning state

Now you should be able to navigate into the folder you created earlier and see the newly created document, as shown in figure 3.2.

The document you created doesn't have any content, and there are times when you might need to create a document that includes a file. For example, a `Company` or an `Employee` object might only have metadata associated with it and no file content. In fact, in chapter 2 you learned that CMIS 1.1 includes a new type called `cmis:item` that can be used specifically for this purpose. If you were using CMIS 1.1, you might choose to create your `Company` or `Employee` objects as instances of `cmis:item` instead of instances of `cmis:document`.

Figure 3.2 The newly created document sitting in the folder you created earlier

Not all repositories support contentless document objects

Some repositories require document instances to always have a content stream. For example, the OpenCMIS InMemory Repository and Alfresco don't require content streams, but SharePoint does. You can check whether or not your repository requires documents to have a content stream by inspecting the type definition for `cmis:document`.

You'll learn about type definitions in chapter 4, but for now just know that the `cmis:document` type definition has an attribute called `contentStreamAllowed`. If the value of the attribute is `required`, then all instances of a document must have a content stream. Of course, you could work around this by creating a content stream with an empty string.

If you're developing an application that's exclusively made up of contentless objects, you might need to rethink your decision to use a content repository to persist your data. More often, most of your objects will have files associated with them, so let's see how to create a document that includes a file.

The key difference is that you have to create a content stream and then pass that to the `createDocument` method. In listing 3.3, you can see a content stream being created from a local file. In this example, it's a PDF.

Listing 3.3 Creating a document with a content stream

```
def someFolder = session.getObjectByPath('/my first folder')

def file = new File('/users/jpotts/Documents/sample/sample-a.pdf')    <-- Set path to point to sample file

def name = file.getName()

def mimetype = 'application/pdf'    <-- Hardcode mimetype

// create a map of properties
def props = ['cmis:objectTypeId': 'cmis:document',
             'cmis:name' : name]

def contentStream = session.getObjectFactory().createContentStream(name,
                                            file.size(),
                                            mimetype,
                                            new FileInputStream(file))
    <-- Instantiate a ContentStream

def someDoc = someFolder.createDocument(props, contentStream, null)    <-- Pass properties and contentStream to createDocument method

println("Doc created!")
println("id:" + someDoc.id)
println("name:" + someDoc.name)
println("length:" + someDoc.contentStreamLength)
```

If you run that code in the Groovy console, you should see the new document in the CMIS Workbench (you may have to re-enter the folder or click Go to refresh the list). If you click the link in the right-hand pane (see figure 3.3), you'll launch the document in its native application.

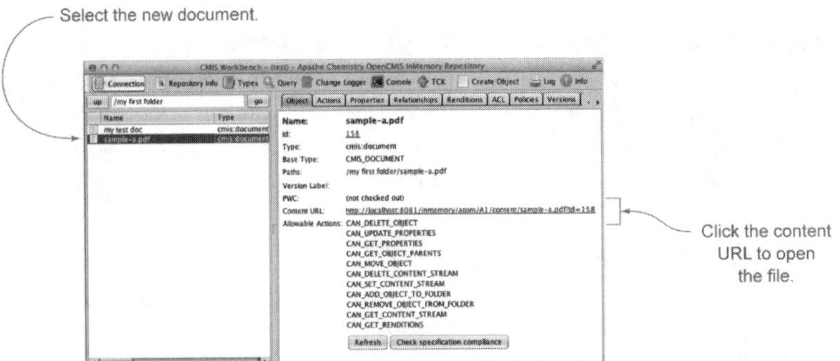

Figure 3.3 After creating a document that has a content stream, you can click the content URL to open the file.

You might be looking at listing 3.3 and thinking, "That seems like a lot of work just to add a file to the repository," and you're absolutely right. There is a shorter way to do it. The CMIS Workbench ships with a set of helper scripts that can be accessed from the Groovy console. The helper scripts include a function called `createDocumentFromFile`, which does the work of figuring out the mimetype, setting up the properties, establishing a `contentStream`, and creating the document. The result, shown next, is much more succinct.

Listing 3.4 Creating a document from a file by using the CMIS helper scripts

```
cmis = new scripts.CMIS(session)                    <-- Load CMIS helper scripts

def someFolder = session.getObjectByPath('/my first folder')

def file = new File('/users/jpotts/Documents/sample/sample-b.pdf')

def someDoc = cmis.createDocumentFromFile(someFolder,
                                          file,
                                          "cmis:document",
                                          null)

println("Doc created!")
println("id:" + someDoc.id)
println("name:" + someDoc.name)
println("length:" + someDoc.contentStreamLength)
```

Use a file with different name from before—InMemory server requires objects in same folder to be uniquely named

Set up properties, mimetype, and contentStream, and create document with a single call

Either way, the result is the same—the document object is created and the local file is uploaded to the repository and set as the content stream on the document object.

Now you know how to create folders and documents, both with and without content. If you stopped here, you could do quite a lot. Got a fileshare full of contracts and legal documents? You could write a script to bulk load those into your company's ECM repository. Or how about an imaging application to feed scanned invoices into the repository (which then might trigger an approval workflow if your repository supports it). That's some decent process automation, and the beauty is that it works regardless of the repository you have now or decide to switch to at some point in the future, because you're coding against an industry-standard API.

> **What other CMIS helper scripts are available?**
>
> You saw how the CMIS helper scripts distributed with the CMIS Workbench can make your Groovy code more succinct. What other shortcuts are available? If you take a look at the source code for the CMIS Workbench, you'll find the Groovy file that defines the CMIS helper scripts in /src/main/resources/scripts/CMIS.groovy. Consult that file for the full list.
>
> These are a few you might be interested in:
>
> - `getObject(id)`,`getFolder(id)`, `getDocument(id)`—Retrieve a CMIS object, folder, or document given its object ID.
> - `printProperties(id)`,`printChildren(id)`,`printRelationships(id)`, `printRenditions(id)`, `printObjectSummary(id)`—Dump information about the object for the ID specified to the console.
> - `createFolder()`, `createTextDocument()`, `createRelationship()`—Shortcut methods for creating documents, folders, and relationships. See the code for the method signatures.
> - `download(id, destination)`—Downloads the file associated with the document represented by the specified ID to the specified destination.
>
> These helper scripts will only work with your code running in the Groovy console. They aren't part of the OpenCMIS API.

3.1.5 *Things to think about when creating documents*

There are a few things you may want to keep in mind when creating documents.

COPYING DOCUMENTS

It's possible to create new document objects using objects that already exist in the repository. The document object has a method called `copy` that takes a target folder as its only argument. If you want to copy sample-b.pdf to another folder called *target folder*, the code would look like the following.

```
def someDoc = session.getObjectByPath("/my first folder/sample-b.pdf")

def targetFolder = session.getObjectByPath("/target folder")

def copiedDoc = someDoc.copy(targetFolder)
```

Grab a reference to the document to copy ...

... and the folder to copy it to (this code assumes the folder exists).

Execute the copy.

Notice that the `copy` method doesn't give you the opportunity to make any changes on the source object, including the name. If you need to do that, use `createDocumentFromSource` instead.

ONLY WORKS WITH THE WEB SERVICES BINDING In CMIS version 1.0, `createDocumentFromSource` isn't supported by the AtomPub binding—it only works when using the Web Services binding. The `copy` method relies on `createDocumentFromSource`. Unfortunately, this is one of the differences that exist between the two bindings. You'll learn more about bindings later in the book. If you can't wait to try out the Web Services binding, click the Connection button, select the Web Services binding, and specify http://localhost:8080/chemistry/services/DiscoveryService as the service URL.

IS A PARENT FOLDER ALWAYS REQUIRED?

In the examples you've seen so far, you've been calling the `createDocument` method on the folder object where the document is to be stored. But some ECM repositories support the notion of *unfiled* documents. These documents are free-floating—they don't live in a folder. To figure out whether or not your repository supports unfiled documents, you can query its capabilities, as follows:

```
session.repositoryInfo.capabilities.unfilingSupported
```

If this returns `true` and you need to create an unfiled document object, use the `createDocument` method on `session` instead of `folder` and pass in null as the folder ID.

ARE YOU ALLOWED?

As you saw earlier when creating folder objects, the repository might not always allow you to create a new document. Similar to `Action.CAN_CREATE_FOLDER`, you can check the folder's allowable actions for `Action.CAN_CREATE_DOCUMENT` before attempting to create a document. Here's an example:

```
if (Action.CAN_CREATE_DOCUMENT in
    someFolder.allowableActions.allowableActions) {
    ...set up the properties, create the folder, etc.
}
```

Now that you know how to create objects, it's time to learn how to make changes to them after they've been created. That's where we're headed next.

3.2 Updating objects

Some content-centric applications are used only for archival purposes—they never need to change the documents once they're stored in the repository. Most often, though, your content application will need to make updates to objects in the repository.

In the previous section, you saw that a document object has both metadata and a content stream. When updating objects, you can update only the properties, only the content, or both.

Let's look at examples of both of these types of updates. In the first example, you'll see how to change the name of one of the sample documents you created earlier. In the second, you'll see how to update the content stream.

3.2.1 Try it—rename a document or a folder

The name of an object is stored in a property called `cmis:name`. To rename an object, all you have to do is provide a new value for that property. Let's change the name of sample-a.pdf to sample-c.pdf. If you no longer have a document called sample-a.pdf, no problem. You should be able to use what you learned in the previous section to create one using code, or you can create one using the CMIS Workbench.

Recall from section 3.1.4 that one of the things you provided when creating a document was a properties map. To change the name of a document, you'll provide a map of the properties you want to update, and then call `updateProperties`, as shown in the next listing.

Listing 3.5 Renaming a document by updating its `cmis:name` property

```
def someDoc = session.getObjectByPath("/my first folder/sample-a.pdf")
println("Before: " + someDoc.name)
def props = ['cmis:name': 'sample-c.pdf']
someDoc.updateProperties(props, true)
println("After: " + someDoc.name)
```

Setting refresh to true refreshes the object so updated values are in object instance

That's it. Now you know how to rename a document. You can use this approach to change any property value.

> **GET DEFENSIVE** Just like in the earlier creation examples, you can add a defensive check (`Action.CAN_UPDATE_PROPERTIES`) before doing the update if you want to. Defensive checks of the allowable actions allow you to not only head off error messages before they are thrown, but also to adapt the user interface based on what the server will allow. Hiding invalid choices from users is a good usability practice.

3.2.2 Try it—update the content stream

You've renamed the PDF sample-a.pdf to sample-c.pdf. But if you open the file associated with that document, it's still sample-a content, as shown in figure 3.4.

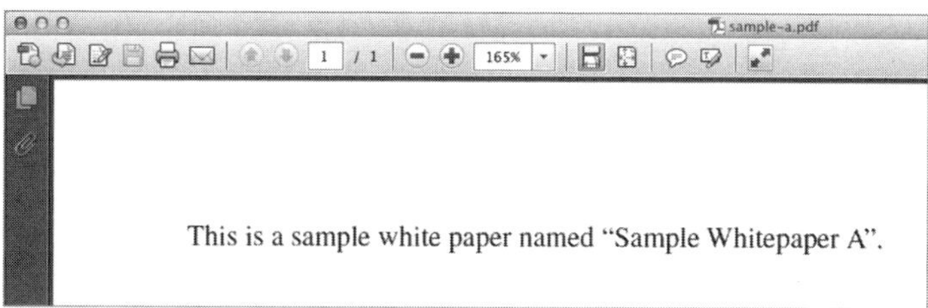

Figure 3.4 You renamed the sample-a.pdf document to sample-c.pdf, but it still contains the original file content.

You can fix that by updating the content stream with a file from the local filesystem called sample-c.pdf.

This works much like creating a document. You need to set up a content stream and then call `setContentStream` on an existing document. This is shown in the following listing.

Listing 3.6 Updating the content stream of a document with a local file

```
def someDoc = session.getObjectByPath("/my first folder/sample-c.pdf")

def file = new File('/users/jpotts/Documents/sample/sample-c.pdf')    <- Grab existing document

def name = file.getName()

def mimetype = 'application/pdf'

def contentStream = session.getObjectFactory().createContentStream(name,
                                                file.size(),
                                                mimetype,
                                                new FileInputStream(file))
                                                                      <- Set up contentStream

someDoc.setContentStream(contentStream, true, true)                   <- Update content stream

println("Name:  " + someDoc.name)
println("Length:  " + someDoc.contentStreamLength)
```

When you update the content stream, the first flag tells the method to overwrite the existing stream. If the document already has a content stream set, this must be set to `true`. The second flag tells it to refresh the object, which is the same concept you saw when updating the properties.

Now when you open the PDF associated with sample-c.pdf, it will contain the content from the sample-c.pdf file, as shown in figure 3.5.

Excellent. You can now change the content stream on a document when you need to update its content.

There's an important caveat related to setting content streams. Different ECM repositories have different rules concerning when content streams can be updated. If you look at your repository's capabilities, you'll see that the InMemory Repository allows content stream updates any time (as shown in figure 3.6).

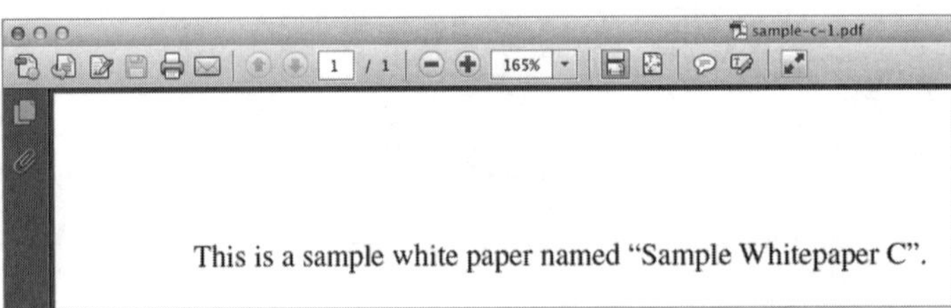

Figure 3.5 The sample-c.pdf document now contains the content from the local file named sample-c.pdf.

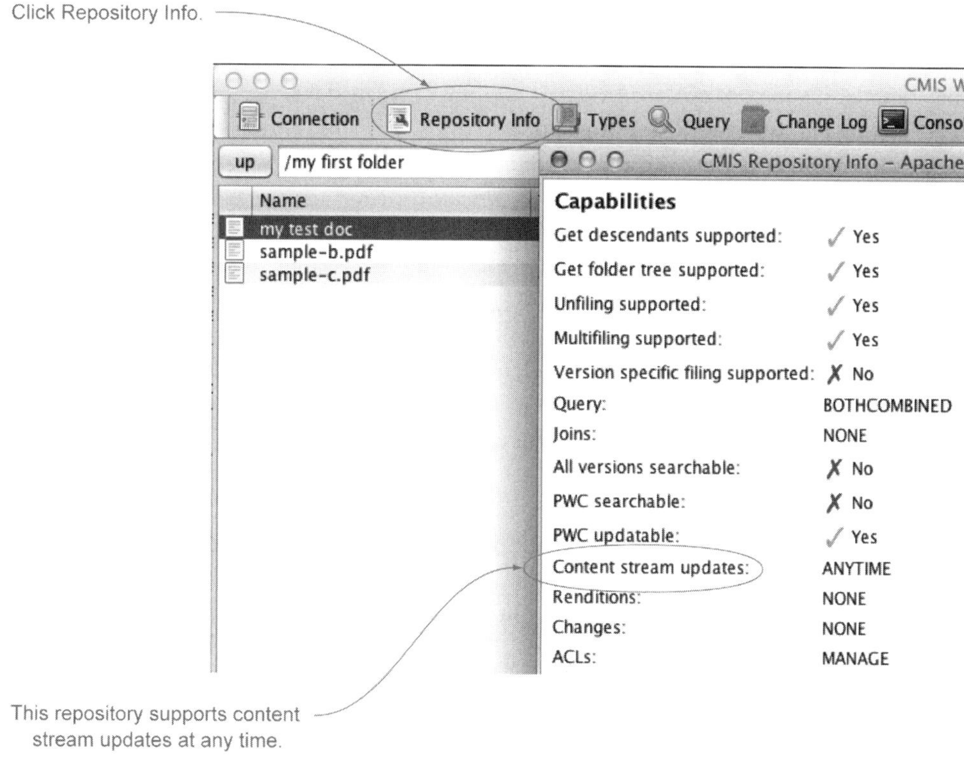

Figure 3.6 Some repositories don't always allow content stream updates, but the InMemory Repository allows them at any time.

You can also perform this check through code, as follows:

```
session.repositoryInfo.capabilities.contentStreamUpdatesCapability
```

The other two possible values for the content stream updates capability are `none` and `pwconly`. `none` means what you think it means: once you set the content stream, you can never update it. Yikes! `pwc` refers to the Private Working Copy, and it has to do with versioning, which you'll learn about in the next section. For now, know that when a repository supports content stream updates to the PWC only, it means that to make a change to the content stream, you'll have to do a checkout on the document first, which returns a PWC. Then you can update the PWC and do a check-in to commit the change.

Now you know how to determine if and when, generally speaking, content streams can be updated in your repository. To check whether a specific content stream can be updated, inspect the allowable actions on the document. You've seen multiple examples of this, so it should be very familiar to you now. The allowable action you're looking for is called `CAN_SET_CONTENT_STREAM`, and a conditional check would look something like the following:

```
if (Action.CAN_SET_CONTENT_STREAM in
    someDoc.allowableActions.allowableActions) {
    //...update the content stream
}
```

You can now create and update documents in your content repository, which is great.

Now suppose you're a developer in a law firm. Using what you know so far, you could develop an application to help the firm's attorneys collaboratively author contracts. You can imagine that a given contract might go through several iterations before it's final. These are lawyers, after all. Inevitably, one of them is going to want to undo a change (or multiple changes). Setting the content stream directly, like you've been doing in this section, overwrites the file content—there's no history, so the lawyers wouldn't be able to go back to an earlier version. Wouldn't it be nice if you could maintain older versions?

You can, and that's the subject of the next section.

3.2.3 *Understanding versioning*

Have you ever seen a file with a name something like potts_contract_v2_jtp_jb_fm_legal_final_signed.pdf?

This may seem like an extreme example, but it's quite common. What's going on here is that multiple people are reviewing, updating, and approving the document. The people involved in the process are attempting to keep track of the different versions of the document by adding things to the name of the file, like a version number (*v2*), or their initials (*jtp*), or the fact that this is the *final* round of edits for this document. It's symptomatic of the fact that a plain filesystem isn't rich enough to help you track the multiple rounds of edits that documents and other digital assets go through during routine business processes.

A CMIS repository that supports versioning fixes this problem. Documents go through their normal business process, and as they're revised, the repository maintains a version history, as shown in figure 3.7.

Users can revert back to previous versions at any time. Now the document's name can stay simple and descriptive, because the repository is keeping track of the version history.

Before we try a versioning example, let's talk about the mechanics of creating a version and some of the terminology that goes with it. Going back to the law firm example, suppose rather than one lawyer working on a contract, there's a full legal team. If the legal team is working on the contract, and the contract lives in the CMIS repository, how would you make sure that two lawyers don't edit the contract simultaneously? This problem is

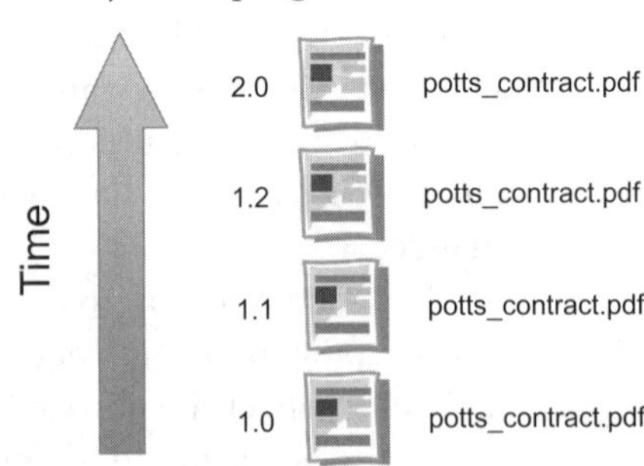

Figure 3.7 CMIS repositories can keep track of versions so you don't have to.

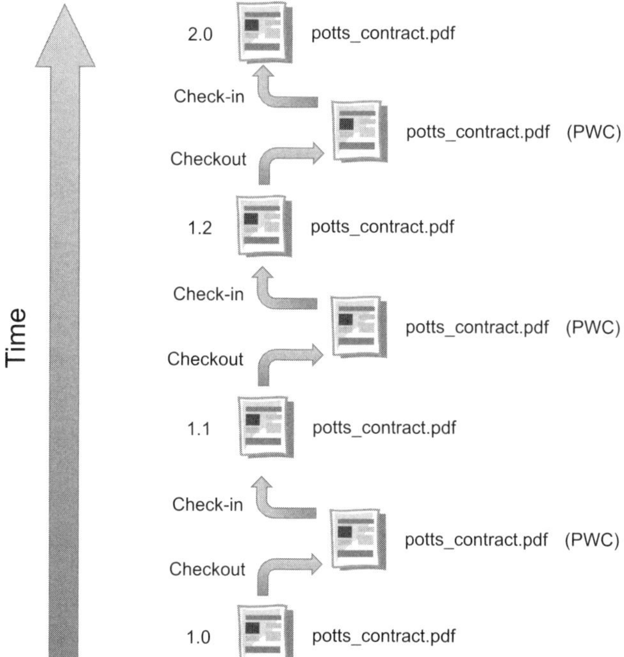

Figure 3.8 Checkouts create PWCs that are edited and then checked in to create new versions.

handled with checkout and check-in. Before making a change, the lawyer does a checkout on the contract. When it's checked out, no other members of the legal team can make changes. When the changes are made, the lawyer does a check-in. Now it's available to others to make their changes.

When you check out a document, you create a private working copy (PWC). As the name suggests, this is a copy of the document that only the person performing the checkout can change. It only exists as long as the document is checked out. Once the document is checked in, the PWC is no longer needed. Figure 3.8 shows a series of checkouts and check-ins happening over time, resulting in the version history you saw previously.

Now refer to figure 3.9. Notice that each version in the version history is identified with a number. This is called the *version label*. Also notice that the version labels follow a dot syntax and that there's a gap between 1.2 and 2.0. Version labels that are not whole numbers (like "1.2") are said to be *minor versions*, whereas version numbers that are whole numbers (like "2.0") are called *major versions*. When you check in a document, you can tell CMIS whether you're checking in a minor version or a major version. The decision is usually business-specific. Typically, documents that contain a small number of changes are checked in as minor versions, whereas more significant changes are checked in as major versions. The most recent version in a version history is called the *latest version*.

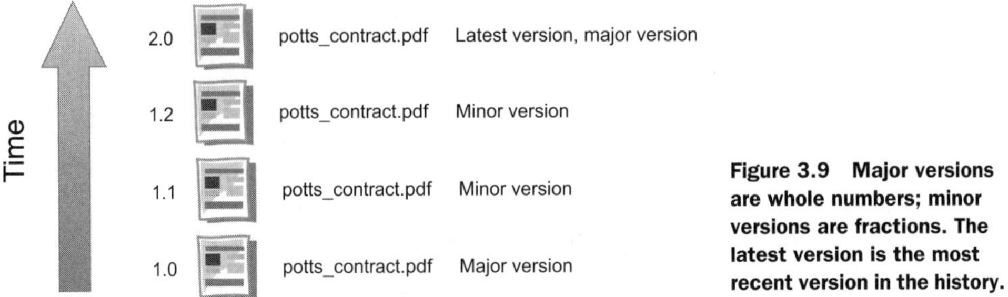

Figure 3.9 Major versions are whole numbers; minor versions are fractions. The latest version is the most recent version in the history.

You may be curious as to why the PWCs in figure 3.8 don't have version labels. That's because a PWC isn't a version. It's a special kind of object that only exists while the object is checked out, so it doesn't have a version label.

Now that you know how useful versioning can be and the terminology that goes with it, it's time to jump back into the CMIS Workbench and learn how to create versions in Groovy.

3.2.4 *Try it—upload a new version of a document*

The best way to understand how versions work is to try it yourself. In this section, you'll create a new document that you can then check out, modify, and check back in. We'll break this into three separate scripts that you'll run from the Groovy console in the CMIS Workbench as you've done in previous examples. First, you'll write a script to create the initial version of a document, then one to check out the document, and finally one to check in a new version of the document.

CREATE A NEW DOCUMENT

This listing shows how to create the initial version of the document.

Listing 3.7 Creating the initial version of a document

```
import org.apache.chemistry.opencmis.commons.enums.*

cmis = new scripts.CMIS(session)

def someFolder = session.getObjectByPath('/my first folder')

def f = new File('/users/jpotts/Documents/sample/potts_contract.docx')

def someDoc = cmis.createDocumentFromFile(someFolder,
                                          f,
                                          "cmisbook:officeDocument",
                                          VersioningState.MAJOR)

println("Doc created!")
println("Id:" + someDoc.id)
println("Name:" + someDoc.name)
println("Length:" + someDoc.contentStreamLength)
println("Version:" + someDoc.versionLabel)
println("Is Latest?" + someDoc.latestVersion)
println("Is Major?" + someDoc.majorVersion)
```

Specify any sample document that you can edit.

The VersioningState.MAJOR argument tells CMIS to create this version as a major version.

Specify a versionable type.

The version label, latest version flag, and major version flag return information about the version.

You may have noticed that we used a custom type called `cmisbook:officeDocument` in the `createInitialVersion.groovy` script. In the OpenCMIS InMemory Repository, `cmis:document` isn't versionable by default. In the InMemory Repository bundled with this book, we've included a versionable type called `cmisbook:officeDocument`, so we're using that. If you're building OpenCMIS from source, you can use `VersionableType`, which is a versionable type shipped with that repository.

CHECK OUT AND DOWNLOAD THE DOCUMENT

Now you have an initial version of a document stored in the repository. It's time to check it out and download the Private Working Copy locally.

> **YOU MUST AUTHENTICATE TO PERFORM A CHECKOUT** The OpenCMIS InMemory Repository doesn't require authentication, but if you don't provide a username and password, the server won't let you perform a checkout. If you haven't done so already, go back to the connection dialog box and provide a username and password before you run the checkout code. Any values will work.

Listing 3.8 shows how to do the checkout. It's one method call. Once the document is checked out, you can use the `cmis.download` shortcut script to download the file to the local machine.

Listing 3.8 Checking out the document and downloading it from the repository

```
cmis = new scripts.CMIS(session)

def someDoc = session.
        getObjectByPath('/my first folder/potts_contract.docx')

def pwcId = someDoc.checkOut()                 <-- Call checkOut method, which returns object ID of the PWC


println("Is checked out?" + someDoc.versionSeriesCheckedOut)
println("PWC ID:" + pwcId)

cmis.download(pwcId,                           <-- CMIS helper includes download method that downloads

          '/users/jpotts/Desktop/potts_contract.docx')
```

Make sure the target directory exists before you run this example, or you may end up with a checked-out file that doesn't exist locally. If this happens to you, use the CMIS Workbench to cancel the checkout of the document, which is an action on the Actions tab.

After running this example, the document in the repository will be checked out and a copy of the document will be placed on the local filesystem in the path specified.

MODIFY THE LOCAL FILE AND CHECK IT IN

The document in the repository is now checked out—that will keep others from making changes to it while you've got the PWC downloaded to your machine. You don't have to modify the file, of course, but in real life you probably wouldn't check it in unless it had been modified.

The next listing shows how to check in the modified local file as a new version.

Listing 3.9 Checking in a modified local file as a new version

```
def someDoc = session.
        getObjectByPath("/my first folder/potts_contract.docx")

println("id:" + someDoc.id)
println("name:" + someDoc.name)

if (!someDoc.latestVersion) {
    someDoc = someDoc.getObjectOfLatestVersion(false)
}

println("Version:" + someDoc.versionLabel)
println("Is Major?" + someDoc.majorVersion)

def pwcId
if (someDoc.versionSeriesCheckedOut) {
    pwcId = someDoc.versionSeriesCheckedOutId
} else {
    pwcId = someDoc.checkOut()
    someDoc.refresh()
}
def pwc = session.getObject(pwcId)

println("Checked out?" + someDoc.versionSeriesCheckedOut)
println("Checked out by:" +
          someDoc.versionSeriesCheckedOutBy)

def file = new File('/users/jpotts/Desktop/potts_contract.docx')

def name = file.getName()

def mimetype = someDoc.contentStreamMimeType

def contentStream = session.getObjectFactory().createContentStream(name,
                                                      file.size(),
                                                      mimetype,
                                                      new FileInputStream(file))

def newDocId = pwc.checkIn(false,
               null,
               contentStream,
               "Made a minor change")

println("Checked in new version")

def newDoc = session.getObject(newDocId)
newDoc.refresh()
println("Version:" + newDoc.versionLabel)
println("Is Latest?" + newDoc.latestVersion)
println("Is Major?" + newDoc.majorVersion)
```

Check makes sure you're working with the latest version

versionSeriesCheckedOutId property returns object ID of the PWC

Otherwise, document wasn't checked out, so example won't work

Dumps the name of the person who checked out the document

File being opened is the locally modified document that will be checked in as new version

Pass in null for properties map because no properties are being changed

In the preceding example, you pass a value of `false` to the `checkIn` method to indicate that the document should be checked in as a minor version. The check-in comment summarizes what's changed.

After running this code, you should be able to use the CMIS Workbench to see that the version has been incremented. If you click the content URL, you should see that the file contains the new version of the content.

CMIS 1.1: BATCH UPDATES All of the updates shown in this section have been against one object at a time. If you're processing a large list of objects, this results in more network traffic than you would probably like. New in CMIS 1.1 is the ability to perform bulk updates of properties. The new `bulkUpdateProperties` method takes an array of object IDs to update, as well as a map of properties to set on every object in the list. The method returns a list of object IDs that were successfully updated.

3.3 Deleting objects

You now know how to create and update objects in the repository. At some point, you'll need to know how to delete objects. Let's cover some requirements for deleting objects, and then you can try it yourself. After that we'll discuss some special considerations to think about when deleting objects.

3.3.1 Requirements for deleting objects

It's quite easy to delete an object from the repository—you call the object's `delete` method. If the object's allowable actions include `CAN_DELETE_OBJECT`, the call should succeed and the object will be deleted. The only decision you need to make is whether you want to delete all versions of the object or only the version you call the `delete` method on.

DELETED OBJECTS CAN'T BE RETRIEVED Once you delete an object, that object is gone. You can't get it back. Some repositories have the notion of *soft deletes*, and there are systems, like many source code repositories, that allow you to revert or undo a delete. But there is nothing in the CMIS specification that provides for this type of functionality. Even in CMIS repositories that support versioning, if you delete a specific version of an object, it's gone forever. So be careful with that `delete` method.

Deleting documents differs slightly from deleting folders. Let's delete the contract you created in the previous section, and then delete the folder it was sitting in.

3.3.2 Try it—delete an object

In section 3.2.4, you probably created a file called potts_contract.docx. If you didn't, and you want to work through this example, create a test document—it doesn't matter what it is because it isn't going to be around for long. The next listing shows how to delete it.

Listing 3.10 Deleting a document

```
import org.apache.chemistry.opencmis.commons.enums.*
import org.apache.chemistry.opencmis.
        commons.exceptions.CmisObjectNotFoundException;

def targetPath = "/my first folder/potts_contract.docx"
def someDoc
try {
```

```
    someDoc = session.
        getObjectByPath(targetPath)
} catch (CmisObjectNotFoundException confe) {
    println("Could not find document to delete: " + targetPath)
    return
}

println("id:" + someDoc.id)
println("name:" + someDoc.name)

if (!someDoc.latestVersion) {
    someDoc = someDoc.getObjectOfLatestVersion(false)
}

someDoc.delete(true)
```

Throws exception if you try to get an object by path and that object doesn't exist

Passes in true to delete all versions of the document, not only this specific version

If you go into the CMIS Workbench and refresh the folder, you should see that your document is no longer in the repository.

Now let's delete the folder. If you've been following along, the folder named *my first folder* isn't yet empty. Like the document class, `folder` has a `delete` method. But if you call `delete` on a non-empty folder, you'll get an exception. If you want to delete a folder and all of its descendents, call `deleteTree` instead of `delete`, as shown in this listing.

Listing 3.11 Deleting a folder

```
import org.apache.chemistry.opencmis.commons.enums.*
import org.apache.chemistry.opencmis.
        commons.exceptions.CmisObjectNotFoundException;

def targetPath = "/my first folder"
def someFolder
try {
    someFolder = session.
        getObjectByPath(targetPath)
} catch (CmisObjectNotFoundException confe) {
    println("Could not find folder to delete: " + targetPath)
    return
}


//someFolder.delete(true)
someFolder.deleteTree(true, UnfileObject.DELETE, true)

println("Deleted folder")
```

The delete method won't work, in this case, because the folder isn't empty.

Instead, deleteTree will delete the folder and all of its descendents.

Note that when you call `deleteTree`, you must decide whether or not to delete all versions. You must also tell CMIS whether to delete or unfile the objects in the tree, if unfiling is supported by the repository. The last argument passed to `deleteTree` indicates what should happen if a failure occurs. In the preceding code, you pass in `true` so that if one object in the tree fails to get deleted, the delete operation continues with the rest of the objects in the tree.

After running this code, *my first folder* and everything in it will be completely removed from the repository.

3.3.3 Things to think about when deleting objects

We should mention a few things you might want to think about when deciding how to handle deletes in your CMIS application. We've already talked about `delete` versus `deleteTree` when deleting folders, and the fact that you can delete either specific versions of an object or every version. Let's look at two other points.

DELETE VERSUS UNFILE

Repositories that support unfiling will allow you to *unfile* rather than delete an object, if that's what you want to do. If you want to unfile a document, use the `removeFromFolder` method instead of the `delete` method.

Once a document is unfiled, you can't navigate to it through the folder structure because it no longer lives in a folder. The document can be retrieved by its object ID, or by search, or, if you're using the AtomPub binding, by asking the repository for its unfiled documents collection.

DELETING THE CONTENT STREAM

You may want the object to stick around but to get rid of the content that's associated with the object. In that case you don't have to delete the entire object—you can delete only the content stream by calling `deleteContentStream` on the `document` object.

3.4 Summary

We've covered a lot of ground in this chapter. You can now create new folders and documents, with or without content. You also saw a few different ways to update documents. You can update them in place by updating properties or the content stream directly. But if you do that, the version history will be lost. One way to address that problem is to check out documents before checking them back in as new versions. This also prevents others from making changes to the same document at the same time.

Last, we talked about deletes. You learned that when folders are deleted, you can either delete only the folder, if it's empty, or you can delete the folder as well as all of its descendents by using `deleteTree` instead of `delete`. When deleting an object with a version history, you can delete every version of the object or you can delete objects individually. For some repositories, you can choose to unfile an object to remove it from a folder instead of deleting it completely.

You can automate a lot of document processing in your organization, armed with what you've learned in this chapter. But so far you've only worked with generic types: folder and document. In reality, you'll likely want to work with types that are specific to your business requirements. Diving deeper into types, properties, and other advanced metadata topics is the subject of the next chapter.

4 CMIS metadata: types and properties

This chapter covers

- General metadata concepts
- CMIS types and property definitions
- Constraints on property definitions
- Type discovery using Chemistry
- Type mutability (CMIS 1.1)
- Secondary types (CMIS 1.1)

Up to this point, we've been working in the realm of data. This chapter will bring us up a level into a discussion of metadata. We'll start with a brief explanation of what exactly metadata is and how it relates to data in general. Then we'll cover all of the basic types of CMIS metadata, including how they're categorized and discovered. Along the way, we'll go through some exercises that show all of these concepts in action. By the end of this chapter, you'll have a good understanding of CMIS metadata and the new metadata-related features that are coming in CMIS 1.1.

4.1 What is metadata and why do we need it?

Simply put, metadata is *data about data.* Perhaps a slightly more helpful definition in this case would be *data about the containers of data.* If that makes no sense to you, don't worry. It'll all be clear in time. If you have a good grasp of metadata already and want to get right to CMIS metadata, you can jump ahead to section 4.2.

A good place for us to start is to relate metadata to what you already know—data. Let's take a library's catalog (an old card catalog or a digital database) as an example. Somewhere you have a book sitting on a shelf—the book is the object in this example. The book also has an associated catalog record (physical or digital) that contains data about the object. The data in this record is the metadata, and it includes items like the title of the book, the author's name, and so on. Finally, there's an archetype for the catalog records—a catalog record will have to conform to certain requirements regarding the data it contains. In some cases, this description of what the cards in the card catalog should look like may only exist in the mind of the librarian. In other cases, it might be written down in an operations manual. Either way, that archetype can be considered the schema. Figure 4.1 illustrates this relationship.

For the rest of this book, when we refer to *metadata*, we'll be talking about metadata in content management systems specifically, unless otherwise noted. When we talk about *types*, we're using the CMIS name for the *schema.* In section 4.2, we'll talk about what this all looks like from a CMIS perspective, which means *types* and *property definitions.*

> **THE SCHEMA IS METADATA, TOO** Remember that because the schema is also data-describing data, the schema is also metadata in the general sense. But this doesn't mean that all metadata is same as the schema. It's OK to loosely refer to both metadata and the schema as metadata, in cases where the distinction isn't important.

Now that we've addressed what metadata is, we're left with the question of why we need it. Metadata is a key part of making objects searchable. In the case of the library, the most important thing you're going to be doing with those catalog records is using

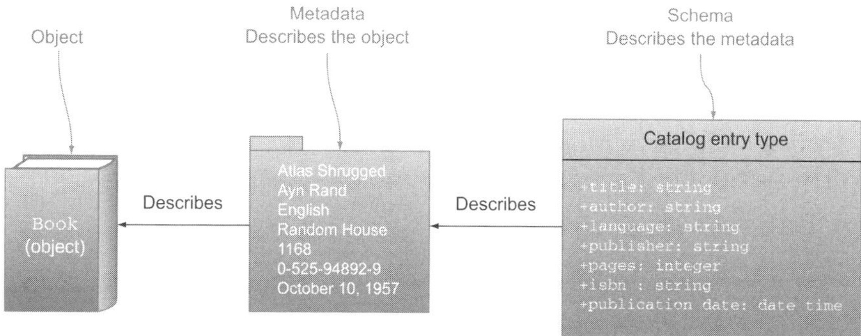

Figure 4.1 The schema describes metadata, which describes data.

them to find what you want. Compare that with a CMIS example: Say you were trying to find a photo in a CMIS repository that contained 100 million or more objects. Without metadata, you could visually search through them all sequentially until you found the one you were seeking. Maybe you could even sort by filename to help out a bit if you knew something about what the photo was called. But with proper types defined on your repository, finding a specific image can be trivial.

Imagine you want to see all of the images that were created after 2007 and updated sometime between 2009 and 2011. You could further restrict this search to only those images that have a resolution of 1024 by 768 pixels and have a description field that contains the words "elephant" *and* "Swahili." Now that 100-million-result set has shrunk by quite a bit. Even if you found a few photos that matched this criteria, it's likely you wouldn't have to visually or manually scan very many.

That's the power of CMIS Query, and that's precisely what we'll talk about in detail in chapter 5. But remember, it's metadata that makes this all possible.

4.2 Metadata in CMIS

Taking the library analogy a bit further, you can imagine that a library might store more types of media than just books. It might have books on tape, CDs, DVDs, magazines, eBooks, and perhaps even microfiche, among others. Each of these different types of objects will have different types of metadata associated with them. This is also typically the case with ECM systems, so it applies to CMIS. ECM repositories generally have a large variety of objects, each with their own associated types. Later in this chapter, you'll see how CMIS manages the organization, storage, and retrieval of these schema objects.

Type is the name used in the CMIS specification to identify the objects that hold the schema for normal data objects in the repository. Recall that data objects are made up of instances of these types. Folders and documents are the most common examples of data objects. *Type* objects contain collections of *property definitions* that define what properties will be present on an object instance of that *type*, as figure 4.2 shows. This is directly analogous to how data objects contain collections of properties.

As you can see in figure 4.2, all objects have one type object to describe them. Also, for every property on that object, there's a corresponding property definition object on the type to describe that property. If you recall, in chapter 2 (section 2.4.2) you saw all of the properties that are present for all objects as well as all of the additional properties that are present on all document objects. The CMIS metadata functions that we'll discuss in this chapter are what you use to find out which properties you should expect to see on any object.

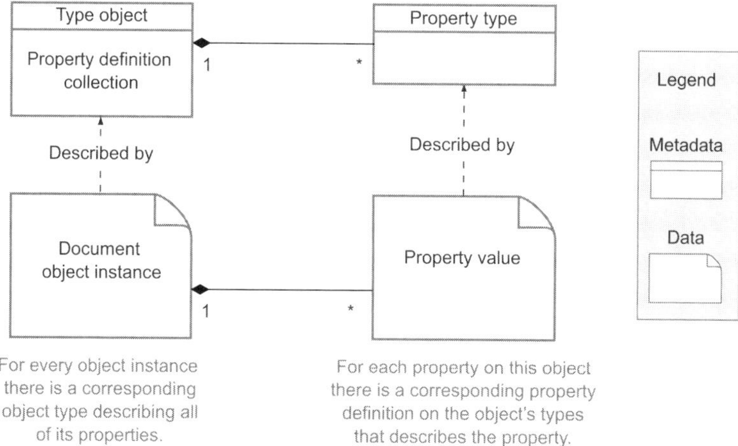

Figure 4.2 CMIS metadata types and property definitions describe objects and properties, respectively.

4.2.1 Type definitions are hierarchical and attributes are inherited

Just like the objects they describe, type objects and property definition objects have properties themselves, but if we also called these *properties*, we could mistake them for normal properties on regular instance objects, and things would get a little confusing. As if they're not already, right? To avoid this unfortunate verbal tangle, the CMIS specification refers to properties on metadata objects as *attributes*. This way it's clear that if we say *property*, we're talking about a value on an object, and if we say *attribute*, we mean a value on a type or property definition. Attribute is shorter to say than metaproperty anyway.

All of these type objects in CMIS inherit attributes from their parent type objects. Therefore, the document type will inherit all of the attributes that are common to all CMIS objects, and it will then add in additional ones that are only present for documents. The same is true for the attributes on property definitions. Figure 4.3 shows the complete base metadata hierarchy for the five base types and the eight CMIS data types we introduced you to in sections 2.3 and 2.4.

A sixth base type (`cmis:secondary`) isn't shown in figure 4.3. This is due to its special secondary/optional nature, which will be explained in section 4.4.2.

4.2.2 Try it—view the types and property definitions using Workbench

Now that you have a good picture of what all of this metadata looks like on paper, let's go into the CMIS Workbench and take a look at the types and property definitions in the test InMemory server. In order to bring up the Types viewer in the Workbench,

Note the spec does not mention a true base type for these objects, but since these hierarchies share the same common attributes, we find it convenient to picture it as if there is (shown).

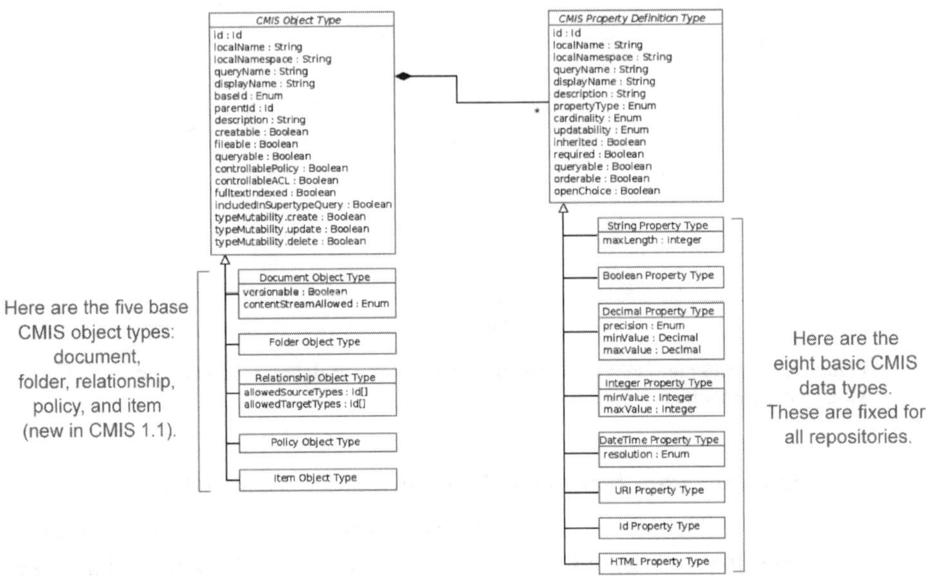

Figure 4.3 CMIS metadata base hierarchy for types and property definitions showing each one's attributes

locate the Types button at the top of the window, as shown in figure 4.4. Clicking this button will load up the Types dialog box that's shown in figure 4.5.

Figure 4.5 shows the CMIS Types view with the `cmis:document` object selected in the left pane, and the `cmis:name` property selected in the properties pane. Note that the Apache Chemistry InMemory Repository we used in this example has multiple child types of `cmis:document`, some of which have further subtypes, which the open

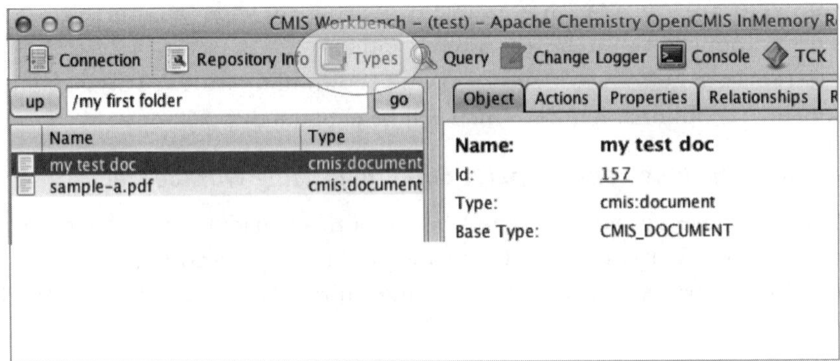

Figure 4.4 Types button (circled), which launches Workbench's Types viewer window

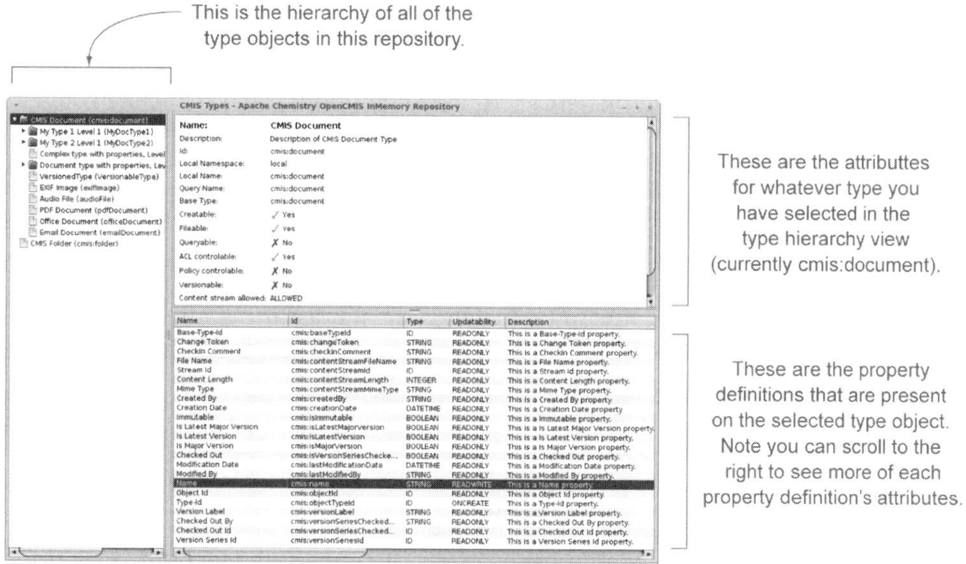

This is the hierarchy of all of the type objects in this repository.
These are the attributtes for whatever type you have selected in the type hierarchy view (currently cmis:document).
These are the property definitions that are present on the selected type object. Note you can scroll to the right to see more of each property definition's attributes.
CMIS Types - Apache Chemistry OpenCMIS InMemory Repository

Figure 4.5 The CMIS Types window in CMIS Workbench showing the attributes and associated property definitions for `cmis:document`

folder icons indicate for each one. The version of the InMemory Repository that you're using may have different child types of `cmis:document`, because the binary package that comes with this book will continue to be updated. Also note that in this property definition view, there's a separate movable column for each of the attributes on that property definition. This makes it easy to move the columns that you're most interested in to the left (and more visible) portion of the window.

In the property definitions pane in figure 4.5 (lower right), you can see that the `cmis:name` property is highlighted. Although only a few of the property's attributes are shown here (scroll right to see more), you can see that the `cmis:name` property for all `cmis:document` objects is of type `STRING` and its updateability is `READWRITE`. That is, it's settable by CMIS clients when they're creating or editing the object. In contrast, the `cmis:objectId` property on the line below it has an `ID` type and shows as `READONLY` to all clients.

4.3 Type collections and hierarchies

ECM repositories often have a lot of types defined—hundreds in extreme cases. This means that there needs to be a scalable way to organize and retrieve them. Some repository designs treat these type collections as a large flat list, and others treat them as a hierarchy. As you saw earlier in this chapter, CMIS defines a hierarchy to organize all of the type objects. If an underlying repository only has a flat list, it would be exposed through CMIS as a hierarchy with a depth of one.

CUSTOM APPLICATION DEVELOPERS TAKE HEED This section is of particular importance to custom application developers. We'll cover type collections and how to navigate them with two code examples that show each of the main methods for retrieving types. Property definitions will be explained, and we'll also discuss the constraints that CMIS permits on properties, followed by a final example that shows how to access choice lists. You'll use the techniques you learn here repeatedly as you code more complex CMIS applications in this chapter, as well as in part 2 of this book.

Recall the default type hierarchy in figure 4.3. This isn't meant to be the sum of the hierarchy, but rather the tip (as in an iceberg) or a starting point that's common to all repositories. Each of these base types can have child and grandchild types going down as deep and as wide as is necessary for each application. Later, in part 2 of the book, you'll use a custom subclass of `cmis:document` that will be tailored for the metadata in the music mashup example application.

4.3.1 Try it—traversing the type hierarchy

Understanding how all of these types are laid out was the first step. Now that you have that down, it's time to look at how your application can programmatically discover anything it needs to know about the metadata in a repository. For this, we're going back to our trusty Groovy console and we'll show you how simple this seemingly complex operation can be.

In this section, you'll traverse the hierarchy of objects, looking at their attributes along the way. You'll even display attributes that are only present on documents so that you can see how easy it is to determine the types of these objects. Although we won't examine all the attributes that are available in this short example, you'll notice that all of the attributes listed in the CMIS specification are accessible as getter methods on the various classes of `type` objects.

Listing 4.1 shows the code for traversing the type hierarchy. For more examples, please see the Javadocs for OpenCMIS (http://chemistry.apache.org/java/0.8.0/maven/apidocs/). In part 2 of the book, you'll see these attribute values being used in a real application to give them a bit more context.

Listing 4.1 `getTypeDescendants` code example (type walker)

```
import org.apache.chemistry.opencmis.client.api.*
import org.apache.chemistry.opencmis.commons.enums.*

      boolean includePropertyDefinitions = true;
      for (t in session.getTypeDescendants(
            null,                        // start at the top of the tree
            -1,                          // infinite depth recursion
            includePropertyDefinitions   // include prop defs
            )) {
         printTypes(t, "");
      }
```

```
static void printTypes(Tree<ObjectType> tree, String tab) {

   ObjectType objType =  tree.getItem();
   println(tab + "TYPE:" + objType.getDisplayName() +
         " (" + objType.getDescription() + ")");
   // Print some of the common attributes for this type
   print(tab + "   Id:" + objType.getId());
   print(" Fileable:" + objType.isFileable());
   print(" Queryable:" + objType.isQueryable());

   if (objType instanceof DocumentType) {
      print(" [DOC Attrs->] Versionable:" +
         ((DocumentType)objType).isVersionable());
      print(" Content:" +
         ((DocumentType)objType).getContentStreamAllowed());
   }
   println("");  // end the line
   for (t in tree.getChildren()) {
      // there are more - call self for next level
      printTypes(t, tab + "  ");
   }
}
```

This is like the code in chapter 2 for recursing the directory hierarchy.

Print some attributes common to all types.

Show contentStreamAllowed and isVersionable if the type is DocumentType.

If you look at the output from listing 4.1 (shown in figure 4.6), you'll see the same information you saw in figure 4.5 with all of the child levels expanded and each level indented to show the hierarchy visually.

Now that you know something about types and their attributes, let's move on to the next exercise, where we'll expand the example to show property definitions and their attributes as well.

```
TYPE:CMIS Folder (Description of CMIS Folder Type)
   Id:cmis:folder Fileable:true Queryable:true
TYPE:CMIS Document (Description of CMIS Document Type)
   Id:cmis:document Fileable:true Queryable:true [DOC Attrs->] Versionable:false Content:ALLOWED
  TYPE:Taggable (Taggable document)
     Id:cmisbook:taggable Fileable:true Queryable:true [DOC Attrs->] Versionable:true Content:ALLOWED
    TYPE:Image (Image)
       Id:cmisbook:image Fileable:true Queryable:true [DOC Attrs->] Versionable:true Content:ALLOWED
    TYPE:Media (Media)
       Id:cmisbook:media Fileable:true Queryable:true [DOC Attrs->] Versionable:true Content:ALLOWED
      TYPE:Audio File (Audio Content (compressed or uncompressed))
         Id:cmisbook:audio Fileable:true Queryable:true [DOC Attrs->] Versionable:true Content:ALLOWED
      TYPE:Video File (Video Content)
         Id:cmisbook:video Fileable:true Queryable:true [DOC Attrs->] Versionable:true Content:ALLOWED
      TYPE:Album (Album)
         Id:cmisbook:album Fileable:true Queryable:true [DOC Attrs->] Versionable:false Content:NOTALLOWED
  TYPE:PDF Document (PDF Document)
     Id:cmisbook:pdf Fileable:true Queryable:true [DOC Attrs->] Versionable:true Content:ALLOWED
  TYPE:Office Document (Document of type Office)
     Id:cmisbook:officeDocument Fileable:true Queryable:true [DOC Attrs->] Versionable:true Content:ALLOWED
  TYPE:Text Document (Text Document)
     Id:cmisbook:text Fileable:true Queryable:true [DOC Attrs->] Versionable:true Content:ALLOWED
    TYPE:Lyrics (Lyrics)
       Id:cmisbook:lyrics Fileable:true Queryable:true [DOC Attrs->] Versionable:true Content:ALLOWED
    TYPE:Poem (Poem)
       Id:cmisbook:poem Fileable:true Queryable:true [DOC Attrs->] Versionable:true Content:ALLOWED
  TYPE:Note (Note)
     Id:cmisbook:note Fileable:true Queryable:true [DOC Attrs->] Versionable:true Content:ALLOWED
Execution complete. Result was null.                                    38:1
```

Figure 4.6 Output from the `getTypeDescendants` code (type walker)

4.3.2 Try it—examining property definitions on types

Now you'll modify the type walker example and add in some code to walk through the property definitions for each type. You'll display a few key attributes for each type, like each property's ID, data type, and updateability.

Listing 4.2 shows the modified version of the code, type walker v2. This version adds a new method, `printPropDefsForType`, that's called in the `type` loop. As you can see, it's trivially easy to get this information from the `type` object using OpenCMIS.

Listing 4.2 `getTypeDescendants` with property definitions (type walker v2)

```
import org.apache.chemistry.opencmis.client.api.*
import org.apache.chemistry.opencmis.commons.enums.*
import org.apache.chemistry.opencmis.commons.definitions.*

boolean includePropertyDefinitions = true;
for (t in session.getTypeDescendants(
    null,                         // match all types
    -1,                           // infinite depth recursion
    includePropertyDefinitions    // include prop defs
    )) {
    printTypes(t, "");
}

static void printTypes(Tree<ObjectType> tree, String tab) {
  ObjectType objType =  tree.getItem();
  println(tab + "TYPE:" + objType.getDisplayName() +
        " (" + objType.getDescription() + ")");
  // Print some of the common attributes for this type
  print(tab + "   Id:" + objType.getId());
  print(" Fileable:" + objType.isFileable());
  print(" Queryable:" + objType.isQueryable());

  if (objType.getBaseTypeId().equals(BaseTypeId.CMIS_DOCUMENT)) {
     print(" [DOC Attrs->] Versionable:" +
        ((DocumentType)objType).isVersionable());
     print(" Content:" +
        ((DocumentType)objType).getContentStreamAllowed());
  }
  println("");  // end the line
  printPropDefsForType(objType, tab);

  for (t in tree.getChildren()) {
     // there are more - call self for next level
     printTypes(t, tab + "  ");
  }
}

static void printPropDefsForType(ObjectType type, String tab) {
  Map<String, PropertyDefinition<?>> mapDefs =
     type.getPropertyDefinitions();

  for (key in mapDefs.keySet()) {
     print(tab + "      " + key + "->");
```

Add one more include for the PropertyDefinition object from OpenCMIS because it's referenced in the printPropDefsForType method.

Hook in a call to the printPropDefsForType method after the type attributes are done printing but before recursing further.

Returns a map of the property definitions for this type, keyed by the associated property name.

```
      PropertyDefinition defn = mapDefs.get(key);
      print(" Id:[" + defn.getId() + "]");
      print(" dataType:[" + defn.getPropertyType() + "]");
      println(" updateable:[" + defn.getUpdatability()+"]");
   }
}
```

Figure 4.7 shows the output of type walker v2. The figure shows the complete output for the type named `audioFile`; the other types are omitted for space reasons.

This example has two parts because you can get at the `Type` and `PropertyDefinition` objects in OpenCMIS in two different ways. In listing 4.2, you retrieved the types from the types collection and walked the types tree directly. But sometimes it's more convenient to get the `Type` object and/or corresponding `PropertyDefinition`

```
TYPE:Audio File (Audio Content (compressed or uncompressed))
  Id:cmisbook:audio Fileable:true Queryable:true [DOC Attrs->] Versionable:true Content:ALLOWED
    cmisbook:artist-> Id:[cmisbook:artist] dataType:[STRING] updateable:[READWRITE]
    cmisbook:album-> Id:[cmisbook:album] dataType:[STRING] updateable:[READWRITE]
    cmisbook:title-> Id:[cmisbook:title] dataType:[STRING] updateable:[READWRITE]
    cmisbook:comment-> Id:[cmisbook:comment] dataType:[STRING] updateable:[READWRITE]
    cmisbook:genre-> Id:[cmisbook:genre] dataType:[STRING] updateable:[READWRITE]
    cmisbook:length-> Id:[cmisbook:length] dataType:[INTEGER] updateable:[READWRITE]
    cmisbook:track-> Id:[cmisbook:track] dataType:[INTEGER] updateable:[READWRITE]
    cmisbook:composer-> Id:[cmisbook:composer] dataType:[STRING] updateable:[READWRITE]
    cmisbook:discNo-> Id:[cmisbook:discNo] dataType:[STRING] updateable:[READWRITE]
    cmisbook:audioFormat-> Id:[cmisbook:audioFormat] dataType:[STRING] updateable:[READWRITE]
    cmisbook:sampleRate-> Id:[cmisbook:sampleRate] dataType:[INTEGER] updateable:[READWRITE]
    cmisbook:audioChannelType-> Id:[cmisbook:audioChannelType] dataType:[STRING] updateable:[READWRITE]
    cmisbook:noChannels-> Id:[cmisbook:noChannels] dataType:[INTEGER] updateable:[READWRITE]
    cmisbook:compressorVersion-> Id:[cmisbook:compressorVersion] dataType:[STRING] updateable:[READWRITE]
    cmisbook:sourceURL-> Id:[cmisbook:sourceURL] dataType:[URI] updateable:[READWRITE]
    cmisbook:license-> Id:[cmisbook:license] dataType:[STRING] updateable:[READWRITE]
    cmisbook:year-> Id:[cmisbook:year] dataType:[INTEGER] updateable:[READWRITE]
    cmisbook:artwork-> Id:[cmisbook:artwork] dataType:[ID] updateable:[READWRITE]
    cmisbook:tags-> Id:[cmisbook:tags] dataType:[STRING] updateable:[READWRITE]
    cmis:name-> Id:[cmis:name] dataType:[STRING] updateable:[READWRITE]
    cmis:objectId-> Id:[cmis:objectId] dataType:[ID] updateable:[READONLY]
    cmis:objectTypeId-> Id:[cmis:objectTypeId] dataType:[ID] updateable:[ONCREATE]
    cmis:baseTypeId-> Id:[cmis:baseTypeId] dataType:[ID] updateable:[READONLY]
    cmis:createdBy-> Id:[cmis:createdBy] dataType:[STRING] updateable:[READONLY]
    cmis:creationDate-> Id:[cmis:creationDate] dataType:[DATETIME] updateable:[READONLY]
    cmis:lastModifiedBy-> Id:[cmis:lastModifiedBy] dataType:[STRING] updateable:[READONLY]
    cmis:lastModificationDate-> Id:[cmis:lastModificationDate] dataType:[DATETIME] updateable:[READONLY]
    cmis:changeToken-> Id:[cmis:changeToken] dataType:[STRING] updateable:[READONLY]
    cmis:description-> Id:[cmis:description] dataType:[STRING] updateable:[READWRITE]
    cmis:secondaryObjectTypeIds-> Id:[cmis:secondaryObjectTypeIds] dataType:[ID] updateable:[READWRITE]
    cmis:isImmutable-> Id:[cmis:isImmutable] dataType:[BOOLEAN] updateable:[READONLY]
    cmis:isLatestVersion-> Id:[cmis:isLatestVersion] dataType:[BOOLEAN] updateable:[READONLY]
    cmis:isMajorVersion-> Id:[cmis:isMajorVersion] dataType:[BOOLEAN] updateable:[READONLY]
    cmis:isLatestMajorVersion-> Id:[cmis:isLatestMajorVersion] dataType:[BOOLEAN] updateable:[READONLY]
    cmis:versionLabel-> Id:[cmis:versionLabel] dataType:[STRING] updateable:[READONLY]
    cmis:versionSeriesId-> Id:[cmis:versionSeriesId] dataType:[ID] updateable:[READONLY]
    cmis:isVersionSeriesCheckedOut-> Id:[cmis:isVersionSeriesCheckedOut] dataType:[BOOLEAN] updateable:[READONLY]
    cmis:versionSeriesCheckedOutBy-> Id:[cmis:versionSeriesCheckedOutBy] dataType:[STRING] updateable:[READONLY]
    cmis:versionSeriesCheckedOutId-> Id:[cmis:versionSeriesCheckedOutId] dataType:[ID] updateable:[READONLY]
    cmis:checkinComment-> Id:[cmis:checkinComment] dataType:[STRING] updateable:[READONLY]
    cmis:contentStreamLength-> Id:[cmis:contentStreamLength] dataType:[INTEGER] updateable:[READONLY]
    cmis:contentStreamMimeType-> Id:[cmis:contentStreamMimeType] dataType:[STRING] updateable:[READONLY]
    cmis:contentStreamFileName-> Id:[cmis:contentStreamFileName] dataType:[STRING] updateable:[READONLY]
    cmis:contentStreamId-> Id:[cmis:contentStreamId] dataType:[ID] updateable:[READONLY]
    cmis:isPrivateWorkingCopy-> Id:[cmis:isPrivateWorkingCopy] dataType:[BOOLEAN] updateable:[READONLY]
TYPE:Video File (Video Content)
  Id:cmisbook:video Fileable:true Queryable:true [DOC Attrs->] Versionable:true Content:ALLOWED
Execution complete. Result was null.
```

Figure 4.7 Truncated output from `getTypeDescendant` with property definitions included (type walker v2)

objects for a particular instance object that you have in hand, and not worry about its type's location in the types hierarchy. Listing 4.3 shows how to do this using the root folder object as a generic example. This technique will work for any CMIS object you encounter.

SYSTEM AND CUSTOM PROPERTIES When developers talk about properties in CMIS, some will refer to *custom* and *system* properties. These terms can have different meanings in different contexts, but in the purest CMIS context, *system properties* usually refer to those properties that are defined in the specification, namely, the properties that look like `cmis:xxx`, such as `cmis:objectId`. Custom properties are everything else. Because custom properties aren't defined by the specification, they're repository- and type-specific. For example, later in the book we'll work with a subclass of `cmis:document` named `audioFile`. This type has many custom properties relating to audio tracks, like `Album`, which is a custom string property that holds the album name. Repository developers should note that you shouldn't use the `cmis:` prefix for naming any of your custom repository's properties. That prefix is reserved for properties defined in the specification.

Listing 4.3 Retrieving type and property definitions directly from the object

```
import org.apache.chemistry.opencmis.commons.*
import org.apache.chemistry.opencmis.commons.data.*
import org.apache.chemistry.opencmis.commons.enums.*
import org.apache.chemistry.opencmis.client.api.*
import org.apache.chemistry.opencmis.commons.definitions.*

// obtain the root folder instance object from the session
   Folder rootFolder = session.getRootFolder();

// this is how you get its type directly from the instance object
ObjectType typeObj = rootFolder.getType();

println("Id of folder's type:" + typeObj.getId());

int DefCount = typeObj.getPropertyDefinitions().entrySet().size();
println("Prop definition total:" + DefCount);

// how to get property definitions directly from the property instance
// by just looking at the defs for the properties that are present
List<Property<?>> props = rootFolder.getProperties();
int propCount = props.size();

println("Property count:" + propCount);
for (prop in props) {
   PropertyDefinition<?> propDef = prop.getDefinition();

   println("  property:" + prop.getDisplayName() +
         " id[" + propDef.getId() + "]");
}
```

Any time you have an object instance, you can always grab its type directly with the getType() method. By default OpenCMIS will retrieve this for you from cache if it's already present.

The amount of properties and property definitions are the same here, but this won't always be the case. There often can be more definitions than properties if you have unset (and not required) properties, or you used a property filter to omit select properties.

Much like getType(), getDefinition() can be called on any Property object and the definition will be retrieved from cache if possible.

```
Id of folder's type:cmis:folder
Prop definition total:12
Property count:12
  property:Allowed Child Types id[cmis:allowedChildObjectTypeIds]
  property:Path id[cmis:path]
  property:Modified By id[cmis:lastModifiedBy]
  property:Type-Id id[cmis:objectTypeId]
  property:Created By id[cmis:createdBy]
  property:Name id[cmis:name]
  property:Object Id id[cmis:objectId]
  property:Creation Date id[cmis:creationDate]
  property:Change Token id[cmis:changeToken]
  property:Base-Type-Id id[cmis:baseTypeId]
  property:Parent Id id[cmis:parentId]
  property:Modification Date id[cmis:lastModificationDate]
Execution complete. Result was null.    7:1
```

Figure 4.8 Output showing type and property definition information retrieved directly from the instance object

If you take a look at the output in figure 4.8, you can see that the number of property definitions that were defined on the `cmis:folder` type matches the number of properties that were on the instance of the folder object. See the callouts in the example for a discussion of why this isn't always the case.

Now that you've seen how to get to the `PropertyDefinition` objects, let's look at all of the types of constraints that are permitted on them.

4.3.3 Constraints on property definitions

The last aspect of property definitions that we need to explore (before we're ready to talk about the new CMIS 1.1 metadata features) is the concept of constraints. Aside from specifying what type of data the property holds and its cardinality, a property definition may also place constraints on the potential values.

Constraints break down into two main groups, as explained in the next section.

COMMON CONSTRAINTS ON PROPERTY DEFINITIONS

Here's a quick rundown of the constraints that can be present on any of the eight property definition object types. For a more detailed discussion of these, see section 2.1.3.3.2 of the CMIS 1.1 specification.

- `choices`—An explicit ordered set of values that are permissible for this property. For example, a string property definition named `PrimaryColors` might have `choices = [Red, Green, Blue]`. Each choice includes a `displayName` and a `value`. The `displayName` may be used by clients for presentation purposes.
- `openchoice (boolean)`—This attribute is only applicable to properties that provide a value for the `choices` attribute. If it's `FALSE`, the data value for the property must only be one of the values specified in the `choices` attribute. If it's `TRUE`, values other than those included in the `choices` attribute may be set for the property.

- defaultvalue—Contains the value that the repository must set for the property if one isn't provided at object creation time. If a property is set to required and doesn't have a default value, any attempt to create an object when this property hasn't been set will result in a constraint exception being thrown.

PROPERTY-SPECIFIC TYPES OF CONSTRAINTS

There are four additional types of constraints for specific property types. For a more detailed discussion of these, see sections 2.1.3.3.3–2.1.3.3.5 of the CMIS 1.1 specification. These are the four type-specific constraints:

- minValue and maxValue—Apply to Integer and Decimal property types only and specify the minimum and maximum values permitted for this property. If an application tries to set this property to a value outside of this range, the repository must throw a constraint exception.
- maxLength—Applies to String property types only and specifies the maximum length (in characters) allowed for a value of this property. If an application attempts to set the value of this property to a string longer than the specified maximum length, the repository must throw a constraint exception.
- resolution—This is an enum that applies only to DateTime property definitions. Each value in the following list implies all of the values above it, like bit flags. For example, if the value of time is present, this implies that time, date, and year are persisted. The permitted values for this enum are as follows:
  - year—Year resolution is persisted. The date and time portion of the value should be ignored.
  - date—Date resolution is persisted. The time portion of the value should be ignored.
  - time—Time resolution is persisted.
- precision—This is an enum that applies to property definitions of Decimal only. The permitted values for this enum are as follows:
  - 32—Use 32-bit precision ("single" as specified in IEEE-754-1985)
  - 64—Use 64-bit precision ("double" as specified in IEEE-754-1985)

Next up, we'll exercise some of these constraints using the Groovy console in the CMIS Workbench.

4.3.4 Try it—examining constraints on property definitions

Ready to see how this all looks in code? Let's go back to the CMIS Workbench again and have a look at listing 4.4. It augments the type walker v2 example to also show choice lists, default values, and the integer-specific constraint maxValue.

Listing 4.4 Examining the constraints on property definitions

```
import org.apache.chemistry.opencmis.client.api.*
import org.apache.chemistry.opencmis.commons.enums.*
import org.apache.chemistry.opencmis.commons.definitions.*
```

```
ObjectType complex = session.getTypeDefinition("cmisbook:audio"); //
printPropDefsForTypeWithContraints(complex, "");

static void printPropDefsForTypeWithContraints(ObjectType type,
      String tab) {
   Map<String, PropertyDefinition<?>> mapDefs = type
         .getPropertyDefinitions();
   for (key in mapDefs.keySet()) {
      print(tab + "      " + key + "->");
      PropertyDefinition defn = mapDefs.get(key);
      print(" Id:[" + defn.getId() + "]");
      print(" dataType:[" + defn.getPropertyType() + "]");
      println(" updateable:["+defn.getUpdatability()+"]");

      // show min max constraint test on integer type
      if (defn.getPropertyType().equals(PropertyType.INTEGER)) { //
         PropertyIntegerDefinition propDefInt =
               (PropertyIntegerDefinition) defn;
         if (propDefInt.getMaxValue() != null) {
            println("      Max value:"
              + propDefInt.getMaxValue());
         }
      }

      // list default value if present
      if (defn.getDefaultValue() != null) {
         println("      default value:["
               + defn.getDefaultValue().get(0) + "]"); //
      }

      // list choices if present
      if (defn.getChoices().size() > 0) {
         // there are choices on this property
         print("      choice present: values:[");
         List<Choice> choices = defn.getChoices();
         Cardinality card = defn.getCardinality();
         for (choice in choices) {
            if (card.equals(Cardinality.SINGLE)) {
               print(choice.getValue().get(0) + " "); //
            } else {
               // code to iterate through all values in
               // choice.getValue() if this was a
               // multivalued choice.
            }
         }
         println("]");
      }
   }
}
```

Grab the type for this example directly by its ID property, rather than navigating for it.

Check for type-specific constraints by determining the data type of the definition and casting it into the specific definition type to get at the data type–specific methods.

For brevity, assume the default value is a single value.

Get the value.

Figure 4.9 shows the output pane from the Groovy console window.

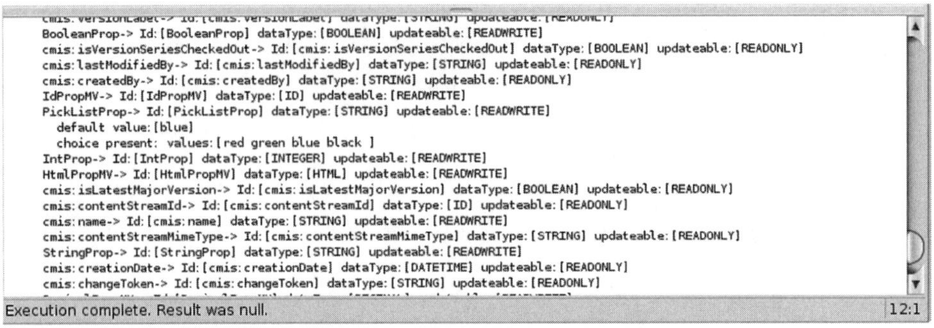

```
BooleanProp-> Id:[BooleanProp] dataType:[BOOLEAN] updateable:[READWRITE]
cmis:isVersionSeriesCheckedOut-> Id:[cmis:isVersionSeriesCheckedOut] dataType:[BOOLEAN] updateable:[READONLY]
cmis:lastModifiedBy-> Id:[cmis:lastModifiedBy] dataType:[STRING] updateable:[READONLY]
cmis:createdBy-> Id:[cmis:createdBy] dataType:[STRING] updateable:[READONLY]
IdPropMV-> Id:[IdPropMV] dataType:[ID] updateable:[READWRITE]
PickListProp-> Id:[PickListProp] dataType:[STRING] updateable:[READWRITE]
  default value:[blue]
  choice present: values:[red green blue black ]
IntProp-> Id:[IntProp] dataType:[INTEGER] updateable:[READWRITE]
HtmlPropMV-> Id:[HtmlPropMV] dataType:[HTML] updateable:[READWRITE]
cmis:isLatestMajorVersion-> Id:[cmis:isLatestMajorVersion] dataType:[BOOLEAN] updateable:[READONLY]
cmis:contentStreamId-> Id:[cmis:contentStreamId] dataType:[ID] updateable:[READONLY]
cmis:name-> Id:[cmis:name] dataType:[STRING] updateable:[READWRITE]
cmis:contentStreamMimeType-> Id:[cmis:contentStreamMimeType] dataType:[STRING] updateable:[READONLY]
StringProp-> Id:[StringProp] dataType:[STRING] updateable:[READWRITE]
cmis:creationDate-> Id:[cmis:creationDate] dataType:[DATETIME] updateable:[READONLY]
cmis:changeToken-> Id:[cmis:changeToken] dataType:[STRING] updateable:[READONLY]
Execution complete. Result was null.                                    12:1
```

Figure 4.9 Truncated output from listing 4.4, showing choice lists and default values

4.3.5 Attribute and attribute value inheritance

Before we get to the new CMIS 1.1 metadata features, we need to clarify one more thing related to inheritance and attributes. You may recall (from earlier in this chapter) the hierarchy of the CMIS type definitions and the attributes that are inherited from the base CMIS object type. An object type will inherit all of its parent type's attributes, but the values of the attribute aren't inherited.

Let's consider the `versionable` attribute of `cmis:document` to illustrate this. All subtypes of `cmis:document` in a repository must have the `versionable` attribute that was introduced at the `cmis:document` level. But the specific Boolean value of `versionable` for each of those subtypes is set independently. Therefore, in a particular repository, `cmis:document` might have `versionable=true` and still have a subtype named `invoiceDocument` that has `versionable=false`.

4.4 CMIS 1.1 metadata features

CMIS 1.1 adds two powerful tools that extend what clients can do with metadata:

- *Type mutability*—Allows CMIS clients to create, read, update, and delete (CRUD) type definitions, which means a CMIS installer application can set up the required types in a repository-agnostic manner. Another way of looking at this is that the manual steps required for an administrator to create a type definition through the repository-specific interfaces are no longer necessary.
- *Secondary types*—These special types can be attached to (or detached from) an object at any point during its life. They allow you to dynamically add or remove lists of additional properties during the lifetime of an object.

We'll describe these tools in the following sections.

4.4.1 Type mutability

The process for creating and deleting types can be surprisingly simple. Nevertheless, type updates have to follow a strictly defined set of rules (for the detailed list, see section 2.1.10.1 in the CMIS 1.1 specification), which we'll explain in this section.

The CMIS specification doesn't allow you to create new base types, only subtypes of existing ones. You can check whether or not a given type allows subtypes by inspecting its type definition.

CONSTRAINT (SECURITY)

As you might expect, only special users can create types for a given repository. The `typeMutability.create` flag for a given type isn't to be interpreted as rights for the current user. Rather, it states whether or not an administrator (or the repository equivalent of the administrator) may create a subtype of this type. This is generally true for all rights associated with type mutability. They refer to the repository as a whole in the context of an administrator. Put another way, `typeMutability.create` indicates whether the repository permits an administrator to create subtypes.

The type mutability settings for a specific type are shown later in figure 4.12. Each type may have any of these three optional Boolean values set. These flags are defined in the CMIS 1.1 spec (section 2.1.3.2.1, "Attributes common to ALL Object-Type Definitions") as follows:

- `typeMutability.create`—Indicates whether new child types may be created with this type as the parent
- `typeMutability.update`—Indicates whether clients may make changes to this type per the constraints defined in this specification
- `typeMutability.delete`—Indicates whether or not clients may delete this type if the repository contains no instances of it

CONSTRAINT (TYPE AND PROPERTY ID VALUES)

Another point often missed is that the type `ID` returned by the `createType` operation might not be the same as what was requested. Because the underlying repository may have other restrictions on the `ID` value, you may only suggest rather than specify. If the repository can use the `ID` you suggested, that's what will be returned. Otherwise it may be slightly modified or even entirely different. The same is true for new property type `ID`s on new or existing object types. For more on this, see the constraint section later in this chapter about order of the properties returned.

CONSTRAINT (NEW SETTABLE ATTRIBUTES)

Section 2.1.3.2.1 of the CMIS 1.1 specification lists the attributes that are common to all object type definitions. As a quick refresher, they are the following:

- `id`
- `localName`
- `localNamespace`
- `displayName`
- `queryName`
- `description`
- `creatable`
- `fileable`
- `queryable`
- `fulltextIndexed`
- `includedInSupertypeQuery`
- `controllablePolicy`
- `controllableACL`

It's important to note that you may not necessarily be able to set all (or any) of these attributes when creating a type. The correct way to find out for certain is to refer to the `capabilityNewTypeSettableAttributes` list. This will indicate which of the attributes this particular repository will accept for new types. Don't be surprised if your repository doesn't allow setting any of these. Often these will be internally generated based on other attributes of (or on inheritance from) the type.

Figure 4.10 shows the `capabilityNewTypeSettableAttributes` list for the InMemory Repository. If you look towards the bottom of the figure, you'll see that the repository hasn't permitted any settable attributes, which isn't correct. At the time of this writing, the InMemory server wasn't populating this list.

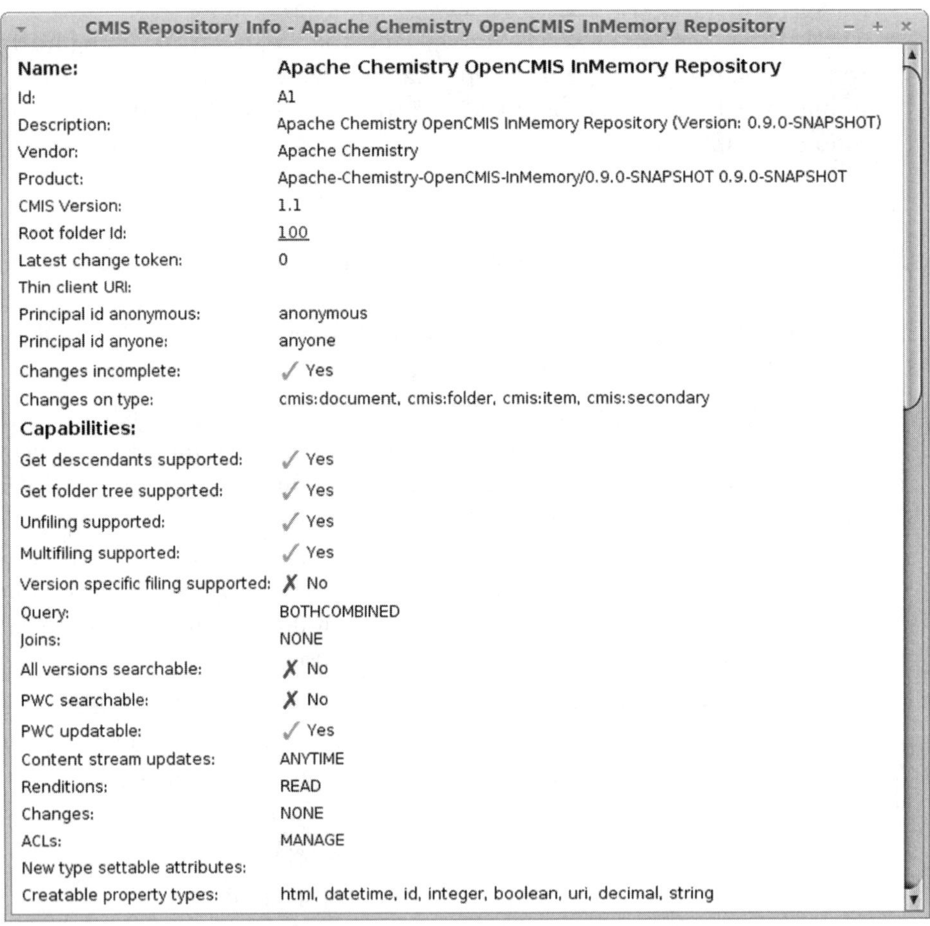

Figure 4.10 CMIS 1.1 repository information settings related to type mutability (partial)

CONSTRAINT (CREATEABLE PROPERTY TYPES)

When you're adding properties to your new type (or adding them to existing types) you must also be aware that a repository may not let you create properties of all of the CMIS-defined property types, even if they're in use elsewhere in the repository. To make this clear for clients, the repository information will contain a list of `capabilityCreatablePropertyTypes`. This is a list of all of the CMIS-defined property types (`boolean`, `id`, `integer`, `datetime`, `decimal`, `html`, `string`, and `uri`) with an associated Boolean indicating whether or not it's OK to create properties of each type in object types.

Figure 4.10 shows these settings for the InMemory Repository. If you look at the last line in the figure, you can see that this InMemory Repository supports creating properties for all eight of the CMIS-defined property types.

CONSTRAINT (ORDER OF RETURNED PROPERTIES)

The order of property types returned from the server is important. When an object type is created or updated, the repository's response will return the new type's properties in the exact same order in which they were listed in the input (the create or update) request. This is necessary so that clients can tell which properties correspond to their requested properties in cases where the `ID`s are different from what was requested. Remember that earlier we said that the value you pass for the type and property `ID` is only a suggestion. The repository may change it if necessary, so always use the returned value.

TYPE CREATION

To create a type, you have to provide the type definition and all of its new property definitions. Because that's generally a repetitious, lengthy, and error-prone piece of code, OpenCMIS provides the `TypeUtils` class, which can read and write type definitions from and to XML and JSON. The XML and JSON format is the same format that's defined in the specification to send type definitions over the wire. The simplest way to create a new type is to save an existing type as XML or JSON from the CMIS Workbench (by clicking the Save Type Definition button at the top of the Types screen), edit this file, and then create the new type.

To speed things up, we'll include a working sample that you can use for the upcoming examples, as well as a template for additional types you may want to create as you're trying things out.

Listing 4.5 shows the XML for a new `cmis:document` subtype named `my-document`. It has one additional integer property defined with the `IDmy-int`.

Listing 4.5 Sample XML to import for a new `my-document` type

```
<?xml version="1.0" encoding="UTF-8" standalone="yes"?>
<ns3:type xmlns="http://docs.oasis-open.org/ns/cmis/core/200908/"
   xmlns:ns2="http://docs.oasis-open.org/ns/cmis/messaging/200908/"
   xmlns:ns3="http://docs.oasis-open.org/ns/cmis/restatom/200908/"
   xmlns:xsi="http://www.w3.org/2001/XMLSchema-instance"
   xsi:type="cmisTypeDocumentDefinitionType">
```

```
<id>my-document</id>
<localName>my-document</localName>
<localNamespace>local</localNamespace>
<displayName>CMIS Document</displayName>
<queryName>my-document</queryName>
<description>Description of My Document Type</description>
<baseId>cmis:document</baseId>
<parentId>cmis:document</parentId>
<creatable>true</creatable>
<fileable>true</fileable>
<queryable>true</queryable>
<fulltextIndexed>false</fulltextIndexed>
<includedInSupertypeQuery>true</includedInSupertypeQuery>
<controllablePolicy>false</controllablePolicy>
<controllableACL>true</controllableACL>
<versionable>false</versionable>
<contentStreamAllowed>allowed</contentStreamAllowed>
  <propertyIntegerDefinition>
    <id>my-int</id>
    <localName>my-int</localName>
    <localNamespace>local</localNamespace>
    <displayName>Int</displayName>
    <queryName>my-int</queryName>
    <description>Int</description>
    <propertyType>integer</propertyType>
    <cardinality>single</cardinality>
    <updatability>readwrite</updatability>
    <inherited>false</inherited>
    <required>false</required>
    <queryable>true</queryable>
    <orderable>true</orderable>
    <openChoice>false</openChoice>
  </propertyIntegerDefinition>
</ns3:type>
```


Now that the XML input file is sorted out, let's take a look at that code. Listing 4.6 shows the steps for using `TypeUtils` to parse that XML into a `TypeDefinition` object and then using the `CreateType` method to create the type. At the end of the listing, we've commented out a section that shows how you'd do the same thing if your type export file was in JSON format.

Listing 4.6 Code for creating a new subtype of `cmis:document` using `TypeUtils`

```
import org.apache.chemistry.opencmis.commons.*
import org.apache.chemistry.opencmis.commons.data.*
import org.apache.chemistry.opencmis.commons.definitions.*
import org.apache.chemistry.opencmis.commons.enums.*
import org.apache.chemistry.opencmis.client.api.*
import org.apache.chemistry.opencmis.client.util.*

if (session.getRepositoryInfo().getCmisVersion() ==
      CmisVersion.CMIS_1_0) {
  println("CMIS 1.0 does not support the creation of types!");
}
```

```
else {
  ObjectType parentType = session.getTypeDefinition("cmis:document");
  TypeMutability typeMutability = parentType.getTypeMutability();

  if (typeMutability != null &&
      Boolean.TRUE.equals(typeMutability.canCreate())) {

    // fix your path here
    InputStream stream1 = new FileInputStream("./my-document.xml");
    TypeDefinition type1 = TypeUtils.readFromXML(stream1);
    ObjectType createdType1 = session.createType(type1);

    // if we wanted to use json instead
    //InputStream stream2 = new FileInputStream("./my-document.json");
    //TypeDefinition type2 = TypeUtils.readFromJSON(stream2);
    //ObjectType createdType2 = session.createType(type2);
  }
}
```

Once the code has completed running, you can restart your Chemistry Workbench (or at least reconnect so that the metadata will be refreshed) and have a look at the new type, which is shown in figure 4.11. The figure shows `my-document` selected in the type tree and the `my-int` property highlighted at the bottom of the properties pane.

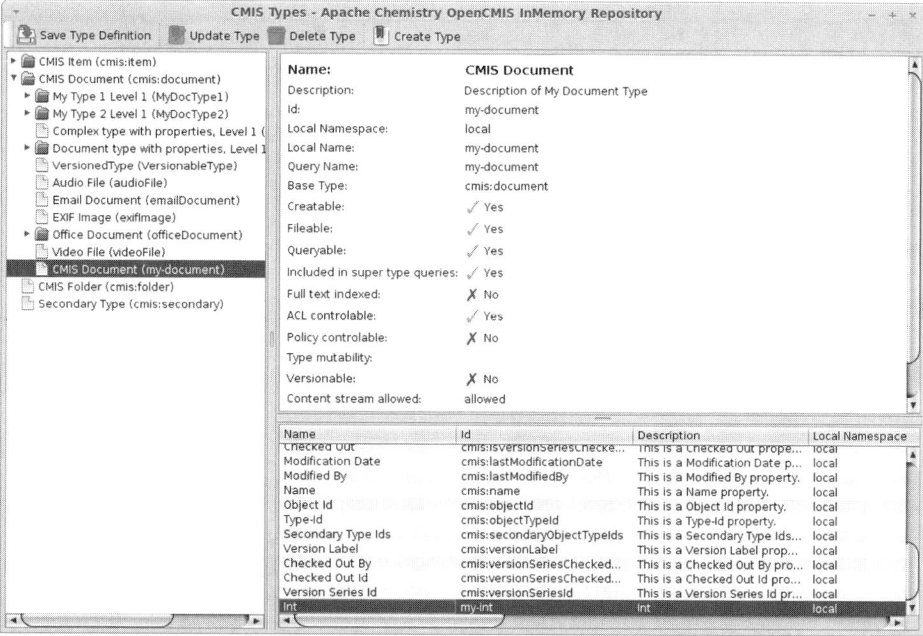

Figure 4.11 CMIS Types screen showing off our newly minted `my-document` type

TYPE DELETION

Unused types can be deleted subject to these constraints:

- The `type delete` flag in the type definition is set to `true`.
- The type has no subtypes currently defined in the repository.
- No objects (instances) of this type currently exist in the repository.

The first of these constraints is discovered by inspecting the type definition for the object in question. Figure 4.12 shows the Chemistry Workbench type mutability settings for the `VersionedType`. Note that this type supports create, update, and delete. Recall that we already showed you how to programmatically check this in listing 4.6, where we checked to see if we could create.

To determine if the type has subtypes, you'll have to navigate the type tree as we showed you earlier in this chapter. Lastly, you can use Query to discover if any objects of a given type currently exist. Alternatively, you can try to do the delete type operation, and if any of these constraints isn't satisfied, the repository will let you know with the corresponding error.

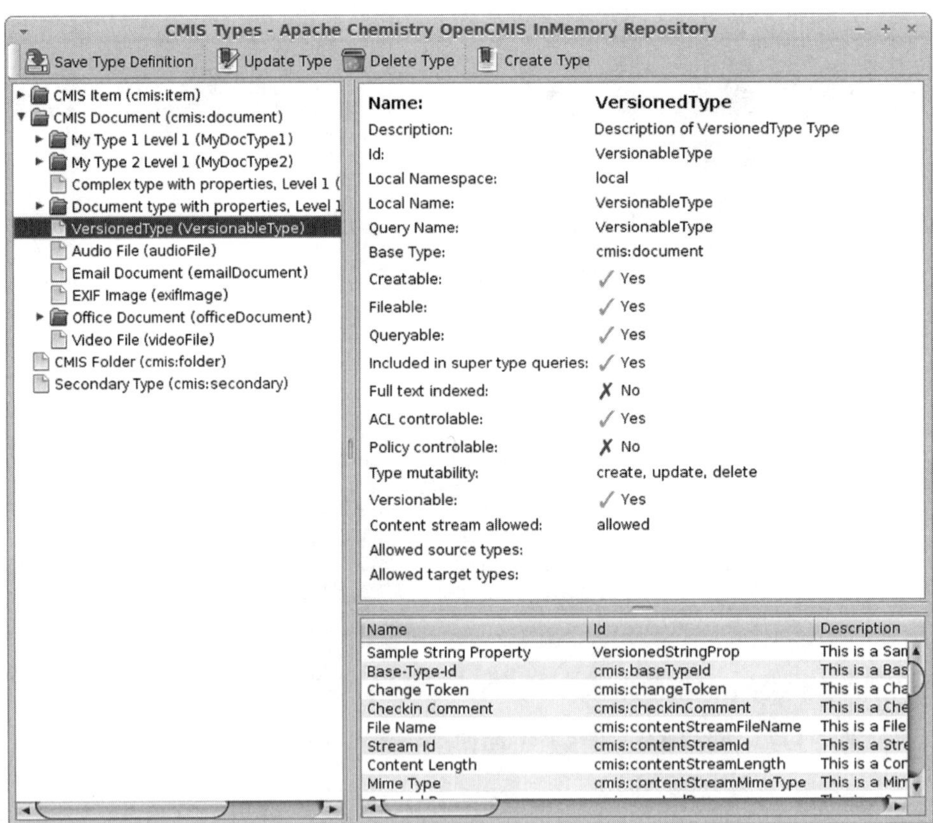

Figure 4.12 Type information for `VersionedType` showing the type mutability options available

The following example shows type deletion:

```
import org.apache.chemistry.opencmis.commons.*
import org.apache.chemistry.opencmis.commons.data.*
import org.apache.chemistry.opencmis.commons.definitions.*
import org.apache.chemistry.opencmis.commons.enums.*
import org.apache.chemistry.opencmis.client.api.*

ObjectType type = session.getTypeDefinition("my:type");
TypeMutability typeMutability = type.getTypeMutability();

if (typeMutability != null &&
     Boolean.TRUE.equals(typeMutability.canDelete())) {
  session.deleteType(type.getId());
}
```

With deletion covered, we have one more modification operation to go. Update finishes off the set and is up next.

Type updates

The logic behind updating a type is similar to creating a type, so we won't waste space here with a complete listing. A type definition has to be provided that contains the changes (usually additions) that you wish to have committed. Then you commit the change with the `updateType` method, as you did with `createType` in the first type creation example.

The code is simple, but the restrictions on when you can update a type are a bit more complicated. Section 2.1.10.1 of the CMIS 1.1 specification covers all of the constraints for metadata updates. The following list highlights these important items:

- Inherited properties *must not* be modified. This includes constraints of any kind.
- Properties defined by the CMIS specification *must not* be modified. This includes constraints of any kind.
- Only leaf types may be modified. That is, if a type already has child types defined, then it (and all of its properties and constraints) *must* be considered read-only.
- Any added properties marked as "required" *must* have a default value.
- Required properties *may* be changed to optional.
- Optional properties *must not* be changed to required.
- Property definitions *must not* be removed.
- Property choice constraints *may* be changed in the following ways:
  - Open choice *may* change from `false` to `true`.
  - Open choice *must not* change from `true` to `false`.
  - Choices *may* be added or removed if open choice is `true`.
  - Choices *must not* be removed if open choice is `false`. Validation constraints (min/max length, min/max value, and so on) on existing properties *may* be relaxed, but they *must not* be further restricted.

For example, an integer property value that originally had a minimum constraint of 100 and a maximum constraint of 1,000 could change as follows:
  - The minimum could be changed to 50 but couldn't be changed to 150.
  - The maximum could be changed to 1,100 but couldn't be changed to 900.
- An existing property type's data type and cardinality *must not* be changed. For example, an `Integer` property type *must not* be changed to a `String`.

That covers the basics of create, update, and delete for types. Next up are the new secondary types.

4.4.2 Secondary types

Support for secondary types is new in CMIS 1.1. We'll first explain what a secondary type is and then talk about how creating secondary types differs from what you already know about creating normal content types. Finally, you'll see how easy it is to add secondary types to and remove them from the objects in your CMIS repository.

WHAT IS A SECONDARY TYPE?

Suppose you're building a case management system and you're persisting the documents the system manages into a CMIS repository. If these are legal cases, you might have a content type called `complaint` and another called `deposition transcript`. You might also use an `image` content type for images related to the case, and these content types might appear on different branches of the content type hierarchy. This leads to the question of what you would do if you need to define metadata that's common across all of these types. To keep it simple, we'll use a case number as an example.

One option would be to define the property in a common ancestor type, but then you'd end up potentially inheriting that property in places where it isn't needed. Another option would be to define the property redundantly—every type that needs it would define its own case number property. Neither of these is a great option. To address this problem, some content repositories support the concept of a free-floating type that can be arbitrarily attached to any object in the repository. Different repositories use different names to describe these special types. For example, in Alfresco, they're called *aspects*. In CMIS they're called *secondary types*.

Using the example of the legal case management system, a document that stores the transcript of a deposition would be created as an instance of a `deposition transcript`, and because it's related to a specific case, you can add the `case-related` secondary type to it. Now the object has all of the metadata defined by the primary type, as well as the `case-related` secondary type.

Now suppose the CMIS repository will also be used to archive email. Some email might be related to a specific case, and some may not. Email will be created using an `email` content type, because that's fundamentally what that object is, and only those emails related to a specific case will be given the `case-related` secondary type. If someone later decides that an email isn't case-related, the `case-related` secondary type can be removed without changing its primary content type.

Later, someone might decide to add a tagging capability to the case management system. A `taggable` secondary type makes it easy to add tag-related metadata to all of the objects that need to be tagged. Now objects can be both `case-related` and `taggable`. In this way, secondary types provide a means to achieve multiple inheritance, which can't be accomplished with primary content types alone.

Therefore, secondary types are often used to group together properties that define characteristics that many different content types might exhibit, in an effort to simplify or more efficiently implement the content model. They have the added benefit of being easy to add to and remove from an object without altering its fundamental type.

As we mentioned, not all repositories support secondary types. We'll discuss a special base type called `cmis:secondary` in the next section. If your repository returns `cmis:secondary` in the list of type definitions returned by `getTypeChildren`, your repository supports secondary types.

CREATING SECONDARY TYPES

Creating a secondary type is nearly identical to creating a normal content type with CMIS. You define your content type using XML or JSON, and then upload the definition to the repository. An important difference is that the base type must be the special `cmis:secondary` base type—that's what distinguishes secondary types from normal types.

Here are the constraints that must be followed when creating secondary types:

- `creatable`—Must be set to `false`. That's because creating instances of secondary types isn't allowed. All objects must be instances of primary types.
- `fileable`, `controllablePolicy`, and `controllableACL`—Must also be set to `false`. The repository uses these values set on the primary type to decide whether or not an object instance is fileable, controllable by a policy, or controllable by an ACL.
- `parentId`—Must not be set. Unlike primary types, secondary types aren't defined in a hierarchy.

USING SECONDARY TYPES

Once you've defined a secondary type in the repository, it's easy to add it to or remove it from an object. Objects in a repository that support secondary object types have a system property called `cmis:secondaryObjectTypeIds`. This is a read-write, multivalue field that lists the type IDs of the secondary types present on that specific object.

To add a secondary type to an object, you update the property by adding the desired secondary type's type ID to the list. Once added, you can set the properties defined by the secondary type as you would any other property. In fact, you can add a secondary type and set the properties it defines simultaneously in a single `updateProperties` call.

To remove a secondary type from an object, remove the secondary type ID from the list. The properties (and values) will be removed from the object.

Now you know all there is to know about the new type mutability and secondary types features in CMIS 1.1, which brings us to the end of our adventures in the world of metadata.

4.5 Summary

In this chapter, you learned all of the basic concepts of metadata in typical ECM systems, as well as how those concepts map to CMIS terms. In addition, you discovered how to exercise those features programmatically in OpenCMIS. Specifically, you learned about CMIS *types* and *property definitions* and the attributes that describe them. This chapter also covered the different types of constraints that can be present on these types. Finally, you walked through the new advanced CMIS 1.1 metadata features: type mutability and secondary types.

Now that you understand these metadata basics, you're ready to effectively use one of the most powerful features of the entire specification. That feature is *Query*, and we'll talk about it in great detail in the next chapter.

5 Query

This chapter covers

- Query overview
- CMIS Query syntax
- Advanced Query functions
- Full-text search syntax

In the last chapter, we spent a lot of time describing types in order to prepare you for this chapter. As we mentioned at the beginning of chapter 4, without metadata you wouldn't have an elegant method for narrowing your searches. Remember the example from the beginning of chapter 4, where we were searching for a specific photo of an elephant? Flexible query capabilities might not be a big deal when you're shuffling through your filing cabinet at home, but wait until you're searching on the scale of Enterprise Content Management systems, where you might be talking about billions of documents. At that scale, you'd better be packing some powerful tools for query, or have a *lot* of free time.

Luckily, CMIS defines a powerful and flexible way to describe searches, and it does this using a syntax that you've probably already been using for years—SQL. As you get deep into this chapter, you may start to feel a little dizzy, but don't be discouraged. This chapter is hands-down the most difficult one in part 1, and one of the most difficult in the whole book. The concepts introduced here are equally powerful and complex. The chapter includes a lot of detail that you may not need at this moment, but we'll cover the subject comprehensively. We packed this chapter with tons of examples so that later, when you need to know the syntax of something tricky, odds are you'll be able to find something here to copy and paste to get you up and running.

Therefore, don't worry about absorbing all of this in the first pass. The chapter is broken up into many small chunks so you'll be able to find what you're looking for later. But if you read it all the way through, we believe the path we're taking you on is the best route for a clear understanding. We'll start with the basics and finish up with the extensions CMIS has added to make certain ECM functions more natural when used as part of a SQL query.

5.1 Query: a familiar face on search

As you may have guessed by now, this chapter will teach you everything you need to know in order to produce an effective CMIS query. Or, stated a different way, you'll understand how to use CMIS to filter out all of the other noise in order to find the data you're looking for.

One of the stated goals of the CMIS specification was to take advantage of technologies and standards that were mature and accepted, wherever possible. We don't want to reinvent the wheel. At the time the CMIS Technical Committee began work on this specification in 2008, SQL had already been around as a standard for decades. It was for this reason that the nearly universally known (at least among developers) SQL syntax was chosen as the way to describe these queries. This is likely one of the reasons that CMIS adoption has been so successful across the industry.

5.1.1 Prerequisite for this chapter: SQL basics

CMIS 1.0 and 1.1 Query is based on SQL-92 (ISO/IEC 9075). In order to avoid droning on about a subject that most readers of this book will consider basic knowledge, we'll make one assumption: that you have a high-level understanding of SQL query syntax. Nothing advanced is required. As long as you can look at a simple SELECT statement without crossing your eyes, you'll be OK.

If you're saying to yourself "SELECT what?" you might want to take a few minutes to read a brief introduction to SQL. A quick internet search will turn up plenty of information, because we're talking about a standard that's been firmly established for nearly 30 years. Even the introduction to SQL in Wikipedia (http://en.wikipedia.org/wiki/SQL) will suffice to explain the key concepts.

5.1.2 Exercises in this chapter and the InMemory server

For most of the exercises in this chapter, we'll continue to use the CMIS InMemory Repository package that you downloaded in chapter 1. You may remember from the previous chapter that quite a bit of sample metadata comes preinstalled with the InMemory server for audio files and other common document types, such as PDFs.

We'll base our queries around these types so you can run the same queries locally, rather than viewing only static examples.

5.2 Introduction to the CMIS Query language

For a quick review, let's look at the components of a typical database. A relational database is composed of tables, columns, and rows. You can also envision the object type as a spreadsheet grid, with the vertical columns as the properties and the horizontal rows as the individual objects. Finally, the row headings are part of the schema. Figure 5.1 shows such a view.

	A	B	C	D	E	F
1	cmis:name	cmis:objectId	cmis:createdBy	cmis:versionLabel	custom int prop	custom string
2	docname1	234324	admin	first version	5	foo
3	invoice doc	233445	johnsmith		4	sff
4	smith loan doc	342443	janesmith	legal hold	6	3re

Figure 5.1 Viewing a list of documents as a spreadsheet with columns as properties and rows as object instances

This table analogy maps easily to the CMIS data model, where object types have property definitions and the data is the instances of objects. By mapping a relational view on the CMIS data model, you can see why the CMIS specification has defined its Query language based on, and extended from, the SQL-92 grammar. It fits perfectly.

CMIS also has extended the Query grammar to make it easier to filter your query results based on multivalued properties, full-text search, and folder membership. Don't worry about the details of these extensions for now. We'll go into each one later in the chapter, with examples, and you'll see how powerful these queries can be.

> **CMIS SQL IS READ-ONLY** Only a subset of the SQL-92 grammar related to SELECT is included in the CMIS Query language. Specifically, you won't be able to do data manipulation to modify the result set data directly.

5.2.1 Reviewing clauses of the SELECT statement

Because we'll work with examples of all of these, the following list contains the four basic clauses of the `SELECT` statement. Think of this as a refresher and the start of an agenda for the next few sections.

- `SELECT`—The properties that will be returned for each object in the result set; you can call them "virtual columns."
- `FROM`—The queryable object type; you can call it a "virtual table."
- `WHERE`—An optional clause to specify the conditions on the virtual columns.
- `ORDER BY`—An optional clause to specify how the objects in the result set will be sorted based on the virtual columns.

Most developers are familiar with these clauses, and that's the point. If you're a developer, you're already familiar with large parts of CMIS before you've even read the first page of the specification.

5.2.2 Checking Query capabilities on a service

In the previous chapter, you learned about object type definitions, including their attributes, property definitions, and the inheritance hierarchy. Some of this information is directly applicable to the repository's ability to support querying on the object type. Before trying to construct a query, though, you'll need to check two things: the level of the CMIS repository's Query support, and whether or not the particular object type has been enabled for query.

You might remember that one of the repository's data fields is `capabilityQuery`. As long as its value isn't set to `none`, the repository supports metadata queries and/or text search. Once you know that Query is supported by your CMIS repository, you'll need to know a few object type attributes in order to construct a CMIS Query. Here are the attributes you should be aware of:

- `queryable`—This Boolean attribute must be `true` to be able to use the object type in a CMIS Query and have the objects from this type be returned as part of the Query result set. For example, the CMIS specification includes an object type called `cmis:relationship`, which is used to establish relationships or associations between objects. If you look at the type definition for `cmis:relationship`, you'll see that it's not queryable. Therefore, you can never have a query that says `SELECT * FROM cmis:relationship`.
- `includedInSuperTypeQuery`—If this Boolean attribute is `true`, then the objects of this object type may be returned when you query against one of its ancestor object types. If this attribute is `false`, the objects in the object type may still be returned when its `queryable` attribute (see the previous item in this list) is `true`. For example, included among the sample object types in the InMemory server that accompanies this book is a type called `cmis:lyrics`. Its parent type is `cmisbook:text`, whose parent is `cmis:document`. Because `includedInSuperTypeQuery` is set to `true` for `cmis:lyrics` and `cmisbook:text`, queries that select from `cmis:document` may return instances of `cmis:lyrics` because `cmis:document` is a supertype of `cmis:lyrics`.
- `queryName`—The `queryName` of an object type is equivalent to the table name used in the `FROM` clause to identify the object type. This is case sensitive. For example, an object type might have an ID of `cmisbook:recordLabel`, but its `queryName` might be `cmisbook:label`. When writing CMIS queries, you must always use the value of the type definition's `queryName`, not its type ID, in the `FROM` clause.

SETTING UP SAMPLE DATA If you haven't done this already, now is a good time to add a few of the audio files into the InMemory server, so you can experiment with more varieties of queries. If you don't, you can still work with the documents that already exist in the server, but the query results may not be as interesting without the diversity of property values to query on.

In the next section, we'll look at these attributes in the CMIS Workbench.

5.2.3 Try it—checking the Query capabilities of a CMIS service

For this exercise, take a quick look at the repository info for the InMemory Repository (CMIS Workbench > Repository Info). Under Capabilities, you'll see that Query is BOTHCOMBINED. That means you can create powerful queries with metadata queries and full-text searches together in one single SQL query statement.

Because you're working in CMIS Workbench, you can take a look at the attributes of the object types. Go to the CMIS Workbench > Types. Click on Audio File (`cmisbook:audio`) in the left pane, and you can see its attributes in the upper-right pane, with queryable set to Yes (see figure 5.2). This means that the Audio File object type can be used in your CMIS SQL. Also note the `queryName` is `cmisbook:audio`, so that's the "virtual table" name you'll use in your SQL query. In the same upper-right pane, you can see that Included in Super Type Queries is set to Yes for object type Audio File. Recall that in chapter 4, you ran code to programmatically examine the attributes for each of the types in the hierarchy. These are the same type attributes you're looking at now.

5.2.4 Try it—your first CMIS Query

Even though you're starting to see how Query works, we'll start with the simplest query possible. This will give you a taste of what to expect later as we fill in the blanks.

In this exercise, you'll query on the base object type, `cmis:document`. Note that it isn't a good idea to run this query on a large production-sized system with document objects in the millions, or more.

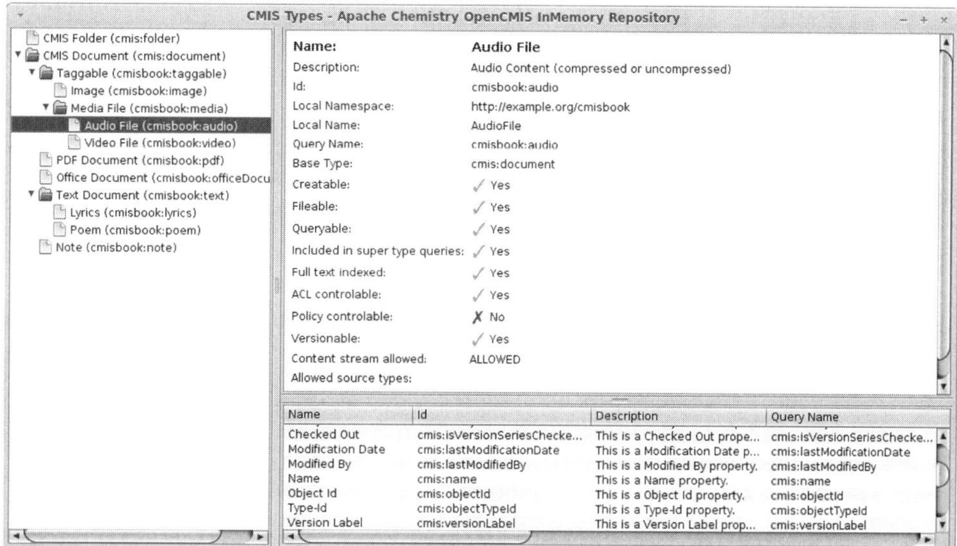

Figure 5.2 Examine the type attributes for `cmis:audio` using the CMIS Workbench Types view.

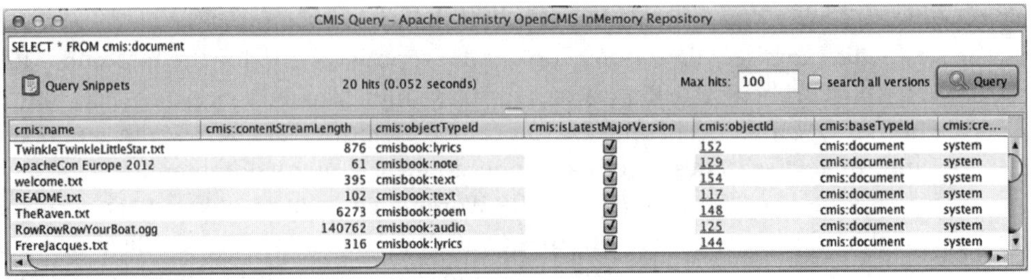

CMIS Query – Apache Chemistry OpenCMIS InMemory Repository

SELECT * FROM cmis:document

Query Snippets — 20 hits (0.052 seconds) — Max hits: 100 — search all versions — Query

cmis:name	cmis:contentStreamLength	cmis:objectTypeId	cmis:isLatestMajorVersion	cmis:objectId	cmis:baseTypeId	cmis:cre...
TwinkleTwinkleLittleStar.txt	876	cmisbook:lyrics	✓	152	cmis:document	system
ApacheCon Europe 2012	61	cmisbook:note	✓	129	cmis:document	system
welcome.txt	395	cmisbook:text	✓	154	cmis:document	system
README.txt	102	cmisbook:text	✓	117	cmis:document	system
TheRaven.txt	6273	cmisbook:poem	✓	148	cmis:document	system
RowRowRowYourBoat.ogg	140762	cmisbook:audio	✓	125	cmis:document	system
FrereJacques.txt	316	cmisbook:lyrics	✓	144	cmis:document	system

Figure 5.3 Simple query results executed in CMIS Workbench

If you go to the CMIS Workbench and click on Query, you can run the default SQL that's in the Query pane. Click the Query button, and you'll see query results with all the document properties:

```
SELECT * FROM cmis:document
```

Figure 5.3 shows the output of this query.

Take a minute to scroll right in the query output to see the object property values for the query results. You may have to widen the columns to see the column names and values. You can also change the order of the columns by dragging them to the right or left. Stop when you get to the `cmis:objectTypeId` column. You can see that the objects that have been returned are of many different object types, such as `cmisbook:note` and `cmisbook:audio`.

Even though you searched for `cmis:document` objects, because `cmisbook:note` is a subtype of `cmis:document`, and its `includedInSuperTypeQuery` attribute is `true`, objects of `cmisbook:note` are also returned. Had `includedInSuperTypeQuery` been `false`, the query wouldn't have returned any `cmisbook:note` objects. As for `cmisbook:audio`, it's a subtype of `cmisbook:media`, which is itself a sub-subtype of `cmis:document`, the object type in the SQL query.

Try the following queries to see that you can specify non-CMIS object types. First, try this (results shown in figure 5.4) :

```
SELECT * FROM cmisbook:note
```

CMIS Query – Apache Chemistry OpenCMIS InMemory Repository

SELECT * FROM cmisbook:note

Query Snippets — 5 hits (0.099 seconds) — Max hits: 100 — search all versions — Query

cmis:con...	cmis:object...	cmis:ver...	cmis:ver...	cmis:ver...	cmis:ver...	cmis:isLa...	cmisbook:noteReminders	cmis:isV...	cmis:last...	cmis:cre...	cmisboo...	c
61	cmisbook:note			130	V 1.0	✓	2011-11-05 03:00:00 -0500	☐	system	system	☐	
52	cmisbook:note			139	V 1.0	✓	2013-05-01 14:00:00 -0500	☐	system	system	☐	
195	cmisbook:note	system	137	134	V 2.1	✓		✓	system	system	☐	
68	cmisbook:note			141	V 1.0	✓	2011-02-09 12:30:00 -0600	☐	system	system	☐	
35	cmisbook:note			132	V 1.0	✓	0064-07-20 17:00:00 -0600	☐	system	system	✓	

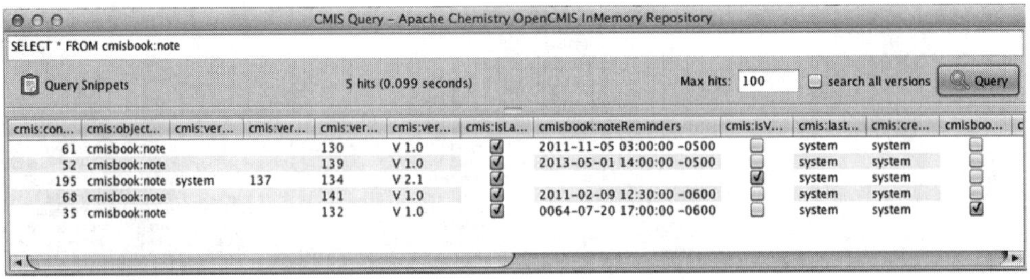

Figure 5.4 Simple Query for `cmisbook:note` objects executed in CMIS Workbench

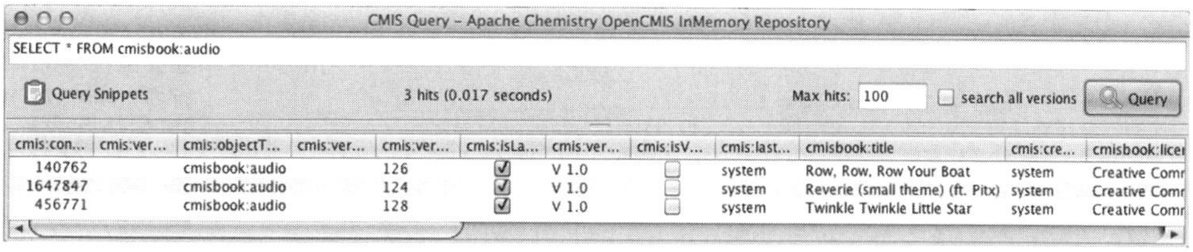

CMIS Query – Apache Chemistry OpenCMIS InMemory Repository

SELECT * FROM cmisbook:audio

Query Snippets | 3 hits (0.017 seconds) | Max hits: 100 | search all versions | Query

cmis:con...	cmis:ver...	cmis:objectT...	cmis:ver...	cmis:ver...	cmis:isLa...	cmis:ver...	cmis:isV...	cmis:last...	cmisbook:title	cmis:cre...	cmisbook:licer
140762		cmisbook:audio		126	☑	V 1.0	☐	system	Row, Row, Row Your Boat	system	Creative Comr
1647847		cmisbook:audio		124	☑	V 1.0	☐	system	Reverie (small theme) (ft. Pitx)	system	Creative Comr
456771		cmisbook:audio		128	☑	V 1.0	☐	system	Twinkle Twinkle Little Star	system	Creative Comr

Figure 5.5 Simple Query for `cmisbook:audio` objects executed in CMIS Workbench

Next, try this one (results shown in figure 5.5):

```
SELECT * FROM cmisbook:audio
```

Now that you're getting comfortable executing these queries from the graphical comfort of CMIS Workbench, let's move into making queries programmatically.

5.2.5 *Try it—running a query from code*

We showed you how easy it is to execute a simple query from CMIS Workbench using the Query GUI. But how hard is this to do with OpenCMIS in code? It turns out to be as easy as you'd have hoped. In this example, you'll run the same query you saw in figure 5.3, but run it in the Groovy console to give you a chance to compare and contrast. You'll see that you're still able to submit the query in much the same way in most cases. Listing 5.1 shows this same simple query, but it's limited to five results to save space.

Listing 5.1 Generating a query with OpenCMIS code in the Groovy console

```
import org.apache.chemistry.opencmis.commons.*
import org.apache.chemistry.opencmis.commons.data.*
import org.apache.chemistry.opencmis.client.api.*

RepositoryInfo info = session.getRepositoryInfo();

RepositoryCapabilities caps =
  session.getRepositoryInfo().getCapabilities();
println("Query capability=" + caps.getQueryCapability());

String query = "SELECT * FROM cmis:document";
boolean searchAllVersions = false;
int count = 1;
ItemIterable<QueryResult> queryResult =
    session.query(query, searchAllVersions);
for (qr in queryResult) {
```

Check to see what level of Query is supported.

Pass in a query as a string.

This simple form of session.query takes two parameters: the query string and a Boolean indicating whether or not you want to include all of the versions of documents in your search or only the most current ones. If the repository doesn't support the optional AllVersionsSearchable capability, this parameter value must be set to FALSE. This version returns an ItemIterable collection of QueryResult items. QueryResult is a generic holder of property results that you specified in your SELECT clause. If you look at the Javadocs for session.query, you'll see that there's another version of Query that returns CmisObjects. This alternative version will be discussed and used in part 2 of this book.

```
    println("-------------------------");
    println("");
    println(count + ": "
    + qr.getPropertyByQueryName("cmis:objectTypeId")
      .getFirstValue() + " , "
    + qr.getPropertyByQueryName("cmis:name")
      .getFirstValue() + " , "
    + qr.getPropertyByQueryName("cmis:createdBy")
      .getFirstValue() + " , "
    + qr.getPropertyByQueryName("cmis:objectId")
      .getFirstValue() + " , "
    + qr.getPropertyByQueryName("cmis:contentStreamFileName")
      .getFirstValue() + " , "
    + qr.getPropertyById("cmis:contentStreamLength")
      .getFirstValue());

    // limit the output to 5 results
    if (count++ >= 5) break;

}
```

Because QueryResults must be able to hold single- or multivalued properties, we need to specify which value we want. In the case of single-valued properties, we can always call this shortcut method to get us the first value. In part 2 you'll see examples of retrieving multivalued properties from a QueryResult.

Retrieve a property by its queryName (previous line) or by the property's ID (this line).

Figure 5.6 shows the output of this code in the bottom output pane of the Groovy console.

Now you can see the direct correlation between running a query string in the Query GUI and running a query from code. We'll focus strictly on the query syntax for the rest of this chapter, but you'll have plenty of opportunities to see query code in part 2 of the book.

Next we'll dig a bit deeper into the queryable aspects of the properties themselves.

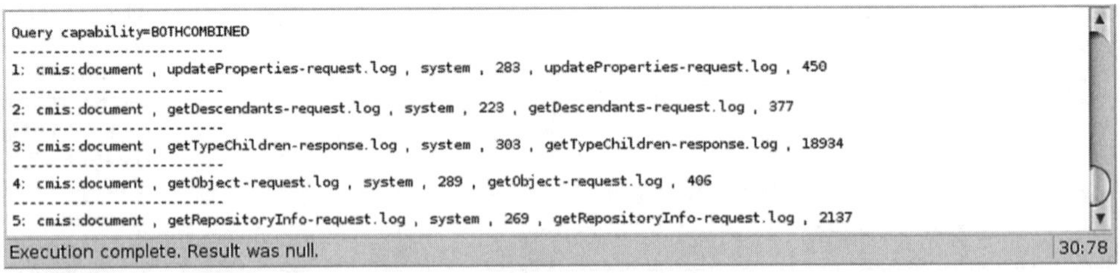

```
Query capability=BOTHCOMBINED
-------------------------
1: cmis:document , updateProperties-request.log , system , 283 , updateProperties-request.log , 450
-------------------------
2: cmis:document , getDescendants-request.log , system , 223 , getDescendants-request.log , 377
-------------------------
3: cmis:document , getTypeChildren-response.log , system , 303 , getTypeChildren-response.log , 18934
-------------------------
4: cmis:document , getObject-request.log , system , 289 , getObject-request.log , 406
-------------------------
5: cmis:document , getRepositoryInfo-request.log , system , 269 , getRepositoryInfo-request.log , 2137
Execution complete. Result was null.                                                          30:78
```

Figure 5.6 Output from the simple query example in listing 5.1

5.2.6 Checking query-related attributes for properties

Now that you've played with object types as "virtual tables" in the FROM clause, we can move on to the second set of information that you'll need to check on—the object type properties and their definitions. The property definitions are involved in the other three clauses in the SELECT statement: SELECT, WHERE, and ORDER BY.

Before using a particular object type property as a virtual column in the query, you'll need to check whether or not the property can be used in the query. Here are the relevant object type property definitions:

- queryable—This Boolean attribute must be true to be able to use this property in the WHERE clause and have the values be returned. If this attribute is false, you can still specify the property in the SELECT clause to return the property values, but it can't be in the WHERE clause.
- queryName—The queryName of this property. You can think of it as the name of the virtual column from the spreadsheet example at the beginning of this chapter. The property can be directly defined or inherited by the object type in the FROM clause. You can also specify the CMIS properties that are defined in the root object types, such as cmis:name and cmis:creationDate. Note that the name is case sensitive.
- orderable—This Boolean attribute must be true to be able to use this property in the ORDER BY clause. A common, sometimes required, DBMS practice is that the properties used in the ORDER BY clause must also be in the SELECT clause.

It's easy to see these attributes from the Workbench. Go back to the Types pane, expand CMIS Document, and click on the Note (cmisbook:note) type. In the bottom-right pane are the object properties ordered alphabetically by their ID and their attribute definitions. Locate one of the predefined CMIS properties, such as cmis:name, that exists for all document object types and descendant types. Examine its attributes to make sure you can use cmis:name in your SQL query. Figure 5.7 shows the Types window displaying the cmis:name information for cmisbook:note.

Scrolling toward the end of the properties, find the property names with the prefix of cmisbook:—these are the custom properties defined for Note. The other properties are inherited from cmis:document and exist for all documents in the repository. Locate the Archived property from the list, and then scroll to the right to see its property definition attributes. Familiarize yourself with the property and how you can use it in your queries.

That's it for property attributes. Next we'll look at the hierarchical relationships between the types and how that relates to the search scope.

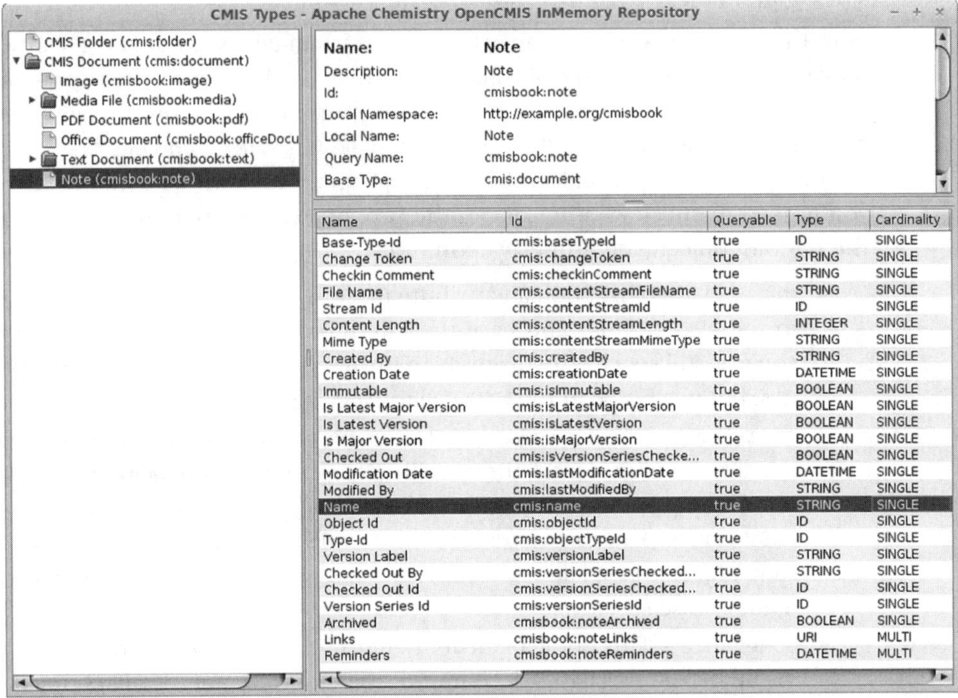

Figure 5.7 Examining the `queryable` attribute for `cmis:name`

5.2.7 *Search scope*

Now that you understand the basics of which object types and which properties can be queried, you'll need to determine the scope of your queries. We briefly touched on scoping and inheritance when we described the object type's `includedInSuperTypeQuery` attribute. You'll also recall the type inheritance we discussed in chapter 4. This also applies to Query.

We can elaborate on this concept using the existing document object types in the InMemory server, as shown in figure 5.8.

Querying on CMIS Document (A) will return matches from its own object type (A) and also all of its descendant object types, (B) and (C). Querying on Text Document (B) will return matches from Text Document (B) and Lyrics (C) object types.

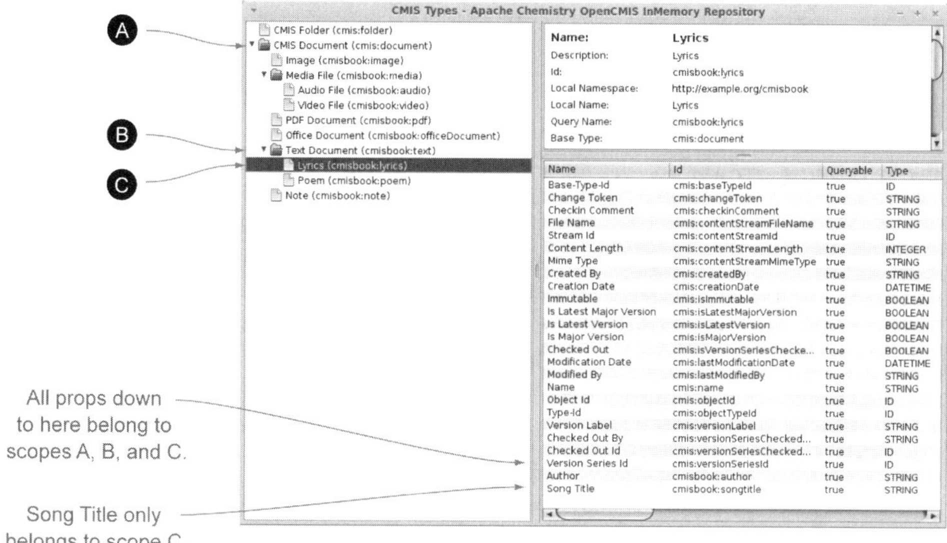

A `cmis:document` base type

B `cmisbook:author` comes from `cmisbook:text`, so it also belongs to all items in scopes B and C.

C `cmisbook:lyrics` adds the Song Title property to the list of inherited props it gets from A and B.

Figure 5.8 Three Query scopes, A, B, and C, each with more properties

5.3 Components of a query

Armed with the basics of object types and properties as tables and columns, and knowing when you can use them in a CMIS Query, you're ready to take a look at the syntax of the supported SQL grammar. Because we'll be talking in terms of SQL with its relationship database references, we'll mix the jargon and refer to object types as tables and properties as columns. The CMIS data model does map nicely to the relational model, and it helps to think in terms of tables and columns.

For those of you brave enough to read the Backus-Naur Form (BNF) grammar for the CMIS SQL query syntax, we have it in appendix B for your reference in graphical form. You'll also find the BNF grammar in section 2.14.2.1 of the CMIS 1.1 specification document as plain text. One look and you'll agree—it's not for the faint of heart. In the rest of this chapter, we'll explain the syntax in more user-friendly terms, along with lots of examples. We hope that you'll only need to refer to the BNF grammar for the more complex queries. Take your time to explore the query syntax by entering the SQL examples that follow into the CMIS Workbench Query editor.

BNF GRAMMAR BNF (Backus-Naur Form) is a computer science term for a notation technique used to describe the syntax of various languages. It's necessary for official language specifications like the OASIS CMIS specification, which must be precise in its definitions in order to avoid any misunderstandings among vendors.

5.3.1 The SELECT clause

The `SELECT` clause describes the virtual columns or properties that will be included in the result set. It can be a comma-separated list of one or more property `queryNames`, or `*` to return all single-valued properties. Some CMIS repositories may also return multivalued properties for the `*`, but it's not a required implementation.

You can specify properties defined specifically for the object type and also the predefined CMIS properties from which the object type inherits.

Aliases can be defined by adding the string `AS` and the alias name to the property `queryName`. As you can see from the following example 4, you can alias the table name (`L`), and then reference the qualified property with another alias (`myTitle`). Using aliases makes it easier to refer to tables and properties in later parts of the query.

Here are the examples:

1. `SELECT * FROM cmis:folder`
2. `SELECT D.* FROM cmis:document D`
3. `SELECT cmisbook:author, cmisbook:songtitle, cmis:objectId FROM cmisbook:lyrics`
4. `SELECT L.cmisbook:author, L.cmisbook:songtitle AS myTitle FROM cmisbook:lyrics L`

QUERY RESULT SETS

Any time you submit a successful query, a set of zero to many objects (or rows) is returned. These objects only consist of properties that you've specified in your `SELECT` clause. For each of the properties, the name of the property will be the same as the `queryName` of the property definition. If an alias is used for the `SELECT` property, the alias will be the name in the result set.

For example, query 4 from the previous list will return `cmisbook:author` and `myTitle` as the names of the properties in the result rows, as shown in figure 5.9.

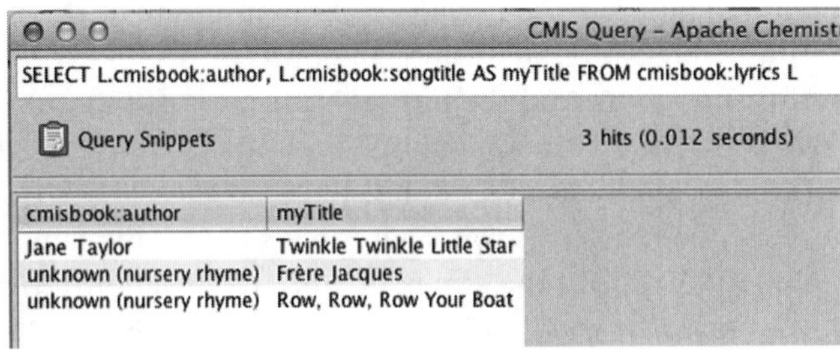

Figure 5.9 Query with aliases on the type and column

FROM CLAUSE, QUERYABLE, AND JOINCAPABILITY

At this point, you should be familiar with the FROM clause. The FROM clause describes the virtual table(s) or object type(s) against which you want to run your query. The object type must have its queryable attribute set to TRUE in order to use its queryName in the FROM clause. As in the SELECT clause, aliases can be defined for the object type by adding the string AS and the alias name to the table queryName.

If you want to query against data from multiple object types by specifying more than one object type in the FROM clause, you must first check that the joinCapability is supported on your CMIS repository. Not all CMIS repositories support the joinCapability. See section 5.3.4 on the JOIN clause for more details.

5.3.2 *WHERE clause*

The WHERE clause adds the constraints and conditions that objects must satisfy to be returned as a result for the query. As with the SELECT clause, you must specify the queryNames of the properties defined as queryable.

The CMIS query syntax supports the following restricted set of SQL-92 query predicates for single-valued queryable properties (see table 5.1). But you can't use all of the predicates for all of the property data types. The rules are logical for each data type. For example, in table 5.1, you can see that Boolean properties can only use the equality (=) comparison test. It's either equal to TRUE or equal to FALSE.

PREDICATES In case this term is new to you, a *predicate* is another query condition that evaluates to TRUE or FALSE.

Table 5.1 Supported SQL-92 predicates, associated operators, and data types

Predicate	Operators	Data types
Comparison	=, <>, <, <=, >, >=	DateTime, Decimal, Integer
	=, <>	ID, String, URI
	=	Boolean
IN	[NOT] IN	DateTime, Decimal, ID, Integer, String, URI
LIKE	[NOT] LIKE	String, URI
NULL	IS [NOT] NULL	All data types

Instead of describing the format of the data type literals, we'll show them through our cookbook-style example queries in the following sections. They follow the SQL convention as follows:

- Numeric literals aren't quoted.
- Character literals are quoted.

The timestamp literal is a little different and we may need to reference the syntax now and then. What follows now are examples for all of the predicates listed in table 5.1. We'll start out with the predicate syntax for single-valued properties, and then follow that with multivalued property predicates.

> **SQL EXAMPLES IN THIS CHAPTER** It's important to note that the many examples shown in this chapter are designed to give examples of syntactically correct queries. Many of them will return nonzero results when executed against the sample InMemory server, and others will not. All are valid, however. We encourage you to experiment and add additional objects to the repository to address specific queries that are of interest.

COMPARISON PREDICATE

You've seen in table 5.1 the basic comparison operators that the CMIS Query language supports (`=`, `<>`, `<`, `<=`, `>`, `>=`). They're the common SQL comparison operators that you can use on single-valued properties.

The following are some additional specifications about the operators with respect to the data types. (Again, the syntax here is for single-valued properties. Multivalued property comparisons will be discussed later in the chapter.)

- Boolean comparisons are only equality tests, either equal to `true` or equal to `false`. The Boolean literal doesn't need to be quoted and the case of the literals doesn't matter (`TRUE` or `true`, `FALSE` or `false`).
- String, ID, and URI comparisons are case sensitive and limited to equal or not equal. These literals will need to be enclosed in single quotes.
- DateTime comparisons are chronological, and the granularity of the time portion of the timestamp may be repository-dependent, based on how the timestamp is represented in the database.

  A DateTime literal has this format: `TIMESTAMP 'YYYY-MM-DDThh:mm:ss.SSSZ'`. The *SSS* part of the timestamp is for fractions of a second. The *Z* stands for Zulu time, otherwise known as GMT.

  Instead of specifying a time in GMT, the time zone offset can be provided using this syntax: `TIMESTAMP 'YYYY-MM-DDThh:mm:ss.SSS{+hh:mm | -hh:mm}'`.

TRY IT—COMPARISON PREDICATE

Please try the following examples in your local CMIS Workbench for the six different types, or play around with your own variations:

- Boolean:

```
SELECT * from cmisbook:note where cmisbook:noteArchived = true
```

- DateTime using GMT time or time zone offset:

```
SELECT * FROM cmis:document WHERE cmis:lastModificationDate >
TIMESTAMP '2012-07-27T16:23:02.390Z'
SELECT * FROM cmis:document WHERE cmis:creationDate < TIMESTAMP '2013-
07-27T16:23:02.390+07:00'
```

- Decimal:

```
SELECT cmis:name, cmisbook:videoDuration FROM cmisbook:video
WHERE cmisbook:videoDuration > 120.0
```

- ID:

```
SELECT cmis:name, cmis:objectId FROM cmis:folder
WHERE cmis:objectId <> '100'
```

- Integer:

```
SELECT cmis:name, cmis:contentStreamLength FROM cmis:document
WHERE cmis:contentStreamLength >= 34000
```

- String:

```
SELECT cmis:name, cmis:objectId FROM cmis:document
WHERE cmis:name = 'welcome.txt'
```

IN PREDICATE

The `IN` predicate is used to specify a set of values for a single-valued property, any of which can be matched, and the owning object is returned as a result.

If you're familiar with SQL, you know that the `IN` predicate is different from `BETWEEN`, which is used to specify a range with a starting and an ending value. CMIS Query doesn't support `BETWEEN` directly, but you can construct a query with similar results by using both the less than/equal to (<=) and the greater than/equal to (>=) comparison operators. For example, to return all objects created on a specific date based on the GMT, you can use two comparisons with two timestamps. Depending on the CMIS client, you may see the timestamp property values displayed in current time, and not GMT time:

```
SELECT * FROM cmis:document WHERE cmis:creationDate >=
     TIMESTAMP '2012-07-27T00:00:00.000Z'
     AND cmis:creationDate < TIMESTAMP '2012-07-28T00:00:00.000Z'
```

SOME ADDITIONAL SPECIFICATIONS ABOUT THE IN OPERATOR AND THE DATA TYPES

- `Boolean` properties can't be used.
- `String`, `ID`, and `URI` literals are case sensitive.
- The `NOT` operator can be used in conjunction with the `IN` predicate for a negative test.

TRY IT—IN PREDICATE EXAMPLES

Try the following examples in your local CMIS Workbench for these five different types, or play around with your own variations:

- String:

```
SELECT * FROM cmisbook:text where cmisbook:author
IN ('Jane Taylor', 'Geoffrey Chaucer')
```

- DateTime:

```
SELECT * FROM cmisbook:image WHERE cmis:creationDate
NOT IN ( TIMESTAMP '2011-06-30T12:00:00.000Z',
TIMESTAMP '2012-06-30T12:00:00.000+00:00')
```

- ID:

  ```
  SELECT * FROM cmis:document WHERE cmis:objectId IN
  ('130','131','132','133')
  ```

- Integer:

  ```
  SELECT * FROM cmisbook:audio WHERE cmisbook:year
  NOT IN (1988, 1990)
  ```

- Decimal:

  ```
  SELECT * FROM cmisbook:video WHERE cmisbook:videoDuration
  NOT IN (0, 60.0, 120.0)
  ```

LIKE PREDICATE

Using wildcards with a `LIKE` predicate, you can query for specific patterns in String and URI properties. The `NOT` operator can be used in conjunction with the `LIKE` predicate for a negative test.

The most commonly used wildcard is the percent symbol (`%`). In a `LIKE` predicate, `%` means zero or more occurrences of any character. Another wildcard is the underscore (_), which matches exactly one character.

Depending on how the String and URI properties are defined in the repository, their values may be padded with spaces, which means you may need to add a trailing wildcard for a match.

Wildcard queries are powerful, but they do incur performance costs, so you shouldn't overuse the `LIKE` predicate. You should also try not to have a wildcard at the beginning of your pattern, and try to be as specific as you can.

ESCAPING RULES

Escaping rules for your `LIKE` operations can be a bit tricky at times. Here are a few cookbook examples that may come in handy next time you're crafting some tricky `WHERE` clauses.

To match a percent sign or underscore in a `LIKE` predicate, the escape character backslash (\) must precede the `%` or _. This example returns all of the lyrics for song titles that start with "Sacred_":

```
SELECT cmisbook:songtitle FROM cmisbook:lyrics
WHERE cmisbook:songtitle LIKE 'Sacred\_%'
```

This example returns all of the lyrics in which the author name ends with "%Bleu":

```
SELECT cmisbook:author FROM cmisbook:lyrics
WHERE cmisbook:author LIKE '%\%Bleu'
```

You can add new documents in the InMemory server with string properties that have `%` or _ in their values, such as in the `cmisbook:songtitle` or `cmisbook:author` properties, and try the `LIKE` queries out. Remember that `LIKE` queries are case sensitive, so your case must match to get results returned.

In case you're wondering about matching quotation marks, you don't need any escaping for double quotes. This example returns all of the lyrics for song titles that start with "My":

```
SELECT cmisbook:songtitle FROM cmisbook:lyrics
WHERE cmisbook:songtitle LIKE '"My%'
```

You'll need to add an escape character before single quotes. The CMIS specification states that the escape character can be either a backslash or the other common escape character for a single quote—another single quote. The following two examples should both work to return all of the lyrics for documents where the song titles start with "David's":

```
SELECT cmisbook:songtitle FROM cmisbook:lyrics
WHERE cmisbook:songtitle LIKE 'David''s%'
```

```
SELECT cmisbook:songtitle FROM cmisbook:lyrics
WHERE cmisbook:songtitle LIKE 'David\'s%'
```

Finally, if you want to match the backslash character itself, add another backslash. This example matches "back\slash" in the song title:

```
SELECT cmisbook:songtitle FROM cmisbook:lyrics
WHERE cmisbook:songtitle LIKE 'back\\slash%'
```

TRY IT—LIKE PREDICATE EXAMPLES

Try the following examples in your local CMIS Workbench, or play around with your own variations:

- Percent symbol wildcard (`%`) example #1:
  ```
  SELECT * FROM cmisbook:media WHERE cmis:contentStreamMimeType
  LIKE 'audio%'
  ```
- Percent symbol wildcard (`%`) example #2:
  ```
  SELECT * FROM cmis:document WHERE cmis:name LIKE '%Document%'
  ```
- Underscore (_) wildcard:
  ```
  SELECT * FROM cmisbook:lyrics WHERE cmis:createdBy LIKE 'syste_'
  ```
- NOT LIKE:
  ```
  SELECT * FROM cmisbook:note WHERE cmis:versionLabel NOT LIKE 'V 0._'
  ```

NULL PREDICATE

The `NULL` predicate tests whether or not a property's value has been set. CMIS doesn't allow properties with a `NULL` value, so this predicate will only test whether or not the property has been set. The `NOT` operator can be used in conjunction with the `NULL` predicate for a negative test.

You can use this predicate for both single- and multivalued properties. Here are some examples of a `NULL` predicate on a single String property and a multi-DateTime property:

```
SELECT * FROM cmisbook:note WHERE cmis:checkinComment IS NULL
SELECT * FROM cmisbook:note WHERE cmisbook:noteReminders IS NOT NULL
```

You can also add a `NULL` condition in your query for inequality comparison. For example, if you want to see all Note documents that don't have a link of resource.txt, you'll probably also expect to see documents that didn't set this property to any value. Try running the following two SQL queries, and you'll see what we mean:

```
SELECT * FROM cmisbook:note WHERE cmis:versionLabel <> 'comment'
SELECT * FROM cmisbook:note WHERE cmis:versionLabel <> 'comment'
     OR cmis:versionLabel IS NULL
```

Or try testing a Boolean property for `FALSE`, or not set at all:

```
SELECT * from cmisbook:note where cmis:isVersionSeriesCheckedOut is null OR
     cmis:isVersionSeriesCheckedOut = FALSE
```

Some CMIS repositories may have already taken this into account, and you don't need to add a `NULL` predicate in those cases, but it's nice to know that this is how you can accomplish the same effect. Another useful reason to add a `NULL` condition is to test for an empty String property.

Some repositories allow you to store an empty String as a valid value, whereas others treat it as not set. You can accommodate both implementations with a query like the following:

```
SELECT * FROM cmis:document WHERE cmis:lastModifiedBy = ''
     OR cmis:lastModifiedBy IS NULL
```

MULTIVALUE PREDICATE

You may have noticed that the previous sections describe query syntax only for single-valued properties. What if you want to query on a multivalued property? Multivalued properties can have more than one value, and not all CMIS repositories support them. You can always check the cardinality of the object type property definition to find out whether a property is single-valued (`single`) or multivalued (`multi`). You saw earlier in the CMIS Workbench Types window how you can select an object type and see the property definition attributes in the lower-right pane.

The Query syntax is a bit more limited for multivalued properties. You can perform equality tests to find a specific value in any of the multiple values of the property. More complex queries for ranges and wildcard searches aren't applicable here.

CMIS syntax extends the SQL-92 syntax to use the `ANY` quantifier for multivalue properties (see table 5.2). If you're already familiar with SQL-92, you'll recognize the syntax. We'll discuss the quantified comparison predicate and the quantified `IN` predicate next. The syntax for the `NULL` predicate is the same for both single-valued and multivalued properties—please refer to the previous section on the `NULL` predicate.

Table 5.2 Supported SQL-92 multivalue predicates, associated operators, and data types

Predicate	Operator	Data types
Quantified comparison	`= ANY`	Multivalued properties of all data types
`Quantified IN`	`[NOT] IN`	Multivalued properties of all data types except Boolean
`NULL`	`IS [NOT] NULL`	Multivalued properties of all data types

QUANTIFIED COMPARISON PREDICATE

The following syntax for the quantified comparison predicate is only used for querying a multivalued property for any of its values matching a literal. In addition, you can only use the equality test (=). Unlike the single-valued property queries, the literal is on the left side of the equal sign, and ANY followed by the property queryName is on the right side of the equal sign. Here are two examples:

```
SELECT * FROM cmisbook:image WHERE -7 = ANY cmisbook:timeZoneOffset
SELECT * FROM cmisbook:pdf WHERE 'rome' = ANY cmisbook:pdfKeywords
```

QUANTIFIED IN PREDICATE

If you want to compare a multivalued property with a list of values, you can use the quantified IN predicate in your query. This syntax is only used for querying a multivalued property for any of its values matching one of the literal values in the IN list. The SQL does exactly what it says: return the object as a match when any of the multivalued property values is among the specified values.

The same data types that support the IN predicate for single-valued properties are allowed for the multivalued properties—that is, this predicate doesn't support Boolean multivalued properties. The NOT operator can be used in conjunction with the quantified IN predicate for a negative test, where none of the multivalued property values matched the list of literals. Here are two examples:

```
SELECT * FROM cmisbook:note WHERE ANY cmisbook:noteLinks
     IN ('http://www.apachecon.eu/','http://www.ibm.com')
SELECT * FROM cmisbook:officeDocument WHERE ANY cmisbook:keywords
     NOT IN ('rome', 'raven', 'cmis') OR cmisbook:keywords IS NULL
```

LOGICAL OPERATORS (), AND, OR, AND NOT

You've seen the logical operator NOT used for negating the condition that comes next (IN, LIKE, IS, NULL). In one of the examples, we also snuck in the use of the OR operator to expand the returned query result set if the row satisfied either of the two conditions. You can also use the AND logical operator to restrict the result set to rows that satisfy both of the two conditions.

The following example will return all cmisbook:note documents except the ones that have a cmisbook:noteLinks with the value of resource.txt or test.txt, including the ones that didn't set a property value for cmisbook:noteLinks:

```
SELECT * FROM cmisbook:note WHERE ANY cmisbook:noteLinks
    NOT IN ( 'resource.txt' , 'test.txt') OR cmisbook:noteLinks IS NULL
```

The next example uses the AND operator to return all documents that are checked out by user abrown:

```
SELECT * FROM cmis:document WHERE cmis:isVersionSeriesCheckedOut = true AND
     cmis:versionSeriesCheckedOutBy = 'abrown'
```

If you want to have more than two conditions that mix the ANDs and ORs, you need to use parentheses to clarify the order in which these conditions are evaluated. CMIS query syntax doesn't specify any implied order of precedence, although the standard order is parentheses first, then NOT, AND, and OR last. Because it'll be up to the CMIS server implementation, it's safest to use parentheses in your SQL to ensure that the conditions are evaluated in the order you've specified.

In the first of the following two examples, you might think you're looking for notes that aren't 287, but the archived document 287 will be returned because you've evaluated the AND operator first. In contrast, the second example won't return document 287:

```
SELECT * FROM cmisbook:note where cmisbook:noteArchived = TRUE
     OR cmisbook:noteArchived = FALSE AND cmis:objectId <> '287'
SELECT * FROM cmisbook:note where (cmisbook:noteArchived = TRUE
     OR cmisbook:noteArchived = FALSE) AND cmis:objectId <> '287'
```

Also note that the objectId values may be different in your own InMemory Repository, so you may have to adjust the queries accordingly.

5.3.3 Ordering and limiting query results

With all the query results that are returned, you probably want to see them in some order that makes sense to you. This calls for adding an ORDER BY clause to your query. The ORDER BY clause comes at the end of the query, after the WHERE clause. It consists of tuples of sorting information—namely, what property you want to sort by, and how you want the results to be sorted, either in ascending or descending order. You can have more than one sorting property in the ORDER BY clause. The first tuple is the primary sort specification, the next tuple is the secondary, and so on.

The properties in the ORDER BY clause must have their attribute orderable set to TRUE, and they must also be specified in the SELECT clause. Some CMIS server implementations may be more lenient about these two requirements.

Because the orderable attribute for a property is supposed to apply to all queries, getChildren, and getCheckedOutDocs, the orderable attribute might be set to false if the CMIS implementation doesn't support sorting on the property in getChildren (for example).

As for requiring sorting properties to be in the SELECT clause, some CMIS implementations may allow the sorting of CMIS properties and/or custom properties without returning their values in SELECT. But it's a good practice to have the sorting property returned, as you're probably interested in seeing the values of the property anyway.

You can order in ascending (ASC) order or in descending (DESC) order. The collation order is repository-specific, and the repository determines the ascending and descending rules. If the collation order isn't specified, the repository will use the default sort order.

The CMIS Workbench shows the orderable attribute in the object type property definitions. You can also find out programmatically by requesting the type definition for an object type. Recall that we've done this using the Groovy console in chapter 4. Only single-valued properties of all data types can be orderable. It makes sense that multivalued properties aren't orderable.

Here are two ORDER BY examples:

```
SELECT cmis:name, cmis:contentStreamLength FROM cmisbook:media
     ORDER BY cmis:contentStreamLength ASC
SELECT cmis:name, cmis:objectId FROM cmis:document
     ORDER BY cmis:name ASC, cmis:objectId DESC
```

5.3.4 Joins and determining repository support

A powerful query feature we've yet to cover is the capability to join object types based on a common property key value. Using relational database table jargon, we can say that a join allows you to combine and associate tables dynamically during a SELECT query, so that the rows from multiple tables can be treated as if from the same table, and a single set of query results can be returned.

This is the SQL JOIN feature, but not all CMIS repositories support JOIN queries. That's why you have to check for the support in the repository's capabilities list. You'll even find a couple of levels of support within the list of those that support JOINs.

In our earlier exercises viewing InMemory capabilities, recall that the simple InMemory server doesn't support JOINs (capabilityJoin = NONE). Therefore, you won't be able to run any JOIN queries on the InMemory server. But we'll continue to use the familiar object types, such as cmisbook:media and cmisbook:text and their properties in our JOIN examples.

If you do have access to a CMIS server that supports JOIN queries, it's a good idea to learn more about this advanced topic of SQL JOINs in relational databases. Here, we'll assume you have a basic knowledge of JOINs, and we'll go through the CMIS-specific syntax, which is more limited in features than the variations allowed in SQL-92. Once you're familiar with the JOIN syntax and the data model specific to your CMIS server, you can use the CMIS Workbench to create documents and objects that can be joined, and test your JOIN queries.

The descriptions in this section will use the relational database jargon, such as rows and tables, because it's easier to visualize joining tables, as opposed to joining object types and objects.

The next three subsections will iterate through the three levels of repository JOIN support you're likely to encounter. These three levels are called none, inneronly, and innerandouter.

CAPABILITYJOIN = NONE

The JOIN clause isn't allowed in a query when a server has capabilityJoin set to none. If you try to run a JOIN query, the server will return an error.

CAPABILITYJOIN = INNERONLY

Only INNER JOINs are allowed in the query if capabilityJoin is set to inneronly. For INNER JOINs, only the rows that satisfy the JOIN condition are included in the results. You can abbreviate INNER JOIN to JOIN in the SQL. Here's an example:

```
SELECT M.*, T.cmis:name textname FROM cmisbook:media
AS M JOIN cmisbook:text AS T ON M.cmis:createdBy = T.cmis:lastModifiedBy
```

CAPABILITYJOIN = INNERANDOUTER

Both INNER JOINs and LEFT OUTER JOINs are supported when `capabilityJoin` is set to `innerandouter`. For LEFT JOIN queries, all of the rows from the left table are returned, regardless of whether or not the JOIN condition (`ON`) is `true`. When a row has unmatched columns, these columns will still be included in the result set if they're SELECTed but with a `NULL` value. You can abbreviate `LEFT OUTER JOIN` to `LEFT JOIN` in the SQL.

In the following example, we'll change our previous INNER JOIN SQL to a LEFT OUTER JOIN. More results will be returned, and they'll now include all the `cmisbook:media` documents in the system, even if their creator never modified a `cmisbook:text` file (`ON` condition). In those cases, the text name for the resulting row will be `NULL`. Look at this example:

```
SELECT M.*, T.cmis:name textname FROM cmisbook:media
AS M LEFT JOIN cmisbook:text AS T ON M.cmis:createdBy
    = T.cmis:lastModifiedBy
```

MULTIPLE JOINS

As in relational database SQL, you can have more than one JOIN in your SELECT query to JOIN with more than one table. The syntax rule for nested JOINs follows the basic SQL rules. But parentheses are required around the `JOIN-ON` syntax (for example, `table2 JOIN table3 ON t2.A = t3.B`), as in this example:

```
SELECT M.cmis:name AS mName, M.cmis:objectId AS mID, T.cmis:createdBy
     AS creatorName, N.cmis:name AS noteName FROM (cmisbook:media AS M JOIN
     cmisbook:text AS T ON M.cmis:createdBy = T.cmis:lastModifiedBy) INNER
     JOIN cmisbook:note AS N ON N.cmis:createdBy = T.cmis:createdBy WHERE
     N.cmisbook:noteArchived = TRUE
```

PERFORMANCE OF JOINS JOINs can be resource intensive and may degrade your system performance, which means you should always try to minimize the number of tables you JOIN, particularly in frequently run queries.

GENERAL JOIN LIMITATIONS IN CMIS

Here are some more notes and limitations you should know for the CMIS JOIN syntax:

- Only explicit JOINs are supported, using the `JOIN ... ON` syntax. Don't use the implicit JOIN syntax, where you only specify multiple tables in the `FROM` clause; for example, `SELECT * FROM Object1, Object2`. The implicit JOIN syntax isn't supported.
- Only equijoin is supported, where the JOIN condition in the `ON` clause can only be an equality test between the object properties. The object properties can be of any data type. The object properties in the `JOIN` condition don't have to have the same name, but the comparison operator must be the equal sign (`=`). Here's an example:

  ```
  SELECT M.*, T.cmis:name textname FROM cmisbook:media AS M JOIN
  cmisbook:text AS T ON M.cmis:createdBy = T.cmis:lastModifiedBy WHERE
  M.cmis:createdBy <> 'unknown'
  ```

- The object properties used in the ON clause to JOIN the tables can only be single-valued properties. You can't specify a multivalued property. It wouldn't make sense anyway.
- RIGHT JOIN and FULL JOIN aren't supported.

That's it for all of the portions of CMIS SQL that are part of the standard SQL-92. Up to this point, if you're experienced with using SQL in general, this should all have felt familiar—we hope even natural. Now that we've finished covering the standard parts of CMIS SQL, all we have left are a few small parts that have been extended for ECM. Hang on, we're almost finished.

5.4 CMIS SQL extension functions

As we mentioned earlier in the chapter, CMIS extends SQL-92 in a few ways that make sense for ECM systems. Specifically, these extensions are `CONTAINS()`, `SCORE()`, `IN_FOLDER()`, and `IN_TREE()`. This section will cover each of them with examples. We'll start with `CONTAINS()` and full-text searching.

5.4.1 CONTAINS(): full-text search

One of the most powerful CMIS query features is the ability to search against the document content, sometimes called *full-text search*. The `CONTAINS()` function is used to express the text-search conditions for the query. You can search for words or phrases with wildcards for matches on substrings. It's much more powerful than the `=` and `LIKE` predicates, which require exact patterns and are case sensitive.

> **ABOUT CMIS INMEMORY REPOSITORY AND CONTAINS()** Although InMemory reports `BOTHCOMBINED`, its ability to do full-text search is greatly exaggerated. It's more of a test/static implementation than the type of full-text search you'll find in any enterprise-level content management system. If you want to exercise all of the stuff you'll be learning in this section, it'll be better to try the examples with a real server. Consult table 1.1 in chapter 1 for a list of available CMIS ECM servers. The same is true for the static nature of the InMemory's `SCORE()` function, which we'll cover shortly.

REPOSITORY-LEVEL FULL-TEXT SEARCH CAPABILITIES

Full-text search capabilities require the CMIS repository to have a text-search engine to perform the indexing of the documents, and to search against the index. Not all CMIS repositories support full-text search. You should check the repository capability, `capabilityQuery`, to see what types of queries are supported.

At the beginning of this chapter, you checked the InMemory Repository information and determined that your server supports `BOTHCOMBINED`. Here are those `capabilityQuery` attribute values as they relate to full-text search:

- `capabilityQuery = none`—The `CONTAINS()` function isn't supported and can't be used in the CMIS SQL queries for this repository.

- `capabilityQuery = metadataonly`—The `CONTAINS()` function isn't supported and can't be used in the CMIS SQL queries for this repository.
- `capabilityQuery = fulltextonly`—The `CONTAINS()` function is the only condition allowed in the `WHERE` clause. The CMIS queries are limited to full-text search of document contents.

  Example: `SELECT cmis:name, cmis:objectId FROM cmis:document WHERE CONTAINS('document')`
- `capabilityQuery = bothseparate`—The repository supports full-text searching against the document content and querying against object properties, but they can't be in the same SQL query. Somehow the CMIS client must manage the query results separately with separate SQL queries.

  Example: `SELECT * FROM cmis:document WHERE CONTAINS('document')` `SELECT cmis:name, cmis:objectId FROM cmis:document WHERE cmis:name LIKE 'update%'`
- `capabilityQuery=bothcombined`—The repository supports full-text searching against the document content and querying against object properties, and they can be in the same SQL query, joined together with `AND`.

  Example: `SELECT cmis:name, cmis:objectId FROM cmis:document WHERE CONTAINS('document') AND cmis:name LIKE 'update%'`

TYPE-LEVEL FULL-TEXT SEARCH SUPPORT

Besides checking that the CMIS repository supports full-text search, you'll need to know whether the particular object type that you want to search on has been defined to be text-searchable. This information has been set in the object type definition attribute, `fulltextindexed`. If the value of this Boolean attribute is `TRUE`, the document content is text-indexed and can be searched using the `CONTAINS()` function.

The CMIS Workbench shows the `fulltextindexed` attribute for all document object types, but you can also check this value programmatically using the techniques we covered in chapter 4.

Depending on the implementation and support of the repository, some repositories may also text-index the object properties along with the document content. This means that you can use the `CONTAINS()` function and the powerful text-search engine to search on the property values (mostly String properties).

The text-search grammar defined in the CMIS query is deliberately small and generic to account for the many text-search engines and their varying levels of search capabilities. You should find that the syntax is sufficient for the average user who's accustomed to the Google keyword search.

> **ABOUT TEXT-SEARCH ENGINE IMPLEMENTATIONS** Because the CMIS specification is meant to be generic, the text-search results returned from different repositories are dependent on the underlying text-search server, how it's configured, and how the CMIS server has chosen to implement the CMIS text-search syntax. If you want to learn more about text search in relational databases,

and how it uses linguistic processing to determine the matches, see the documentation for your particular search engine for the details.

CONTAINS() SYNTAX

Because `CONTAINS()` is a function, we'll start off with a normative description of its input and output, and then we'll follow up with plenty of examples.

Here's the syntax:

```
CONTAINS ( [ <qualifier> ,] ' <text search expression> ' )
```

In this statement, `qualifier` is an optional parameter for the name of the "virtual table" or object type's `queryName`. Usually the table is implied from the `FROM` clause of the SQL. If the query is a JOIN, you must specify in which table the `CONTAINS()` function is to be applied.

The text-search expression is a character string enclosed in single quotes that specifies the text-search criteria. You enter words (or terms) in order to find documents that contain the words. You can also refine your searches with some additional options:

- Phrases are denoted by enclosing words in double quotes.
- Terms separated by whitespace are `AND`ed together. `AND` is implied, and it has a higher precedence than `OR`.
- Terms separated by `OR` are `OR`ed together. `OR` is a reserved word and shouldn't be used as a search term.

USE OF OR IN SEARCHES "Or" shouldn't be used as a search term. But even if you think you want to search for the word "or," you probably wouldn't find it because text indexers often filter out common words to improve storage and performance.

- Use the minus sign (`-`) as a modifier to exclude documents that contain the word. You can prefix a word or a phrase with the minus sign.
- Terms can contain wildcards. The wildcard character `*` substitutes for zero or more characters. The wildcard character `?` substitutes for exactly one character.
- Use the backslash (`\`) as the escape character when you want to search for special characters, such as the following, in your text-search SQL:
  - Minus sign (`-`)
  - Asterisk sign (`*`)
  - Question mark (`?`)
  - Double quote (`"`)
  - Single quote (`'`)
  - Backslash (`\`)

Now let's look at some examples.

CONTAINS() EXAMPLES

For the following examples, you can create a few documents using the Workbench, or update the content stream of existing documents with a file of your own (in the CMIS Workbench main window, click on a document, click on the Actions tab, and then specify your own local file to be used for Set Content Stream). Then experiment with the text-search syntax by adding modifiers and operators (see table 5.3) to your own terms in the `CONTAINS()` SQL query.

Table 5.3 `CONTAINS()` modifiers and operators

Modifiers and operators	Example	Query returns documents that contain the following
Implied AND	`CONTAINS('document folder')`	Both terms, "document" and "folder"
`OR`	`CONTAINS('document OR folder')`	Either "document" or "folder"
`-`	`CONTAINS('document -folder')`	"Document" but not "folder"
`*`	`CONTAINS('class*')`	Words matching the combinations of the wildcard pattern, such as "class" or classic"
`*`	`CONTAINS('c*ss')`	Words matching the combinations of the wildcard pattern, such as "class" and cross"
`*`	`CONTAINS('*lass')`	Words matching the combinations of the wildcard pattern, such as "lass" and class"
`?`	`CONTAINS('clas?')`	Words matching the combinations of the wildcard pattern, such as "class" and clasp"
`?`	`CONTAINS('temp?r')`	Words matching the combinations of the wildcard pattern, such as "temper"
`?`	`CONTAINS('?olor')`	Words matching the combinations of the wildcard pattern, such as "color" and dolor"
Double-quoted phrase	`CONTAINS(' "class hierarchy" ') '`	The exact phrase, "class hierarchy"

CONTAINS() ESCAPING

Escape characters are needed in a text-search string whenever you want to search on a particular character that has a special use in text search. For example, we talked about using the minus sign as an exclusion character. If you want to search for the minus sign, you'll need to add the escape character (the backslash) before the minus sign.

Between CMIS specification versions 1.0 and 1.1, the list of characters that need escaping, and the requirements for constructing the text-search string with respect to escaping, have changed. Even in version 1.0–compliant servers, there may be implementation differences for the use of escape characters in text search because of the generality of the specifications.

Another consideration when searching for a special character that needs escaping is that depending on the configuration of the text-search server, these characters might be considered delimiters and might not be text-indexed at all, resulting in no match even if it's properly escaped.

In version 1.0, only two characters need escaping in a text-search string: the single quote and the backslash. Any other occurrence of the backslash is an error. It's left to the individual CMIS server implementations to interpret how to handle other special characters used in `CONTAINS()`, such as the minus sign.

In version 1.1, you'll need to think of the entire `CONTAINS()` SQL as having two separate grammars: a query statement–level grammar, and a text-search expression–level grammar. The statement-level grammar will parse through SQL, identifying the `SELECT`, the `FROM`, the `WHERE`, and the `CONTAINS()` functions, and their parameters. At this level, the grammar knows about single-quoted character strings. Like the CMIS 1.0 specifications says, you'll need escape characters for single quotes and backslashes at this level.

The second level is the text-search expression. Once the text-search expression is isolated, you'll realize that this expression has some more special characters that will need to be escaped, including `*`, `?`, `-`, plus the original `\` and `'`.

Now it's definitely time for some examples. Let's look in table 5.4 at the list of special characters that need escaping, and their corresponding syntax according to CMIS 1.0 and CMIS 1.1. Some of the characters don't have CMIS 1.0 examples because it depends on the CMIS server implementation.

Table 5.4 Table of `CONTAINS()` escape examples

Special character	Query result contains	`CONTAINS()` syntax
Single quote (`'`)	`d'Aconia`	CMIS 1.0: `CONTAINS('d\'Aconia')` CMIS 1.1: `CONTAINS('d\\\'Aconia')`
Backslash (`\`)	`\root`	CMIS 1.0: `CONTAINS('\\root')` CMIS 1.1: `CONTAINS('\\\\root')`
Asterisk (`*`)	`*atlas`	CMIS 1.1: `CONTAINS('\\\*atlas')`
Question mark (`?`)	`shrugged?`	CMIS 1.1: `CONTAINS('shrugged\\\?')`
Dash (`-`)	`value-for-value`	CMIS 1.1: `CONTAINS('value\\\-for\\\-value')`

ADDITIONAL CONSTRAINTS ON CONTAINS()

The CMIS specification doesn't dictate whether the text search is case sensitive or not (whether searching for "TEST" and "test" will return different matches). Most of the text-search servers in the market aren't case sensitive, but it will be up to the repository implementation.

The CONTAINS() function returns TRUE when the document object is considered relevant with respect to the text-search expression, and it returns FALSE when the object isn't relevant.

The CONTAINS() function call can only be ANDed with the combined result of all the other conditions. Here's an example:

```
SELECT * FROM cmis:document WHERE CONTAINS('documents') AND (cmis:createdBy =
    'system' OR cmis:lastModifiedBy = 'system')
```

In one SQL query statement, you can only have one CONTAINS() function call. One of the reasons for this is because of the syntax of the CMIS Score() function. Because the Score() function doesn't take any parameters, it's implicitly tied to one and only one CONTAINS() function in the same query. This is the perfect lead-in to our next topic, the Score() function.

5.4.2 Score()

The Score() function allows you to quantify how relevant your search result is in matching the criteria in the CONTAINS() text-search function.

This function returns a floating point relevance score between 0 and 1 to show how well the document satisfies the text-search portion of the query. How the score is calculated depends on the repository and text-search server. If the Score() for a particular document is 0, then it didn't satisfy the CONTAINS() function's criteria. In practice, you'll never see any documents with a 0 text-search score in your query results.

The Score() function doesn't take any parameters, and it returns a numeric representation of the relevance of all the documents that satisfy the CONTAINS() function in the query. There can only be one CONTAINS() function, which means there can be at most one Score() function call in a text-search query, too.

The CMIS specification has a limitation on how the Score() function can be used in a query. It can only be part of the SELECT clause. This doesn't mean you can't use the document score in other parts of the query, though, such as the ORDER BY clause. After all, this is probably the most common way to use the relevance score—to order the query results so that the most relevant results are returned first in the results. To do that, you need to define an alias for the Score() function, and use the alias in the ORDER BY clause.

Try this example query:

```
SELECT cmis:name, cmis:objectTypeId, SCORE() AS myscore
    FROM cmis:document WHERE CONTAINS('row') ORDER BY myscore DESC
```

SCORE() IMPLEMENTATION IN THE CMIS INMEMORY REPOSITORY You may notice that the scores all come back with the same number in your InMemory server. Again, this is repository-specific, and the ability of the CMIS repository to perform text searches doesn't always mean that they're also able to return a conversion of the back-end text-search engine's relevance score into a range from 0 to 1. Because InMemory is only a test server, it returns a static value for all cases. Also note that not all text-search engines use the range of 0 to 1; some use 0 to 100, and others may use 0 to 1,000. It's possible that the scores are therefore implemented to always return the full score for all of the matches in the query results. But be assured that the query results you receive will be sorted by their relevance, as you specified in the `ORDER BY` clause.

The default `queryName` for the `Score()` function is `SEARCH_SCOPE`, so if you don't specify an alias, the scores will be returned under the alias name of SEARCH_SCOPE. Here's an example:

```
SELECT SCORE() FROM cmis:document WHERE CONTAINS('row')
```

The CMIS specification doesn't specifically prohibit the use of the alias of `Score()` in the `WHERE` clause.

5.4.3 Navigational functions

We're getting to the end now—only two more functions left to discuss. Both of these are CMIS extensions, like `CONTAINS()` and `Score()`, but these deal with folder containment. They're `In_Folder()` and `In_Tree()`.

IN_FOLDER()

`In_Folder()` is an interesting extension to the SQL syntax, tailored to the content management crowd. The `In_Folder()` function can be used to return all matches that reside in a specific folder. This is a powerful scoping feature for querying under a particular folder.

Here's the syntax:

```
IN_FOLDER( [ <qualifier>, ] <folder id> )
```

The first input parameter, `<qualifier>`, is an optional parameter that indicates the virtual table to which the `In_Folder()` function should be applied. This is the `queryName` of the type of objects you want to return, which should be one of the object types in the `FROM` clause. The same table alias should be used here as when it's specified in the `FROM` clause.

For example, if you want the first-level documents of the folder /texts, whose `cmis:objectId` is 118, the following three SQL examples will return the same results. (Again, please note that the `objectId` values may be different in your local InMemory Repository.)

```
SELECT * FROM cmis:document WHERE IN_FOLDER('118')
SELECT * FROM cmis:document WHERE IN_FOLDER(cmis:document,'118')
SELECT D.* FROM cmis:document AS D WHERE IN_FOLDER(D,'118')
```

The `<qualifier>` becomes a mandatory parameter when the query is a JOIN query and the SQL has more than one virtual table. For JOINs, you'll get an error message if you don't specify the table name in the `In_Folder()` function:

```
SELECT D.* FROM cmis:document AS D JOIN cmis:folder AS F ON D.cmis:createdBy
    = F.cmis:createdBy WHERE IN_FOLDER(D,'118')
```

In the previous example, IN_FOLDER(D, '118') will return cmis:document objects residing in folder 118. If you change the qualifier to the other table, IN_FOLDER(F, '118') will return cmis:folders in folder 118.

Note that In_Folder() isn't only limited to returning base cmis:document or cmis:folder object types. You can restrict the object type to any object type in FROM, and type inheritance still applies. The following example SQL will return all cmisbook:text objects and their descendant object types, including cmisbook:lyrics and cmisbook:poem in the folder /texts.

```
SELECT cmis:name, cmis:objectTypeId FROM cmisbook:text WHERE IN_FOLDER('118')
```

The second parameter for In_Folder() is the <folder id>. This should be the cmis:objectId of a folder. Remember that this is an ID parameter, and not the folder name or the path name.

Even though this is a useful function extension and it has a simple syntax, as always, you should take care to construct a concise query. The In_Folder() function isn't necessarily easy for a CMIS repository to implement, and it may be performance intensive—like our next CMIS extension, the In_Tree() predicate function.

IN_TREE()

The In_Tree() function is even more powerful than its In_Folder() cousin. This function will return all descendant objects under the specified folder tree. For example, if the specified folder has three more levels of subfolders, In_Tree() will return matches from all three levels. Here's the syntax:

```
IN_TREE( [ <qualifier>, ] <folder id> )
```

In_Tree() has the same syntax as In_Folder(), with two parameters. <qualifier> is the optional virtual table queryName or alias, and <folder id> is the cmis:objectId of the relative root folder that you want to scope your query to. You can go back to the In_Folder() section to review the details of the parameters and the examples.

Let's compare the two functions In_Folder() and In_Tree() against the InMemory server. The first of the two following SQL statements calls In_Folder() to return all folders in the root folder, /, which has a cmis:objectId equal to 100. The second changes the function call to In_Tree(), and it returns all folders and subfolders under the same root folder:

```
SELECT cmis:path FROM cmis:folder WHERE IN_FOLDER('100') ORDER BY cmis:path
SELECT cmis:path FROM cmis:folder WHERE IN_TREE('100') ORDER BY cmis:path
```

One thing you might've noticed about In_Folder() and In_Tree() is that you can only return query results of the same object type, such as all folders or all documents. This means SQL can't return both folders and documents. You'll have to make separate SQL statements to get each object type.

This same limitation affects all CMIS queries, where the results are bound by the same object type and its descendant object types. It's more obvious with these folder function calls because you're used to browsing a directory structure, opening folders, and seeing all their content. For those simple scenarios, you should use the folder API calls, such as `getChildren()`, to get all the object type instances in the folder.

Again, we'll repeat our warning about the performance implications of the `In_Tree()` function call. This is one of the more powerful query capabilities that all CMIS repositories must implement, and it could also require more database processing. Please be careful and monitor your use of the `In_Folder()` and `In_Tree()` function calls.

5.5 Summary

In this chapter, you were introduced to the key high-level concepts of SQL queries, and along the way you were shown how these ideas map to CMIS SQL concepts. We then dove down into all of the details of Query, from the main clauses that make up a CMIS query, to grinding through all of the predicates, to reviewing the extension functions that were added for CMIS. We also used the CMIS Workbench's query panel to interactively execute queries and view their results, and we ran queries from the Groovy console.

If you understood the ideas presented in this chapter, you're now competent in CMIS Query functionality. Congratulations! We know this chapter was no cakewalk. The concepts you've learned here, when added to the repository basics you learned in chapters 1 through 4, make you fully prepared to do some real work (and have some real fun) in part 2, where we'll build a music server.

Part 2

Hands-on CMIS client development

By now you have a general familiarity with CMIS, and it's time to apply what you've learned. In this part of the book, you'll build a custom, content-centric application called The Blend. In chapter 6, you'll learn more about the project and the architecture of the solution. Then, over the next few chapters, you'll apply what you've learned about CMIS to implement the solution using Apache Chemistry and some JSP pages. Toward the end of this part of the book, you'll have the opportunity to try out a few other CMIS client libraries that extend The Blend to work with SharePoint, PHP, and mobile operating systems, like Android and iOS.

Meet your new project: The Blend

6

This chapter covers

- Previewing the functionality of The Blend
- Establishing a technical design based on business requirements
- Setting up your development environment
- Configuring the InMemory server with custom content types
- Adding login/logout to The Blend and connecting to the repository

This chapter introduces you to the project you're going to tackle using CMIS and Apache Chemistry. The project is a collaborative music- and art-sharing application called The Blend. By the end of the chapter, you'll understand the business requirements and the technical design of the application. You also will have set up your development environment and configured the OpenCMIS InMemory Repository to be ready to store the content for the application. Finally, you'll take the first steps toward coding the application by creating a new web application project and writing the code necessary to log in, connect to the repository, and log out.

6.1 Understanding the business requirements and technical approach

Before we start knocking out code, let's take a minute to talk about some of the application's requirements and discuss a high-level approach to the project.

6.1.1 Business requirements

The Blend is a web application that artists can use to collaborate with others and to organize their work. The idea is for different types of artists—musicians, graphic designers, and sound engineers—to upload, share, and remix their work. Rather than doing this using email or simple cloud file-sharing applications, The Blend is a purpose-built, content-centric application aimed specifically at fulfilling the needs of these types of artists. Specifically, users of The Blend need to be able to do the following:

- Upload audio, lyrics, artwork (such as album covers), and videos.
- Group one or more songs into an album of orderable tracks.
- Tag songs, artwork, albums, and videos.
- Create new versions of audio or video files and keep track of version history. (This is particularly important for these artists, who create lots of derivative works as they riff on each other's ideas.)
- Associate artwork (such as an album cover) with an album or an individual song.
- Search the entire repository for tags or keywords that appear within lyrics, song titles, album names, and so on.
- Organize any of these creative assets in a folder structure that makes sense to end users. This includes the ability not only to create an arbitrary folder structure, but also to move assets between folders and rename assets.
- Play audio and video files within the web page without requiring the intermediate step of downloading the file first.

In addition, it'd be nice if the system could take advantage of some existing libraries that know how to extract metadata from audio and video files as they're uploaded so end users don't have to rekey metadata that's already contained in existing files.

It's also important to get something done quickly and to implement a solution that's as portable and open as possible.

That's it for the requirements. Don't you wish all of your projects were this straightforward? Now that you know what you're about to build from a functional perspective, let's talk about the technical approach.

6.1.2 Establishing the technical design

You don't need to go overboard to design this application, but it does make sense to discuss an approach or an overall technical design. At a high level, the application architecture looks like figure 6.1.

To cover all the bases, we'll need to talk about the repository, the web application framework, security, the organization of the data, and the data model.

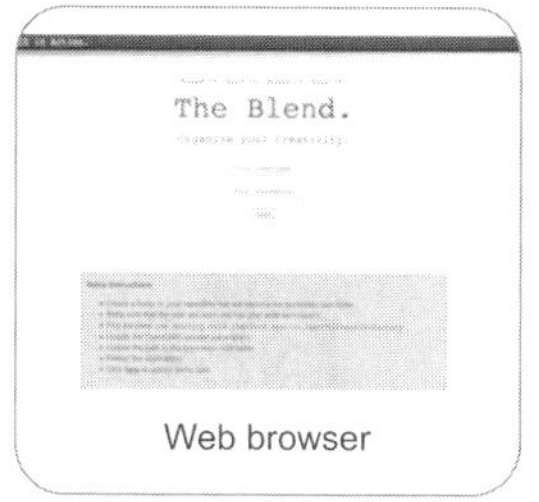

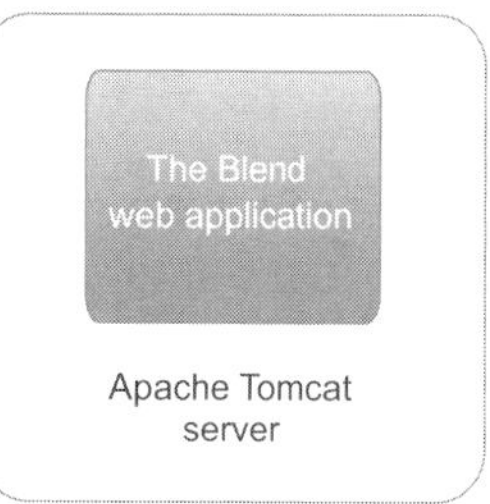

Figure 6.1 High-level architecture of The Blend

THE REPOSITORY

To the surprise of no one reading this book, the technical team decides that the repository that will hold The Blend's data needs to be CMIS-compliant for all of the reasons we discussed in part 1. Because you've already got it set up, you'll use the OpenCMIS InMemory Repository as the CMIS repository for this project, but you could as easily use Alfresco, FileNet, SAP, or any other CMIS-compliant server as the backend for The Blend.

THE WEB APPLICATION FRAMEWORK

You can't throw a stick without hitting a web application framework these days. They're as ubiquitous as dry cleaning and frozen yogurt shops are in my little part of the world—there's one on every corner. Even if you decide to narrow your scope to Java-based web application frameworks, you'll still be faced with hundreds to choose from.

For this simple application, most any framework would be fine—Grails, Spring MVC, or anything. And as much as we'd like to pick something trendy and new, we decided that it would be best to keep things as simple as possible and go with an approach that won't distract you from the task at hand—learning how to write CMIS applications. We chose to use no framework at all and to write the application using good old Java servlets and JSPs. If you're old enough to remember writing apps with servlets, we'll give you a second to reminisce. If you're not, well, you're about to kick it old school.

Using this approach, every page in the application will have a corresponding servlet that uses OpenCMIS to talk to the CMIS repository, and each servlet will have a corresponding JSP page that's used to show the CMIS repository data to the end user. This one-to-one mapping between servlets and JSP pages is shown in figure 6.2.

Bear in mind that you're likely to have additional Java classes that aren't servlets. And the application will include additional resources that aren't JSPs, such as images, style sheets, and JavaScript files.

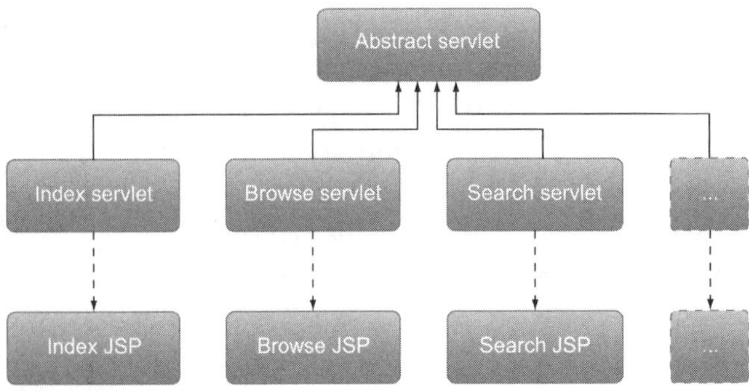

Figure 6.2 Every page in the application will have one servlet and one JSP.

SECURITY

It's always a good idea to talk about security up front. You'll notice that the business requirements were silent on this subject, and that's primarily because this application is about sharing, remixing, and reusing these creative assets freely. This means the application doesn't require much in the way of security.

Depending on the capabilities of your repository, you could have certain users or groups who could modify certain object types (like Graphic Designers can modify Album Covers but not Songs). But for our purposes, we'll assume that users who can log in to the application have full rights to everything stored in the repository.

The Blend will have a login page, and it will use the CMIS repository to validate the user's credentials. All pages except the login page will require a session to be established.

DATA ORGANIZATION

In many content-centric applications, the physical organization of the data is critically important, either because the organization of the data helps the humans who have to work with it, or because the organization has semantic meaning to the system that's working with it, or both. For example, if you were building a system to manage expense reports, you might choose to model the expense report as a folder and the receipts as images stored in that folder. Both the human using the application and the system get some efficiency in being able to assume that anything they find in that expense report folder will be an expense receipt image.

In some repositories, the security requirements may also drive folder structure. It may be optimal, for example, to store everything with similar security settings in a common root folder in cases where access control lists are inherited from parent to child. Grouping objects with similar security profiles makes it easy to manage security settings in fewer places.

In The Blend, the songs, videos, lyrics, and other assets will be typed. We'll talk about the types in the next section, but for now that means that the system doesn't need a specific folder structure to know what an object is—it can look at the object's type.

The Blend's folder structure will be purely for the convenience of its human users. The exception to this is the application's root folder. The Blend application will let users browse the folder structure, but it's not safe to assume that the repository is used solely for The Blend. What's more likely is that one folder in the repository will be designated as the application's root folder. In our setup, we'll use /blend as the application's root folder.

The default folder structure is shown in figure 6.3.

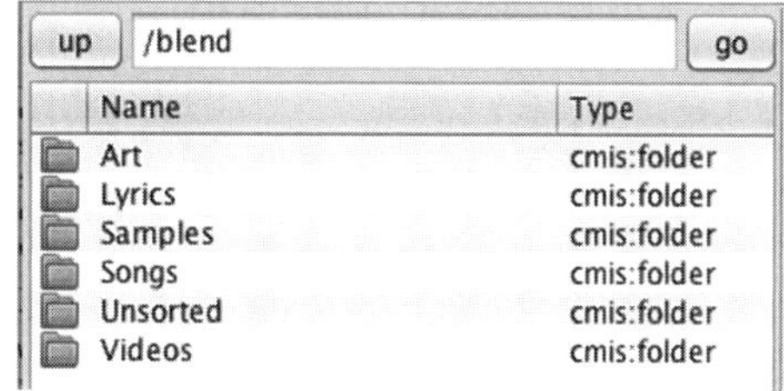

Figure 6.3 Default folder structure for The Blend

DATA MODEL

As mentioned in the previous section, every object The Blend works with will be of a type specific to this application. The first step is to identify the types that are needed. Next, the types need to be organized in a type hierarchy. Then properties can be added to each type. The result is the data or content model.

Identifying types

One way to identify types is to look back at the requirements and look for words that describe the kind of content being managed. If you do that now, you'll likely come up with a list that includes audio, video, lyrics, artwork, album covers, albums, and songs.

A song is a specific type of audio. But there's nothing special you need to do to a song compared to a piece of audio, so there's no need to have two different types. Let's start with a type called *audio,* and later it can be specialized to *song* if needed.

Similarly, an album cover is a specific kind of artwork, and a more general form of artwork is an image. That gives us the types shown in figure 6.4.

Organizing the types into a hierarchy

The types we'll work with have been identified, but they need to be organized into a hierarchy. That's because some of these types may have characteristics in common, so it's helpful to group them under a common ancestor. For example, audio, video, and album are all types of media. The application might want to display a media player that can deal with any of these types, so it makes sense to group those.

Now consider the tagging requirement. You have a lot of ways to implement this. The easiest way is to create a "taggable" type that has a multivalue property that keeps

Figure 6.4 Types of content users will work with in The Blend

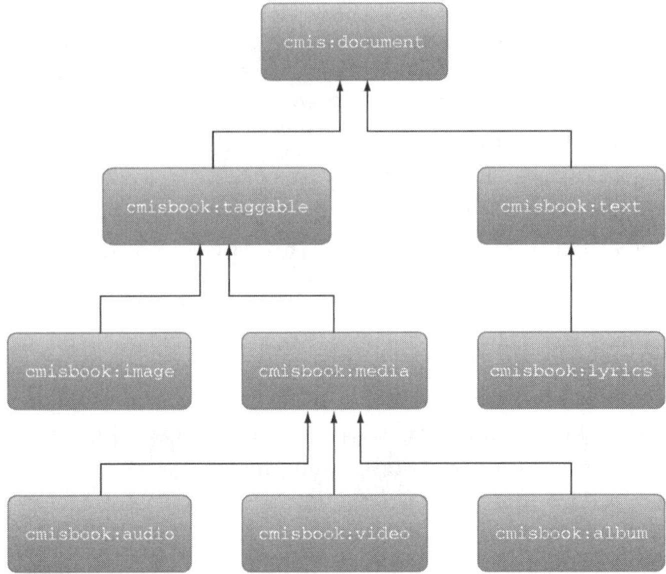

Figure 6.5 The basic content type hierarchy for The Blend

track of tags, and then have the types that need to support tags inherit from the taggable type.

All of these types ultimately have a file associated with them, so they all share `cmis:document` as a common ancestor.

When you prepend the type names with the `cmisbook` namespace and organize them as discussed, you get the content type hierarchy shown in figure 6.5.

Identifying each type's properties

The content types are identified and are organized in a hierarchy. The last thing you need in order to create the complete content model is to know the properties defined for each type. The tables that follow (tables 6.1 through 6.8) show the properties that will be defined for each type.

The `cmis:taggable` type (table 6.1) needs a single property to keep track of the tags assigned to an object. Any other type that needs to have tags associated can inherit from this type.

Table 6.1 Properties of `cmis:taggable`

ID	Type	Multivalue?
`cmisbook:tags`	String	Yes

The `cmisbook:image` type (table 6.2) contains properties typical of digital images, and many of these properties are part of a standard called EXIF. Most digital cameras will set some or all of these properties when they capture the images.

Table 6.2 Subset of properties of `cmisbook:image`

ID	Type	Multivalue?
`cmisbook:imageWidth`	Integer	No
`cmisbook:imageHeight`	Integer	No
`cmisbook:bitsPerSample`	Integer	No
`cmisbook:compression`	Integer	No
`cmisbook:photometricInterpretation`	Integer	No
`cmisbook:imageDescription`	String	No
`cmisbook:make`	String	No
`cmisbook:model`	String	No
`cmisbook:orientation`	Integer	No
`cmisbook:xResolution`	Decimal	No
`cmisbook:yResolution`	Decimal	No
`cmisbook:resolutionUnit`	Integer	No

The `cmisbook:media` type (table 6.3) contains properties common to media such as audio, video, and albums.

Table 6.3 Properties of `cmisbook:media`

ID	Type	Multivalue?
`cmisbook:sourceURL`	URI	No
`cmisbook:license`	String	No
`cmisbook:year`	Integer	No
`cmisbook:artwork`	ID	No

Table 6.4 Subset of properties of `cmisbook:audio`

ID	Type	Multivalue?
`cmisbook:artist`	String	No
`cmisbook:album`	String	No
`cmisbook:title`	String	No
`cmisbook:comment`	String	No
`cmisbook:genre`	String	No
`cmisbook:length`	Integer	No

Table 6.4 Subset of properties of `cmisbook:audio` *(continued)*

ID	Type	Multivalue?
`cmisbook:track`	Integer	No
`cmisbook:composer`	String	No
`cmisbook:discNo`	String	No
`cmisbook:audioFormat`	String	No
`cmisbook:sampleRate`	Integer	No

Table 6.5 Properties of `cmisbook:video`

ID	Type	Multivalue?
`cmisbook:videoHeight`	Integer	No
`cmisbook:videoWidth`	Integer	No
`cmisbook:hasVideo`	Boolean	No
`cmisbook:hasAudio`	Boolean	No
`cmisbook:datasize`	Integer	No
`cmisbook:audiosize`	Integer	No
`cmisbook:videoDuration`	Decimal	No
`cmisbook:videoFramerate`	Decimal	No

An album is a collection of songs ordered into tracks, so the `cmisbook:album` type (table 6.6) needs a single multivalued property that contains the IDs of songs that make up the album.

Table 6.6 Properties of `cmisbook:album`

ID	Type	Multivalue?
`cmisbook:tracks`	ID	Yes

Table 6.7 Properties of `cmisbook:text`

ID	Type	Multivalue?
`cmisbook:author`	String	No

Lyrics are blocks of text with a song title, so the `cmisbook:lyrics` type (table 6.8) needs only a song title property.

Table 6.8 Properties of `cmisbook:lyrics`

ID	Type	Multivalue?
`cmisbook:songtitle`	String	No

Now you've got everything you need to define a content model. This wraps up the high-level approach. In the next section, you'll see what the finished application looks like. In the real world, this would be a set of mockups or a prototype. After that you'll have a better idea of what it is you're building, and you'll be ready to prepare your development environment so you can start to implement The Blend step by step with your own code.

6.2 Walking through the finished product

We hate to spoil the surprise, but we thought it might be helpful for you to see the finished product before you build it. So here, as they say, is the nickel tour.

Before starting the tour, you have a choice. You can either read through the tour of the finished product in this section and then move on to the next section, which shows you how to get the application running on your machine, or you can get the application running on your machine first, and then follow along click by click as we walk through the application. To get the application running first, jump ahead to section 6.3, and then come back.

When you first go to the application's home page, you'll see the page shown in figure 6.6.

Figure 6.6 Click the link to load sample data into the OpenCMIS InMemory Repository.

The application ships with some demo data that needs to be loaded into the repository before you use it. To load the demo data into the OpenCMIS InMemory Repository, follow these steps:

1. Click the Here link to load sample data into the OpenCMIS InMemory Repository.
2. Specify a username and password. Anything will do. How about *admin* and *admin*? Then, click Install. The application will load some sample data into the InMemory server and will tell you when it's done.

REPEAT THE SETUP AFTER EVERY RESTART Because the InMemory server stores everything in memory, any time you shut down the OpenCMIS InMemory Repository, you'll have to repeat this process.

Now that the InMemory server has some sample data, you can click around the application and see what it can do. That will give you a good idea of the functionality you'll be building in the rest of part 2 of this book.

Navigate back to the application's home page, http://localhost:8080/the-blend, to log in. Again, you can use *admin* and *admin*. After logging in, you'll see The Blend's dashboard, as shown in figure 6.7.

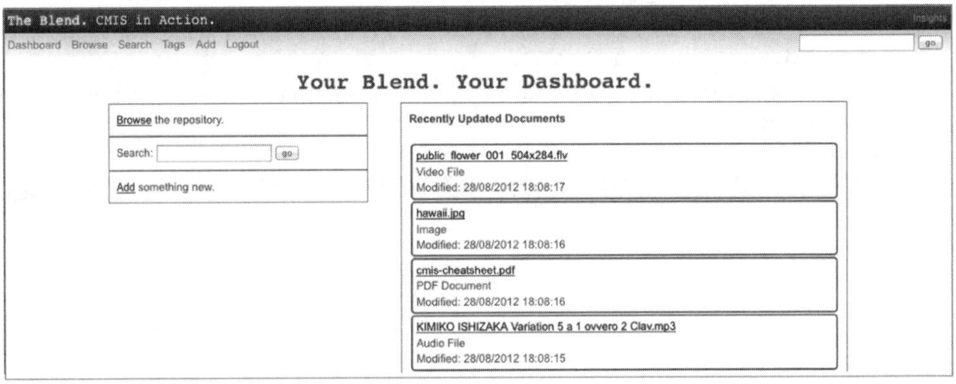

Figure 6.7 The Blend's dashboard

Clicking Browse shows the children of the Blend root directory (see figure 6.8).

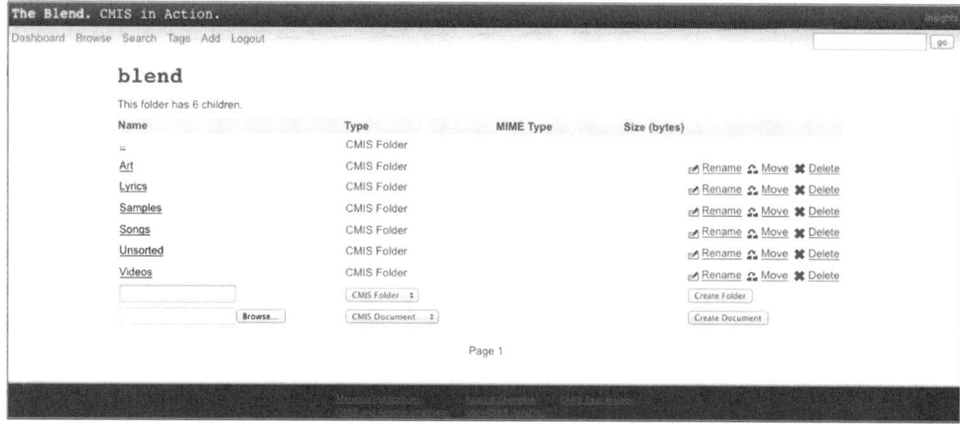

Figure 6.8 Viewing the children of the Blend root directory

If you navigate to the Videos folder, you'll see a list of sample videos. You'll notice that the file named public_flower_001_504x284.flv has two tags associated with it: "video" and "flower" (see figure 6.9).

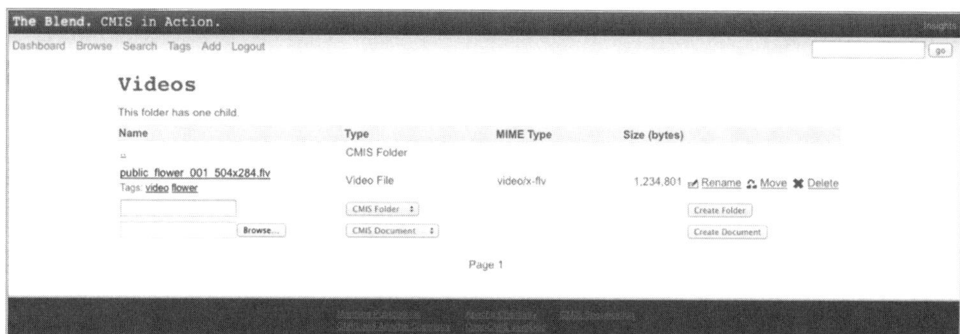

Figure 6.9 The Blend supports tags on certain content types.

The Blend supports creating new objects. In figure 6.10, you've navigated to the Unsorted folder. You can create a new folder by specifying a folder name in the empty folder name field and then clicking Create Folder.

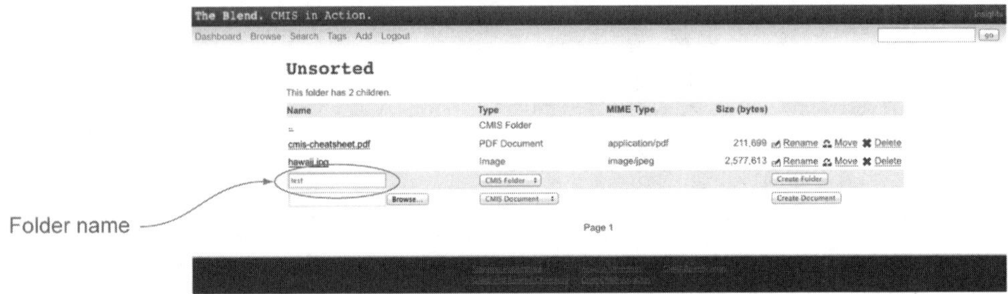

Figure 6.10 The Blend allows users to create new folders easily.

Suppose you want to create a new document in the test folder created in figure 6.10. You can navigate into the folder, browse for a test document to upload, select Taggable from the dropdown list, and then click Create Document (see figure 6.11). By specifying Taggable as the content type, you allow the document to have multiple tags associated with it.

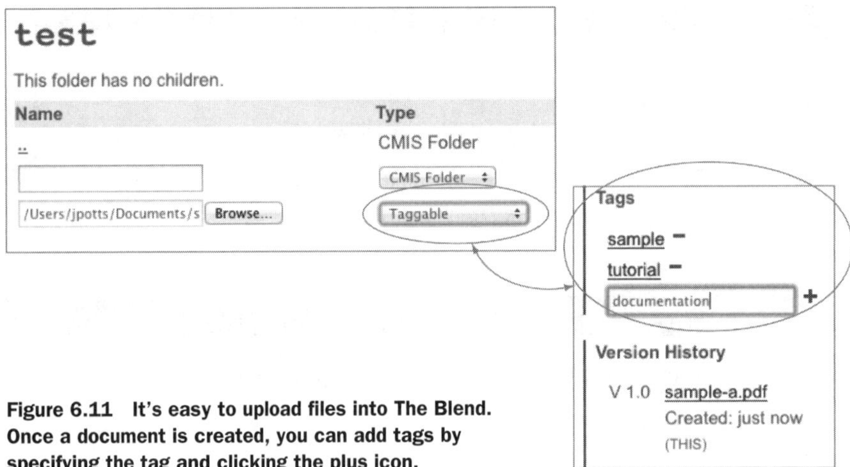

Figure 6.11 It's easy to upload files into The Blend. Once a document is created, you can add tags by specifying the tag and clicking the plus icon.

Searching is also easy. Just click the Search link. In figure 6.12, we typed the name of the sample document uploaded earlier, and it shows up in the search results list.

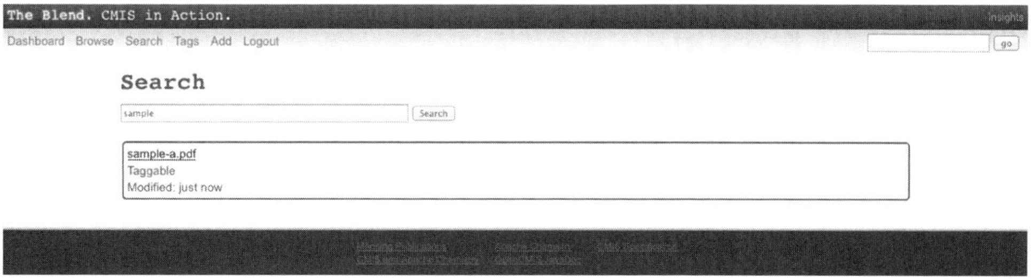

Figure 6.12 The Blend allows users to search the repository for content.

You can also search for documents by tag. If you click the Tags link, then type the name of one of the tags added to the test document, and then click Search (as figure 6.13 shows), the document shows up in the search results.

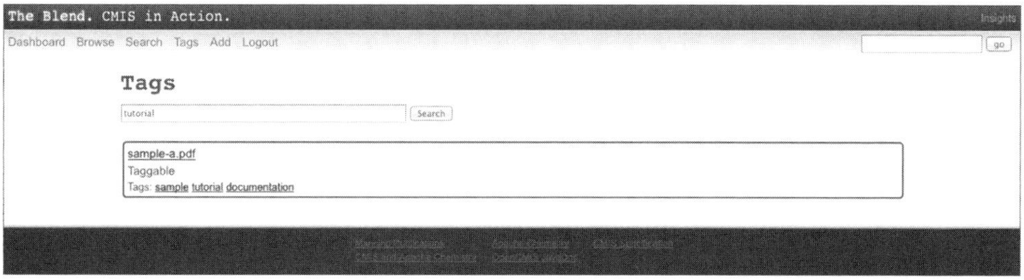

Figure 6.13 The Blend allows users to search the repository for documents with a particular tag.

An alternative to adding a document from within a folder is to add it by clicking Add in the main navigation, and then specifying the path where the document should be created and browsing for the file on your desktop to upload to that path.

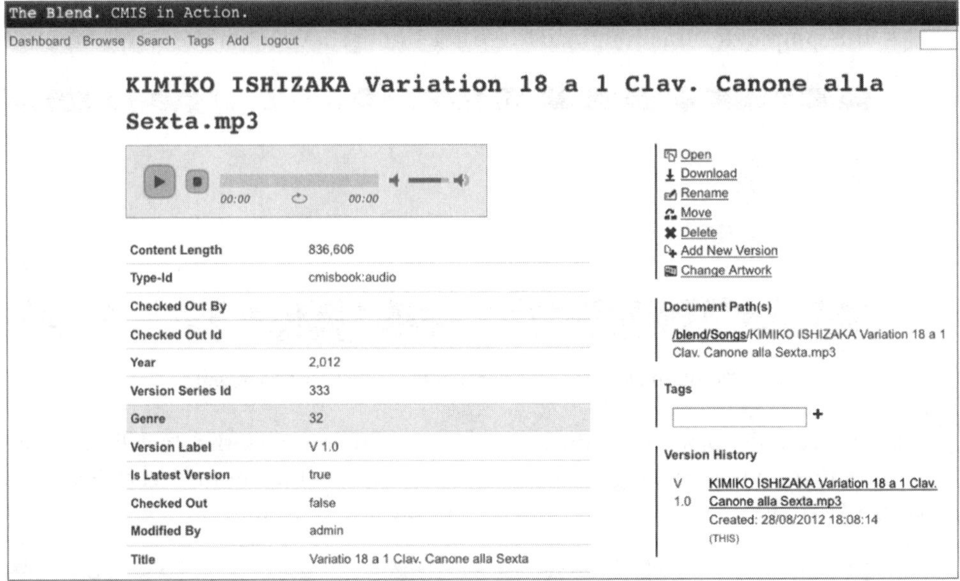

Figure 6.14 The detail page features an embedded media player, which can play songs that reside in the repository.

The Blend features an embedded audio player. You can see this by navigating to the Songs folder and clicking on one of the songs in the list, as shown in figure 6.14.

Notice that the song's detail page includes an embedded player, as shown in figure 6.14. If you scroll down (figure 6.15), you'll see that the song object's properties have been populated with metadata taken from the song file. This happens automatically when a song is uploaded.

Audio Channel Type	Stereo
Name	KIMIKO ISHIZAKA Variation 18 a 1 Clav. Canone alla Sexta.mp3
Mime Type	audio/mpeg
Creation Date	28/08/2012 18:08:14
Comment	
Change Token	1346195294915
Disc Number	
Checkin Comment	
Sample Rate	44,100
Object Id	332
Audio Format	MP3
Is Major Version	true
Immutable	false
Base-Type-Id	cmis:document
Number Channels	2
File Name	KIMIKO ISHIZAKA Variation 18 a 1 Clav. Canone alla Sexta.mp3
Modification Date	28/08/2012 18:08:14

Figure 6.15 The Blend leverages an open source project called Apache Tika to extract metadata from certain file types and set that metadata as properties on the document.

Songs can have a piece of artwork associated with them, as figure 6.16 shows, but it's a little clumsy in this demo app. You first have to navigate to the Art folder to pick out a

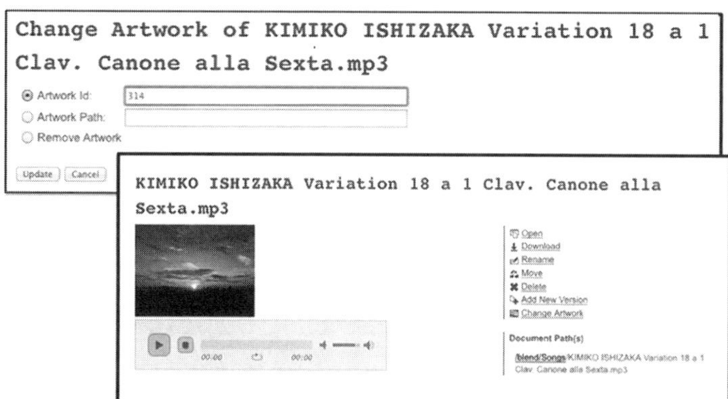

Figure 6.16 Songs can have artwork associated with them if you know the object ID for the image you want to set as the artwork.

nice piece of artwork, and then click on it to find its object ID. For example, the object ID for Sunset.jpg is 314 (yours may be different). Now you go back into the song's detail page and click Change Artwork, paste the ID into the Artwork ID field, making sure Artwork Id is selected, and then click Update to save the change.

You've now seen the finished product. It's time to learn how it's built. In the next section, you'll set up your development environment so you can do that.

6.3 Setting up the development environment

If you're going to follow along and build the application, which we definitely recommend, you'll need to have a few things installed on your machine. First, review the prerequisites to make sure you have everything you need, and then go through the steps to build the project and run it from Eclipse. By the end of this section, you'll have the finished product running so you can get a feel for what you'll build in subsequent chapters.

Here's what you'll need to build The Blend on your own:

- Apache Maven 3.x or higher. If you need to install Apache Maven, go to http://maven.apache.org/.
- Eclipse IDE for Java EE Developers. You can use another IDE or no IDE at all, but these instructions and screenshots assume you're running Eclipse. We used Eclipse Juno, but any fairly recent version should work fine.
- Apache Tomcat. Any servlet container will work, but our instructions will assume Apache Tomcat 6.x or 7.x. If you need to download and install Tomcat, go to http://tomcat.apache.org/.
- The code that accompanies this book. We'll assume you've expanded it in a directory we'll refer to as $CODE_HOME. The completed project resides in $CODE_HOME/the-blend.
- Optionally, you can bookmark the OpenCMIS Javadoc on the Apache Chemistry website, which resides at http://chemistry.apache.org/.

With those prerequisites in place, you're ready to use Maven to build and "Eclipsify" the project. To do that, follow these steps:

1 On the command line, switch to $CODE_HOME/the-blend.
2 Tell Maven to clean, install, and Eclipsify the project. You can combine these three commands into a single command, like this:

```
mvn clean install eclipse:eclipse
```

The results will look something like figure 6.17.

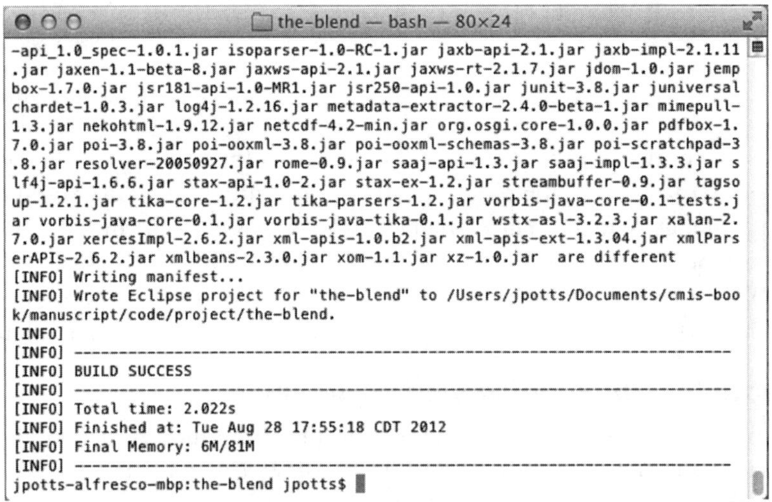

the-blend — bash — 80×24
-api_1.0_spec-1.0.1.jar isoparser-1.0-RC-1.jar jaxb-api-2.1.jar jaxb-impl-2.1.11
.jar jaxen-1.1-beta-8.jar jaxws-api-2.1.jar jaxws-rt-2.1.7.jar jdom-1.0.jar jemp
box-1.7.0.jar jsr181-api-1.0-MR1.jar jsr250-api-1.0.jar junit-3.8.jar juniversal
chardet-1.0.3.jar log4j-1.2.16.jar metadata-extractor-2.4.0-beta-1.jar mimepull-
1.3.jar nekohtml-1.9.12.jar netcdf-4.2-min.jar org.osgi.core-1.0.0.jar pdfbox-1.
7.0.jar poi-3.8.jar poi-ooxml-3.8.jar poi-ooxml-schemas-3.8.jar poi-scratchpad-3
.8.jar resolver-20050927.jar rome-0.9.jar saaj-api-1.3.jar saaj-impl-1.3.3.jar s
lf4j-api-1.6.6.jar stax-api-1.0-2.jar stax-ex-1.2.jar streambuffer-0.9.jar tagso
up-1.2.1.jar tika-core-1.2.jar tika-parsers-1.2.jar vorbis-java-core-0.1-tests.j
ar vorbis-java-core-0.1.jar vorbis-java-tika-0.1.jar wstx-asl-3.2.3.jar xalan-2.
7.0.jar xercesImpl-2.6.2.jar xml-apis-1.0.b2.jar xml-apis-ext-1.3.04.jar xmlPars
erAPIs-2.6.2.jar xmlbeans-2.3.0.jar xom-1.1.jar xz-1.0.jar are different
[INFO] Writing manifest...
[INFO] Wrote Eclipse project for "the-blend" to /Users/jpotts/Documents/cmis-boo
k/manuscript/code/project/the-blend.
[INFO]
[INFO] --
[INFO] BUILD SUCCESS
[INFO] --
[INFO] Total time: 2.022s
[INFO] Finished at: Tue Aug 28 17:55:18 CDT 2012
[INFO] Final Memory: 6M/81M
[INFO] --
jpotts-alfresco-mbp:the-blend jpotts$

Figure 6.17 Results of telling Maven to clean, install, and Eclipsify the project

3 Start Eclipse.
4 Specify a new workspace for this book. We'll use workspace-cmis-book.
5 Close the Welcome page.

6 From the menu, select File > Import > General > Existing Projects into Workspace, and then click Next, as shown in figure 6.18.

Figure 6.18 Import the project into your Eclipse workspace.

7 Select $CODE_HOME/the-blend, and then click Finish.

8 Right-click on the project and select Run As > Run on Server, as shown in figure 6.19.

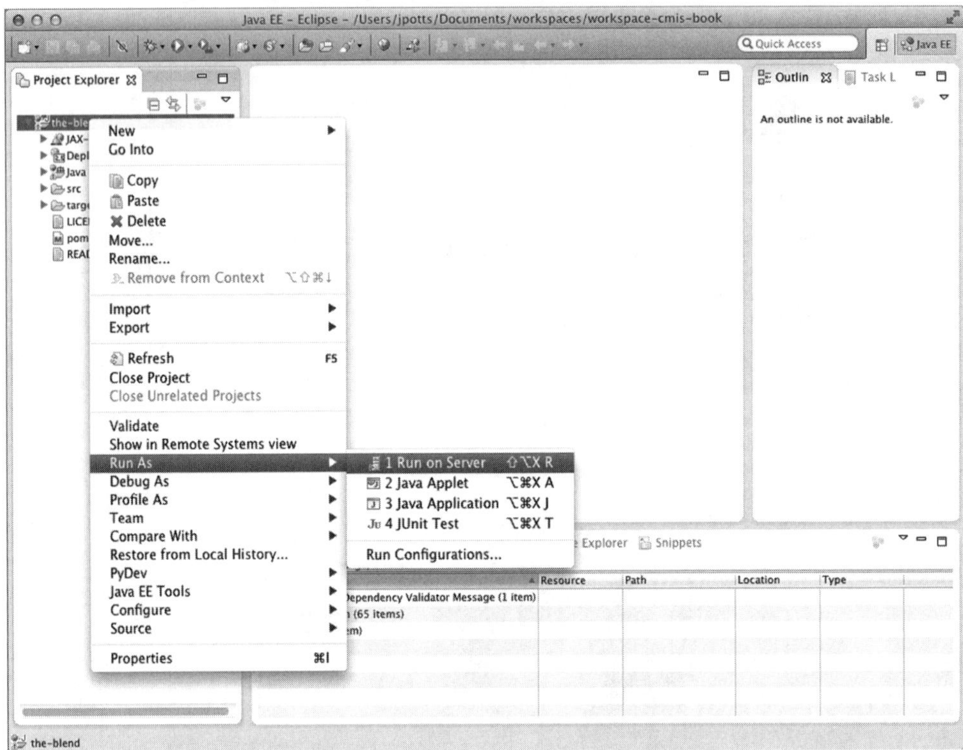

Figure 6.19 Run the project using Eclipse's built-in Tomcat integration.

9 Manually configure a new server.

10 Specify Apache Tomcat and tell Eclipse where to find the Tomcat installation on your machine.

DON'T SEE APACHE TOMCAT? Is Apache Tomcat missing from the list? One reason could be that you're running Eclipse IDE for Java Developers instead of Eclipse for Java EE Developers. See the Eclipse site (www.eclipse.org) for more details.

Eclipse will start the web application and render the home page in the built-in browser, as shown in figure 6.20.

At this point, you've got an Eclipse project set up with the finished product. You can make changes to the servlets and JSPs in the Eclipse project, and those changes will be reflected in the running application.

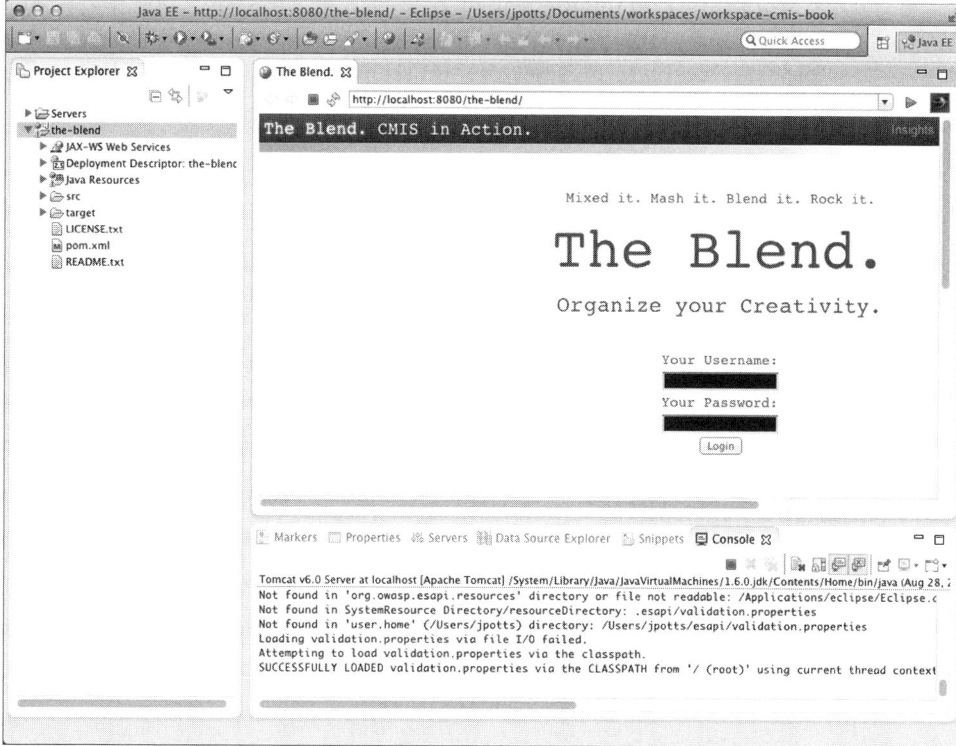

Figure 6.20 The Blend running in the browser built into Eclipse

You may prefer to hit the web application with a "real" web browser instead of the one embedded in Eclipse. That's not a problem. Open your preferred browser and navigate to http://localhost:8080/the-blend.

6.4 Configuring the InMemory server

The InMemory server that accompanies this book has already been configured with a content model for The Blend, but you might be curious how the content model is defined. If so, read on; otherwise, feel free to skip this section.

TYPE MUTABILITY IN CMIS 1.1 In CMIS 1.0, the specification doesn't provide for the creation of new type definitions. That's left up to the underlying repository. This makes it a little tough on CMIS application developers and their customers, because it complicates the installation process. Developers have to provide repository-specific content models and installation instructions. In CMIS 1.1, this will change. The 1.1 version of the specification provides for *type mutability*, which means that the CMIS API can be used to create new types and modify existing types. With CMIS 1.1, applications ought to be able to inspect the repository and install the content model they require, regardless of the underlying repository.

When you run the InMemory server that accompanies this book, the server webapp gets expanded to $SERVER_HOME/cmis/webapps/inmemory. If you look in the WEB-INF folder within that, you'll see the webapp's web.xml file. That file contains the following context parameter:

```
<context-param>
  <param-name>
    org.apache.chemistry.opencmis.REPOSITORY_CONFIG_FILE
  </param-name>
  <param-value>/inmemory-repository.properties</param-value>
</context-param>
```

This context parameter tells the InMemory server to use a file called inmemory-repository.properties for configuration. The InMemory server that accompanies this book is configured to run using several of its assets compressed into zip files. That inmemory-repository.properties file resides in $SERVER_HOME/inmemory-cmis-server-sources.zip. If you were to unzip the file and look inside, you'd see the following properties:

```
# InMemory Server Settings
InMemoryServer.RepositoryId=A1
InMemoryServer.TypeDefinitionsFile=inmemory-types.xml
InMemoryServer.MaxSize=20971520
```

The `InMemoryServer.TypeDefinitionsFile` setting tells the InMemory server that its type definitions reside in a file called inmemory-types.xml. That file also resides in the inmemory-cmis-server-sources.zip file, and if you were to browse it, you'd see that it contains several type definitions.

The type definitions should look familiar to you from the type definition discussion in chapter 4. Here's one example of a type definition in inmemory-types.xml:

```
<cmisra:type xsi:type="cmisTypeDocumentDefinitionType">
  <id>cmisbook:taggable</id>
  <localName>Taggable</localName>
  <localNamespace>http://example.org/cmisbook</localNamespace>
  <parentId>cmis:document</parentId>
  <displayName>Taggable</displayName>
  <queryName>cmisbook:taggable</queryName>
  <description>Taggable document</description>
  <baseId>cmis:document</baseId>
  <creatable>true</creatable>
  <fileable>true</fileable>
  <queryable>true</queryable>
  <fulltextIndexed>true</fulltextIndexed>
  <includedInSupertypeQuery>true</includedInSupertypeQuery>
  <controllablePolicy>false</controllablePolicy>
  <controllableACL>true</controllableACL>
  <versionable>true</versionable>
  <contentStreamAllowed>allowed</contentStreamAllowed>
  <propertyStringDefinition>
    <id>cmisbook:tags</id>
    <localName>Tags</localName>
```

```
    <displayName>Tags</displayName>
    <queryName>cmisbook:tags</queryName>
    <description>Tags</description>
    <localNamespace>http://example.org/cmisbook</localNamespace>
    <propertyType>string</propertyType>
    <cardinality>multi</cardinality>
    <updatability>readwrite</updatability>
    <inherited>false</inherited>
    <required>false</required>
    <queryable>true</queryable>
    <orderable>false</orderable>
    <openChoice>false</openChoice>
  </propertyStringDefinition>
</cmisra:type>
```

The inmemory-types.xml file tells the InMemory server everything it needs to know about the types you need to support The Blend.

Every content repository defines its content model in a different way. If you want to run The Blend on top of a different CMIS repository, you should be able to translate this content model into one that your CMIS repository understands. A version of this content model that will work with Alfresco is provided with the code that accompanies this book.

6.5 Taking first steps with The Blend

Now that you understand the business requirements and the high-level technical approach, and you've seen the complete system in action, it's time to begin your own development effort. By the end of this section, you'll have your own start on The Blend, which you'll build upon in subsequent chapters.

6.5.1 Setting up the Eclipse project

The first step is to create an Eclipse project. You'll use Eclipse's Dynamic Web Project wizard, and then you'll configure Maven for the project. After this bit of yak shaving, the real work of coding can begin.

CREATE THE PROJECT

The first step is to create a new project in Eclipse. To do that, follow these steps:

1. In Eclipse, select File > New > Other > Web > Dynamic Web Project, and then click Next.
2. Name the project something other than *the-blend*, such as *my-blend*, and then click Next.
3. Remove the src folder from the build path, click Add Folder to add src/main/java as the new source folder, and then click Next.
4. Leave the context root alone, but change the content directory to src/main/webapp, and then click Finish.

You should now have a project that looks roughly like figure 6.21.

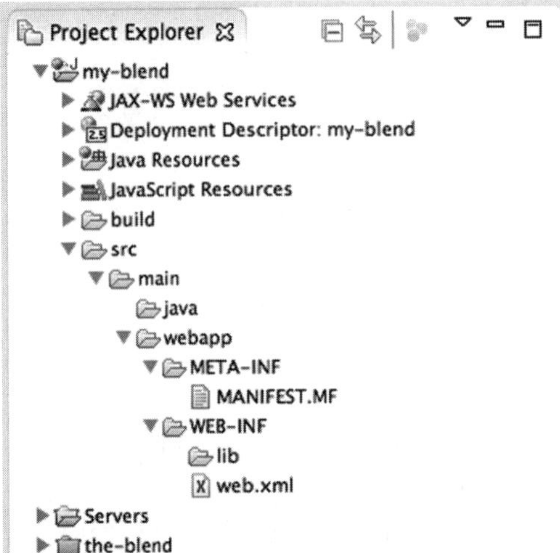

Figure 6.21 The my-blend project structure after it's first created

CONFIGURE MAVEN FOR THE PROJECT

Configuring Maven for the project means you won't have to go searching for the OpenCMIS JARs or any other dependencies. You'll tell Maven what the project depends on, and Maven will take care of the rest. To do that, follow these steps:

1. Right-click the my-blend project and select Configure > Convert to Maven Project.
2. Specify `com.manning` for the Group Id, `my-blend` for the Artifact Id, and `war` for Packaging, and then click Finish.
3. Eclipse should automatically open the pom.xml file. If it doesn't, edit it now. It should open in the Maven POM Editor.
4. Click the Dependencies tab, and then click Add. Specify `org.apache.chemistry.opencmis` for the Group Id, `chemistry-opencmis-client-impl` for the Artifact Id, and `${opencmis.version}` for the Version. Then click OK.
5. Click Add again. This time specify `javax.servlet` as the Group Id, `servlet-api` as the Artifact Id, `2.5` as the Version, and change the Scope to `provided`. Then click OK.
6. Two final dependencies need to be added. You won't need them until chapter 8, but let's add them now. Click Add. Specify `commons-fileupload` as the Group Id and as the Artifact Id. Specify `1.2.2` as the Version and `compile` as the Scope. Click OK. Click Add again. This time specify `commons-io` as the Group Id and as the Artifact Id, `2.2` as the Version, and `compile` as the Scope. Click OK again.
7. Go back to the Overview tab and expand the Properties section. Use the Create button to add the following properties and their values: `project.build.sourceEncoding: UTF-8`, `maven.compile.source: 1.6`, `maven.compile.target: 1.6`, `opencmis.version: 0.9.0-beta-1`.

8 Go to the pom.xml tab and add the following additional plugin:

```
<plugin>
  <groupId>org.apache.maven.plugins</groupId>
  <artifactId>maven-eclipse-plugin</artifactId>
  <version>2.9</version>
  <configuration>
    <projectNameTemplate>the-blend-ch06</projectNameTemplate>
    <wtpmanifest>true</wtpmanifest>
    <wtpapplicationxml>true</wtpapplicationxml>
    <wtpversion>2.0</wtpversion>
    <manifest>
      \$\{basedir\}/src/main/webapp/META-INF/MANIFEST.MF
    </manifest>
    <downloadSources>true</downloadSources>
    <downloadJavadocs>true</downloadJavadocs>
    <workspace>..</workspace>
  </configuration>
</plugin>
```

9 Save the pom.xml file.

Now that you've configured Maven with the project's dependencies, Eclipse shouldn't have any problem finding the OpenCMIS JARs as you start to add code in the next section.

6.5.2 Creating a session factory

Nearly everything the application does is going to need an OpenCMIS session. Creating sessions is expensive—you should only do it once for each user and then store it on the user's HTTP session for reuse. So let's create a session factory that knows how to establish a session with the OpenCMIS repository. In the next section, you'll see how to persist the OpenCMIS session to the HTTP session when you set up the servlets.

1 Right-click Java Resources and select New > Package. Specify `com.manning.cmis.theblend.session`, and click Finish.
2 Right-click the package you created and select New > Class. Specify `OpenCMISSessionFactory` as the class name.
3 The class only needs a single static method called `createOpenCmisSession` that takes a username and a password and returns an instance of `org.apache.chemistry.opencmis.client.api.Session`, as you can see here:

```
public static Session createOpenCMISSession(
        String username, String password) {
    Map<String, String> parameter = new HashMap<String, String>();

    parameter.put(SessionParameter.USER, username);
    parameter.put(SessionParameter.PASSWORD, password);

    parameter.put(SessionParameter.ATOMPUB_URL,
            "http://localhost:8081/inmemory/atom");
    parameter.put(SessionParameter.BINDING_TYPE,
            BindingType.ATOMPUB.value());
    parameter.put(SessionParameter.REPOSITORY_ID, "A1");
```

In the real world, pull this out into configuration.

Use the AtomPub binding.

```
        SessionFactory factory = SessionFactoryImpl.newInstance();

        return factory.createSession(parameter);
    }
```

You may have noticed that the ID of the repository is hardcoded with a value of "A1" and passed in via the `SessionParameter.REPOSITORY_ID` parameter. Servers have one or more repositories—here we're making an assumption about the ID of the repository we want to use. This is also a good candidate for configuration.

4 Resolve the imports and save the class.

6.5.3 *Creating the servlets*

As discussed earlier in the chapter, each page of The Blend will be implemented with a servlet and a JSP. All of the servlets share some common functionality, and that functionality will be implemented in an abstract class that all servlets will extend. Let's implement the abstract servlet and the servlet for the index page, as well as some utility classes on which those servlets will rely.

IMPLEMENT THE ABSTRACT SERVLET

The abstract servlet will make it easy for subsequent servlets to work with the CMIS repository by grabbing the OpenCMIS session from the HTTP session and handing it to the concrete servlet along with the request and response. To implement the abstract servlet, follow these steps:

1 Create a new package called `com.manning.cmis.theblend.servlets`.
2 In the package you created, create a new abstract class called `AbstractTheBlendServlet` that extends `HttpServlet`.
3 Add some constants:

```
public static final String JSP_DIRECTORY = "/WEB-INF/jsp/";

public static final String PAGE_INDEX = "";

public static final String ATTR_TITLE = "title";

private static final String HTTP_SESSION_SESSION = "session";

private static final long serialVersionUID = 1L;
```

4 Implement doGet, like this:

```
protected void doGet(HttpServletRequest request,
        HttpServletResponse response)
        throws ServletException, IOException {

    // get OpenCMIS Session
    Session session = getOpenCMISSession(request, response);
    if (session == null) {
        // no session -> forward to index (login) page
        redirect("", request, response);
        return;
    }
```

You'll implement this method shortly.

If there's no session, redirect to the login page.

Call doGet with an OpenCMIS session.

```
        try {
            doGet(request, response, session);
        } catch (TheBlendException tbe) {
            error(tbe.getMessage(), tbe.getCause(), request, response);
        } catch (Exception e) {
            error(e.getMessage(), e, request, response);
        }
    }
```

5 Set up an overloaded version of doGet that accepts an OpenCMIS session as an argument in addition to the request and response. Because the "normal" doGet calls this doGet, any servlets that need a session can implement this method:

```
protected void doGet(HttpServletRequest request,
        HttpServletResponse response, Session session)
        throws ServletException, IOException, TheBlendException {
}
```

6 As with doGet, you'll need two doPost methods that follow this same pattern:

```
protected void doPost(HttpServletRequest request,
        HttpServletResponse response)
        throws ServletException, IOException {

    // get OpenCMIS Session
    Session session = getOpenCMISSession(request, response);
    if (session == null) {
        // no session -> forward to index (login) page
        redirect("", request, response);
        return;
    }

    try {
        doPost(request, response, session);
    } catch (TheBlendException tbe) {
        error(tbe.getMessage(), tbe.getCause(), request, response);
    } catch (Exception e) {
        error(e.getMessage(), e, request, response);
    }
}

protected void doPost(HttpServletRequest request,
        HttpServletResponse response, Session session)
        throws ServletException, IOException, TheBlendException {
}
```

7 The getOpenCMISSession method is going to look at the HTTP session and attempt to retrieve the OpenCMIS session from it. The setOpenCMISSession method sets the OpenCMIS session on the HTTP session. It will get called on a successful login, as follows:

```
protected Session getOpenCMISSession(
        HttpServletRequest request,
        HttpServletResponse response)
        throws ServletException, IOException {
    Session session = null;
```

Get the HTTPSession from the request.

Get the OpenCMISSession from the HTTPSession.

```
        HttpSession httpSession = request.getSession(false);
        if (httpSession != null) {
            session = (Session) httpSession.
                    getAttribute(HTTP_SESSION_SESSION);
        }

        return session;
    }

    protected void setOpenCMISSession(
            HttpServletRequest request,
            Session session) {
        HttpSession httpSession = request.getSession();
        httpSession.setAttribute(HTTP_SESSION_SESSION, session);
    }
```

Set the OpenCMIS-Session on the HTTPSession.

8 Drop in a helper method for retrieving parameter values:

```
protected String getStringParameter(
        HttpServletRequest request,
        String name) {
    return request.getParameter(name);
}

protected int getIntParameter(
        HttpServletRequest request,
        String name, int defValue) {
    String value = getStringParameter(request, name);
    if (value == null) {
        return defValue;
    }

    try {
        return Integer.parseInt(value);
    } catch (NumberFormatException nfe) {
        return defValue;
    }
}
```

9 The final chunk of code is some helper methods for dispatching and redirecting to JSP pages and showing the error JSP page:

```
protected void dispatch(String jsp, String title,
        HttpServletRequest request,
        HttpServletResponse response)
        throws ServletException, IOException {

    request.setAttribute(ATTR_TITLE, title);

    RequestDispatcher dispatcher = request
            .getRequestDispatcher(JSP_DIRECTORY + jsp);
    dispatcher.include(request, response);
}

protected void redirect(String url,
        HttpServletRequest request,
        HttpServletResponse response)
        throws ServletException, IOException {
```

```
        response.sendRedirect(url);
    }

    /**
     * Forwards to an error message.
     *
     * @throws IOException
     * @throws ServletException
     */
    protected void error(String msg, Throwable t,
            HttpServletRequest request,
            HttpServletResponse response)
            throws ServletException, IOException {

        request.setAttribute("message", msg);
        request.setAttribute("exception", t);

        // show error page
        dispatch("error.jsp", "Error.", request, response);
    }
```

10 Resolve the imports and save the class.

Now you have an abstract servlet that the rest of the servlets in the application can extend, reducing the code that has to be repeated in each servlet.

IMPLEMENT THE INDEX SERVLET

Every page in The Blend will have a corresponding servlet, so let's create one for the index page. It'll display the login page. If the login is successful, we'll display some information about the repository for now:

1 Create a new class named `IndexServlet` in the `com.manning.cmis.theblend.servlets` package that extends `AbstractTheBlendServlet`.

2 Set up parameters for the username, password, and logout:

```
private static final String PARAM_LOGOUT = "logout";
private static final String PARAM_USERNAME = "username";
private static final String PARAM_PASSWORD = "password";
```

3 Implement `doGet`. It needs to display the login page, unless the user is trying to log out, in which case the session needs to be invalidated:

```
protected void doGet(HttpServletRequest request,
        HttpServletResponse response)
        throws ServletException, IOException {
    if (getStringParameter(request, PARAM_LOGOUT) != null) {
        HttpSession httpSession = request.getSession(false);
        if (httpSession != null) {
            httpSession.invalidate();
        }
    }

    // just show index page
    dispatch("index.jsp", "The Blend.", request, response);
}
```

If the logout argument exists, invalidate the session.

4 Implement doPost, which is what will attempt to use the OpenCMISSession-Factory to try to log in:

```
protected void doPost(HttpServletRequest request,
        HttpServletResponse response)
        throws ServletException, IOException {

    String username = getStringParameter(request, PARAM_USERNAME);
    String password = getStringParameter(request, PARAM_PASSWORD);

    try {
        Session session = OpenCMISSessionFactory.
                createOpenCMISSession(
                        username, password);
        setOpenCMISSession(request, session);
    } catch (Exception e) {
        error("Could not create OpenCMIS session: " + e,
                e,
                request,
                response);
        return;
    }

    // show index page
    dispatch("echo.jsp", "The Blend.", request, response);
}
```

Grab the username and password from the form.

Use the username and password to create a CMIS session.

Redirect to the echo page to display basic repository information.

5 Resolve the imports and save the class.

CREATE AN APPLICATION-SPECIFIC EXCEPTION CLASS

Sometimes it's nice to be able to throw an exception that's more specific than java.lang.Exception. Let's create one called TheBlendException. It can live in the same package as the servlet classes:

1 Create a new class named TheBlendException in the com.manning.cmis.theblend.servlets package that extends java.lang.Exception.
2 The contents of the new class are as follows:

```
public class TheBlendException extends Exception {

    private static final long serialVersionUID = 1L;

    public TheBlendException(String message) {
        super(message);
    }

    public TheBlendException(String message, Throwable cause) {
        super(message, cause);
    }
}
```

3 Resolve the imports and save the class.

CONFIGURE THE WEB.XML FILE

Like any other Java web application, the web.xml file is used to declare the servlets used within the application. For now, you have only one servlet to configure—the index servlet—but you'll add to this file in subsequent chapters.

In the project structure, the web.xml file goes in src/main/webapp/WEB-INF, as shown in the following listing.

Listing 6.1 The Blend's web.xml file

```
<display-name>The Blend</display-name>

<servlet>
 <servlet-name>IndexServlet</servlet-name>
 <servlet-class>
    com.manning.cmis.theblend.servlets.IndexServlet
 </servlet-class>
 </servlet>
<servlet-mapping>
 <servlet-name>IndexServlet</servlet-name>
 <url-pattern>/index</url-pattern>
</servlet-mapping>

<welcome-file-list>
 <welcome-file>index</welcome-file>
</welcome-file-list>
```

6.5.4 Creating the JSPs

The first JSP to create is an index JSP to show the login form and an echo JSP to display some information about the repository after successful login. Every page in the application will have a header and a footer, and you need a generic error-handling page, so now is a good time to set those up as well.

CREATE THE INDEX JSP

In the src/main/webapp/WEB-INF/jsp directory, create a file called index.jsp (create the directory if it doesn't exist). This JSP doesn't do much—it displays the login form.

Listing 6.2 Display the login form

```
<%@ page language="java" contentType="text/html; charset=UTF-8"
pageEncoding="UTF-8" trimDirectiveWhitespaces="true" %>
<%@ include file="header.jsp"  %>

<div class="monospace" style="text-align: center; margin: 30px;">
<div style="font-size: 15px;">
  Mix it. Mash it. Blend it. Rock it.
</div>
<div style="font-size: 60px;">The Blend.</div>
<div style="font-size: 23px;">Organize your Creativity.</div>
</div>

<div class="monospace" style="text-align: center;">

<form method="POST" action="">
```

```
 Your Username:<br>
 <input type="text" name="username"><br>
    Your Password:<br>
 <input type="password" name="password"><br>
 <input type="submit" value="Login">
</form>

</div>

<br><br><br><br><br>

<%@ include file="footer.jsp" %>
```

CREATE THE ECHO JSP

The echo JSP is temporary—its purpose is only to test out the login logic and to ensure that the application can connect to the back-end CMIS repository without any problem. The contents of echo.jsp need to be as shown in the following listing.

Listing 6.3 A temporary JSP that echoes some basic information about the repository

```
<%@ page language="java" contentType="text/html; charset=UTF-8"
    pageEncoding="UTF-8" trimDirectiveWhitespaces="true" %>
<%@ page import="org.apache.chemistry.opencmis.client.api.*" %>
<%@ page import="org.apache.chemistry.opencmis.commons.enums.*" %>
<%@ page import="java.util.*" %>
<%@ include file="header.jsp"  %>

<div class="monospace" style="text-align: center;">

<%
Session cmisSession = (Session) request.
                                 getSession().
                                 getAttribute("session");
if (cmisSession != null) {%>
  <ul>
    <li><%=cmisSession.getRepositoryInfo().getVendorName() %></li>
    <li><%=cmisSession.getRepositoryInfo().getProductName() %></li>
    <li>
      <%=cmisSession.getRepositoryInfo().getProductVersion() %>
    </li>
  </ul>
<%
}
%>

</div>

<br><br><br><br><br>

<%@ include file="footer.jsp" %>
```

We realize it's bad form to put Java code in the JSP, but we're doing it anyway here and in later chapters to keep the examples manageable.

CREATE THE HEADER, FOOTER, AND ERROR JSPs

The header, footer, and error JSPs are barely worth mentioning at this point. They provide some basic information that will be expanded on in later chapters. They don't make any CMIS calls, so rather than include them here, we'll let you copy them from the completed project into your project.

The header JSP relies on a CSS file. Copy the CSS file from the completed project into your project. It belongs under src/main/webapp/stylesheets/main.css.

6.5.5 Try it—testing The Blend

You've got your OpenCMIS session factory, the abstract servlet, a concrete servlet for the index page, and the index JSP page implemented. You've also set up a basic header, footer, error page, and style sheet. Now all that's left is to run the code and see if the echo JSP properly connects to the InMemory server and responds with some basic repository information.

To test out what you have so far, follow these steps:

1. The web application's manifest needs to be updated—if you don't do this, when you run the application in the embedded Tomcat server, Tomcat won't be able to find your dependent classes. The easiest way to do this is to open up a command line, `cd` to the project's root directory (where the pom.xml lives), and run `mvn eclipse:eclipse`. Then you can go back into Eclipse, refresh the project, and the manifest file (MANIFEST.MF) will be up to date.
2. Run the application, as you did during the walk-through. Right-click on the project, and then select Run As > Run on Server. The index page should display in Eclipse's embedded browser, as shown in figure 6.22.

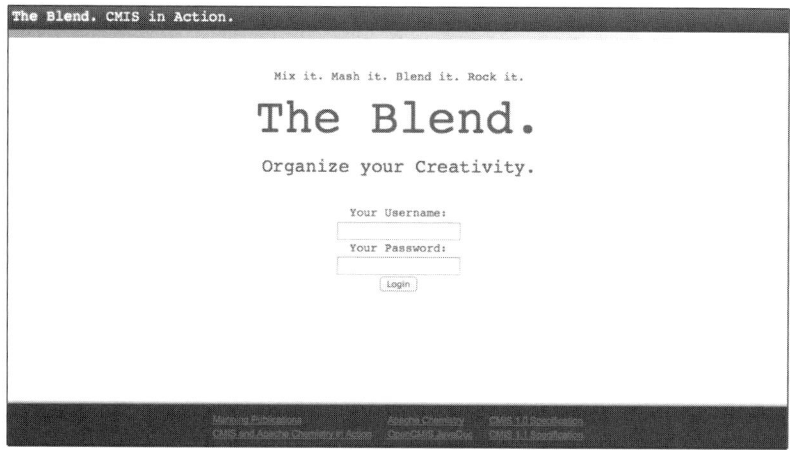

Figure 6.22 The index page of the first iteration of The Blend

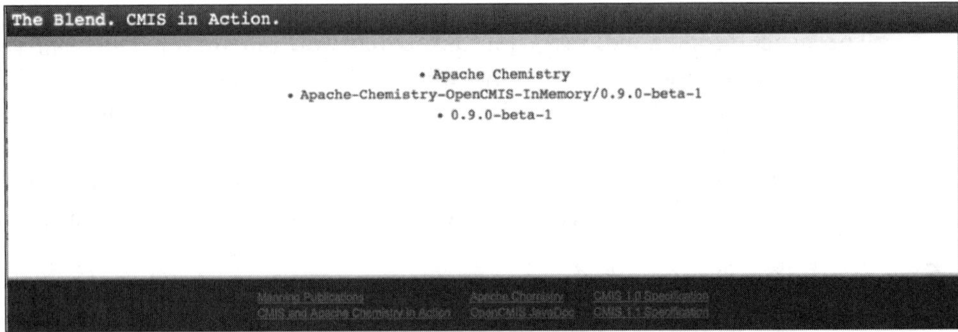

Figure 6.23 If all goes well, this iteration of The Blend should echo back some repository information.

Provide a username and password. If the web application connects successfully to the repository, you should see the echo page, and it should look something like figure 6.23.

Your own work-in-progress copy of The Blend is off to a good start. You've set up the abstract servlet and you've implemented one concrete servlet and its associated JSP, which is the pattern you'll follow for the rest of the pages. As it stands, the application doesn't do much with the CMIS repository, but the echo page proves you can connect and retrieve some basic repository information. Now you can start to work on pages that retrieve and display music and artwork from the back end.

6.6 Summary

This chapter introduced you to The Blend, a web application that artists can use to mix and mash-up music, sounds, and artwork. After reviewing the business requirements, the chapter took a look at the technical approach. Key aspects of the approach include

- The obvious choice of a CMIS server as the back-end data repository.
- Keeping the web application as simple as possible. The application will be built with servlets and JSPs so that you can focus on the details around using OpenCMIS to write web applications.
- Other than the ability to handle authentication and making sure all your pages can only be accessed when a session has been established, this application has no other security features.
- The application's data will be stored in a single root folder called /blend. Below that, the folder structure is arbitrary, but when you import some test data, it's likely to be organized into a default folder structure that'll help end users find their content.
- All objects will be typed. The types are organized in a hierarchy, and each type has a set of properties specific to that type.

You also got a tour of the finished product. In the real world, this product likely would have been a screen mockup or a prototype of some sort. In this chapter, you saw the fully baked pie first, in the hope that you'd be motivated to start slicing some apples.

Then you started to do some work. The rest of the chapter showed you how to use XML to define the content model for the InMemory server. Then you implemented enough code to support login, a connection to the repository, and logout.

With this foundation in place, you can now move on to the next chapter, in which you'll implement all of the browse functions of The Blend.

7 The Blend: read and query functionality

This chapter covers

- Retrieving metadata and content with OpenCMIS
- Error handling and mapping to OpenCMIS exceptions
- Paging and skipping lists
- Working with version series
- Queries

In part 1 of this book, you took your first steps with the OpenCMIS client library in the Groovy console. In this (and the next) chapter, you'll learn how to develop an application with OpenCMIS. You'll fill the framework that you set up in chapter 6 and build your own version of The Blend, step by step. By the end of chapter 8, you'll have all the knowledge you need to build a complete CMIS solution in Java.

In this chapter, we'll focus on the basics: reading and querying data.

About .NET and the mobile version of OpenCMIS

The API we'll cover in the next two chapters is the same for the Java SE version and the Android version of OpenCMIS. The differences between the two OpenCMIS versions are under the hood. For example, the Android version doesn't support the Web Services binding. Chapter 10 includes more details on Android development.

DotCMIS is another Apache Chemistry subproject that provides a CMIS client library for .NET. Its interfaces and behavior are similar to OpenCMIS. You can transfer most of the concepts in this and the next chapter to DotCMIS. If you're a .NET developer, keep reading; chapter 9 offers more on DotCMIS.

ObjectiveCMIS is yet another Apache Chemistry subproject. This CMIS client library for Objective-C loosely follows the OpenCMIS concepts. Although the interfaces are different, the basic design principles are the same. Chapter 10 has more on ObjectiveCMIS.

7.1 Building a browse page

Let's start with something common in content-centric applications: folder browsing. The Blend has a basic browse page that displays the children of a folder with the following features:

- If the page has more than ten children, it provides links to navigate to the next or to the previous pages.
- If the user clicks on a child that's a subfolder, the browse page is reloaded for this folder.
- If the displayed folder isn't the root folder, the page will have a link to navigate to the parent folder.

These features are what you'd expect from a typical browse page, so we'll build that first. Figure 7.1 shows the browse page in The Blend displaying the root folder's children.

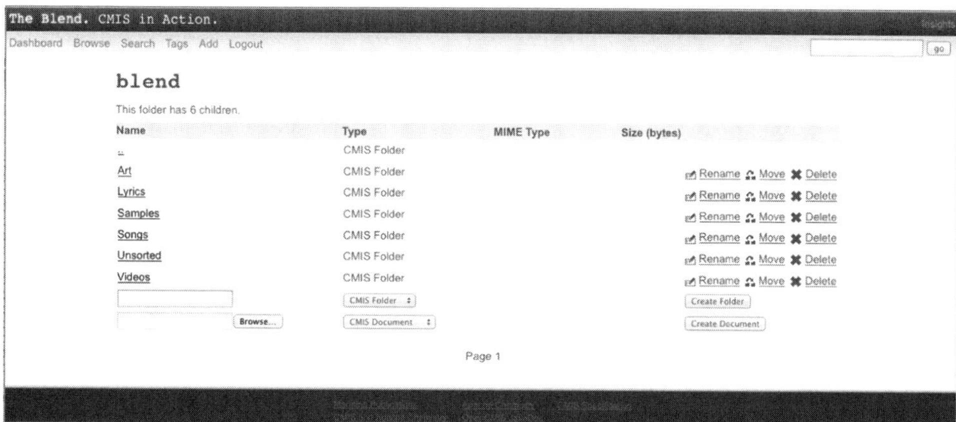

Figure 7.1 The Blend's browse page showing the root folder

Besides the basic functions we've listed, the code behind this page will be able to handle error conditions. Also, access to the repository will be optimized to retrieve only the data required to populate the page.

7.1.1 Preparing the HTML part of the browse page

Copy the echo JSP from chapter 6 (listing 6.3), rename it to browse.jsp, and put it into the jsp folder. Next, remove everything between the line that includes the header JSP and the line that includes the footer JSP. The pseudo HTML between the header and the footer will be similar to the following listing.

Listing 7.1 Pseudocode for the browse JSP page

```
<h1>[name of the folder]</h1>

Path: [path of the folder]<br>
Number of children: [total number of children]<br>

<table>

[if folder has a parent folder]
<tr>
  <td>[link to parent folder]</td>
  <td></td>
  <td></td>
<tr>
[end if]

[loop over children]
<tr>
  <td>[name and link to the child]</td>
  <td>[if child is a document][MIME type][end if]</td>
  <td>[if child is a document][content size][end if]</td>
<tr>
[end loop]

</table>

[if there is a previous page][link to the previous page][end if]
[if there is a next page][link to the next page][end if]
```

You have a few things to do now. You have to find the folder you want to browse to learn its name and its path and to retrieve the children. For each child, you need its name (the `cmis:name` property) and its object ID for the link you'll generate. If the child is a document, you also need its MIME type and content size. Finally, you have to determine whether you have previous and next pages. Let's create a servlet that does that.

In the package `com.manning.cmis.theblend.servlets`, create a new class called `BrowseServlet` that extends `AbstractTheBlendServlet`, and then add the following XML snippet to the web.xml file:

```
<servlet>
 <servlet-name>BrowseServlet</servlet-name>
 <servlet-class>
   com.manning.cmis.theblend.servlets.BrowseServlet
```

```
  </servlet-class>
</servlet>
<servlet-mapping>
  <servlet-name>BrowseServlet</servlet-name>
  <url-pattern>/browse</url-pattern>
</servlet-mapping>
```

The servlet has two `doGet` methods, and you want to override the one that has three parameters. The last parameter is the OpenCMIS session that you'll need to communicate with the CMIS repository.

The browse page needs two pieces of information: which folder and which page it should display. Let's assume you accept the ID of the folder as a parameter. If it isn't present, you'll fall back to the application root folder. For paging, you accept a `skip` parameter that defines how many children should be skipped before the displayed page starts. If that isn't present, assume the user wants the first page.

The first lines of the `doGet` method should look like the next listing.

Listing 7.2 Changes for the `doGet` method

```
String id = getStringParameter(request, "id");
if (id == null) {
  id = session.getRepositoryInfo().getRootFolderId();
}

int skip = getIntParameter(request, "skip", 0);
if (skip < 0) {
  skip = 0;
}
```

Falls back to the root folder if no ID is provided

Falls back to 0 if the skip parameter is invalid (negative)

Now you're ready for the CMIS-specific part of this business: getting the folder object.

7.1.2 Getting the folder object

The OpenCMIS folder interface provides the `getChildren` method that you'll call to get the children of the folder. First, you need the OpenCMIS folder object for the folder.

CMIS and OpenCMIS provide two ways to retrieve an object: the `getObject` operation and the `getObjectByPath` operation. These operations are similar to each other, with some subtle differences.

`getObject` takes an object ID as its parameter. Because all CMIS objects have a unique, unchangeable object ID, `getObject` can retrieve any of them.

`getObjectByPath`, on the other hand, can only retrieve filed objects—objects that are filed in a folder. This is because, as the name implies, it takes a path as its parameter, and only filed objects have a path. More specifically, this excludes relationship objects and unfiled documents, policies, and item objects. Because CMIS folders are always filed, `getObjectByPath` can reach all folder objects. Document, policy, and item objects that reside in more than one folder (multifiled objects) can be reached by more than one path.

A few repositories support version-specific filing, which means different versions of a document can reside in one or more folders. If version-specific filing isn't supported, getObjectByPath usually returns the latest version of a document. It isn't possible to retrieve an older version with getObjectByPath unless it's explicitly filed. getObject, on the other hand, can retrieve older versions because all versions have a unique object ID.

Let's get back to the folder object. Folders are easy, because they're always filed, they have exactly one path, and they can't be versioned. This means getObject and getObjectByPath would both work fine for the browse page. We'll use the folder ID for uniformity.

In the doGet method, you already have a few lines that provide the folder ID. Let's use them:

```
CmisObject object = session.getObject(id);
```

That doesn't look like a folder object, does it? The CmisObject interface provides access to properties and operations that are common to all primary CMIS base types. To get access to the properties and operations that are specific to a base type, you have to cast it to the document, the folder, the relationship, the policy, or the item interface. Have a look at the OpenCMIS Javadoc to get an idea of the differences. You'll find the URL in appendix E.

Before you do that cast, it's always better to check whether the object is what you've expected. The code now looks like this:

```
CmisObject object = session.getObject(id);

Folder folder = null;
if (object instanceof Folder) {
  folder = (Folder) object;
}
else {
  throw new TheBlendException("Object is not a folder!");
}
```

Now you have a valid folder object that you can use for a getChildren call. Is there anything else about this folder that would be interesting for the browse page? As it turns out, you'll only need the name and the path of the folder, so you should be good.

If you were to use a debugger (or the CMIS Workbench Groovy console) to inspect the folder object, you'd see that quite a lot of data is held in this object. At the least, you'll see a lot of properties, and there can also be the allowable actions—data that you don't need for the browse page. It took time and resources to compile that data on the repository side, transmit it, and parse it on the client side. You might argue that for most repositories, we're only talking about a millisecond or two. Nothing to be concerned about, you might also say. But what if your browse page gets used by thousands of users simultaneously—every little bit of extra (and unnecessary) server work becomes magnified. If you don't need it, you're better off not asking for it. This leads us into the next topic, `OperationContext`.

7.1.3 Taking advantage of the OperationContext

The `OperationContext` object defines what data about the object(s) should be requested from the repository. Fetching as little data as possible is obviously better, as we've discussed. OpenCMIS gives you a nice set of knobs you can adjust to precisely control what you get back with every round trip to the server. For example, you can define a properties filter and a rendition filter. You can also turn on and off ACLs, allowable actions, policies, and path segments. Finally, you can define the order of items for operations like `getChildren` that return lists of objects.

Let's set up an `OperationContext` to fetch the folder object so you can see exactly what this all looks like. The next listing shows your first `OperationContext` creation.

Listing 7.3 Creating your first `OperationContext`

```
OperationContext folderOpCtx = session.createOperationContext();
folderOpCtx.setFilterString("cmis:name,cmis:path");
folderOpCtx.setIncludeAcls(false);
folderOpCtx.setIncludeAllowableActions(false);
folderOpCtx.setIncludePolicies(false);
folderOpCtx.setIncludeRelationships(IncludeRelationships.NONE);
folderOpCtx.setRenditionFilterString("cmis:none");
folderOpCtx.setIncludePathSegments(false);
folderOpCtx.setOrderBy(null);
folderOpCtx.setCacheEnabled(true);
```

Filter out everything except the name and path properties.

Don't include any of the allowable actions for this object.

Property and rendition filters can be set either as a comma-separated string or as a `Set` of strings. Remember, whenever properties are referenced, you have to use the query names of the properties. OpenCMIS automatically adds the properties `cmis:objectId`, `cmis:baseTypeId`, and `cmis:objectTypeId` to the property filter because it always needs these values internally to build a minimal and valid `CmisObject`.

Finally, our next listing shows how you could make use of the `OperationContext` in code.

Listing 7.4 Using your `OperationContext`

```
CmisObject object = null;
try {
  object = session.getObject(id, folderOpCtx);
}
catch (CmisBaseException cbe) {
  throw new TheBlendException("Could not retrieve folder!", cbe);
}

Folder folder = null;
if (object instanceof Folder) {
  folder = (Folder) object;
}
```

Use folderOpCtx created in previous listing

```
else {
  throw new TheBlendException("Object is not a folder!");
}
```

If no `OperationContext` is provided, OpenCMIS falls back to the default `OperationContext` of the session. For example, `getObject(id)` would use the default `OperationContext`. You can modify the default `OperationContext`, but it's strongly recommended that you do this only between session creation and making the first call to the repository. Changing the default `OperationContext` later may have side effects in multithreaded environments.

You can get the default context like this and then modify it:

```
OperationContext context = session.getDefaultContext();
```

You can also set a completely new default context if you want, like this:

```
session.setDefaultContext(context);
```

But now back to that browse page. Let's get those folder children.

7.1.4 Getting the folder children

With the folder object in hand, you can now call `getChildren` like so:

```
ItemIterable<CmisObject> children = folder.getChildren();
```

OpenCMIS hasn't contacted the repository yet. It's only created an object that knows how to contact the repository. You can now use this `children` object to iterate over the children of the folder.

Let's do a quick test. You can try this in the CMIS Workbench:

```
for (CmisObject child : children) {
  System.out.println(child.getName());
}
```

That looks easy. When the `children` object is asked for the first object in the list, it contacts the repository and asks for a certain number of list entries. When this batch is consumed and the repository has more entries, the `children` object fetches the next batch until the application stops the loop or all list entries have been consumed. As you can see, the application code doesn't notice that at all. It iterates over the children.

You can control the batch size if you want. The `OperationContext` is your friend if you need to do this, as shown here:

```
OperationContext childrenOpCtx = session.createOperationContext();
childrenOpCtx.setMaxItemsPerPage(10);
```

The `OperationContext` also provides control over the order of the returned list. For example, the following line requests the list to be ordered by the names of the objects. (Check the repository info first to determine whether the repository supports this feature or not. Most repositories do.)

```
childrenOpCtx.setOrderBy("cmis:name");
```

The syntax follows the `ORDER BY` clause of the CMIS Query language. That is, you can also sort by multiple properties and define whether they should be sorted in ascending or descending order.

And while you're here, you can define which fields of the children you want back. How about the object ID, the object's base type, the name, the content length, the MIME type, and the allowable actions? That should be enough to populate the browse page. The following listing shows how to create this `OperationContext` and shows its use in the `getChildren` call.

Listing 7.5 Using a filtering `OperationContext` with `folder.getChildren()`

```
OperationContext childrenOpCtx = session.createOperationContext();
childrenOpCtx.setFilterString(
   "cmis:objectId,cmis:baseTypeId," +
   "cmis:name,cmis:contentStreamLength," +
   "cmis:contentStreamMimeType");
childrenOpCtx.setIncludeAcls(false);
childrenOpCtx.setIncludeAllowableActions(true);
childrenOpCtx.setIncludePolicies(false);
childrenOpCtx.setIncludeRelationships(IncludeRelationships.NONE);
childrenOpCtx.setRenditionFilterString("cmis:none");
childrenOpCtx.setIncludePathSegments(false);
childrenOpCtx.setOrderBy("cmis:name");
childrenOpCtx.setCacheEnabled(false);
childrenOpCtx.setMaxItemsPerPage(10);

ItemIterable<CmisObject> children = folder.getChildren(childrenOpCtx);
for (CmisObject child : children) {
  System.out.println(child.getName());
}
```

Use CMIS Query names for filter.

Include allowable actions details.

Order by cmis:name property.

Set batch size to 10.

You've already created your second `OperationContext`. You might be thinking that you're going to have to create a bunch of these, but this generally isn't the case. Most applications only need a handful of `OperationContexts`. You can create those in one place, and then reuse them elsewhere in the application.

Finally, let's not forget the exception handling, shown next.

Listing 7.6 Exception handling example for `folder.getChildren()`

```
ItemIterable<CmisObject> children = folder.getChildren(childrenOpCtx);

try {
  for (CmisObject child : children) {
    System.out.println(child.getName());
  }
}
catch (CmisBaseException cbe) {
  throw new TheBlendException("Could not fetch children!", cbe);
}
```

This line doesn't contact the repository, so it doesn't throw an exception.

The repository may be contacted several times here; each time an exception might be thrown.

Hierarchical navigation

The getChildren method has two siblings. The getDescendants method and the getFolderTree method can return more than one level of children. getDescendants returns all children (documents, folders, policies, and items), whereas getFolderTree only returns the subfolders. Both take a parameter called depth that defines how many levels should be returned. A depth of 1 is similar to getChildren. The special reserved depth value of -1 means you're asking for the whole subtree (infinite depth).

Not all repositories support these two methods. You can check the repository capabilities to find out if the repository you're talking to supports them, as shown in this snippet:

```
if (Boolean.TRUE.equals(
   session.getRepositoryInfo().
     getCapabilities().isGetDescendantsSupported())) {

   // getDescendants() is supported here
}

if (Boolean.TRUE.equals(
   session.getRepositoryInfo().
     getCapabilities().isGetFolderTreeSupported())) {

   // getFolderTree() is supported here
}
```

Generally, these methods are expensive operations. Use them with care. Calling getDescendants on the root folder of a populated repository with a depth of -1 may return hundreds of megabytes of data—or worse, an exception if the result set becomes too big for the repository.

Neither method supports paging or ordering. But you can and should set an OperationContext to narrow down the data that comes back from these calls.

So far, so good. But this returns all of the children, and the browse page should support paging. Something is missing. Next, let's see how to get only a page at a time.

7.1.5 Paging

To extract a page from the list of children, you have to define at which offset the page should start and how long the page should be. The offset is the skip parameter that you've already extracted in the doGet method.

Let's set the page size to 10:

```
ItemIterable<CmisObject> children = folder.getChildren(childrenOpCtx);

ItemIterable<CmisObject> page = children.skipTo(skip).getPage(10);
```

Skip over (skip) items and get a page with next 10 entries

That's all you have to do for paging. The `skipTo` method lets you set any offset. If the offset is greater than the total number of children, the repository returns an empty list. The `getPage` method creates an `ItemIterable` object that will stop an iteration when the provided number of objects has been processed.

The `skipTo` and `getPage` methods don't change the original `ItemIterable` object; the `children` object stays untouched. Instead, they create new `ItemIterable` objects with a different behavior.

The whole paging code now looks like the following snippet—note that the `for` loop only iterates over the page, as opposed to the whole children collection:

```
ItemIterable<CmisObject> children = folder.getChildren(childrenOpCtx);

ItemIterable<CmisObject> page = children.skipTo(skip).getPage(10);

try {
  for (CmisObject child : page) {
    System.out.println(child.getName());
  }
}
catch (CmisBaseException cbe) {
  throw new TheBlendException("Could not fetch children!");
}
```

The batch size in the `OperationContext` and the page size should be the same, to reduce the number of calls and the amount of transferred data.

Now let's look at the paging navigation links. If the user is on the first page, you obviously don't need to provide a link to a previous page. But is there a second page? Luckily, the `page` object knows the answer. The repository returns the `hasMoreItems` flag, which can be retrieved with the `getHasMoreItems` method, shown here:

```
if (page.getHasMoreItems()) {
  // prepare link to next page
}
else {
  // this is the last page
}
```

Another useful piece of information would be the total number of children in the folder. The `page` object provides this number as well. You only need to call `getTotalNumItems`. It's important to note that returning this number is optional for repositories. Some repositories always return this number, some repositories never return it, and some repositories return it sometimes. If the repository didn't provide this number, `getTotalNumItems` returns `-1`:

```
if (page.getTotalNumItems() > -1) {
  // repository returned the total number of children
}
```

Now you're close to completing this browse page. You have the name and path of the folder. You can get a page from the list of all children of the folder, and you know which paging links you have to provide. You have the IDs of the children to create navigation links to subfolders. But you can't navigate up yet. You have no information about the parent folder. Let's look at how you can go about getting that next.

7.1.6 Getting the folder parent

All folders have exactly one parent folder. Only the root folder is the exception, which never has a parent. The CMIS specification defines two operations that deal with the parents of an object: `getFolderParent` returns the parent of a folder and throws an exception for the root folder; `getObjectParents` returns the list of all parents for fileable, nonfolder objects. If the object is unfiled, this list is empty. If the object is multi-filed, the list contains two or more parents.

OpenCMIS combines these two operations into one. All fileable types provide a `getParents` method, which returns a list of `Folder` objects. For folders, this list contains exactly one object. For the root folder, this list is empty. Let's use the `getParents` method to get information about the parent folder:

```
Folder parent = null;

if (!folder.isRootFolder()) {              <- Don't try to get the parent of the root folder.
   parent = folder.getParents().get(0);    <- Get the first (and only) parent.
}
```

You can optimize this. `getParents` uses the default `OperationContext`, so you can reuse the `OperationContext` for the `getChildren` call, like this:

```
Folder parent = null;
if (!folder.isRootFolder()) {
   parent = folder.getParents(childrenOpCtx).get(0);
}
```

Now you have all the pieces together. Let's assemble the browse page.

7.1.7 Assembling the browse page

First, gather all of the code snippets from the previous sections and compile the `doGet` method. In a real application, it's better to create the `OperationContext` objects in a central place and reuse them. But for demonstration purposes, we'll leave them as shown in the following listing.

Listing 7.7 The doGet() method for the browse page, all in one place

```
protected void doGet(HttpServletRequest request,
  HttpServletResponse response, Session session)
    throws ServletException, IOException, TheBlendException {

  // --- get parameters ---
  String id = getStringParameter(request, "id");
  if (id == null) {
    id = session.getRepositoryInfo().getRootFolderId();
  }

  int skip = getIntParameter(request, "skip", 0);
  if (skip < 0) {
```

```
  skip = 0;
}

request.setAttribute("skip", skip);

// --- fetch folder object ---
OperationContext folderOpCtx
         = session.createOperationContext();
folderOpCtx.setFilterString("cmis:name,cmis:path");
folderOpCtx.setIncludeAcls(false);
folderOpCtx.setIncludeAllowableActions(false);
folderOpCtx.setIncludePolicies(false);
folderOpCtx.setIncludeRelationships(IncludeRelationships.NONE);
folderOpCtx.setRenditionFilterString("cmis:none");
folderOpCtx.setIncludePathSegments(false);
folderOpCtx.setOrderBy(null);
folderOpCtx.setCacheEnabled(true);

CmisObject object = null;
try {
  object = session.getObject(id, folderOpCtx);
} catch (CmisBaseException cbe) {
  throw new TheBlendException("Could not retrieve folder!", cbe);
}

Folder folder = null;
if (object instanceof Folder) {
  folder = (Folder) object;
} else {
  throw new TheBlendException("Object is not a folder!");
}

request.setAttribute("folder", folder);

// --- fetch children ---
OperationContext childrenOpCtx = session.createOperationContext();
childrenOpCtx.setFilterString("cmis:objectId,cmis:baseTypeId,"
    + "cmis:name,cmis:contentStreamLength,"
    + "cmis:contentStreamMimeType");
childrenOpCtx.setIncludeAcls(false);
childrenOpCtx.setIncludeAllowableActions(true);
childrenOpCtx.setIncludePolicies(false);
childrenOpCtx.setIncludeRelationships(IncludeRelationships.NONE);
childrenOpCtx.setRenditionFilterString("cmis:none");
childrenOpCtx.setIncludePathSegments(true);
childrenOpCtx.setOrderBy("cmis:name");
childrenOpCtx.setCacheEnabled(false);
childrenOpCtx.setMaxItemsPerPage(10);

ItemIterable<CmisObject> children =
    folder.getChildren(childrenOpCtx);
ItemIterable<CmisObject> page = children.skipTo(skip).getPage(10);

List<CmisObject> childrenPage = new ArrayList<CmisObject>();

try {
  for (CmisObject child : page) {
    childrenPage.add(child);
  }
```

```
    } catch (CmisBaseException cbe) {
      throw new TheBlendException("Could not fetch children!");
    }

    request.setAttribute("page", childrenPage);
    request.setAttribute("total", page.getTotalNumItems());

    // --- determine paging links ---
    request.setAttribute("isFirstPage", skip == 0);
    request.setAttribute("isLastPage", !page.getHasMoreItems());

    // --- fetch parent ---
    Folder parent = null;
    if (!folder.isRootFolder()) {
       try {
          parent = folder.getParents(childrenOpCtx).get(0);
        } catch (CmisBaseException cbe) {
          throw new TheBlendException("Could not fetch parent folder!");
        }
    }

    request.setAttribute("parent", parent);

    // --- show browse page ---
    dispatch("browse.jsp", folder.getName() + ". The Blend.",
        request, response);
}
```

You might've noticed that the servlet calls `request.setAttribute()` a few times and hands over the results of the CMIS requests. You need those to transfer the objects to the JSP.

The second step is to retrieve the objects again in the JSP, shown next.

Listing 7.8 JSP code for getting the folder children data

```
<%
  int skip = (Integer) request.getAttribute("skip");
  Folder folder = (Folder) request.getAttribute("folder");      <-- The Folder object

  List<CmisObject> childrenPage =                                <-- The list of children to display
     (List<CmisObject>) request.getAttribute("page");
  long total = (Long) request.getAttribute("total");             <-- The total number of children
  boolean isFirstPage = (Boolean) request.getAttribute("isFirstPage");
  boolean isLastPage = (Boolean) request.getAttribute("isLastPage");
  Folder parent = (Folder) request.getAttribute("parent");       <-- The parent Folder object
%>
```

Finally, you need to change the HTML pseudocode to real code. For clarity, we're using the values that the repository delivers without encoding. In a real application, you should never do that because it can be abused for cross-site scripting (XSS) and other attacks. Make sure you always encode all values.

Security considerations with HTML and JavaScript

If you neglect to test the data that comes back from a CMIS repository, you make XSS attacks too easy. Property values can contain HTML and JavaScript snippets that are executed in the user's browser. Because they're running in the context of your CMIS application, they have access to everything the user has access to and the potential to add, remove, modify, or steal data.

You can find a lot of information on the internet about how to counteract such attacks. A good starting point is The Open Web Application Security Project (OWASP; www.owasp.org). It also provides libraries that help lower the risk of an attack; one of these libraries is used in The Blend code.

Compare the JSP code in listing 7.9 with the pseudocode listing 7.1.

Listing 7.9 JSP code for folder browse

```
<h1><%= folder.getName() %></h1>

Path: <%= folder.getPath() %><br>
Number of children:
  <%= (total == -1 ? "unknown" : String.valueOf(total)) %><br>

<table>

<% if (parent != null) { %>
<tr>
  <td><a href="browse?id=<%= parent.getId() %>">..</a></td>
  <td></td>
  <td></td>
<tr>
<% } %>

<% for (CmisObject child: childrenPage) { %>
<tr>
  <% if (child instanceof Folder) { %>

  <td>
    <a href="browse?id=<%= child.getId() %>"><%= child.getName() %></a>
  </td>
  <td></td>
  <td></td>

  <% } else if (child instanceof Document) { %>
  <%
       Document doc = (Document) child;

       String mimeType = doc.getContentStreamMimeType();
       if (mimeType == null) {
         mimeType = "";
       }

       String contentLength = "";
       if (doc.getContentStreamLength() > 0) {
         contentLength =
           String.valueOf(doc.getContentStreamLength()) + " bytes";
```

```
            }
      %>

      <td><a href="show?id=<%= doc.getId() %>"><%= doc.getName() %></a></td>
      <td><%= mimeType %></td>
      <td><%= contentLength %></td>

      <% } else { %>

      <td><%= child.getName() %></td>
      <td></td>
      <td></td>

      <% } %>
  <tr>
  <% } %>

  </table>

  <% if (!isFirstPage) { %>
  <% String skipParam = (skip < 10 ? "0" : String.valueOf(skip - 10)); %>
  <a href="browse?id=<%= folder.getId() %>&skip=<%= skipParam %>">
  Previous Page<a>
  <% } %>

  <% if (!isLastPage) { %>
  <a href="browse?id=<%= folder.getId() %>&skip=<%= skip + 10 %>">
  Next Page<a>
  <% } %>
```

That's it. Your browse page should be working now. Follow the instructions in chapter 6 to restart the server and open the web application in a web browser. After you've logged in, append /browse to the URL in the address bar, and the browse page should appear. It should look like the screenshot in figure 7.2.

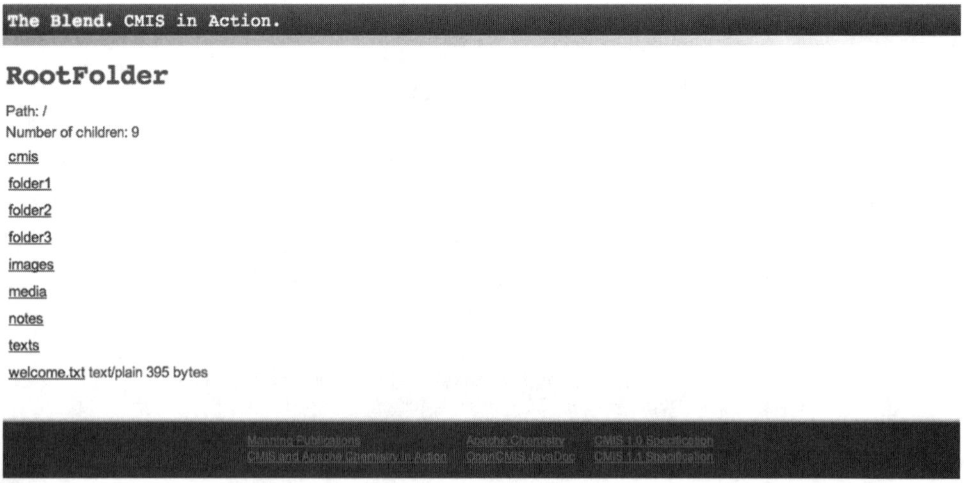

Figure 7.2 Your first simple browse page

Before we move on, we have a few things to note. Just as you checked to see if the requested object was a folder or a document, you also need to check each child in the JSP. If it's a folder, you generate a link to the browse page with the ID of this folder. If the object is a document, you cast to the OpenCMIS document interface, which provides convenience methods to access document-specific properties. Here, you're accessing the MIME type and the content length. You also generate a link to a page that's supposed to display details about the document. We'll build this page next.

A CHALLENGE FOR .NET DEVELOPERS If you're a .NET expert, we offer a challenge: try turning this into an ASP.NET application. We think you'll be surprised by how similar the code will be. If you do this, let us know how it turned out on the Author Online forum. We love to hear feedback from readers, as well as stories of how you used CMIS to solve your own real-world problems.

7.2 Building a document page

Now you can browse folders. But you also want to handle documents, and in this section we'll focus on only that. When you click on a document in The Blend, whether it's an audio file, an image, or something similar, a page will load that displays details about the document. You're now going to build a stripped-down version of that page.

Figure 7.3 shows a screen from The Blend displaying document details for a song document object.

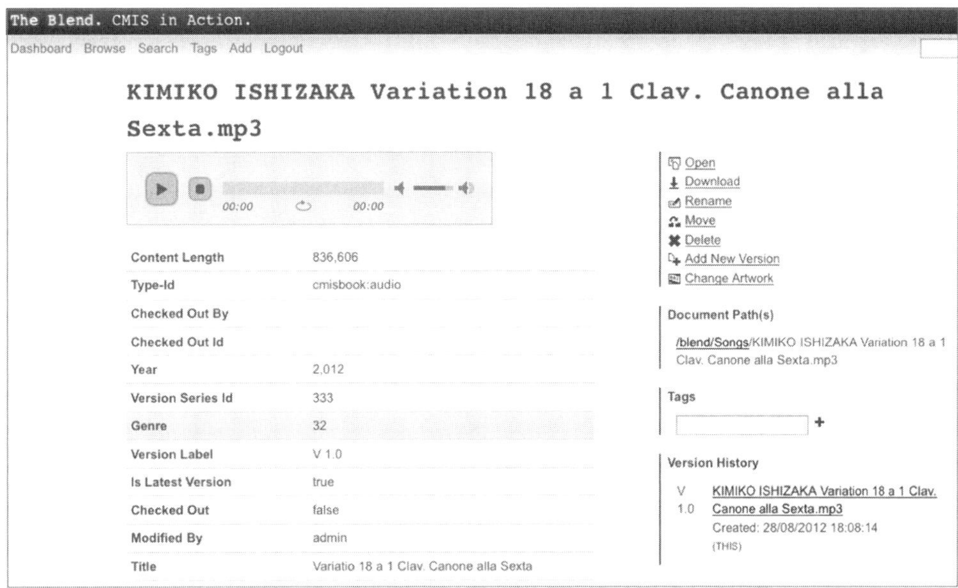

Figure 7.3 The Blend document (song) object details page

7.2.1 Preparing the HTML part of the document page

Similar to the previous section, we'll prepare HTML pseudocode first. Copy the echo JSP from chapter 6, and rename it to show.jsp.

This time the page should have the name of the document, a thumbnail if available, a download link, a list of paths to the document, its allowable actions, and finally, all of its properties. The pseudocode for this is shown in the following listing.

Listing 7.10 JSP pseudocode for document detail page

```
<h1>[name of document]</h1>

[if document has thumbnail]
  [display thumbnail]
[end if]

[if document has content]
  [if current user is allowed to download content]
    [download link]
  [end if]
[end if]


<h2>Paths</h2>

<ul>
[loop over paths]
  <li>[path]</li>
[end loop]
</ul>


<h2>Allowable Actions</h2>

<ul>
[loop over allowable actions]
  <li>[allowable action]</li>
[end loop]
</ul>


<h2>Properties</h2>

<table>
[loop over properties]
<tr>
  <td>[property display name]</td>
  <td>[property value]</td>
</tr>
[end loop]
</table>
```

Again, you also need a servlet that prepares all that data. In the package `com.manning.cmis.theblend.servlets`, create a new class called `ShowServlet` that extends `AbstractTheBlendServlet`, and add the following XML snippet to the web.xml file:

```
<servlet>
 <servlet-name>ShowServlet</servlet-name>
```

```
 <servlet-class>
   com.manning.cmis.theblend.servlets.ShowServlet
 </servlet-class>
</servlet>
<servlet-mapping>
 <servlet-name>ShowServlet</servlet-name>
 <url-pattern>/show</url-pattern>
</servlet-mapping>
```

Similar to the browse page, you need to know which document to display. Again, you can use the ID to identify the document. That allows this page to display older versions of a document, not only the latest one. If the user doesn't provide an ID, you can't do anything except return an error message. These are the first lines of the doGet methods:

```
String id = getStringParameter(request, "id");
if (id == null) {
  throw new TheBlendException("No document id provided!");
}
```

Excellent. Now that you have the ID, you need to get this document.

7.2.2 Retrieving documents

From section 7.1, you already know how to fetch an object from a CMIS repository. For a quick start, let's borrow and slightly modify some code from there, as shown in the next listing.

Listing 7.11 Retrieving a document with an appropriate OperationContext

```
OperationContext docOpCtx = session.createOperationContext();
docOpCtx.setFilterString("*");                  <- Select all of the properties to display all the details.
docOpCtx.setIncludeAcls(false);
docOpCtx.setIncludeAllowableActions(true);      <- Allowable actions are included.
docOpCtx.setIncludePolicies(false);
docOpCtx.setIncludeRelationships(IncludeRelationships.NONE);
docOpCtx.setRenditionFilterString("cmis:thumbnail");   <- Include the thumbnail, if it's available.
docOpCtx.setIncludePathSegments(false);
docOpCtx.setOrderBy(null);
docOpCtx.setCacheEnabled(true);

CmisObject object = null;
try {
  object = session.getObject(id, docOpCtx);     <- Use the object context created for document details.
}
catch (CmisBaseException cbe) {
  throw new TheBlendException("Could not retrieve document!", cbe);
}

Document document = null;                       <- The object should be a document in this context.
if (object instanceof Document) {
```

```
  document = (Document) object;
}
else {
  throw new TheBlendException("Object is not a document!");
}
```

The first thing you probably noticed is that this time the code tests whether the object is a document. The second important change is in the `OperationContext`. The filter is set to `"*"`, which forces the repository to return all properties. This is different than not setting a filter at all. If no filter is set, the repository decides which properties are returned. It might exclude, for example, properties that are resource intensive to compute. Because the page that you'll develop should display all properties, the filter must be `"*"`.

The browse page didn't distinguish between different CMIS errors, and the borrowed code doesn't either. Let's fix that before we move on.

EXCEPTION HANDLING

The CMIS specification defines 13 exceptions. Five of them are general exceptions that might be thrown at any time. The others are specific exceptions that should only be thrown by certain operations. You might have noticed the word "should" in the last sentence. In reality, you should be prepared for all 13 exceptions at any time. Most CMIS repositories follow the specification, but a few don't.

All CMIS exceptions have a counterpart in OpenCMIS with a similar name. For example, the CMIS exception `invalidArgument` is mapped to the `CmisInvalidArgumentException` in OpenCMIS. CMIS and OpenCMIS exceptions have a message and a code. The code isn't used by many repositories and usually isn't relevant. The quality of the messages depends on the repository. Some repositories provide only a generic error message, and some repositories provide detailed information.

Now let's do a little exception handling and catch the case where the document doesn't exist:

```
CmisObject object = null;
try {
   object = session.getObject(id, docOpCtx);
}
catch (CmisObjectNotFoundException onfe) {
   throw new TheBlendException("The document does not exist!", onfe);
}
catch (CmisBaseException cbe) {
   throw new TheBlendException("Could not retrieve document!", cbe);
}
```

Catch the "not found" exception.

Handle all other CMIS exceptions.

Because all CMIS exceptions are derived from `CmisBaseException`, the second catch block covers all other error cases.

Apart from the exceptions defined in the specification, there are a few other exceptions to cover in OpenCMIS dealing with connection and authorization issues. The most prominent example is the `CmisConnectionException`, which is thrown if the repository can't be reached anymore. For a list of all exceptions, refer to the OpenCMIS Javadoc and the CMIS specification.

GETTING DETAILS ABOUT THE EXCEPTIONS WITH GETERRORCONTENT OpenCMIS exceptions have a `getErrorContent` method that provides the content that was sent with the exception. What that content is depends on the repository and the binding. In many cases, it contains valuable information. A server stack trace, for example, may tell you more than the error message. This content is nothing you can present to an end user, but it helps find issues during development.

Now you're equipped with the tools to handle CMIS errors. You have a document object with all the properties and the allowable actions. What's missing is the document, and the content.

HANDLING CONTENT STREAMS

The OpenCMIS document interface provides a few `getContentStream` methods. The simplest `getContentStream` method requires no parameters and returns a `ContentStream` object, or `null` if the document has no content. If you want to check in advance whether the document has content, look at the content length:

```
if (document.getContentStreamLength() < 0) {
  // the document has no content
}
else if (document.getContentStreamLength() == 0) {
  // the document has an empty content
}
else {
  ContentStream content = document.getContentStream();
  InputStream stream = content.getStream();
  String name = content.getFileName();
  String mimeType = content.getMimeType();
  long length = content.getLength();
 }
```

getLength() should return the same number as getContentStreamLength() but in some cases returns -1.

The `ContentStream` object carries the stream, a filename, the MIME type of the stream, and the stream length. The filename should be the value of the `cmis:contentStreamFileName` property. The stream length isn't always set, so don't rely on it.

DANGLING SOCKETS, A WARNING This is really important. If you've requested the content, consume and close the stream! Always. Even if it turns out that you don't need it, consume it and close it. If you don't do that, you'll have a dangling socket connection to the repository. Depending on your environment, only a certain number of connections are allowed to the same host, and you'll get stuck or get an exception in a subsequent call.

Before we move on, let's look at the other `getContentStream` methods. There's one that accepts an offset and a length parameter, and it allows you to retrieve an excerpt of the content. That helps you deal with big documents, or resume a download, or something similar. Before using it, check if the repository supports it. Some repositories ignore these parameters and always present the full stream. To test this, run one of the following lines in the CMIS Workbench console and count the bytes that come back:

```
offset = BigInteger.valueOf(10);
length = BigInteger.valueOf(200);
document.getContentStream(offset, length);      <- Get 200 bytes, starting at offset 10

length = BigInteger.valueOf(1024)
document.getContentStream(null, length);        <- Get first 1024 bytes

offset = BigInteger.valueOf(4096);
document.getContentStream(offset, null);        <- Get all bytes from offset 4096 to end
```

> **OPENCMIS TCK** The OpenCMIS TCK (Test Compatibility Kit) also checks whether the repository supports content ranges. You start it in the CMIS Workbench by clicking the TCK button. You can either run all tests or select the Content Ranges Test. Note that the support for content ranges may work with one binding but not with another. To be sure, test all bindings. The TCK is covered in more detail in chapter 14.

Let's look at another `getContentStream` method that takes a stream ID. If the stream ID isn't set (is `null`), then it returns the content of the document. Other values represent renditions of the document or additional content streams depending on the repository.

How do you get to such a rendition stream ID? You may recall requesting the document thumbnails via the `OperationContext`:

```
docOpCtx.setRenditionFilterString("cmis:thumbnail");
```

If the document has a thumbnail, you can find it in the renditions list:

```
List<Rendition> renditions = document.getRenditions();
```

In the `OperationContext`, you've defined that you're only interested in thumbnails, but it's also possible to request all renditions (`"*"`) or renditions of a certain MIME type. See the "Rendition Filter Grammar" section in the CMIS specification (section 2.2.1.2.4.1) for details.

A document can have none, one, or multiple thumbnails. If the document has more than one, they usually differ by their size. The `Rendition` object contains the width and height of the thumbnail and several other details, including the stream ID that you can use to get the content of the thumbnail. Or you use the `getContentStream` method provided by the `Rendition` object:

```
InputStream stream = null;
List<Rendition> renditions = document.getRenditions();
if (renditions != null) {
  for (Rendition rendition: renditions) {
    if (rendition.getHeight() == 16) {            <- Look for thumbnail that's 16 pixels high
      String streamId = rendition.getStreamId();
      stream = rendition.getContentStream().getStream();   <- Get content stream of the rendition, in this case the thumbnail
      break;
    }
  }
}

...
```

```
if (stream != null) {
  stream.close();        <-- Always close stream
 }
```

FOLDER RENDITIONS The CMIS specification defines that folders can also have renditions. A repository could, for example, provide a thumbnail as an icon for the folder. It's also possible for a repository to provide a zip file that contains the contents of the folder and that's created on the fly, as a rendition.

PATHS

Next on the list and in the HTML pseudocode are the document's paths—yes, plural. If the repository supports multifiling, documents can reside in more than one folder. To make it a bit more confusing, the last segment of the document's paths might not match the `cmis:name` property.

Let's illustrate that with an example. Suppose the document's `cmis:name` property value is "Budget 2013" and it resides in two folders with the paths /engineering/development and /engineering/budgets/2013. The document might be filed under the paths /engineering/development/Budget 2013_01 and /engineering/budgets/2013/Budget 2013.pdf, as shown in figure 7.4.

As you can see, it's the same single document, but the last path segment is different. This isn't common, but a repository can do that, for example, to avoid name clashes. Combining the path of a folder with the `cmis:name` property of the document

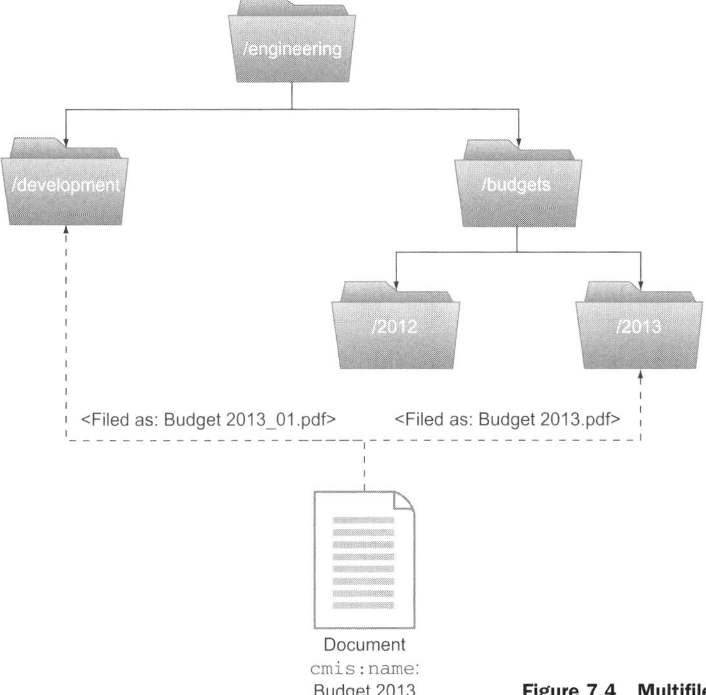

Figure 7.4 Multifiled document example

doesn't necessarily generate a valid path to the document, but OpenCMIS knows how to build the correct path.

Do you remember the `IncludePathSegments` flag in the `OperationContext`? It controls whether the repository should provide the document's path segments when the children lists or parents lists are requested for an object. Luckily, that's nothing you have to deal with. OpenCMIS hides all these details, and you can (and should) set the `IncludePathSegments` flag to `false`. All you need to call is `getPaths` on the object:

```
List<String> paths = document.getPaths();
```

It returns a list of all paths to the document with the correct path segments. But be careful with that method. It talks to the repository every single time you call it.

ALLOWABLE ACTIONS

Allowable actions are next in line. The allowable actions define what the current user can do with this object at this point in time. They help user interfaces to activate or to deactivate features. On the page, you'll use them to decide whether or not to display a download link. A user might be allowed to know about the existence of a document, but might not be allowed to see its content. For demonstration purposes, we'll also list all allowable actions.

In CMIS, the allowable actions are represented by a long list of Boolean values. In OpenCMIS they're represented as a `Set` of `Action` enum values. You can check if an allowable action is set for an object by testing it in that set:

```
Set<Action> allowableActions =
   document.getAllowableActions().getAllowableActions();

if (allowableActions.contains(Action.CAN_DELETE_OBJECT)) {
   // the current user is allowed to delete the object
}
```

PROPERTIES

Finally, let's look at the properties. Our web page doesn't concern itself with the differences between the properties, so it lists them all. A `CmisObject` object provides the following three methods to access properties and property values:

- `getProperties()`—Returns a list of all properties that have been retrieved
- `getProperty(String id)`—Returns the property object for the given property ID
- `getPropertyValue(String id)`—A shortcut that directly obtains the value of a property

The `CmisObject` object contains only the properties that have been defined in the property filters of the `OperationContext` used when the object was fetched. Only if the property filter was set to `"*"` can you be sure to get all of the properties. But use `"*"` with care. Some repositories return more than 100 properties for a simple document, so only choose the ones you need.

Both getProperties and getProperty return Property objects. Those objects hold all kinds of information about the property, and it's worth having a look into the OpenCMIS Javadoc. The most important data points are the data type of the property, a flag indicating if it's a single-value or a multivalue property, and the property value itself. As we noted in chapter 4, the Property object carries both metadata about the property and the property itself.

Under the hood, all CMIS properties are transferred as lists of values. Single-value properties are lists that must not have more than one value. You can see these echoes of the original CMIS specification in various places in OpenCMIS. For example, the Property object provides a getValues method, which returns a list of values. It also provides a helper method primarily for single-valued properties named getFirstValue, which returns the first value in the list if the list isn't empty. But both work for single- and multivalue properties.

The simplest way to get the value of a property is to call getValue on the Property object or use the shortcut and call getProperyValue on the CmisObject. In both cases, you only have to cast the right Java data type. If it's a multivalue property, cast to a List of the Java data type. If the property isn't set—that is, it has no value—OpenCMIS returns null. Here are a few examples:

```
String name1 = document.getProperty("cmis:name").getValue();      // CMIS data types: String, Id, URI, HTML
String name2 = document.getPropertyValue("cmis:name");            // This line equivalent to preceding line

BigInteger width = document.getPropertyValue("picture:width");    // CMIS data type: Integer

BigDecimal height = document.getPropertyValue("scan:height");     // CMIS data type: Decimal

Boolean archived = document.getPropertyValue("xray:archived");    // CMIS data type: Boolean

GregorianCalendar dueDate =
   document.getPropertyValue("invoice:dueDate");                  // CMIS data type: DateTime

Property<String> tagsProp = document.<String>getProperty("my:tags");   // Multivalue String property
if (tagsProp != null) {
  List<String> tags = tagsProp.getValue();    // If there's no tag set, null is returned. There are no empty lists in CMIS. Lists are either null or have at least one entry.
}
```

That's all you need for this web page. But something is different here, compared to the browse page. For this page you don't just need the JSP that displays all of this data—you also need something that serves the content. Let's assemble the JSP first and build a servlet that deals with the content later.

7.2.3 Assembling the document page

The code for the servlet is straightforward and speaks for itself. The `OperationContext` is in this code again, but you're already an expert now, and you know that it should go in a central place and would be reused in a real application. The code for the `doGet` method is shown in the next listing.

Listing 7.12 `doGet` method for the document page

```
protected void doGet(HttpServletRequest request,
  HttpServletResponse response, Session session)
    throws ServletException, IOException, TheBlendException {

  // --- get parameters ---
  String id = getStringParameter(request, "id");
  if (id == null) {
    throw new TheBlendException("No document id provided!");
  }

  // --- fetch document object ---
  OperationContext docOpCtx = session.createOperationContext();
  docOpCtx.setFilterString("*");
  docOpCtx.setIncludeAcls(false);
  docOpCtx.setIncludeAllowableActions(true);
  docOpCtx.setIncludePolicies(false);
  docOpCtx.setIncludeRelationships(IncludeRelationships.NONE);
  docOpCtx.setRenditionFilterString("cmis:thumbnail");
  docOpCtx.setIncludePathSegments(false);
  docOpCtx.setOrderBy(null);
  docOpCtx.setCacheEnabled(true);

  CmisObject object = null;
  try {
    object = session.getObject(id, docOpCtx);
  }
  catch (CmisObjectNotFoundException onfe) {
    throw new TheBlendException("The document does not exist!", onfe);
  }
  catch (CmisBaseException cbe) {
    throw new TheBlendException("Error getting document!", cbe);
  }

  Document doc = null;
  if (object instanceof Document) {
    doc = (Document) object;
  }
  else {
    throw new TheBlendException("Object is not a document!");
  }

  request.setAttribute("document", doc);

  // --- get thumbnail stream id ---
  String thumbnailStreamId = null;

  List<Rendition> renditions = doc.getRenditions();
  if (renditions != null && !renditions.isEmpty()) {
    thumbnailStreamId = renditions.get(0).getStreamId();     <- Blindly take first rendition
```

```
  }

  request.setAttribute("thumbnail", thumbnailStreamId);

  // --- show the page ---
  dispatch("show.jsp", doc.getName() + ". The Blend.",
    request, response);
}
```

Next stop: JSP, which is shown in listing 7.13. Here, you fill in the blanks with the document data. Again, we haven't encoded the data here for code clarity and brevity, but it would be careless to do this in a real-world application.

Listing 7.13 JSP code for loading the document

```
<%
  Document doc = (Document) request.getAttribute("document");   <-- Document object that you have to load

  Set<Action> allowableActions =
     doc.getAllowableActions().getAllowableActions();   <-- Extract document's allowable actions

  String thumbnailStreamId = (String) request.getAttribute("thumbnail");
%>

<h1><%= doc.getName() %></h1>

<% if (thumbnailStreamId != null) { %>
  <img src="download?id=<%= doc.getId() %>&stream=
     <%= thumbnailStreamId %>">
<% } %>

<% if (doc.getContentStreamLength() > 0) { %>
  <% if (allowableActions.contains(Action.CAN_GET_CONTENT_STREAM)){ %>   <-- Make sure user is permitted to download content

    <a href="download?id=<%= doc.getId() %>">download</a>
  <% } %>
<% } %>


<h2>Paths</h2>

<ul>
<% for (String path: doc.getPaths()) { %>
  <li><%= path %></li>
<% } %>
</ul>


<h2>Allowable Actions</h2>

<ul>
<% for (Action action: allowableActions) { %>
  <li><%= action.value() %></li>
<% } %>
</ul>


<h2>Properties</h2>

<table>
<% for (Property<?> prop: doc.getProperties()) { %>
<tr>
```

```
  <td><%= prop.getDefinition().getDisplayName() %></td>
  <td>
    <% if (prop.isMultiValued()) { %>

      <ul>
        <% if (prop.getValues() != null) { %>
          <% for(Object value: prop.getValues()) { %>
            <li><%= value %></li>
          <% } %>
        <% } %>
      </ul>
    <% } else { %>
      <%= prop.getValue() %>
    <% } %>
</tr>
<% } %>
</table>
```

Check if this is multivalued property, and if it is, display list of values

When you run the code you've built up to this point, you'll notice that DateTime values aren't nicely formatted, as you can see in figure 7.5. Also, if properties aren't set,

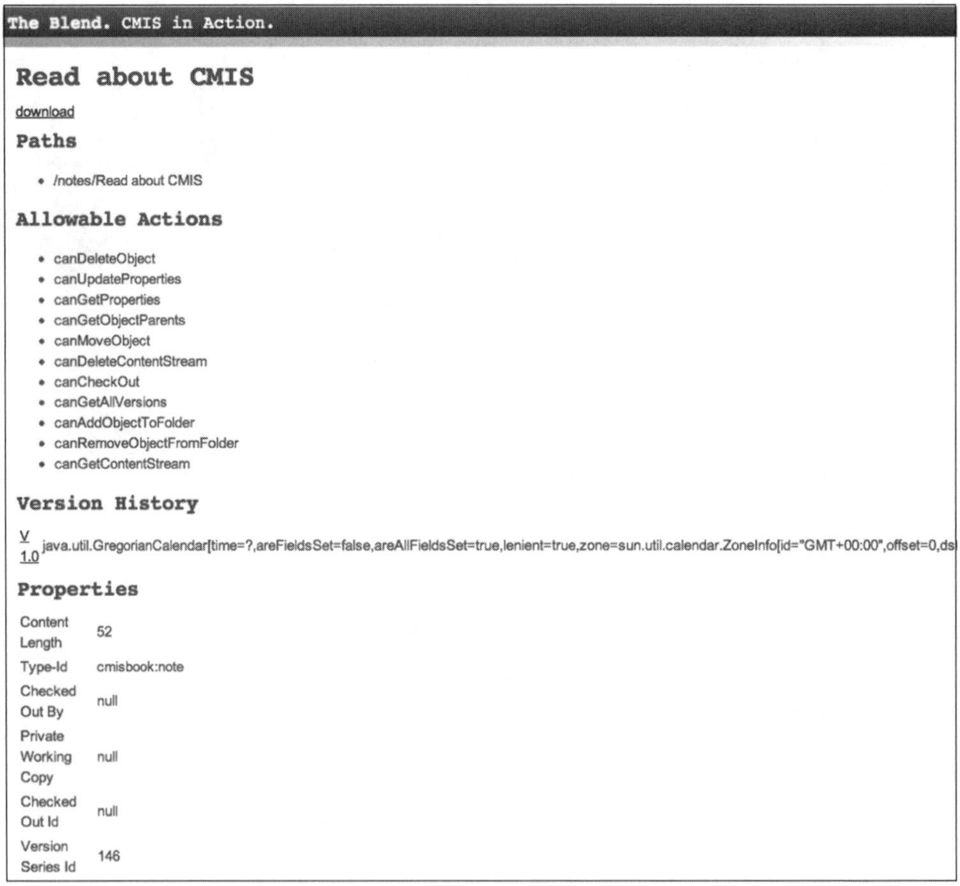

The Blend. CMIS in Action.

Read about CMIS

download

Paths

- /notes/Read about CMIS

Allowable Actions

- canDeleteObject
- canUpdateProperties
- canGetProperties
- canGetObjectParents
- canMoveObject
- canDeleteContentStream
- canCheckOut
- canGetAllVersions
- canAddObjectToFolder
- canRemoveObjectFromFolder
- canGetContentStream

Version History

V 1.0 java.util.GregorianCalendar[time=?,areFieldsSet=false,areAllFieldsSet=true,lenient=true,zone=sun.util.calendar.ZoneInfo[id="GMT+00:00",offset=0,ds

Properties

Content Length	52
Type-Id	cmisbook:note
Checked Out By	null
Private Working Copy	null
Checked Out Id	null
Version Series Id	146

Figure 7.5 The document page

you'd like to see something other than "null" displayed. But because you have to encode these values anyway (remember the XSS attack issue), you can also use that code to nicely format property values. That's an exercise for you to complete on your own if you wish. If you need some inspiration, have a look at the `HTMLHelper` class in The Blend code.

The last missing piece now is the content stream. Next up, we'll build the download servlet.

7.2.4 The download servlet

For the download servlet, we don't need HTML or a JSP. We want to stream the content from the repository directly to the browser.

About document URLs

As you now know, CMIS is based on HTTP, so why not use the content URLs that the CMIS repository provides? Why do we need our own download servlet?

In some scenarios it's possible to use the CMIS content URLs, but let's look at some of the downsides to that:

- The Web Services binding doesn't provide a content URL. Only the AtomPub and the Browser bindings do. If your application should be binding-agnostic, the CMIS content URL isn't an option. You'll find more about the differences between the bindings in chapter 11.
- Usually, users have to provide their username and password again because the content URL doesn't carry any authentication information. From a user-experience point of view, that's a bad thing.
- Depending on the server setup, the end user's web browser may not be able to contact the CMIS repository directly. In these cases, your content URL wouldn't work.

You can see that use of URLs in this way is too fragile to rely on. But if you want to do it anyway, here's the line of code you need to get to the URL:

```
String contentURL =
  ((LinkAccess)session.getBinding().getObjectService()).
    loadContentLink(session.getRepositoryInfo().getId(), documentId);
```

OK, wait. What happened here? That code looks complicated. A little background explanation is necessary.

The OpenCMIS client library consists of two layers: a high-level and a low-level API. Up to this point, you've only seen the high-level API. It provides a lot of conveniences and hides the cumbersome details. The low-level API is a bit more difficult to use, but it lets you access and control every CMIS detail, including the content URL. You'll find more on these two APIs in chapter 11.

The `loadContentLink` method on the `LinkAccess` interface provides the content URL. If the current binding is the Web Services binding, it returns `null`. It needs the

> ***(continued)***
> repository ID and the document ID to compile the URL. The repository ID can be found in the repository info. The `LinkAccess` interface is provided by all low-level services. To get hold of one of the service objects (in this example, it's the object service), you have to get the entry point to the low-level API. The `getBinding` method on the session object provides this convenient entry point.

Now you'll prepare the new `DownloadServlet`, as you did for the `BrowseServlet` earlier in this chapter. In the package `com.manning.cmis.theblend.servlets`, create a new class called `DownloadServlet` that extends `AbstractTheBlendServlet`, and then add the following XML snippet to the web.xml file:

```
<servlet>
 <servlet-name>DownloadServlet</servlet-name>
 <servlet-class>
   com.manning.cmis.theblend.servlets.DownloadServlet
 </servlet-class>
</servlet>
<servlet-mapping>
 <servlet-name>DownloadServlet</servlet-name>
 <url-pattern>/download</url-pattern>
</servlet-mapping>
```

You've already added two links from the document page to this servlet. One link provided only the document ID as a parameter. The second link provided the document ID and a stream ID to access a rendition: the thumbnail.

Next, let's create the first half of the `doGet` method. Note the `setFilterString` in the following listing. You only select the `cmis:contentStreamFileName` property. This is because `cmis:objectId`, `cmis:baseTypeId`, and `cmis:objectTypeId` are added by OpenCMIS automatically, as we discussed earlier. The filename helps OpenCMIS in some cases to return the right filename in the `ContentStream` object.

Listing 7.14 First half of the download `doGet()` method

```
String id = getStringParameter(request, "id");
String streamId = getStringParameter(request, "stream");

OperationContext docOpCtx = session.createOperationContext();
docOpCtx.setFilterString("cmis:contentStreamFileName");
docOpCtx.setIncludeAcls(false);
docOpCtx.setIncludeAllowableActions(false);
docOpCtx.setIncludePolicies(false);
docOpCtx.setIncludeRelationships(IncludeRelationships.NONE);
docOpCtx.setRenditionFilterString("cmis:none");
docOpCtx.setIncludePathSegments(false);
docOpCtx.setOrderBy(null);
docOpCtx.setCacheEnabled(true);
```

```
CmisObject cmisObject = null;
try {
  cmisObject = session.getObject(id, docOpCtx);
} catch (CmisObjectNotFoundException onfe) {
  response.sendError(HttpServletResponse.SC_NOT_FOUND,
    "Document not found!");
  return;
} catch (CmisBaseException cbe) {
  response.sendError(HttpServletResponse.SC_INTERNAL_SERVER_ERROR,
    "Error: " + cbe.getMessage());
  return;
}

if (!(cmisObject instanceof Document)) {
  response.sendError(HttpServletResponse.SC_BAD_REQUEST,
    "Object is not a document!");
 return;
}

Document document = (Document) cmisObject;
```

You might've noticed that the error handling in the previous listing is different. It's not throwing an exception that's finally turned into a human-readable error page. Instead, it returns the proper HTTP status codes. That helps web browsers and other clients to distinguish real content from errors.

The code block in the next listing shows how to handle the `ContentStream`.

Listing 7.15 Second half of the download `doGet()` method

```
ContentStream contentStream = null;
if (streamId == null) {
  contentStream = document.getContentStream();
}
else {
  contentStream = document.getContentStream(streamId);
}

if (contentStream == null) {
  response.sendError(HttpServletResponse.SC_NOT_FOUND, "No content!");
  return;
}

InputStream in = contentStream.getStream();
try {
  String mimeType = contentStream.getMimeType();
  if (mimeType == null || mimeType.length() == 0) {
    mimeType = "application/octet-stream";
  }

  response.setContentType(mimeType);
  OutputStream out = response.getOutputStream();

  byte[] buffer = new byte[64 * 1024];
  int b;
  while ((b = in.read(buffer)) > -1) {
```

A document that has no content or stream ID is invalid

Repository didn't send a MIME type, so use a generic one

```
      out.write(buffer, 0, b);
    }

    out.flush();
  } finally {
    in.close();                                 <-- Always close stream
  }
```

The second half of the doGet certainly isn't surprising. If the stream ID has been provided, it will be used. If the return content stream is null, the document has no content or the stream ID wasn't valid. Finally, the stream is forwarded to the web browser and the content stream is closed. Closing the stream is important in order to release all resources that are attached to it.

Now the document page is working, and you can finally download content. Great. Are you in the mood for more? How about also showing the version history of the document on the document page? Let's do that next.

7.2.5 *Adding the version series to the document page*

Whether or not a document can have multiple versions depends on the type of the document. All versions of a document share the same version series. Following that logic, sorting all documents of a version series by their creation dates produces the version history.

If you want to attach the version history to the document's page JSP, you need a bit of HTML code first. Here's a pseudocode version of what that would look like:

```
[if versionable]
<h2>Version History</h2>

<table>
[loop over versions]
<tr>
  <td>[version label and link to version]</td>
  <td>[version creation date]</td>
  <td>[if major version] major [else] minor [end if]</td>
</tr>
[end loop]
</table>
[end if]
```

You only want to do this if the document is a versionable type. If it is, you list the version label with a link and the version's creation date. Then display whether it's a major or minor version. Checking if the document is versionable is easy:

```
DocumentType doctype = (DocumentType) document.getType();

if (Boolean.TRUE.equals(doctype.isVersionable())) {
  // document is versionable
} else {
  // document is not versionable
}
```

Getting all versions also isn't difficult, as you can see here:

```
List<Document> versions = null;
try {
  versions = document.getAllVersions();
}
catch (CmisBaseException cbe) {
  throw new TheBlendException("Couldn't fetch doc versions!", cbe);
}
```

The method getAllVersions returns all members of the version series in reverse order by their creation date. That is, the latest version is at the top of the list; the first version is at the bottom of the list. If the version series is checked out, then the Private Working Copy (PWC) is on top of this list, followed by the latest version.

You see that getAllVersions returns a list of document objects. Does this ring a bell? Yes, you can use an OperationContext here. Note that you can't change the order of the returned list. The order is defined, in this case, by the CMIS specification:

```
OperationContext versOpCtx = session.createOperationContext();

versOpCtx.setFilterString("cmis:versionLabel,cmis:creationDate," +
   "cmis:isLatestVersion");                          <-- Properties you want to display
versOpCtx.setIncludeAcls(false);
versOpCtx.setIncludeAllowableActions(false);
versOpCtx.setIncludePolicies(false);
versOpCtx.setIncludeRelationships(IncludeRelationships.NONE);
versOpCtx.setRenditionFilterString("cmis:none");
versOpCtx.setIncludePathSegments(false);
versOpCtx.setOrderBy(null);
versOpCtx.setCacheEnabled(false);

List<Document> versions = null;
try {
  versions = document.getAllVersions(versOpCtx);
}
catch (CmisBaseException cbe) {
  throw new
    TheBlendException("Could not fetch document versions!", cbe);
}
```

Let's assemble this all together. First, add the previous code to the doGet method in ShowServlet.java, somewhere between getting the thumbnail and the dispatch call, and add this snippet:

```
List<Document> versions = null;

DocumentType doctype = (DocumentType) doc.getType();

if (Boolean.TRUE.equals(doctype.isVersionable())) {
    OperationContext versOpCtx = session.createOperationContext();
    versOpCtx.setFilterString("cmis:versionLabel,cmis:creationDate," +
       "cmis:isMajorVersion");
    versOpCtx.setIncludeAcls(false);
    versOpCtx.setIncludeAllowableActions(false);
    versOpCtx.setIncludePolicies(false);
    versOpCtx.setIncludeRelationships(IncludeRelationships.NONE);
    versOpCtx.setRenditionFilterString("cmis:none");
```

```
    versOpCtx.setIncludePathSegments(false);
    versOpCtx.setOrderBy(null);
    versOpCtx.setCacheEnabled(false);

    try {
      versions = doc.getAllVersions(versOpCtx);
    }
    catch (CmisBaseException cbe) {
      throw new
       TheBlendException("Could not fetch document versions!", cbe);
    }
}

request.setAttribute("versions", versions);
```

Next, extend the show.jsp. In the first block, you have to extract the versions for the attributes again, like this:

```
List<Document> versions = (List<Document>) request.getAttribute("versions");
```

Finally, append the snippet that displays the version history to the JSP, like so:

```
<% if (versions != null) { %>
<h2>Version History</h2>

<table>
<% for (Document version: versions) { %>
<tr>
  <td><a href="show?id=<%= version.getId() %>">
       <%= version.getVersionLabel() %></a></td>
  <td><%= version.getCreationDate() %></td>
  <td><% if (Boolean.TRUE.equals(version.isMajorVersion())) {
       %>major<% } else { %>minor<% } %> </td>
</tr>
<% } %>
</table>
<% } %>
```

If it works correctly, you should now be able to jump between different versions by clicking on the version labels. Each version is a full-blown document that will supply both metadata and content. But have a look at the allowable actions. Most repositories don't allow you to change a document that isn't the latest version. Some don't even allow deleting an earlier version. Each version of a document carries additional information as well. For example, flags will help you find out if the version is the latest version or the latest major version, if it's checked out, and if so by whom. Have a look at the Javadoc to discover the applicable methods.

Note that all versioning-related properties are often calculated properties. That is, the repository has to compute these properties values for each document every time. For many repositories, this is a relatively expensive operation, so you should only request those properties when, and if, you need them.

With the code you've seen up to this point, you can browse folders, show documents, and traverse the version history of a document. Indeed those are all critical

> **About is...() methods in OpenCMIS**
>
> Here's one final remark on the code you've seen so far. Have a look at this line:
>
> ```
> if (Boolean.TRUE.equals(version.isMajorVersion()) { ... }
> ```
>
> That looks a bit cumbersome, doesn't it? When you look through the OpenCMIS Javadoc, you'll notice that most Boolean values are Boolean objects. The reason for this is that it's possible that the repository won't return a value. There are two reasons why this could happen: either the repository doesn't follow the CMIS specification, or you haven't requested the properties that back these methods. If you want the method `isMajorVersion` to return a non-null value, for example, you have to include the `cmis:isMajorVersion` property in your property filter. The same is true for similar methods like `isLatestVersion` and `isVersionSeriesCheckedOut`.

features. But the most powerful way to discover content in a CMIS repository is a query. Let's build a query page next.

7.3 Building a query page

Chapter 5 explained the CMIS Query language, and you've probably played with it already in the CMIS Workbench. In this section, you'll learn how to use it in an application. Let's build a simple web page that allows the user to find documents by their names or parts of their names. A CMIS query can do much more than this, but we'll start with the basics. This section provides only a blueprint for many other interesting, Query-based use cases.

> **Checking query capabilities**
>
> In this example, we don't check if the repository supports queries. We assume it does because our included repository does. But you can find this information in the repository capabilities and test it for your own use cases. Recall from chapter 2 how this is done:
>
> ```
> if (session.getRepositoryInfo().getCapabilities().
>   getQueryCapability() != CapabilityQuery.NONE) {
>     // queries are supported
> }
> ```

By this point in the chapter, creating a new page should be routine for you. Following the same pattern you've used for the previous new pages, prepare the new `SearchServlet`. In the package `com.manning.cmis.theblend.servlets`, create a new class called `SearchServlet` that extends `AbstractTheBlendServlet`, and then add the following XML snippet to the web.xml file:

```
<servlet>
 <servlet-name>SearchServlet</servlet-name>
 <servlet-class>
   com.manning.cmis.theblend.servlets.SearchServlet
```

```
 </servlet-class>
</servlet>
<servlet-mapping>
 <servlet-name>SearchServlet</servlet-name>
 <url-pattern>/search</url-pattern>
</servlet-mapping>
```

Next, you need an HTML skeleton. This has to be a simple form that takes the partial name and a list of results. Here's the pseudocode:

```
<h1>Search</h1>

<form method="GET">
Enter the name of the document:
<input type="text" name="q" value="[query]">
<input type="submit" value="Search">
</form>

[if query performed]
<ul>
[loop over results]
  <li>[document name and link to show page]<li>
[end loop]
</ul>
[end if]
```

The form provides a parameter `q` to the servlet that's backing this JSP. Getting this parameter is first thing to do in the `doGet` method:

```
String q = getStringParameter(request, "q");
```

The query that you want to execute looks like this:

```
SELECT cmis:objectId, cmis:name FROM cmis:document
  WHERE cmis:name LIKE '%[value of q]%'
```

You're selecting the ID and the name of the document and looking for documents that contain the value of the parameter `q` in their name. The CMIS `LIKE` predicate works as it does in SQL. The `%` characters are wildcards for any character sequence. For more details on Query syntax, please refer back to chapter 5.

7.3.1 Ways to query: there be three

Sorry about that heading. We were temporarily possessed either by a pirate or an 1890s prospector. Anyway, OpenCMIS gives you three choices for how to build and execute the query. We'll show you all of them in this section. They all have their advantages and disadvantages, so it's up to you to pick the one that makes the most sense in your application. Let's start with the most generic query call.

THE QUERY METHOD

The OpenCMIS session object provides a `query` method. It takes two parameters: the query statement and a flag indicating whether all versions should be included in the query. Not many repositories support querying all versions; you can look up whether it's supported in the repository capabilities. Also, not many application scenarios need it. In most cases, this flag will be set to `false`:

```
String statement = "SELECT cmis:objectId, cmis:name " +
  "FROM cmis:document " +
  "WHERE cmis:name LIKE '%" + q + "%'";

ItemIterable<QueryResult> results = session.query(statement, false);
```

First you assemble the query statement, and then you call the `query` method. The result is an `ItemIterable` object of type `QueryResult`.

You already know `ItemIterable` objects. They're also returned by the `getChildren` method that we explained at the beginning of this chapter. Everything you've learned about skipping, paging, and iterating works here too. The `query` method doesn't perform the query—it only creates an object that knows how to perform the query. You can then use this object to extract the page from the result set that you need:

```
ItemIterable<QueryResult> page = results.skipTo(20).getPage(10);

try {
  for (QueryResult result : page) {
    System.out.println(
      result.getPropertyValueByQueryName("cmis:name"));
  }
}
catch (CmisBaseException cbe) {
  throw new TheBlendException("Could not perform query!");
}
```

Skip to 20th result in result set and return a page of 10 results

A `QueryResult` object represents one row in the result set. It doesn't necessarily represent an object, though. For example, if the query contained a JOIN of multiple primary types, the `QueryResult` object would be a mix of data from multiple objects.

You can access the properties and the property values in a `QueryResult` object by property ID and by query name or alias:

```
PropertyData<?> nameProp1 = result.getPropertyById("cmis:name");

PropertyData<?> nameProp2 = result.getPropertyByQueryName("cmis:name");

String name1 = result.getPropertyValueById("cmis:name");
String name2 = result.getPropertyValueByQueryName("cmis:name");

List<String> tags1 =
  result.getPropertyMultivalueById("cmisbook:tags");
List<String> tags2 =
  result.getPropertyMultivalueByQueryName("cmisbook:tags");
```

Query name or alias as defined in SELECT clause of the query

As you'll recall, it's recommended that you always use the query name for queries and filters. The CMIS specification makes it optional for repositories to send the property IDs, but repositories must always send the query names or aliases. Query names and aliases make particular sense if JOINs are involved. If two objects with the same properties are JOINed, the property ID can be ambiguous and all overlapping properties would be available twice with the same property ID. The aliases, on the other hand, are always unambiguous. If you try to use the same alias for two properties, the query would be invalid and wouldn't be executed in the first place.

That all looks straightforward, but there's an issue. Did you spot it? Look again at this query statement:

```
String statement = "SELECT cmis:objectId, cmis:name FROM cmis:document
  WHERE cmis:name LIKE '%" + q + "%'";
```

What if the parameter `q` contains a single quote? The query would break. A user could even use this flaw to extend the query with additional clauses. It's your responsibility as an application developer to escape this value according to the CMIS Query language specification.

In the SQL world, this is known as "SQL injection." It's the same principle here, but the consequences aren't as severe for two reasons. First, the CMIS Query language can't change data, so an attacker can't use it to add, remove, or modify data. Second, the repository only returns results that the user is allowed to see. Even if this attack was successfully used, it's not possible to get data that the user doesn't already have permissions to read. Attacks like this might break the application, though, or open other security holes. It's for this reason (and others) that we've the `createQueryStatement` method, which we'll cover in the next section.

THE CREATEQUERYSTATEMENT METHOD

Once again, OpenCMIS has the "SQL injection" issue handled with the `QueryStatement` object. The following code shows how to create and use one:

```
QueryStatement stmt = session.createQueryStatement(
   "SELECT cmis:objectId, cmis:name
    FROM cmis:document WHERE cmis:name LIKE ?");
stmt.setStringLike(1, "%" + q + "%");

ItemIterable<QueryResult> results = stmt.query(false);
```

If you're familiar with JDBC `PreparedStatements`, you'll probably recognize the idea. You create a query statement with placeholders, which are question marks (`?`). The placeholders can then be replaced by values. In this example, the `LIKE` predicate has a placeholder whose value is set by the `setStringLike` method. The first parameter of `setStringLike` determines which question mark should be replaced. The numbering starts with 1, following the example of the JDBC `PreparedStatement` class. This method not only replaces the placeholder, it also escapes the value according to the CMIS specification. There's nothing extra you have to do.

Let's look at more of these `set...()` methods for other data types. The particularly convenient methods are those that format DateTime values. Check the Javadoc of the `QueryStatement` interface. Let's look at a few more examples.

This example sets String and DateTime values:

```
GregorianCalendar cal = new GregorianCalendar(2012, 7, 21, 10, 0, 0);

QueryStatement stmt = session.createQueryStatement(
```

```
  "SELECT * FROM cmisbook:poem
   WHERE cmisbook:author = ? AND cmis:creationDate < ?");
stmt.setString(1, "Edgar Allan Poe");
stmt.setDateTimeTimestamp(2, cal);

ItemIterable<QueryResult> results = stmt.query(false);
```

The following example sets a list of values:

```
QueryStatement stmt = session.createQueryStatement(
"SELECT * FROM cmisbook:media WHERE cmisbook:year IN (?)");

stmt.setNumber(1, new Integer[] { 2010, 2011, 2012 });

ItemIterable<QueryResult> results = stmt.query(false);
```

To populate IN list, use array of values

Finally, this example sets properties, types, and values:

```
QueryStatement stmt = session.createQueryStatement(
   "SELECT ?, ? FROM ? WHERE ? = ?");
stmt.setProperty(1, "cmisbook:audio", "cmisbook:track");
stmt.setProperty(2, "cmisbook:audio", "cmisbook:title");
stmt.setType(3, "cmisbook:audio");
stmt.setProperty(4, "cmisbook:audio", "cmisbook:year");
stmt.setNumber(5, 2012);

ItemIterable<QueryResult> results = stmt.query(false);
```

This last example looks a bit funny. Even the properties and the type are set with placeholders. This technique is handy in some situations. You know that in queries, only query names of properties and types must be used. All CMIS specification–defined properties and types use the property ID duplicated as the query name, but that might not be the case for custom types because it isn't required by the specification. For example, if the property ID doesn't comply with the rules for query names, the repository must use a different value for the query name. As input, the `setProperty` method takes the type and property ID and then determines the query name for this property and sets it. That's a task that you, as an application developer, don't have to worry about anymore. The `setType` method works similarly. It takes the object type ID, determines the correct query name, and sets it.

The `query` method of the `QueryStatement` interface works exactly like the `query` method of the `Session` interface. It takes a flag specifying whether older versions should be included in the query and returns an `ItemIterable` object that can be used for skipping and paging. It also returns `QueryResult` objects.

THE QUERYOBJECTS METHOD

As you can imagine, the `QueryResult` object is only a data container and doesn't necessarily represent an object. But in some cases, they happen to also be relatively complete objects as well, and in those cases it would be handy to use them like `CmisObjects`. That is, use them to update properties, change permissions, delete them, and so on.

There's no way to convert `QueryResult` objects into `CmisObjects` after the fact, but you can perform a query that returns `CmisObjects` in the first place. It's called `queryObjects`, and here's how you use it:

```
OperationContext queryCtx = session.createOperationContext();
queryCtx.setFilterString("cmis:objectId, cmis:name");
queryCtx.setIncludeAcls(false);
queryCtx.setIncludeAllowableActions(false);
queryCtx.setIncludePolicies(false);
queryCtx.setIncludeRelationships(IncludeRelationships.NONE);
queryCtx.setRenditionFilterString("cmis:none");
queryCtx.setIncludePathSegments(false);
queryCtx.setOrderBy(null);
queryCtx.setCacheEnabled(false);

ItemIterable<CmisObject> results = session.queryObjects(
   "cmis:document", "cmis:name LIKE '%" + q + "%'", false, queryCtx);
```

Query SELECT clause

Query ORDER BY clause

The important change in the previous code is that `queryObjects` returns an `ItemIterable` of full-blown `CmisObjects`. To get there, the query statement has been broken into multiple parts. The first parameter of `queryObjects` takes the type ID (not the query name). The second parameter takes the `WHERE` clause of the query, and it suffers from the same escaping issue that the vanilla `query` method has. We'll solve this issue in a moment. The third parameter specifies whether older versions should be included in the query or not. Finally, the fourth parameter takes an `OperationContext` object that defines the `SELECT` clause and the `ORDER BY` clause of the query statement.

To get the `WHERE` clause escaping properly, you can combine a `QueryStatement` with the `queryObject` method, like so:

```
QueryStatement stmt =
  session.createQueryStatement("cmis:name LIKE ?");
stmt.setStringLike(1, "%" + q + "%");

String whereClause = stmt.toQueryString();

ItemIterable<CmisObject> results = session.queryObjects(
  "cmis:document", whereClause, false, queryCtx);
```

Statement doesn't have to be a complete SELECT ... FROM

Instead of executing the query, get complied query statement

The only limitation of `queryObjects` is that you can't use JOINs or aliases. But they wouldn't make sense here anyway.

Let's get back to building the query page. The `QueryStatement` option seems to work well for the page:

```
QueryStatement stmt = session.createQueryStatement(
  "SELECT cmis:objectId, cmis:name
   FROM cmis:document WHERE cmis:name LIKE ?");
stmt.setStringLike(1, "%" + q + "%");

ItemIterable<QueryResult> queryResults = stmt.query(false);

ItemIterable<QueryResult> page = queryResults.skipTo(0).getPage(10);
```

Get only first 10 results

All you have to do now is gather the results. Because you only need the object ID and the name of the documents, you don't need a sophisticated data structure. A `LinkedHashMap` is sufficient, and it keeps the order of the query results. Let's use the object ID as the key and put the document name into the value:

```
LinkedHashMap<String, String> results =
  new LinkedHashMap<String, String>();

try {
  for (QueryResult result : page) {
    String docId = result.getPropertyValueByQueryName("cmis:objectId");
    String name = result.getPropertyValueByQueryName("cmis:name");
    results.put(docId, name);
  }
}
catch (CmisBaseException cbe) {
  throw new TheBlendException("Could not perform query!");
}
```

OK, that's it. Next, let's assemble the parts and build the search page.

7.3.2 Assembling the search page

Keeping up the pace on this marathon tour, and without any further ado, our next listing shows the servlet `doGet` code.

Listing 7.16 Search servlet `doGet()` code

```
protected void doGet(HttpServletRequest request,
    HttpServletResponse response, Session session)
    throws ServletException, IOException, TheBlendException {

String q = getStringParameter(request, "q");

if (q != null) {                                    <-- If page is called for the first time, then q is not set

  request.setAttribute("q", q);

  QueryStatement stmt =
  session.createQueryStatement(
    "SELECT cmis:objectId, cmis:name FROM cmis:document " +
    "WHERE cmis:name LIKE ?");
  stmt.setStringLike(1, "%" + q + "%");

  ItemIterable<QueryResult> queryResults = stmt.query(false);

  ItemIterable<QueryResult> page = queryResults.skipTo(0).getPage(10);   <-- Get first 10 results

  LinkedHashMap<String, String> results =
    new LinkedHashMap<String, String>();

  try {
    for (QueryResult result : page) {
      String docId =
        result.getPropertyValueByQueryName("cmis:objectId");
      String name =
        result. getPropertyValueByQueryName("cmis:name");
```

```
        results.put(docId, name);
      }
    }
    catch (CmisBaseException cbe) {
      throw new TheBlendException("Could not perform query!");
    }

    request.setAttribute("results", results);
  }

  // --- show the search page ---
  dispatch("search.jsp", "Search. The Blend.",
    request, response);
}
```

The JSP code is equally straightforward, as shown next.

Listing 7.17 JSP code for the search page

```
<%
  String q = (String) request.getAttribute("q");
  Map<String, String> results =
    (Map<String, String>) request.getAttribute("results");
%>

<h1>Search</h1>

<form method="GET">
Enter the name of the document:
<input type="text" name="q" value="<%= (q == null ? "" : q) %>">
<input type="submit" value="Search">
</form>

<% if (results != null) { %>
<ul>
<% for (Map.Entry<String, String> result: results.entrySet()) { %>
  <li>
    <a href="show?id=<%= result.getKey() %>">
      <%= result.getValue() %></a>
  </li>
<% } %>
</ul>
<% } %>
```

Now you have a blueprint for all kinds of search pages. You can, for example, extend the HTML form and add more criteria to the query. You can display the thumbnail for each query result on the page. If you want to add paging for the query results, follow the pattern that we described for the browse page. It's exactly the same here.

Searching and browsing are ways of finding objects in a CMIS repository. The CMIS specification also defines relationships to interconnect objects. In the next section, you'll see to how to traverse relationships.

7.3.3 Accessing and traversing relationships

This section will be a dry run without an example page in The Blend because not many repositories support relationships. To check if a repository supports relationships, call `getTypeChildren`:

```
ItemIterable<ObjectType> types = session.getTypeChildren(null, false);
```

`getTypeChildren` returns all child types of a given type. The second parameter defines that you want the type definitions without all the property definitions. If the first parameter, the type, is set to `null`, the repository returns all supported base types. A CMIS repository must return at least the two types `cmis:document` and `cmis:folder`. A CMIS 1.0 repository might also return the `cmis:relationship` and `cmis:policy` types, if they're supported. A CMIS 1.1 repository can additionally return the types `cmis:item` and `cmis:secondary`. To test whether the repository supports relationships, call `getTypeChildren` and check if `cmis:relationship` is in the list. If it is, then this repository supports relationships.

A relationship is an object, similar to a document or a folder, that connects two objects: a source and a target object. A relationship object has its own object ID and has (from a CMIS point of view) its own lifecycle. That is, if the source or target object disappears, the relationship object might still exist with a dangling link. It's up to the repository to clean up dangling relationships where that makes sense, but it's not required by the specification.

A relationship object can't be filed, which means it can't reside in a folder. You can access such a relationship object by knowing its object ID, performing a query, or discovering it from a source or target object.

The `OperationContext` is the key to getting hold of the relationships of an object. You can set the `includeRelationships` flag to the self-explanatory values `NONE`, `SOURCE`, `TARGET`, or `BOTH`:

```
docOpCtx.setIncludeRelationships(IncludeRelationships.BOTH);
```

If you need more fine-grained control over the list of relationships of an object, call `getRelationships`:

```
ItemIterable<Relationship> relationships =
  session.getRelationships(objectId, true,
    RelationshipDirection.EITHER, null, context);
```

The first parameter is the ID of the source or target object. The second and fourth parameters define which relationship types should be considered. In this example, all relationship types are selected. The third parameter defines whether the object is considered to be the source, the target, or either. The last parameter sets the `OperationContext` for the relationship objects. Here you could, for example, set a property filter.

Once you have a relationship object, you can get hold of the source and the target objects of the relationship:

```
try {
  CmisObject source = relationship.getSource();
  CmisObject target = relationship.getTarget();
}
catch (CmisObjectNotFoundException onfe) {
  ...
}
```

Because the source or target object might not exist anymore, be prepared for an exception. There are also `getSource` and `getTarget` methods that take an `OperationContext`. If you're only interested in the IDs of the source and the target objects, you can get those as well:

```
ObjectId sourceId = relationship.getSourceId();
ObjectId targetId = relationship.getTargetId();
```

All four methods are backed by the properties `cmis:sourceId` and `cmis:targetId`. If you haven't selected them in the `OperationContext` that was used to fetch the relationship object, these methods will return `null`. When you create a relationship, you have to set those two properties to create a proper relationship object.

7.4 Summary

This chapter has covered all of the read-only operations you usually need in a CMIS application. We only have a few things left to talk about now.

We haven't mentioned permissions, ACLs, or policies yet. Chapter 12 will cover these areas. But in most scenarios, the allowable actions that were described in this chapter are probably the preferable path.

We also want to mention a feature called Change Log that falls into the read-only category. It provides the history of changes in a repository, and search engines can use it to index the repository, or tools can use it to synchronize content between repositories.

CMIS also provides a way to get a list of all documents that are checked out in a repository or in a specific folder. The next chapter covers how to do this.

Finally, to summarize what we've done in this chapter, you first learned how to gain access to content and metadata in a CMIS repository. You also learned how to use the OpenCMIS API to browse a folder, obtain metadata, stream the content of a document, fetch the version series of a document, and perform queries. In addition, you learned how to integrate these skills into a typical web application.

None of these operations have created, modified, or removed data in the repository. In the next chapter, you'll learn how to do that.

8 The Blend: create, update, and delete functionality

This chapter covers

- Creating folders, documents, and document versions
- Working with primary and secondary types
- Updating properties and content
- Optimistic locking and change tokens
- Copying, moving, and deleting objects

In the last chapter, you learned how to read metadata and content from a CMIS repository. In this chapter, you'll learn about adding, updating, and removing data. You'll enhance the web pages that you built in the previous chapter and add new web pages to your version of The Blend.

8.1 Creating folders

In the previous chapter, we started out with folder browsing; in the opening section of this chapter we'll tie in with that. We'll extend the browse page with the capability to create a new subfolder in the folder that's displayed.

The operations that create objects in CMIS need at least two pieces of information: the type of the object and a name for the object. If the object should be filed (and folders are always filed), they also need a parent folder. To let the user provide these details about the new folder, you'll have to extend the browse page starting with this HTML, which you can place wherever you want on the page:

```
<h2>Create new folder</h2>

<form method="POST" action="browse">
  <input type="hidden" name="parent" value="<%= folder.getId() %>">
  Folder name:
  <input type="text" size="20" name="name"><br>
  Folder type:
  <input type="text" size="20" name="type" value="cmis:folder"><br>
  <input type="submit" value="create">
</form>
```

Let's note a few things about this code:

- The form points back to the browse servlet using HTTP `POST`, which means the folder creation logic will be in the browse servlet.
- There's a hidden field called `parent` that gets the ID of the current folder. Remember, in a real application, you'd want to encode the ID. The repository may use characters like double quotes in its IDs that must be encoded here.
- There are input fields for the name and type, and the type field is prefilled with the value `cmis:folder`. It's inconvenient for the end user that the type field is a text field. Typically, users don't know which types are available, and even if they know, it's inconvenient (and error prone) to enter a potentially long value. Keep that in mind; we'll fix it later.

On the browse servlet side, you have to override the `doPost` method, which provides the OpenCMIS session as the third parameter. Before you can do anything else, you have to get the values from the form like this:

```
String parentId = getStringParameter(request, "parent");
String name = getStringParameter(request, "name");
String typeId = getStringParameter(request, "type");
```

You might recall from chapter 3 that you need all three of these values to create a folder. You can proactively check them here, but to keep the code short and readable, we'll let the repository throw exceptions later if something is missing.

8.1.1 Two ways to create folders

OpenCMIS offers two ways to create new objects:

- The `Session` object provides create methods for all the primary base types. If you want to create an unfiled object, this is your only option. (Set the parent folder ID to `null`.) These methods only return the object ID and nothing else about the newly created object. If you want to create and forget an object, this is your best choice. If you want to do something with the newly created object, the next option will make more sense.

- The OpenCMIS folder interface provides create methods for all fileable base types (which means there's no create method for relationships). Objects created in this manner are created already filed in this folder. Also, these create methods return complete objects, so you can provide an `OperationContext` to control what these objects should contain.

Let's look at examples of both techniques.

SESSION.CREATEFOLDER()

This first example is straightforward—it calls the `createFolder` method on the OpenCMIS `Session` object. This method takes two parameters: a set of properties and the parent folder ID. It returns the ID of the new folder:

```
Map<String, Object> properties = new HashMap<String, Object>();

properties.put(PropertyIds.NAME, name);
properties.put(PropertyIds.OBJECT_TYPE_ID, typeId);

ObjectId parentFolderId = session.createObjectId(parentId);

ObjectId newFolderId = session.createFolder(properties, parentFolderId);
```

> **PROPERTY NAME CONSTANTS** The class `PropertyIds` has constants for the property names that are defined by the CMIS specification. For example, `PropertyIds.NAME` maps to `cmis:name` and `PropertyIds.OBJECT_TYPE_ID` maps to `cmis:objectTypeId`.

The two properties, name and type ID, are always required to create an object. You can also set any other property that isn't read-only. OpenCMIS filters read-only properties for you, and if you set them, they have no effect. Other libraries forward them to the repository, and you should be prepared for an exception if you send values for read-only properties.

You'll need to make sure that the data types are correct, though. OpenCMIS automatically converts common Java data types into appropriate CMIS data types. For example, `Date` and `Calendar` objects are converted to the CMIS DateTime data type, and all Java integer types are converted to the CMIS Integer data type. But if you supply an integer for a CMIS String property, OpenCMIS throws an exception. And multivalue properties must always be supplied as a `List`, as the following shows:

```
List<String> colors = new ArrayList<String>();
colors.add("red");
colors.add("green");
colors.add("blue");

properties.put("colors", colors);
```

Remember, per the specification, this list *must not* contain any null values. The list itself can be null, but not empty (although OpenCMIS takes care of empty lists and treats them like a null value).

FOLDER.CREATEFOLDER()

For the second way to create a folder, you have to get the parent Folder object first. To simplify the following example, we'll use the repository's root folder:

```
Folder root = session.getRootFolder();

Map<String, Object> properties = new HashMap<String, Object>();
properties.put(PropertyIds.NAME, name);
properties.put(PropertyIds.OBJECT_TYPE_ID, typeId);

Folder newFolder = root.createFolder(properties);
```

That looks similar to the first example. The (parent) Folder object provides a createFolder method that takes the properties. The main difference here is that it returns a real Folder object for the newly created folder. This variant of createFolder uses the default OperationContext of the session to fetch the new folder. As you'd expect by now, there's also a second createFolder method that lets you specify your own OperationContext, among other details.

This second option has a few advantages. For example, you can check the allowable actions of the parent folder to see if the current user is allowed to create a subfolder here. If not, you can provide an error message without even making a round trip to the server. Repositories can also restrict which object types can be filed in a specific folder. The IDs of the allowed types are provided in the multivalue property cmis:allowedChildObjectTypeIds. If this list isn't set, all object types are allowed. You can check this list before you create the folder or any other object.

Even with all of this careful capability checking, folder creation can fail for many other reasons. For example, the nameConstraintViolation exception can be thrown for two reasons:

- The name is empty or contains characters that the repository doesn't support.
- An object with this same name already exists in the folder.

If this happens, the repository is allowed to change the name or use a different path segment. But most repositories throw an exception in this case.

8.1.2 Create folder: doPost()

Getting back to the browse servlet, you now have all the parameters you need, and you know how to create a folder. Let's put that all together in the doPost method, shown in the next listing.

Listing 8.1 doPost method for creating a folder

```
protected void doPost(HttpServletRequest request,
   HttpServletResponse response, Session session)
   throws ServletException, IOException, TheBlendException {
```

```
    // --- gather input ---
    String parentId = getStringParameter(request, "parent");
    String name = getStringParameter(request, "name");
    String typeId = getStringParameter(request, "type");

    // --- fetch the parent folder ---
    CmisObject parentObject = null;
    try {
       parentObject = session.getObject(parentId);
    } catch (CmisBaseException cbe) {
       throw new TheBlendException(
         "Could not retrieve parent folder!", cbe);
    }

    // --- safety check for parent object ---
    Folder parent = null;
    if (parentObject instanceof Folder) {
       parent = (Folder) parentObject;
    } else {
       throw new TheBlendException("Parent is not a folder!");
    }

    // --- create new folder ---
    try {
       Map<String, Object> properties = new HashMap<String, Object>();
       properties.put(PropertyIds.NAME, name);
       properties.put(PropertyIds.OBJECT_TYPE_ID, typeId);

       parent.createFolder(properties);
    } catch (CmisNameConstraintViolationException cncve) {
       throw new TheBlendException(
         "Please choose a different name and try again!", cncve);
    } catch (CmisBaseException cbe) {
       throw new TheBlendException(
         "Could not create the folder!", cbe);
    }

    // --- redirect to browsc page ---
    try {
       StringBuffer url = request.getRequestURL();
       url.append("?id=");
       url.append(URLEncoder.encode(parent.getId(), "UTF-8"));

       redirect(url.toString(), request, response);
    }
    catch(UnsupportedEncodingException e) {
       throw new ServletException(e);
    }
}
```

Use an OperationContext here.

The returned Folder object isn't used, so an OperationContext that selects the bare minimum properties is advisable here.

The doPost method goes through four steps. It first gets the servlet parameters, and then it fetches the parent folder to check that it's a real folder. Next, it creates the new subfolder, and finally it redirects to the browse page of the parent folder. The page should now display the new subfolder in the list of children.

Folder creation should work now, but you still have this annoying text field for the folder type. Before we move on, let's turn that into a more convenient and mouse-friendly select box.

8.1.3 Enumerating the creatable folder types

When you create a folder, you have to provide an object type that's either `cmis:folder` or a type derived from `cmis:folder`. The descendants of `cmis:folder` form a hierarchy, and to reflect that on the web page you'd have to provide some kind of a tree selection box. Let's keep it simple and collapse this tree down to a flat list. This list should only contain types that can be used to create a folder, because a repository might provide types that aren't "creatable," such as abstract types that serve as parents for other types but can't have objects associated with them.

Let's look at the methods that turn the types tree into a flat list. The `getCreateableTypes` method (see listing 8.2) requires an OpenCMIS `Session` object and a root type ID, which can be any valid type ID. That is, you can use this to get the list of creatable folder types and reuse this code later to retrieve the creatable document types.

For now, copy the methods in listing 8.2 into the browse servlet. In a real application, you'd want to get that list only once when the application starts up and cache it. Type information usually doesn't change in a production environment, and it isn't necessary to retrieve the type hierarchy over and over again unless you have special circumstances.

Listing 8.2 `getCreatableTypes()` helper methods

```
public List<ObjectType> getCreatableTypes(Session session,
    String rootTypeId) {

    List<ObjectType> result = new ArrayList<ObjectType>();

    ObjectType rootType = null;
    try {
        rootType = session.getTypeDefinition(rootTypeId);
    }
    catch (CmisObjectNotFoundException e) {
        return result;
    }

    boolean isCreatable =
        (rootType.isCreatable() == null ? true :
            rootType.isCreatable().booleanValue());

    if (isCreatable) {
        result.add(rootType);
    }

    List<Tree<ObjectType>> types =
        session.getTypeDescendants(rootTypeId, -1, false);
    addType(types, result);

    return result;
}
```

Get type definition of the provided root type

If given type doesn't exist, return an empty list

Determine whether type is creatable or not

If root type is creatable, add it to the list

Call getTypeDescendants to get types tree

Hand tree to addType method, which recursively walks tree and adds creatable types to the list

```
private void addType(List<Tree<ObjectType>> types,
    List<ObjectType> resultList) {

    for (Tree<ObjectType> tt : types) {
        if (tt.getItem() != null) {
            boolean isCreatable =
                (tt.getItem().isCreatable() == null ? true :
                    tt.getItem().isCreatable().booleanValue());

            if (isCreatable) {
                resultList.add(tt.getItem());
            }

            addType(tt.getChildren(), resultList);
        }
    }
}
```

The `getCreateableTypes` method calls `getTypeDescendants`. It returns the descendant types of the given root type. The method takes three parameters:

- The ID of the root type.
- The depth of the tree that should be returned. The depth here is set to `-1`, which means that the whole tree should be retrieved.
- A Boolean that indicates whether the property definitions should be retrieved as well. In this case, it's set to `false` because you're not interested in the properties.

To make the list of folder types available on the web page, add the following lines at the top of the `doGet` method of the servlet:

```
List<ObjectType> folderTypes =
  getCreatableTypes(session, "cmis:folder");
request.setAttribute("folderTypes", folderTypes);
```

Next, load the folder types and put the list into an attribute that can be retrieved in the JSP, like so:

```
List<ObjectType> folderTypes =
  (List<ObjectType>) request.getAttribute("folderTypes");
```

Now you can replace this line,

```
<input type="text" size="20" name="type" value="cmis:folder">
```

with this snippet:

```
<select name="type">
  <% for(ObjectType type: folderTypes) { %>
    <option value="<%= type.getId() %>"<%=
      ("cmis:folder".equals(type.getId()) ? " selected" : "") %>>
  <%= type.getDisplayName() %>
  </option>
  <% } %>
</select>
```

This snippet generates a select box with all the folder types, and it preselects `cmis:folder`. The user sees the display names of types instead of the type IDs. That's much more convenient than the text box with the type ID.

If you're connecting to the InMemory Repository, the list of folder types is short. In fact, `cmis:folder` is the only one. It gets more interesting when you look at the document types, though. Let's create some documents next.

8.2 Creating documents

Creating documents is similar to creating folders. The main difference is that you have to handle the content in addition to the properties.

Let's add another web page to create documents. The user has to specify the folder in which the document should be created, a name for the document, the type of the document, and the content. The JSP in the following listing contains a form that asks for all this data. Copy it to the other JSPs and call it add.jsp.

Listing 8.3 add.jsp code for creating a new document

```
<%@ page language="java" contentType="text/html; charset=UTF-8"
    pageEncoding="UTF-8" trimDirectiveWhitespaces="true" %>
<%@ page import="org.apache.chemistry.opencmis.client.api.*" %>
<%@ page import="org.apache.chemistry.opencmis.commons.enums.*" %>
<%@ page import="java.util.*" %>
<%@ include file="header.jsp"  %>

  <h1>Create new document</h1>

  <form method="POST" action="add" enctype="multipart/form-data">
    Path to the parent folder:
    <input type="text" size="20" name="path"><br>
    Document name:
    <input type="text" size="20" name="name"><br>
    Document type:
    <input type="text" size="20" name="type" value="cmis:document"><br>
    File:
    <input name="content" type="file"><br>
    <input type="submit" value="create">
  </form>

<%@ include file="footer.jsp" %>
```

The HTML for creating the document starts here.

The <form> tag gets the attribute enctype with the value multipart/form-data. This is necessary to transmit the content of the file to your servlet.

Input field of type file allows user to pick a file from their desktop.

We'll keep it simple. The user has to enter the path of the parent folder, and by now you should know how to navigate folders and provide a more convenient way to let the user pick a folder, so we won't repeat that in this example. The user also has to enter the type ID here. In the last section, you built a type select box for folder types, and the same code will work here for document types. Next we'll prepare the servlet.

In the package titled `com.manning.cmis.theblend.servlets`, create a new class called `AddServlet` that extends `AbstractTheBlendServlet`, and then add the following XML snippet to the web.xml file:

```
<servlet>
 <servlet-name>AddServlet</servlet-name>
 <servlet-class>
   com.manning.cmis.theblend.servlets.AddServlet
 </servlet-class>
</servlet>
<servlet-mapping>
 <servlet-name>AddServlet</servlet-name>
 <url-pattern>/add</url-pattern>
</servlet-mapping>
```

8.2.1 Creating doGet() and doPost() for document creation

With all of the previous preparations completed, you're ready to tackle the doGet and doPost methods of the servlet. You don't have much to do in the doGet method except call the JSP shown here:

```
protected void doGet(HttpServletRequest request,
  HttpServletResponse response, Session session)
    throws ServletException, IOException, TheBlendException {
      dispatch("add.jsp", "Add a new document", request, response);
}
```

The doPost method requires a bit more code. Let's start from the beginning. As we mentioned in the previous section, you can create documents in one of two ways. You can use the createDocument method on the Session object or the createDocument method on a Folder object. Because they're similar, we'll only look at the createDocument method on the Session object, as shown in the next listing.

Listing 8.4 createDocument() example

```
Map<String, Object> properties = new HashMap<String, Object>();
properties.put(PropertyIds.NAME, name);
properties.put(PropertyIds.OBJECT_TYPE_ID, typeId);

ObjectId parentFolderId = session.createObjectId(parentId);

File file = new File("my-content.txt");

ContentStream contentStream =
  session.getObjectFactory().createContentStream(file.getName(),
    file.length(), "text/plain", new FileInputStream(file));

VersioningState versioningState = null;

ObjectId newDocumentId =
```

The property collection must at least contain a name for the document and the type of the document.

To create an unfiled document, set the parent folder ID to null.

Create the ContentStream object.

Don't set the VersioningState—let the repository pick one that matches the document type.

```
session.createDocument(properties, parentFolderId,
  contentStream, versioningState);
```

Creating a document with content requires the ContentStream and the properties.

The first few lines of this listing should look familiar to you. The `createDocument` method needs properties and a parent folder ID. The property collection must at least contain a name for the document and the type of the document. The type ID must be `cmis:document` or the ID of a type derived from `cmis:document`.

Testing getContentStreamAllowed() constraints

Some repositories don't support documents without content. To be safe, you can test for this using the following code:

```
DocumentType docType =
  (DocumentType) session.getTypeDefinition(typeId);

if (docType.getContentStreamAllowed() ==
  ContentStreamAllowed.REQUIRED) {
  // document must always have content
}
else if (docType.getContentStreamAllowed() ==
  ContentStreamAllowed.NOTALLOWED) {
  // document must never have content
}
else {
  // document may or may not have content
}
```

Creating a ContentStream

`ContentStream` is an interface, which means you can implement it yourself. Use the `ContentStreamImpl` class that comes with OpenCMIS, or use the factory method, as shown in listing 8.4. You have to provide an input stream and we strongly recommend you also provide a name, length, and MIME type for the stream.

If you don't know the MIME type, set `application/octet-stream`. If you don't know the length, set it to `null` (or `-1` if you're using the object factory). The length is only a number that's transmitted to the repository; OpenCMIS doesn't verify it. If this number and the length of the stream don't match, you may or may not get an exception from the repository.

If you want to create a document without content, don't provide a `ContentStream` object at all—set it to `null`. That's entirely different from a `ContentStream` object with an empty stream, because an empty stream still has a length (`0`), a MIME type, and a name.

A document without content: cmis:item

CMIS 1.1 introduced a new base type called `cmis:item`. This type is similar to an unversionable, contentless document type. An `Item` object only carries properties.

`Item` objects can be used to model data (think complex types) that are obviously not documents. Think of a project modeled as an item. It may have properties for a project name, a project ID, a start and end date, project members, and so on. You can attach documents and folders to this project object with relationships. Or you can discover a connection between documents using a query that takes the properties of a project item into account. The project object itself is neither a document nor a folder. An object type derived from `cmis:item` is the best choice for a such a case.

Chapter 7 explained how you can check if the repository supports relationships. The same works for items. Call `getTypeChildren()` and check if `cmis:item` is in the returned list. If it is, the repository supports items. You can then use the `createItem` method to create `cmis:item` objects.

The last parameter to explain from the `createDocument` call is the `versioningState`. It specifies whether the new document should become a major version, a minor version, or a Private Working Copy (PWC) when the document is created. If the document type isn't versionable, only the fourth state, `none`, is valid. If you don't set the `versioningState`, as in this example, the repository will make it a major version if the document type is versionable.

To play it safe, you can check whether the type is versionable and set a concrete `versioningState` like this:

```
VersioningState versioningState = VersioningState.NONE;
DocumentType docType =
  (DocumentType)session.getTypeDefinition(typeId);
if (Boolean.TRUE.equals(docType.isVersionable()) {
  versioningState = VersioningState.MAJOR;
}
```

8.2.2 Performing file uploads

You've now got all you need to create a CMIS document. But in a web application, you don't want to read the content from a file. You want to get the content from your user's web browser. The Apache Commons FileUpload library can help with that, as the following listing shows.

Listing 8.5 File upload

```
boolean isMultipart = ServletFileUpload.isMultipartContent(request);
if (!isMultipart) {
  throw new TheBlendException("Invalid request!");
}
```

ServletFileUpload is provided by Apache Commons FileUpload

```
Map<String, Object> properties = new HashMap<String, Object>();
File uploadedFile = null;                                   <-- Temporary file for the content

String mimeType = null;                             <-- MIME reported by the web browser
String parentPath = null;        <-- Path of the documents parent folder

try {
  DiskFileItemFactory factory = new DiskFileItemFactory();

  ServletFileUpload upload = new ServletFileUpload(factory);
  upload.setSizeMax(50 * 1024 * 1024);        <-- Limit size of the uploaded file to 50 MB

  @SuppressWarnings("unchecked")
  List<FileItem> items = upload.parseRequest(request);

  Iterator<FileItem> iter = items.iterator();
  while (iter.hasNext()) {
    FileItem item = iter.next();

    if (item.isFormField()) {
      String name = item.getFieldName();

      if ("path".equalsIgnoreCase(name)) {
        parentPath = item.getString();        <-- Use value of the path field as parent folder path
      }
      else if ("name".equalsIgnoreCase(name)) {
        properties.put(PropertyIds.NAME, item.getString());    <-- Use value of the name field as the name of document to create
      }
      else if ("type".equalsIgnoreCase(name)) {
        properties.put(PropertyIds.OBJECT_TYPE_ID, item.getString());    <-- Use value of the type field as the document type
      }
    }
    else {
      uploadedFile = File.createTempFile("blend", "tmp");

      item.write(uploadedFile);        <-- Write received content to a temporary file

      mimeType = item.getContentType();        <-- Get MIME type of the content
      if (mimeType == null) {
        mimeType = "application/octet-stream";    <-- If browser didn't provide a MIME type, fall back to octet-stream
      }
    }
  }
} catch (Exception e) {
  throw new TheBlendException("Upload failed: " + e, e);
}

if (uploadedFile == null) {        <-- Check if user provided content, and if not, throw an exception
  throw new TheBlendException("No content!");
}
```

Let's take a quick tour through this code. First, the servlet checks whether the request is a multipart request. If not, it hasn't been sent from the web page and you return an error message. If everything looks good, the code iterates over all of the form fields and gathers the field values. The content is written to a temporary file that you'll later have to delete. If no content was transmitted, the code returns an error message.

Next, the doPost method needs to perform the following functions:

- Get the properties, path, and content from the request
- Get the parent folder by path because you need the ID of the folder to create the document
- Create the document with the right `versioningState`
- Delete the temporary file
- Redirect to the show page to display only the uploaded document

The following listing puts this all together for you.

Listing 8.6 `doPost()` method for creation of document

```
protected void doPost(HttpServletRequest request,
  HttpServletResponse response, Session session)
  throws ServletException, IOException, TheBlendException {

  // --- get parent folder, properties, and content ---
  boolean isMultipart = ServletFileUpload.isMultipartContent(request);
  if (!isMultipart) {
    throw new TheBlendException("Invalid request!");
  }

  Map<String, Object> properties = new HashMap<String, Object>();
  File uploadedFile = null;
  String mimeType = null;
  String parentPath = null;
  ObjectId newDocId = null;

  try {
    DiskFileItemFactory factory = new DiskFileItemFactory();
    ServletFileUpload upload = new ServletFileUpload(factory);
    upload.setSizeMax(50 * 1024 * 1024);

    @SuppressWarnings("unchecked")
    List<FileItem> items = upload.parseRequest(request);

    Iterator<FileItem> iter = items.iterator();
    while (iter.hasNext()) {
      FileItem item = iter.next();

      if (item.isFormField()) {
        String name = item.getFieldName();

        if ("path".equalsIgnoreCase(name)) {
          parentPath = item.getString();
        }
        else if ("name".equalsIgnoreCase(name)) {
          properties.put(PropertyIds.NAME, item.getString());
        }
        else if ("type".equalsIgnoreCase(name)) {
          properties.put(PropertyIds.OBJECT_TYPE_ID,
            item.getString());
        }
      }
      else {
        uploadedFile = File.createTempFile("blend", "tmp");
        item.write(uploadedFile);
```

```
        mimeType = item.getContentType();
        if (mimeType == null) {
          mimeType = "application/octet-stream";
        }
      }
    }
  } catch (Exception e) {
    throw new TheBlendException("Upload failed: " + e, e);
  }

  if (uploadedFile == null) {
    throw new TheBlendException("No content!");
  }

  FileInputStream stream = null;

  try {

    // --- fetch the parent folder ---
    CmisObject parentObject = null;
    try {
      parentObject = session.getObjectByPath(parentPath);
    } catch (CmisBaseException cbe) {
      throw new
        TheBlendException("Could not retrieve parent folder!", cbe);
    }

    Folder parent = null;
    if (parentObject instanceof Folder) {
      parent = (Folder) parentObject;
    }
    else {
      throw new TheBlendException("Parent is not a folder!");
    }

    // --- determine the VersioningState ---
    VersioningState versioningState = VersioningState.NONE;

    String typeId = (String)properties.get(PropertyIds.OBJECT_TYPE_ID);
    DocumentType docType =
      (DocumentType) session.getTypeDefinition(typeId);

    if (Boolean.TRUE.equals(docType.isVersionable())) {
      versioningState = VersioningState.MAJOR;
    }

    // --- prepare the content ---
    stream = new FileInputStream(uploadedFile);
    String name = (String) properties.get(PropertyIds.NAME);
    ContentStream contentStream =
      session.getObjectFactory().createContentStream(name,
        uploadedFile.length(), mimeType, stream);

    // --- create the document ---
    newDocId = session.createDocument(properties, parent,
         contentStream, versioningState);
  }
  finally {
    if (stream != null) {
```

Close and delete temporary file

```
      try {
        stream.close();
      }
      catch (IOException ioe) {
        // ignore
      }
    }

    uploadedFile.delete();
  }

  // --- redirect to show page ---
  try {
    String url = request.getRequestURL().toString();
    int lastSlash = url.lastIndexOf('/');

    url = url.substring(0, lastSlash) + "/show?id=" +
      URLEncoder.encode(newDocId.getId(), "UTF-8");

    redirect(url, request, response);
  }
  catch(UnsupportedEncodingException e) {
    throw new ServletException(e);
  }
}
```

Congratulations! Your application now creates documents in a CMIS repository. Restart the server, log in, and append/add to the URL in the address bar of your web browser.

The web page you've built is simple, though. In real applications, you know the domain the user is dealing with—be it invoices, photos, or CAD drawings—and you know the object type of those documents.

Properties become more important with specific types, because they let you use the CMIS query in much more powerful ways. Your users will expect you to set more property values at creation time. Also important is updating these properties. That's the topic of the next section.

APACHE TIKA If you've played with The Blend version that comes with this book, you may have noticed that many property values are magically set when you upload a file. For example, when you upload an MP3 file, the title and artist are retrieved from the file and set. When you upload an image, the height and width are set. This works for PDFs, Office files, and various types of media files as well. The magic behind this is the Apache Tika library, which can extract metadata and text from many different file formats. Before we create the document in the CMIS repository, we let Apache Tika scan the temporary file in the servlet. It delivers a set of metadata that we then map to properties of the object type the user has specified. Apache Tika can also detect the MIME type of a file, which is handy if you have content but no idea what type of content it is. If you want to learn more about Apache Tika, check out *Tika in Action* by Chris Mattmann and Jukka Zitting (Manning, 2011).

8.3 Updating properties

As you'll recall, the CMIS specification defines a bunch of properties for the base object types. You've seen most of them already in previous chapters. Most properties defined in the specification are read-only, and you can only change their values indirectly by doing something with the object. But only one property is modifiable for almost all repositories and all types: the object's name, also known as `cmis:name`. In this section, you'll build a web page that allows you to rename objects.

To rename an object, the user has to specify the object and provide a new name. The HTML form could look like this:

```
<h1>Rename object</h1>

<form method="POST" action="rename">
 Object path:
 <input type="text" size="20" name="path"><br>
 New name: <input type="text" size="20" name="name"><br>
 <input type="submit" value="rename">
</form>
```

To specify the object, we'll use the object's path this time. That excludes unfiled objects, but you know already how to modify the code to accept the object ID.

As in previous sections, copy the echo JSP from chapter 6 and rename it (to rename.jsp). Remove everything between the line that includes the header JSP and the line that includes the footer JSP, and copy in the previous HTML fragment. The result should look like the next listing.

Listing 8.7 rename.jsp with inserted HTML form

```
<%@ page language="java" contentType="text/html; charset=UTF-8"
    pageEncoding="UTF-8" trimDirectiveWhitespaces="true" %>
<%@ page import="org.apache.chemistry.opencmis.client.api.*" %>
<%@ page import="org.apache.chemistry.opencmis.commons.enums.*" %>
<%@ page import="java.util.*" %>
<%@ include file="header.jsp"  %>

  <h1>Rename object</h1>                    <-- HTML for Rename object form inserted here

  <form method="POST" action="rename">
    Object path:
    <input type="text" size="20" name="path"><br>
    New name: <input type="text" size="20" name="name"><br>
    <input type="submit" value="rename">
  </form>

<%@ include file="footer.jsp" %>
```

In the package titled `com.manning.cmis.theblend.servlets`, create a new class called `RenameServlet` that extends `AbstractTheBlendServlet`, and then add the following XML snippet to the web.xml file:

```
<servlet>
  <servlet-name>RenameServlet</servlet-name>
```

```
  <servlet-class>
    com.manning.cmis.theblend.servlets.RenameServlet
  </servlet-class>
</servlet>
<servlet-mapping>
  <servlet-name>RenameServlet</servlet-name>
  <url-pattern>/rename</url-pattern>
</servlet-mapping>
```

CMIS has no explicit rename operation. The object's name is stored in the `cmis:name` property. To rename an object, you only have to modify this property and persist the change:

```
String path = "/path/to/some/object.txt";
String newName = "newname.txt";
try {
  CmisObject object = session.getObjectByPath(path);

  Map<String, Object> properties = new HashMap<String, Object>();
  properties.put(PropertyIds.NAME, newName);

  CmisObject newObject = object.updateProperties(properties);
}
catch (CmisBaseException cbe) {
  // handle error
}
```

You must first acquire a `CmisObject`. Then you create a `Map` with all the properties you want to update and their new corresponding values. If you want to unset a property, set the value to `null`. Don't add any properties here that you don't want to modify. At this point, calling `updateProperties` will update the object on the server.

As always, exception handling is important because the update could fail. For example, the object might not exist anymore, or a property value might be invalid. You'll want to be careful about handling the `CmisNameConstraintViolationException` when changing the `cmis:name` property.

The `updateProperties` method on `CmisObject` doesn't only update the properties in the repository, it also refreshes the Java object afterward. This means the property values in the `CmisObject` are up to date after this call, including properties that have been changed indirectly, such as the last modification date.

Note that the `CmisObject` you get back may be an entirely new one, and not merely the same object with a couple of different properties. The reason for this is that a few repositories have autoversioning for certain document types, so that whenever you change a property, the repository automatically creates a new version. If that's the case, `updateProperties` returns this new version. In all other cases, including all nondocument objects, it returns the original `CmisObject`.

If you think there's too much going on with refreshing the object and possibly fetching a new version, here's a second `updateProperties` method. You can do an update-and-forget operation like this:

```
String path = "/path/to/some/object.txt";
String newName = "newname.txt";
try {
  CmisObject object = session.getObjectByPath(path);

  Map<String, Object> properties = new HashMap<String, Object>();
  properties.put(PropertyIds.NAME, newName);

  ObjectId newObjectId = object.updateProperties(properties, false);
 } catch (CmisBaseException cbe) {
  // handle error
}
```

Second parameter defines whether object should be refreshed after the update

This updateProperties method only returns the object ID rather than the whole replacement object. The second parameter indicates whether or not the Java object should be refreshed. In this example, the object isn't refreshed, which is the least expensive way to update properties.

8.3.1 *Concurrent access and locking*

When multiple people work on the same object at the same time, they may not see each other's modifications, and updates could get lost when overwritten. Some sort of locking mechanism is required to prevent this.

CMIS doesn't support pessimistic locking. That is, you can't reserve an object only for you, and do something with it, while forcing everybody else to wait until you unreserve it.

But CMIS does support optimistic locking. That is, a repository can send a *change token* with each object. It's transmitted as the property `cmis:changeToken`. When you update an object to include this change token, the repository can check whether someone else has updated the object since you got your copy. If it has been updated, the repository throws a `CmisUpdateConflictException`. You can then reload the object and either reapply or merge your changes with the new object and its corresponding fresh change token.

OpenCMIS takes care of sending the change token along—if it's available. The token isn't available if the repository doesn't support optimistic locking. It's also not available if you didn't select the property `cmis:changeToken` when you fetched the object. This property needs to be in the property filter of your `OperationContext` if you want to use this feature.

That covers everything you need to know about updating the name of an object. Let's now implement the rename servlet. The `doGet` method has only to call the JSP, as shown here:

```
protected void doGet(HttpServletRequest request,
  HttpServletResponse response, Session session)
    throws ServletException, IOException, TheBlendException {
  dispatch("rename.jsp", "Rename an object", request, response);
}
```

The doPost method, shown in listing 8.8, does all of the hard work. It gets the path and name parameters, fetches the object, and updates the properties. Note that the OperationContext selects the cmis:changeToken property.

Listing 8.8 doPost method for updating properties

```
protected void doPost(HttpServletRequest request,
    HttpServletResponse response, Session session)
    throws ServletException, IOException, TheBlendException {

    String path = getStringParameter(request, "path");
    String name = getStringParameter(request, "name");

    OperationContext opCtx = session.createOperationContext();
    opCtx.setFilterString("cmis:changeToken");          <-- Select change token
    opCtx.setIncludeAcls(false);                            to allow support for
    opCtx.setIncludeAllowableActions(false);                optimistic locking
    opCtx.setIncludePolicies(false);
    opCtx.setIncludeRelationships(IncludeRelationships.NONE);
    opCtx.setRenditionFilterString("cmis:none");
    opCtx.setIncludePathSegments(false);
    opCtx.setOrderBy(null);
    opCtx.setCacheEnabled(false);

    // --- get the object and update its name ---
    CmisObject object = null;

    try {
        object = session.getObjectByPath(path, opCtx);

        Map<String, Object> properties = new HashMap<String, Object>();
        properties.put(PropertyIds.NAME, name);

        object.updateProperties(properties, false);
    }
    catch (CmisObjectNotFoundException nfe) {
        throw new TheBlendException("The object doesn't exist.", nfe);
    }
    catch (CmisNameConstraintViolationException ncve) {
        throw new TheBlendException("The name is invalid. " +
            "Please try a different name.", ncve);
    }
    catch (CmisUpdateConflictException uce) {
        throw new
          TheBlendException("Somebody else updated the object. " +
          "Please try again.", uce);
    }
    catch (CmisBaseException cbe) {
        throw new
          TheBlendException("Could not update the object!", cbe);
    }

    // --- find the parent folder to redirect to the browse page ---
    String parentId = null;

    if (object instanceof FileableCmisObject) {         <-- Only fileable object
       List<Folder> parents =                               can have parents
```

```
            ((FileableCmisObject) object).getParents();      <- getParents also accepts
                                                                OperationContexts
        if (parents.size() > 0) {                               object
            parentId = parents.get(0).getId();    <- Choose first parent
        }
    }

    if (parentId == null) {
        throw new TheBlendException("Object is unfiled. " +
            "Don't know where to go.");
    }

    // --- redirect to the parents browse page ---
    try {
        String url = request.getRequestURL().toString();
        int lastSlash = url.lastIndexOf('/');

        url = url.substring(0, lastSlash) + "/browse?id=" +
            URLEncoder.encode(parentId, "UTF-8");

        redirect(url, request, response);     <- Redirect to browse page of parent folder of this object
    }
    catch(UnsupportedEncodingException e) {
          throw new ServletException(e);      <- Handle error cases
    }
}
```

A warning about caching

You may have noticed this line in listing 8.8:

```
opCtx.setCacheEnabled(false);
```

The `OperationContext` explicitly disabled the OpenCMIS cache for the `getObjectByPath` method. The reason is simple. If `getObjectByPath()` always got the object data from the cache, there's a chance that it might get an outdated change token, which would cause all update attempts to fail. Chapter 13 explains how caching works in detail and how to deal with this situation more elegantly.

As we've shown, updating properties isn't difficult. What works for the `cmis:name` property also works for any properties with updatability equal to `read-write`. For details on property constraints, choices, default values, and other factors that might affect a property's writeability, take a quick pass through chapter 4 again.

8.3.2 Properties from CMIS 1.1 secondary types

CMIS 1.1 introduced two new features that have to do with properties. We'll touch on them briefly in this section because they're worth mentioning, although they're not used in The Blend.

When we've talked about properties up to this point, the type of the object defined them. But the type doesn't only define the properties of an object, it also defines its behavior and the operations that you can perform on the object. These primary types aren't changeable after an object has been created. You can't turn a document into a folder, just as you couldn't turn an x-ray image into an invoice.

CMIS 1.1 adds secondary types, which gives you more flexibility. A secondary type defines a discrete bag of properties. With secondary types you can add additional properties to an object that aren't defined by its primary object type. You can't use a secondary type like a primary type to create an object, but you can attach secondary types to or detach them from an existing object whenever you want, where they're supported. You can even attach a secondary type as an additional type when the object is created. Attaching a secondary type means that the object gains the properties that are defined by that secondary type. If a secondary type is detached from an object, the object loses these properties and the associated property values.

The secondary types are managed in the multivalue property `cmis:secondaryObjectTypeIds` at the object. Adding a secondary type ID to that list attaches the secondary type. Removing a type ID detaches the secondary type.

You use the `updateProperties` and `checkIn` methods to attach and detach types. When you attach a secondary type, you can also supply values for the new properties, as shown here:

```
try {
  CmisObject object = session.getObject(id);

  List<String> secondaryTypes =
    object.getPropertyValue("cmis:secondaryObjectTypeIds");

  if (secondaryTypes == null) {
    secondaryTypes = new ArrayList<String>();
  }

  Map<String, Object> properties = new HashMap<String, Object>();

  if (!secondaryTypes.contains("project")) {
    secondaryTypes.add("project");
    properties.put("cmis:secondaryObjectTypeIds", secondaryTypes);
  }

  properties.put("project_name", "The Big Building");
  properties.put("project_id", "000000001");

  CmisObject newObject = object.updateProperties(properties);
} catch (CmisBaseException cbe) {
  // handle error
}
```

Get current list of attached secondary types

If no secondary types are attached yet, create new empty list of secondary types

Only attach secondary type project if it's not already attached

Set some properties of secondary type

Update object with secondary type properties

The other new CMIS 1.1 addition is the `bulkUpateProperties` operation. As the name suggests, it updates a bunch of objects with the same property values in one call. That's handy if you have to attach a secondary type to multiple objects.

Let's say you have a secondary type that holds data about projects. You could have properties for the project name, a project number, the team members working on the project, the project start date, and so on. If you have documents that belong to that project already, you can identify them and attach the secondary type with all of that data in one go, as in this example:

```
List<CmisObject> objects = new ArrayList<CmisObject>();
objects.add(session.getObject("123"));
objects.add(session.getObject("456"));
objects.add(session.getObject("789"));

Map<String, Object> properties = new HashMap<String, Object>();
properties.put("projectName", "THE project");
properties.put("projectNumber", "123456");
properties.put("projectMembers", Arrays.asList("Bob", "Fred", "Lisa"));

List<String> addSecondaryTypes =
   Collections.singletonList("projectType");

List<BulkUpdateObjectIdAndChangeToken> updated =
  session.bulkUpdateProperties(objects, properties,
    addSecondaryTypes, /* remove secondary type */ null);
```

Set up list of objects to update

Set up properties to update

Also add secondary type to all objects

Note that the bulkUpateProperties operation isn't an atomic operation. If something goes wrong mid-operation and this method throws an exception, some objects might be updated and others might not. Usually, bulkUpateProperties doesn't throw an exception. It returns a list of all objects that have been updated. The application has to figure out which objects haven't been updated, if any, by comparing the input list and the output list.

In addition to properties, documents also have content that can be updated. Let's look at that next.

8.4 Updating and deleting content

The content of documents can be replaced, deleted, and, since CMIS 1.1, appended. The Blend doesn't have any real use case for doing any of those operations, which means this section will be a dry run. The Blend uses document versions to add new content, and we'll talk about that in the next section.

8.4.1 Deleting content

You won't find anything simpler than deleting the content of a document, as you can see in this example:

```
try {
  Document doc = (Document) session.getObject(id);
  Document newVersion = doc.deleteContentStream();
}
catch(CmisBaseException e) {
  // handle error
}
```

Be prepared for exceptions, though. This example uses the change token as well, which means you may encounter a `CmisUpdateConflictException`. To check in advance if you can delete the content at all, examine the allowable actions of the document.

Similar to the `updateProperties` method, `deleteContentStream` refreshes the Java object and returns a new version of the object if one has been created. A delete-and-forget variant of this method also is available, and is shown here:

```
try {
  Document doc = (Document) session.getObject(id);

  ObjectId newVersionId = doc.deleteContentStream(false);
}
catch(CmisBaseException e) {
  // handle error
}
```

Parameter indicates whether the Java object should be refreshed after content is deleted

8.4.2 Replacing content

You can replace content with the `setContentStream` method:

```
try {
  Document doc = (Document) session.getObject(id);

  ContentStream contentStream =
    session.getObjectFactory().createContentStream(name,
      length, mimeType, stream);

  Document newVersion = doc.setContentStream(contentStream, true);
 }
catch(CmisBaseException e) {
  // handle error
}
```

Second parameter defines whether existing content should be overwritten

The second parameter of this method specifies whether or not to overwrite existing content. If it's set to `false` and you already have content, the repository throws a `CmisContentAlreadyExistsException`. If it's set to `false` and you don't have any content, the provided content will be set. You can't use this method to remove content by not setting a `ContentStream` object. Use `deleteContentStream` instead.

The remaining behavior is similar to `deleteContentStream`. It refreshes the Java object and returns a new version if one has been created. Note that there's an allowable action available, which you can use to check whether new content can be set. Again, there's a set-and-forget variant of this method:

```
try {
  Document doc = (Document) session.getObject(id);

  ContentStream contentStream =
    session.getObjectFactory().createContentStream(name,
      length, mimeType, stream);

  ObjectId newVersionId =
    doc.setContentStream(contentStream, true, false);
}
```

```
catch(CmisBaseException e) {
  // handle error
}
```

8.4.3 Appending content

Appending content is new in CMIS 1.1. It was added to support uploads of huge documents in multiple steps. Think of a video that consists of several gigabytes. Such an upload can take some time, and the longer the time needed for such a connection, the greater the probability of a connection failure between client and repository during that time.

The appendContentStream operation allows clients to upload partial chunks of the content. Applications can, for example, chop a video into smaller chunks, say 100 megabytes, and upload them sequentially in a batch. If the connection fails, only the last chunk has to be repeated. This operation isn't intended to support parallel uploads from one or multiple users. The behavior of the repository in this case isn't defined by the specification and may vary from repository to repository. The change token can prevent some of these types of collisions, but not all:

```
byte[][] chunks = new byte[][] {
  "First line\n".getBytes(),
  "Second line\n".getBytes(),
  "Third line\n".getBytes()
};

try {
  Document doc = (Document) session.getObject(id);
  doc.deleteContentStream();

  for (int i = 0; i < chunks.length; i++) {

    ByteArrayInputStream stream = new ByteArrayInputStream(chunks[i]);

    ContentStream contentStream =
      session.getObjectFactory().createContentStream("lines.txt",
        chunks[i].length, "text/plain", stream);

    boolean isLastChunk = (i == chunks.length - 1);

    doc.appendContentStream(contentStream, isLastChunk, false);
  }
} catch (CmisBaseException e) {
  // handle error
}
```

The second parameter tells the repository whether this chunk is the last chunk of the document. For some repositories, that can be important information, because it might trigger some content processing in the background. For example, the repository might create low-resolution renditions of videos, but generating such a rendition would only make sense when the video is fully uploaded, so the repository has to know what the last chunk is. If you define a chunk as the last chunk and then try to append yet another chunk, the repository may throw a CmisConstraintException. You can also start over by calling setContentStream and providing the first chunk of the content.

When you call `deleteContentStream` or `setContentStream`, you don't leave a trace of the content that's been there before—you're not able to switch back or recover a previous state of the document. But versioning of the documents makes that possible. The next section focuses on how to accomplish versioning.

8.5 Versioning

Chapter 3 described how versioning works in CMIS. Let's put that into practice and build a web page that creates a new version of a document. We can borrow quite a bit of code from section 8.2.

The user has to specify the document and the new content. To keep it simple, we won't update any properties when we create this new version. Here's the HTML form we'll use:

```
<h1>Add a new version</h1>

<form method="POST" action="addversion" enctype="multipart/form-data">
  Path to the document:
  <input type="text" size="20" name="path"><br>
  File:
  <input name="content" type="file"><br>
  <input type="submit" value="add version">
</form>
```

Copy the echo JSP from chapter 6 and rename it to addversion.jsp. Remove everything between the line that includes the header JSP and the line that includes the footer JSP, and copy in the preceding HTML fragment.

In the package `com.manning.cmis.theblend.servlets`, create a new class called `AddVersionServlet` that extends `AbstractTheBlendServlet`, and then add the following XML snippet to the web.xml file:

```
<servlet>
 <servlet-name>AddVersionServlet</servlet-name>
 <servlet-class>
  com.manning.cmis.theblend.servlets.AddVersionServlet
 </servlet-class>
</servlet>
<servlet-mapping>
 <servlet-name>AddVersionServlet</servlet-name>
 <url-pattern>/addversion</url-pattern>
</servlet-mapping>
```

Good. Now add the code for the `doGet` method. It only redirects to the JSP:

```
protected void doGet(HttpServletRequest request,
    HttpServletResponse response, Session session)
    throws ServletException, IOException, TheBlendException {
  dispatch("addversion.jsp", "Add a new version", request, response);
}
```

8.5.1 Creating a new version

This last piece of code looks familiar, doesn't it? If you're thinking that the doPost method will be a bit longer, you're absolutely right.

But first things first. This next snippet shows you how to create the new version of the specified document:

```
try {
  Document doc = (Document) session.getObject(id);

  ObjectId pwcId = doc.checkOut();

  Document pwc = (Document) session.getObject(pwcId);

  // ... do something with the Private Working Copy ...

  ObjectId newVersionId =
    pwc.checkIn(true, properties, contentStream, "a new version");

  Document newVersion = (Document) session.getObject(newVersionId);
}
catch(CmisBaseException e) {
  // handle error
}
```

Creating a version is a two-step process: check out and check in. First, you have to check out a document. The document must also be versionable. If it isn't, the repository will return a CmisConstraintException. Usually, repositories only allow you to check out the latest version, but that's not a strict rule. Inspect the allowable actions to verify that you can do a checkout. If you can't, you might want to get the latest version and try again.

The following code snippet shows how to check if the document is the latest version, and if it isn't, how to retrieve the latest document version. The Boolean parameter that getObjectOfLatestVersion accepts defines whether you want the latest major version. Here, you want the very last version, even if it's a minor version, so you set this parameter to false:

```
if (!Boolean.TRUE.equals(doc.isLatestVersion())) {
  doc = doc.getObjectOfLatestVersion(false);
}
```

Keep in mind that you have to select the cmis:isLatestVersion property when you fetch the object to make that snippet work.

The checkOut method returns the ID of the Private Working Copy (PWC). As the name suggests, this working copy might only be visible to you. (There are exceptions to this rule. For example, a few repositories provide ways to make the PWC also visible to other users by changing the ACL of the PWC.)

When a version series is checked out, it can't be checked out a second time. There can be exactly one PWC per version series, and CMIS only supports linear versioning. You and other users can test whether the version series is checked out with the following piece of code:

```
if (!Boolean.TRUE.equals(doc.isVersionSeriesCheckedOut())) {
  String user = doc.getVersionSeriesCheckedOutBy();
  String pwcId = doc.getVersionSeriesCheckedOutId();
}
```

The `getVersionSeriesCheckedOutBy` method returns the user that owns the PWC. This information is optional, and some repositories don't provide it. The `getVersionSeriesCheckedOutId` method returns the ID of the PWC. If you checked out the version series, you should get the ID. Other users may not get this ID, but that depends on the repository. Again, make sure you've selected all of the properties that are backing these methods.

You can also retrieve the list of all checked-out documents. The `Session` interface and the `Folder` interface both provide a `getCheckedOutDocs` method for this purpose, though their scopes are different. The variant at the `Session` interface covers the whole repository, whereas the `Folder` variant only covers one folder. You're probably going to see only the documents that you've checked out, but they are repository-specific. A superuser might see all checked out documents:

```
ItemIterable<Document> checkedOutDocs = session.getCheckedOutDocs();

for (Document pwc : checkedOutDocs) {            // Skipping and paging works here too.
   System.out.println(pwc.getName());
}
```

With the PWC ID, you can now retrieve the PWC object. This object is a copy of the checked-out document, though a few system properties like the creation date may be different. Most repositories also copy the content during checkout, but to be sure, examine the content properties, length, and MIME type.

This `Document` object can now be updated. You can change the properties and content as often as you want. In fact, in some cases you can change more properties than when the document isn't checked out. The updatability of a property can be one of the following four states:

- `READONLY`—Property is a system property and can't be changed directly.
- `READWRITE`—Property can be updated at any time.
- `WHENCHECKEDOUT`—Property can be updated only when the document is checked out (it can only be updated on a PWC instance).
- `ONCREATE`—Property can only be set during object creation.

Content also has a similar flag. The repository capability `ContentStreamUpdatability` tells applications when content can be updated. These are the possible values:

- `ANYTIME`—Content can always be updated.
- `PWCONLY`—Content can only be updated when the document is checked out.
- `NONE`—Content can never be updated.

At some point, you'll have to decide whether or not you want to keep your changes and make a new version, or discard all of your changes. If you want to discard them, you can cancel the checkout like this:

```
pwc.cancleCheckOut();
```

That deletes the Private Working Copy and all your changes are lost. The version series can always be checked out again.

8.5.2 The checkIn() method

If you want to create the new version, you have to check it in:

```
ObjectId newVersionId =
  pwc.checkIn(true, properties, contentStream, "a version comment");
```

The first parameter defines whether this new version should become a major or a minor version. The second parameter changes properties, and the third parameter sets new content. You can see that you can work with a PWC in one of two ways. You can update a PWC object, and when you check it in, set the properties and content parameters to `null`. The current state of the PWC then becomes the new version. You can also get the PWC object and not change anything. When you call `checkIn`, you provide all property updates and/or the new content. It's up to you what makes more sense for your application.

The fourth parameter is a comment that's associated with the version and is stored in the property `cmis:checkinComment`. Some repositories don't support it and therefore won't set this property even when you supply it. Not supporting this property is allowed in the specification for repositories that don't have a `checkIn` comment.

The `checkIn` method returns the ID of the newly created version, allowing you to fetch it from the repository if you need it again. The Java object that represented the PWC is now invalid. The new version provides a version label property, `cmis:versionLabel`. This property should reflect the version number. The format of the version is repository-specific, though.

CMIS doesn't specify how long a version series can be checked out. That's repository-specific, and most repositories don't have a limit. A version series can be blocked forever if nobody cancels a checkout or checks in the PWC. There are use cases that require a version series to be checked out for a longer period of time, but in most cases the time between checkout and check-in is short, and both operations are controlled by the same application. It's good practice to clean up the version series if something goes wrong. For example, if a check-in fails, the application should try to cancel the checkout. That enables the next application to work with the version series.

Creating a version is straightforward, and so is the `doPost` method of the servlet, which is shown in the next listing.

Listing 8.9 doPost method for checkIn()

```
protected void doPost(HttpServletRequest request,
  HttpServletResponse response, Session session)
  throws ServletException, IOException, TheBlendException {

  boolean isMultipart = ServletFileUpload.isMultipartContent(request);
  if (!isMultipart) {
    throw new TheBlendException("Invalid request!");
  }

  // --- get the content for the next version ---
  File uploadedFile = null;
  String mimeType = null;
  String docPath = null;
  ObjectId newVersionId = null;

  try {
    DiskFileItemFactory factory = new DiskFileItemFactory();
    ServletFileUpload upload = new ServletFileUpload(factory);
    upload.setSizeMax(50 * 1024 * 1024);

    @SuppressWarnings("unchecked")
    List<FileItem> items = upload.parseRequest(request);

    Iterator<FileItem> iter = items.iterator();
    while (iter.hasNext()) {
      FileItem item = iter.next();

      if (item.isFormField()) {
        String name = item.getFieldName();

        if ("path".equalsIgnoreCase(name)) {
          docPath = item.getString();
        }
      }
      else {
        uploadedFile = File.createTempFile("blend", "tmp");
        item.write(uploadedFile);

        mimeType = item.getContentType();
        if (mimeType == null) {
          mimeType = "application/octet-stream";
        }
      }
    }
  } catch (Exception e) {
    throw new TheBlendException("Upload failed: " + e, e);
  }

  if (uploadedFile == null) {
    throw new TheBlendException("No content!");
  }

  FileInputStream stream = null;

  try {
    // --- fetch the document ---
    CmisObject cmisObject = null;
```

```
  try {
    cmisObject = session.getObjectByPath(docPath);
  } catch (CmisBaseException cbe) {
    throw new TheBlendException(
      "Could not retrieve the document!", cbe);
  }

  Document doc = null;
  if (cmisObject instanceof Document) {
    doc = (Document) cmisObject;
  } else {
    throw new TheBlendException("Object is not a document!");
  }

  // --- prepare the content ---
  stream = new FileInputStream(uploadedFile);
  ContentStream contentStream =
    session.getObjectFactory().createContentStream(
      doc.getContentStreamFileName(), uploadedFile.length(),
        mimeType, stream);

  // --- do the check out ---
  Document pwc = null;
  try {
    ObjectId pwcId = doc.checkOut();
    pwc = (Document) session.getObject(pwcId);
  } catch (CmisBaseException cbe) {
    throw new TheBlendException(
      "Could not check out the document!", cbe);
  }

  // --- do the check in ---
  try {
    newVersionId = pwc.checkIn(true, null, contentStream, null);
  } catch (CmisBaseException cbe) {
    throw new TheBlendException(
      "Could not check in the document!", cbe);
  }
}
finally {
  if (stream != null) {
    try {
      stream.close();
    }
    catch (IOException ioe) {
      // ignore
    }
  }

  uploadedFile.delete();
}

// --- redirect to show page ---
try {
  String url = request.getRequestURL().toString();
  int lastSlash = url.lastIndexOf('/');
```

Create a new major version with new content, but without changing properties and without a comment.

The check-in failed; this would be a good place to call cancelCheckOut() and thereby remove the PWC.

```
    url = url.substring(0, lastSlash) + "/show?id=" +
      URLEncoder.encode(newVersionId.getId(), "UTF-8");

    redirect(url, request, response);
  }
  catch(UnsupportedEncodingException e) {
    throw new ServletException(e);
  }
}
```

There shouldn't be any surprises in the `doPost` and `checkIn` code. If performs the following steps:

- Gathers the input parameters and the new content
- Fetches the document and checks it out
- Fetches the Private Working Copy and checks it in (creating a new version)
- Redirects to the show page where the user can gaze in awe at the new version

Now, restart the server, log in, and append /addversion to the URL in the web browser. When you're testing it, make sure that the document is versionable. Otherwise the repository will throw an exception. The document type `cmis:document` in the InMemory Repository isn't versionable. You'll have to choose another type when you're creating your test document.

Sometimes creating a new version isn't exactly what you want. Sometimes you'll need an independent copy of a document with its own version series. Let's look into copying documents next.

8.6 Copying documents

CMIS has no discrete copy operation, but you can use a `createDocumentFromSource` operation, which is a close second. In this section, you'll build a web page that makes use of `createDocumentFromSource` to let the user copy a document.

Let's start building the copy web page. The HTML form could look like this:

```
<h1>Copy document</h1>

<form method="POST" action="copy">
  Document path:
  <input type="text" size="20" name="path"><br>
  Target folder path:
  <input type="text" size="20" name="target"><br>
  <input type="submit" value="copy">
</form>
```

The user has to specify the document to copy and the target folder. It's possible to create a copy in the same folder, but we'll discuss that later.

Now copy the echo JSP from chapter 6 and rename it to copy.jsp. Remove everything between the line that includes the header JSP and the line that includes the footer JSP, and copy in the preceding HTML fragment. In the package `com.manning.cmis.theblend.servlets`, create a new class called `CopyServlet` that extends `AbstractTheBlendServlet`, and then add the following XML snippet to the web.xml file:

```
<servlet>
 <servlet-name>CopyServlet</servlet-name>
 <servlet-class>
  com.manning.cmis.theblend.servlets.CopyServlet
 </servlet-class>
</servlet>
<servlet-mapping>
 <servlet-name>CopyServlet</servlet-name>
 <url-pattern>/copy</url-pattern>
</servlet-mapping>
```

Here's the code for the doGet method:

```
protected void doGet(HttpServletRequest request,
  HttpServletResponse response, Session session)
    throws ServletException, IOException, TheBlendException {
  dispatch("copy.jsp", "Copy a document.", request, response);
}
```

You know the pattern. It calls the JSP.

Before we jump into the doPost method, let's cover the basics. As mentioned previously, CMIS has no copy operation, and if you want to copy folders or other nondocument objects, you're on your own. CMIS only provides a createDocumentFromSource operation.

createDocumentFromSource is similar to createDocument. The only difference is that it doesn't accept a ContentStream object but instead copies the content of an already existing document in the repository. You can provide properties, a versioning state, an ACL, and policies if you want. If you don't, the repository will copy those, too. In the case of the properties, you only have to provide the property values you want to change. All other properties are copied as they are in the source document. The repository might adjust the ACL depending on the parent folder of the new document.

The main advantage of the createDocumentFromSource operation is that the content isn't transferred to the application and then back to the repository. The content is copied inside the repository, which saves time and bandwidth. That sounds good, but there's a hitch—the AtomPub binding doesn't support this operation. If you want or need to build a binding-agnostic application, you'll have to handle that yourself.

Luckily, OpenCMIS already has a solution. The Document interface provides two copy methods. The simplest one makes a straight copy:

```
try {
  ObjectId targetFolderId = session.createObjectId(folderId);

  Document newDocument = doc.copy(targetFolderId);    <- Copy method returns newly created document
 }
catch(CmisBaseException e) {
  // handle error
}
```

If you set the target folder to a folder that the source document already resides in, the execution is likely to fail. The new document is created with the same name, and most repositories reward the attempt to have two documents with the same name in the same folder with a `CmisNameConstraintViolationException`.

You're still left with the AtomPub binding problem. OpenCMIS detects whether or not `createDocumentFromSource` is supported, and if it isn't, OpenCMIS loads the properties and the content from the source document and creates a new document with that data. That is, it streams the content from the repository to the application and back. That can be an expensive operation if it's a big document. The advantage is that you don't have to care about this problem anymore in your business logic.

If you want to duplicate a document in the same folder, you have to use the second method, which lets you, among other things, define the properties that should be changed. You only have to choose a different name:

```
try {
  Map<String, Object> properties = new HashMap<String, Object>();
  properties.put(PropertyIds.NAME, "newDocumentName");

  ObjectId targetFolderId = session.createObjectId(folderId);

  Document newDocument = doc.copy(
    targetFolderId,
    properties,
    null, null, null, null,
    session.getDefaultContext());
}
catch(CmisBaseException e) {
  // handle error
}
```

Look up other parameters in OpenCMIS Javadoc

This method gives you full control over the new document.

For the servlet's `doPost` method, we'll go for the first simple option, shown in the following listing.

Listing 8.10 `doPost` method for copying document

```
protected void doPost(HttpServletRequest request,
   HttpServletResponse response, Session session)
   throws ServletException, IOException, TheBlendException {

   String path = getStringParameter(request, "path");
   String target = getStringParameter(request, "target");

   // --- fetch the document ---
   CmisObject object = null;
   try {
     object = session.getObjectByPath(path);
   } catch (CmisBaseException cbe) {
      throw new TheBlendException(
         "Could not retrieve the document!", cbe);
   }

   Document doc = null;
   if (object instanceof Document) {
     doc = (Document) object;
```

```
    }
    else {
      throw new TheBlendException("Object is not a document!");
    }

    // --- fetch the target folder ---
    CmisObject targetObject = null;
    try {
      targetObject = session.getObjectByPath(target);

    } catch (CmisBaseException cbe) {
       throw new TheBlendException(
          "Could not retrieve target folder!", cbe);
    }

    if (!(targetObject instanceof Folder)) {
      throw new TheBlendException("Target is not a folder!");
    }

    Document newDoc = null;
    try {
      newDoc = doc.copy(targetObject);
    } catch (CmisBaseException cbe) {
      throw new TheBlendException("Could not copy the document!", cbe);
    }

    // --- redirect to show page ---
    try {
      String url = request.getRequestURL().toString();
      int lastSlash = url.lastIndexOf('/');

      url = url.substring(0, lastSlash) + "/show?id=" +
          URLEncoder.encode(newDoc.getId(), "UTF-8");

      redirect(url, request, response);
    }
    catch(UnsupportedEncodingException e) {
      throw new ServletException(e);
    }
}
```

Again, it's a simple buildup. Get the parameters, fetch the document and the target folder, copy the document, and redirect to the show web page to display the copy of the source document.

Copying is easy, but what about moving? Can we move a document to a different folder? Of course we can. Read on.

8.7 Moving objects

The move operations in CMIS are slightly different than what you're used to in a file-system, because you have to take multifiled objects into account. In this section, you'll build a web page that lets a user move an object from one folder to another.

You start as always with the web page:

```
<h1>Move object</h1>

<form method="POST" action="move">
```

```
  Object path:
  <input type="text" size="20" name="path"><br>
  Target folder path:
  <input type="text" size="20" name="target"><br>
  <input type="submit" value="move">
</form>
```

This time you definitely want to use the path to the object. You'll understand why in a moment. The user must also define the target folder.

Again, copy the echo JSP from chapter 6 and rename it to move.jsp. Remove everything between the line that includes the header JSP and the line that includes the footer JSP, and copy in the preceding HTML fragment. Our next listing shows the result.

Listing 8.11 Move.jsp with inserted HTML form

```
<%@ page language="java" contentType="text/html; charset=UTF-8"
    pageEncoding="UTF-8" trimDirectiveWhitespaces="true" %>
<%@ page import="org.apache.chemistry.opencmis.client.api.*" %>
<%@ page import="org.apache.chemistry.opencmis.commons.enums.*" %>
<%@ page import="java.util.*" %>
<%@ include file="header.jsp"  %>

  <h1>Move object</h1>                      <- HTML for move form inserted here

  <form method="POST" action="move">
    Object path:
    <input type="text" size="20" name="path"><br>
    Target folder path:
    <input type="text" size="20" name="target"><br>
    <input type="submit" value="move">
  </form>

<%@ include file="footer.jsp" %>
```

In the package `com.manning.cmis.theblend.servlets`, create a new class called `MoveServlet` that extends `AbstractTheBlendServlet`, and then add the following XML snippet to the web.xml file:

```
<servlet>
 <servlet-name>MoveServlet</servlet-name>
 <servlet-class>
  com.manning.cmis.theblend.servlets.MoveServlet
 </servlet-class>
</servlet>
<servlet-mapping>
 <servlet-name>MoveServlet</servlet-name>
 <url-pattern>/move</url-pattern>
</servlet-mapping>
```

Here's the code for the `doGet` method:

```
protected void doGet(HttpServletRequest request,
  HttpServletResponse response, Session session)
    throws ServletException, IOException, TheBlendException {
```

```
  dispatch("move.jsp", "Move an object", request, response);
}
```

You don't have anything else to do here except call the JSP.

CMIS provides three methods that you can use to move objects around: `move`, `addToFolder`, and `removeFromFolder`.

The `move` method moves an object from one folder to another folder, as the following example shows:

```
try {
  CmisObject object = session.getObjectByPath(path);

  if (!(object instanceof FileableCmisObject)) {
    throw new TheBlendException("Object is not fileable!");
  }

  FileableCmisObject fileableCmisObject = (FileableCmisObject) object;

  ObjectId sourceFolderId = session.createObjectId(moveFromFolderId);
  ObjectId targetFolderId = session.createObjectId(moveToFolderId);

  FileableCmisObject movedObject =
    fileableCmisObject.move(sourceFolderId, targetFolderId);
}
catch(CmisBaseException e) {
  // handle error
}
```

The previous code snippet has three interesting aspects to it.

First, to move an object it must be fileable. OpenCMIS classes that represent fileable objects implement the interface `FileableCmisObject`. Because the `move` method is declared on that interface, you have to cast to that interface first.

The second interesting aspect is that you have to provide the ID of the source folder when you move an object. That makes sense if the object is filed in multiple folders, because the repository has to know from which folder it should move the object. If the object is only filed in one folder, it's unambiguous, but you have to provide the source folder ID anyway.

The third interesting aspect is that the `move` method returns the moved object after it has been moved. There's only one rare use case for this object. A repository might implement the move operation by deleting the original object and creating a new one in the target folder. In that case, the new object would have a new ID, and that would be the only reliable way to get to the new ID. Because all serious repositories have native support for move, this isn't generally a concern.

Another way to move an object would be to remove it from the source folder first and then add it to the target folder:

```
fileableCmisObject.removeFromFolder(sourceFolderId);
fileableCmisObject.addToFolder(targetFolderId, true);
```

Second parameter specifies whether all versions of a document should be added or just the one that's calling addToFolder

But that requires that the repository supports unfiled objects, because the object could be potentially unfiled for a moment. It also works the other way round:

```
fileableCmisObject.addToFolder(targetFolderId, true);
fileableCmisObject.removeFromFolder(sourceFolderId);
```

The object is added to the target folder first and then removed from the source folder. In this case, the repository has to support multifiling because the object would reside in multiple folders for a moment. If you have to deal with unfiled and multifiled objects, these are the two methods you want to look into. For our servlet, we'll stick with the `move` method.

The following listing shows the completed `doPost` with the move logic.

Listing 8.12 `doPost` method for move document

```
protected void doPost(HttpServletRequest request,
   HttpServletResponse response, Session session)
   throws ServletException, IOException, TheBlendException {

   String path = getStringParameter(request, "path");
   String target = getStringParameter(request, "target");

   // --- fetch the object ---
   CmisObject object = null;
   try {
      object = session.getObjectByPath(path);
   } catch (CmisBaseException cbe) {
      throw new TheBlendException(
         "Could not retrieve the object!", cbe);
   }

   if (!(object instanceof FileableCmisObject)) {
      throw new TheBlendException("Object is not fileable!");
   }

   FileableCmisObject fileableCmisObject = (FileableCmisObject) object;

   // --- fetch the source folder ---
   CmisObject sourceObject = null;
   try {
      int lastSlash = path.lastIndexOf('/');
      String parentPath = path.substring(0, lastSlash);
      if (parentPath.length() == 0) {
         parentPath = "/";
      }

      sourceObject = session.getObjectByPath(parentPath);
   } catch (CmisBaseException cbe) {
      throw new TheBlendException(
      "Could not retrieve target folder!", cbe);
   }

   // --- fetch the target folder ---
   CmisObject targetObject = null;
   try {
      targetObject = session.getObjectByPath(target);
```

That shouldn't happen because you just received the object by path, so it must be fileable.

Extract the path of the parent folder from the object's path.

```
    } catch (CmisBaseException cbe) {
        throw new TheBlendException(
            "Could not retrieve target folder!", cbe);
    }

    if (!(targetObject instanceof Folder)) {
        throw new TheBlendException("Target is not a folder!");
    }

    try {
      fileableCmisObject.move(sourceObject, targetObject);
    } catch (CmisBaseException cbe) {
      throw new TheBlendException("Could not move the object!", cbe);
    }

    // --- redirect to browse page ---
    try {
      String url = request.getRequestURL().toString();
      int lastSlash = url.lastIndexOf('/');

      url = url.substring(0, lastSlash) + "/browse?id=" +
          URLEncoder.encode(targetObject.getId(), "UTF-8");

      redirect(url, request, response);
    }
    catch(UnsupportedEncodingException e) {
      throw new ServletException(e);
    }
}
```

Let's do a quick rundown of what happens in this code. The method gets the parameters, fetches the object, and checks if the object is fileable. Then it gets the parent folder of the object because this path already contains the parent from which the object should be moved. Even if the object is multifiled, the parent is unambiguous here. To get to the parent object, you remove the last path segment and fetch the folder object. Then the target folder is fetched and checked. The object is moved and the web browser is redirected to the browse page of the new parent of the object.

You can now create and manipulate objects with CMIS, but one important operation is missing. Let's talk about deleting objects.

8.8 Deleting objects

It should come as no surprise that CMIS objects can be deleted, after all of these other operations we've been performing on them in this chapter. Let's build a web page that deletes objects and handles the deletion of folder trees.

The only input you need is an object. We'll go with the path again, as follows:

```
<h1>Delete object</h1>

<form method="POST" action="delete">
  Object path:
  <input type="text" size="20" name="path"><br>
  <input type="submit" value="delete">
</form>
```

8.8.1 Deleting documents

For unfiled objects and document versions, you'd need the object ID because they don't have a path. Modifying this web page to accept an ID should be a simple exercise for you at this point.

Next (and for the final time), copy the echo JSP from chapter 6 and rename it to delete.jsp. Then remove all lines between the line that includes the header JSP and the line that includes the footer JSP, and copy in the preceding HTML fragment, shown in the next listing.

Listing 8.13 delete.jsp with inserted HTML form

```
<%@ page language="java" contentType="text/html; charset=UTF-8"
    pageEncoding="UTF-8" trimDirectiveWhitespaces="true" %>
<%@ page import="org.apache.chemistry.opencmis.client.api.*" %>
<%@ page import="org.apache.chemistry.opencmis.commons.enums.*" %>
<%@ page import="java.util.*" %>
<%@ include file="header.jsp"  %>

<h1>Delete object</h1>                              HTML for delete
                                                    form inserted here
  <form method="POST" action="delete">
    Object path:
    <input type="text" size="20" name="path"><br>
    <input type="submit" value="delete">
  </form>

<%@ include file="footer.jsp" %>
```

In the package com.manning.cmis.theblend.servlets, create a new class called DeleteServlet that extends AbstractTheBlendServlet, and then add the following XML snippet to the web.xml file:

```
<servlet>
 <servlet-name>DeleteServlet</servlet-name>
 <servlet-class>
  com.manning.cmis.theblend.servlets.DeleteServlet
 </servlet-class>
</servlet>
<servlet-mapping>
 <servlet-name>DeleteServlet</servlet-name>
 <url-pattern>/delete</url-pattern>
</servlet-mapping>
```

The doGet method only has to call the JSP:

```
protected void doGet(HttpServletRequest request,
  HttpServletResponse response, Session session)
    throws ServletException, IOException, TheBlendException {
  dispatch("delete.jsp", "Delete an object", request, response);
}
```

The `CmisObject` interface has a delete method that we'll use here:

```
try {
  CmisObject object = session.getObject(id);
  object.delete(true);
}
catch(CmisBaseException e) {
    // handle error
}
```

The Boolean parameter is only relevant for documents. It indicates whether this one version (`false`) or all versions in the version series (`true`) should be deleted. Before you delete an object, you should check the allowable actions to check whether you're allowed to do that. The Java object becomes invalid after you've called `delete`. All subsequent calls to the repository are likely to fail, and the object also removes itself from the OpenCMIS cache.

8.8.2 Deleting folders

Folders can be deleted with the `delete` operation if they're empty. When you call it on a non-empty folder, the repository returns a `CmisConstraintException`. To delete a non-empty folder, use the `deleteTree` method on the `Folder` interface:

```
try {
  Folder folder = (Folder) session.getObject(id);
  List<String> failedToDelete =
    folder.deleteTree(true, UnfileObject.DELETE, true);
}
catch(CmisBaseException e) {
  // handle error
}
```

The first parameter again defines what should happen to documents and document versions. The second parameter lets you choose whether nonfolder children of this folder should be deleted or unfiled. Three possible options are available:

- `UNFILE`—Objects aren't deleted, only unfiled. This option is available only if the repository supports unfiling and/or multifiling.
- `DELETESINGLEFILED`—Objects are deleted only if they're not filed in another folder.
- `DELETE`—Objects are deleted even if they're also filed in another folder.

The third parameter defines whether or not the operation should continue if the deletion of a child fails. If you set it to `true`, the repository deletes everything it can delete in the context of the current user. If you set it to `false`, it stops when it hits the first object the current user can't delete. Other objects might be already deleted by then. The deletion-processing order is repository-specific, but you can't predict which object in the folder tree is deleted first and which is deleted last.

The `deleteTree` method returns a list of IDs of objects that couldn't be deleted. If this list is empty or `null`, the delete operation was successful. If the list contains IDs, objects were left undeleted. This list doesn't need to be complete, though. If many objects are left, some repositories truncate the list.

That's all you need for the `doPost` method; here it is in the next listing.

Listing 8.14 `doPost` method for deleting objects

```
protected void doPost(HttpServletRequest request,
   HttpServletResponse response, Session session)
   throws ServletException, IOException, TheBlendException {

   String path = getStringParameter(request, "path");

   // --- fetch the object ---
   CmisObject object = null;
   try {
     object = session.getObjectByPath(path);

   } catch (CmisBaseException cbe) {
      throw new TheBlendException(
        "Could not retrieve the object!", cbe);
   }

   // --- delete the object ---
   try {
     if (object instanceof Folder) {
         Folder folder = (Folder) object;
         List<String> failedToDelete =
           folder.deleteTree(true, UnfileObject.DELETE, true);

         if (failedToDelete != null && !failedToDelete.isEmpty()) {
             throw new TheBlendException("Deletion failed!");
         }
     }
     else {
         object.delete(true);
     }
   }
   catch (CmisBaseException cbe) {
     throw new TheBlendException("Could not delete the object!", cbe);
   }

   // --- redirect to browse page of the root folder ---
   String url = request.getRequestURL().toString();
   int lastSlash = url.lastIndexOf('/');
   url = url.substring(0, lastSlash) + "/browse";

   redirect(url, request, response);
}
```

You won't find any magic in this code. It fetches the object and checks if it's a folder or something else. If it's a folder, it calls `deleteTree` and checks if all children have been deleted. If it isn't a folder, it calls only the `delete` method.

With this final step, you've rebuilt the most important parts of The Blend. Now it's up to you to tidy it up, add new features, and develop your own user interface.

As a final recap, let's look at all of the functionality we've implemented in chapters 6, 7, and 8.

- *Login/connection*—Chapter 6
- *Folder browsing (includes paging logic)*—Chapter 7
- *Document display (metadata) and retrieval (includes version series information)*—Chapter 7
- *Query*—Chapter 7
- *Creating folders and documents*—Chapter 8
- *Updating properties*—Chapter 8
- *Updating and deleting content*—Chapter 8
- *Copying, moving, and deleting objects*—Chapter 8

8.9 Summary

This and the previous chapter covered the bigger part of the OpenCMIS API. You were introduced to all the major CMIS create, read, update, and delete (CRUD) operations as you rebuilt a stripped-down version of The Blend.

With this knowledge, you're now able to build CMIS applications in Java for the desktop, for the web, and for Android. These chapters were also a blueprint for .NET developers, because the Apache Chemistry DotCMIS API is similar to the OpenCMIS API.

In the next chapters, you'll learn more about other CMIS libraries for other programming languages and environments. The general principles, such as type system, properties, content, versioning, exceptions, filing, and so on, are the same for all of the other libraries, which makes jumping between them much easier.

9 Using other client libraries

This chapter covers

- Overview of other CMIS client libraries
- Connecting to SharePoint with CMIS
- Using C#, Python, and PHP to write CMIS applications

This chapter will review some of the CMIS client libraries that are available beyond OpenCMIS. These libraries are useful if your preferred language is something other than Java, or if OpenCMIS doesn't meet the specific needs of the solution you're building (see figure 9.1). By the end of the chapter, you'll have a working knowledge of the capabilities of these libraries. Optionally, you can work through the "Try it" sections for each client library to add functionality to the solution you've developed in previous chapters—The Blend.

We realize you may not have an immediate need for all of these libraries, but we recommend that you read the entire chapter because it introduces you to what's available and gives you an idea of when each of these libraries might be appropriate to use. But if you have zero interest in a particular language, feel free to skip that section.

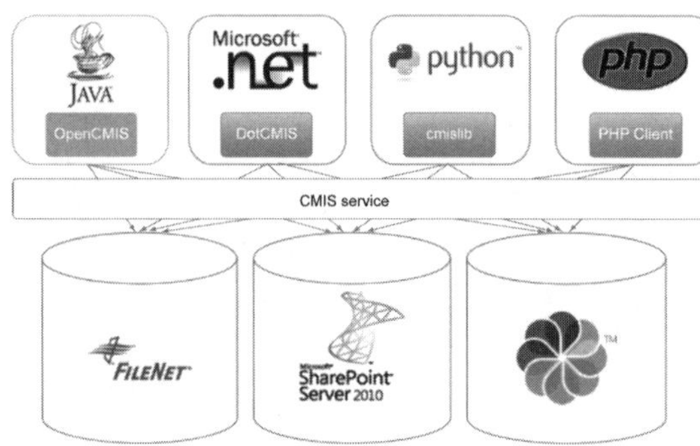

Figure 9.1 Other client libraries give non-Java developers access to any CMIS-compliant repository.

9.1 Working with other client libraries

If you're a Java developer, you might have the luxury of developing your applications using only the OpenCMIS client library, depending on the type of applications you build. But the real world is rarely that homogeneous, which is a good thing—it keeps life interesting.

Luckily, CMIS is language-independent, which means that if you prefer another language, or if Java isn't a good match for the task at hand, it's highly likely that another client library is available that will meet your needs.

Let's take a look at some common CMIS client libraries other than OpenCMIS.

9.1.1 Common client libraries

The first place to start when seeking out another client library is the Apache Chemistry project (http://chemistry.apache.org). This project isn't only home to OpenCMIS; it also hosts CMIS projects for .NET, Python, PHP, and Android. Each of these subprojects has its own page on the Apache Chemistry site, which is where you'll find download packages and documentation.

Apache Chemistry isn't the only place to find CMIS client libraries. When developers need to work with a CMIS repository in their preferred language and a client library doesn't already exist, often a new client library is born. Table 9.1 lists some of the more common client libraries.

Table 9.1 At a glance: popular non-Java libraries for working with CMIS

Library	Language	Project home	Bindings supported	Install method	Key dependencies
DotCMIS	.NET	Apache Chemistry	AtomPub and Web Services	Manual	Microsoft OS
cmislib	Python	Apache Chemistry	AtomPub only	Python setup-tools or manual	Python 2.6 or 2.7
PHP Client	PHP	Apache Chemistry	AtomPub only	Manual	None

In this chapter, we'll spend some time looking at each of these. You'll learn a little bit about each one, including how it compares to OpenCMIS, what the requirements are for using the library, and how to install it. Once you have a feel for a given library, you can work through a hands-on example that further expands on The Blend. By the end of the chapter, you'll have a better idea of what's available and how to use each one.

9.2 Coding in .NET with DotCMIS

The first client library we'll look at is DotCMIS, which is used when writing C#, PowerShell, and web parts that need to talk to a CMIS repository. By the end of this section, you'll know how DotCMIS compares with OpenCMIS, and you'll have a web part that can browse The Blend. Toward the end of this section, there will also be a discussion of how to use Microsoft SharePoint as a CMIS provider.

9.2.1 Comparing DotCMIS and OpenCMIS

.NET provides a formidable platform for CMIS client applications targeting Windows users. Not only do you get the opportunity to take advantage of the strongly typed, object-oriented C# programming language, which provides comforts such as garbage collection, operator overloading, optional arguments, and C-like syntax, but also the opportunity to take advantage of the powerful, flexible, command-line shell and scripting language that's PowerShell.

Imagine you're in the early exploratory stages of developing the next grand slam CMIS client application. You want to know how best to solve a problem with your algorithm, but on this particular implementation detail the specification is intentionally vague, and no other relevant documentation solves your problem. Coding up a whole program to test your various rival theories on the best solution could take forever, but luckily you remember that you have a PowerShell window open, with a session already connected to a test server equipped with a CMIS producer. You type in a few method calls using your session instance, and upon inspecting the results you come to a solid conclusion as to which theory holds water. Now that experimentation has yielded a solid, sanity-tested plan, you can get to work creating a high-quality compiled C# program—using the same API that you experimented with.

DotCMIS, as its name implies, is the .NET CMIS client library. It's similar in architecture to the OpenCMIS client library, and it's tightly based on the CMIS domain model. It's a full-featured library, including caching of CMIS objects and bindings, but it's limited in the area of authentication. Whereas OpenCMIS provides support for both NTLM and Basic authentication, DotCMIS includes only Basic authentication. On the bright side, it's extensible to other authentication methods, as we'll discuss shortly.

In the following sections, you'll see a demonstration of the basic use of the DotCMIS library in both C# and PowerShell and how to use PowerShell to change the metadata of songs in The Blend's repository.

9.2.2 *Getting started with DotCMIS*

In this section, you'll see how to connect to the repository and perform basic CRUD functions against it using DotCMIS.

Regardless of whether you seek to take advantage of DotCMIS in PowerShell or C#, your first step is the same: you must create a reference to the DotCMIS binary. In C#, this is as simple as clicking Add a Reference for your Visual Studio project and browsing to the DotCMIS binary. In PowerShell, you'll need to run the following command:

```
[Reflection.Assembly]::LoadFile("C:\example\path\DotCMIS.dll")
```

Within the DotCMIS API, the `Session` object is the star of the show. You need to create a `Session` instance as the first step in any CMIS client program, and once you have it, you can use it for a myriad of different tasks, including creating and retrieving ACLs, documents, folders, policies, relationships, and type definitions—for a full list, see figure 9.2.

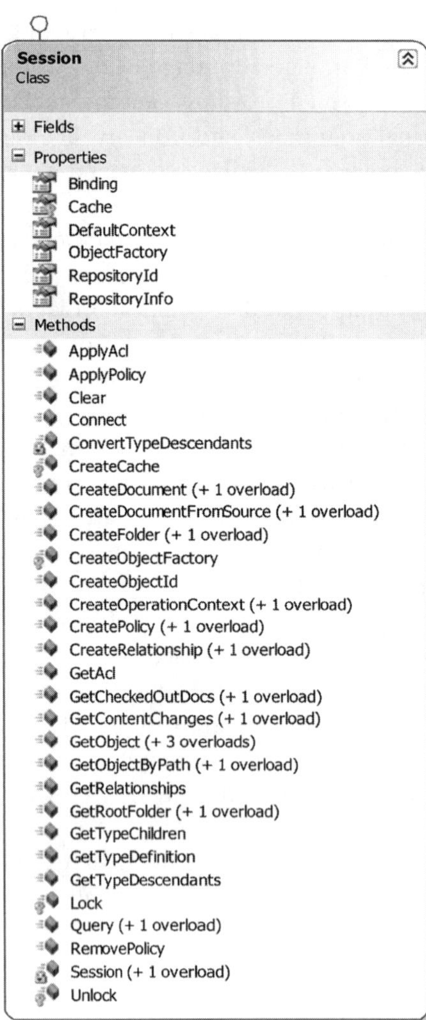

Figure 9.2 DotCMIS methods

Here's what creating an AtomPub session looks like in C#:

```
Dictionary<string, string> parameters =
     new Dictionary<string, string>();

parameters[SessionParameter.BindingType] = BindingType.AtomPub;
parameters[SessionParameter.AtomPubUrl] =
     "http://exampleServer/service/cmis/rest";
parameters[SessionParameter.User] = "exampleUser";
parameters[SessionParameter.Password] = "examplePassword";

SessionFactory factory = SessionFactory.NewInstance();
ISession session = factory.GetRepositories(parameters)[0].
     CreateSession();
```

And here's what it looks like in PowerShell:

```
#helper function
function New-GenericDictionary([type] $keyType, [type] $valueType) {
    $base = [System.Collections.Generic.Dictionary``2]
    $ct = $base.MakeGenericType(($keyType, $valueType))
    New-Object $ct
}
$sp = New-GenericDictionary string string
$sp["org.apache.chemistry.dotcmis.binding.spi.type"] = "atompub"
$sp["org.apache.chemistry.dotcmis.binding.atompub.url"] =
     "http://exampleServer/service/cmis/rest"
$sp["org.apache.chemistry.dotcmis.user"] = "exampleUser"
$sp["org.apache.chemistry.dotcmis.password"] = "examplePassword"

$factory = [DotCMIS.Client.Impl::SessionFactory]::NewInstance()
$session = $factory.GetRepositories($sp)[0].CreateSession()
```

Creating a SOAP Web Services session in either language is slightly different, because it requires the endpoints not only of the repository service, but of every service. To connect with Web Services instead of AtomPub, change the value of the binding type, and replace the line setting the AtomPub URL with the endpoints for each service. Here's what that looks like in C#:

```
Dictionary<string, string> parameters =
     new Dictionary<string, string>();

parameters[SessionParameter.BindingType] = BindingType.WebServices;
parameters[SessionParameter.WebServicesAclService] =
     "https://exampleServer/cmis/soap/aclservice?wsdl";
parameters[SessionParameter.WebServicesDiscoveryService] =
     "https://exampleServer/cmis/soap/discoveryservice?wsdl";
parameters[SessionParameter.WebServicesMultifilingService] =
     "https://exampleServer/cmis/soap/multifilingservice?wsdl";
parameters[SessionParameter.WebServicesNavigationService] =
     "https://exampleServer/cmis/soap/navigationservice?wsdl";
parameters[SessionParameter.WebServicesObjectService] =
     "https://exampleServer/cmis/soap/objectservice?wsdl";
parameters[SessionParameter.WebServicesPolicyService] =
     "https://exampleServer/cmis/soap/policyservice?wsdl";
parameters[SessionParameter.WebServicesRelationshipService] =
```

```
     "https://exampleServer/cmis/soap/relationshipservice?wsdl";
parameters[SessionParameter.WebServicesRepositoryService] =
     "https://exampleServer/cmis/soap/repositoryservice?wsdl";
parameters[SessionParameter.WebServicesVersioningService] =
     "https://exampleServer/cmis/soap/versioningservice?wsdl";
parameters[SessionParameter.User] = "exampleUser";
parameters[SessionParameter.Password] = "examplePassword";

SessionFactory factory = SessionFactory.NewInstance();
ISession session = factory.GetRepositories(parameters)[0].
     CreateSession();
```

And here's what creating a SOAP Web Services `Session` looks like in PowerShell:

```
#helper function
function New-GenericDictionary([type] $keyType, [type] $valueType) {
    $base = [System.Collections.Generic.Dictionary``2]
    $ct = $base.MakeGenericType(($keyType, $valueType))
    New-Object $ct
}
$sp = New-GenericDictionary string string
$sp["org.apache.chemistry.dotcmis.binding.spi.type"] = "webservices"
$sp["org.apache.chemistry.dotcmis.binding.webservices.ACLService"] =
     "https://exampleServer/service/cmis/soap/aclservice?wsdl"
$sp[
"org.apache.chemistry.dotcmis.binding.webservices.DiscoveryService"
] = "https://exampleServer/service/cmis/soap/discoveryservice?wsdl"
$sp[
"org.apache.chemistry.dotcmis.binding.webservices.MultiFilingService"
] = "https://exampleServer/service/cmis/soap/multifilingservice?wsdl"
$sp[
"org.apache.chemistry.dotcmis.binding.webservices.NavigationService"
] = "https://exampleServer/service/cmis/soap/navigationservice?wsdl"
$sp["org.apache.chemistry.dotcmis.binding.webservices.ObjectService"] =
     "https://exampleServer/service/cmis/soap/objectservice?wsdl"
$sp["org.apache.chemistry.dotcmis.binding.webservices.PolicyService"] =
     "https://exampleServer/service/cmis/soap/policyservice?wsdl"
$sp[
"org.apache.chemistry.dotcmis.binding.webservices.RelationshipService"
] = "https://exampleServer/service/cmis/soap/relationshipservice?wsdl"
$sp[
"org.apache.chemistry.dotcmis.binding.webservices.RepositoryService"
] = "https://exampleServer/service/cmis/soap/repositoryservice?wsdl"
$sp[
"org.apache.chemistry.dotcmis.binding.webservices.VersioningService"
] = "https://exampleServer/service/cmis/soap/versioningservice?wsdl"
$sp["org.apache.chemistry.dotcmis.user"] = "exampleUser"
$sp["org.apache.chemistry.dotcmis.password"] = "examplePassword"

$factory = [DotCMIS.Client.Impl::SessionFactory]::NewInstance()
$session = $factory.GetRepositories($sp)[0].CreateSession()
```

If your server requires authentication, you'll need to provide an authentication provider class, which should implement the `AbstractAuthenticationProvider` interface. Out of the box, DotCMIS provides Basic authentication for the AtomPub REST binding, and Basic-over-SSL authentication for the Web Services SOAP binding, contained within the `DotCMIS.Binding.StandardAuthenticationProvider` class. Assuming you've decided on an appropriate authentication provider class, you can set it along with the rest of your preconnection `Session` settings. Here it is in C#:

```
parameters[SessionParameter.AuthenticationProviderClass] =
     "ExampleNamespace.ExampleAuthenticationProvider";
```

And here's how to set the authentication provider in PowerShell:

```
$sp["org.apache.chemistry.dotcmis.binding.auth.classname"] =
     "ExampleNamespace.ExampleAuthenticationProvider"
```

Note that in the previous examples, you get the list of repositories (through the call to `factory.getRepositories`) and pick the first one. If you wish to choose a known repository by ID rather than choosing whichever repository happens to be first in the returned list, you can specify the repository ID as a session parameter, and change the factory method call from `getRepositories` to `getRepositoryInfo`, as shown here in C#:

```
Dictionary<string, string> parameters =
     new Dictionary<string, string>();

parameters[SessionParameter.BindingType] = BindingType.AtomPub;
parameters[SessionParameter.AtomPubUrl] =
     "http://exampleServer/service/cmis/rest";
parameters[SessionParameter.RepositoryId] =
     "01234567-89ab-cdef-0123-456789abcdef";
parameters[SessionParameter.User] = "exampleUser";
parameters[SessionParameter.Password] = "examplePassword";

SessionFactory factory = SessionFactory.NewInstance();
ISession session = factory.GetRepositoryInfo(parameters)[0].
     CreateSession();
```

And here's the same thing shown in PowerShell:

```
#helper function
function New-GenericDictionary([type] $keyType, [type] $valueType) {
    $base = [System.Collections.Generic.Dictionary``2]
    $ct = $base.MakeGenericType(($keyType, $valueType))
    New-Object $ct
}
$sp = New-GenericDictionary string string
$sp["org.apache.chemistry.dotcmis.binding.spi.type"] = "atompub"
$sp["org.apache.chemistry.dotcmis.binding.atompub.url"] =
     "http://exampleServer/service/cmis/rest"
$sp["org.apache.chemistry.dotcmis. session.repository.id"] =
     "01234567-89ab-cdef-0123-456789abcdef"
$sp["org.apache.chemistry.dotcmis.user"] = "exampleUser"
$sp["org.apache.chemistry.dotcmis.password"] = "examplePassword"

$factory = [DotCMIS.Client.Impl::SessionFactory]::NewInstance()
$session = $factory.GetRepositoryInfo($sp).CreateSession()
```

At this point, you should be able to create a session appropriate for your situation. This enables you to, among other things, implement basic CRUD (create, read, update, and delete) operations. From your session instance, you can either retrieve the root folder or get another object by ID or path, as shown in C# in a later section (from this point on, we'll omit the PowerShell version):

```
IFolder rootFolder = session.GetRootFolder();                    <-- Get root folder
ICmisObject objectById = session.GetObject(new ObjectId("exampleID"));   <-- Get another object by ID
ICmisObject objectByPath = session.GetObjectByPath(
     "/examplePath/exampleFile");                  <-- Get another object by path
```

Once you have an ICmisObject instance, you may find it more useful to further define it as an IFolder, IDocument, IPolicy, or IRelationship after checking its base type, as follows:

```
if (objectByPath.BaseTypeId == BaseTypeId.CmisDocument)
{
     IDocument document = (IDocument)objectById;

     //do something
}
else if (objectByPath.BaseTypeId == BaseTypeId.CmisFolder)
{
     IFolder folder = (IFolder)objectById;

     //do something else
}
```

When creating an object, you have the choice between specifying the folder ID explicitly through the session instance, or by calling the creation method from that folder's IFolder instance directly:

```
Dictionary<string, object> properties = new Dictionary<string,object>()
{
     {"cmis:name", "exampleName" },
     {"cmis:objectType", "cmis:document"},
};
string filePath = "C:\\examplePath\\exampleFile";
string fileName = "exampleFile";
FileStream stream = File.Create(filePath);
IObjectFactory objectFactory = session.ObjectFactory;
IContentStream contentStream = session.ObjectFactory.
     CreateContentStream(fileName, stream.Length, "text/plain", stream);

IDocument firstDoc = folder.CreateDocument(properties, contentStream,
     VersioningState.Major);           <-- Create document through the folder instance

properties["cmis:name"] = "exampleName2";
IDocument secondDoc = session.CreateDocument(properties, folder.Id,
     contentStream, VersioningState.Major);      <-- Create document through the session
```

Suppose you want to delete the first file and then rename the second file so it has the first file's name. You can do that as follows:

```
firstDoc.Delete(true);

Dictionary<string, object> properties = new Dictionary<string,object>()
{
     {"cmis:name", "exampleName" },
};
secondDoc.UpdateProperties(properties);
```

Finally, one of the most useful abilities of CMIS is its query functionality. In order to perform some action on all documents retrieved by a query, you'd do something like this:

```
foreach (ICmisObject cmisObject in session.Query(
     "SELECT * FROM cmis:document", false))
{
     //do something
}
```

Now that you know how to connect to a CMIS repository to perform basic operations using DotCMIS, it's time to revisit The Blend to see how you can expand on that example with .NET.

9.2.3 Try it—building a web part with .NET and CMIS to browse The Blend

In prior chapters, you wrote a Java-based web application to work with music and art objects in sophisticated ways. Now suppose you have a new requirement to access The Blend from a web part running within SharePoint. In this section, you'll learn how to do that. When you've finished, the CMIS Browser web part will look like figure 9.3.

A .NET web part can be a simple and powerful means of displaying CMIS-powered information on a web page. We'll use a web part to browse The Blend within the web browser. The user should see a list of the files in The Blend's CMIS repository and be able to navigate the repository's folder hierarchy within the page. For the purposes of this example, we'll use Microsoft Visual Studio 2012 paired with Microsoft SharePoint Server 2013.

Figure 9.3 CMIS Browser web part as it appears after working through this section

In order to create a SharePoint 2013 Web Part Project in Visual Studio, you're required to have installed the Microsoft Office Developer Tools for Visual Studio 2012 (available from Microsoft at http://mng.bz/2qzs) and the SharePoint Server 2013 Client Components SDK (available at http://mng.bz/h2T0). After you've created the project in Visual Studio, you'll need to add a reference to the DotCMIS binary as instructed earlier. There's also an extra step when dealing with web parts: because this web part will be dependent on the third-party DotCMIS binary, you must go to the

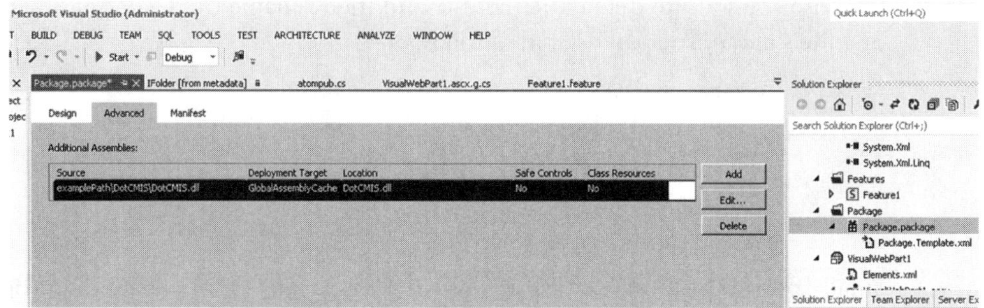

Figure 9.4 Adding an additional assembly to your package

Package file, click on the Advanced tab, and add the binary as an Additional Assembly, as shown in figure 9.4. Don't worry, you can keep the binary where it is; Visual Studio will automatically deploy it to the GAC or an alternate appropriate location.

Peering into the project, you should see the first several lines of listing 9.1 already added into your .ascx file. Because this project calls for user-controlled dynamic navigation from the contents of one folder to another, it will require postbacks to the server to get that new content—but the web part would hardly be smooth if it required a full-page refresh for every click. In order to handle this issue, you can use an `UpdatePanel` to restrict the postback to within the bounds of that single DOM element. You'll also need a server-side `Placeholder` to serve as a container for the list of files to be displayed, and a `HiddenField` to store the current folder ID that the user has browsed to in the `ViewState` of the page.

Listing 9.1 User interface for the DotCMIS-based CMIS Browser

```
<%@ Assembly
    Name="$SharePoint.Project.AssemblyFullName$" %>
<%@ Assembly Name="Microsoft.Web.CommandUI, Version=15.0.0.0,
    Culture=neutral, PublicKeyToken=71e9bce111e9429c" %>
<%@ Register Tagprefix="SharePoint"
    Namespace="Microsoft.SharePoint.WebControls"
    Assembly="Microsoft.SharePoint,
    Version=15.0.0.0,
    Culture=neutral,
    PublicKeyToken=71e9bce111e9429c" %>
<%@ Register Tagprefix="Utilities"
    Namespace="Microsoft.SharePoint.Utilities"
    Assembly="Microsoft.SharePoint,
    Version=15.0.0.0,
    Culture=neutral,
    PublicKeyToken=71e9bce111e9429c" %>
<%@ Register Tagprefix="asp"
    Namespace="System.Web.UI"
    Assembly="System.Web.Extensions,
    Version=3.5.0.0,
    Culture=neutral,
```

This entire block is automatically generated.

```
    PublicKeyToken=31bf3856ad364e35" %>
<%@ Import Namespace="Microsoft.SharePoint" %>
<%@ Register Tagprefix="WebPartPages"
    Namespace="Microsoft.SharePoint.WebPartPages"
    Assembly="Microsoft.SharePoint,
    Version=15.0.0.0,
    Culture=neutral,
    PublicKeyToken=71e9bce111e9429c" %>
<%@ Control Language="C#" AutoEventWireup="true"
    CodeBehind="VisualWebPart1.ascx.cs"
    Inherits="CMIS_Web_Part_Project.VisualWebPart1.VisualWebPart1" %>

<asp:UpdatePanel
    id="CMISBrowser_UpdatePanel"
    UpdateMode="Conditional"
    ChildrenAsTriggers="true"
    runat="server">
  <ContentTemplate>
    <div id="CMISBrowser_Files_Area">
        <asp:Placeholder
            id="CMISBrowser_Files" runat="server" />
    </div>
    <asp:HiddenField
        id="CMISBrowser_Id"
        runat="server"
        value=""/>
  </ContentTemplate>
  <Triggers>
  </Triggers>
</asp:UpdatePanel>
```

Postbacks will be restricted to within this web part.

Placeholder contains the list of files being browsed.

Saves the ID of the folder being browsed between page loads.

Next, we'll look into the code behind the web part. This web part will have an `ISession` member variable in order to maintain its connection to the repository for the entire ASP .NET lifecycle, initialized as shown in listing 9.2. Whenever a folder (or the Up One Level link) is clicked in the web part's user interface, the `CMISBrowser_File_Click` event handler will fire, triggering a postback and refreshing the web part with that folder's ID as the new parent folder ID.

Listing 9.2 Logic for the DotCMIS-based web part

```
using DotCMIS;
using DotCMIS.Binding;
using DotCMIS.Client;
using DotCMIS.Client.Impl;
using System;
using System.Collections.Generic;
using System.ComponentModel;
using System.Web;
using System.Web.UI.WebControls;
using System.Web.UI.WebControls.WebParts;

namespace CMIS_Web_Part_Project.CMISBrowserWebPart
{
    [ToolboxItemAttribute(false)]
```

```
    public partial class CMISBrowserWebPart: WebPart
    {
        protected ISession session;

        protected override void OnInit(EventArgs e)
        {
            base.OnInit(e);
            InitializeControl();

            //instantiate a session
        }

        protected override void OnLoad(EventArgs e)
        {
            base.OnLoad(e);

            EnumerateFiles();
        }

        protected void CMISBrowser_File_Click(object sender,      Handles the
             EventArgs e)                                        Up One Level
        {                                                        link click
            LinkButton link = (LinkButton)sender;

            CMISBrowser_Id.Value = link.Attributes["cmisObjectId"];
            EnumerateFiles();
        }

        protected void Page_Load(object sender, EventArgs e)
        {
        }
    }
}
```

The lion's share of the logic resides in the `EnumerateFiles` method (shown in listing 9.3), whose purpose is to fill the `CMISBrowser_Files` control with the contents of the parent folder pointed to by `CMISBrowser_Id`. Because the `ViewState` of the `CMISBrowser_Id` is necessary for this method to work properly (and hence for the proper folder's contents being displayed), the `EnumerateFiles` method must be invoked after the `ViewState` has been defined during the ASP .NET lifecycle, which means no earlier than the `OnPreLoad` event. Even in cases where a folder has been clicked and the `CMISBrowser_File_Click` event has been queued to run, the call to `EnumerateFiles` inside of `OnLoad` is necessary, so that it can recreate the control that initiated the call to `CMISBrowser_File_Click`. This allows the event handler to fire correctly and triggers the second call to `EnumerateFiles`. Similarly, if the `LinkButtons` didn't have DOM IDs specified, the control's ID wouldn't be recreated consistently, meaning the event handler would end up firing an unreliable portion of the time.

Listing 9.3 The `EnumerateFiles` method of the DotCMIS-based web part

```
protected void EnumerateFiles()
{
    CMISBrowser_Files.Controls.Clear();
```

```
ICmisObject cmisObject =
   string.IsNullOrEmpty(CMISBrowser_Id.Value) ?
     session.GetRootFolder() :
     session.GetObject(new ObjectId(CMISBrowser_Id.Value));

if (cmisObject.BaseTypeId ==
    DotCMIS.Enums.BaseTypeId.CmisFolder)
{
    IFolder cmisFolder = (IFolder)cmisObject;
    if (cmisFolder.FolderParent != null)
    {
        string folderParentId = cmisFolder.FolderParent.Id;
        LinkButton upLink = new LinkButton();
        upLink.Click += new EventHandler(CMISBrowser_File_Click);
        upLink.Text = "Up One Level";
        upLink.Attributes["cmisObjectId"] = folderParentId;
        upLink.ID = "cmisObjectId" + folderParentId;
        CMISBrowser_Files.Controls.Add(upLink);
    }
    foreach (ICmisObject cmisChild in cmisFolder.GetChildren())
    {
        if (cmisChild.BaseTypeId ==
            DotCMIS.Enums.BaseTypeId.CmisFolder)
        {
            IFolder cmisChildFolder = (IFolder)cmisChild;
            LinkButton childLink = new LinkButton();
            childLink.Click +=
                 new EventHandler(CMISBrowser_File_Click);
            childLink.Text =
                 HttpUtility.HtmlEncode(cmisChildFolder.Name);
            childLink.Attributes["cmisObjectId"] =
                 cmisChildFolder.Id;
            childLink.ID = "cmisObjectId" + cmisChildFolder.Id;
            CMISBrowser_Files.Controls.Add(childLink);
        }
        else
        {
            Literal childText = new Literal();
            childText.Text =
                 "<span class='CMISBrowser_Document'>" +
                 HttpUtility.HtmlEncode(cmisChild.Name) +
                 "</span>";
            childText.ID = "cmisObjectId" + cmisChild.Id;
            CMISBrowser_Files.Controls.Add(childText);
        }
    }
}
}
```

The Up One Level link is added as long as the parent folder isn't the root of the repository.

The ID must be specified; otherwise, event handlers won't trigger properly.

folder.getChildren() is called and, for each child, if it's a folder, it's made into a link allowing the user to drill down into the contents of that folder.

The ID must be specified; otherwise, event handlers won't trigger properly.

If the child is a document, only the title is displayed and it doesn't link to anything.

This sample is obviously not production-ready, and many more improvements upon it could be made, such as adding metadata other than the names of the files and folders (artist, track time, album date, and so on) and including a visual of the album thumbnail next to the album title. We won't discuss the styling of the CSS for the user interface here, either, as that's likely to be implementation-specific.

Now you know how to create a web part that uses CMIS to talk to a content repository. This should serve as a solid starting point for any CMIS-powered web part, and it hopefully illustrates how the ASP lifecycle and client-server paradigm interact with DotCMIS.

9.2.4 Using SharePoint as a CMIS repository

You can use DotCMIS with any CMIS-compliant repository. But if you're doing .NET development, the chances are high that you also have access to Microsoft SharePoint Server. In this section, you'll learn about special considerations when using SharePoint as a CMIS server, and you'll see an example of how to connect to Microsoft SharePoint Server 2013 using CMIS.

The first thing to consider is which authentication protocol your client application will implement—if it isn't also supported by SharePoint 2013, you won't be able to connect. In an effort to be flexible and allow as many different clients to work with SharePoint as possible, SharePoint 2013's CMIS Producer supports the following authentication protocols:

- Basic
- NTLM
- Digest
- Kerberos
- Windows-Claims
- Claims-Multiprotocol

SHAREPOINT SERVER 2013 Note that this section refers only to Microsoft SharePoint Server 2013, not SharePoint Foundation 2013, which doesn't include support for CMIS.

The second thing to consider is which optional capabilities within the CMIS specification you'll use within your client application. Table 9.2 lists some of the capabilities and limitations of the SharePoint 2013 CMIS Producer.

Table 9.2 Optional capabilities of the SharePoint 2013 CMIS Producer

Capability	Value
`capabilityACL`	`Manage`
`capabilityAllVersionsSearchable`	`false`
`capabilityChanges`	`objectidsonly`
`capabilityContentStreamUpdatability`	`anytime`
`capabilityGetDescendants`	`false`
`capabilityGetFolderTree`	`true`
`capabilityMultifiling`	`false`

Table 9.2 Optional capabilities of the SharePoint 2013 CMIS Producer *(continued)*

Capability	Value
`capabilityPWCSearchable`	`true`
`capabilityPWCUpdatable`	`true`
`capabilityQuery`	`bothseparate`
`capabilityRenditions`	`none`
`capabilityUnfiling`	`false`
`capabilityVersionSpecificFiling`	`false`
`capabilityJoin`	`none`
`cmisVersionSupported`	`1.0`

Beyond the list in table 9.2, the SharePoint 2013 CMIS Producer development team made other choices regarding optional parts of the CMIS 1.0 specification. For example, the SharePoint ACL model is more complex than the CMIS ACL model that it emits: SharePoint supports custom permission levels, which can be applied to dynamic user groups and applied to any subset of the full set of repositories on a site. Within a repository, folders and even documents can have their own unique set of permissions. But when the CMIS Producer is asked for all possible permission levels, it only returns `cmis:read`, `cmis:write`, and `cmis:all`, as required by the specification. Each of these CMIS permission levels is mapped to a native SharePoint permission level that has the same relevant permissions.

Another nuance to consider is SharePoint 2013's support for CMIS Query. SharePoint supports the `CONTAINS` predicate as long as `CONTAINS` predicates are only used in queries that don't contain comparison predicates. For example, consider the following queries:

```
SELECT cmis:name, cmis:contentStreamLength
      FROM cmis:document
     WHERE cmis:contentStreamLength > 31337
SELECT cmis:name, cmis:contentStreamLength
      FROM cmis:document
     WHERE CONTAINS('Hackers')
SELECT cmis:name, cmis:contentStreamLength
      FROM cmis:document
     WHERE cmis:contentStreamLength > 31337 AND CONTAINS('Hackers')
```

❶ These two queries are supported by SharePoint's CMIS provider.

❷ This query is not supported by SharePoint because it combines CONTAINS and predicate branches.

The first two queries ❶ are both supported by SharePoint 2013, yet the third query ❷ isn't, because it combines `CONTAINS` and comparison predicates.

Another query-related item is the fact that SharePoint 2013 supports table aliases, as demonstrated by the `t` in the following query, which is functionally equivalent to the first of the three previous queries, but with aliases inserted appropriately. These aliases are meaningless due to SharePoint's lack of support for JOINs, so they're ignored:

```
SELECT t.cmis:name, t.cmis:contentStreamLength FROM cmis:document t
    WHERE t.cmis:contentStreamLength > 31337
```

With these capabilities and limitations in mind, let's see how to make the connection to SharePoint.

9.2.5 Connecting to SharePoint

Now that you understand the capabilities of SharePoint 2013's CMIS Producer, let's move on to see how exactly you could go about setting up and connecting to it. Let's assume you have your SharePoint server up and running, and you know which SharePoint libraries you want to use as CMIS repositories.

SharePoint 2013's CMIS capabilities are all wrapped up in a SharePoint site feature called Content Management Interoperability Services (CMIS) Producer. This means that for every site that contains a library you want to use as a CMIS repository, you must follow these steps to make the library accessible via CMIS:

1. Navigate to any page on your site.
2. Click on the gear in the upper-right corner and select Site Settings (figure 9.5).

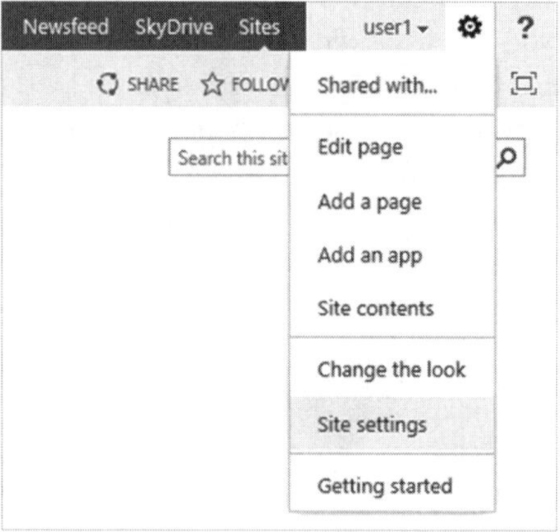

Figure 9.5 SharePoint site settings

3. Click on Manage Site Features under the Site Actions header.
4. Look for the feature entitled Content Management Interoperability Services (CMIS) Producer, and click the Activate button to the right of it.

With these steps completed, the CMIS Producer is ready to go.

Let's assume that you want to connect to a SharePoint site with a URL of www.example.com/cmis. SharePoint 2013's CMIS Producer provides both the AtomPub binding and the Web Services binding, which means you can connect in several ways. A typical CMIS client will connect to the AtomPub binding by calling the `getRepositories` or `getRepositoryInfo` methods. The `getRepositories` method can be used to get a list of all CMIS-appropriate repositories on the SharePoint site, but, as you saw earlier, if you already know the GUID of your repository, you can skip right to that repository using the `getRepositoryInfo` method. Here are two examples:

http://www.example.com/cmis/_vti_bin/cmis/rest?getRepositories
http://www.example.com/cmis/_vti_bin/cmis/rest/
156939c0-7a4d-48ef-9bed-82741ccd785f?getRepositoryInfo

On the other hand, if the client application needs to use the Web Services binding, it can connect using the WSDL file, which (if we continue our imaginary example) should be available at the following address: http://www.example.com/cmis/_vti_bin/cmissoapwsdl.aspx.

Note that the preceding file, unlike some WSDLs, isn't anonymously accessible—you'll need to authenticate in order to access it.

This WSDL file will provide a list of endpoints for the various CMIS services, which might look like these:

http://www.example.com/cmis/_vti_bin/cmis/soap/ACLService.svc
http://www.example.com/cmis/_vti_bin/cmis/soap/DiscoveryService.svc
http://www.example.com/cmis/_vti_bin/cmis/soap/NavigationService.svc
http://www.example.com/cmis/_vti_bin/cmis/soap/ObjectService.svc
http://www.example.com/cmis/_vti_bin/cmis/soap/RepositoryService.svc
http://www.example.com/cmis/_vti_bin/cmis/soap/VersioningService.svc

From this point on, interacting with the SharePoint 2013 CMIS Producer is like working with any other CMIS server.

Now you know how to connect to Microsoft SharePoint Server using CMIS.

9.3 Coding in Python with cmislib

Picture yourself as a digital archivist. It's 5:30 p.m. on a Friday, and you're about to start your weekend when you get an instant message from your boss. Against your better judgment, you accept the video chat (see figure 9.6). One look at her frantic face is enough to send chills down your spine. It seems that a major acquisition is happening and you've got to sift and sort through a pile of files and metadata, organizing and storing them in the corporate digital asset repository so they can be tagged and served up by the website before the press release goes out on Monday.

Figure 9.6 Handing out last-minute assignments—like a boss. Luckily, Python and cmislib can automate repetitive tasks like bulk content loading.

After making your boss squirm for a few minutes, you assure her it's all good. You're confident you can knock this out quickly. Why? Because you aren't just any digital archivist. You're a digital archivist who knows Python. And Python is one bad-ass programming language. You can use Python to productively code all kinds of things—from desktop applications to full-featured, consumer-grade web applications—but it's particularly good at command-line scripting, which is where compiled languages like Java can't compare.

In addition to its clear syntax, and the fact that it's cross-platform (it's installed by default on Mac OS X and most Linux- and Unix-based operating systems), another great thing about Python is that thousands of modules are freely available for a broad spectrum of functionality, ranging from imaging libraries to web application frameworks and everything in between. One such module is cmislib, which, as the name suggests, is a CMIS client library for Python.

Using cmislib, anyone can make quick work of repetitive tasks. For example, suppose that the pile of digital artifacts you need to sort through needs to be organized in the CMIS repository based on some metadata the files contain rather than the current folder structure. As shown in figure 9.7, a Python script could traverse the folder structure, and, using one of several freely available modules, read the metadata on the files (maybe it's EXIF or IPTC, for example, which are two common metadata sets for images), and then upload the files into the repository, renaming them and setting properties on the new documents along the way.

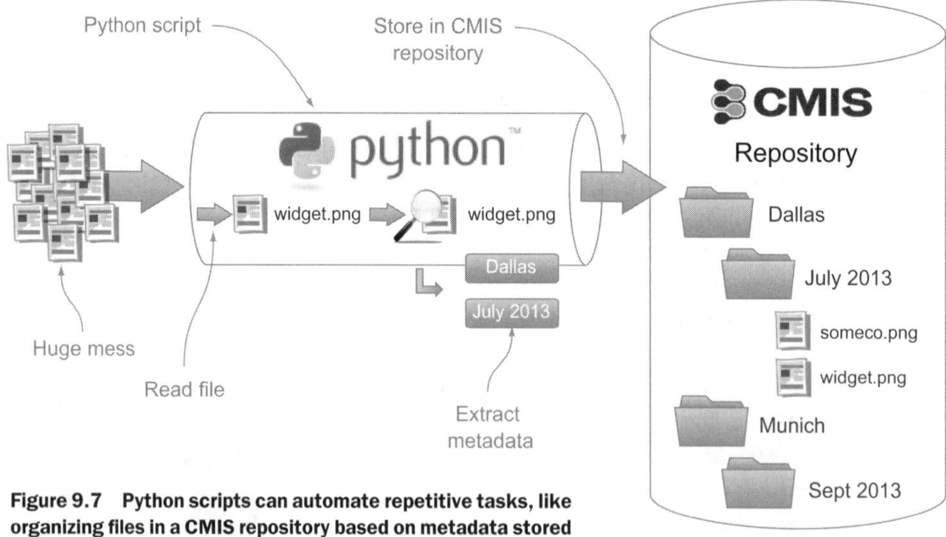

Figure 9.7 Python scripts can automate repetitive tasks, like organizing files in a CMIS repository based on metadata stored in the file itself.

Python, cmislib, and a CMIS-compliant repository are a powerful and productive combination for people who need to automate content-centric tasks.

Let's take a look at how cmislib compares to what you already know about OpenCMIS and also at how to install cmislib. Once that's done, you'll see how to use it from the command line and how to write a script that can copy objects from one CMIS repository to another.

9.3.1 Comparing cmislib and OpenCMIS

The motivation for the creation of the cmislib project was to make it easy for people to learn CMIS and to explore different CMIS server implementations without having to slog through all of the XML that's returned by the AtomPub binding. A secondary motivation was that the original developer loved Python and wanted to encourage the creation of simple web applications built on top of CMIS repositories using Python frameworks like Django and Pyramid.

As a result, cmislib is easy for developers to pick up—its API follows the CMIS domain model as closely as possible. Remember the domain model discussed in chapter 2 and shown in figure 9.8? Well, in cmislib you'll find `CmisClient`, `Repository`, `Folder`, and `Document` classes, as well as others named as you'd expect based on what you know about the CMIS specification.

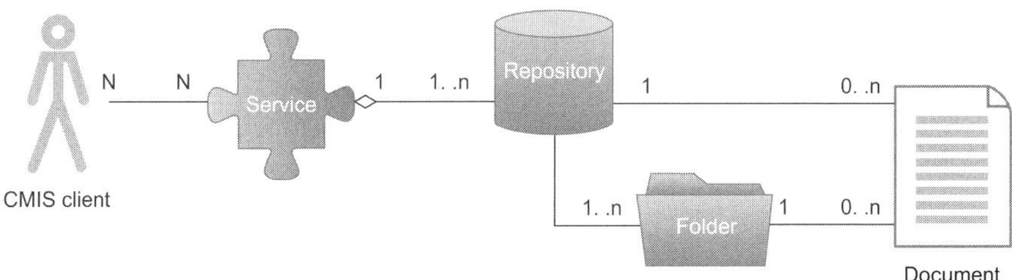

Figure 9.8 The CMIS domain model

Additionally, the creator made a conscious decision to minimize the number of dependencies, to make it as easy to install as possible. Table 9.3 summarizes cmislib at a high level.

Table 9.3 At a glance: cmislib

Library	Language	Project home	Bindings supported	Install method	Key dependencies
cmislib	Python	Apache Chemistry	AtomPub only	Python setuptools or manual	Python 2.6 or 2.7

This pragmatic approach means you'll have a few limitations when compared to a more full-featured library, such as the one included in OpenCMIS. These are some of the limitations:

- cmislib supports only the AtomPub binding, although support for the new Browser binding is a work in progress.
- cmislib offers no sophisticated level of caching.
- cmislib uses Python's built-in XML parsing library, which is slower than other available XML libraries.
- cmislib is maintained by a smaller development team.

Despite these potential limitations, cmislib is still valuable for a variety of uses.

9.3.2 *Installing cmislib*

We'll assume you already have Python 2.6 or 2.7 installed. We also highly recommend you use virtualenv to create and activate a virtual environment directory to keep cmislib, its dependencies, and the code you write isolated from other libraries that may exist on your system. If you need help installing Python or virtualenv, see http://python.org.

The easiest way to install cmislib is to use a Python package installer called setuptools. Using setuptools to install cmislib is as easy as `typing easy_install cmislib`. The package manager does the work of finding the latest version, downloading it, installing it, and making it available on the system path. It also does the same for each of cmislib's dependencies (and their dependencies, and so on).

If you can't or don't want to use setuptools, it's still easy to download and install cmislib. Download the egg file from the Apache Chemistry website and add it to Python's system path.

9.3.3 *Connecting to a CMIS repository using the interactive shell*

Let's slowly slither into the weeds by launching the Python interactive shell and using it to connect to a CMIS repository. This will validate that cmislib is installed correctly. It has the added benefit of providing instant feedback as you explore the library.

LAUNCH THE SHELL

First, launch the Python interactive shell by typing `python` at the command line. You should see the Python version followed by three right angle brackets (>>>), as shown in figure 9.9.

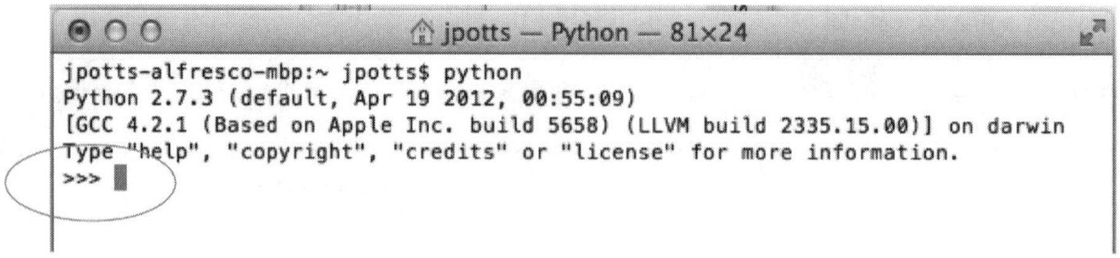

```
jpotts — Python — 81x24
jpotts-alfresco-mbp:~ jpotts$ python
Python 2.7.3 (default, Apr 19 2012, 00:55:09)
[GCC 4.2.1 (Based on Apple Inc. build 5658) (LLVM build 2335.15.00)] on darwin
Type "help", "copyright", "credits" or "license" for more information.
>>> 
```

Figure 9.9 The Python interactive shell patiently waiting to do your bidding

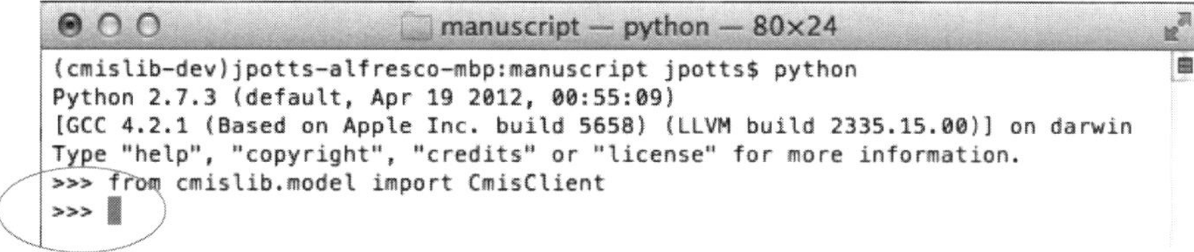

Figure 9.10 No news is good news: once the client successfully imports, it's easy to connect to the repository.

IMPORT CMISLIB

Next, import cmislib by typing `from cmislib.model import CmisClient`, as shown in figure 9.10. If you get another three angle brackets, it means Python has found the library and you're ready to move on.

If you took our earlier advice and used virtualenv and setuptools to install cmislib, it's highly likely that when you import CmisClient on your machine, Python will import cmislib successfully. If so, you're ready to connect to the repository.

But if Python complains, it means cmislib isn't installed on your system path properly. If this happens to you, it might be a good idea to do an `import sys` followed by `print sys.path` to start your troubleshooting.

We'll assume everything is looking good and you're ready to connect to the repository.

In earlier chapters, you learned that when using OpenCMIS you might need to specify many parameters before you can get a session. With cmislib it's much easier. Everything starts with a `CmisClient` object. You instantiate that by specifying the AtomPub service URL, a username, and a password:

```
>>>from cmislib.model import CmisClient
>>>client = CmisClient('http://localhost:8081/inmemory/
     atom', '', '')
```

If the import succeeds, nothing will be returned.

The CmisClient constructor takes three arguments: the AtomPub service URL, a username, and a password (but the in-memory CMIS server doesn't require a username or password).

Once you have a `CmisClient` object, you can get a handle to the repository:

```
>>> repo = client.defaultRepository
>>> type(repo)
<class 'cmislib.model.Repository'>
>>> repo.id
 u'A1'
>>> repo.name
 u'Apache Chemistry OpenCMIS InMemory Repository'
```

Returns the first repository in the server's list of repositories.

Methods used frequently, like getRepositoryId and getRepositoryName, are exposed as if they were properties of the object.

The Repository object is like the lobby in a grand hotel. You can learn a lot about the services a hotel offers from standing in the lobby. Is there a concierge desk? Maybe a car rental counter? A four-star restaurant? A hopping lobby bar? Or is there only a scary-looking guy in a stained T-shirt staring at you from behind bulletproof glass, offering to rent you a bath towel by the hour? Different hotels offer different capabilities and qualities of service that you can often summarize with a quick glance at the lobby.

Similarly, the Repository object tells you information about that particular CMIS server and about the capabilities the server offers. For example, if you call getRepositoryInfo(), you'll get a dictionary of metadata about the repository. The next listing shows how to iterate over the items in the dictionary to see what kind of metadata is returned.

Listing 9.4 Iterating over repository information

```
>>> for (k,v) in repo.getRepositoryInfo().items():
 ... print "%s: %s" % (k,v)
 ...
aclCapability: None
principalAnyone: anyone
cmisVersionSupported: 1.0
principalAnonymous: anonymous
thinClientURI: None
repositoryDescription: Apache Chemistry OpenCMIS InMemory
    Repository (Version: 0.9.0-beta-1)
changesIncomplete: true
productVersion: 0.9.0-beta-1
rootFolderId: 100
latestChangeLogToken: 0
repositoryId: A1
repositoryName: Apache Chemistry OpenCMIS InMemory Repository
vendorName: Apache Chemistry
productName: Apache-Chemistry-OpenCMIS-InMemory/0.9.0-beta-1
```

Repository information is returned as a Python dictionary.

Similarly, the Repository object can tell you what the capabilities of this particular repository are, as shown in the following listing.

Listing 9.5 Retrieving the repository's capabilities

```
>>> for (k,v) in repo.getCapabilities().items():

 ... print "%s: %s" % (k,v)
 ...

PWCUpdatable: True
VersionSpecificFiling: False
Join: None
ContentStreamUpdatability: anytime
AllVersionsSearchable: False
Renditions: None
Multifiling: True
GetFolderTree: True
GetDescendants: True
```

cmislib returns converted values to Python primitives so they're easier to work with in a Pythonic way.

```
ACL: manage
PWCSearchable: False
Query: bothcombined
Unfiling: True
Changes: None
>>> repo.getCapabilities()['Multifiling']
True
```

Continuing with the hotel lobby analogy, just as the lobby leads to the elevators and the elevators to the rooms, the `Repository` object is your gateway to other objects in the system. It contains methods for things like retrieving the root folder, getting an object by ID, getting an object by path, and running queries.

For example, try printing the name of every child in the repository's root folder:

```
>>> root = repo.rootFolder                       <-- Get repository's root folder
>>> for child in root.getChildren():             <-- Ask root folder for its children
 ... child.name                                  <-- Print name of each child
 ...
u'cmis'
u'folder1'
u'folder2'
u'folder3'
u'images'
u'media'
u'notes'
u'texts'
u'welcome.txt'
```

Use the built-in dir() function to help learn the API

If you ever forget or don't know what you can do with an object, Python's built-in `dir()` function will help. When you call `dir` with any Python object, it'll respond with a list of the properties and methods of the object, like so:

```
>>> child = root.getChildren()[0]           <-- Ask root for its first child
>>> type(child)                             <-- Ask Python what child object is an instance of
 <class 'cmislib.model.Folder'>
>>> for func in dir(child):                 <-- Use dir function to find out what you can do with object
 ... func
 ...
'ACL'
'addObject'
'allowableActions'
'applyACL'
'applyPolicy'
'createDocument'
'createDocumentFromString'
'createFolder'
'createRelationship'
'delete'
'deleteTree'
'getACL'
...snip...
```

> ***(continued)***
> If the `dir()` function doesn't tell you enough about what you can do with an object, you can try the `help()` function. It spits out the documentation for that object. You can also always browse the full documentation online at the Apache Chemistry website or generate the documentation yourself locally using a tool called Sphinx.

CREATING OBJECTS WITH CMISLIB

Now that you know how to connect to the repository and can use cmislib to navigate the repository, you're probably anxious to learn how to create new objects in the repository. Let's look at how to create a new folder and then a new document within that. Then you'll be ready to do something useful, like polling for changed objects to copy from one repository to another.

Creating objects is straightforward. If you do a `dir(root)`, you'll see a method called `createFolder` (figure 9.11).

```
>>> dir(root)
['ACL', '__class__', '__delattr__', '__dict__', '__doc__', '__format__', '__geta
ttribute__', '__hash__', '__init__', '__module__', '__new__', '__reduce__', '__r
educe_ex__', '__repr__', '__setattr__', '__sizeof__', '__str__', '__subclasshook
__', '__weakref__', '_allowableActions', '_cmisClient', '_getLink', '_getSelfLin
k', '_initData', '_kwargs', '_name', '_objectId', '_properties', '_repository',
'addObject', 'allowableActions', 'applyACL', 'applyPolicy', 'createDocument', 'c
reateDocumentFromString', 'createFolder', 'createRelationship', 'delete', 'delet
eTree', 'getACL', 'getAllowableActions', 'getAppliedPolicies', 'getChildren', 'g
etChildrenLink', 'getDescendants', 'getDescendantsLink', 'getName', 'getObjectId
', 'getObjectParents', 'getParent', 'getPaths', 'getProperties', 'getRelationshi
ps', 'getTitle', 'getTree', 'id', 'logger', 'move', 'name', 'properties', 'reloa
d', 'removeObject', 'removePolicy', 'title', 'updateProperties', 'xmlDoc']
>>>
```

Figure 9.11 Using `dir(root)` to find the `createFolder` method

If you do a `help(root.createFolder)`, you'll see that the `createFolder` method takes a name and, optionally, a dictionary of properties (see figure 9.12).

That means creating a new folder called *test* as an instance of `cmis:folder` is as easy as typing `root.createFolder('test')`.

But what if you didn't want to create the folder as an instance of `cmis:folder`, but instead wanted to use some other folder type? The object type of a folder is one of the properties you can specify when you call the `createFolder` method. To create a new folder as an instance of `F:mm:expenseReport`, a completely made-up type for this example, you'd do this:

```
>>> props = {'cmis:objectTypeId': 'F:mm:expenseReport'}
>>> folder = root.createFolder('test2', props)
>>> folder.id '137'
>>> folder.name u'test2'
>>> folder.properties['cmis:objectTypeId']
 'F:mm:expenseReport'
```

Create dictionary of properties to set

Call createFolder method with folder name and

Inspect folder's cmis:objectTypeId property

```
Help on method createFolder in module cmislib.model:

createFolder(self, name, properties={}) method of cmislib.model.Folder instance
    Creates a new :class:`Folder` using the properties provided.
    Right now I expect a property called 'cmis:name' but I don't
    complain if it isn't there (although the CMIS provider will). If a
    cmis:name property isn't provided, the value passed in to the name
    argument will be used.

    To specify a custom folder type, pass in a property called
    cmis:objectTypeId set to the :class:`CmisId` representing the type ID
    of the instance you want to create. If you do not pass in an object
    type ID, an instance of 'cmis:folder' will be created.

    >>> subFolder = folder.createFolder('someSubfolder')
    >>> subFolder.getName()
    u'someSubfolder'

    The following optional arguments are not supported:
     - policies
     - addACEs
     - removeACEs
(END)
```

Figure 9.12 Using the built-in `help()` function to determine the syntax of `createFolder`

Creating a document is similar—a name for the new document is required. The object type is also required, but cmislib will use `cmis:document` if one isn't provided as part of a properties dictionary. If a name is the only thing provided, the result will be a new `Document` object that has a zero-byte content stream. You might hear people call these *content-less* objects:

```
>>> doc = folder.createDocument('contentless-example')      <-- Call createDocument with only a name
>>> doc.id
'139'
>>> doc.name
u'contentless-example'
>>> doc.properties['cmis:contentStreamLength']
>>>                                                         <-- Result is None—this document doesn't have a content stream
```

Another option is to use the `createDocumentFromString` method. This is useful if your code is generating plain text to store as content. The next listing shows how to use this method.

Listing 9.6 Creating a document using a string as content

```
>>> doc = folder.createDocumentFromString(        <-- Call createDocumentFromString to provide inline content
 'fromstring-example',                            <-- Provide a name
 contentString='The Dude abides.',                <-- Provide content as a string
 contentType='text/plain')                        <-- Specify MIME type of the content
>>> doc.name

u'fromstring-example'

>>> doc.properties['cmis:contentStreamLength']

16

>>> doc.properties['cmis:contentStreamMimeType']

u'text/plain'
```

The most common case is that a file needs to be set as the content stream:

```
>>> f = open('/Users/jpotts/sample/mydoc.pdf', 'rb')     <-- Open file as read-only
>>> doc = folder.createDocument('mydoc.pdf',             <-- Name doesn't necessarily have to match the filename
 contentFile=f,                                          <-- Pass file to createDocument
 contentType='application/pdf')
>>> doc.name
u'mydoc.pdf'
>>> doc.id
'142'
>>> doc.properties['cmis:contentStreamLength']
117249
```

You now know how to use Python to connect to a CMIS repository, navigate among the objects stored there, and even create new objects. You can do several things with the repository that we didn't cover. In short, if it's in the CMIS specification and implemented in the AtomPub binding, cmislib can do it. Remember to use `dir()`, `help()`, and the documentation if you get stuck.

Now let's look at a more useful example: using Python to synchronize objects between two CMIS repositories.

9.3.4 *Using cmislib to synchronize objects between two CMIS repositories*

Suppose you've been using The Blend with one CMIS repository and you'd like to migrate those images, songs, and videos to another CMIS repository. You might be moving objects from "test" to "production." Or maybe you've decided to move to a different vendor's CMIS implementation. Whatever the reason, Python is up to the task.

FUNCTIONAL OVERVIEW

Given two repositories, a source repository and a target repository, the goal is to copy all new and changed objects from the source repository to the target repository. This includes the content and the metadata.

Here are some additional requirements for the synchronization example:

- The synchronization process should be incremental. You don't want to have to copy the entire source repository to the target repository every time the script runs.
- The source and target repositories may have different content models. For example, The Blend has a type called `cmisbook:image` in the InMemory Repository, but in Alfresco, the same type has an ID of `D:cmisbook:image`. Similarly, properties writable in one repository may not be writable in another repository.
- The synchronization process should run constantly, polling for changes periodically. If the process is stopped and restarted, it should pick up where it left off.
- Two CMIS repositories from different vendors will have two different object ID implementations, so if an object in the source repository has an object ID of

ABCD, there's no way to use that object ID to find the equivalent object in the target repository without maintaining some sort of mapping. For this example, we'll use the object's path as the unique identifier that's common across repositories. The implication of this is that if an object moves in the source repository, this simplified approach won't have a way to move the equivalent object in the target repository.

- Deletes in the source repository are going to be ignored. There's no technical reason to ignore deletes in the source—we're just trying to keep it simple.
- The synchronization is one-way, from the source to the target. If something changes on the target, the source won't be updated, and if a subsequent change happens in the source, the equivalent object in the target repository will be overwritten.

The high-level approach

CMIS has a built-in mechanism that will make finding the incremental changes easy. It's called a *change token*. A CMIS repository that supports changes (check the repository's Changes capability) will return the changes that have occurred since the time the change token was generated. If you persist the change token after you process a set of changes, you can provide that change token later and get all of the changes that have occurred since then.

The high-level algorithm will be as follows:

1. If this is the first sync, ask the repository for its changes. Otherwise, ask the repository for the changes for a specific change token.
2. Process each change. This might involve creating new objects in the target repository if they don't exist, or updating existing objects in the target repository with the modified objects from the source repository.
3. After processing all of the changes, save the latest change token.
4. Go to sleep for a configurable amount of time, and then wake up and repeat.

The code

The goal is to synchronize changes in the source repository to a target repository. We'll take advantage of CMIS change tokens to get a list of incremental changes to process since the last time the script processed changes. Let's walk through some of the code.

The main polling and processing loop

Listing 9.7 shows the two functions: `main` and `sync`. There isn't much to the `main` function—it starts an infinite loop that calls the `sync` function, goes to sleep, and then repeats.

The `sync` function connects to the source and target repositories, asks the source repository for its changes, and persists the change token to be used the next time `sync` gets called. The function calls `processChange` for every object that has been created or updated in the source repository.

Listing 9.7 The main and sync functions

```
def main():
    while True:
        sync()
        print "Polling for changes every %d seconds" %
            settings.POLL_INTERVAL
        print "Use ctrl+c to quit"
        print "Sleeping..."
        sleep(settings.POLL_INTERVAL)

def sync():
    # Connect to the source repo
    sourceClient = CmisClient(settings.SOURCE_REPOSITORY_URL,
                              settings.SOURCE_USERNAME,
                              settings.SOURCE_PASSWORD)
    sourceRepo = sourceClient.defaultRepository
    dumpRepoHeader(sourceRepo, "SOURCE")

    # Make sure it supports changes, bail if it does not
    if sourceRepo.getCapabilities()['Changes'] == None:
        print "Source repository does not support changes:%s" %
            sourceRepo.getCapabilities()['Changes']
        sys.exit(-1)
    latestChangeToken = sourceRepo.info['latestChangeLogToken']
    print "Latest change token: %s" % latestChangeToken

    # Connect to the target repo
    targetClient = CmisClient(settings.TARGET_REPOSITORY_URL,
                              settings.TARGET_USERNAME,
                              settings.TARGET_PASSWORD)
    targetRepo = targetClient.defaultRepository
    dumpRepoHeader(targetRepo, "TARGET")
    print "    Path: %s" % settings.TARGET_ROOT

    # Get last token synced from savefile
    # Using the repository IDs so that you can use this script against
    # multiple source-target pairs and it will remember where you are
    syncKey = "%s><%s" % (sourceRepo.id, targetRepo.id)
    lastChangeSynced = {}
    changeToken = None
    if (os.path.exists(SAVE_FILE)):
        lastChangeSynced = pickle.load(open(SAVE_FILE, "rb" ))
        if lastChangeSynced.has_key(syncKey):
            print "Last change synced: %s" % lastChangeSynced[syncKey]
            changeToken = lastChangeSynced[syncKey]
        else:
            print "First sync..."
    else:
        print "First sync..."

    if changeToken == latestChangeToken:
        print "No changes since last sync so no work to do"
        return

    # Ask the source repo for changes
```

Annotations:
- **Connect to source repository** (sourceClient = CmisClient(...))
- **Make sure repository supports changes; bail out if it doesn't** (if sourceRepo.getCapabilities()...)
- **Connect to target repository** (targetClient = CmisClient(...))
- **Get token from a previous synchronization** (lastChangeSynced = pickle.load(...))

```
    changes = None
    if changeToken != None:
        changes = sourceRepo.
            getContentChanges(changeLogToken=changeToken)
    else:
        changes = sourceRepo.getContentChanges()

    # Process each change
    for change in changes:
        if change.changeType == 'created' or
           change.changeType == 'updated':
            processChange(change, sourceRepo, targetRepo)

    lastChangeSynced[syncKey] = latestChangeToken
    pickle.dump(lastChangeSynced, open(SAVE_FILE, "wb"))
    return
#
```

Ask source repository for changes

Process each change

Processing each change

The processChange function in listing 9.8 gets called for every object created or updated in the source repository. It's responsible for retrieving the source object and then attempting to retrieve the corresponding object in the target repository. If it finds the object in the target repository, it knows it needs to do an update. If it doesn't find it, it knows the object needs to be created.

Listing 9.8 The `processChange` function

```
def processChange(change, sourceRepo, targetRepo):
    """
    Processes a given change by replicating the change from the source
    to the target repository.
    """

    print "Processing: %s" % change.objectId

    # Grab the object
    sourceObj = None
    try:
        sourceObj = sourceRepo.getObject(change.objectId,
                                         getAllowableActions=True)
    except ObjectNotFoundException:
        print "Warning: Changes included an object that "
              "no longer exists"
        return

    if (sourceObj.properties['cmis:objectTypeId'] != 'cmis:document' and
        sourceObj.properties['cmis:objectTypeId'] != 'cmis:folder' and
        not(mapping.mapping.has_key(
            sourceObj.properties['cmis:objectTypeId']))):
        return

    try:
        sourcePath = sourceObj.getPaths()[0]
    except NotSupportedException:
        return
```

Find source object

Assume one path for this example

```
    print "Source Path: %s" % sourcePath
    targetPath = settings.TARGET_ROOT + sourcePath.encode('utf-8')

    sourceProps = sourceObj.properties

    # Determine if the object exists in the target
    targetObj = None
    try:
        targetObj = targetRepo.getObjectByPath(targetPath)

        if type(targetObj) == Document:
            targetObj = targetObj.getLatestVersion()
            print "Version label:%s" %
                targetObj.properties['cmis:versionLabel']

        # If it does, update its properties
        props = getProperties(targetRepo, sourceProps, 'update')

        if (len(props) > 0):
            print props
            targetObj = targetObj.updateProperties(props)

    except ObjectNotFoundException:
        print "Object does not exist in TARGET"
        props = getProperties(targetRepo, sourceProps, 'create')
        targetObj = createNewObject(targetRepo, targetPath, props)
        if targetObj == None:
            return

    if type(sourceObj) == Folder:
        return

    # Then, update its content if that is possible
    targetObj.reload()
    if sourceObj.allowableActions['canGetContentStream'] == True:
        if targetObj.allowableActions['canSetContentStream'] == True:
            print "Setting content stream on target"
            try:
                targetObj.setContentStream(
                    sourceObj.getContentStream(),
                    contentType=sourceObj.
                        properties['cmis:contentStreamMimeType'])
            except CmisException:
                print "Could not set content stream on target "
                    "object: %s (%s)" % (targetObj.name, targetObj.id)
        elif targetObj.allowableActions['canCheckOut'] == True:
            print "Updating content stream in target object ver.:%s" %
                targetObj.properties['cmis:versionLabel']
            pwc = targetObj.checkout()
            pwc.setContentStream(
                sourceObj.getContentStream(),
                contentType=sourceObj.
                    properties['cmis:contentStreamMimeType'])
            pwc.checkin(major=False)
            print "Checkin is done, version:%s" %
                targetObj.properties['cmis:versionLabel']
        else:
            print "Cannot update content stream"
#
```

Try to get target object by path

Get target object if it exists

Create object if it doesn't exist

Update content on object, if possible

Determining the properties to set

Listing 9.9 shows the `getProperties` function. Its job is to figure out what properties need to be sent to the target repository when a given object is created or updated based on the source object's type and the corresponding type definition in the target repository. This is the function that figures out that a given type in the source repository maps to a given type in the target repository. The function also makes sure that every property is writable in the target repository.

Listing 9.9 The `getProperties` function

```
def getProperties(targetRepo, sourceProps, mode):
    sourceTypeId = sourceProps['cmis:objectTypeId']
    props = {}

    if mode == 'create':
        props['cmis:name'] = sourceProps['cmis:name']
        props['cmis:objectTypeId'] = sourceTypeId

    # if the source type is cmis:document,
    # don't move any custom properties
    # set the type and return
    if sourceTypeId == 'cmis:document' or
        sourceTypeId == 'cmis:folder':
        return props

    # otherwise, get the target object type from the mapping
    targetObjectId = mapping.mapping[sourceTypeId]['targetType']
    if mode == 'create':
        props['cmis:objectTypeId'] = targetObjectId
    print "Target object id: %s" % targetObjectId

    targetTypeDef = targetRepo.getTypeDefinition(targetObjectId)

    # get all of the target properties
    for propKey in mapping.mapping[sourceTypeId]['properties'].keys():
        targetPropId = mapping.
            mapping[sourceTypeId]['properties'][propKey]
        if sourceProps[propKey] != None:
            if targetTypeDef.properties[targetPropId].
                    getUpdatability() == 'readwrite':
                props[targetPropId] = sourceProps[propKey]
                print "target prop: %s" % targetPropId
                print "target val: %s" % sourceProps[propKey]
            else:
                print "Warning, property changed but isn't writable "
                    "in target:%s" % targetPropId

    return props
#
```

If source type is cmis:document or cmis:folder, don't move any custom properties

Otherwise, find target type from mapping

Notice how the last block uses the type definition to make sure that the property is writable in the target. If it isn't, there's no need to attempt to write the value, so the property isn't added to the list of properties to sync and a warning is printed.

Running the sync

To test the script, we created an instance of The Blend that persisted its data to Alfresco. If you want to try this, see the code zip download that comes with the book for the instructions on building and deploying The Blend's content model to Alfresco. We chose Alfresco because it's freely available and because it supports change tokens.

> **Configuring Alfresco for change support**
>
> Out of the box, Alfresco isn't configured to support changes, but it's easy to turn on. Edit your alfresco-global.properties file and add the following:
>
> ```
> #
> # Auditing
> #
> # Enable audit in general
> audit.enabled=true
>
> # Enable the alfresco-access audit application
> audit.alfresco-access.enabled=true
>
> # Enable CMIS change log
> audit.cmischangelog.enabled=true
> ```
>
> Now when you start the server and invoke `getCapabilities()`, you'll see that `Changes` has a value of `objectidsonly`.

We created a mapping file that maps Alfresco's content types and properties to the InMemory server's content types and properties.

With that in place, we started the sync and watched as the script mirrored the data stored in the local Alfresco repository into the InMemory Repository. After the initial pass, the script went to sleep. The output in the next listing shows what happens when we subsequently modified a property on an image in the source Alfresco repository.

Listing 9.10 Output of cmis-sync when it sees a change that needs to be synced

```
==================================
SOURCE repository info:
----------------------------------
    Name: Main Repository
      Id: 068e0de6-434e-4106-99c2-a08c5ef4016d
  Vendor: Alfresco
 Version: 4.2.0 (4428)
Latest change token: 1022
==================================
TARGET repository info:
----------------------------------
    Name: Apache Chemistry OpenCMIS InMemory Repository
      Id: A1
  Vendor: Apache Chemistry
 Version: 0.8.0-SNAPSHOT
```

```
    Path: /cmis-sync
Last change synced: 1021
Processing: workspace://SpacesStore/1f9acfdf-d438-42c3-9bf4-2
69bb37d1617;1.0
Source Path: /blend/Art/Sunset.jpg
Version label:V 1.25
Target object id: cmisbook:image
Warning, target property changed but isn't writable in target:
  cmisbook:imageHeight
target prop: cmisbook:xResolution
target val: 72.0
Warning, target property changed but isn't writable in target:
  cmisbook:imageWidth
target prop: cmisbook:make
target val: Research In Motion
target prop: cmisbook:model
target val: BlackBerry 8900
target prop: cmisbook:copyright
target val: test value updated alfresco eight
target prop: cmisbook:yResolution
target val: 72.0
Updating content stream in target object version:V 1.25
Polling for changes every 10 seconds
Use ctrl+c to quit
Sleeping...
```

You can see that when the script woke up and asked Alfresco for its latest changes, the script saw the change to Sunset.jpg, and then determined which properties to set on the target object. Because `cmisbook:imageHeight` and `cmisbook:imageWidth` are marked as `createonly` in the target repository instead of `readwrite`, the script tosses those properties out and sets the rest. The script isn't smart enough to know exactly which properties have changed or whether or not the content stream was modified, so a single change triggers the entire object and all of its properties to get updated in the target.

You now have what you need to run Python against any CMIS-compliant repository, and you've seen how Python and change tokens can help you write a CMIS synchronization daemon. Let's now turn our attention to another one of the "P" languages: PHP.

9.4 Apache Chemistry PHP API

PHP is one of the most widely used languages for web applications. PHP is one of the Ps that can be attributed to the LAMP stack (Perl and Python are the other Ps). Many of the most widely used web development frameworks use PHP, including Drupal, Moodle, Joomla, WordPress, and CakePHP. Providing a PHP client library allows developers to take advantage of CMIS-compliant content repositories as a part of their web solutions. Currently, Drupal and WordPress have CMIS integrations that take advantage of the CMIS PHP Client. You'll see Drupal and CMIS in action in later sections.

The next section discusses the PHP Client and how it maps CMIS objects into PHP objects. You'll learn how to install the PHP Client, see how it compares to OpenCMIS, and then see some simple PHP examples before moving on to a Drupal example that builds on The Blend.

9.4.1 Installing the PHP Client

You can install the client in one of two ways. The preferred way is to follow these two steps:

1. Add the location of the cmis-lib to the include_path.
2. Include the following line in your code:

```
require_once ('cmis-lib.php');
```

Alternatively, you can add the following line:

```
require_once('<fullpath to cmis-lib>/cmis-lib.php'); .
```

9.4.2 About the PHP Client library

The Apache Chemistry PHP API provides access to a CMIS-compliant repository using a structure that will make sense to PHP developers. The main access is provided by instantiating a `CMISService` object that accepts a CMIS endpoint, authentication information, and some optional settings.

All of the operations performed against a CMIS repository using the PHP Client are executed by calling methods on the `CMISService`. Not all of the methods are functional—some have yet to be implemented. The methods that aren't yet functional will throw a `CmisNotImplementedException($functionName)`.

You'll want to keep a couple of things in mind with regard to arguments passed in to `CMISService` methods:

- The CMIS server expects a repository ID with every method call (except `getRepositories`). The PHP Client caches the repository ID in the `CMISService` object, so developers don't need to repeat it with each call.
- All of the required input parameters for `CMISService` methods are included in the method signature. All of the optional parameters for those methods are passed in an associative array.

9.4.3 PHP Client architecture

The PHP Client is divided into two classes: `CMISRepositoryWrapper` and `CMISService`, as shown in figure 9.13.

The `CMISRepositoryWrapper` handles the HTTP connection and has all of the logic to marshal and unmarshal AtomPub XML to PHP objects.

The `CMISService` provides an interface that implements the CMIS domain-level methods. Rather than separating the client into the seven individual services you learned about in part 1, the `CMISService` class implements all of the services you might call.

Table 9.4 highlights the supported return types.

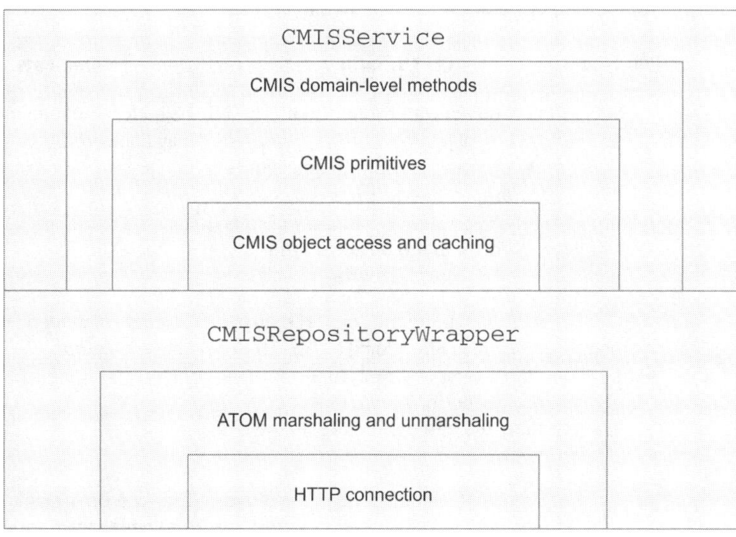

Figure 9.13 PHP Client architecture

Table 9.4 Mapping of AtomPub types and PHP types

Return type	AtomPub type	PHP structure	Comments
Repository definition	Workspace	An object with the following five arrays: 1 Links (used by the client to navigate the repository) 2 URI templates (used by the client to navigate the repository) 3 Collections (used by the client to navigate the repository) 4 Capabilities 5 Repository information	
CMIS object	Entry	An object containing two scalars and three arrays: 1 Links (used by the client to navigate the repository) 2 Properties 3 Allowable actions 4 UUID (`atom:id`) 5 ID (Object ID) The following members will be added in the future: 1 Relationships 2 Policy IDs 3 Renditions 4 ACLs	A CMIS object can refer to ▪ Document ▪ Folder ▪ Policy ▪ Relationship ▪ Object ID ▪ Object ID + change token

Table 9.4 Mapping of AtomPub types and PHP types *(continued)*

Return type	AtomPub type	PHP structure	Comments
List of CMIS objects	Feed	PHP object with two arrays of `Entry` objects: ■ `objectsById`—An associative array of the `Entrys` ■ `objectList`—An array of references to the objects in the `objectsById` array	Objects in the feed may not be fully populated.
Tree of CMIS objects	Feed with CMIS hierarchy extensions	Array similar to previous. Hierarchy is achieved by adding a `Children` object to each `Entry` that has children. The `Children` object contains the same structure as the feed.	Objects in the feed may not be fully populated.
Type definition	Entry	An object with three arrays and one scalar: ■ Links (used by the client to navigate the repository) ■ Properties ■ Attributes ■ ID (object type ID)	The Type Definition data structure needs work for completion. Currently, it has enough to support the needs of the Object Services.
List of type definitions	Feed	PHP object with two arrays of `Entry` objects: ■ `objectsById`—An associative array of the `Entrys` ■ `objectList`—An array of references to the objects in the `objectsById` array	Objects in the feed may not be fully populated.
Tree of type definitions	Feed with CMIS hierarchy extensions	Array similar to previous. Hierarchy is achieved by adding a `Children` object to each `Entry` that has children. The `Children` object contains the same structure as the feed.	Objects in the feed may not be fully populated.
Content stream	Content	Content	

9.4.4 *Differences between OpenCMIS and the PHP Client*

OpenCMIS and the PHP Client have several differences between them. Let's look at some functional differences and then see some simple code examples to further illustrate the differences.

FUNCTIONAL DIFFERENCES

In Java-based web applications, you can cache information from one request for future requests. In many PHP installations, PHP is run in the CGI mode, which means that server memory has no means of caching content for access by future requests. As a result, the PHP Client places less emphasis on caching. Most of the caching is centered around retaining information that will be used in a single HTTP request to the web application.

In the OpenCMIS implementation, CMIS objects have methods. In the PHP Client, only the `CMISService` object has methods; the CMIS objects contain only data—they have no methods.

The PHP Client only supports the AtomPub binding. Currently, work is under way that will add a SOAP binding to the PHP Client.

The current implementation doesn't support CMIS endpoints with multiple repositories.

CODE COMPARISON

It's helpful to see a few PHP examples of things you learned to do with OpenCMIS in earlier chapters. In this section, you'll see how to get a session, how to run a query, and how to update the properties on an object.

Initiating a session

In PHP, initiating a session requires you to call the `CMISService` constructor with the CMIS endpoint and login credentials. The `CMISService` session will return a new object that's connected to the repository. Currently, only Basic authentication is supported:

```
require_once ('cmis-lib.php');

$client = new CMISService("http://localhost:8081/inmemory/atom",
                          "admin",
                          "admin");
```

Executing a query

You can execute queries by passing the CMIS SQL to the query method, which will return a list of objects, like this:

```
$query = "SELECT * FROM cmisbook:taggable AS t
          WHERE 'soul' = ANY t.cmisbook:tags";
$objs = $client->query($query);
foreach ($objs->objectList as $obj) {
    print $obj->properties['cmis:name'] . "\n";
}
```

Updating a multivalued property

Updating a property is a matter of creating an array of properties, and then passing that to the `updateProperties` method:

```
# Set $objectId
$item = $client->getObject($objectId);
$tags = $client->getMultiValuedProp($item,'cmisbook:tags');
$tags[] = "gospel";
$changeToken = $item->properties['cmis:changeToken'];
$properties = array('cmisbook:tags' => $tags);
$client->updateProperties($objectId,$properties);
```

The underlying code ensures that the changeToken is sent along if necessary.

The array helper function forces a property to be an array.

You may have noticed a difference in how OpenCMIS handles multivalued properties compared to the PHP library. The PHP library doesn't change all multivalued properties into a list/array. If you want to do that, you have to use the `array` helper function. The maintainers of the PHP Client library might remove the need for this at a later date, but it would involve parsing the type definition when retrieving the properties.

That gives you a rough feel for what it's like to work with CMIS from PHP. Let's move on to a more real-world example by returning to The Blend.

9.4.5 Using PHP to browse The Blend

We've created a module that allows users to tag content, mark content as favorites, and search for content. We built the module as a custom Drupal 7 module on top of the PHP CMIS library, and we used Drupal 7's library feature to add the PHP CMIS library as a shared library. Using PHP CMIS as a shared library allows the developer to create multiple CMIS-based modules using the same library.

The custom module for The Blend doesn't use the CMIS API module that's part of Drupal 6. The CMIS module is still in development form for Drupal 7 and will probably need to be reworked to take advantage of the shared library.

Let's look at some of the details of the Drupal module for The Blend.

FUNCTIONAL OVERVIEW

The Drupal module for The Blend, shown in figure 9.14, allows a visiting user to add tags to any taggable object and to list objects that are tagged with a specific term. The module also allows users to create their own collections of taggable objects (for example, playlists and photo galleries). Finally, the module allows users to store saved searches.

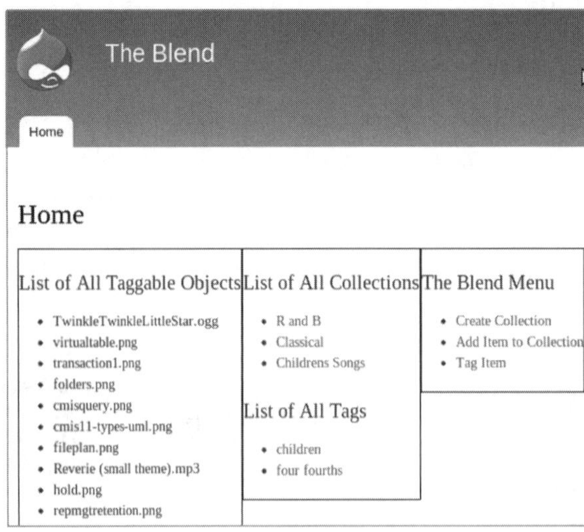

Figure 9.14 The Blend as a Drupal module

TAGGING TAGGABLE ITEMS

In The Blend, tags are implemented using a multivalue property called cmisbook:tags on a type called cmisbook:taggable. Tags on a given object are added by updating the tags property with the new tag:

```
function theblend_add_tag_to_item($objectId,$tag_name) {
    $client = theblend_get_cmis_client();
    $item = $client->getObject($objectId);
    $tags = $client->getMultiValuedProp($item, 'cmisbook:tags');
    $properties = array('cmisbook:tags' => $tags);
    $properties['cmisbook:tags'][] = $tag_name;
    $client->updateProperties($objectId,$properties);
}
```

The Drupal form for adding a tag to an item is shown in figure 9.15.

Figure 9.15 Adding a tag to a taggable object

LISTING ITEMS TAGGED WITH A SPECIFIC TAG

You'll use a CMIS query with an ANY clause to find objects with a specific tag, as this code shows:

```
function theblend_list_items_with_tag($tag_name) {
    $client = theblend_get_cmis_client();
    $query = "SELECT * FROM cmisbook:taggable AS t WHERE '" .
               $tag_name . "' = ANY t.cmisbook:tags";
    $objs = $client->query($query);
    $output = "<h2>$query</h2>";
    $output .= "<ul>";
    foreach ($objs->objectList as $obj) {
        $output .= "<li>" . $obj->properties['cmis:name'] . "</li>";
```

```
    }
    $output .= "</ul>";
    return $output;
}
```

From Drupal, searching for a list of items with a specific tag looks like figure 9.16.

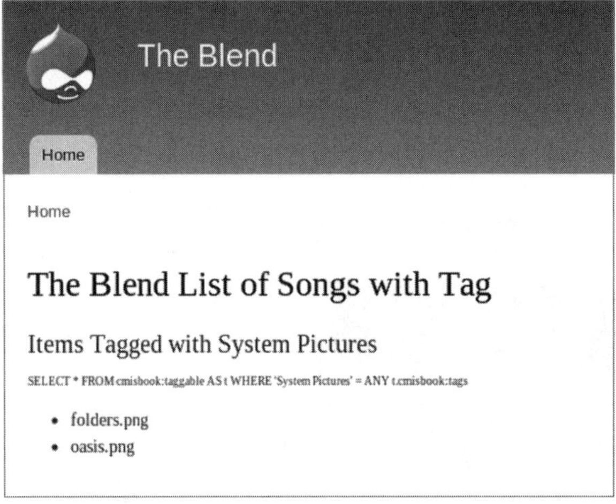

Figure 9.16 Querying for taggable objects with a specific tag

ADVANCED SEARCHES AND SAVED QUERIES

In order to store a user's saved searches, we created a folder called /user_content. This folder will have a subfolder for each user. The queries for the saved searches are stored in the queries subfolder for the user. This means if joeschmoe is a user, his queries would be stored in /user_content/joeschmoe/queries. The next listing shows how the queries are saved, retrieved, and run.

Listing 9.11 Saving, retrieving, and executing saved searches

```
function theblend_run_query($query_name) {
    return $client->query(theblend_get_query($query_name));
}

// Get the saved queries folder for the user
function theblend_get_queries_folder() {
    $client = theblend_get_cmis_client();

    $user_content = $client->getObjectByPath("/user_content");
    try {
        $my_content = $client->getObjectByPath("/user_content/" .
                  $client->username);
    } catch (Exception $exception) {
        $my_content = $client->createFolder($user_content->id,
                  $client->username);
    }
    try {
```

All user content is under /user_content/<user_name>, and all saved queries are in a subfolder called queries; the code creates any required folders that aren't already there.

```
        $my_queries = $client->getObjectByPath("/user_content/" .
                    $client->username . "/queries");
    } catch (Exception $exception) {
        $my_queries = $client->createFolder($my_content->id,
                    "queries");
    }
    return $my_queries;
}

// get Named Query
function theblend_get_query($query_name) {
    $client = theblend_get_cmis_client();

    $my_queries = theblend_get_queries_folder();
    $my_query = false;
    try {
        $my_query = $client->getObjectByPath("/user_content/" .
                    $client->username . "/queries/" . $query_name);
    } catch (Exception $exception) {
        return "";
    }

    return $client->getContentStream($my_query->id);
}
```

Call get_queries_folder and then get the named query.

Return contents of the query.

CREATING COLLECTIONS OF TAGGABLES (PLAYLISTS, GALLERIES)

Collections of taggables are implemented by creating folders in which taggable items can be multifiled. A collection for a user is stored in a subfolder of a user-content folder called collections. For example, if our user, joeschmoe, wants to create a collection called "classics," that folder would be located at /user_content/joeschmoe/collections/classics/. The functions that deal with creating and retrieving collections of taggables are shown in the following listing.

Listing 9.12 Creating and retrieving collections of taggables

```
function theblend_get_collection($collection_name,$create=false) {
    $client = theblend_get_cmis_client();

    $my_collections = theblend_get_collections_folder();
    $my_collection = false;

    try {
        $my_collection = $client->getObjectByPath(
                    "/user_content/" .
                    $client->username .
                    "/collections/" .
                    $collection_name);
    } catch (Exception $exception) {
        if ($create) {
            drupal_set_message("creating my collection");
            $my_collection = $client->createFolder(
                        $my_collections->id,$collection_name);
        }
```

Get collections folder, which is the container for all collections

Get named collection folder (or create it if necessary)

```
    }
    return $my_collection;
}

// Add item to collection
function theblend_add_item_to_collection($objectId,$collection_name) {
    $client = theblend_get_cmis_client();
    $collection=theblend_get_collection($collection_name);
    $client->addObjectToFolder($objectId,$collection->id);
}

// Get members of a collection
function theblend_view_collection($collection_name) {
    $client = theblend_get_cmis_client();

    // Get children of named collection folder
    $collection=theblend_get_collection($collection_name);
    return $client->getChildren($collection->id);
}
```

When adding an item to collection, first get named collection

Then add item to the folder as a secondary parent

Now you've seen how PHP and CMIS can be used together—in this case, to build a Drupal module—and how they can work with content in a CMIS repository.

9.5 Summary

You should now have a good feel for some of the other client libraries available to you. If you read the entire chapter and worked through all of the examples, congratulations! Your laptop is now a veritable CMIS Swiss Army knife.

Table 9.5 summarizes the client libraries we reviewed in this chapter.

Table 9.5 At a glance: popular non-Java libraries for working with CMIS

Library	Language	Project home	Bindings supported	Install method	Key dependencies
DotCMIS	.NET	Apache Chemistry	AtomPub and Web Services	Manual	Microsoft OS
cmislib	Python	Apache Chemistry	AtomPub only	Python setuptools or manual	Python 2.6 or 2.7
PHP Client	PHP	Apache Chemistry	AtomPub only	Manual	None

All of the libraries you saw in this chapter are available as part of the Apache Chemistry project. Developers typically use these libraries to build desktop applications and web applications. But what if you're a mobile developer? Whether your platform of choice is iOS or Android, the next chapter shows you how to build mobile applications that work with CMIS repositories.

10 Building mobile apps with CMIS

This chapter covers

- Setting up an OpenCMIS development environment for Android
- Tips for writing a mobile application with OpenCMIS for Android
- Setting up an ObjectiveCMIS development environment
- Using ObjectiveCMIS to enhance an iOS application

The emergence of modern mobile smartphones and tablets has fundamentally changed how people interact with their mobile devices. Every day, more and more users access and consume websites, music, email, and video directly from these devices regardless of their physical location. Now, for both personal and professional reasons, they want their documents too.

In this chapter, we'll use projects from Apache Chemistry to create native mobile applications on both the Android and Apple iOS platforms. The applications will show how easy it is to create mobile applications that store content to and retrieve it from a CMIS repository.

10.1 Writing mobile apps with OpenCMIS for Android

This section will introduce you to developing mobile applications that need to work with CMIS repositories on Android devices. We'll start by talking a little bit about Android and about a port of the OpenCMIS library built specifically for Android. Then we'll show you how to set up a local development environment before taking some initial steps with a simple one-screen application. Finally, we'll wrap up by looking at an Android application written specifically for The Blend.

10.1.1 Android and CMIS

Android is a Linux-based operating system for mobile devices such as smartphones and tablet computers, developed by Google in conjunction with the Open Handset Alliance. It is one of the world's most popular mobile platforms. Every day more than one million Android devices are activated.

Android's programming interface is Java-oriented. You may have already tried to import Apache Chemistry OpenCMIS libraries as dependencies into an Android project and found that it doesn't work. That's because OpenCMIS relies on some dependencies that aren't available in the Android platform. Although the Android SDK is Java-based, it's different than the JDK. They share some common packages, but they don't share all of them, and Android lacks several packages necessary to use straight OpenCMIS in an Android application.

That's why, starting with version 0.8.0-SNAPSHOT of Apache Chemistry, a subproject named chemistry-opencmis-android-client was added. This project allows Android developers to use OpenCMIS. It's a merge of the opencmis-client-* and opencmis-commons-* projects into a single JAR file.

The OpenCMIS Android Client supports Android 2.3 and later. The coverage of the CMIS specification is not yet complete—for example, you can't use OpenCMIS Android to manage ACLs or policy objects.

The OpenCMIS Android Client is a *synchronous* library. What does this mean to you as a developer? By default, all components of an Android application run in the same process—running code, graphical user interface, and input events are all managed from a single thread, generally called the *main thread* or the *UI thread*. This is not usually a problem if developers don't require any time-consuming operations. When you do need to perform a long-running operation, such as retrieving information from the internet, the screen interface of the application will be blocked until the code has finished running. Android will kill the application if it doesn't react within five seconds of the user's input, so to provide a good user experience, all potentially long-running operations in an Android application should run asynchronously, which developers can achieve by encapsulating all operations in a background thread.

Android has a few different objects that can help:

- `Service`—An application component representing either an application's desire to perform a longer-running operation while not interacting with the user or to supply functionality for other applications to use.

- `AsyncTask`—Helps perform asynchronous work in the user interface. The `AsyncTask` performs the blocking operations in a worker thread and then publishes the results on the UI thread.
- `Loader`—Available since Android HoneyComb, a `Loader` gives the developer a mechanism for loading data asynchronously for an activity or fragment. A `Loader` is usually easier to use than an `AsyncTask`.

It's up to the developer to determine which object and overall approach is best for a given application.

Now that you know a little bit about the library and how it's used in Android applications, it's time to set up a development environment.

10.1.2 Setting up an Android environment

Before you can create your first Android project, you need to set up the Android SDK, configure Eclipse, and install an emulator. So let's do that now.

Requirements

One of the nice things about Android development is that the dependencies are freely available and will run on any platform. Here's what you need:

- Java Development Kit (JDK)
- Java Integrated Development Environment (IDE)
- Android SDK
- Android Development Tools (ADT) Eclipse Plugin (optional, but this book assumes you're using the ADT with Eclipse)
- Android emulator (or a real Android device)
- OpenCMIS Android Client library

Installing the Android SDK

The Android SDK includes all the tools and APIs you need to write mobile applications. You can download the latest version for your platform from the Android developer website at http://developer.android.com/sdk/index.html. Follow the instructions to install the SDK from the Android developer website at http://developer.android.com/sdk/installing/index.html.

Before you begin development, you need to download at least one SDK platform release. The Android SDK Manager will do this for you. If you're on Windows, run the SDK Manager.exe file (at the root of the Android SDK directory). If you're on Mac OS X or Linux, run the android executable (in the /tools directory in the Android SDK). Either way, when you open the Android SDK Manager, it will automatically select a set of recommended packages. Then, when you click Install (see figure 10.1), the Android SDK Manager will launch the download and installation.

For more information, please refer to Android's "Adding Platforms and Packages" page: http://developer.android.com/sdk/installing/adding-packages.html.

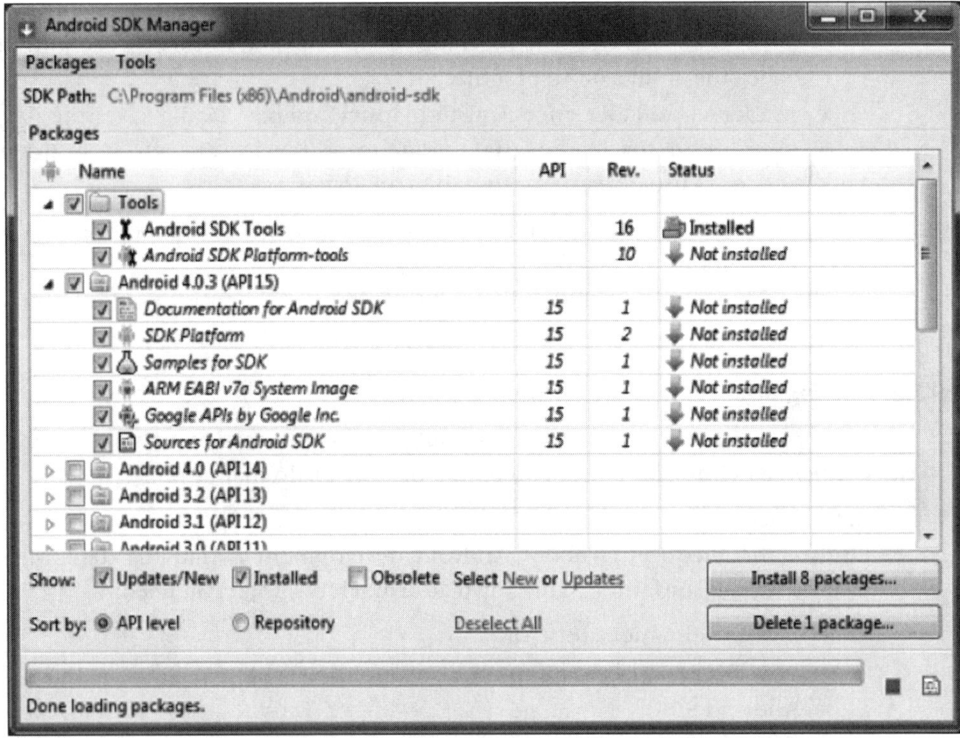

Figure 10.1 Android SDK Manager

INSTALLING ECLIPSE AND THE ANDROID ADT

You probably already have Eclipse installed from your work with OpenCMIS in earlier chapters. If not, Eclipse is available for download from the Eclipse foundation website: www.eclipse.org/downloads. Installing Eclipse consists of uncompressing the installation package file onto your filesystem.

Android offers a custom plugin for the Eclipse IDE called Android Development Tools (ADT). It extends the capabilities of Eclipse to let you quickly set up new Android projects, build an application UI, use an emulator, debug your app, and export signed (or unsigned) application packages (APKs) for distribution. To install this plugin from Eclipse, follow these steps:

1. Select Help > Install New Software.
2. Click Add, in the top-right corner.
3. In the next dialog box, enter "Android Plugin" for the name and the following URL for the location: https://dl-ssl.google.com/android/eclipse/. Then click OK.
4. In the Available Software dialog box, select the check box next to Developer Tools, and click Next.

5 Read and accept the license agreements, and then click Finish.
6 When installation is complete, restart Eclipse and update the ADT preferences.
7 After restart, in the "Welcome to Android Development" window that appears, select Use Existing SDKs.
8 Browse and select the location of the Android SDK directory you recently downloaded.
9 Click Next. You're finished.

The Android SDK is now installed and running in Eclipse. If you don't have a physical Android device (or even if you do), you may want to configure one or more virtual devices for testing and debugging. That's covered in the next section.

SETTING UP AN ANDROID EMULATOR

The Android SDK includes an Android Virtual Device (AVD) Manager. As the name implies, the AVD can create, use, and delete a virtual mobile device that runs on your computer to emulate what end users will see when they run your application on a physical device. You can create as many AVDs as you need.

To create an AVD, follow these steps:

1 In Eclipse, select Window > AVD Manager, or click the AVD Manager icon in the Eclipse toolbar. If you don't see the AVD Manager window, you can launch it as you did earlier.
2 In the Virtual Devices panel, you'll see a list of existing AVDs. Click New to create a new AVD. The Create New AVD dialog box appears, as shown in figure 10.2.
3 Fill in the details for the AVD.
4 Give it a name, a platform target, an SD card size, and a skin (HVGA is the default). You can also add specific hardware features of the emulated device by clicking New and selecting the feature.

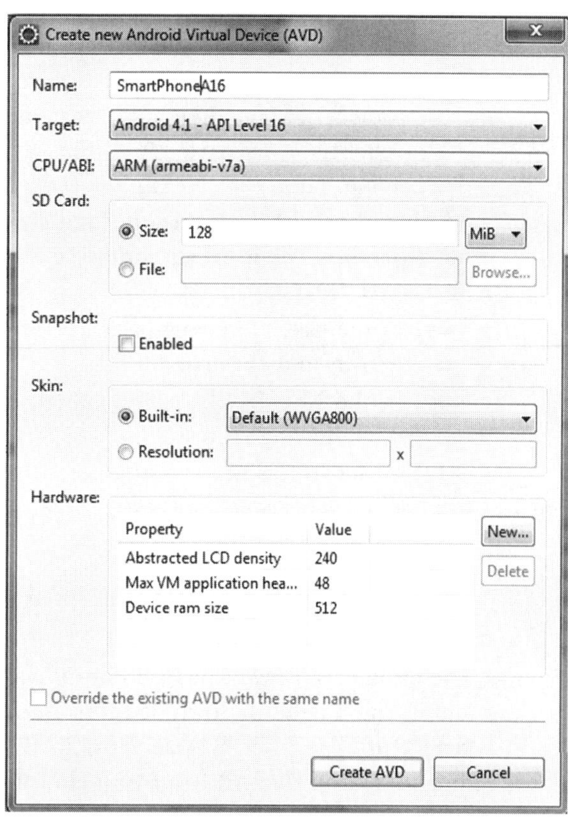

Figure 10.2 The Create New AVD dialog box

5 Click Create AVD.
6 Your AVD is now ready, and you can either close the AVD Manager, create more AVDs, or launch an emulator with the AVD by selecting a device and clicking Start.

You now have an Android development environment set up. It's time to start working with CMIS from an Android application.

10.1.3 Writing your first Android CMIS application

Let's start with something simple. Let's create a one-screen application that iterates over the children in the media folder of a CMIS repository. Then we can look at a more complex example.

CREATING AN ANDROID PROJECT

To create an Android Project, follow these steps:

1 In Eclipse, select File > New > Other.
2 In the Wizard List panel, select Android > Android Application Project and click Next.
3 Fill in the details for the project. Use `The Blend` for the application name and project name. Use `com.manning.cmis.theblend.android` for the package name. Then click Next.
4 In the Configure Custom Launcher Icon panel, let your artistic side free and then click Next.
5 In the Create Activity panel, select Blank Activity and click Next.
6 In the New Blank Activity panel, change the following values:
   - Activity Name: `FirstOpenCMISActivity`
   - Layout Name: `activity_opencmis`
7 Click Finish.

Figure 10.3 Android project structure for The Blend

Your Android project is now ready, and it should look like the one shown in figure 10.3.

ADDING LIBRARIES

The build path of your project doesn't yet contain the OpenCMIS Android Client. To add it, you'll need to download it from the Apache Chemistry OpenCMIS downloads page (http://chemistry.apache.org/java/download.html), unzip it, and then either drag and drop the JAR from your download folder to YourProject > libs, or you can right-click on the libs folder and select Import > File System > Browse > Path to download folder, and then select the JAR and click Finish.

You'll also need to add slf4j-android-1.6.1-RC1. If you don't already have it, you can download SLF4J Android from www.slf4j.org/android/.

USING APACHE MAVEN If you prefer to use the build tool Maven, it's also possible to import the Android client as a Maven dependency by adding the following to your pom.xml file: `<dependencies><dependency> <groupId>org.apache.chemistry.opencmis</groupId> <artifactId>chemistry-opencmis-android-client</artifactId> <version>0.8.0</version> <dependency> </dependencies>`. This requires the use of the Android Maven plugin. For more information on how to use the Android Maven plugin, see the "Android Maven Plugin" page: http://code.google.com/p/maven-android-plugin/.

CREATING THE FIRST SCREEN

First of all, you need to modify the default layout of your screen. A layout in Android is a type of resource that defines what's drawn on the screen. Layouts are implemented as XML files in the /res/layout resource directory for the application.

By default, your application already has a layout named activity_opencmis.xml. Let's modify it:

1. In Eclipse, from an Explorer view, navigate to Blend/res/layout, then right-click the file named activity_open_cmis.xml, and then click Open With > XML Editor.
2. Edit the file as follows:

```
<RelativeLayout
    xmlns:android="http://schemas.android.com/apk/res/android"
    xmlns:tools="http://schemas.android.com/tools"
    android:layout_width="match_parent"
    android:layout_height="match_parent" >

    <TextView
        android:id="@+id/opencmis_text"
        android:layout_width="wrap_content"
        android:layout_height="wrap_content"
        android:layout_centerHorizontal="true"
        android:layout_centerVertical="true"
        android:text="@string/hello_world"
        />

</RelativeLayout>
```

This line needs to be added. The rest should already exist.

Now it's time to change the main activity of your application to use the Android OpenCMIS Client. An *Android activity* is an application component that provides a screen with which users can interact in order to do something, such as dial the phone, take a photo, send an email, or view a map. Each activity is given a window in which to draw its user interface. The window typically fills the screen, but it may be smaller than the screen and can float on top of other windows.

In your current project, you already have an activity called `FirstOpenCMIS-Activity`. Let's modify it to display the list of all documents inside the media folder. This requires two things:

- A `Session` object, which can be used to list the children of the media folder
- An asynchronous mechanism to respect the UI/Background Thread model

In this example, you'll use an `AsyncTask` to do the job. Here's how:

1. In Eclipse, from an Explorer view, navigate to Blend/src/com.manning.cmis.theblend.android and select the file named FirstOpenCMISActivity.java.
2. Edit the file and replace it with the contents of listing 10.1. The content of FirstOpenCMISAsyncTask may look familiar—it's exactly the same logic that you used in chapter 7 to iterate over the children in a folder with OpenCMIS.

Listing 10.1 FirstOpenCMISActivity.java

```
public class FirstOpenCMISActivity extends Activity {

@Override
public void onCreate(Bundle savedInstanceState) {
    super.onCreate(savedInstanceState);
    setContentView(R.layout.activity_opencmis);
    new FirstOpenCMISAsyncTask().execute();
}

private class FirstOpenCMISAsyncTask
  extends AsyncTask<Void, Void, String> {

@Override
protected String doInBackground(Void... arg0) {

    // Initiates a Session Factory
    SessionFactory sessionFactory = SessionFactoryImpl.newInstance();

    // Initiates connection session parameters.
    Map<String, String> parameter = new HashMap<String, String>();
    parameter.put(SessionParameter.USER, "admin");
    parameter.put(SessionParameter.PASSWORD, "admin");
    parameter.put(
      SessionParameter.ATOMPUB_URL,
      "http://192.168.1.36:8081/inmemory/atom/");
    parameter.put(
      SessionParameter.BINDING_TYPE,
      BindingType.ATOMPUB.value());

    // Retrieves repository information and create the session object.
    Repository repository = sessionFactory.getRepositories(parameter)
      .get(0);
    parameter.put(SessionParameter.REPOSITORY_ID, repository.getId());
    Session session = sessionFactory.createSession(parameter);

    // Retrieves media folder and list all its children.
    String listChildren = "";
    Folder mediaFolder = (Folder) session.getObjectByPath("/media");
    ItemIterable<CmisObject> children = mediaFolder.getChildren();
    for (CmisObject o : children) {
        listChildren += o.getName() +
          " - " +
          o.getType().getDisplayName() +
```

Change this to your local IP address; using the loopback address (127.0.0.1) won't work.

```
                " - " +
                o.getCreatedBy() +
                "bn";
        }

        return listChildren;
    }

    @Override
    protected void onPostExecute(String result) {
        TextView tv = (TextView) (FirstOpenCMISActivity.this)
          .findViewById(R.id.opencmis_text);
        tv.setText(result);
    }}}
```

CONFIGURING PERMISSIONS

By default, an Android application has no permission to do much of anything. To make use of the protected features of the device, you must include one or more `<uses-permission>` tags declaring the permissions that your application needs in your AndroidManifest.xml.

The internet access permission is mandatory for the Android OpenCMIS Client. An Android application that needs to connect to a CMIS server isn't going to get very far without it. Here's how to give your application the permission:

1. In Eclipse, from an Explorer view, select the file named AndroidManifest.xml that resides in The Blend.
2. Add the following internet permission after the `uses-sdk` element and before the `application` element:

   ```
   <uses-permission android:name="android.permission.INTERNET"/>
   ```

RUNNING YOUR APPLICATION

Now it's time to run the application. To do that, follow these steps:

1. In Eclipse, right-click the project folder.
2. Click Run as > Android Application.
3. If you don't use a real device, an Android emulator will start. If you use a real device, plug in the device to your development machine with a USB cable. You might need to install the appropriate USB driver for your device. Ensure that USB debugging is enabled in the device settings.
4. After a few seconds, your device/emulator will display a screen that looks like figure 10.4.

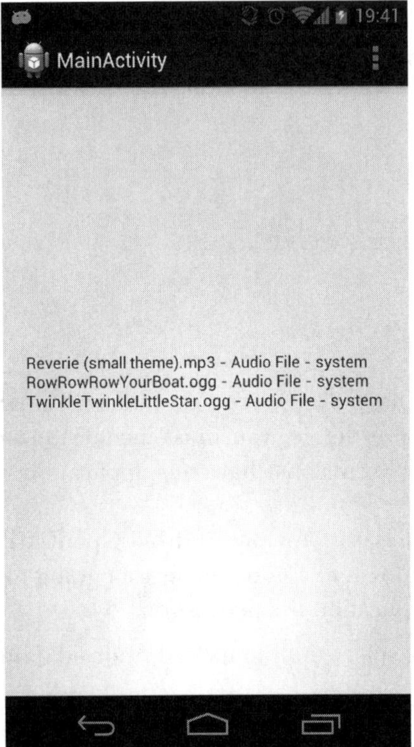

Figure 10.4 A simple Android application that iterates over a folder's children

Now you've created a simple Android application that has successfully connected to a CMIS server and iterated over a folder's children. The next step is to create a full-blown Android application for The Blend.

10.1.4 Try it—writing an Android application for The Blend

You know the basics of how to use and incorporate CMIS in an Android application. It's now time to go further. Let's build an Android application for The Blend. It will be a simple mobile application that allows users to connect to a CMIS repository, retrieve information about their favorite songs, and plays those songs. The full source code for this application accompanies this book. Figure 10.5 shows mockups of what The Blend for Android will look like.

This application is divided into three main screens:

- The *Login* screen is responsible for requesting information about the CMIS repository where the music is being stored.
- The *Album List* screen displays a list of all albums stored in the repository.
- The *Album Details* screen provides information on a specific album and a list of the tracks that make up the album.

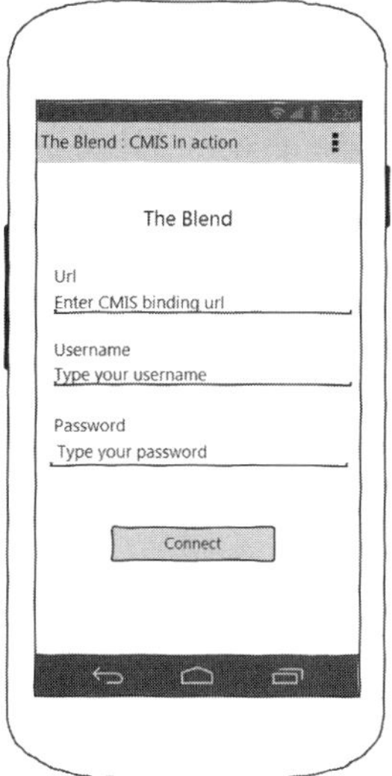

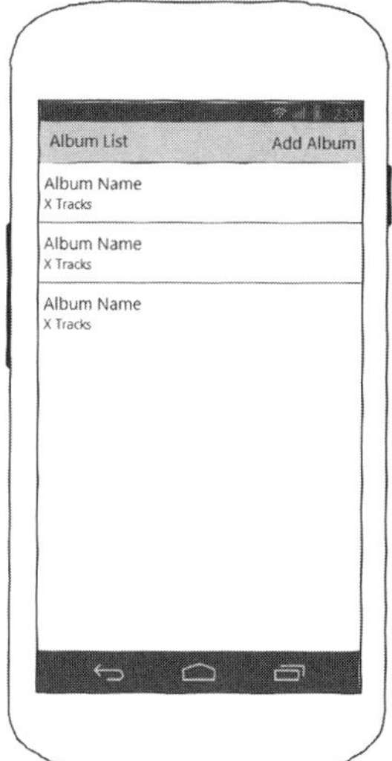

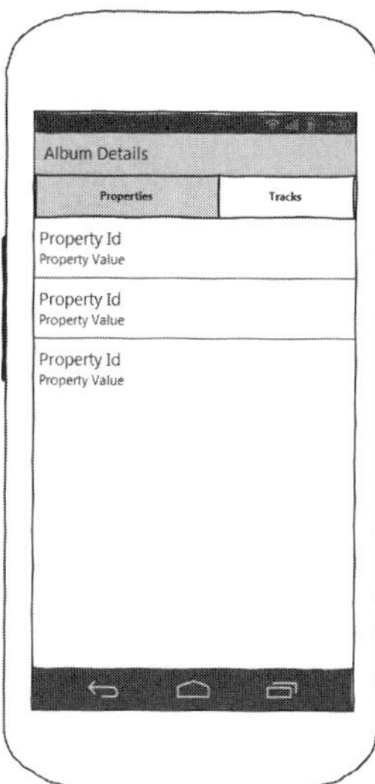

Figure 10.5 Mockups of The Blend for Android

Each screen includes actions associated with the page context, such as "create album" or "download a track."

Now that you've seen a high-level overview of the application, let's look at how you can get the source code set up in Eclipse. Then we'll walk through how the Login and Album List screens are built and complete the section by giving you some suggestions for tackling some of the functionality on your own.

SETTING UP THE PROJECT IN ECLIPSE

The easiest way to step through the code and to run the application is to import the source code that accompanies the book into Eclipse. To import the Android project, follow these steps:

1. In Eclipse, Select File > Import > Android > Existing Android Code Into Workspace.
2. Browse to the chapter10 folder and validate the choice by clicking Finish.

You should now have a project that looks like figure 10.6. Take a few minutes to get familiar with the project structure:

- The components and settings are described in the AndroidManifest.xml file.
- The src folder contains Java class files. They implement the screens and behaviors of the application. Activities (application screens) and tasks (background tasks to retrieve information from the server) are inside this folder. They're divided into a logical package structure.
- The libs folder contains all of the libraries the project depends on. This is the same set of dependencies you configured in section 10.1.3. If this folder doesn't

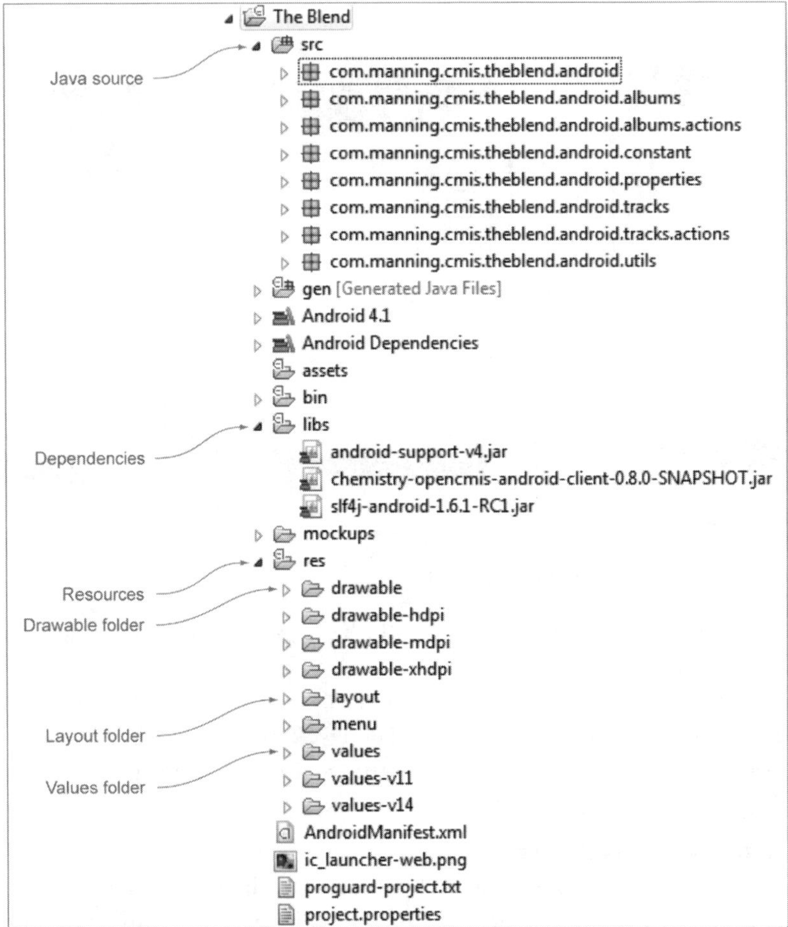

Figure 10.6 The Blend after importing the source code into Eclipse

exist in your project after importing, create it, and import the same three JARs you used earlier.

- The res folder contains all of the resources files, including these:
  - *Drawable folders*—Images in different sizes to support different Android device screen sizes
  - *Layout folder*—XML file that describes files used to define the user interface
  - *Values folder*—XML files used to define strings, colors, dimensions, styles, and static arrays of strings or integers

Now that you know your way around the project, let's take a look at the Login page.

THE BLEND: LOGIN PAGE

The main goal of the Login screen is to create the CMIS `Session` object and share it with all of the other screens in the application.

The implementation of the screen is found inside `com.manning.cmis.theblend.android`. It's composed of two classes:

- `LoginActivity`—Displays the form and manages user interactions. It allows the user to provide information about the CMIS server, retrieves information from the server, and creates the `SessionTask`.
- `SessionTask`—Creates the CMIS `Session` object in a background thread and displays the Album List screen when the session is created.

In an Android application, each screen or activity is totally independent of other screens/activities. Each activity has its own context and its own lifecycle. If your application is composed of more than one screen, you must exchange important information, like the `Session` object, between screens. The CMIS `Session` object is critical to The Blend. Without this object, the application can't do anything. For this reason, it's important to keep it safe and to share it with all of the components that need it.

In Android there's a mechanism called an *intent*. An intent is an object that provides a runtime binding between separate components (such as two activities). The intent represents an app's *intent to do something*. You can use intents for a wide variety of tasks, but most often they're used to start another activity.

An example of this is the `SessionTask`. After successfully creating a `Session` object, the task creates an intent to display the Album List screen and uses it to transfer the session, like this:

```
public class SessionTask extends AsyncTask<Bundle, Void, Session> {
...
@Override
protected void onPostExecute(String result) {
    Bundle b = new Bundle();
    b.putSerializable(BundleConstant.KEY_SESSION, result);
    Intent i = new Intent(activity, AlbumsActivity.class);
    i.putExtra(BundleConstant.KEY_EXTRAS, b);
    activity.startActivity(i);
}}
```

Then, in `AlbumsActivity` it's possible to retrieve the object with the `getIntent().getExtras()` method and use it inside your new screen, like so:

```
public class AlbumsActivity extends Activity{
...
@Override
public void onCreate(Bundle savedInstanceState){
...
    // Retrieves informations from Intent
    if (getIntent().getExtras() != null) {
       Bundle b = getIntent().getExtras().
                  getBundle(BundleConstant.KEY_EXTRAS);
       session = (Session) b.getSerializable(
                             BundleConstant.KEY_SESSION);
    }
...
}}
```

This same pattern can be repeated by any other screen in the application that needs to use the Session object.

THE BLEND: ALBUM LIST SCREEN

The Album List screen displays all of the CMIS album objects present in the CMIS repository. The implementation for this screen is found inside com.manning.cmis.theblend.android.albums. It consists of the following:

- AlbumsActivity—Displays the list of all of the cmisbook:album objects. The user sees a list of albums and can scroll through them and select one to display more information.
- AlbumsTask—First creates a CMIS request to retrieve all cmisbook:album objects in a background thread. Then it transforms the result object into a CMIS Document object and transfers this information to the AlbumsActivity.
- AlbumsAdapter—Used by AlbumsActivity to receive data and populate an Android listView component. It's responsible for creating a row for each cmisbook:album object.

The Blend uses wireless networking to retrieve its information. But during this transfer, there's a risk of latency caused by a problem with the network, user interaction, an incoming phone call, or any number of things. The application needs to catch and manage errors that prevent it from getting data. A common way to address this is to wrap information from an AsyncTask into a high-level result object. This object encapsulates information (data expected, exceptions, and other data) from the server side and allows other parts of the application to display the right information. In a normal case, the code displays the information as expected. If an exception occurs, the code can handle it gracefully and display a user notification that explains why the action hasn't been executed.

In The Blend, the CmisResult class, which resides in the com.manning.cmis.theblend.android.utils package, is responsible for implementing this pattern.

AlbumsTask uses CmisResult to change the behavior on its onPostExecute method. If the albums list is retrieved, AlbumsTask pushes the information to the activity. If not, it displays a user notification that contains the exception message. You can see this happening in the following listing.

Listing 10.2 AlbumsTask.java

```
public class AlbumsTask
  extends AsyncTask<Void, Void, CmisResult<List<Document>>> {

    private static final String QUERY_ALL_ALBUMS =
      "SELECT * FROM cmis:document" .
      " where cmis:objectTypeId = 'cmisbook:album'";

...

   @Override
   protected CmisResult<List<Document>> doInBackground(Void... arg0) {
```

```
        List<Document> listAlbums = null;
        Exception exception = null;

        // Try to execute a CMIS Query
        // to retrieve all albums from the Server.
        try {
            ItemIterable<QueryResult> results =
              session.query(QUERY_ALL_ALBUMS, false);
            listAlbums = new ArrayList<Document>(
              (int) results.getTotalNumItems());
            Document album = null;

            // Create a list of Albums (Document object)
            // based on the result.
            for (QueryResult result : results) {
                album = (Document) session.getObject(
                  session.createObjectId((String) result.
                    getPropertyById(PropertyIds.OBJECT_ID).
                    getFirstValue()));
                listAlbums.add(album);
            }
        } catch (Exception e) {
            exception = e;
        }
        return new CmisResult<List<Document>>(exception, listAlbums);
    }

    @Override
    protected void onPostExecute(CmisResult<List<Document>> results) {
        // In case of exception, displays
        // informations for debugging purpose.
        if (results.hasException()) {
            Toast.makeText(
              activity,
              results.getException().getMessage(),
              Toast.LENGTH_LONG).show();
            Log.e(TAG, Log.getStackTraceString(results.getException()));
        } else if (activity instanceof AlbumsActivity) {
            // Display albums inside the listview.
            ((AlbumsActivity) activity).listAlbums(results.getData());
        }
    }
...

}
```

CmisResult gets passed to OnPostExecute method

Display message if there's a problem

All AsyncTasks inside The Blend use this principle. Instead of returning the expected object, they return a CmisResult object that contains the information.

THE BLEND: THINGS TO TRY ON YOUR OWN

As you may have noticed, OpenCMIS Android mobile development is really similar to OpenCMIS Java development. Just remember to respect these three rules:

1. Always take care of your Session object by using an intent to share it across all of the screens in your application.
2. Use a background thread to execute any OpenCMIS code.

3 Encapsulate your data into a high-level result object.

To practice what you've learned about OpenCMIS Android development, try to implement one or more of these features inside The Blend:

- Create an action that allows a user to create a new album
- Create an action that allows a user to add a track to an album based on a track ID
- Create a screen that displays the track list for an album
- Create a screen that displays the track object's properties

That's it! Now let's turn our attention from Java and Android to Objective-C and iOS.

10.2 Writing iOS apps with ObjectiveCMIS

This section introduces you to ObjectiveCMIS, an Objective-C client library for CMIS, and to iOS application development using ObjectiveCMIS. We'll also look at ObjectiveCMIS and how it compares to Apache Chemistry's OpenCMIS client library. We'll then take a look at how you can incorporate ObjectiveCMIS into your existing project and review several code snippets for a few different CMIS operations. Finally, we'll walk you through an example that builds a very simple audio-capture application that can be used to upload audio to The Blend.

DON'T KNOW OBJECTIVE-C OR ARE NEW TO IOS DEVELOPMENT? A good place to begin your adventures with Objective-C and iOS application development is by starting at Apple's iOS Dev Center (https://developer.apple.com/ios). Apple provides excellent resources (documentation, videos, sample code projects, and so on) for anyone interested in iOS development. All you need to do is register as an Apple Developer.

10.2.1 What is ObjectiveCMIS?

ObjectiveCMIS is an open source project that provides a CMIS client API written in Objective-C for iOS. It's part of the Apache Chemistry project. The goal behind the ObjectiveCMIS project is to provide a robust CMIS client library for iOS applications.

ObjectiveCMIS is implemented as a Cocoa Touch static library for iOS development and links against Apple's Foundation framework. What this means to you is that there are no third-party APIs or frameworks being used by the library. It also means that the library is built for iOS usage—if you want to develop Mac OS X applications, you can't do that with ObjectiveCMIS out of the box. The library is thread-safe, and calls to a CMIS repository are asynchronous. The asynchronous operations in ObjectiveCMIS are provided by the extensive use of Objective-C blocks.

OBJECTIVE-C BLOCKS ObjectiveCMIS uses Objective-C blocks to provide callback handlers (completion blocks) for all asynchronous calls. Objective-C blocks are also known as *closures*. If you're unfamiliar with the concept, an introduction to blocks can be found in the iOS Developer Library at http://mng.bz/6Fz6.

ObjectiveCMIS is essentially an Objective-C port of the OpenCMIS Java client library you already know so much about. Like the OpenCMIS client library, ObjectiveCMIS is implemented so that it closely follows the CMIS domain model. Just like OpenCMIS, ObjectiveCMIS provides two APIs: a high-level object-oriented API and a low-level bindings API. The high-level object-oriented API is the API that you'll most likely want to use whenever possible—it's much easier to use than the low-level binding API, which will be used only when you need more fine-grained control of how your application talks to the CMIS repository.

WHY ARE ALL CLASSES IN OBJECTIVECMIS PREFIXED WITH CMIS? When you dive into the ObjectiveCMIS API, you'll notice that all classes in ObjectiveCMIS are prefixed with *CMIS*. This is a common pattern recommended by Apple. It's necessary because Objective-C doesn't have namespaces.

Table 10.1 summarizes ObjectiveCMIS at a high level in its current state.

Table 10.1 ObjectiveCMIS at a high level

Library	Language	Project home	Bindings supported	Install method	Key dependencies
ObjectiveCMIS	Objective-C	Apache Chemistry	AtomPub only	Manual	iOS SDK 5.1+, Xcode 4.3+

ObjectiveCMIS is a fairly new client library. As such, there are a few limitations you should know about up front before deciding if it's right for your project:

- Supports CMIS 1.0 only
- Supports the RESTful AtomPub binding only
- Doesn't yet provide support for CMIS policies, relationships, change logs, or full access control functionality
- Provides no caching features, other than a link cache
- Can't be used to create OS X desktop applications out of the box

Over time, some of these limitations may go away. The project is always looking for more contributors, so if you're interested, reach out to the Chemistry Dev List (dev@chemistry.apache.org).

Although there are limitations in features and capabilities, ObjectiveCMIS is capable of performing most of the common use cases for acting upon documents and folders, search, and versioning. It's used in multiple production applications.

10.2.2 Comparing ObjectiveCMIS with OpenCMIS

As we mentioned earlier, ObjectiveCMIS is essentially an Objective-C port of the OpenCMIS Java client library, and it's implemented so that it closely follows the CMIS domain model. If you understand the OpenCMIS Java client library, you should be able to quickly understand how to use the ObjectiveCMIS static library—the biggest difference between the two is the programming language.

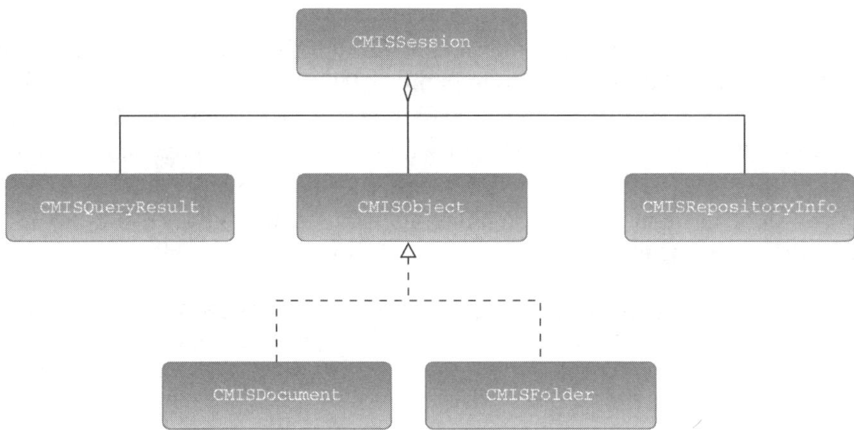

Figure 10.7 ObjectiveCMIS object model

Because of the similarity between the two, it shouldn't surprise you that the main entry point when interacting with a CMIS repository is the `CMISSession`. Once you get a `CMISSession`, you can start making calls against either the high-level client API or the low-level client binding API. However, in ObjectiveCMIS you'll find that not all the core CMIS domain model classes are available. ObjectiveCMIS includes support for documents, folders, query results, and repository info objects. CMIS policy and relationship objects aren't yet available. That leaves us with an object model that looks like figure 10.7.

It's encouraging that the API is so close to OpenCMIS. If you already know how to work with Xcode to develop mobile applications, that may be all you need to know. If that's the case for you, you might want to skip ahead to section 10.2.4 to learn how to generate the ObjectiveCMIS documentation before you move on to the "Try it" section. Otherwise, keep reading to learn how to set up the library in your local Xcode environment.

10.2.3 Getting started with ObjectiveCMIS

Now that you have a general understanding of ObjectiveCMIS and its current capabilities and limitations, it's time to see how to use it in your own project. This section describes the requirements for using the library, how to include ObjectiveCMIS in your project, and finally how to build the documentation for ObjectiveCMIS.

MINIMUM REQUIREMENTS

Because ObjectiveCMIS makes use of Automatic Reference Counting (ARC) and ObjectiveCMIS blocks, there are a few technical requirements that need to be met before you can use ObjectiveCMIS as part of your iOS application:

- Xcode 4.3 or newer
- iOS SDK 5.1 or newer
- iOS deployment target of iOS 5.1 or above

Where to find the source code

The ObjectiveCMIS source code and other resources you'll need to work through the examples in this section are provided in the zip archive that accompanies this book. If you would prefer to work with the latest release of ObjectiveCMIS, the release packages can be found on the Apache Chemistry ObjectiveCMIS web page at http://chemistry.apache.org/objective-c/objectivecmis.html. The ObjectiveCMIS source code is kept in a Subversion repository located at http://svn.apache.org/repos/asf/chemistry/objectivecmis/trunk/.

In the next few sections, we'll go through the process of building the ObjectiveCMIS library, adding it to an Xcode project using two different approaches, and, finally, generating the documentation. If you want to follow along, identify a folder where you'll unzip the ObjectiveCMIS source code archive file, ObjectiveCMIS-src.zip. We'll call this location $IOS_DEV_HOME. If you haven't done so already, go ahead and extract ObjectiveCMIS-src.zip to $IOS_DEV_HOME. You should now have the ObjectiveCMIS Xcode project available at $IOS_DEV_HOME/ObjectiveCMIS.

Now let's look at how you can incorporate the ObjectiveCMIS library into your project.

Incorporating ObjectiveCMIS into your application project

There are two options for incorporating the static library into your new or existing iOS application. The first option is to compile ObjectiveCMIS into a universal static library and then add the compiled universal static library and header files to your project. The second option is to add the ObjectiveCMIS Xcode project to an existing Xcode workspace, and allow Xcode to properly build the explicit and implicit dependencies required.

Let's look at each of these two options.

Using the compiled universal library file and public headers directly

The simplest way to incorporate the ObjectiveCMIS library into your mobile application project is to directly add the compiled universal static library and public headers to your project. For convenience, the compiled universal library file and public headers are made available in the archive ObjectiveCMIS-UniversalLib.zip that accompanies this book. If you want to use the precompiled files from the zip, jump to step 5. Otherwise, you must manually compile the library file and headers. To do that, follow these steps:

1. Change to the root folder for the ObjectiveCMIS Xcode project located at $IOS_DEV_HOME/ObjectiveCMIS.
2. Execute the shell script `build_universal_lib.sh` to start the build.
3. The script will output something similar to the following:

   ```
   ...I will output a universal build to: /Users/dev/Code/
   ObjectiveCMIS/build/Debug-universal
   ```

4. Copy the folder path the script spit out. This folder contains ObjectiveCMIS compiled as a universal library and it's ready to be included in an Xcode project.

Open the folder using the open command and the path, which will likely be different on your machine:

```
open /Users/dev/Code/Objective-CMIS/build/Debug-universal
```

5 Add the generated universal library file and header files to your application project by dragging and dropping the folder into your Xcode project or by using the Add Files to ProjectName action from the Navigator and selecting the folder Debug-universal. When you're prompted for the Add options for the new files (as shown in figure 10.8), make sure that you add the files to the target of your iOS application.

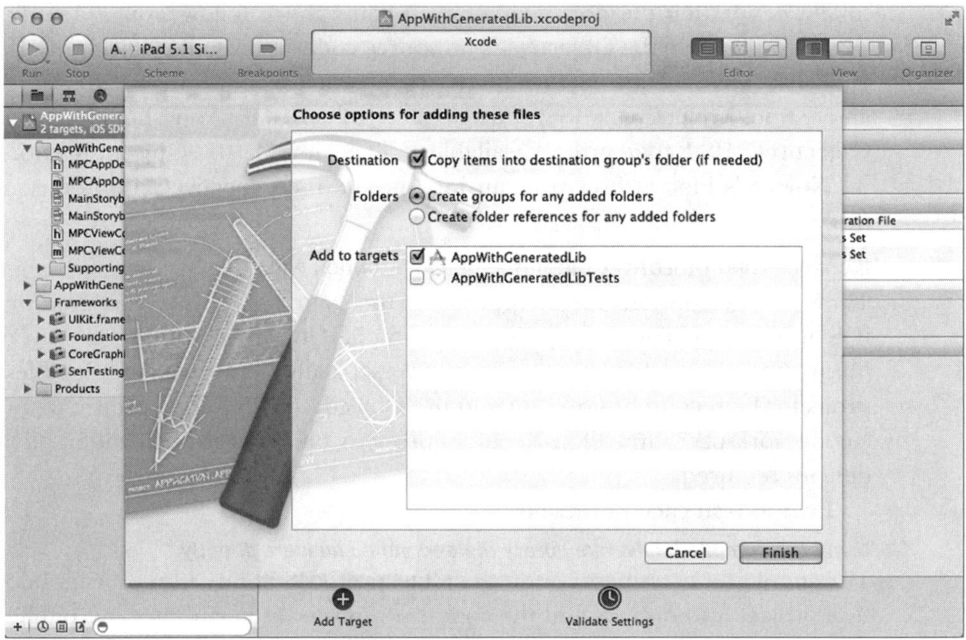

Figure 10.8 Adding the library to the Xcode project

6 The ObjectiveCMIS universal library has been added, and you can verify that the static library is available. Open the Target Summary view for your mobile application and find libObjectiveCMIS.a as a linked library, as shown in figure 10.9.

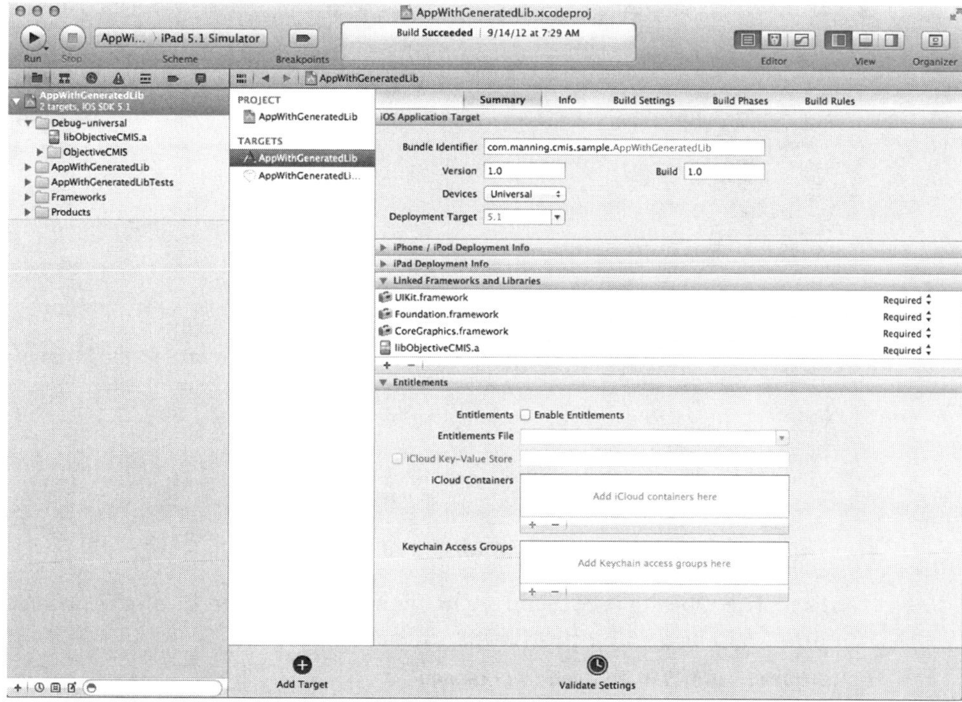

Figure 10.9 Verifying that the static library is available

7 Finally, you'll need to set the flags `-ObjC -all_load` in the Other Linker Flags setting available in the Target Build Settings (see figure 10.10). The `-ObjC` flag must be set because ObjectiveCMIS uses categories. The flag `-all_load` must be set to work around a linker bug in iOS applications (see Apple's Technical Q&A QA1490 for complete details—http://developer.apple.com/library/mac/#qa/qa1490/_index.html).

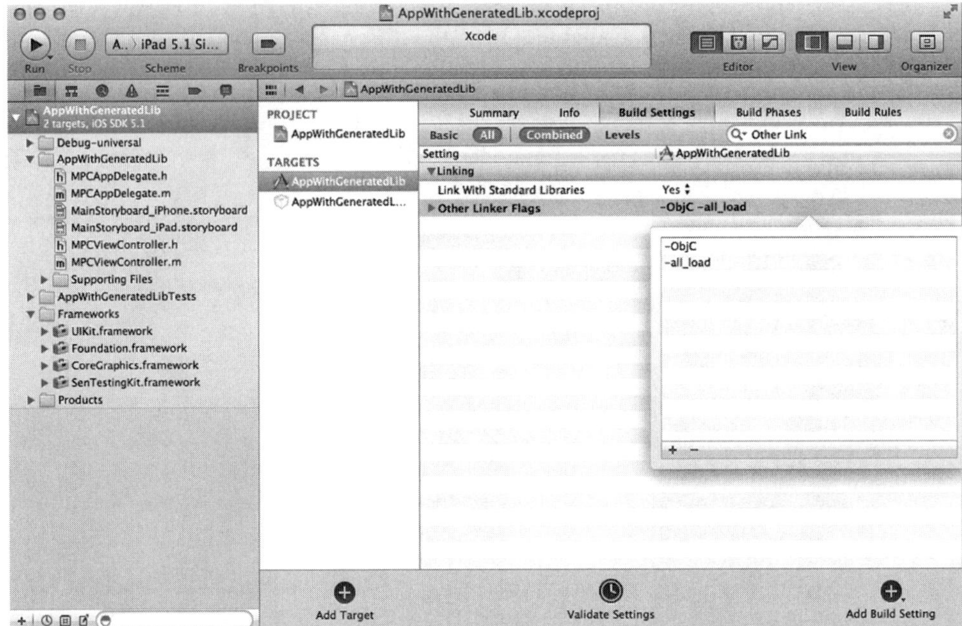

Figure 10.10 Setting the Other Linker Flags in build settings

That's it! The ObjectiveCMIS library has been incorporated into your project and you can now begin using ObjectiveCMIS!

Using ObjectiveCMIS in an Xcode workspace

You've seen the first option for making the ObjectiveCMIS library available to your iOS application. Now let's take a look at the second option, which is to add the entire ObjectiveCMIS source code project to your Xcode project. Xcode then builds ObjectiveCMIS and its dependencies when it builds your project. The advantage to this approach is that it gives you full access to the ObjectiveCMIS source code and any other files and projects added to the workspace. The disadvantage is that the ObjectiveCMIS project will be built more often than you might prefer, and it requires some additional configuration that isn't required for the first option.

For our purposes, the positives outweigh the negatives, so if you're following along, go ahead and incorporate ObjectiveCMIS into your workspace. To do that, follow these steps:

1 Open or create a workspace with your existing project. If you don't know about Xcode workspaces, Apple provides excellent documentation in the iOS Developer Library. Go to http://developer.apple.com/library/ios and search for *workspaces*.
2 Add the ObjectiveCMIS Xcode project to your workspace by adding the ObjectiveCMIS Xcode project file, ObjectiveCMIS.xcodeproj. ObjectiveCMIS

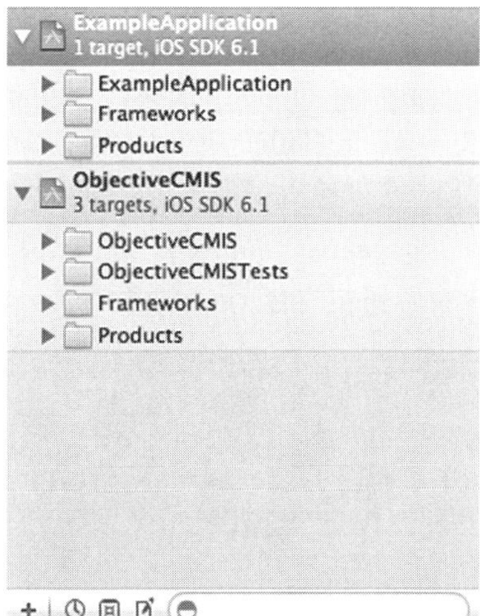

Figure 10.11 ObjectiveCMIS added to a workspace

should be added to the workspace as a sibling project to your other Xcode projects. Figure 10.11 shows the project navigator pane with ObjectiveCMIS and another Xcode project.

3 Add the libObjectiveCMIS.a library from the workspace, so that it's a linked library. After linking libObjectiveCMIS.a, the library should now be in your list of linked frameworks and libraries, as shown in figure 10.12.

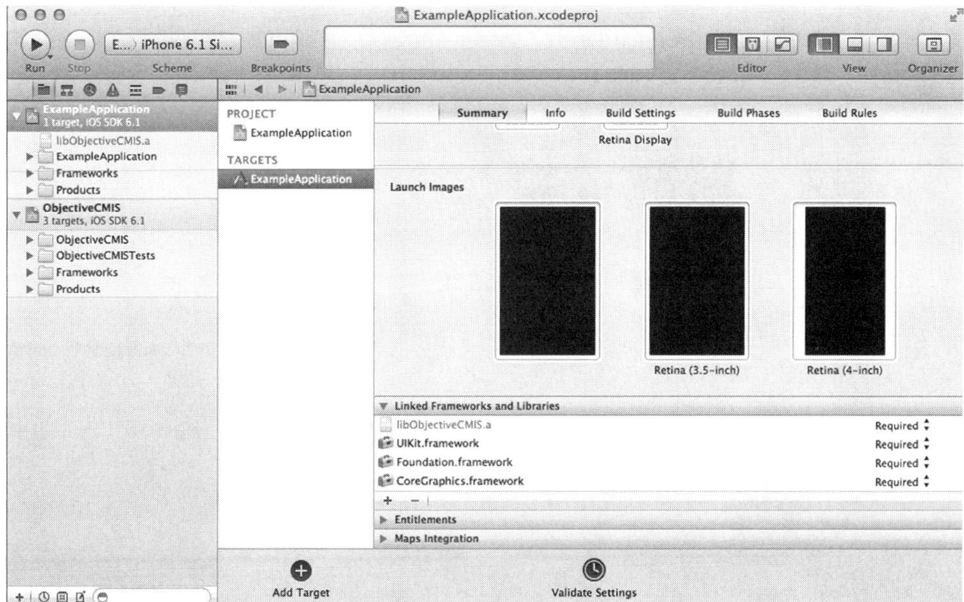

Figure 10.12 Summary view showing ObjectiveCMIS as a linked library

4 Configure the settings User Header Search Paths and Other Linker Flags in the Target Build Settings for the mobile application. You must configure these settings so that the target is able to locate the ObjectiveCMIS public headers.

- Configure the User Header Search Paths setting with value `$(BUILT_PRODUCTS_DIR)`, and make sure to check the recursive flag, as shown in figure 10.13.

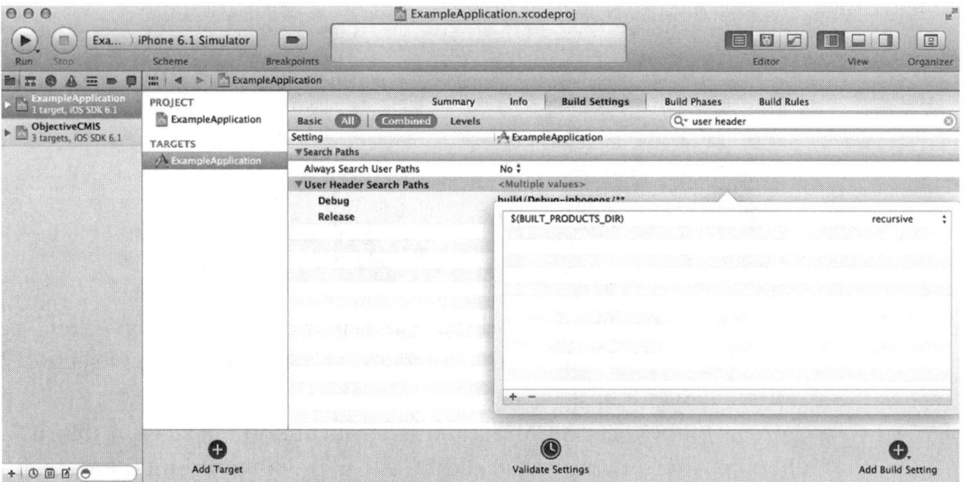

Figure 10.13 Setting User Header Search Paths

- Set Other Linker Flags by adding the following flags: `-ObjC -all_load`. These flags are required. Figure 10.14 shows the setting correctly configured.

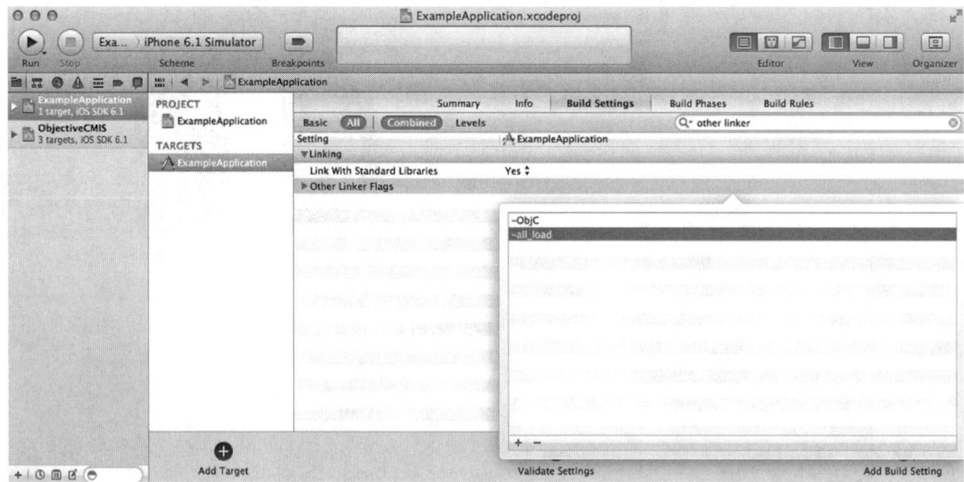

Figure 10.14 Setting Other Linker Flags

> **CAN'T GET OBJECTIVECMIS TO BUILD?** If you encounter a problem where ObjectiveCMIS fails to build, try updating the project scheme for the target that you're building so that the ObjectiveCMIS build target is explicitly built before your application is built.

Well done! If you've made it this far, you've successfully incorporated ObjectiveCMIS into your workspace. Now other targets within the workspace can leverage the ObjectiveCMIS library.

GENERATING THE OBJECTIVECMIS DOCUMENTATION

ObjectiveCMIS provides the capability to output Apple-like source code documentation that's fully indexed and browsable as an Xcode documentation set. That's because the ObjectiveCMIS project has a Documentation build target. However, if you want to generate the documentation, you must have the appledoc tool installed and available on your path. You can find instructions from the appledoc home page on GitHub at https://github.com/tomaz/appledoc.

It's probably a good idea to generate the documentation so you can use it later when you build The Blend's mobile application. Here's how:

1. If you don't have appledoc installed, download and install appledoc from GitHub as mentioned previously.
2. Run the Documentation target available in the ObjectiveCMIS Xcode project.
3. Once the Documentation target build completes, open the Xcode documentation and you should see the ObjectiveCMIS documentation, as shown in figure 10.15.

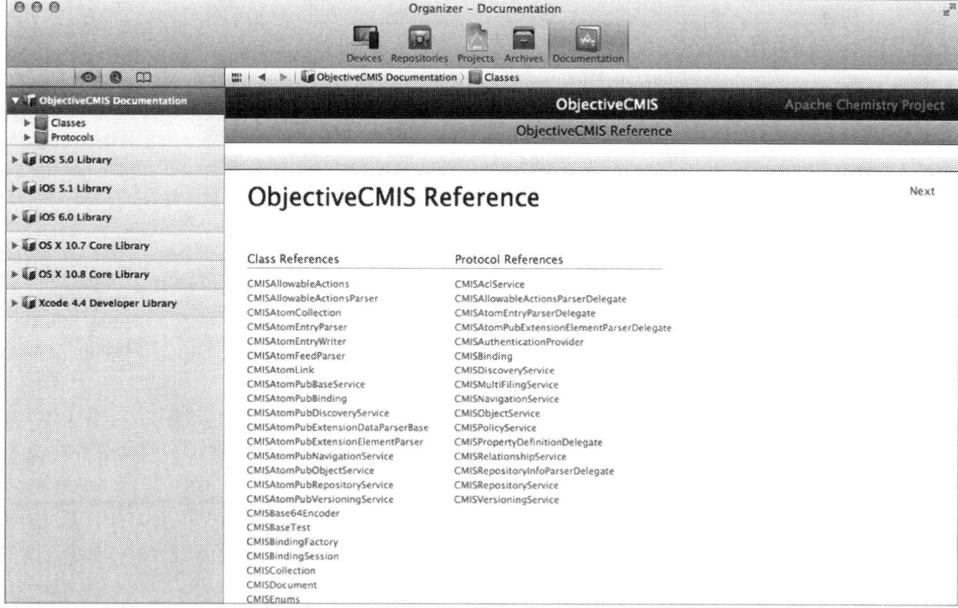

Figure 10.15 Browsing ObjectiveCMIS documentation in Xcode

Great! You've got the library set up in your Xcode workspace, and you have some documentation to refer to. You're now ready to begin developing a CMIS-based mobile app for iOS.

10.2.4 Using ObjectiveCMIS

Now that you've incorporated ObjectiveCMIS into your project, let's see how you can use ObjectiveCMIS to do something simple, like grabbing a session and retrieving a folder. Then we'll knock out the application.

CREATING A CMISSESSION

As discussed earlier in the section, the `CMISSession` object is the main entry point to interacting with a CMIS repository, just as it is in OpenCMIS. To create a `CMISSession`, you must first provide session parameters for the session. The next listing shows a simple scenario of setting up a `CMISSession` for the AtomPub binding.

Listing 10.3 Setting up a `CMISSession` for the AtomPub binding

```
CMISSessionParameters *sessionParams = [[CMISSessionParameters alloc]
  initWithBindingType:CMISBindingTypeAtomPub];                    <- Set up
sessionParams.atomPubUrl =                                           session
  [NSURL URLWithString:@"http://localhost:8080/service/atom"];       parameters
sessionParams.username = @"bogusUser";
sessionParams.password = @"bogusPassword";
sessionParams.repositoryId = @"repo1";

[CMISSession connectWithSessionParameters:sessionParams completionBlock:   <-

     ^(CMISSession *session, NSError *error)                    Connect using
     {                                                          those session
         if (nil == session)                                    parameters
         {
             // Error during authentication, handle gracefully
             if (error) {
                 NSLog(@"Failed to connect the session");
             }
         }
         else
         {
             // CMIS Session successfully connected
             self.cmisSession = session;                 <- Successfully
         }                                                  connected; store
     }];                                                    session for later use
/
```

Once you've got a session, you're standing in the CMIS hotel lobby (remember that analogy from chapter 9?). With what you know already, together with the documentation, you're probably good to go, but before building the app, let's look at the differences between the ObjectiveCMIS Object API and Binding API. Let's see how retrieving a folder and iterating over its children differs between the two.

RETRIEVING A FOLDER

Let's use ObjectiveCMIS to grab a folder and iterate over its children using the two different client APIs available in ObjectiveCMIS: the Object API and the Binding API. For both examples, assume that the `CMISSession` object you instantiated in listing 10.3 has been authenticated successfully and is still valid.

Object API

Using the Object API to get a folder is straightforward. Use `retrieveObject` on the `CMISSession` object. Once you have a handle on the `CMISFolder`, you can use the Object API to retrieve the folder's children, as shown in the next listing.

Listing 10.4 Getting the children of a folder

```
NSString *folderId = <some folder ObjectId>

[self.cmisSession retrieveObject:folderId completionBlock:      <-- Retrieve specified object
  ^(CMISObject *object, NSError *error)
  {
    if (nil == object) {
      // Handle Error
    }
    else {
      // Folder successfully retrieved, do something
      CMISFolder *aFolder = (CMISFolder *)object;            <-- Cast object to a CMISFolder
      [aFolder retrieveChildrenWithCompletionBlock:
      ^(CMISPagedResult *result, NSError *error)
      {
        if (nil == result) {
          // Handle error
        }
        else {
          for (CMISObject *childObject in result.resultArray)    <-- Iterate over paged result set
            {
              // retrieveChildren completion block
            }
      }
    }];
  }
}];
/
```

Binding API

Now let's see how you'd retrieve the same folder object using the Binding API. The Binding API deals with each of the CMIS services you learned about in chapter 2, so to get a folder and iterate over its children, the first step is to use the `getObject` service available on the Object Services to retrieve the folder object. The second step is to call `getChildren` on the Navigation Services to retrieve the children objects for the specified folder, shown next.

Listing 10.5 Using the Binding API to retrieve the children objects of a specific folder

```
void (^listChildrenObjects)(CMISObjectData *objectData,
  NSError *error) =
    ^(CMISObjectData *objectData, NSError *error)
    {
        if (nil == objectData) {
            // Handle error gracefully
            return;
        }

        [self.cmisSession.binding.navigationService
         retrieveChildren:objectData.identifier
         orderBy:nil
         filter:nil
         relationships:CMISIncludeRelationshipNone
         renditionFilter:nil
         includeAllowableActions:NO
         includePathSegment:NO
         skipCount:0
         maxItems:nil
         completionBlock:^(CMISObjectList *objectList, NSError *error) {
             if (nil == objectList) {
                 // Handle Error state
                 return;
             }

             for (CMISObjectData *childObjectData in
               objectList.objects) {
                 // Do something with the children
             }

         }];
    };

[self.cmisSession.binding.objectService retrieveObject:folderId//
                                               filter:nil
    relationships:CMISIncludeRelationshipNone
    includePolicyIds:NO
    renditionFilder:nil
    includeACL:NO
    includeAllowableActions:NO
    completionBlock:listChildrenObjects];
/
```

Create a completion block named listChildrenObjects that will list children objects.

Call the retrieveChildren (getChildren) method from within the listChildrenObjects completion block.

Iterate over the children objects in the completion block for RetrieveChildren.

Retrieve the specified object and provide the listChildrenObjects completion block.

That example was very basic, but it gives you a feel for the two APIs available in ObjectiveCMIS. It's time to move on to something a little more involved. You'll add an iOS app to The Blend.

10.2.5 *Try it—writing an iOS application to capture new tracks for The Blend*

Alright, it's time for a real-world example. Suppose that the artists using The Blend to create, share, and remix audio, video, and other artwork are happy, but they'd like more options to capture content and load it into the repository. Specifically, they want to be able to use their iPhones and iPads to record music or even cool sounds while they're out and about.

Let's take everything that you learned in this section and put it into action by creating a mobile application for The Blend's users. As luck would have it, some kind soul has created an audio capture application called "Blend Capture" and made it available as open source. But it isn't CMIS-aware. So we'll take that app and enhance it so that after a user captures audio on their mobile device, they can easily upload it to the CMIS repository used by The Blend. Sound cool? We think so too.

Before we begin, you must have The Blend web application and the InMemory Repository running on Tomcat. If you followed along in chapter 6, you're already good to go. If not, flip back to that chapter, get the base web application and repository working, and then come back.

> **DON'T FORGET TO RELOAD YOUR TEST DATA!** Remember that the InMemory Repository loses its data every time Tomcat restarts, so before you continue you might need to reload the test data. See chapter 6 if you forget how to do that.

For the remainder of this section, we'll assume that the InMemory CMIS Repository is running on the same ports you set up in chapter 6. As a reminder, the InMemory Repository should be available at http://localhost:8081/inmemory/ and The Blend web application is available at http://localhost:8080/the-blend/.

GETTING STARTED WITH THE BLEND CAPTURE XCODE PROJECT

Let's begin by opening up the Xcode workspace for the Blend Capture mobile application. To do that, follow these steps:

1. Unzip BlendCapture.zip to $IOS_DEV_HOME. After extracting the archive, you should find the folder $IOS_DEV_HOME/BlendCapture.
2. Open the Xcode workspace file found at $IOS_DEV_HOME/BlendCapture/BlendCaptureWorkspace.xcworkspace.
3. Xcode should now launch with the Blend Capture workspace and project available. The Xcode workspace will look like figure 10.16.

Now that you have the project open, you can see that the project uses Apple's AV Foundation framework for the audio capture and playback capabilities. The audio is captured using the AAC encoding, as the MP3 encoding is not available out of the box on iOS. As you look through the project, you'll see that the application is very simple—it's an iPhone application with a single view, nothing more.

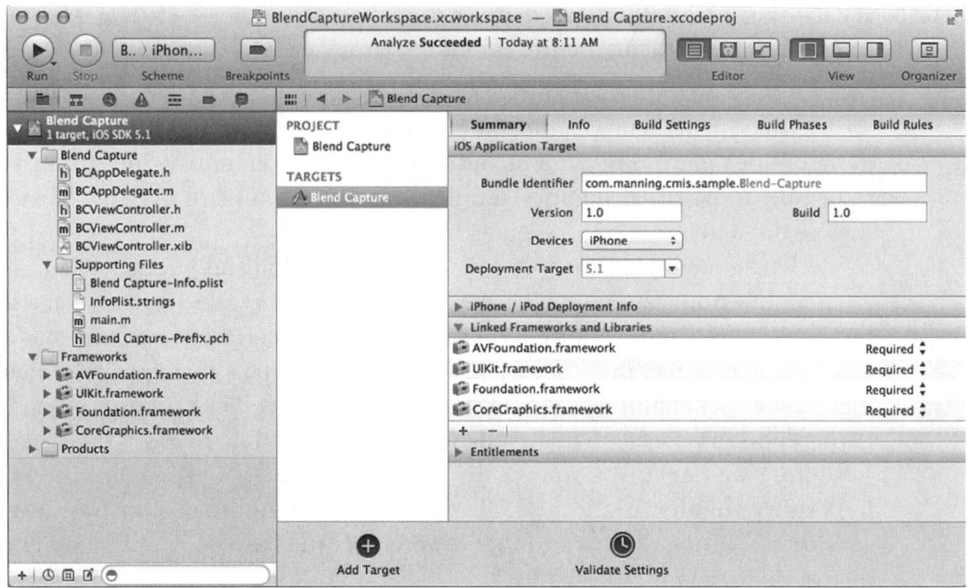

Figure 10.16 Blend Capture workspace and project

Go ahead and run the Blend Capture application in the iOS simulator. If everything builds successfully, your simulator should look like the one shown in figure 10.17.

Go ahead and play with the application. You should find that it's a very simple audio recorder that can play back the audio it most recently captured.

Figure 10.17 Blend Capture application running in the iOS simulator

Using ObjectiveCMIS to extend Blend Capture

Great! Now that you've explored the project and tested the application in the simulator, it's time to enhance the application so that it exposes the ability for the user to upload captured audio to The Blend's CMIS repository. You'll do the following:

- Incorporate ObjectiveCMIS into the project or workspace.
- Update the application so that it provides the user the ability to upload the audio that has been captured. You'll use ObjectiveCMIS to do the upload.

Incorporating ObjectiveCMIS

ObjectiveCMIS is a dependency for your project. You can either incorporate it using the same steps you followed earlier in section 10.2.3, or you can include ObjectiveC-MIS as a workspace project.

If you want to include ObjectiveCMIS as a workspace project, follow these steps:

1. Add the ObjectiveCMIS Xcode project to the workspace so that it's a sibling project to the Blend Capture project.
2. Add the Objective CMIS static library to the Blend Capture as a linked static library.
3. Update the User Header Search Paths setting so that it searches the `$(BUILT_PRODUCTS_DIR)` path recursively.
4. Add the flags `-ObjC -all_load` to the Other Linker Flags.

Enhancing Blend Capture to upload captured audio

Let's now go ahead and update the Blend Capture application so that it can be used to upload audio to The Blend application using ObjectiveCMIS. To provide this functionality, you'll need to add a new button to the view. This new button, when pressed, will attempt to upload the captured audio to the path /blend/Unsorted.

The following steps will walk you through the implementation:

1. Add a new `UIButtonIBOutlet` named `uploadButton` that has an `IBAction` linked to `-(IBAction)uploadButtonPressed`.
2. Update the nib file for the view controller by adding a new `UIButton` with the text `Upload to The Blend`, and then use interface builder to wire up the new `IBOutlet` and `IBAction` defined in the previous step. Thus, when the new `UIButton` receives a touch event, the `IBAction -uploadButtonPressed` will be messaged. The updated nib should look similar to figure 10.18.

Figure 10.18 Updated view showing The Blend upload button

Now that the view and view controller are wired up, you can implement the upload logic that will allow you to upload the captured audio to the CMIS server used by The Blend. Begin by initializing a `CMISSession` and retrieving the `cmis:objectId` for the folder /blend/Unsorted. The folder /blend/Unsorted will be the default location to which you upload the captured audio. The following listing implements this requirement in the `viewDidLoad` method of the view controller.

Listing 10.6 Determining the `objectId` of the target folder for the upload

```
CMISSessionParameters *sessionParams = [[CMISSessionParameters alloc]
  initWithBindingType:CMISBindingTypeAtomPub];
sessionParams.atomPubUrl =
  [NSURL URLWithString:@"http://localhost:8081/inmemory/atom"];
sessionParams.repositoryId = @"A1";

[CMISSession connectWithSessionParameters:sessionParams completionBlock
  ^(CMISSession *session, NSError *error)
  {
    if (nil == session)
    {
      // Handle Error
      if (error) {
        NSLog(@"Failed to connect session - %@",
          error.localizedDescription);
      }
    }
    else
    {
      self.cmisSession = session;

      // Authentication Success!
      [self.cmisSession retrieveObjectByPath:@"/blend/Unsorted"
        completionBlock:
      ^(CMISObject *object, NSError *error)
      {
        if (nil == object)
        {
          if (error) {
            NSLog(
              @"Failed to retrieve Folder Object by path: %@",
              error.localizedDescription);
          }
        }
        else
        {
          self.uploadFolderId = object.identifier;
        }
      }];
    }
  }];
/
```

Callouts: Create session parameters object; Initialize and authenticate CMISSession; Retrieve cmis:objectId for the folder at path /blend/Unsorted; Successfully retrieved folder for path /blend/Unsorted; store cmis:objectId for later

Now that you have the `cmis:objectId` for the Unsorted folder, you can implement the upload logic for the newly added `UIButton`. The upload logic should be implemented in the `uploadButtonPressed IBAction` method. The next listing shows an implementation of the upload logic using the ObjectiveCMIS object-oriented API.

Listing 10.7 Upload logic

```
- (void)uploadButtonPressed
{
    // Helper block to enable all buttons
    void (^reenableButtonsBlock)() = ^()
    {
        ... snip ...
    };

    void (^completionBlock)(NSString *objectId, NSError *error) =
    ^(NSString *objectId, NSError *error)
    {
        if (nil == objectId)
        {
            self.messageLabel.text = @"Upload Failed";
        }
        else
        {
            self.messageLabel.text = @"Upload Success";
        }

        reenableButtonsBlock();
    };

    // Disable and hide all buttons while upload is in progress
    ... snip ...

    // Update the message to inform the user
    // that an upload is in progress.
    self.messageLabel.text = @"Upload in Progress...";

    NSString *documentName =
      [NSString stringWithFormat:@"audio-captured-%f.aac",
      [[NSDate date] timeIntervalSince1970]];

    NSMutableDictionary *documentProperties =
      [NSMutableDictionary dictionary];
    [documentProperties setObject:documentName forKey:@"cmis:name"];
    [documentProperties setObject:@"cmis:document"
      forKey:@"cmis:objectTypeId"];

    [self.cmisSession
      createDocumentFromFilePath:self.capturedAudioFilePath
      mimeType:@"audio/aac"
      properties:documentProperties
      inFolder:self.uploadFolderId
      completionBlock:completionBlock
      progressBlock:NULL];
}
/
```

Annotations:
- Upload completion block
- Generate cmis:name for the uploaded audio file
- Set name and objectType for the document being created
- Create document

Now that you've enhanced the Blend Capture mobile application, test it against your CMIS repository used by The Blend. (If you weren't able to successfully enhance the Blend Capture mobile application, you can find an enhanced working version of the mobile application in the archive BlendCaptureEnhanced.zip).

To test it, follow these steps:

1. Capture some audio that you want to upload to The Blend.
2. Upload the audio to The Blend.
3. Open The Blend web application and navigate to the Unsorted directory.
4. If the upload was successful, you should find a new audio file in the Unsorted directory. Figure 10.19 shows two audio files that were captured and uploaded by the Blend Capture mobile application.

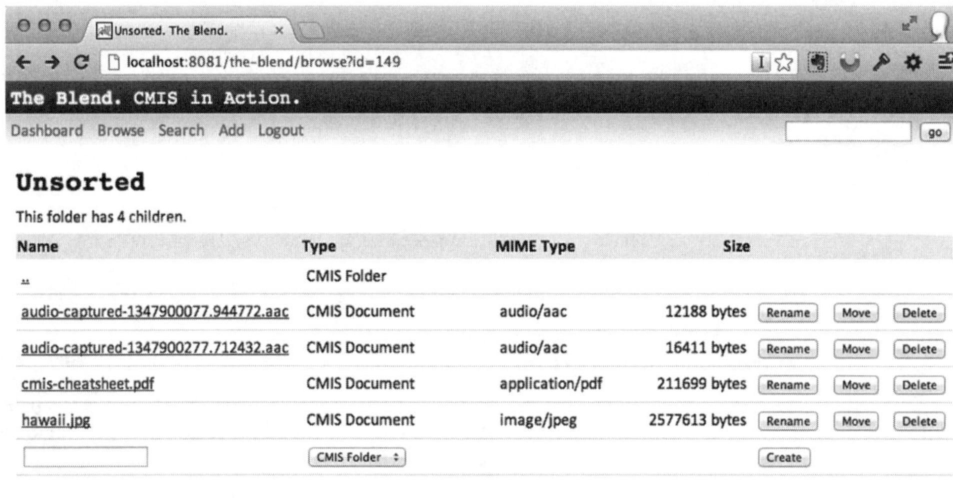

Figure 10.19 The two .aac files shown here were captured and uploaded by the Blend Capture iOS application.

In this section, you learned about ObjectiveCMIS, the new CMIS library for Objective-C and iOS. You should now have a fundamental overview of and the basic know-how for developing iOS applications using ObjectiveCMIS.

10.3 Summary

Android and iOS are the two dominant mobile platforms today. Regardless of which one is right for your solution, you saw in this chapter that applications on each platform can work with CMIS repositories. You saw that, in both cases, the libraries are fairly close ports of OpenCMIS, so a lot of what you've learned about OpenCMIS in earlier chapters applies to OpenCMIS for Android and for ObjectiveCMIS.

In the Android section, you saw that you can easily develop Android applications directly in Eclipse with minimal setup. These are the keys to success with OpenCMIS for Android:

- Use intents to share the CMIS session.
- Use a background thread to execute OpenCMIS code.
- Encapsulate your data in a higher-level object.

The iOS side is a little more involved in terms of setup and dependencies, and you have to use Objective-C, which is not that difficult for people who already know Java or C, but it requires a completely different toolchain. Hopefully, you saw that once you make that adjustment, writing a CMIS application for iOS is very similar to writing a Java application with OpenCMIS.

This also concludes part 2 of the book and our client-side programming examples. In part 3, we'll turn our attention to more advanced topics like bindings, security, performance considerations, and server-side implementations.

Part 3

Advanced topics

In this part of the book, we'll pick up the pace even further and take you through some of the thornier issues of CMIS development. Because this section is the most advanced, we'll make further assumptions about the extent of your technical background. You'll see this in the brevity of our background explanations for topics that are not specifically related to CMIS.

This part will start with a peek under the covers as we look at the wire protocol in chapter 11 (CMIS bindings), followed by the often-overlooked subject of security in chapter 12. In chapter 13, we'll cover performance issues. Finally, we'll give you a tour of the major parts involved in building your own CMIS server, leveraging OpenCMIS to make this process much easier, in chapter 14.

You may not need this level of information right away, but we think you'll find it helpful to look over, and then you can come back to it when needed.

11 CMIS bindings

This chapter covers

- The CMIS bindings: Web Services, AtomPub, and Browser
- Capturing CMIS traffic
- CMIS schema

So far you've become acquainted with the CMIS domain model and with APIs for several programming languages. But we haven't yet shown you how CMIS clients and CMIS repositories communicate with each other over the wire.

A big part of the CMIS specification describes how the CMIS domain model is mapped to the bytes that are transferred. These mappings are called *bindings*. CMIS 1.0 defines two bindings, the Web Services binding and the AtomPub binding; and CMIS 1.1 adds a third, the Browser binding.

The big advantage of using a CMIS library is that it hides most of the binding details. You don't need to know how your request is serialized into XML or JSON, and you don't need to know how to parse the response from the repository. Nevertheless, having a basic understanding of how the bindings work can help when you're debugging your application. It's also necessary when you're reading the following chapters about security and performance, because the different bindings have different strengths and characteristics.

For this chapter, you need a basic understanding of XML and JSON. You should also have some high-level understanding of HTTP, Web Services, SOAP, AtomPub, HTML, and JavaScript.

> **GETTING THE SPECIFICATIONS** If you haven't done so yet, now is the time to download the CMIS specifications:
>
> - CMIS 1.0: http://docs.oasis-open.org/cmis/CMIS/v1.0/
> - CMIS 1.1: http://docs.oasis-open.org/cmis/CMIS/v1.1/
>
> The specification document is available in an HTML version and a PDF version. The PDF version is the better choice because it contains a complete rendering of the document, including diagrams. The specification also includes schema files and a set of sample requests and responses for each binding. They're useful to have around as you read this chapter.

11.1 CMIS binding overview

Usually, the first question when we start talking about the bindings is, "Why are there three bindings and not just one?" CMIS has been designed to work in enterprise environments. It turned out to also work well in other scenarios—for example, over the internet—but the design focus was on enterprise environments.

Many companies invested in big and often expensive Web Services infrastructures a few years ago. They want to, and sometimes *have* to, use features such as authentication, logging, and auditing that they have in place. To be accepted in such an environment, CMIS had to speak Web Services and tie into these existing IT landscapes. Integrating a RESTful service into such an environment can be difficult, tedious, and expensive.

11.1.1 The RESTful trend

In spite of this long history, there has been a trend over the last few years to move away from Web Services and to use RESTful interfaces instead. CMIS also had to provide an answer for environments that banned Web Services and their complexity. It's debatable how RESTful the CMIS AtomPub binding is, but it follows REST principles and the AtomPub specification. As a result, any AtomPub client can interact with a CMIS repository. Today, the CMIS AtomPub binding is more popular than the Web Services binding.

11.1.2 The need for JavaScript support

After CMIS 1.0 was released, applications of all kinds emerged; CMIS worked well for desktop, mobile, and web applications. Only one scenario wasn't covered by the two bindings: consuming CMIS directly from a JavaScript application in a web browser turned out to be very difficult. If you've ever tried using Web Services from a JavaScript application, you know that it's problematic and not a fun experience. The AtomPub binding had two major issues. First, the XML parsers in some web browsers had major difficulties with XML namespaces. Second, AtomPub works by walking through links. For example, to get to the download link from a document, a client has to make several calls and follow the chain of links. Libraries like OpenCMIS avoid most of the calls by caching those links, but doing that in a stateless JavaScript application is a major effort and not a feasible approach.

CMIS 1.1 introduced the Browser binding for that reason. The Browser binding has been tailored for JavaScript applications in web browsers. It uses JSON and HTML forms for communication between application and repository. It turns out that this binding is more efficient, faster, and easier to implement than the other two bindings and has the potential to replace at least the AtomPub binding in the long run.

A CMIS-compliant repository must expose the Web Services and AtomPub bindings. Support for the Browser binding is optional, and it will take a while for most repositories to expose this new binding.

Before we dive into the details of each binding, let's first look at the traffic between a CMIS client and a CMIS repository. The next section explains how to capture the traffic.

11.1.3 Capturing CMIS traffic for inspection

The best way to get an impression of the CMIS bindings is to see them in action (as the book title implies). Because all CMIS bindings are based on HTTP, any HTTP debug proxy should be able to capture CMIS requests and responses as long as they aren't encrypted.

CAPTURE TOOLS If you don't already have a favorite capture tool in your programmer's toolbox, either of these will help you capture CMIS traffic:

- Fiddler (Windows)—www.fiddler2.com/fiddler2
- Charles (Windows, Mac OS, Linux)—www.charlesproxy.com

The CMIS client has to be configured to use the proxy. If you want to capture the traffic to and from the CMIS Workbench, open the Workbench's start script (`workbench.bat` or `workbench.sh`, depending on your OS) in a text editor and add the following parameters to the `JAVA_OPTS` environment variable:

```
-Dhttp.proxyHost=localhost -Dhttp.proxyPort=8888
```

The host and port values depend on your debug proxy setup. If you run the client and the repository on the same machine, make sure you don't use localhost as the host name in the CMIS binding URL. Use the name of your machine or your IP address instead. If you use localhost, the traffic isn't routed through your proxy (although in some cases you may find that localhost works).

After the Workbench is properly configured, the debug proxy shows you all of its HTTP requests and responses.

11.1.4 Try it—tracing requests from part 1

If you would like to dig in further for more detail, try rerunning any of the examples from part 1 under your new trace configuration. While doing so, try to identify which

API call maps to which HTTP call. Try changing the binding in the example, and see the differences across the wire.

The OpenCMIS client library can also log all URLs it calls when the log level is set to DEBUG. In the Workbench, you can see the log and change the log level by clicking the Log button on the toolbar. Doing so opens a log window with a drop-down menu at the bottom where you can change the log level. Try copying the logged URLs and opening them in a web browser.

If you don't want to set up a debug proxy, you can also use the request-recording facility of the InMemory Repository. Open the InMemory start script (run.bat or run.sh) in a text editor, and find this parameter:

```
-Dcmis.server.record=false
```

Change the value to true, and restart the server.

Doing so creates a directory named *record* in the server directory. Each request or response from this point on is written to a separate file in that location. The InMemory server applies some XML and JSON formatting on output, so these files don't exactly reflect what is sent over the wire. But the formatted files are easier to read than the real (raw) traffic.

The next sections explain in more detail what you'll observe in that output.

11.2 A close look at the three bindings

For space considerations, we can't cover all aspects of the three CMIS bindings in this book. That would require a full book itself. But the following sections provide the basics and entry points that will make you familiar enough to solve most problems. Note that each subsection gives you an example of what that binding looks like over the wire. Refer to the CMIS specification for the full normative details.

11.2.1 The Web Services binding

The Web Services binding is what you probably expected. It maps CMIS operations directly to SOAP calls.

This binding covers the entire CMIS specification. That is, everything defined in the specification can be done with this binding. In addition to the operation parameters defined in the specification, some operations have an extra extension parameter. This parameter lets you send and receive extra, repository-specific data. The other bindings have different means to add extra data. There's also a way to add binding-agnostic extensions. We'll explain those when we talk about the CMIS schema a bit later in this chapter.

THE NINE WEB SERVICES AND ASSOCIATED WSDL The CMIS specification divides all operations into nine different services. This is reflected in the CMIS Web Services Description Language (WSDL; www.w3.org/TR/wsdl). For these services, nine different endpoints are defined. For the sake of simplicity, most repositories have only one WSDL that consolidates all these services, but a few have one WSDL per service.

MTOM ENCODING

All communications using the CMIS Web Services binding must be Message Transmission Optimization Mechanism (MTOM) encoded. MTOM (www.w3.org/TR/soap12-mtom/) defines how binary data is attached to SOAP messages. The CMIS specification defines that MTOM must also be used for operations and services that don't transport content.

Web Services tools should be able to generate stubs from the CMIS WSDL, but in some cases you have to manually enable MTOM support for all operations. If you're familiar with SOAP and Web Services, there shouldn't be any surprises, except for the following: Many Web Services toolkits aren't designed to handle big messages that contain content and may load them into main memory. That can be fatal if the document you want to send or receive is bigger than available memory or if the toolkit discards the request due to its size. Libraries like OpenCMIS are crafted to avoid loading messages to main memory and can handle documents of arbitrary size when this binding is used.

EXCEPTIONS IN WEB SERVICES

SOAP faults indicate CMIS exceptions. They must include the type of the exception and a message. They also contain an error code (a number), which is repository-specific and not used by many repositories. The exception types map to the exception types in the CMIS domain model and consequently map to Java exceptions in OpenCMIS and .NET exceptions in DotCMIS.

One of the biggest challenges with the Web Services binding is user authentication. We'll cover that in chapter 12, because it's a subject worthy of deeper discussion.

EXAMPLE OF A GETOBJECTS RESPONSE OVER THE WIRE

Listing 11.1 shows a complete example of a typical `getObjects` call to retrieve a document. Note that we inserted lots of extra page breaks to accommodate book formatting restrictions, so you can ignore those. Remember that these responses can be void of any line breaks in their raw transmitted form. As you examine the listing, note the length of these XML responses for comparison to the length of the JSON responses you'll see later.

Listing 11.1 Example of an XML response for a typical `getObjects` request

```
<?xml version="1.0" encoding="UTF-8"?>
<S:Envelope xmlns:S="http://schemas.xmlsoap.org/soap/envelope/">
  <S:Body>
    <ns2:getObjectResponse
    xmlns="http://docs.oasis-open.org/ns/cmis/core/200908/"
    xmlns:ns2="http://docs.oasis-open.org/ns/cmis/messaging/200908/">
      <ns2:object>
        <properties>
          <propertyBoolean
           queryName="cmis:isLatestMajorVersion"
           displayName="Is Latest Major Version"
           localName="cmis:isLatestMajorVersion"
```

Object's properties are listed starting here

```
 propertyDefinitionId="cmis:isLatestMajorVersion">
    <value>true</value>
</propertyBoolean>
<propertyInteger queryName="cmis:contentStreamLength"
 displayName="Content Length"
 localName="cmis:contentStreamLength"
 propertyDefinitionId="cmis:contentStreamLength">
    <value>395</value>
</propertyInteger>
<propertyString queryName="cmis:contentStreamId"
 displayName="Stream Id" localName="cmis:contentStreamId"
 propertyDefinitionId="cmis:contentStreamId"/>
<propertyId queryName="cmis:objectTypeId"
 displayName="Type-Id" localName="cmis:objectTypeId"
 propertyDefinitionId="cmis:objectTypeId">
    <value>cmisbook:text</value>
</propertyId>
<propertyString
 queryName="cmis:versionSeriesCheckedOutBy"
 displayName="Checked Out By"
 localName="cmis:versionSeriesCheckedOutBy"
 propertyDefinitionId="cmis:versionSeriesCheckedOutBy"/>
<propertyId queryName="cmis:versionSeriesCheckedOutId"
 displayName="Checked Out Id"
 localName="cmis:versionSeriesCheckedOutId"
 propertyDefinitionId="cmis:versionSeriesCheckedOutId"/>
<propertyString queryName="cmisbook:author"
 displayName="Author" localName="author"
 propertyDefinitionId="cmisbook:author"/>
<propertyString queryName="cmis:name" displayName="Name"
 localName="cmis:name" propertyDefinitionId="cmis:name">
    <value>welcome.txt</value>
</propertyString>
<propertyString queryName="cmis:contentStreamMimeType"
 displayName="Mime Type"
 localName="cmis:contentStreamMimeType"
 propertyDefinitionId="cmis:contentStreamMimeType">
    <value>text/plain</value>
</propertyString>
<propertyId queryName="cmis:versionSeriesId"
 displayName="Version Series Id"
 localName="cmis:versionSeriesId"
 propertyDefinitionId="cmis:versionSeriesId">
    <value>162</value>
</propertyId>
<propertyDateTime queryName="cmis:creationDate"
 displayName="Creation Date"
 localName="cmis:creationDate"
 propertyDefinitionId="cmis:creationDate">
    <value>2012-11-17T19:21:04.169Z</value>
</propertyDateTime>
<propertyString queryName="cmis:changeToken"
 displayName="Change Token"
 localName="cmis:changeToken"
 propertyDefinitionId="cmis:changeToken">
```

MIME type of content on this document is text/plain

```
        <value>1353180064169</value>
    </propertyString>
    <propertyString queryName="cmis:versionLabel"
     displayName="Version Label"
     localName="cmis:versionLabel"
     propertyDefinitionId="cmis:versionLabel">
        <value>V 1.0</value>
    </propertyString>
    <propertyBoolean queryName="cmis:isLatestVersion"
     displayName="Is Latest Version"
     localName="cmis:isLatestVersion"
     propertyDefinitionId="cmis:isLatestVersion">
        <value>true</value>
    </propertyBoolean>
    <propertyBoolean
     queryName="cmis:isVersionSeriesCheckedOut"
     displayName="Checked Out"
     localName="cmis:isVersionSeriesCheckedOut"
     propertyDefinitionId="cmis:isVersionSeriesCheckedOut">
        <value>false</value>
    </propertyBoolean>
    <propertyString queryName="cmis:lastModifiedBy"
     displayName="Modified By"
     localName="cmis:lastModifiedBy"
     propertyDefinitionId="cmis:lastModifiedBy">
        <value>system</value>
    </propertyString>
    <propertyString queryName="cmis:createdBy"
     displayName="Created By" localName="cmis:createdBy"
     propertyDefinitionId="cmis:createdBy">
        <value>system</value>
    </propertyString>
    <propertyString queryName="cmis:checkinComment"
     displayName="Checkin Comment"
     localName="cmis:checkinComment"
     propertyDefinitionId="cmis:checkinComment"/>
    <propertyId queryName="cmis:objectId"
     displayName="Object Id"
     localName="cmis:objectId"
     propertyDefinitionId="cmis:objectId">
        <value>161</value>
    </propertyId>
    <propertyBoolean queryName="cmis:isMajorVersion"
     displayName="Is Major Version"
     localName="cmis:isMajorVersion"
     propertyDefinitionId="cmis:isMajorVersion">
        <value>true</value>
    </propertyBoolean>
    <propertyBoolean queryName="cmis:isImmutable"
     displayName="Immutable" localName="cmis:isImmutable"
     propertyDefinitionId="cmis:isImmutable">
        <value>false</value>
    </propertyBoolean>
    <propertyId queryName="cmis:baseTypeId"
     displayName="Base-Type-Id" localName="cmis:baseTypeId"
```

```
   propertyDefinitionId="cmis:baseTypeId">
      <value>cmis:document</value>
  </propertyId>
  <propertyString queryName="cmis:contentStreamFileName"
   displayName="File Name"
   localName="cmis:contentStreamFileName"
   propertyDefinitionId="cmis:contentStreamFileName">
      <value>welcome.txt</value>
  </propertyString>
  <propertyDateTime queryName="cmis:lastModificationDate"
   displayName="Modification Date"
   localName="cmis:lastModificationDate"
   propertyDefinitionId="cmis:lastModificationDate">
      <value>2012-11-17T19:21:04.169Z</value>
  </propertyDateTime>
</properties>
```

Allowable actions for the document

```
<allowableActions>
  <canDeleteObject>true</canDeleteObject>
  <canUpdateProperties>true</canUpdateProperties>
  <canGetFolderTree>false</canGetFolderTree>
  <canGetProperties>true</canGetProperties>
  <canGetObjectRelationships>false
   </canGetObjectRelationships>
  <canGetObjectParents>true</canGetObjectParents>
  <canGetFolderParent>false</canGetFolderParent>
  <canGetDescendants>false</canGetDescendants>
  <canMoveObject>true</canMoveObject>
  <canDeleteContentStream>true</canDeleteContentStream>
  <canCheckOut>true</canCheckOut>
  <canCancelCheckOut>false</canCancelCheckOut>
  <canCheckIn>false</canCheckIn>
  <canSetContentStream>false</canSetContentStream>
  <canGetAllVersions>true</canGetAllVersions>
  <canAddObjectToFolder>true</canAddObjectToFolder>
  <canRemoveObjectFromFolder>true
   </canRemoveObjectFromFolder>
  <canGetContentStream>true</canGetContentStream>
  <canApplyPolicy>false</canApplyPolicy>
  <canGetAppliedPolicies>false</canGetAppliedPolicies>
  <canRemovePolicy>false</canRemovePolicy>
  <canGetChildren>false</canGetChildren>
  <canCreateDocument>false</canCreateDocument>
  <canCreateFolder>false</canCreateFolder>
  <canCreateRelationship>false</canCreateRelationship>
  <canDeleteTree>false</canDeleteTree>
  <canGetRenditions>false</canGetRenditions>
  <canGetACL>false</canGetACL>
  <canApplyACL>false</canApplyACL>
</allowableActions>
<acl>
  <permission>
      <principal>
          <principalId>anyone</principalId>
      </principal>
      <permission>cmis:all</permission>
```

```
                <direct>true</direct>
              </permission>
            </acl>
             <policyIds/>
          </ns2:object>
        </ns2:getObjectResponse>
      </S:Body>
    </S:Envelope>
```

11.2.2 The AtomPub binding

The AtomPub binding is built on the AtomPub specification (http://tools.ietf.org/html/rfc5023). AtomPub was mainly designed for publishing and simple editing of resources. The CMIS specification extends AtomPub to support features like hierarchies, versioning, renditions, permissions, and so on.

The AtomPub binding follows the REST paradigm by using the HTTP methods `GET`, `POST`, `PUT`, and `DELETE` in the following manner:

- `GET` requests fetch data.
- `POST` requests create new objects.
- `PUT` requests update data and objects.
- `DELETE` requests remove objects.

This binding covers most of the CMIS specification. Note, though, that it doesn't support the `createDocumentFromSource` operation. Other unsupported operations such as `getRenditions` are implicitly covered by `getObject`. There are also a few values this binding doesn't return. If you need details, refer to the AtomPub section in the official CMIS specification. The operation `applyACL` works slightly different from the description in the CMIS domain model; we'll cover the details in chapter 12. The specification also doesn't define how the filename (`cmis:contentStreamFileName`) can be set with this binding when a document is created. OpenCMIS and DotCMIS add an extra `<filename>` tag to the document creation request. Note that this isn't part of the CMIS standard but is understood by all OpenCMIS-based servers.

Exceptions in AtomPub

Exceptions are expressed by HTTP status codes. Unfortunately, some exceptions share the same status code. For example, a constraint exception and a versioning exception aren't distinguishable by a CMIS client. Therefore, the OpenCMIS server framework sends additional information that clients can use to figure out the right exception type. This isn't part of the CMIS standard, but the OpenCMIS and the DotCMIS client libraries interpret this additional information, if they're present; thus, this is more of a recommendation at this point.

The AtomPub service document and URL templates

The entry point for CMIS clients is the service document. This XML document lists all available repositories, describes their capabilities, and provides URLs and URL templates for Atom collections, feeds, and entries. A CMIS client can navigate from here, for example, to the root folder or the types collection. The URL templates allow clients to directly access the Atom entry of a CMIS object by its ID or its path.

Let's assume the URL template to get an object by ID looks like this:

```
http://example.com/repository/id?id={id}&filter={filter}
          &includeAllowableActions={includeAllowableActions}
          &includeACL={includeACL}
          &includePolicyIds={includePolicyIds}
          &includeRelationships={includeRelationships}
          &renditionFilter={renditionFilter}
```

The parts in curly brackets have to be replaced by the client with parameter values. If a client doesn't provide a value for a parameter (that is, it sends an empty string), the repository has to assume the default value for this parameter, which is defined in the specification.

Let's look at a specific example. To select the document with the object ID 123456 with all default parameter values, the client must generate this URL:

```
http://example.com/repository/id?id=123456
          &filter=&includeAllowableActions=&includeACL=&
          includePolicyIds=&includeRelationships=&renditionFilter=
```

The repository returns an Atom entry with the details of this document. (See the example in listing 11.2.)

AtomPub links

Most CMIS operations aren't directly accessible from the service document. For example, to access the content of a document, the client must first get the document's Atom entry. The Atom entry contains a link to the content. What this content link looks like is repository-specific and can't be guessed by the client (and therefore must be treated by clients as opaque). That is, two HTTP calls are necessary to access the content. Libraries like OpenCMIS cache these links and drastically reduce the number of repeat calls to the repository.

If you know AtomPub, you're already familiar with CMIS requests and responses. You'll notice a few additional CMIS-specific links, though. You can look them up in the specification, but most of them are self-explanatory. You might also notice the XML namespace `http://docs.oasis-open.org/ns/cmis/restatom/200908/`, which is often used with the namespace prefix `cmisra`. XML tags with this namespace encapsulate CMIS-specific data structures, which are defined in the CMIS XML schema. We'll talk about this schema a bit later in this chapter.

CRUD operations (create, read, update, and delete)

To update properties or delete an object, the client has to get the Atom entry and use the URL of the `self` link in the entry to make an HTTP `PUT` (or, respectively, an HTTP `DELETE`) request. The payload of the HTTP `PUT` request is an Atom entry that contains all the properties that should be updated.

To create an object, the client must send an HTTP `POST` request either to the URL of the prospective parent folder or to the Unfiled Collection if the object shouldn't be filed. (You can find the URL of the Unfiled Collection in the service document.) The payload of the HTTP POST request is an Atom entry that describes the new object. If the object is a document, the content can optionally be embedded as a Base64-encoded string into this entry to prevent the need for a second PUT request dedicated to sending the binary content.

Clients and repositories can extend an Atom entry with additional data that is specified neither in Atom nor in the CMIS specification. For example, a repository could expose a link in an Atom entry to a feature that is repository-specific. If a client or a repository doesn't understand such an extension, it should ignore it. We'll talk more about extensions in the upcoming schema section. Listing 11.2 shows the AtomPub version of the same response we showed you for Web Services in listing 11.1.

Listing 11.2 Example of an XML response for a typical `getObjects` request (AtomPub)

```
<?xml version="1.0" encoding="UTF-8"?>
<atom:entry xmlns:atom="http://www.w3.org/2005/Atom"
   xmlns:cmis="http://docs.oasis-open.org/ns/cmis/core/200908/"
   xmlns:cmisra="http://docs.oasis-open.org/ns/cmis/restatom/200908/"
   xmlns:app="http://www.w3.org/2007/app">
   <atom:author>
     <atom:name>system</atom:name>
   </atom:author>
   <atom:id>http://chemistry.apache.org/MTYx</atom:id>
   <atom:published>2012-11-17T19:21:04Z</atom:published>
   <atom:title>welcome.txt</atom:title>
   <app:edited>2012-11-17T19:21:04Z</app:edited>
   <atom:updated>2012-11-17T19:21:04Z</atom:updated>
   <atom:content
     src="http://localhost:8081/inmemory/atom/A1/content/welcome.txt
       ?id=161" type="text/plain"/>
   <cmisra:object
    xmlns:ns3="http://docs.oasis-open.org/ns/cmis/messaging/200908/">
     <cmis:properties>
      <cmis:propertyBoolean
         queryName="cmis:isLatestMajorVersion"
         displayName="Is Latest Major Version"
         localName="cmis:isLatestMajorVersion"
         propertyDefinitionId="cmis:isLatestMajorVersion">
           <cmis:value>true</cmis:value>
      </cmis:propertyBoolean>
      <cmis:propertyInteger queryName="cmis:contentStreamLength"
         displayName="Content Length"
         localName="cmis:contentStreamLength"
         propertyDefinitionId="cmis:contentStreamLength">
           <cmis:value>395</cmis:value>
      </cmis:propertyInteger>
      <cmis:propertyString queryName="cmis:contentStreamId"
         displayName="Stream Id" localName="cmis:contentStreamId"
         propertyDefinitionId="cmis:contentStreamId"/>
      <cmis:propertyId queryName="cmis:objectTypeId"
         displayName="Type-Id" localName="cmis:objectTypeId"
         propertyDefinitionId="cmis:objectTypeId">
```

First big difference from Web Services example: includes Atom (http://www.w3.org/2005/Atom), APP (www.w3.org/2007/app), and CMIS restatom (http://docs.oasis-open.org/ns/cmis/restatom/200908/) namespaces

Those versed in ATOM see familiar elements like atom:author

CMIS object starts here with all its properties up first

```
    <cmis:value>cmisbook:text</cmis:value>
</cmis:propertyId>
<cmis:propertyString queryName="cmis:versionSeriesCheckedOutBy"
   displayName="Checked Out By"
   localName="cmis:versionSeriesCheckedOutBy"
   propertyDefinitionId="cmis:versionSeriesCheckedOutBy"/>
<cmis:propertyId queryName="cmis:versionSeriesCheckedOutId"
   displayName="Checked Out Id"
   localName="cmis:versionSeriesCheckedOutId"
   propertyDefinitionId="cmis:versionSeriesCheckedOutId"/>
<cmis:propertyString queryName="cmisbook:author"
   displayName="Author" localName="author"
   propertyDefinitionId="cmisbook:author"/>
<cmis:propertyString queryName="cmis:name" displayName="Name"
   localName="cmis:name" propertyDefinitionId="cmis:name">
    <cmis:value>welcome.txt</cmis:value>
</cmis:propertyString>
<cmis:propertyString queryName="cmis:contentStreamMimeType"
   displayName="Mime Type" localName="cmis:contentStreamMimeType"
   propertyDefinitionId="cmis:contentStreamMimeType">
    <cmis:value>text/plain</cmis:value>
</cmis:propertyString>
<cmis:propertyId queryName="cmis:versionSeriesId"
   displayName="Version Series Id"
   localName="cmis:versionSeriesId"
   propertyDefinitionId="cmis:versionSeriesId">
    <cmis:value>162</cmis:value>
</cmis:propertyId>
<cmis:propertyDateTime queryName="cmis:creationDate"
   displayName="Creation Date"
   localName="cmis:creationDate"
   propertyDefinitionId="cmis:creationDate">
    <cmis:value>2012-11-17T19:21:04.169Z</cmis:value>
</cmis:propertyDateTime>
<cmis:propertyString queryName="cmis:changeToken"
   displayName="Change Token" localName="cmis:changeToken"
   propertyDefinitionId="cmis:changeToken">
    <cmis:value>1353180064169</cmis:value>
</cmis:propertyString>
<cmis:propertyString queryName="cmis:versionLabel"
   displayName="Version Label" localName="cmis:versionLabel"
   propertyDefinitionId="cmis:versionLabel">
    <cmis:value>V 1.0</cmis:value>
</cmis:propertyString>
<cmis:propertyBoolean queryName="cmis:isLatestVersion"
   displayName="Is Latest Version"
   localName="cmis:isLatestVersion"
   propertyDefinitionId="cmis:isLatestVersion">
    <cmis:value>true</cmis:value>
</cmis:propertyBoolean>
<cmis:propertyBoolean queryName="cmis:isVersionSeriesCheckedOut"
   displayName="Checked Out"
   localName="cmis:isVersionSeriesCheckedOut"
   propertyDefinitionId="cmis:isVersionSeriesCheckedOut">
    <cmis:value>false</cmis:value>
```

```
  </cmis:propertyBoolean>
  <cmis:propertyString queryName="cmis:lastModifiedBy"
     displayName="Modified By" localName="cmis:lastModifiedBy"
     propertyDefinitionId="cmis:lastModifiedBy">
      <cmis:value>system</cmis:value>
  </cmis:propertyString>
  <cmis:propertyString queryName="cmis:createdBy"
     displayName="Created By" localName="cmis:createdBy"
     propertyDefinitionId="cmis:createdBy">
      <cmis:value>system</cmis:value>
  </cmis:propertyString>
  <cmis:propertyString queryName="cmis:checkinComment"
     displayName="Checkin Comment" localName="cmis:checkinComment"
     propertyDefinitionId="cmis:checkinComment"/>
  <cmis:propertyId queryName="cmis:objectId"
     displayName="Object Id" localName="cmis:objectId"
     propertyDefinitionId="cmis:objectId">
      <cmis:value>161</cmis:value>
  </cmis:propertyId>
  <cmis:propertyBoolean queryName="cmis:isMajorVersion"
     displayName="Is Major Version" localName="cmis:isMajorVersion"
     propertyDefinitionId="cmis:isMajorVersion">
      <cmis:value>true</cmis:value>
  </cmis:propertyBoolean>
  <cmis:propertyBoolean queryName="cmis:isImmutable"
     displayName="Immutable" localName="cmis:isImmutable"
     propertyDefinitionId="cmis:isImmutable">
      <cmis:value>false</cmis:value>
  </cmis:propertyBoolean>
  <cmis:propertyId queryName="cmis:baseTypeId"
     displayName="Base-Type-Id" localName="cmis:baseTypeId"
     propertyDefinitionId="cmis:baseTypeId">
      <cmis:value>cmis:document</cmis:value>
  </cmis:propertyId>
  <cmis:propertyString queryName="cmis:contentStreamFileName"
     displayName="File Name" localName="cmis:contentStreamFileName"
     propertyDefinitionId="cmis:contentStreamFileName">
      <cmis:value>welcome.txt</cmis:value>
  </cmis:propertyString>
  <cmis:propertyDateTime queryName="cmis:lastModificationDate"
     displayName="Modification Date"
     localName="cmis:lastModificationDate"
     propertyDefinitionId="cmis:lastModificationDate">
      <cmis:value>2012-11-17T19:21:04.169Z</cmis:value>
  </cmis:propertyDateTime>
 </cmis:properties>
 <cmis:allowableActions>                                  <- AllowableActions start here
  <cmis:canDeleteObject>true</cmis:canDeleteObject>
  <cmis:canUpdateProperties>true</cmis:canUpdateProperties>
  <cmis:canGetFolderTree>false</cmis:canGetFolderTree>
  <cmis:canGetProperties>true</cmis:canGetProperties>
  <cmis:canGetObjectRelationships>false
     </cmis:canGetObjectRelationships>
  <cmis:canGetObjectParents>true</cmis:canGetObjectParents>
  <cmis:canGetFolderParent>false</cmis:canGetFolderParent>
```

```
    <cmis:canGetDescendants>false</cmis:canGetDescendants>
    <cmis:canMoveObject>true</cmis:canMoveObject>
    <cmis:canDeleteContentStream>true</cmis:canDeleteContentStream>
    <cmis:canCheckOut>true</cmis:canCheckOut>
    <cmis:canCancelCheckOut>false</cmis:canCancelCheckOut>
    <cmis:canCheckIn>false</cmis:canCheckIn>
    <cmis:canSetContentStream>false</cmis:canSetContentStream>
    <cmis:canGetAllVersions>true</cmis:canGetAllVersions>
    <cmis:canAddObjectToFolder>true</cmis:canAddObjectToFolder>
    <cmis:canRemoveObjectFromFolder>true
       </cmis:canRemoveObjectFromFolder>
    <cmis:canGetContentStream>true</cmis:canGetContentStream>
    <cmis:canApplyPolicy>false</cmis:canApplyPolicy>
    <cmis:canGetAppliedPolicies>false</cmis:canGetAppliedPolicies>
    <cmis:canRemovePolicy>false</cmis:canRemovePolicy>
    <cmis:canGetChildren>false</cmis:canGetChildren>
    <cmis:canCreateDocument>false</cmis:canCreateDocument>
    <cmis:canCreateFolder>false</cmis:canCreateFolder>
    <cmis:canCreateRelationship>false</cmis:canCreateRelationship>
    <cmis:canDeleteTree>false</cmis:canDeleteTree>
    <cmis:canGetRenditions>false</cmis:canGetRenditions>
    <cmis:canGetACL>false</cmis:canGetACL>
    <cmis:canApplyACL>false</cmis:canApplyACL>
  </cmis:allowableActions>
  <cmis:acl>
     <cmis:permission>
      <cmis:principal>
        <cmis:principalId>anyone</cmis:principalId>
      </cmis:principal>
      <cmis:permission>cmis:all</cmis:permission>
      <cmis:direct>true</cmis:direct>
     </cmis:permission>
  </cmis:acl>
  <cmis:policyIds/>
</cmisra:object>
<atom:link rel="service"
   href="http://localhost:8081/inmemory/atom/A1?repositoryId=A1"
   type="application/atomsvc+xml"/>
<atom:link rel="self"
   href="http://localhost:8081/inmemory/atom/A1/entry?id=161"
   type="application/atom+xml;type=entry" cmisra:id="161"/>
<atom:link rel="enclosure"
   href="http://localhost:8081/inmemory/atom/A1/entry?id=161"
   type="application/atom+xml;type=entry"/>
<atom:link rel="edit"
   href="http://localhost:8081/inmemory/atom/A1/entry?id=161"
   type="application/atom+xml;type=entry"/>
<atom:link rel="describedby"
   href="http://localhost:8081/inmemory/atom/A1/type?
      id=cmisbook%3Atext" type="application/atom+xml;type=entry"/>
<atom:link
   rel="http://docs.oasis-open.org/ns/cmis/link/200908
      /allowableactions" href="http://localhost:8081/inmemory/atom
      /A1/allowableactions?id=161"
      type="application/cmisallowableactions+xml"/>
```

ATOM links; note that some are defined not by Atom but rather by CMIS (such as rel="http://docs.oasis-open.org/ns/cmis/link/200908/acl")

```
    <atom:link rel="up"
       href="http://localhost:8081/inmemory/atom/A1/parents?id=161"
       type="application/atom+xml;type=feed"/>
    <atom:link rel="version-history"
       href="http://localhost:8081/inmemory/atom/A1/versions?
         id=161&amp;versionSeries=162"
         type="application/atom+xml;type=feed"/>
    <atom:link rel="edit-media"
       href="http://localhost:8081/inmemory/atom/A1/content?id=161"
       type="text/plain"/>
    <atom:link rel="http://docs.oasis-open.org/ns/cmis/link/200908/acl"
       href="http://localhost:8081/inmemory/atom/A1/acl?id=161"
       type="application/cmisacl+xml"/>
</atom:entry>
```

11.2.3 The Browser binding

The objective of the Browser binding is to enable a JavaScript application in a web browser to access data in a CMIS repository. The binding only makes use of features that are available in the HTML and JavaScript specifications. It only uses the HTTP methods `GET` and `POST`: `GET` for requests that read data, and `POST` for requests that create, modify, or delete data. CMIS repositories return JSON responses as well as binary contents of documents. CMIS clients use URL parameters and HTML form data to communicate with the repository. Multipart messages are used to transport content from the client to the repository. A simple HTML form is sufficient to create a document in a CMIS repository.

The Browser binding covers the entire specification. There are no restrictions as in AtomPub, so in that respect the feature set is comparable with the Web Services binding. This includes the error handling. The Browser binding uses the same HTTP status codes as AtomPub but additionally sends a JSON response that contains the exception type and a message. HTTP status codes can be tricky in a browser application, but adding the parameter `suppressResponseCodes` with the value `true` to a URL can turn them off. The repository will then always return the HTTP status code 200.

THE SERVICE DOCUMENT

In contrast to those in the AtomPub binding, the URLs of this binding are entirely predictable. That is, the specification defines URL patterns that work for all repositories. Similar to the AtomPub binding, the application must first get the service document. The service document contains information about all repositories available at this endpoint, two base URLs per repository. One URL is called the *repository URL* and the other one is called the *root folder URL*. The repository URL is used for all requests that are independent of the folder hierarchy, such as accessing or changing type definitions, performing a query, or getting content changes. A URL that is derived from the root folder URL always addresses an object, either by its ID or its path. The term *root folder URL* is a bit misleading because unfiled objects can also be addressed with this URL, so don't be confused. To select an object by path, the object's path is attached to the root folder URL.

To select an object by ID, the URL parameter `objectId` with the object's ID is attached to the root folder URL. If the parameter `objectId` is set, it takes precedence over the path.

Let's assume the root folder URL is http://example.com/repository/root. To select the document with the object ID 123456 and the path /myfolder/doc.txt, the following three URLs would work:

This one is by ID:

```
http://example.com/repository/root?objectId=123456
```

This one is by path:

```
http://example.com/repository/root/myfolder/doc.txt
```

In this one, the `objectId` parameter wins over the path:

```
http://example.com/repository/root/another/path?objectId=123456
```

Such URLs are called *object URLs*. If an object URL points to a document, the content of this document is returned by default. If it points to a folder, the children of this folder are the default return type. For all other base types, the object details are returned.

A client can specify which aspect of the object the repository should return by setting the parameter `cmisselector`. For example, a URL that gets the object details of a document could look like this:

```
http://example.com/repository/root?objectId=123456&cmisselector=object
```

And a URL to get the versions of a document could look like this:

```
http://example.com/repository/root/myfolder/doc.txt
        ?cmisselector=versions
```

Other URL parameters are similar to the parameters in the AtomPub URL templates. Property filters can be defined; allowable actions, ACLs, and policies can be turned on and off; a rendition filter can be set; and so on. For operations that return lists, such as `getChildren`, the offset, the length, the order of the list, and other things can be defined. The official CMIS 1.1 specification is the best complete reference for all the supported parameters and operations.

THE SUCCINCT FEATURE

A feature that is unique to the Browser binding is the `succinct` flag. All bindings transport for each property the property ID, the data type, the query name, the display name, the local name, and the value. That makes it easier for clients that don't know the type definition of the object to work with these properties. But if the client knows the type definition, this is extra weight. The `succinct` parameter with the value `true` can be attached to all Browser binding URLs that return objects. The repository then only sends the property ID and the value, which makes the response more compact.

Try capturing a URL from the CMIS Workbench, and open in it a web browser. The Workbench always sets the `succinct` flag. Remove that flag from the URL, and reload the URL in the web browser. You'll see that the response is now considerably larger.

CRUD OPERATIONS

Operations that create, read, update, or delete objects use HTTP `POST` instead of HTTP `GET`. Data is transmitted in the same format that web browsers use to send HTML form data to a server. The form data must be URL encoded or sent as a multipart message. If content is attached to the request, then it *must* be a multipart request. (Thus, that only applies to the operations `createDocument`, `setContentStream`, `appendContentStream`, and `checkIn`.)

To indicate which operation should be invoked, the parameter `cmisaction` must be included. If a new document should be created, the value of `cmisaction` must be `createDocument`. To delete an object, `cmisaction` must be `delete`, and so on. The CMIS specification defines a `cmisaction` value for each operation as well as all other required and optional parameters.

Complex data structures are broken down to multiple parameters and parameter names with indexes. For example, to transmit the two base properties for creating a document (`cmis:name` and `cmis:objectTypeId`), the four properties shown in table 11.1 are required.

Table 11.1 Example parameters and values for `createDocument`

Parameter name	Parameter value
`propertyId[0]`	`cmis:name`
`propertyValue[0]`	`myNewDocument.txt`
`propertyId[1]`	`cmis:objectTypeId`
`propertyValue[1]`	`cmis:document`

You need a parameter pair (`propertyId` and `propertyValue`) to set one single-value property. The indexes indicate which parameters belong together, but the order doesn't matter. This pattern is used for all complex data structures and lists such as ACLs or lists of object IDs or change tokens.

> **TRANSPORTING PARAMETER NAMES AND VALUES** At first glance, it looks unnecessarily complex to split a property into two parameters. Wouldn't it be simpler to use the property ID as the parameter name?
>
> It would, but that could lead to ambiguities. Here's the reason why. The HTML specification says parameter names are case insensitive but property IDs are case sensitive. If a repository provided a type with two properties that differed only in the capitalization of the property ID, the client (such as a web browser) would normalize the parameter names, and it wouldn't be possible to identify which property the application meant. The chance of such a situation occurring isn't very high, but to prevent any kind of ambiguity, the Technical Committee fixed all parameter names.
>
> Apart from that, parameter names in multipart messages should only use 7-bit ASCII characters because they're used in HTTP headers. Property IDs

with characters outside this charset are very likely, so it's better to avoid compatibility issues and use fixed parameter names instead.

As with the other two bindings, you can add JSON structures that aren't defined in the CMIS specification. Clients that don't understand these should ignore them. The names of these extensions should be chosen carefully, though. In the other two bindings, the XML namespace can distinguish an extension tag from a CMIS or an Atom tag. Because JSON has no namespaces, the names should be as unique as possible. Future versions of CMIS may introduce more elements, and a name clash could lead to incompatibilities.

To learn more about the Browser binding and how to use it, see appendix D. It shows how to build a JavaScript application that accesses a CMIS repository. It also demonstrates how to use JSON-P and callbacks to work with a repository that's hosted on a different server. In chapter 12, we cover user authentication and CSRF attack protection.

JSON CREATE REQUEST EXAMPLES

This section shows two examples of JSON requests. The first is an extremely simple example of `createFolder`:

```
cmisaction=createFolder&
  propertyId[0]=cmis%3AobjectTypeId&
  propertyValue[0]=cmis%3Afolder&
  propertyId[1]=cmis%3Aname&
  propertyValue[1]=myFolder&
  succinct=true
```

The second is a more complicated example of a `createDocument` multipart message:

```
--aPacHeCheMIStryoPEncmiS6a5a1a37createDocument13b766ab8a531763c9a
Content-Disposition: form-data; name="cmisaction"
Content-Type: text/plain; charset=utf-8

createDocument
--aPacHeCheMIStryoPEncmiS6a5a1a37createDocument13b766ab8a531763c9a
Content-Disposition: form-data; name="propertyId[0]"
Content-Type: text/plain; charset=utf-8

cmis:objectTypeId
--aPacHeCheMIStryoPEncmiS6a5a1a37createDocument13b766ab8a531763c9a
Content-Disposition: form-data; name="propertyValue[0]"
Content-Type: text/plain; charset=utf-8

cmis:document
--aPacHeCheMIStryoPEncmiS6a5a1a37createDocument13b766ab8a531763c9a
Content-Disposition: form-data; name="propertyId[1]"
Content-Type: text/plain; charset=utf-8

cmis:name
--aPacHeCheMIStryoPEncmiS6a5a1a37createDocument13b766ab8a531763c9a
Content-Disposition: form-data; name="propertyValue[1]"
Content-Type: text/plain; charset=utf-8

myDoc.txt
```

```
--aPacHeCheMIStryoPEncmiS6a5a1a37createDocument13b766ab8a531763c9a
Content-Disposition: form-data; name="versioningState"
Content-Type: text/plain; charset=utf-8

none
--aPacHeCheMIStryoPEncmiS6a5a1a37createDocument13b766ab8a531763c9a
Content-Disposition: form-data; name="content"; filename=myDoc.txt
Content-Type: text/plain
Content-Transfer-Encoding: binary

Hello World!
--aPacHeCheMIStryoPEncmiS6a5a1a37createDocument13b766ab8a531763c9a--
```

JSON OBJECT RESPONSE EXAMPLE

Listing 11.3 shows a typical example of a response for requested CMIS object details via the Browser binding, with the `succinct` flag set to `true`.

Listing 11.3 JSON object response

```
{
    "allowableActions":{                              <-- JSON responses: much smaller and easier to read than other XML responses
        "canGetACL":false,
        "canGetObjectRelationships":false,
        "canGetContentStream":true,
        "canCheckIn":false,
        "canApplyACL":false,
        "canRemoveObjectFromFolder":true,
        "canMoveObject":true,
        "canDeleteContentStream":true,
        "canGetProperties":true,
        "canGetAllVersions":true,
        "canApplyPolicy":false,
        "canGetObjectParents":true,
        "canSetContentStream":false,
        "canCreateRelationship":false,
        "canGetFolderTree":false,
        "canCheckOut":true,
        "canCreateDocument":false,
        "canCancelCheckOut":false,
        "canAddObjectToFolder":true,
        "canRemovePolicy":false,
        "canDeleteObject":true,
        "canGetDescendants":false,
        "canGetFolderParent":false,
        "canGetAppliedPolicies":false,
        "canDeleteTree":false,
        "canUpdateProperties":true,
        "canGetRenditions":false,
        "canCreateFolder":false,
        "canGetChildren":false
    },
    "acl":{                                <-- Passes ACLs
        "aces":[
            {
                "isDirect":true,
```

```
                    "principal":{
                        "principalId":"anyone"
                    },
                    "permissions":[
                        "cmis:all"
                    ]
                }
            ]
        },
        "exactACL":true,
        "succinctProperties":{
            "cmis:isLatestMajorVersion":true,
            "cmis:contentStreamLength":395,
            "cmis:contentStreamId":null,
            "cmis:objectTypeId":"cmisbook:text",
            "cmis:versionSeriesCheckedOutBy":null,
            "cmis:versionSeriesCheckedOutId":null,
            "cmisbook:author":null,
            "cmis:name":"welcome.txt",
            "cmis:contentStreamMimeType":"text/plain",
            "cmis:versionSeriesId":"162",
            "cmis:creationDate":1353180064169,
            "cmis:changeToken":"1353180064169",
            "cmis:isLatestVersion":true,
            "cmis:versionLabel":"V 1.0",
            "cmis:isVersionSeriesCheckedOut":false,
            "cmis:lastModifiedBy":"system",
            "cmis:createdBy":"system",
            "cmis:checkinComment":null,
            "cmis:objectId":"161",
            "cmis:isImmutable":false,
            "cmis:isMajorVersion":true,
            "cmis:baseTypeId":"cmis:document",
            "cmis:lastModificationDate":1353180064169,
            "cmis:contentStreamFileName":"welcome.txt"
        }
    }
```


Properties: notice how concise they are

To build compatible clients and servers, these XML and JSON responses must be clearly defined. The next section explains the CMIS schemas that provide these definitions.

11.3 CMIS schemas and schema extensions

The CMIS specification defines two schemas: an XML schema for the Web Services and AtomPub bindings and the Orderly (JSON) schema for the Browser binding. The schemas define the structure, restrictions, and extension points of the XML and JSON serialization of the CMIS data. The schemas are almost equivalent.

The XML schema was introduced with CMIS 1.0 and slightly extended in CMIS 1.1. The JSON schema came with CMIS 1.1. It's possible to translate any CMIS XML structure into JSON, but not necessarily vice versa because the `succinct` feature exists only for the Browser binding.

11.3.1 XML schema

Reading and understanding the XML schema is straightforward, if you're generally familiar with XML schemas. The XSD files are part of the CMIS specification. The schema is broken into the following three files:

- CMIS-Core.xsd contains the core definitions and is used by the Web Services and AtomPub bindings.
- CMIS-Messaging.xsd adds message definitions for the Web Services binding.
- CMIS-RestAtom.xsd contains XML definitions used only by the AtomPub binding.

JSON schema

JSON has no comparable schema standard. There are a few different initiatives, but none of them have been widely accepted yet. The CMIS Technical Committee decided to adopt and extend Orderly (http://orderly-json.org/). Orderly describes the structure of a JSON document in a simple format. The original Orderly specification by Lloyd Hilaiel wasn't sufficient for CMIS, and the Technical Committee had to add a few features to it. The Orderly specification that is used by CMIS can be found in an appendix of the CMIS specification. To understand the CMIS Orderly schema, it's recommended that you pull down a copy and scan through it.

Schema extension points

The CMIS schema defines several extension points, where clients and repositories can stick extra data. CMIS structures are extensible if they contain an `Any` element in the XML schema or if the structure in the Orderly schema ends with `*`.

These extension points are meant to work across all bindings so a developer can implement a binding-agnostic application with extensions. The other extensions that we've mentioned so far were binding-specific (for example, an additional Atom link) and are of limited use.

Repository extensions

Extensions can be useful for repository vendors to expose additional features that aren't covered by CMIS. Generic CMIS clients ignore them, and specific clients can make use of the features without switching the protocol. But if an additional feature can be mapped to a CMIS structure—for example, to a secondary type—it's usually better to do this. It eases the life of the application developers significantly.

In CMIS 1.0 it wasn't possible for a client to detect up front whether a repository supported a specific non-CMIS feature. That changed with CMIS 1.1. A CMIS 1.1 repository's info may list all additional specifications that are supported by the repository on top of CMIS. Such a feature doesn't necessarily depend on a schema extension. It might, for example, indicate that a specific type is available or define specific semantics for certain properties or secondary types. But if there are schema extensions, a CMIS 1.1 repository should announce those in the repository info.

WHICH BINDING SHOULD I USE? Answering this question properly depends on the repository, the environment, and the library you're using.

The Browser binding is the fastest and most lightweight binding. If it's supported on both ends, it's the best choice for all kinds of applications. The most common binding at the moment (available on all CMIS servers) is the AtomPub binding. It's usually faster than the Web Services binding and supported in environments that don't have a Web Services stack. Note that there are repositories with broken (not conforming 100%) AtomPub binding implementations, most notably SharePoint 2010.

The Web Services binding is the last resort. Most implementations are stable and correct but comparatively slow. On the upside, in environments with a Web Services infrastructure, this binding may be easy to implement and integrate.

Now let's jump back from the level of bytes on the wire and look into the OpenCMIS low-level API.

11.4 The OpenCMIS low-level API

When you compare the bindings with the OpenCMIS, DotCMIS, and ObjectiveCMIS APIs, you might notice a disconnection. The APIs provide an object-oriented interface with a lot of convenience, simplified data structures, and high-level operations that don't exist in CMIS. On the other hand, these APIs hide extension points and access to the data structures that are transferred over the wire.

It turns out that there's a layer between the bindings and these APIs called the *low-level API*. The low-level API provides a set of interfaces and operations that model all the services and operations in the CMIS specification one-to-one. For each of the nine CMIS services, there's an interface. For each operation, there's a method with exactly the same name and the same parameters, in the same order. The data objects are very close to the data structures used on the wire. The semantics and behavior are as described in the CMIS domain model. You can use the CMIS specification as a manual for these interfaces.

The high-level API with which you're now familiar always calls the low-level API. That is, the high-level API never touches the bindings directly. The step from the low-level API to the bindings isn't that big. Method calls are translated to HTTP requests, and the data is transformed to XML or JSON and back.

The low-level API gives you full control over the data you send and receive. It lets you access and exploit all CMIS extension points, for example. But there's a price to pay. The code you have to write to use this API is much longer, and there are no safety nets. No trail markers help you ensure that you're following the CMIS domain model path.

Let's create a new folder in the root folder with the high-level API and then do the same with the low-level API. Here's a typical example of using the high-level API that we've been using throughout the book:

```
Folder root = session.getRootFolder();                  <-- Get root folder

Map<String, Object> properties = new HashMap<String, Object>();   | Set up
properties.put(PropertyIds.OBJECT_TYPE_ID, "cmis:folder");        | properties
properties.put(PropertyIds.NAME, "myFolder");

root.createFolder(properties);                          <-- Create folder
```

Now let's see what's required to do this at the low level:

```
CmisBinding binding = session.getBinding();         <-- Get low-level API entry point
BindingsObjectFactory bof = binding.getObjectFactory();
                                                          Get repository ID
String repositoryId = session.getRepositoryInfo().getId();  <-- and root folder ID
String rootFolderId = session.getRepositoryInfo().getRootFolderId();

PropertyId objectTypeId =                                            <--
  bof.createPropertyIdData(PropertyIds.OBJECT_TYPE_ID, "cmis:folder");
PropertyString name =
  bof.createPropertyStringData(PropertyIds.NAME, "myFolder");
                                                      Set up properties
List<PropertyData<?>> propertiesList =                  (note that you
  new ArrayList<PropertyData<?>>();                     need to know the
propertiesList.add(objectTypeId);                       data types)
propertiesList.add(name);

Properties properties = bof.createPropertiesData(propertiesList);
                                                                       Create
binding.getObjectService().createFolder(repositoryId, properties,  <-- folder
   rootFolderId, null, null, null, null);
```

11.4.1 Reasons to use the low-level API

There's usually no good reason to use the low-level API. The only semi-valid reason is to get hold of or set extension values. Before you start fiddling with the low-level API because you think there's no other way, ask on the Apache Chemistry mailing list; there could be a more elegant way to solve your problem.

If you're starting to get all misty, thinking you'll never see this low-level API again, cheer up. If you're planning to implement your own CMIS server with the OpenCMIS server framework (see chapter 14), your paths will cross again. These are the same interfaces and data classes that are used on the server side. But instead of calling the interface methods, you have to implement them.

With that knowledge about the bindings and the low-level API, you can now dive into the security and performance aspects of CMIS.

11.5 Summary

This chapter provided some high-level insight into the three CMIS bindings and their differences, principles of operation, and use cases. Knowing about the CMIS bindings will help you debug, tune, deploy, and, sometimes, develop CMIS applications. The chapter also described how to capture CMIS wire traffic, which is useful for learning about the bindings and for debugging your application.

The description of the bindings takes up more than 120 pages in the CMIS 1.1 specification plus schema and sample files. Due to space considerations, we could only provide an overview here. The specification itself is always the best and most authoritative reference for all operations, parameters, and patterns not covered here.

The following chapters cover security and performance topics. These can vary for each binding, and a basic understanding of how the bindings work is assumed for some details.

12 Security and control

This chapter covers

- Authentication
- Authorization
- ACLs and policies
- Retentions and holds

This chapter looks into different security- and control-related aspects of CMIS. It starts with some general security considerations and hints for web application developers. We'll then cover authenticating users. The chapter also addresses authorization, ACLs, and policies, and finally it skims through retentions and holds.

12.1 General security considerations

Many CMIS repositories contain confidential data. It's the repository's task to protect this data. It has to check the user's credentials and figure out what this user is allowed to see and do. CMIS is *only* the transport vehicle for that data and responsible for a secure transport.

Because all CMIS bindings are based on HTTP, the easiest and most compatible way to secure the connection is to use SSL everywhere. That sounds obvious and trivial. But many CMIS repositories allow unencrypted access, which can reveal user credentials and confidential documents. And many production CMIS applications don't use HTTPS or have disabled the SSL certificate checks. We strongly recommend that you always use HTTPS in production environments!

Having unencrypted access may help during development, though. In chapter 11, which discusses CMIS bindings, we used it to look directly at the wire protocols. It's handy to find out exactly what the repository returned when you get something unexpected.

Once the data has reached the application, it's the application's responsibility to keep the data secure. In this section, we'll point out two general and repeating issues with web applications: cross-site scripting (XSS) attacks and cross-site request forgery (CSRF) attacks.

12.1.1 Cross-site scripting (XSS) attacks

Web applications should be protected against XSS attacks. That is, they should make sure no foreign and potentially malicious HTML and JavaScript code could be injected into a web page of the application. CMIS applications have to be careful with property values and document content because either may contain HTML or JavaScript fragments. A user might be tricked into looking at the properties of a CMIS document or opening a document that contains malicious code. This code would run in the user's application context and would potentially be able to read and modify data in the CMIS repository.

Whether property values should be HTML-encoded before they're displayed on a web page depends on the application and the properties. CMIS has an HTML property data type to indicate that the property value is an HTML fragment, and it's generally used for a good reason. The application has to decide if it can trust this property. All other string property data types are usually good candidates for encoding.

Dealing with content is a bit more complicated. Many applications provide a means to download a document's content. The user clicks a link, and the content is streamed to the web browser. The web browser then decides whether to open the document in the browser, offer the user a dialog box to open the content in another application, or download the content to a file. Most web browsers open HTML documents in the browser, and that can be a potential attack vector. CMIS repositories provide the content as it was stored. If the content contains malicious JavaScript code, this code is executed in the context of the user who clicked the download link.

There's no perfect solution for this problem. The application could encode or ban HTML and other problematic documents. But that would prohibit a user from downloading the original document, which could be genuine and harmless. The application could send a different MIME type for an HTML document, such as `text/plain`. Most web browsers then show the HTML code and don't interpret it. But this isn't a bulletproof solution either. Some applications store their web pages or parts of them—for example, images—in a CMIS repository. They definitely want the original document from the repository to be loaded by the web browser. So it's up to the application. But being aware of the issue is important.

12.1.2 Cross-site request forgery (CSRF) attacks

The second common issue with web applications is CSRF attacks. This is an issue for both the application and the repository. CSRF attackers take advantage of the fact that web browsers always send cookies and basic authentication information back to the origin website. A malicious web application might use this to send `POST` requests after the user has logged in to the CMIS applications. These malicious requests would be executed in the context of that user.

There are generic solutions for this issue for web applications that we won't explore here. The CMIS 1.1 specification defines how applications and repositories can solve the issue when the browser binding is used directly by a JavaScript application running in a web browser. The idea is to send tokens back and forth that only the CMIS application and the repository know. A malicious web application can't attack without these tokens. We'll cover that later in this chapter.

Repositories that allow authentication via cookies, basic authentication, or single sign-on (SSO) for the AtomPub binding and the Web Services binding must implement their own solution. These bindings aren't intended to be used in a web browser, but they can be exploited by a malicious web application.

But we're tapping into the authentication topic. Let's do that systematically in the next section.

12.2 Authentication

User authentication can be the most difficult topic in a CMIS project. There are many ways to authenticate a user, and they depend on the repository, the environment, business and security constraints, the application itself, and the end-user device. Authentication from a mobile application might be completely different from authentication in a web application.

The CMIS specification doesn't talk much about authentication. It recommends that repositories implement basic authentication (via an HTTP header) for the AtomPub binding and the Browser binding, and UsernameTokens (via a SOAP header) for the Web Services binding. Both mechanisms require a username and password to be sent with each request.

Most CMIS repositories support this recommendation, and all Apache Chemistry libraries support it out of the box. Remember the method in chapter 8 that created the OpenCMIS session? All you had to do was add the username and password to the session parameters, like this:

```
parameter.put(SessionParameter.USER, username);
parameter.put(SessionParameter.PASSWORD, password);
```

OpenCMIS automatically turns this information into an HTTP header or a SOAP header and adds it to all requests. There's nothing else you have to do. A session is always bound to a specific user because of this.

12.2.1 Cookies

Using usernames and passwords to authenticate can be expensive. The repository has to check the username and password for each request. In many cases, it has to contact another system like a user directory (for example, an LDAP server) to do this, and that costs valuable time. Therefore, some repositories return session cookies. It's faster to check whether a cookie is still valid than to authenticate the user with a username and password every time. To make that work, the repository must depend on the client to send back that cookie. Because the CMIS specification doesn't say a word about cookies, a repository vendor must not rely on cookie support on the client side.

Cookie support varies in the different Apache Chemistry libraries. Although cookies are automatically turned on in DotCMIS, they have to be manually activated in OpenCMIS via a session parameter:

```
parameter.put(SessionParameter.COOKIES, "true");
```

It's recommended that you always turn on cookies. It doesn't do any harm if the repository doesn't send cookies. And if it does, the performance gain can be significant.

Authentication with a username and password is simple, but also has its drawbacks. First, the user's credentials are always sent in clear text over the wire. That might not be a big deal if you're using HTTPS in production. But it might be a problem during development when you use unencrypted access. Another common issue is that the client application doesn't (and shouldn't) know the user's password. Think of SSO scenarios, portals, and mobile applications.

Many authentication mechanisms try to solve one or both issues: NTLM, Kerberos, SSL client certificates, SAML tokens, and OAuth, just to name a few. There are also many product-specific and homegrown solutions.

12.2.2 AuthenticationProvider interface

Because the Apache Chemistry CMIS libraries can't implement every flavor of every authentication mechanism, OpenCMIS, DotCMIS, and ObjectiveCMIS provide interfaces that let you plug in your own authentication implementations. We're using OpenCMIS for the following examples. The interfaces of the other libraries are slightly different because of the underlying technologies, but the general idea is the same.

OpenCMIS lets you provide HTTP headers and SOAP headers for the requests to the repository, which can transport authentication details. You can also take control of the SSL socket factory to attach an SSL client certificate to the requests, which identifies the user. All you have to do is to implement the `AuthenticationProvider` interface. To use your implementation, add the class name to the session parameters when you set up a new session, like so:

```
parameters.put(SessionParameter.AUTHENTICATION_PROVIDER_CLASS,
   "org.example.MyAuthenticationProvider");

parameters.put("org.example.user", "cmisuser");
parameters.put("org.example.secret", "b3BlbmNtaXMgdXNlcg==");
```

The example also shows that you can add your own parameters to the session parameters. In your authentication provider implementation, you can access these parameter values and use them as needed.

It's recommended that you *not* implement the `AuthenticationProvider` interface directly, but instead derive your implementation from the `AbstractAuthenticationProvider` class or the `StandardAuthenticationProvider` class. The latter gives you support for the standard authentication recommended in the specification as well as cookie support. You may also want to look at the source code for the `StandardAuthenticationProvider` class; it could be a good starting point for your own implementation.

12.2.3 Example of an authentication provider

The most important method is `getHTTPHeaders`. It's called before each request to the repository for all CMIS bindings and returns the HTTP headers that should be added to the request. Listing 12.1 shows a simple authentication provider implementation that uses the additional parameters from the previous example. The parameter values are sent to the repository as nonstandard HTTP headers.

Listing 12.1 A sample `AuthenticationProvider` implementation

```
public class ExampleAuthenticationProvider extends
    StandardAuthenticationProvider {

  private static final long serialVersionUID = 1L;

  @Override
  public Map<String, List<String>> getHTTPHeaders(String url) {

    Map<String, List<String>> headers = super.getHTTPHeaders(url);
    if (headers == null) {
      headers = new HashMap<String, List<String>>();
    }

    Object exampleUserObject =
      getSession().get("org.example.user");
    if (exampleUserObject instanceof String) {
      headers.put("example-user",
          Collections.singletonList((String) exampleUserObject));
    }

    Object exampleSecretObject =
      getSession().get("org.example.secret");
    if (exampleSecretObject instanceof String) {
      headers.put("example-secret",
          Collections.singletonList((String) exampleSecretObject));
    }

    return headers;
  }
}
```

Gets default headers from the StandardAuthenticationProvider; if it doesn't return headers, creates a new Map

Gets session parameter org.example.user and sets the HTTP header

Gets session parameter org.example.secret and sets the HTTP header

The getSOAPHeaders method works similarly to the getHTTPHeaders method. It returns a SOAP header, which is attached to all Web Services calls. This method is called only once per Web Services service. Therefore, you can't customize every call.

Another (often) important method is putResponseHeaders. It provides the HTTP response headers and the HTTP status code after each call. If the CMIS repository returned something that can be used to authenticate a follow-up request (a token, perhaps), this is the method you should override to extract this information.

The AuthenticationProvider object is kept for the whole session. Because sessions can be used across multiple threads, the AuthenticationProvider object must be thread-safe. So if you get a token back from the repository, make sure you manage it in a thread-safe manner.

The loose definition of how the authentication works can cause some headaches and often requires extra code if a simple username/password combination isn't sufficient. It's even more complicated in web applications that should directly talk to a CMIS repository from a web browser. It not only has to authenticate the user; it also has to prevent CSRF attacks. Fortunately, the Browser binding specification defines this authentication process for web applications. That's the topic of the next section.

12.3 Authentication in web applications using the Browser binding

Web applications that use the Browser binding have another option to authenticate a user, which additionally protects the repository from CSRF attacks. The idea is to let the repository handle authentication. The web application only has to trigger the authentication process and then send tokens with each request that it gets from the repository. Let's start at the beginning with the entry points.

12.3.1 JavaScript entry points

The entry point for the web application is a JavaScript file that's served from the repository server. The application includes the file into its web page, like so:

```
<script src="http://cmis.example.com/cmis.js"/>
```

This JavaScript file defines the following four functions:

- cmisServiceURL()—Returns the URL to the Browser binding service document (see chapter 11)
- cmisLogin(callback)—Triggers a login
- cmisLogout(callback)—Triggers a logout
- cmisNextToken(callback)—Provides a token for the next CMIS request

12.3.2 Sequence: log in, nextToken, ..., log out

When the application starts up, it calls the function cmisLogin. What happens next is repository-specific. It's very likely that the repository will redirect the user to a login page or to a page that handles SSO. If the user authentication was successful, the user is redirected back to the application page. Now the application again calls cmisLogin. It's the repository's responsibility not to run into an endless loop here. If everything works correctly, there's no second redirection, and the application moves on.

Every call the application makes to the repository must be authorized with a token. To get a token, the application calls cmisNextToken and retrieves a token from the repository. Whether this requires another round trip to the repository depends on the underlying implementation. If the next call is a GET request, the application attaches a token parameter to the URL. If the next call is a POST request, the application adds a token field to the HTML form.

Ideally, these are one-time-use tokens. That is, a token works for one request, but a second request with the same token would fail. Tokens may also expire after a preset time. But these rules aren't defined by the CMIS specification. The repository vendor decides how the tokens are generated and managed and when they become invalid.

The application can also log out a user by calling the function cmisLogout. All issued tokens should become invalid, and the function cmisNextToken shouldn't return any more new tokens.

Figure 12.1 shows this sequence of events as an activity diagram.

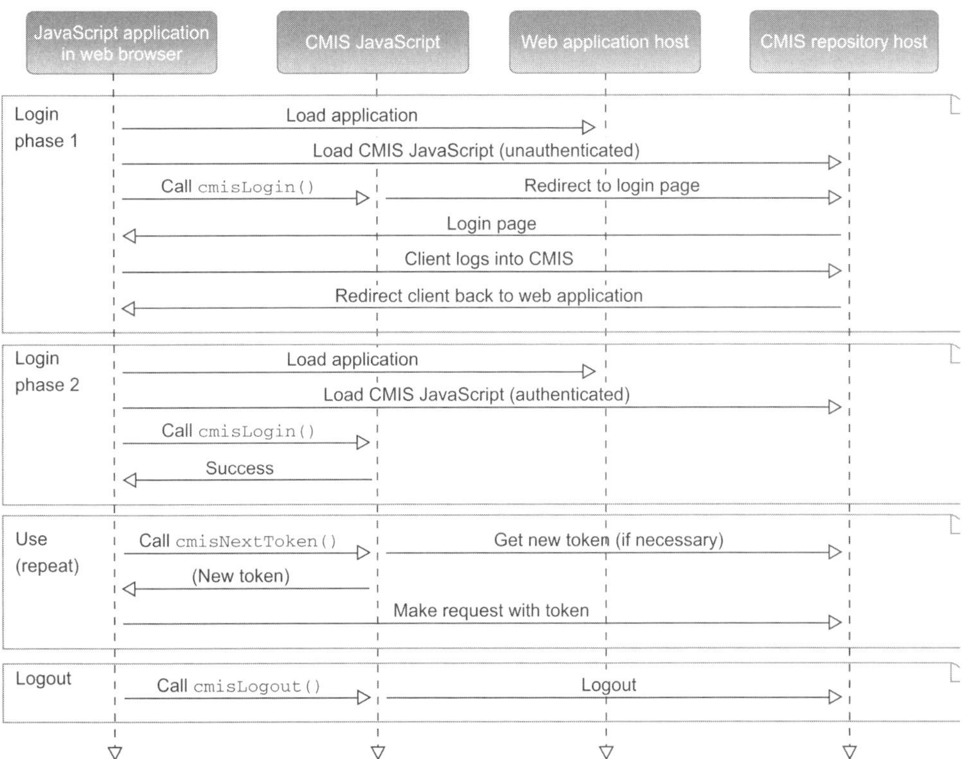

Figure 12.1 Activity diagram of the secure login sequence for the Browser binding

12.3.3 Example JavaScript

Here's a short example taken from the CMIS specification. It calls `cmisLogin` when the web page is loaded. If the login was successful, it calls the `displayRootFolder` function, which is defined here. This function first gets the `next` token and provides it to the `loadChildren` function, which isn't in this example. The `loadChildren` function uses the token to make requests to the CMIS repository. That's the basic pattern for JavaScript applications that use this authentication option:

```
<script src="http://cmis.example.com/cmis.js"/>
<script>
  cmisLogin(function(success) {
    if (success) {
       displayRootFolder();
    } else {
      showLoginErrorMessage();
    }
  });

  function displayRootFolder() {
    cmisNextToken(function(token) {
      loadChildren('/', ..., token);
     });
  }
</script>
```

Boolean variable "success" indicates whether this function was successful the second time it was called

Variable "token" contains the token returned by the repository; CMIS call is done in the callback of cmisNextToken

This procedure should work against all CMIS repositories that support it, without adapting the application code. If one-time tokens are used, it additionally provides protection against CSRF attacks. If you're interested in the details, refer to section 5.2.9.2 of the CMIS 1.1 specification. The OpenCMIS server framework ships a working example of a mini application that uses this authentication procedure.

Once the repository knows who the user is, it can determine what the user is allowed to see and do. The following sections examine authorization and different forms of permissions.

12.4 Authorization and permissions

CMIS knows about two concepts of modeling permissions: policies and access control lists (ACLs). Policies are rules that determine whether a user can do a certain action with an object, whereas ACLs are mappings from users to permissions. Repository vendors map their permission model to either one or both CMIS concepts. It's the repository's responsibility to check and enforce permissions. Remember that CMIS is only the messenger.

12.4.1 Policies

The mechanics of policies are defined in the CMIS specification, but the specific semantics isn't. The idea is that a repository provides a set of policy types, and applications create instances of such types and attach them to objects. Policies can be any type of rules. For example, a policy could restrict access to a document to a certain time of the day. Let's say a document should be accessible only between 8:00 a.m. and 5:00 p.m. Another policy could enforce that a document can be updated only if the user is accessing the repository from a certain network segment. That could restrict editing to a special part of a building. A policy could also take a user's classification level into account and only allow the user to download a document if they have the required security clearance.

To test if a repository supports policies, fetch the CMIS base types from the repository with the operation `getTypeChildren`. If the base type `cmis:policy` is in the list of returned types, the repository supports policies. Not all objects may be controllable by policies, though. All CMIS types have the flag `controllablePolicy`, which indicates whether policies can be applied to objects of that type.

The base policy type is of no direct use because it doesn't represent any rule. Repositories derive their own policy types from that base type. The display name and the type description should be something an end user can understand, because it's usually the end user who picks a policy. A policy type may also define extra properties. A policy that restricts access to a certain time of day may need a start and an end time, for example. Or a policy that restricts edits to a network segment may need an IP address range.

Before a policy can be applied, you must create a policy object and set its properties with the `createPolicy` operation. You then use `applyPolicy` to put an object under the control of a policy. A policy object can be applied to multiple objects. The `removePolicy` operation releases a policy from an object. Policy objects live on when they've been removed from all objects; a policy object can't be deleted while it's applied to at least one object. The next listing shows an example of manipulating policy objects using OpenCMIS.

Listing 12.2 Applying and removing policies with OpenCMIS

```
CmisObject object = ...

Policy workingHoursPolicy =
    (Policy) session.getObject("ab530ca3e7e92ab4");
Policy buildingPolicy =
   (Policy) session.getObject("832ef21cabf71a6c");

object.applyPolicy(workingHoursPolicy);
object.removePolicy(buildingPolicy);
```

Find policies through queries or browsing

12.4.2 ACLs

ACLs are more common than policies. An ACL is an integral part of an object if the repository supports ACLs. A `capability` flag in the repository info indicates whether the repository supports ACLs, as well as the level of support, for example, read-only versus the ability to fully manage ACLs.

An ACL consists of zero or more access control entries (ACEs). Each ACE defines the permissions for a principal. A principal could be a user, a group, a role, or some grouping of that nature. CMIS has no notion of these user-management concepts and treats the principal IDs as opaque strings. The assumption is that the client and the repository share a common understanding of principals, which is transparent to CMIS. For example, both client and repository are using the same LDAP directory or Active Directory, which provides user and group information.

> **ANYONE, ANONYMOUS, AND CURRENT USERS** Repositories that have a notion of "any authenticated user" or "anonymous users" provide the corresponding principal IDs with the repository info. CMIS clients can use those to compile ACEs. The CMIS specification also defines the principal ID `cmis:user`. Repositories that support this macro replace this principal ID with the principal ID of the current user when an ACL is applied.

There should be only one ACE per principal, which collects all permissions for that principal. But some repositories do expose multiple ACEs per principal in some cases.

The CMIS specification defines three basic permissions, but allows repositories to expose additional, repository-specific permissions. The basic permissions are as follows:

- `cmis:read`—A user with this permission can read an object's metadata and content.
- `cmis:write`—A user with this permission has the authorization to update metadata and content. In almost all repositories, the `cmis:write` permission contains the `cmis:read` permission.
- `cmis:all`—A user with this permission has full control of the object. This permission contains the `cmis:write` and `cmis:read` permissions.

There are some fuzzy areas regarding these permissions. For example, does a user need the `cmis:write` or `cmis:all` permission to delete an object or change the ACL of an object? If you want to move an object, what permissions are required on the source folder, the target folder, or the object itself? The repository info provides some general hints: it contains a permission mapping that maps input parameters of CMIS operations to permissions. For concrete objects, you should also check the allowable actions of each involved object. Figure 12.2 shows the CMIS Workbench displaying the ACLs that are set for a selected document. When you look at this, you might wonder about the other permissions it shows. Those repository-specific permissions are discussed next.

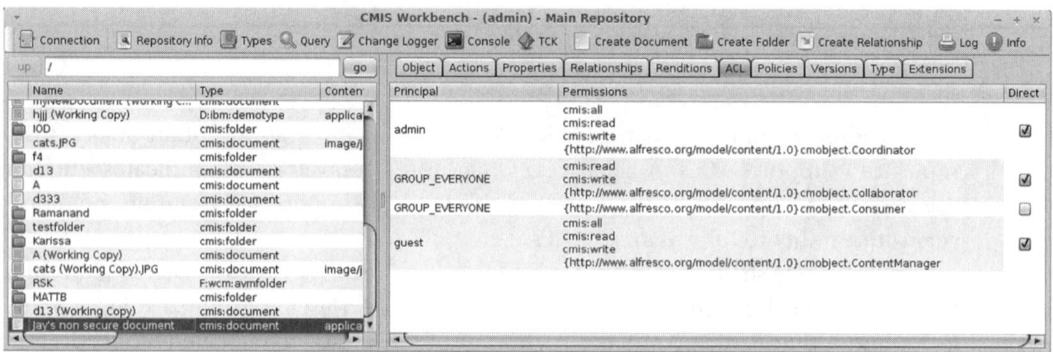

Figure 12.2 CMIS Workbench displaying the ACLs for a document

12.4.3 Repository-specific permissions

Many repositories also provide more fine-grained permissions and permissions that are specific to each repository. For example, a repository might a have special permission for folders that sits between `cmis:read` and `cmis:write` and defines whether a user can file an object in this folder. That would allow a repository to distinguish between users who are only allowed to see the folder, users who are allowed to add new children to the folder, and users who are allowed to add new children and rename the folder. An example of a repository-specific permission could be the right to publish a document. There's no concept of publishing a document in CMIS, but it's possible to see and manage such a repository-specific permission through the CMIS interface. This permission would be orthogonal to the CMIS basic permissions.

A list of all available permissions is also part of the repository info. Each permission should have a human-readable explanation, such that end users can pick the right permission when presented with a choice.

When an application requests the ACL of an object from the repository, it can ask for the full ACL or an ACL that contains only the CMIS basic permissions. If the latter is requested, the repository has to try hard to map all its specific permissions to the basic permissions. It then also returns a flag that indicates whether the mapping is an exact mapping or if the user has more rights that aren't expressed with basic permissions. Let's assume that a user has the permission to file objects in a folder as described earlier. A mapping to the basic permission would return the `cmis:read` permission for this user, because that is the next-lower basic permission. The publishing permission wouldn't show up at all. The returned ACL would be an approximation or best fit.

12.4.4 Changing permissions (applyACL)

Calling the `applyACL` operation can change an object's ACL. This operation takes a list of ACEs that should be added to and a list of ACEs that should be removed from the current ACL of the object. Either list can be empty. The repository takes these lists, calculates and sets a new ACL, and returns it. The resulting ACL may look different than you expect, because the repository has the freedom to change and streamline the ACL based on its internal rules. For example, a repository might decide not to change the ACL if a user already has the `cmis:all` permission and the application tries to add the `cmis:read` permission. But if the application tries to remove the `cmis:write` permission from that user, the repository may remove all permissions for that user or changes the permission to `cmis:read`.

The `applyACL` operation also takes a parameter that tells the repository how to propagate ACL changes. The three available options are as follows:

- `object only`—Tells the repository to change this object only.
- `propagate`—Forces the repository to update all inheriting objects. The repository info provides a `capability` flag that indicates whether the repository supports propagation. Applications should check it before trying to propagate ACL changes.

- `repository determined`—Allows the repository to decide whether the ACL changes should be forwarded to inheriting objects. In this case, *inheriting objects* usually means that if the ACL is changed on a folder, the ACLs of all descendants of this folder are also updated. It might also affect objects that are connected through a relationship.

There are two models of permission propagation, and a repository usually supports just one or the other. Propagation can mean that the ACEs are added to and removed from each descendant. That is, if an ACE is added, the object owns the ACE. This ACE is independent of the same ACE on the parent or a sibling. The CMIS term for such an ACE is *direct ACE*. CMIS ACEs have a flag that indicates whether or not the ACE is a direct ACE.

Nondirect ACEs are defined on a parent, but affect the descendants. They appear in the ACLs of the descendants and have the same impact as direct ACEs, but can only be removed or changed on the parent. For some repositories, that is the definition of permission propagation.

Listing 12.3 shows an example of adding ACEs to an object. You give the principals florian and jeff write permissions and the user jay all permissions for an object. Afterward, all three are allowed to update the object.

Listing 12.3 Adding ACEs to an object with OpenCMIS

```
CmisObject object = ...

ObjectFactory of = session.getObjectFactory();

Ace ace1 = of.createAce("florian",
   Collections.singletonList("cmis:write"));
Ace ace2 = of.createAce("jeff",
   Collections.singletonList("cmis:write"));
Ace ace3 = of.createAce("jay",
   Collections.singletonList("cmis:all"));

List<Ace> addAces = new ArrayList<Ace>();

addAces.add(ace1);
addAces.add(ace2);
addAces.add(ace3);

object.applyAcl(addAces, /* no ACEs to remove*/ null,
   AclPropagation.OBJECTONLY);

Acl acl = session.getAcl(object,
    /* only basic permissions */ true);
```

Get the new ACL, but only the basic permissions

Another obstacle with ACL updates is the AtomPub binding. It works slightly differently for the procedure just described. Instead of taking the two lists of ACEs to add and remove, it requires the client to send a complete ACL to the repository. The repository has to calculate the difference between the retrieved ACL and the current ACL of the object to determine which ACEs should be added and which should be removed.

APPLYACL VERSUS SETACL OpenCMIS provides two methods to change ACLs: `applyAcl` and `setAcl`. `applyAcl` works as described in the CMIS specification. For the AtomPub binding, it calculates the complete ACL under the hood on the client side to make it work like the other two bindings. `setAcl` takes a complete ACL and tries to apply it. If the AtomPub binding is used, the ACL is forwarded as is to the repository. For the other two bindings, OpenCMIS calculates the ACE add list and the ACE remove list and calls `applyACL`. Because that doesn't work with propagation, the ACL can only be set for one object.

ACL management can be repository- and binding-specific. You should carefully test how your repository handles ACL changes. This is an area where switching from one repository vendor to another might require some application code adjustments.

Applications that only need to know what the user is allowed to do and don't change permissions should rely on the allowable actions. They're computed by the repository, which should take all aspects of the object into account. One of these aspects could be the document's retention settings; which we'll cover in the next section.

12.5 Retentions and holds

Retentions and holds were introduced in CMIS 1.1. They control whether documents can be updated and deleted. Before CMIS 1.1, they had to be modeled as policies. Although it was technically possible, the lack of standardization in this area made it difficult to build interoperable applications.

CMIS 1.1 defines two types of retentions:

- Repository-managed retentions
- Client-managed retentions

We'll discuss them next.

12.5.1 Repository-managed retentions

A repository that supports repository-managed retentions provides a hierarchy of secondary types derived from the type `cmis:rm_repMgtRetention`. This hierarchy might be the same as a classification hierarchy or a file plan in a repository. A client that wants to put a document under retention must attach the appropriate secondary type to the document. Some retention types need specific property values, and some need special permissions. Not everyone is allowed to apply a certain retention type.

The semantics of the retention types is transparent to the CMIS client, and the impact on a document is unpredictable from the client point of view. In this regard, repository-managed retentions are similar to policies. But in many cases, applying such a retention means the repository calculates a date until which the document can't be updated or deleted. For example, if invoices have to be kept for seven years starting from the beginning of the next month, the repository calculates the date and makes sure the document can't be altered and the retention can't be removed.

12.5.2 Client-managed retentions

Client-managed retentions allow the client to set the retention date. For this purpose, the client has to attach to the object the secondary type `cmis:rm_clientMgtRetention` or a type derived from it. These types have the `cmis:rm_expirationDate` property, which defines the retention date. This property doesn't have to be set initially. But once it's set, the retention time can only be prolonged and can never be reduced. There's also the `cmis:rm_startOfRetention` property, which takes the start date of the retention. It exists only for documentation purposes and doesn't have any impact on document protection.

Repositories can also provide the secondary type `cmis:rm_destructionRetention`, which is derived from `cmis:rm_clientMgtRetention`. On top of the inherited retention-date property, it adds the `cmis:rm_destructionDate` property. This date defines when the destruction of the document should be triggered. That doesn't necessarily mean the document will be automatically deleted on this date; what happens depends on the repository. Some use cases require an administrator to approve the deletion of every document.

12.5.3 Holds

CMIS 1.1 also introduced holds. Documents that have at least one hold applied can't be update or deleted. But in contrast to retentions, everyone with sufficient permissions can remove holds at any time.

You set a hold by attaching the secondary type `cmis:rm_hold`. This type defines the multivalue string property `cmis:rm_holdIds`. This list contains hold identifiers that are defined somewhere else; they're opaque strings for CMIS. An empty list means that no hold is applied and the hold type can be detached.

You may have noticed that we've only talked about documents in this section. Retentions and holds are only defined for documents. To be precise, they're only defined for document versions and for the content of the document version. Protecting a document version may or may not also protect all other documents in the version series. Some repositories may also freeze property values, not just the content. The semantics of setting a retention or a hold on a folder isn't defined by the CMIS specification, but a repository may allow that.

Retentions and holds again demonstrate that looking at a document's ACL doesn't reveal a user's true permissions. Even if a user has the `cmis:all` permission, they may not be allowed to delete the document because of a retention. But the allowable actions should reflect this fact.

12.6 Summary

This chapter covered authentication and authorization topics and pointed out some general security issues that CMIS applications frequently face. We started with some obvious, but sometimes overlooked, issues in web applications that deal with documents. We then explained that CMIS doesn't define how a client should authenticate an end user against the repository. A short introduction into the implementation of an OpenCMIS authentication provider showed you how to handle authentication in real projects. This was followed by the special authentication mechanism for web applications.

We also looked into policies and access control lists and explained what they're good for and how to use them. Finally, we touched on retentions and holds.

We've reached a major milestone in this book. At this point, we've covered all the functional details of CMIS. The next chapter covers a nonfunctional but important topic: performance.

13 Performance

This chapter covers

- Selecting the optimal data set
- OpenCMIS and DotCMIS caches
- Binding performance
- HTTP tuning

As a developer and end user, you know how important performance is for an application. Creating a folder should take only a few milliseconds. If it takes longer than that, sooner or later somebody will complain. If you've played with multiple CMIS repositories, you might have discovered that some repositories are faster than others.

The performance of a CMIS application depends on many factors. Of course, the repository is a major factor, but often it isn't the culprit when an application seems to be slow. This chapter presents a collection of real-world hints about how to avoid bottlenecks and how to improve the performance of CMIS clients and servers.

13.1 CMIS performance

When the first developers picked up OpenCMIS to build applications, there were mixed reactions. A few blog posts on the internet talk about first experiences with CMIS, and OpenCMIS in particular. Some reported something like this: "I quickly got it running and could connect to Alfresco and SharePoint. That's great! But this CMIS thing is very slow. I don't know if I should use it in my application."

What's the reason for these apparently missed expectations? CMIS looks similar to a filesystem, and people make calls against a repository that are similar to the calls they would make against a filesystem. So on one hand, you have a local filesystem where operations are usually fast. Getting the list of files in a folder or the size of a file takes almost no time. On the other hand, CMIS communicates over a network. Each OpenCMIS method call results in one or more calls to the repository. Each call has to be authenticated, and each request or response must be serialized and parsed. Although almost all of these calls take only a few milliseconds, they add up.

Thus, some of the missed expectations are due to people making an unfair comparison between local filesystem performance and a remote CMIS repository. But other reasons are linked to simple misuse of the library. Here are a few examples:

- A developer with administrator permissions requested all descendants of the root folder, and the repository happily returned them. The response was 170 MB of XML. It worked—both the client and server were able to handle the large response. But it took a moment to transfer this large amount of data. Because the application needed only a fraction of it, the situation was easy to fix. Eventually, the data was reduced to a few kilobytes.
- A development team switched an application from filesystem-based storage to CMIS. They replaced all filesystem operations with CMIS operations. They had one method that returned the file path, one that returned the file size, and one that returned the last modification date. In their CMIS code, each method set up a new OpenCMIS session, fetched the object, and retrieved the requested property. That is, each of these methods performed three or four calls to the repository. They performed 10 calls total per document. With a bit of refactoring, it was easy to reduce this to one call, which saved a few hundred milliseconds per document.
- A developer wanted to display the version histories of a set of documents on a web page. He fetched the version history of each document, grabbed the object ID of each version object, and then fetched the version object. When the documents had many versions, it took a while to load the web page. It turned out that it wasn't necessary to fetch each version object again. The version history already contained all required information about the version objects. With a few code changes, the web page's load performance became acceptable.
- A development team built an application and tested it. It worked fine. But when they deployed it into the production environment, performance was much worse compared to the test environment. The culprit was a reverse proxy server in the production environment, which handled the traffic between the repository and the application. This proxy server closed the socket connection after each request, ignoring HTTP Keep-Alive. After the administrator changed the configuration of the proxy server, performance was on par with the test environment.

CMIS can be fast if the application is properly designed, the runtime environment is correctly set up, and the repository plays along. CMIS client libraries make development easy, but as a developer you still have to understand what's going on under the covers.

The following sections highlight a few critical spots. They're independent of each other, and not all will be applicable to your application. Keep them in the back of your mind when you're building your application.

13.2 Selecting the smallest data set

Do you remember chapters 7 and 8, where `OperationContext` was used everywhere? "Not again!" you might think, but in fact, from a developer's point of view, the `OperationContext` is one of the best tools you have to tune your application's performance.

Here are a few rules of thumb for an efficient CMIS application:

- Only ask for the object details you really, really need. If you can supply filters or, with OpenCMIS and DotCMIS, an `OperationContext`, do it. Never rely on the default values of the repository, because most of them will give you far more details than you need.
- Where possible, avoid properties that the repository has to calculate. Good candidates to avoid are properties that have to do with versioning and paths. For example, to find out if the document is the latest major version, the repository has to go through the version history. That may take only a fraction of a millisecond per object, and that's nothing you would identify as a problem during development. But it might make a difference in production with millions of requests per day.
- Allowable actions are handy if you're implementing a user interface and you want to show users what they can and can't do with an object. But calculating the allowable action values is expensive for almost all repositories. The server has to check the permissions for all operations covered by the allowable actions. So if you don't need them, don't ask for them.
- Fetching the ACL of an object can be expensive for repositories that support inherited permissions. To compile the ACL of an object, the repository has to visit all parents, and the parents of the parents, and so on, until it hits the root.
- When you fetch an object, you can choose to retrieve no relationships, only the relationships where the object is the source or is the target, or all relationships the object is involved in. Some repositories have to filter which relationships the current user is allowed to see. Even if the number of relationships that the repository returns is small, the repository might have touched a greater number of objects, so only pick what you need. Check whether requesting the relationships with a separate `getObjectRelationships` call makes more sense than getting the relationships in the same call as `getObject` or `getObjectByPath`. This provides much better control over the result set. (The CMIS operation

getObjectRelationships is called getRelationships in OpenCMIS and DotCMIS.)

- Prefer getObject to getObjectByPath. getObject is a bit faster for many repositories because many repositories internally organize their objects by object ID, not by path.
- Ask only for objects you really need. Pay special attention to operations that return lists and trees, such as getChildren, query, and getDescendants. With lists and trees, even minimal performance penalties per object multiply quickly. Losing a millisecond per object adds up to a second when a query returns 1,000 results. A second can be a long time for an end user.
- Use paging, and use it wisely. Ask only for the subset you really need. If you present a list to an end user, select only the first few entries. It's not likely that an end user is interested in the thousandth query result. If you need to iterate over the entire list, go for relatively large pages, because that requires fewer round trips.
- If you have to sort a list, let the repository do it. The repository can do it more efficiently than your application. Most operations that return lists have an order by parameter.
- Select a reasonable tree depth for operations that take a depth parameter. Avoid the value -1 (infinite). Repositories can restrict the number of elements returned in a tree. Because these operations don't support paging, asking for too many elements can be counterproductive. An incomplete tree is often useless for an application.
- Never use a SELECT * FROM ... query in a production application. Always provide the list of properties you want back. You don't know how expensive it is for the repository to prepare the result set with all properties.

There shouldn't been any real surprises in this list; we covered most of these items in previous chapters. But it's good to recap them here. You may want to use them as a checklist when you encounter a performance issue.

13.3 Performance notes specific to OpenCMIS and DotCMIS

The list of performance considerations covered so far is applicable regardless of which CMIS client you're using. Here are some items specific to OpenCMIS and DotCMIS:

- When you define a property filter in an OperationContext, OpenCMIS and DotCMIS always add the properties cmis:objectId, cmis:objectTypeId, and cmis:baseTypeId to the filter. This is necessary to construct proper CmisObjects.
- The create methods on the Session object (createDocument, createFolder, and so on) are faster than similar methods on other interfaces. These create methods return only the object ID and not the full-blown new object, which saves a round trip. If you want to create and forget objects, use these methods.

- There's a `getContentStream` method on the `Session` object, which lets you get the content of a document directly without getting the document object. That can save a round trip to the repository.
- There's also a `delete` method, which you can use to delete an object without fetching it first. That can save another round trip.
- In the CMIS specification, you'll find the terms *path segment* and *relative path segment* in conjunction with the `getChildren` and `getObjectParents` operations. You can turn them on and off in the `OperationContext`, but there's no need to turn them on. OpenCMIS and DotCMIS request them automatically if necessary.
- The `OperationContext` has a `setMaxItemsPerPage` method, which lets you define the actual page size that's used when the repository is contacted to retrieve a list. For example, if you iterate over all children in a folder (where the folder has 1,000 children and max items per page is 100), then the library contacts the repository 10 times during the iteration to get a chunk of 100 children. There's a trade-off between responsiveness and the total time to fetch all items in the list. A high max items per page value decreases the total time to fetch all items because it requires fewer round trips. But it also takes longer to retrieve the first item because a longer list must be compiled, transferred, and parsed first. This value depends on your use case.
- If you explicitly select a page with the `getPage` method, the max items per page value still applies. If the selected page size is bigger than the max items per page value, the library makes multiple calls until the data for the page has been completely served. If the selected page size is smaller than the max items per page value, the library makes one call that potentially requests more items than necessary for the page. If your page size is small (for example, you want to display the first 10 hits of a query), the page size and the max items per page value should be the same.

Caching is another way to avoid unnecessary calls. The next two sections explain the OpenCMIS and DotCMIS caches.

13.4 Caching

Caching is a common method to increase performance. OpenCMIS and DotCMIS provide several built-in caches (see figure 13.1). Most of them are invisible to the application, and application developers usually don't need to be familiar with the details. But it helps to know the basics when you debug your application and trace the traffic between client and server.

There are two types of caches. The first type caches static data that's unlikely to change. The second type deals with object data that does change during runtime. The next two sections explain these caches.

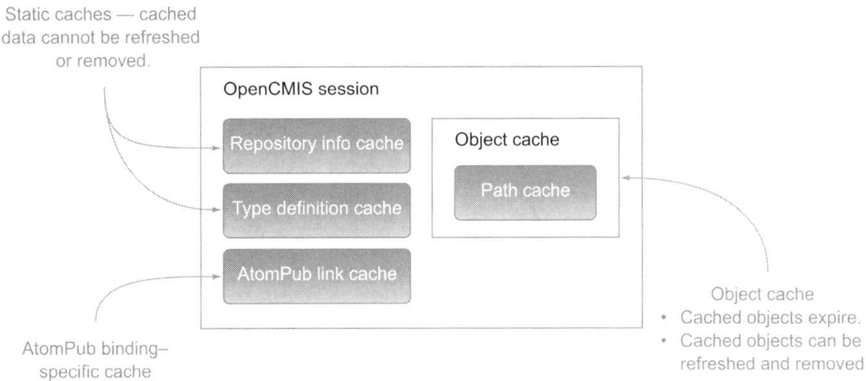

Figure 13.1 Built-in OpenCMIS session caches at a glance

CACHES FOR OTHER CMIS CLIENT LIBRARIES Other client libraries may not provide built-in caches, but applications can build something similar on top. All programming languages provide the means to build a simple cache infrastructure. Web applications could, for example, use the HTML5 Web Storage. Although the following sections talk about the OpenCMIS caches and interfaces, these topics are also relevant for your homemade caches.

13.4.1 Caching static data

In a production environment, several things in CMIS are static and can be cached on the client side without side effects. These are mainly the repository info and the type definitions. This data is needed—directly or indirectly—over and over again in an application. So fetching it only once and caching it makes sense.

OpenCMIS transparently caches repository info and type definitions. The `Session` object manages all caches. You can turn these caches off or change the cache sizes when you set up the session. Usually you don't have to change the cache settings—you can live with the defaults. But if your application deals with more than 100 different object types at the same time, you may want to increase the type definition cache size.

In development environments, type definitions may change while your application is running. New and removed types won't harm your application. New types will be picked up when the application loads an object with this type for the first time. Removed types will stay in the cache, but there shouldn't be any objects referencing them. When type definitions are modified and the type definition is already cached, OpenCMIS may throw exceptions when the first object that uses the changes is loaded. If you find yourself in this situation, you can either clear all caches by calling `clear` on the `Session` object or create a new `Session` object.

A SESSION PER USER

You may wonder why these caches are attached to a session. Wouldn't it be possible to have one repository info cache and one type definition cache for all sessions in the

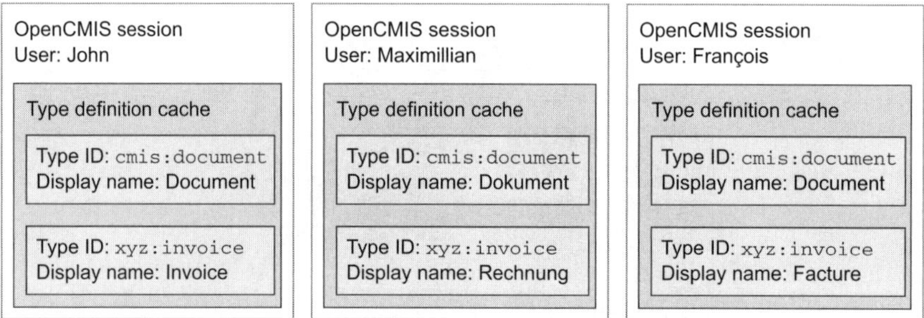

Figure 13.2 An OpenCMIS session is bound to a user. Each user has its own cache because a repository can return user-specific data. Here, three different users retrieved the same type definitions, and the repository returned localized display names.

JVM? Wouldn't that save additional calls and memory? This is a valid idea, but it doesn't work that way. A session is bound to a user. A repository can return different repository info and different type definitions for each user. For example, the display names of type and property definitions can be localized for each user (see figure 13.2). Some users may not be allowed to see certain type definitions. And the repository info may return different repository capabilities if the user has admin privileges.

The `Session` object and the caches belong together. *That's why you should always keep your* `Session` *object.* Create one when you need it, and then reuse it whenever possible. Creating a second `Session` object for the same user is equivalent to throwing away your caches. And that adversely affects application performance.

THE ATOMPUB LINK CACHE

There's another cache in OpenCMIS that you'll probably never notice because it resides deep down the stack. It caches AtomPub links (see section 11.2.2) and is crucial for the performance of the AtomPub binding implementation. This cache is mentioned here for those who want to build their own binding library. You should keep track of the links in Atom entries and feeds; they're required for subsequent calls to the repository.

The cache settings can be adjusted with session parameters when the session is created. In contrast to the other two caches, it's updated very frequently because each entry refers to a CMIS object. The cache size should reflect the number of objects your application is dealing with. The default cache size of 400 entries should work for most scenarios.

Apart from caching Atom links, caching whole objects can drastically increase the application performance. It's a bit more difficult to manage, though. Let's explore the OpenCMIS object cache.

13.4.2 Caching objects

Assume you're developing a web application. It uses Ajax calls to refresh certain areas of your web page. Multiple Ajax calls refer to the same CMIS document. One call

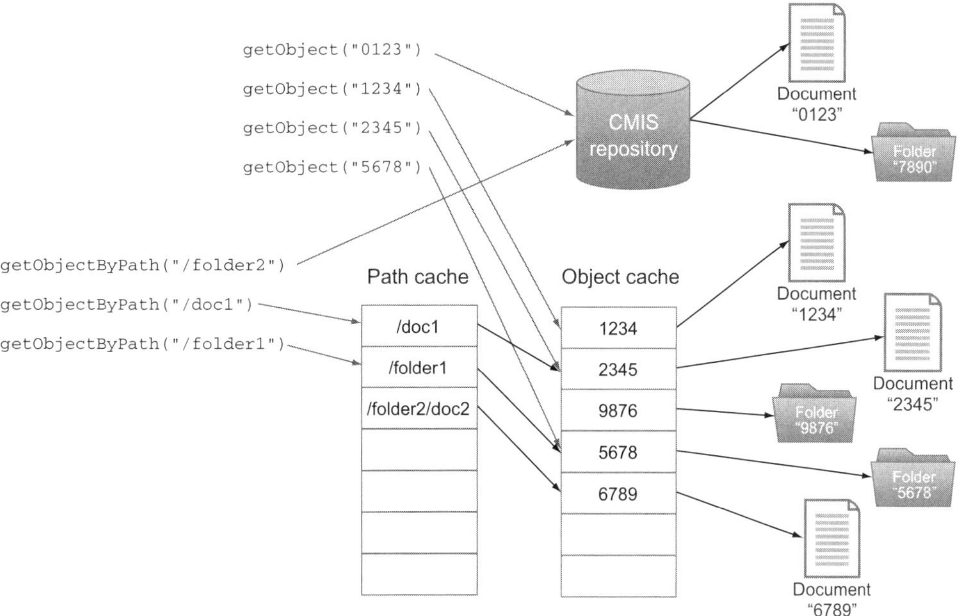

Figure 13.3 Routing `getObject` and `getObjectByPath` calls through the object and path cache. If the requested object isn't in the cache, the request is forwarded to the repository.

updates the properties view, another refreshes the ACL view, and a third lists the document renditions. Usually, different server threads serve each call.

Each thread could load the document data separately, but that would be a waste of time, bandwidth, and memory. Because this is the chapter about performance, we have a solution for you.

OpenCMIS has an object cache. Whenever you call `getObject` or `getObjectByPath`, it will first look into its cache. If the object is available, the method won't fetch it from the repository but will serve it from the cache (see figure 13.3). Because OpenCMIS is thread-safe, you can and should reuse its objects across multiple threads.

An object is the same object in the cache if the object ID is same and the same `OperationContext` (remember chapter 7) was used to retrieve the object. That is, an object can be in the cache more than once with a different set of metadata. This is another reason to keep the number of `OperationContexts` small and to reuse these objects.

The default cache is an LRU cache; each object expires after two hours. An additional cache keeps a mapping from the object path to the object ID; these cache entries time out after 30 minutes. All these characteristics can be adjusted when you create the session. You can even provide your own cache implementation or turn off the cache entirely.

Caches are good for performance, but they have a common problem: they can become stale. Sometimes you want a fresh object, and there are multiple ways to achieve that.

The `OperationContext` has a flag that controls whether the cache should be used (or not) for an operation. That's handy if you repeatedly need fresh data. Set up such an `OperationContext` that turns off the cache, and reuse it, like this:

```
OperationContext context = session.createOperationContext();
context.setFilterString(
  "cmis:objectId,cmis:name,cmis:lastModificationDate"
);
context.setIncludeAllowableActions(false);
context.setCacheEnabled(false);
 ...
CmisObject obj = session.getObject("1234567890", context);
```

Object cache is ignored when this Operation-Context is used

getObject call bypasses the cache and gets the object directly from the repository

If you want to disable the cache for all operations that don't take an `Operation-Context`, you can do this:

```
session.getDefaultContext().setCacheEnabled(false);
```

A more individual way is to call `refresh` on an object. The object will contact the repository and ask for the same set of data it was originally created with. If the object no longer exists in the repository, `refresh` will throw a `CmisObjectNotFoundException`:

```
try {
  doc.refresh();
} catch(CmisObjectNotFoundException notFound) {

}
```

A common misuse of `refresh` is this:

```
try {
  document = (Document) session.getObject("12345678");
  document.refresh();
}
catch(CmisObjectNotFoundException e) {

}
```

Call unnecessary because of the getObject call immediately before it

The first request for the object loads the object and then immediately refreshes it. That is, there are two calls to the repository, and the second one isn't necessary.

Usually you want to refresh an object only after a certain period of time. Each object knows when it was last refreshed. If you need to know that too, call `getRefreshTimestamp`. This timestamp is also used for the `refreshIfOld` method. `refreshIfOld` takes a duration in milliseconds. If the object has been refreshed within this time span, `refreshIfOld` doesn't do anything. Otherwise, it contacts the repository and refreshes the object:

```
Document doc = (Document) session.getObject("1234567890");
...
try {
```

```
  doc.refreshIfOld(2 * 60 * 1000);
} catch(CmisObjectNotFoundException notFound) {
}
```

Refreshes the object only if it hasn't been refreshed within the last 2 minutes

How would you use this? Let's go back to the web page example with the parallel Ajax requests. Each thread can call `refreshIfOld` with a duration of, let's say, 10 seconds. Because Ajax requests are usually pretty close together, only the first call that hits the server refreshes the document data. It doesn't matter which call is first.

Whether 5 seconds, 5 minutes, or 50 minutes is the best duration depends on your application. If your documents don't change often, a long duration may be acceptable. A website with many visitors can reduce the load of the repository and improve the site's performance with an appropriately long duration.

A tricky combination is the cache and the `getObjectByPath` method. The cache maps the path of an object to the object. If somebody deletes the object and creates a new object with the same path, the cache won't recognize this and will return the old object (until it expires in the cache). Calling `refresh` on an object won't help because it tries to reload the object by its ID. Because an object with this ID doesn't exist anymore, you always get a `CmisObjectNotFoundException`. The pattern to deal with this situation is shown in the following listing.

Listing 13.1 Dealing with a deleted and re-created document at the same path

```
Document doc = (Document) session.getObjectByPath("path/to/doc");

...

ContentStream stream = null;
try {
  stream = doc.getContenStream();
}
catch(CmisObjectNotFoundException e) {
  session.removeObjectFromCache(doc);

  try {

    doc = (Document) session.getObjectByPath("/path/to/doc");
    stream = doc.getContenStream();
  }
  catch(CmisObjectNotFoundException e) {
    // there is no object at this path anymore
  }
}
```

Removes old object from the cache before requesting it again

Object is no longer in the cache, so this call will hit the repository

This listing tries to get the content of a document that was retrieved earlier by path. Someone deleted the original document, and now `getContentStream` throws a `CmisObjectNotFoundException` because there's no longer a document with this object ID. That is, the object is invalid, and you can remove it from the cache. Then you try fetching the document again by path. If there's a new document, you get the content stream. If there's nothing at this path, you have to deal with it.

The static data cache described in the previous section resides in the low-level API implementation and therefore is available for both the low-level and high-level APIs of OpenCMIS and DotCMIS. The object cache is a feature of the high-level API. If you're using the low-level API, you have to build your own object data cache.

13.5 Selecting the fastest binding

Performance varies widely among the three bindings. The Web Services binding is the slowest of the three. The AtomPub binding is significantly faster. And the Browser binding is even faster than the AtomPub binding.

To give you a rough idea of the differences, we ran a test set using a typical mix of operations against a fast repository on a fast network without compression. The AtomPub binding run was about three times faster than the Web Services binding run. And the Browser binding run was two times faster than the AtomPub binding run, as shown in figure 13.4.

Figure 13.4 Performance differences of the three CMIS bindings. The Browser binding is the fastest.

The absolute numbers depend on the repository, client, network setup, authentication method, and so on. If you have a choice, test all available bindings. OpenCMIS makes switching the binding pretty easy (see chapter 11).

One last word about the AtomPub binding: the content of a document is Base64-encoded when you're creating a document with `createDocument`. That is, the content size grows by approximately a third when it's transferred over the wire. That doesn't matter when you're uploading typical office documents, but it makes a difference when you're uploading big video files or X-ray images. A workaround is to create an empty document first and then add the content to the document with `setContentStream` or `appendContentStream`, which don't encode the content.

If the repository doesn't allow or support `setContentStream` or `appendContentStream`, you should at least test whether the server supports client compression, because Base64 compresses very well. The next section explains how to turn that on. It also covers other HTTP-related and binding-independent performance hints.

13.6 Tuning HTTP for CMIS

All CMIS bindings are based on HTTP, and thus tuning HTTP performance helps CMIS applications and servers. Let's walk through the most important aspects.

13.6.1 HTTP Keep-Alive

HTTP 1.1 defines that clients and servers should support Keep-Alive connections. That is, a socket connection between client and server should be reused for multiple requests. This is an important feature of CMIS because applications usually send a burst of requests to the repository. Here's a simple example: the application wants to create a document in a folder. This may lead to the following sequence of calls:

1. `getObjectByPath` (get folder object)
2. `getTypeDefinition` (get the folder's type, if not already cached)
3. `getTypeDefinition` (get the document's type, if not already cached)
4. `createDocument` (create the document)
5. `getObject` (retrieve the newly created document to present the metadata to the user)

With Keep-Alive, this can happen over one connection. There's no overhead for establishing multiple connections. This overhead can be considerable, especially if you use HTTPS. Many SSL handshakes can affect application performance.

There's usually nothing you have to do to enable Keep-Alive. Most client libraries and repositories support it out of the box. But be prepared for a nasty surprise when you deploy your repository and your application in your production environment. Load balancers, proxy servers, and firewalls may not have Keep-Alive activated. If you encounter much worse performance after you move your application from the development to the production environment, check whether Keep-Alive is enabled along the way.

13.6.2 Compression

CMIS sends XML and JSON requests and responses over the wire. Both compress very well. The size of an AtomPub feed shrinks between 5% and 95% when it's compressed. Compression can burst application performance, especially on slow networks and over the internet.

How do you enable compression? We have to look at requests and responses separately. Let's start with responses.

Clients can request response compression by setting the HTTP header `Accept-Encoding`. OpenCMIS does that if you turn on compression when you set up the session (see chapter 6, section 6.5.2):

```
parameter.put(SessionParameter.COMPRESSION, "true");
```

That doesn't necessarily mean the repository returns a compressed response. Some repositories support it out of the box, and others don't. Check with the repository vendor as well as the application server vendor. If you can configure it, the following MIME types at least should be compressed:

- `application/atomsvc+xml`
- `application/atom+xml;type=entry`

- application/atom+xml;type=feed
- application/cmisquery+xml
- application/cmisallowableactions+xml
- application/cmisatom+xml
- application/cmistree+xml
- application/cmisacl+xml
- application/json
- application/xml
- text/xml

OpenCMIS can also compress requests. Turn on client compression when you set up the session, like this:

```
parameter.put(SessionParameter.CLIENT_COMPRESSION, "true");
```

OpenCMIS uses gzip to compress the XML and JSON payloads. Only a few repositories can handle compressed requests, though. Check with the repository vendor and application server vendor to find out if the repository you're working with supports this feature.

The CMIS Workbench lets you switch request and response compression on and off in the login dialog box. Use a debug proxy, and watch the traffic as described in chapter 11. You'll see that compression can make a huge difference.

13.6.3 Authentication and cookies

Chapter 12 covered the use of cookies for authentication. It's important to mention it here again in the context of performance. Turning on cookies can drastically boost performance for some repositories because the repository has to check the user credentials only once per session. Try using the CMIS Workbench with and without cookies to test whether it makes a difference for the repository you want to use.

To turn on cookie support in OpenCMIS, use this session parameter:

```
parameter.put(SessionParameter.COOKIES, "true");
```

13.6.4 Timeouts

Connection and read timeouts aren't performance-related. They control how quickly a call should fail if the application can't connect to the repository. The end user's perception of application performance may be related to this aspect.

You can set the timeouts in milliseconds as session parameters, as follows:

```
parameter.put(SessionParameter.CONNECT_TIMEOUT, "20000");    <-- 20 seconds
parameter.put(SessionParameter.READ_TIMEOUT, "10000");       <-- 10 seconds
```

13.7 Summary

In this chapter, we discussed different factors that affect the performance of a CMIS application. Although repository performance plays a big role, several other factors, such as network infrastructure and application design, may have an impact. Read and make sure you understand the hints in this chapter before you start your first real CMIS application. Also be sure to revisit this chapter before you put your application into production.

If you've ever thought about building your own CMIS server, then the next chapter is what you've been waiting for. It covers the OpenCMIS Server Framework.

14 Building a CMIS server

This chapter covers

- Generating a CMIS server stub with the OpenCMIS Server Framework
- Testing a CMIS server for compliance
- Using the OpenCMIS query parser
- Changing the authentication mechanism

In the previous chapters, we looked at CMIS mainly from a client perspective. In this chapter, we're changing sides and explaining how to build a CMIS server. You'll learn how to build a CMIS frontend on top of an existing content repository (or similar data source) with the OpenCMIS Server Framework. For this chapter, you should know how to work with servlets and understand the general concepts relating to building web applications.

14.1 Introduction to the OpenCMIS Server Framework

It's hardly surprising that a CMIS server is an upside-down version of a CMIS client. All the principles we've discussed in this book apply here, too. Similar to a CMIS client, you can either implement the CMIS bindings yourself or use a library or framework. Using a framework obviously saves you time and effort.

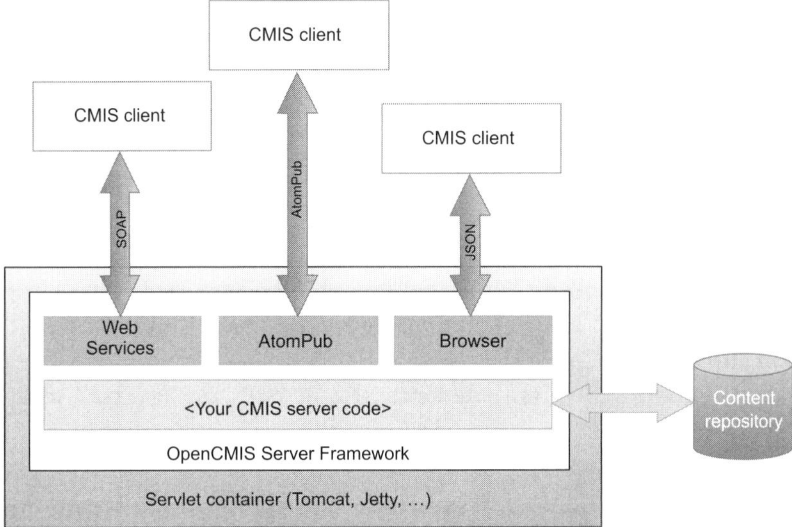

Figure 14.1 The OpenCMIS Server Framework in a servlet engine

In this chapter, we'll discuss the OpenCMIS Server Framework, which is a Java server implementation of CMIS. It runs on top of a servlet engine such as Tomcat or Jetty (see figure 14.1). It implements all CMIS bindings, which means it covers all XML and JSON handling. To connect the framework to the content repository, you have to implement two Java interfaces: `CmisService` and `CmisServiceFactory`. Take a wild guess what we'll be talking about next.

14.1.1 CmisService interface

The main interface is `CmisService`. If you've played with the OpenCMIS client low-level API, this interface should look familiar. The `CmisService` interface is an aggregation of all nine low-level interfaces plus a few extra methods that we'll explain a bit later. This interface covers all CMIS 1.0 and 1.1 operations and has over 50 methods. The methods and parameters are named after the CMIS operations. Implementations of this interface are supposed to behave as described in the specification; that includes throwing the exceptions documented in the specification. The "Services" section of the CMIS specification will become your best friend when you're implementing this interface.

14.1.2 CmisServiceFactory interface

The second interface is `CmisServiceFactory`. As the name suggests, it provides instances of `CmisService` implementations. Apart from the `getService` method that returns such an object, there are some methods that are called at initialization and destruction time of the web application as well as methods that return configuration data.

14.1.3 The framework

The framework consists of five servlets (shown in figure 14.2) and two context listeners. One context listener initializes the `CmisServiceFactory` implementation. The other one sets up the Web Services binding. There are two servlets for the Web Services binding (one for CMIS 1.0, the other for CMIS 1.1), two servlets for the AtomPub binding (again one for CMIS 1.0 and one for CMIS 1.1), and one servlet for the Browser binding (CMIS 1.1 only).

When a servlet receives a CMIS request, it parses the requests, checks if the request is syntactically correct, and turns the input parameters into Java objects. It then asks the `CmisServiceFactory` implementation for an instance of the `CmisService` implementation and calls the appropriate method with the input Java objects. The response of the called method is then translated into XML or JSON and sent back to the client.

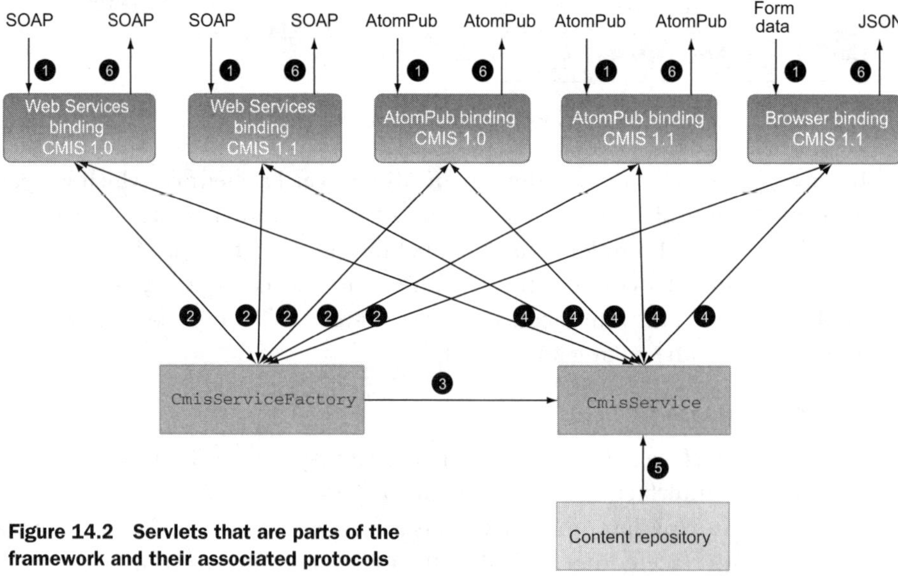

Figure 14.2 Servlets that are parts of the framework and their associated protocols

That is the general mode of operation. The rest of this chapter describes how to implement the two interfaces, set up a CMIS web application, and deploy that application.

14.2 Generating a server stub

You'll use a Maven archetype to generate a Maven project, which in turn creates a server stub. Don't worry if you aren't familiar with Maven; this chapter provides step-by-step instructions. Once the stub has been generated, you can keep the Maven project for further development or move the stub to a different build environment of your choice.

To generate the stub, you need Java 5 (or higher) and Maven 3 installed on your computer. The stub generation is done via command line. First change to the stub's target directory. Then execute the following command:

```
mvn archetype:generate \
-DgroupId=org.example.cmis \
-DartifactId=my-cmis-server \
-Dversion=1.0-SNAPSHOT \
-Dpackage=org.example.cmis.server \
-DprojectPrefix=Example \
-DarchetypeGroupId=org.apache.chemistry.opencmis \
-DarchetypeArtifactId=chemistry-opencmis-server-archetype \
-DarchetypeVersion=0.9.0 \
-DinteractiveMode=false
```

This call accepts the following parameters:

- `groupId`, `artifactId`, and `version`—Maven coordinates for the project you're creating.
- `package`—Java package for your project.
- `projectPrefix`—Prefix for the classes that will be generated. For example, the prefix `Example` generates the classes `ExampleCmisService` and `ExampleCmisServiceFactory`.
- `archetypeGroupId`, `archetypeArtifactId`, and `archetypeVersion`—OpenCMIS archetype and OpenCMIS version that should be used. The archetype was introduced with OpenCMIS 0.9.0. You may choose this version or a later version to generate the stub. This version also defines the runtime OpenCMIS Server Framework version.
- `interactiveMode`—If false, Maven won't prompt you to confirm any of the previous parameters passed in.

Next we'll explore the results generated by this process. As you'll see, this is a real time saver:

```
|--my-cmis-server
|----pom.xml
|----src
  |----main
    |----java
    | |----org
    |   |----example
    |     |----cmis
    |       |----server
    |         |----ExampleCmisService.java
    |         |----ExampleCmisServiceFactory.java
    |----webapp
      |----index.jsp
      |----WEB-INF
        |----classes
          |----repository.properties
```

Here are the five key files:

- *pom.xml*—The pom.xml file for your web project. It contains the configuration you need to build the CMIS server. You can adapt this file if necessary.
- *ExampleCmisService.java*—Stub implementation of the `CmisService` interface. Note that it resides in the package you provided and has the prefix defined previously.
- *ExampleCmisServiceFactory.java*—Stub implementation of the `CmisServiceFactory` interface.
- *index.jsp*—Start page of the web application. It provides the URLs for the three CMIS bindings. You can change or remove this file; it's not required in order to run the server.
- *repository.properties*—Connects the framework with your implementation. It's a Java properties file, which must at least contain the key `class`. The value for this key is the fully qualified class name of the `CmisServiceFactory` implementation. If you rename or move your factory class, you have to adapt this file accordingly.

Now that all the introductions are over, let's build a WAR file for this new project.

14.2.1 Building the CMIS server WAR file

Change to the my-cmis-server directory, and run the following command to build the web application:

```
mvn clean install
```

When the build is done, there should be a subdirectory called target. It contains a ready-to-run WAR file called my-cmis-server-1.0-SNAPSHOT.war. The name is a combination of the `artifactId` and project version. Rename it to something shorter, such as myserver.war, and deploy it to a servlet engine.

For your first tests, use a plain servlet engine like Tomcat or Jetty. Some application servers need a special classloader configuration, which we don't cover here. Once the deployment has finished, open the URL http://localhost:8080/myserver (adjust host and port) in a web browser. You should see the CMIS server start page shown in figure 14.3.

The start page contains links to the three bindings. Copy the URLs, and try them with the CMIS Workbench. You should be able to load the (short) list of repositories, but further requests will fail. Nevertheless, you've just deployed a CMIS server. Congratulations!

Let's look under the hood of the WAR file next.

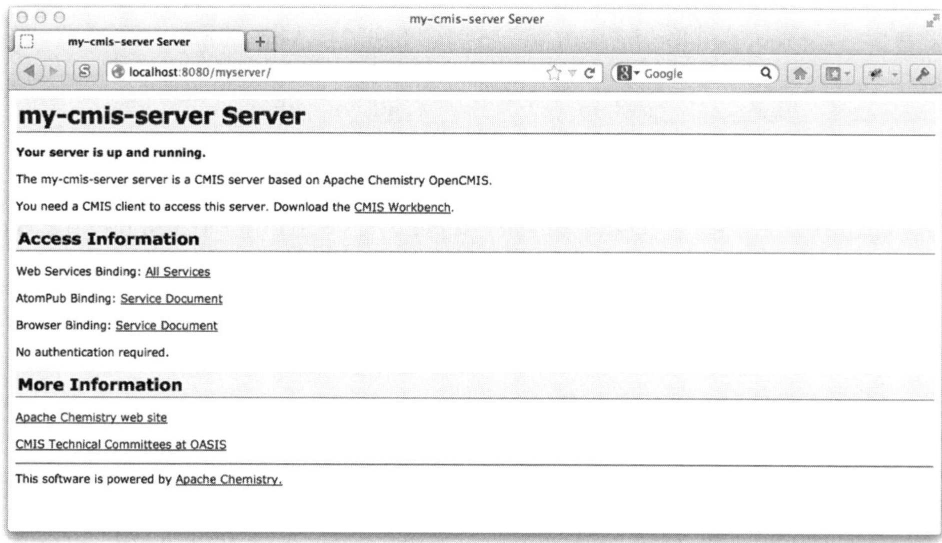

Figure 14.3 The CMIS server start page

14.2.2 Dissecting the CMIS server WAR file

When you unpack the WAR file, you should see something like this:

```
|----index.jsp
|----WEB-INF
  |----classes
  | |----org
  | | |----example
  | |   |----cmis
  | |     |----server
  | |       |----ExampleCmisService.class
  | |       |----ExampleCmisServiceFactory.class
  | |----repository.properties
  |----lib
  | |----...
  |----cmis10
  | |----...
  |----cmis11
  | |----...
  |----sun-jaxws.xml
  |----web.xml
```

Here are the high points of what you see here:

- The index.jsp file and the contents of the WEB-INF/classes directory should look familiar. These are the generated project files.
- The WEB-INF/lib directory contains all libraries that are required to run the CMIS server.

- The WEB-INF/sun-jaxws.xml file and the cmis10 and cmis11 directories are required for the Web Services binding. The WSDL and XSD files are fixed by the specification and shouldn't be modified. We'll come back to the sun-jaxws.xml file a bit later when we talk about authentication.
- The WEB-INF/web.xml file defines all servlets and context listeners.

You can override these files and add new files by putting them in the right place under the src directory. You can also add dependencies to other Maven projects to pom.xml. You'll probably want to embed a library that helps you connect to your underlying content repository.

At this point you have a choice of continuing to use this Maven project or taking the contents of the WAR file plus the source files and moving to a different build environment. The project setup is done now. Next we'll dive into the implementation details.

14.3 Implementing the CmisServiceFactory interface

The main task of a `CmisServiceFactory` implementation is to serve `CmisService` instances. Before we look into this, open the generated class `ExampleCmisServiceFactory` and skim through it. You may notice that it doesn't implement the interface directly but extends the `AbstractServiceFactory` class instead. This abstract class implements all the methods of the `CmisServiceFactory` interface except `getService`, which provides the `CmisService` objects. It's recommended that you use this abstract class because it provides sensible default return values for the interface's other methods.

How the `getService` method creates or manages a `CmisService` object is up to the implementation. The factory can create an object for each request, can pool objects, or can keep an object per thread in a `ThreadLocal`. In the end it depends on how expensive it is to create and maintain such an object.

`CmisService` objects aren't shared across threads by the framework and don't need to be thread-safe. But if they're reused, they must not keep any data from a previous request. That could lead to unpredictable side effects and memory leaks.

14.3.1 CmisServiceWrapper

OpenCMIS provides an optional wrapper for `CmisService` objects. The `CmisServiceWrapper` class checks every request before it's forwarded to the `CmisService` object. If a request obviously violates the CMIS specification, the wrapper throws the appropriate exception. For example, if a client calls the `getObject` operation without an object ID, the wrapper automatically throws a `CmisInvalidArgumentException`, and the actual `CmisService` object isn't bothered with this request.

Additionally, the wrapper sets operation parameters that the client didn't provide if the specification defines a default values for these parameters. For example, if a client calls the `checkIn` operation and doesn't provide the `major` flag, which defines whether the new version should become a major version, the wrapper sets the `major` flag to `TRUE`, because that's the default value defined in the specification. That is, your

`CmisService` implementation always gets a value for such a parameter, even if the client didn't supply one.

Clients don't need to set the `maxItems` parameter for operations that return lists, and they also don't need to set the `depth` parameter for operations that return trees. The specification says the default values for these parameters are repository-specific. The wrapper lets you define these values and fills them in if the client didn't provide the parameters.

In summary, the wrapper helps you build a specification-compliant and more robust server, and it's recommended that you take advantage of it. The generated `ExampleCmisServiceFactory` class demonstrates how to apply this wrapper. But the wrapper is optional—if you want or need to catch all invalid requests yourself, remove it from the code.

14.3.2 *CallContext*

You may also have noticed that the `getService` method gets a parameter of type `CallContext`. This `CallContext` object contains a lot of details about the current call. Just to name a few, it provides the repository ID, the binding the client used, the CMIS version of this call, and the username and password if the standard authentication mechanisms were used. It also provides the call's `HttpServletRequest` and `HttpServletResponse` objects, if you need low-level access.

The `getService` method is also a good place for checking user credentials. The `CallContext` object should provide all the necessary data. We'll cover authentication in detail later in this chapter; but as a rule of thumb, if the credentials are incorrect, throw a `CmisPermissionDeniedException` right here.

14.3.3 *Other CmisServiceFactory methods*

The other methods of the `CmisServiceFactory` interface can be divided into two groups. First are the two lifecycle methods `init` and `destroy`. The names suggest when they're called. The `init` method retrieves a `Map` of values, which represents the content of the repository.properties file. This file can be used to provide repository connection details.

The second group provides several configuration details for the framework. To handle big documents, the framework sometimes has to create temporary files in which to park content for a very short period of time. The following methods control the temporary files:

- `getTempDirectory`—Defines the directory for the temporary files. The default is the system's temp directory.
- `encryptTempFiles`—Documents can contain confidential content, so the temporary files can be encrypted. If this is turned on, plain document content will never touch a hard disk. It's turned off by default for performance reasons. (At the time of writing, the Web Services binding ignores this parameter, but that may change with later OpenCMIS releases.)

- getMemoryThreshold—Document content is written to temporary files only if they're bigger than the threshold value returned by this method. Documents smaller than that are buffered in main memory. The default value is 4,194,304 bytes (4 MB).
- getMaxContentSize—Temporary space isn't infinite. This method defines the size at which the framework should reject the document. The default value is 4,294,967,296 bytes (4 GB). If you're daring, you can return -1, which lifts this restriction entirely. (At the time of writing, the Web Services binding ignores this parameter, but that may change with later OpenCMIS releases.)

The factory is now set up, but the real work happens in the service implementation. Let's look into that next.

14.4 Implementing the CmisService interface

The CmisService interface is huge. We already said it has more than 50 methods. It's probably a good idea to split up the implementation into logical chunks, but how you divide it is up to you. The next few subsections will suggest some logical divisions.

14.4.1 AbstractCmisService

When you look at the generated ExampleCmisService class, you may wonder where all these methods are. The answer is that they're in the AbstractCmisService class, which the ExampleCmisService class extends. The abstract class provides convenience implementations for almost all CMIS operations. Most of them throw a CmisNotSupportedException. A few methods try deriving meaningful responses from other methods. For example, the getAllowableActions method calls the getObject method and extracts the allowable action from the response. That's good enough for a start, but probably not a sustainable solution for a productive system. For the most efficient implementation, you should eventually override all methods with your own code.

There are a few methods that the AbstractCmisService class doesn't implement and that are empty in the ExampleCmisService class. These methods are the bare minimum for a read-only CMIS server. Once those are implemented, you can browse your repository with the CMIS Workbench. The server isn't a fully compliant repository yet, but it's fairly close.

14.4.2 Best practices for implementing the CmisService

The best practices for implementing the CmisService interface work as follows:

1. Pick the next CMIS operation you want to implement, going for the read-only operations first.
2. Read the operation description in the CMIS specification and everything related to it.
3. Check the Javadoc of the AbstractCmisService class for implementation hints. A few CMIS operations map to more than one method because of binding differences. A bit later, you'll learn that the AtomPub binding sometimes needs

special treatment. Whenever you read something about "object info" objects, refer to "AtomPub differences," section 14.6, later in this chapter.

4 Implement the method(s). Note that all input and output parameters are interfaces. You can either implement them yourself or use the implementations provided by OpenCMIS. If you want to use the OpenCMIS implementations, add the suffix `Impl` to the interface names to get the implementation class names. These classes are basic data containers with getter and setter methods. Some parameters are wrapped in a `Holder<>` class; these are input and output parameters at the same time. Make sure you don't forget to set the values of these holders before your method returns.
5 Once in a while, compile and deploy your server and run the OpenCMIS Test Compatibility Kit (TCK), which is discussed in the next section.

THE LOCAL BINDING A fourth, nonstandard binding is mentioned in the `AbstractCmisService` Javadoc: the Local binding. This binding allows OpenCMIS clients to talk to OpenCMIS servers that reside in the same JVM. Instead of making calls over the network, the client directly invokes the server's Java methods.

There are all kinds of use cases for this binding. You'll know them when you see them, but it's particularly handy for tests. It lets you run automated tests outside a servlet engine, which can make testing much easier.

The process of implementing over 50 methods isn't as tedious as it seems. There's a lot of code you'll use over and over. For example, one of the first methods you have to implement is `getObject`. It takes a moment to build this method's bells and whistles, but it pays off when you tackle all the other methods that return `ObjectData` objects—`getChildren`, for example. Depending on the underlying content repository and how well its concepts fit with CMIS, it's possible to build a pretty solid and almost complete proof of concept in about a week.

You may also want to check out the source code of the OpenCMIS FileShare repository. This repository implementation turns a local filesystem directory on your computer into a CMIS repository. The code is straightforward and simple, and you may find some code snippets that you want to borrow—especially the type- and property type–definition code, which should be reusable.

Developing a proof of concept and developing a production server are two different things. The latter needs a lot more testing, and the OpenCMIS TCK should be part of it. We'll cover that in the next section.

14.5 Testing the CMIS server with the OpenCMIS TCK

The CMIS Technical Committee didn't define test cases or provide a certification program. There's no official test that can validate your CMIS server.

OpenCMIS tries to fill this gap with the Test Compatibility Kit (TCK). The TCK is a set of tests that makes a few hundred calls to a repository and checks whether the responses comply with the CMIS specification. It covers almost all aspects of the specification and is an essential tool for the early development stages.

14.5.1 Running the TCK with the CMIS Workbench

The easiest way to run the TCK is with the CMIS Workbench. There's a TCK button on the Workbench toolbar; it opens a dialog box that allows you to choose the tests you would like to execute (see figure 14.4). The TCK session inherits the login details from the Workbench session. When you're doing serious testing, you should run the tests for each binding.

All TCK tests are also JUnit tests, and the OpenCMIS TCK includes an Ant task for automated testing. The OpenCMIS Full Integration Test (FIT) runs the TCK with every OpenCMIS Maven build. If you want to do something similar, you may want to look at the OpenCMIS FIT package.

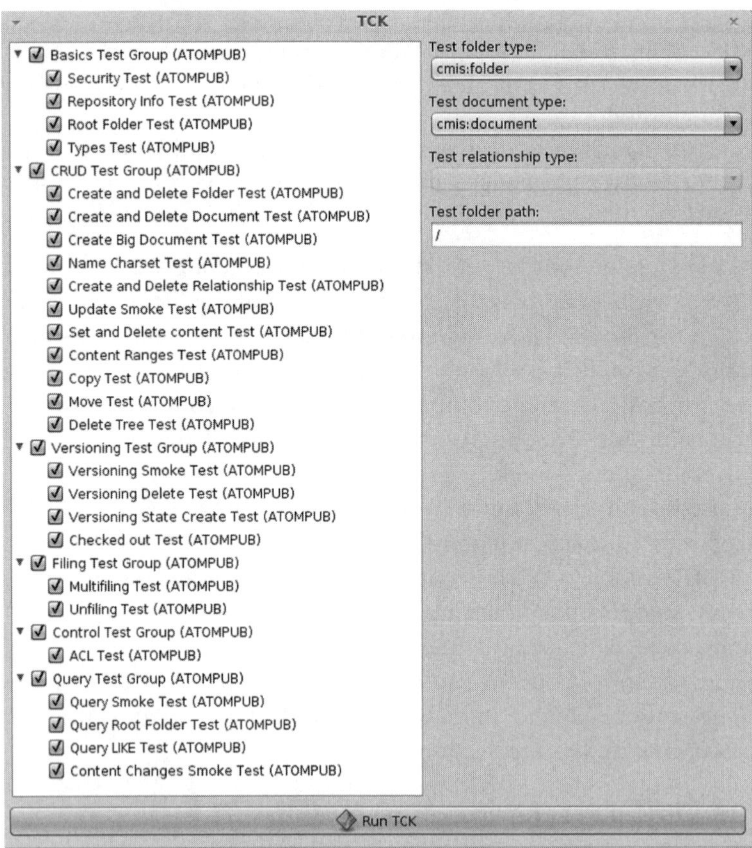

Figure 14.4 Dialog for TCK run options

14.5.2 TCK results breakdown

The TCK can report the results as XML, HTML, or plain text. There are six different message types:

- `INFO`—This type provides additional information about a test or a test result.
- `SKIPPED`—The test was skipped because the repository doesn't support the feature that should be tested.
- `OK`—The repository behaved as expected.
- `WARNING`—The repository didn't behave as expected, but it didn't violate the specification. When you see a warning for the first time, make sure you understand what's going on. Some warnings can be tolerable; others should be fixed to improve interoperability.
- `FAILURE`—The repository violated the specification. This needs to be fixed. There shouldn't be any failures in the final implementation.
- `UNEXPECTED EXCEPTION`—The repository threw an exception that the test didn't expect. It's very likely that there's a bug in the repository implementation.

The TCK tries to point out the exact cause of a problem wherever possible. But in some cases it's helpful to look at the TCK test code and understand exactly what's going on. Each result contains the name of the Java test class and a line number, which should help you track down the issue. Figure 14.5 shows the TCK results screen after a test run in the CMIS Workbench.

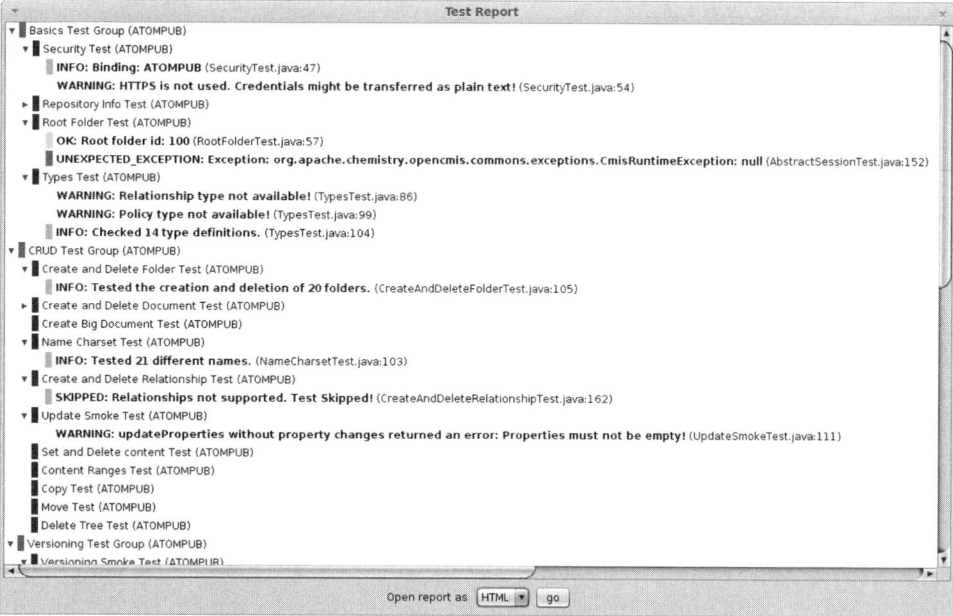

Figure 14.5 TCK results dialog box after a test run, showing first few results

14.5.3 Deeper testing

Although the TCK covers a lot, it can't replace repository-specific tests. Some TCK tests are complete, whereas others are shallow. An example of a more complete test is this: the TCK creates documents, checks that the documents are there, verifies that they're complete and correct, and then deletes the documents and checks that they're gone. Queries, on the other hand, can only be tested superficially. The TCK can perform a query and check whether the response is syntactically correct, but it generally can't verify whether the result set is complete.

The TCK is constantly growing and improving. New tests are added and existing tests are refined with every OpenCMIS release. You may want to follow OpenCMIS development and revalidate your server once in a while. If you have any suggestions for TCK tests, please let the Apache Chemistry development team know (see appendix E).

When you test, test all three bindings. That's because the AtomPub binding is a bit different compared to its two siblings. We'll look into that in the next section.

14.6 AtomPub differences

The Web Services binding and Browser binding are almost one-to-one mappings of the CMIS domain model to the wire protocol. The AtomPub binding is different, though. It also has to comply with the AtomPub specification, and serving these two masters makes life more difficult in some areas. In this section, we'll explain the extra methods in the `CmisService` interface that don't directly map to the CMIS specification.

14.6.1 Providing ObjectInfo

Chapter 11 gave you some insight into the CMIS bindings. One of the main elements of the AtomPub binding is the use of links. A CMIS client has to hop from one link to another to access certain pieces of information about an object or trigger an action. To make that possible, the repository must provide all these links, even if the client hasn't explicitly asked for them. For example, if a client calls `getObject` for a document with a property filter that only contains the document's name, the Web Services binding and the Browser binding can return just that. But the AtomPub binding must also provide a link to the content (if the document has content), a link for the version history (if the document is versioned), links for each rendition (if it has any), a link for the ACLs (if the repository supports ACLs), links to one or more parents (if the document is filed), and so on.

The OpenCMIS framework, which eventually has to compile and send these links, can't know all these details about an object. You have to tell it. The tool to do this is called `ObjectInfo`. For each object the framework delivers to the client, it needs an accompanying `ObjectInfo` object that carries these extra bits of information.

If you've already started building your server and you're wondering why your AtomPub binding magically works when you've never touched any `ObjectInfo` objects, you probably derived your implementation from the `AbstractCmisService` class. This abstract class has convenience code that automatically creates `ObjectInfo` objects on the fly if they're missing. It does that by making several calls to your `CmisService` implementation and extracting the information it needs. It gets the object and its version history, parents, and relationships, and it looks into the repository info to check the capabilities and more. This implementation isn't very efficient, but it's so generic that it works with all repositories. It's good enough to get off the ground, but eventually you should provide your own code optimized for your repository.

The framework asks the `CmisService` object for `ObjectInfo` objects by calling the `getObjectInfo` method. You can either implement this method or let the abstract class manage the `ObjectInfo` objects for you. The abstract class keeps a `Map` in the background that stores all `ObjectInfo` objects for one request and clears this `Map` after each request. You can add your own `ObjectInfo` objects by calling the `addObjectInfo` method. If you don't provide an `ObjectInfo` object for a CMIS object, it will generate one as explained earlier. The framework may ask for the same object multiple times during the XML response generation, so caching these objects per request is advised. Eventually, the framework calls the `close` method to indicate that the request processing is finished and the `CmisService` object isn't needed any more.

The `AbstractCmisService` class Javadoc reveals whether and which `ObjectInfo` objects should be provided for each method. The `CallContext` method `isObjectInfoRequired` specifies whether `ObjectInfo` objects are required at all for the request (it could be a Web Services binding or Browser binding request).

14.6.2 Handling create and delete requests

Create and delete requests can be ambiguous with the AtomPub binding. If a create request comes in, all the framework knows is that an object should be created. It doesn't know if it's a document, a folder, a policy, or an item. (Relationships are slightly different.)

Therefore, the `CmisService` interface has an unspecific `create` method that's only called with the AtomPub binding. The `AbstractCmisService` class provides a convenience implementation of this method that dissects the request and forwards it to the `createDocument`, `createFolder`, `createPolicy`, or `createItem` method. This code might or might not be efficient for your repository. If it isn't, you override the `create` method. For example, your server may have an internal way of determining the type of object by its ID format in some static manner.

Delete requests have a similar issue. They're indistinguishable from `cancelCheckOut` requests. Therefore, the framework calls the `deleteObjectOrCancelCheckOut` method, and the server implementation has to figure out how to deal with it. If the object is a private working copy, then this is definitely a `cancelCheckOut` request. If the object is a document that isn't checked out or any other nondocument object, then this is definitely a `delete` request. The behavior of the repository is undefined if the document is checked out but the referenced object isn't the Private Working Copy. Many repositories don't allow a document to be deleted if it's checked out. In this case, the server should throw an exception.

14.6.3 Dealing with version series

The CMIS domain model defines three operations that receive the version series ID as a parameter:

- `getAllVersions`
- `getObjectOfLatestVersion`
- `getPropertiesOfLatestVersion`

You may have noticed that the AtomPub binding and Browser binding server code don't receive the version series ID when these operations are called. Instead, an object ID of an object that's part of the version series is provided. To deal with that, the corresponding methods in the `CmisService` interface have an extra object ID parameter. This parameter is set if the AtomPub binding or the Browser binding is used. The version series ID isn't set in this case. For the Web Services binding, it's the other way around.

14.6.4 Managing ACLs

In chapter 12, we pointed out that changing ACLs is slightly different with the AtomPub binding. This is reflected in the `CmisService` interface. There's an extra `applyAcl` method, which takes the complete ACL instead of a list of ACEs to add and a list of ACEs to remove. This method is called only for the AtomPub binding, whereas the other `applyAcl` method is called for the other bindings.

These binding differences are annoying but don't make the implementation much more complex. What is truly complex is parsing the CMIS Query language. Luckily, OpenCMIS provides a CMIS query parser, which we discuss next.

14.7 Parsing a CMIS query

At some point you'll reach the `query` method of the `CmisService` interface and want to implement it. It hands you the query statement that the client sent as a string. You now have to parse this string to understand what the client wants. You're free to do whatever you want with the string. The idea of having to implement a parser can be a bit intimidating, but fear not. If you like, OpenCMIS can support you with its own CMIS query parser.

The OpenCMIS query parser uses ANTLR (www.antlr.org/) to do the actual parsing. If you're familiar with ANTLR, you can take the CMIS Query language grammar file and build your own parser; that would be the lowest level of integration. There are a few more layers of convenience on top of that. We'll explore just one here, which should work for most servers.

14.7.1 An example of initialization and use

Listing 14.1 demonstrates how to initialize and use the parser. After we've discussed this code, we'll show you how to work with the individual parsed query parts.

Listing 14.1 Initialization and use of the parser

```
String statement =
  "SELECT x, y AS z FROM demo WHERE x > 10 AND x < 20";

TypeManager tm = new DemoTypeManager();
QueryObject queryObj = new QueryObject(tm);
QueryUtil queryUtil = new QueryUtil();

try {

  CmisQueryWalker walker =
    queryUtil.traverseStatement(statement, queryObj, null);

  List<CmisSelector> select = queryObj.getSelectReferences();
  Map<String, String> from = queryObj.getTypes();
  Tree where = walker.getWherePredicateTree();
  List<SortSpec> orderBy = queryObj.getOrderBys();

  printSelect(select);
  printFrom(from);
  printWhere(where);
  printOrderBy(orderBy);

} catch (RecognitionException e) {
  String errorMsg = queryObj.getErrorMessage();
  throw new CmisInvalidArgumentException(
    "Query parsing failed: " + errorMsg);
} catch (CmisBaseException e) {
  throw e;
} catch (Exception e) {
  throw new CmisInvalidArgumentException(
    "Query parsing failed: " + e);
}
```

❶ **Query parser needs a TypeManager object. DemoTypeManager used here isn't in this example; you have to implement it first.**

❷ **traverseStatement method that does the actual parsing.**

The traverseStatement method ❷ is provided by the QueryUtil class, which hides the complexity that is required to set up the ANTLR parser. The traverseStatement method needs at least two parameters: the query statement that the client sent and a QueryObject object. This object is responsible for interpreting the query statement and managing the parsing result. It needs a TypeManager object in order to work ❶. The TypeManager interface is a small interface that you have to implement first. It gives the QueryObject access to the type system of your repository. It lets you fetch type and property type definitions by their query names and navigate the type hierarchy.

The traverseStatement method returns a CmisQueryWalker object. It contains the abstract syntax tree (AST) of the WHERE clause, which we'll discuss in a second.

14.7.2 Parsing SELECT

First let's look at the SELECT part of the query. As you can see from the previous code, you get the list of selected properties from the QueryObject. Let's iterate through the following code:

```
public void printSelect(List<CmisSelector> select) {
   System.out.println("SELECT:");

  for (CmisSelector property : select) {
    System.out.print("  Query name: " + property.getName());
    System.out.println(" [Alias: " + property.getAliasName() + "]");

    if (property instanceof ColumnReference) {
      ColumnReference colRef = (ColumnReference) property;
      TypeDefinition typeDef = colRef.getTypeDefinition();
      PropertyDefinition<?> propDef = colRef.getPropertyDefinition();

    } else if (property instanceof FunctionReference) {
      FunctionReference funcRef = (FunctionReference) property;
      CmisQlFunction function = funcRef.getFunction();
    }
  }
}
```

List contains a CmisSelector object for each item in the SELECT list, providing the query name and alias name.

If the item is a property, the object is also a ColumnReference and provides the property definition, type definition, etc.

If the item is a function, the object is also a FunctionReference and lets you check which function it is. (Spoiler: CMIS query language defines only one function, SCORE.)

14.7.3 Parsing FROM

Now let's check out the `FROM` part. The `QueryObject` provides a `Map` that maps the alias name to the query name:

```
public void printFrom(Map<String, String> from) {
  System.out.println("FROM:");

  for (Map.Entry<String, String> type : from.entrySet()) {
    System.out.print("  Query name: " + type.getValue());
    System.out.println(" [Alias: " + type.getKey() + "]");
  }
}
```

If you need the type definition, you can call the `getTypeDefinitionFromQueryName` method on the `QueryObject`, which in turn asks for your `TypeManager` object.

14.7.4 Parsing WHERE

The `WHERE` clause is translated into an abstract syntax tree, which you get from the `CmisQueryWalker` object. Here's one way to walk through it:

```
public void printWhere(Tree where) {
  System.out.println("WHERE:");

  if (where == null) {
    return;
  }

  printTree(where, 1);
 }
```

Walk recursively through the tree.

```
private void printTree(Tree tree, int level) {
  StringBuilder sb = new StringBuilder();

  for (int i = 0; i < level; i++) {            <-- Indentations make
     sb.append("  ");                              it look prettier.
  }

  sb.append(tree.getText());                   <-- Print node text
  sb.append(" (" + tree.getType() + ")");          and type.
  System.out.println(sb.toString());

  for (int i = 0; i < tree.getChildCount(); i++) {   <-- Go one level down
     printTree(tree.getChild(i), level + 1);             and visit the children
  }                                                      of this node.
}
```

Your task is now to traverse that tree and turn it into a query that your repository understands. Each tree node has a type and may have children. The `CmisQueryWalker` class provides descriptive constants for node types. You may want to look at the source code of the `AbstractPredicateWalker` class that's part of OpenCMIS; it connects the right dots and could serve as a good starting point for your tree-traversal code.

14.7.5 Parsing ORDER BY

Finally we've arrived at the `ORDER BY` part. The following code gets the list of properties and indicates for each one whether the sort order should be ascending or descending:

```
public void printOrderBy(List<SortSpec> orderBy) {
  System.out.println("ORDER BY:");

    if (orderBy == null) {
      return;
    }

    for (SortSpec property : orderBy) {
      System.out.print("  " + property.getSelector().getName() + " ");
      System.out.println(property.isAscending() ? "ASC" : "DESC");
    }
}
```

14.7.6 Query wrap-up

These are the basics of the OpenCMIS query parser. Implementing the CMIS query is one of the difficult parts of server development and requires a lot of testing. Especially challenging is making sure the current user sees only what they're allowed to see. The permissions for each object have to be checked before the object is added to the result set. But to get to this point, the server must first know who the current user is. The next section explains how authentication works with the OpenCMIS Server Framework.

14.8 Extracting authentication information

The OpenCMIS Server Framework implements the authentication mechanisms that are recommended by the CMIS specification. That is, it supports HTTP Basic Authentication for the AtomPub binding and the Browser binding and UsernameTokens for the Web Services binding. These were discussed in chapter 12.

14.8.1 CallContext

The `CallContext` object delivers the username and password to the server implementation. It's the responsibility of the server to verify the credentials. The framework only provides the values as shown here:

```
String username = context.getUsername();
String password = context.getPassword();
```

Other authentication mechanisms can replace the default implementation. The interface for the Web Services binding is different from the interfaces for the other bindings, though. It's important to replace both.

The implementations of both interfaces are supposed to extract authentication information from the request and enrich the `CallContext` object with this data. Usually, authentication information is transported in a request's HTTP headers or in an SSL client certificate. In case of the Web Services binding, there are also SOAP headers that can contain credentials, keys, signatures, or whatever is used to identify the user.

The `CallContext` object stores key-value pairs. You can add as many entries as you want and use any key you like as long as there's no collision with the predefined keys. Everything you add here is accessible from the `CallContext` object that the framework hands over to the `CmisServiceFactory` object.

14.8.2 CallContextHandler

Let's focus on the AtomPub binding and the Browser binding first. The interface to implement is called `CallContextHandler`. The method to implement it is called `getCallContextMap`. The following listing shows a code example.

Listing 14.2 A sample `CallContextHandler` implementation

```
public class MyCallContextHandler implements CallContextHandler {

  @Override
  public Map<String, String>
    getCallContextMap(HttpServletRequest request) {

    String user = ...
    String password = ...

    Map<String, String> callContextMap =
      new HashMap<String, String>();

    callContextMap.put(CallContext.USERNAME, user);
    callContextMap.put(CallContext.PASSWORD, password);
```

```
    return callContextMap;
  }
}
```

This code tries to extract a username and a password. But again, it could be anything else. The key-value pairs that this method returns are later added to the `CallContext` object.

To activate your call-context handler, you have to change the web.xml file. Find *all* servlets that have a `callContextHandlerinit` parameter, and set the value to the fully qualified class name of your implementation:

```
<servlet>
  <servlet-name>cmisbrowser</servlet-name>
  <servlet-class>org.apache.chemistry.opencmis.server.\
     impl.browser.CmisBrowserBindingServlet</servlet-class>
  <init-param>
    <param-name>callContextHandler</param-name>
    <param-value>org.example.MyCallContextHandler</param-value>
  </init-param>
</servlet>
```

14.8.3 Web services

On the web services end, you use JAX-WS handlers. A lot of documentation and examples are available on the internet, so we don't dive deep here.

> **IMPORTANT ADVICE ABOUT MESSAGEHANDLER** We have one important piece of advice at this point. If you have to access the SOAP headers, extend the non-standard `MessageHandler` interface and not the standard `SOAPHandler` and `LogicHandler` interfaces. The latter two load the entire SOAP message, including the document content, into main memory when you touch the headers. That can be fatal if the content is bigger than the main memory.

The next listing shows a simple example of a handler that processes user credentials.

Listing 14.3 A sample `MessageHandler` implementation

```
public class MyAuthHandler implements
  MessageHandler<MessageHandlerContext> {

  public Set<QName> getHeaders() {
    return null;
  }

  public void close(MessageContext context) {
  }

  public boolean handleFault(MessageHandlerContext context) {
    return true;
  }

  public boolean handleMessage(MessageHandlerContext context) {
    Boolean outboundProperty = (Boolean) context
        .get(MessageContext.MESSAGE_OUTBOUND_PROPERTY);
```

```
    if (outboundProperty.booleanValue()) {
      return true;
    }

    Map<String, String> callContextMap =
      new HashMap<String, String>();

    String user = ...
    String password = ...

    callContextMap.put(CallContext.USERNAME, user);
    callContextMap.put(CallContext.PASSWORD, password);

    context.put(AbstractService.CALL_CONTEXT_MAP,
      callContextMap);

    context.setScope(AbstractService.CALL_CONTEXT_MAP,
      Scope.APPLICATION);

    return true;
  }
}
```

Important line that hands over the key-value pairs to OpenCMIS

To activate your handler, you have to change the sun-jaxws.xml file. Find *all* handler chain entries, and set the fully qualified class name of your handler, as shown here:

```
<handler-chains xmlns="http://java.sun.com/xml/ns/javaee">
  <handler-chain>
    <handler>
      <handler-class>org.examplpe.MyAuthHandler</handler-class>
    </handler>
  </handler-chain>
</handler-chains>
```

14.8.4 Authentication wrap-up

That's how you read and forward authentication information to the server implementation. If you make sure both implementations send the authentication information with the same keys and in the same format, you don't have to distinguish later between the bindings.

14.9 CMIS extensions

We covered CMIS extensions in chapter 12 and explained what they're good for and when to use them. We won't repeat that, but we want to show you how to add extensions with the OpenCMIS Server Framework.

A CMIS extension is a tree of nodes. Each node has a name, a namespace, and attributes. Leaf nodes have a string value, and all other nodes have one or more child nodes. Extensions are eventually converted into XML fragments or JSON objects. When an extension is converted to JSON, the namespaces and attributes of the nodes are ignored, because such concepts don't exist in JSON. To be compatible across all bindings, you shouldn't rely on namespaces and attributes.

All objects that implement the `ExtensionsData` interface can carry extensions. The following example adds an extension to an object:

```
ObjectData object = ...

String ns = "http://example.org/cmis";

List<CmisExtensionElement> extElements =
   new ArrayList<CmisExtensionElement>();

String value = (new Date()).toString();
 CmisExtensionElement extensionLeaf =
  new CmisExtensionElementImpl( ns, "datetime",
     /* no attributes */ null, value);
extElements.add(extensionLeaf);

List<CmisExtensionElement> extensions =
   new ArrayList<CmisExtensionElement>();

CmisExtensionElement extensionRoot =
 new CmisExtensionElementImpl(ns, "exampleExtension",
    /* no attributes */ null, extElements);
extensions.add(extensionRoot);

object.setExtensions(extensions);
```

Find a namespace for the extension that's different from the CMIS namespaces.

Create a list for the first level of the extension.

Add a leaf to the extension.

Set the extension list.

So far, all of this is compliant with CMIS 1.0; but with CMIS 1.1, you can also announce your extension in the `repositoryInfo`. Doing so means clients no longer have to dig around manually in the types and properties to figure out if this particular extension feature is supported. The following code shows how to add this extra 1.1 extension information to your `repositoryInfo`:

```
ExtensionFeatureImpl extensionFeature = new ExtensionFeatureImpl();
extensionFeature.setId("http://example.org/cmis/current-datetime");
extensionFeature.setCommonName("CurrentDateTime");
extensionFeature.setVersionLabel("1.0");
extensionFeature.setDescription(
  "Adds the current date and time to each object.");

List<ExtensionFeature> extensionFeatures =
  new ArrayList<ExtensionFeature>();
extensionFeatures.add(extensionFeature);

repositoryInfo.setExtensionFeature(extensionFeatures);
```

Speaking of CMIS 1.1, the next section explains what you should take into consideration if you want to support CMIS 1.0 and CMIS 1.1 with the same server code.

14.10 Supporting CMIS 1.0 and CMIS 1.1

Because CMIS 1.1 only adds functionality to CMIS 1.0, it makes sense to have one code base for both specifications. To make that work, you must make sure you serve CMIS 1.0 clients only data that is defined in the CMIS 1.0 specification. For example, if your repository supports `cmis:item` objects, you need to suppress them in `getChildren` calls. The `cmis:item` type definition also shouldn't appear in `getTypeChildren` and `getTypeDescendants` responses. Similarly, properties of secondary types must not be included in the property set of an object. You get the idea. The TCK checks quite a bit of that, but don't rely on it.

The CallContext provides the information about which CMIS version the client understands:

```
if (context.getCmisVersion() != CmisVersion.CMIS_1_0) {
  // add CMIS 1.1 stuff here
}
```

14.11 Summary

OpenCMIS provides a server framework to build CMIS servers on top of existing content repositories and data stores. In this chapter, we've outlined how to generate a CMIS server stub and build a web application for the server. We discussed the two Java interfaces that must be implemented and how to test the server for compliance with the CMIS specification.

We focused your attention on the AtomPub binding, which requires some extra coding. We also looked into the OpenCMIS query parser and how to hook nonstandard authentication mechanisms into the server. Finally, we demonstrated how to add CMIS extensions and discussed CMIS 1.0 and CMIS 1.1 support with the same code base.

Many small details and best practices about building a CMIS server didn't made it into this chapter. The subject could probably fill a separate book of its own. If you have any questions, please email the Apache Chemistry mailing list; the community is very active and an ever-evolving source of information on this subject.

This has been a long ride, if you made it all the way to this point. As you can see, the subject of CMIS development is both broad and extremely deep in places. Whether you're building a client or your own server, we (the authors and contributors) hope we've exposed enough of the layers for you to confidently start planning and building your application.

Happy coding!

appendix A Apache Chemistry OpenCMIS components

This appendix discusses where to get the latest Apache Chemistry OpenCMIS components, what they're good for, and how to build them from source. It also covers how to update the InMemory server that we use throughout this book.

A.1 Apache Chemistry OpenCMIS

The Apache Chemistry project provides CMIS libraries and tools for several programming languages. At the time of this writing, there was support for Java (including support for Android), .NET, Python, PHP, and Objective-C. This appendix focuses on the Java tools and libraries that make up the Apache Chemistry OpenCMIS subproject.

A.1.1 OpenCMIS components overview

Figure A.1 provides a high-level overview of the OpenCMIS components. These are the building blocks.

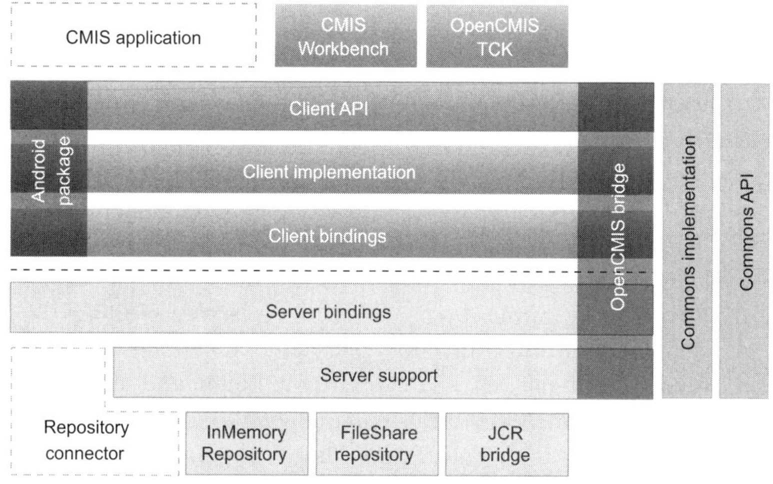

Figure A.1 OpenCMIS components

- *Client library*—The OpenCMIS client library provides the Java code that lets you talk to a CMIS repository. Most of this book is about this library and its counterparts for other programming languages. The OpenCMIS client library depends on a set of third-party libraries that are required in order to build and run applications. We'll explain in a moment how to obtain them.
- The client library consists of the client API, the client implementation, the client bindings, the commons API, and the commons implementation. There are two flavors of this library: the default client library, which works for Java SE applications and on several application servers; and the Android version, which is tailored to run on Android devices (see chapter 10 for details). Both versions support the AtomPub binding and the Browser binding. The Web Services binding is only supported by the default client library. The default library consists of five JARs, one for each component. The Android library is condensed into one JAR.
- *CMIS Workbench*—We use this tool a lot in this book. It's an essential developer tool for CMIS client and server developers. It's built on top of the client library.
- *OpenCMIS TCK*—The OpenCMIS Test Compatibility Kit (TCK) provides a set of tests that checks whether a CMIS repository is compliant with the CMIS specification and compatible with the OpenCMIS client library. You can find more details about the TCK in chapter 14.
- *Server Webapps package*—The Webapps package contains two CMIS test repositories and a web application to browse CMIS repositories. One of these repositories is the InMemory Repository that we use in this book. The other repository is called FileShare and turns a directory on your computer into a CMIS repository. Because it's built on top of the filesystem, it only provides a subset of the CMIS features. There is no versioning or query support, for example.
- The browsing web application is the predecessor of the CMIS Workbench (not shown in figure A.1). It's an obsolete component because the CMIS Workbench does much more and does it better. The browsing application might be useful in environments where the CMIS Workbench doesn't run or only a web browser is available. These three web applications are packaged as WAR files and can be directly deployed into an application server.
- *Server Framework*—Chapter 14 covers in detail how to build a CMIS server with this framework. The framework consists of the server bindings (split into a package that contains the code and a package that contains all auxiliary files), server support, commons API, and commons implementation.
- The OpenCMIS build also creates a complete WAR file that's deployable. If for whatever reason you don't want to use Maven to generate the scaffolding for your server, you can use the contents of the WAR file as a starting point for your server development.
- *OpenCMIS bridge*—The bridge is a server component that routes incoming CMIS requests to another CMIS repository. On the way, it can switch the binding and

filter, enrich, and federate data from the back-end repository. This book doesn't cover the OpenCMIS bridge.

- *OpenCMIS* JCR *bridge*—This component puts a CMIS interface on top of a JCR repository. We don't touch on this topic in this book. If you have questions, please refer to the Apache Chemistry mailing list. (See appendix E.)

Apart from these components, there are also packages that contain the source code and the Javadocs. These packages aren't divided by component but contain the code and documentation for all components.

Let's look next at how to get and build the OpenCMIS components.

A.1.2 Getting and using OpenCMIS components

OpenCMIS provides three ways of delivering its components for your use:

- *Source code*—Each OpenCMIS release provides the full source code, which can be easily built with Maven.
- *Zip, JAR, and WAR packages*—Each OpenCMIS component comes prepackaged and ready to use. The components can be directly deployed into an application server or unpacked and copied into a development project.
- *Maven modules*—The OpenCMIS components can also be referenced via Maven or other build environments that are compatible Maven repositories. This is the preferred way if you're using Maven for your project.

Let's go through the different options.

A.1.3 Building OpenCMIS

There's usually no reason to build OpenCMIS other than getting the latest development version. But doing so is very easy. Here's how you do it.

First you need the source code. Either go to the Apache Chemistry download page and get the source code package or get the source code via SVN. (See appendix E for the URLs.)

All OpenCMIS components are built together with Maven. Go the root directory of the source code, and run the following Maven command: `mvn clean install`. Maven may complain during the build that it doesn't have enough memory. Give it more memory by setting the environment variable `MAVEN_OPTS` to `-Xmx1024m -XX:MaxPermSize=256m`.

After the build is complete, walk through the directories. Under each component directory there should be a target directory that contains a zip, JAR, or WAR package. These are the packages you can download from the Apache Chemistry website. We'll look at them next.

A.1.4 Download packages

The packages you download from the Apache Chemistry website contain everything you need for the corresponding component. This includes all the required JAR files and auxiliary files. If you need to know which dependencies are required, find the DEPENDENCIES file. In zip packages, it should be in the top directory. In JAR and WAR files, it's in the META-INF directory.

For example, if you want to use the OpenCMIS client library, make sure you copy all dependencies to your project. Although your project may compile without them, it may not work or, worse, may do something unexpected at runtime. Depending on the Java version you're using, the JVM provides similar libraries or the same library in a different version, and OpenCMIS might not be compatible with them.

Remember, the simplest (and recommended) way to deal with the dependencies is to use Maven.

A.1.5 Maven modules

Using Maven is the preferred way to use OpenCMIS. The main advantage is that it takes care of the dependencies and transitive dependencies. In chapter 6, we explain how to get the OpenCMIS client library with Maven. Chapter 14 covers the Server Framework and shows how to generate the scaffolding with Maven.

The OpenCMIS components for this book are slightly different from their default OpenCMIS counterparts. The next section explains how to update them.

A.1.6 OpenCMIS components for this book

In this book, we use the CMIS Workbench and the InMemory server. Although it shouldn't be necessary, you can update them with the latest OpenCMIS version.

The CMIS Workbench is the same one you get from the Apache Chemistry website, except for the embedded Groovy code examples from the book. If you want to update, get the CMIS Workbench from Apache Chemistry. The zip file that comes with the book contains all the Groovy examples as simple files. You can open them directly in the Groovy console.

The InMemory server is a bit different. The original InMemory Repository from the Apache Chemistry website comes as a WAR file that you have to deploy into a servlet engine of your choice. When you run it, it contains only a few simple documents and types.

The InMemory Repository that we use in this book embeds the Tomcat servlet engine and is preloaded with documents and types that are used in this book. To update this InMemory Repository with the latest OpenCMIS release, you have to replace the OpenCMIS JARs and dependencies as follows:

1. Remove all JAR files starting with *chemistry-opencmis* from your InMemory Repository directory.
2. Download the InMemory server (OpenCMIS Server Webapps) and the client library (OpenCMIS Client With Dependencies) from the Apache Chemistry website. (See appendix E for the URL.)
3. Unzip the Webapps zip file. Find the InMemory server WAR file, and unzip that, too.

4. Copy all files in the WEB-INF/libs folder into your InMemory Repository directory.
5. Unzip the client library package into the InMemory Repository directory, and overwrite all files.
6. Restart the server.

The InMemory Repository should now be using the OpenCMIS version you've provided. (If you want to rebuild the server from scratch, use the source code available in the inmemory-cmis-server-pack.zip file.)

A.1.7 Using the OpenCMIS client library on an application server

Applications servers like WebLogic, WebSphere, and GlassFish provide environments that are slightly different from each other. The OpenCMIS client library had difficulties working in a few of those environments up to the OpenCMIS version 0.9.0-beta-1. It was necessary to tweak the application server's class loading to get it to run, and there were special packages for WebLogic and WebSphere.

OpenCMIS 0.9.0 reduced the number of dependencies and therefore reduced the chance of potential conflicts. The AtomPub binding and the Browser binding should work without any special configuration. An OpenCMIS session that uses the Web Services binding requires a hint, though. OpenCMIS has to know which JAX-WS implementation the application server uses. Please refer to your application server documentation for this information.

If your application server uses the Oracle/Sun JAX-WS Reference Implementation (RI), add the following parameter to your session parameters when you set up the OpenCMIS session:

```
parameter.put(SessionParameter.WEBSERVICES_JAXWS_IMPL, "sunri");
```

If the application server relies on the JAX-WS implementation that's shipped with an Oracle JRE or a JRE derived from it, use this session parameter:

```
parameter.put(SessionParameter.WEBSERVICES_JAXWS_IMPL, "sunjre");
```

If the application server provides the Apache CXF implementation of JAX-WS, use the following parameter:

```
parameter.put(SessionParameter.WEBSERVICES_JAXWS_IMPL, "cxf");
```

And, finally, on WebSphere 7.0.0.5 and later, use this session parameter:

```
parameter.put(SessionParameter.WEBSERVICES_JAXWS_IMPL, "websphere");
```

If you run into a problem with that, ask about it on the Apache Chemistry mailing list. You'll find the address in appendix E.

appendix B BNF

This appendix contains graphical representations of the BNF grammar that's contained in the CMIS 1.1 specification for Query. There's no additional information here beyond what's in the normative text. These graphics were generated with the Railroad Diagram Generator tool, which you can find at http://railroad.my28msec.com/rr/ui.

CMIS11QueryStatement

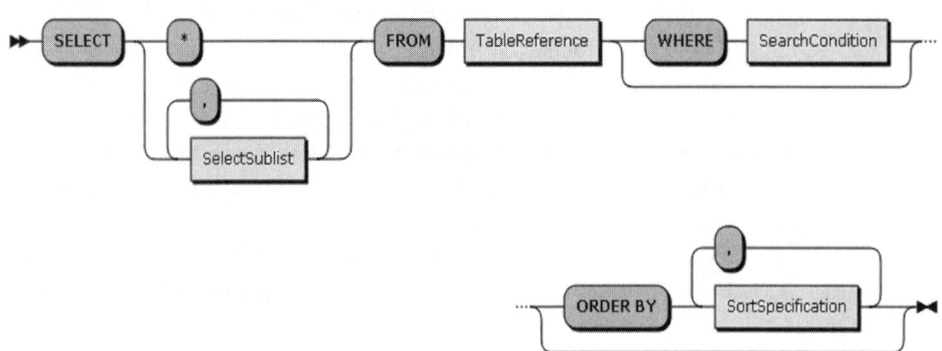


```
CMIS11QueryStatement
         ::= 'SELECT' ( '*' | SelectSublist ( ',' SelectSublist )* ) ➥
          'FROM' TableReference ( 'WHERE' SearchCondition )? ( ➥
          'ORDER BY' SortSpecification ( ',' SortSpecification )* )?
```

No references.

SelectSublist

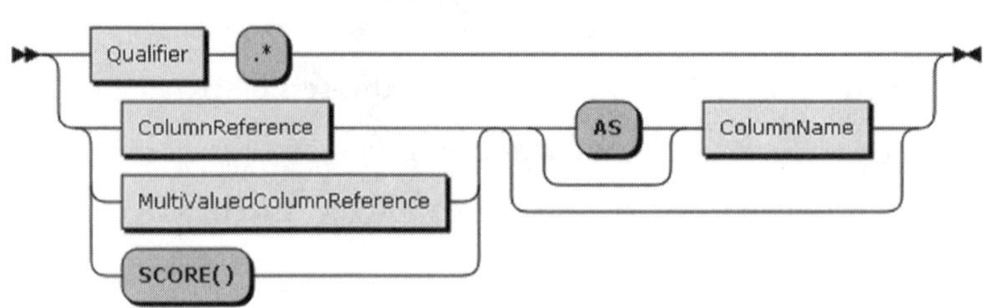

```
SelectSublist
         ::= Qualifier '.*'
           | ( ColumnReference | MultiValuedColumnReference | ➥
            'SCORE()' ) ( 'AS'? ColumnName )?
```

Referenced by

CMIS11QueryStatement

ColumnReference

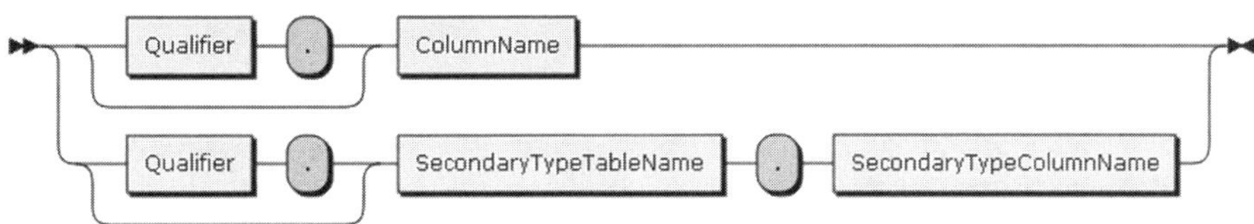


```
ColumnReference
         ::= ( Qualifier '.' )? ColumnName
           | ( Qualifier '.' )? SecondaryTypeTableName '.' ➥
            SecondaryTypeColumnName
```

Referenced by

InPredicate
JoinedTable
LikePredicate
NullPredicate
SelectSublist
SortSpecification

MultiValuedColumnReference

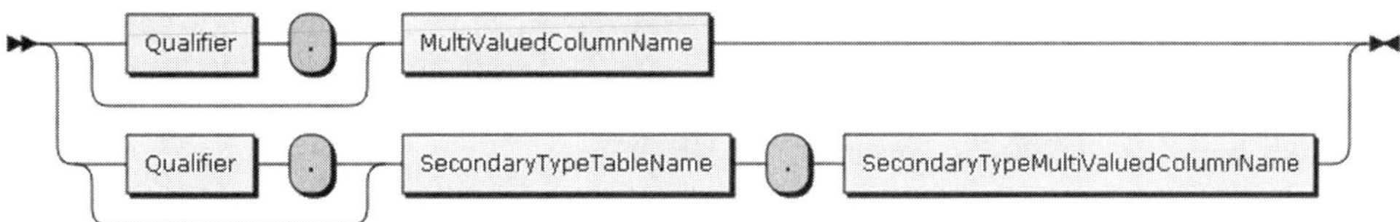


```
MultiValuedColumnReference
         ::= ( Qualifier '.' )? MultiValuedColumnName
           | ( Qualifier '.' )? SecondaryTypeTableName '.' ➥
            SecondaryTypeMultiValuedColumnName
```

Referenced by

NullPredicate
QuantifiedComparisonPredicate
QuantifiedInPredicate
SelectSublist

Qualifier

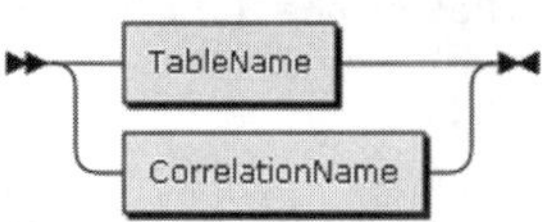


```
Qualifier
        ::= TableName
          | CorrelationName
```

Referenced by

```
ColumnReference
FolderPredicate
MultiValuedColumnReference
SelectSublist
TextSearchPredicate
```

TableReference

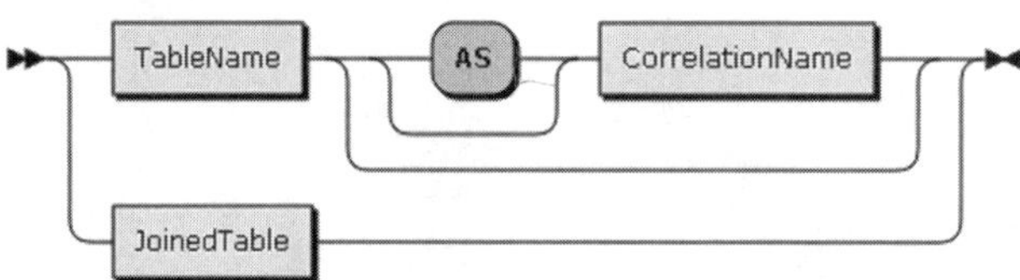


```
TableReference
        ::= TableName ( 'AS'? CorrelationName )?
          | JoinedTable
```

Referenced by

```
CMIS11QueryStatement
JoinedTable
```

JoinedTable

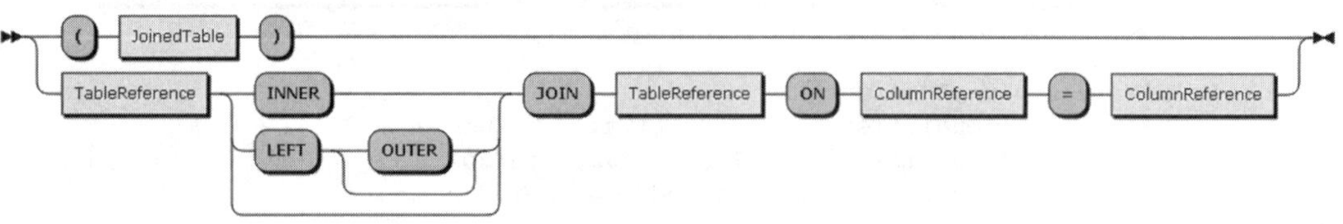


```
JoinedTable
        ::= '(' JoinedTable ')'
          | TableReference ( 'INNER' | 'LEFT' 'OUTER'? )? 'JOIN' ➥
         TableReference 'ON' ColumnReference '=' ColumnReference
```

Referenced by

```
JoinedTable
TableReference
```

SearchCondition

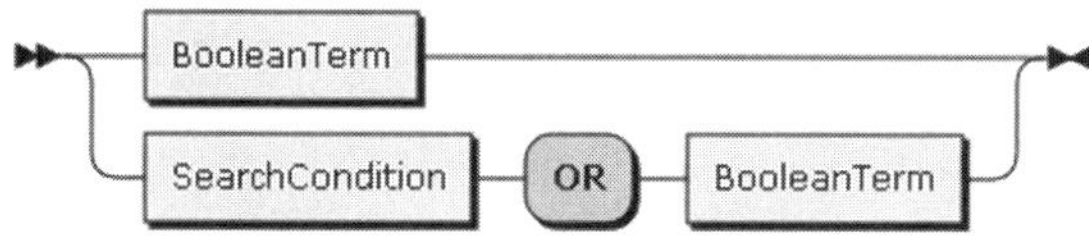


```
SearchCondition
        ::= BooleanTerm
          | SearchCondition 'OR' BooleanTerm
```

Referenced by

BooleanTest
CMIS11QueryStatement
SearchCondition

BooleanTerm

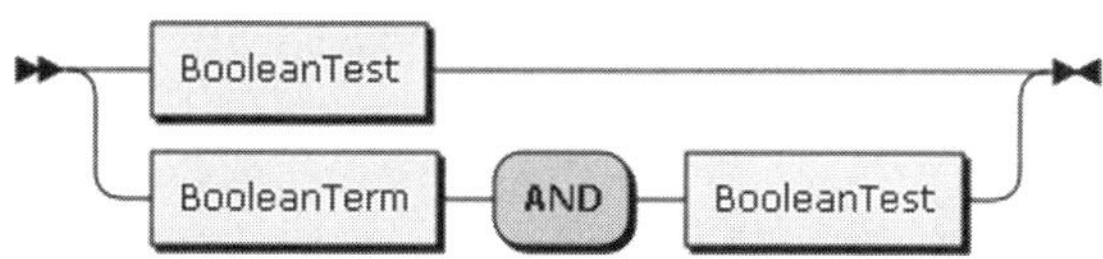


```
BooleanTerm
        ::= BooleanTest
          | BooleanTerm 'AND' BooleanTest
```

Referenced by

BooleanTerm
SearchCondition

BooleanTest

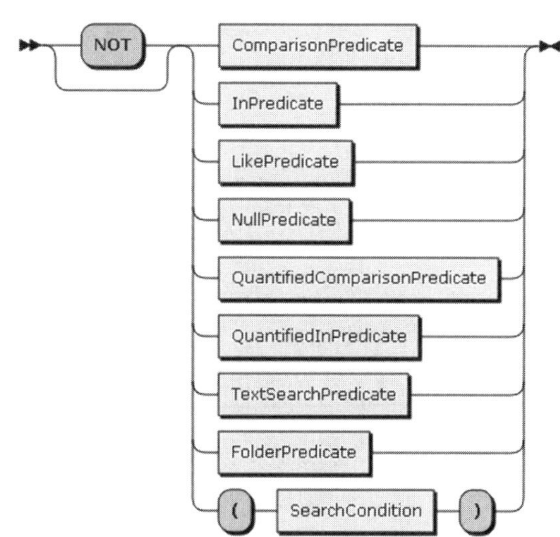

```
BooleanTest
        ::= 'NOT'? ( ComparisonPredicate | InPredicate | LikePredicate➥
         | NullPredicate | QuantifiedComparisonPredicate | ➥
         QuantifiedInPredicate | TextSearchPredicate | FolderPredicate ➥
         | '(' SearchCondition ')' )
```

Referenced by

BooleanTerm

ComparisonPredicate

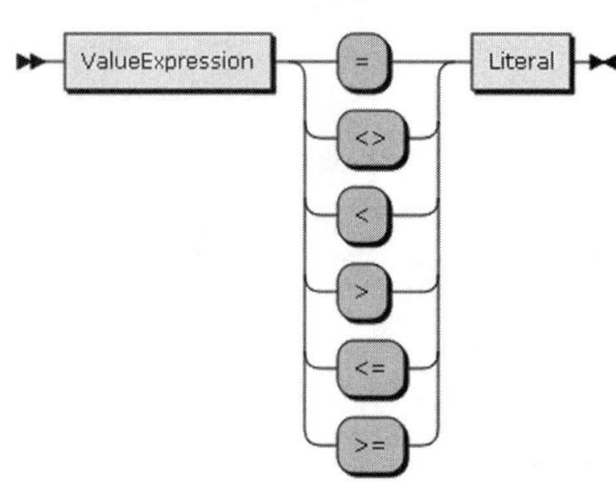


```
ComparisonPredicate
        ::= ValueExpression ( '=' | '<>' | '<' | '>' | '<=' ➥
         | '>=' ) Literal
```

Referenced by

BooleanTest

InPredicate

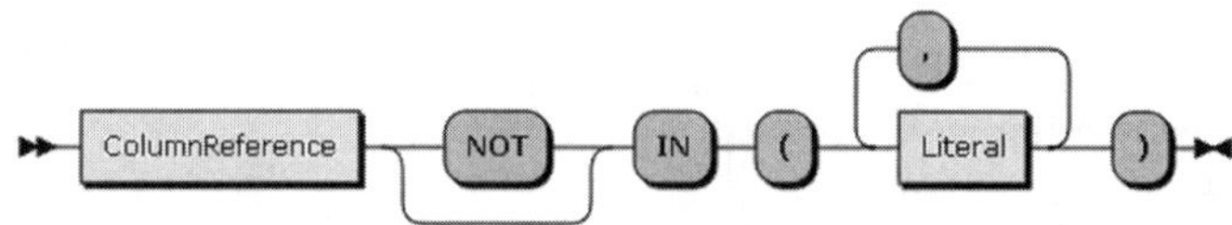


```
InPredicate
        ::= ColumnReference 'NOT'? 'IN' '(' Literal ( ',' Literal ➥
         )* ')'
```

Referenced by

BooleanTest

Literal

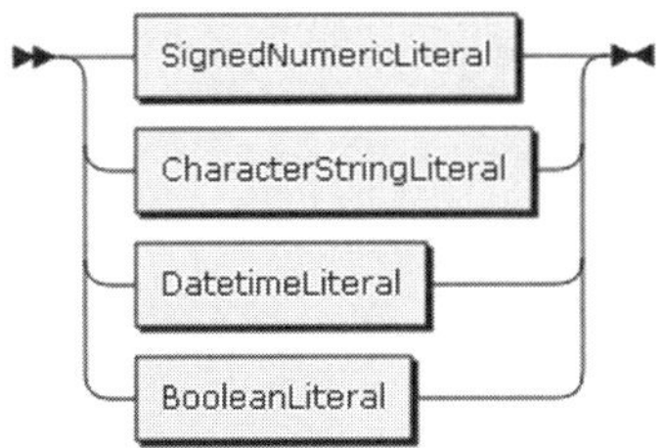


```
Literal  ::= SignedNumericLiteral
           | CharacterStringLiteral
           | DatetimeLiteral
           | BooleanLiteral
```

Referenced by

ComparisonPredicate
InPredicate
QuantifiedComparisonPredicate
QuantifiedInPredicate

LikePredicate

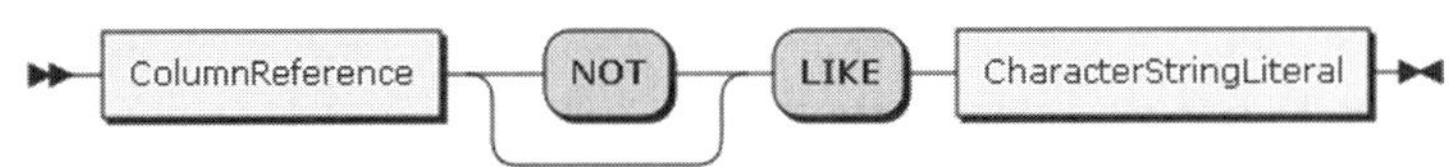


```
LikePredicate
         ::= ColumnReference 'NOT'? 'LIKE' CharacterStringLiteral
```

Referenced by

BooleanTest

NullPredicate

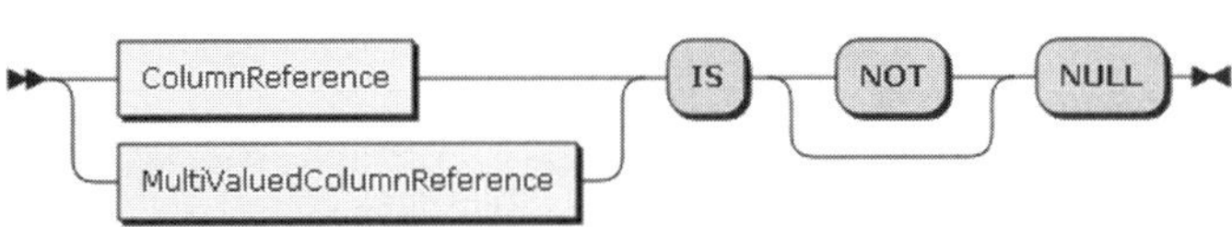


```
NullPredicate
         ::= ( ColumnReference | MultiValuedColumnReference ) 'IS' ➥
          'NOT'? 'NULL'
```

Referenced by

BooleanTest

QuantifiedComparisonPredicate

```
QuantifiedComparisonPredicate
        ::= Literal '=' 'ANY' MultiValuedColumnReference
```

Referenced by

`BooleanTest`

QuantifiedInPredicate

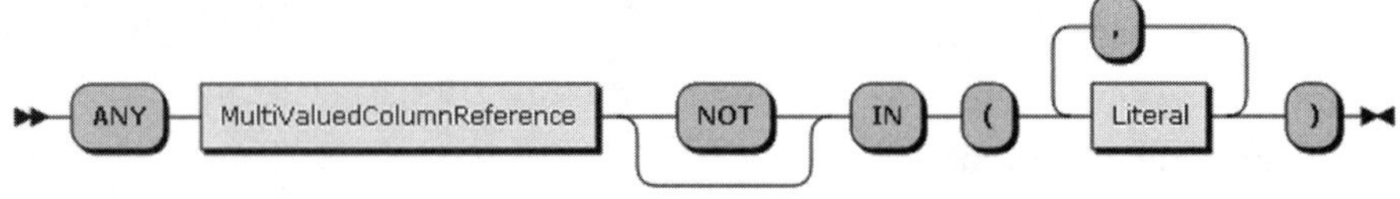


```
QuantifiedInPredicate
        ::= 'ANY' MultiValuedColumnReference 'NOT'? 'IN' '(' Literal
         ( ',' Literal )* ')'
```

Referenced by

`BooleanTest`

TextSearchPredicate

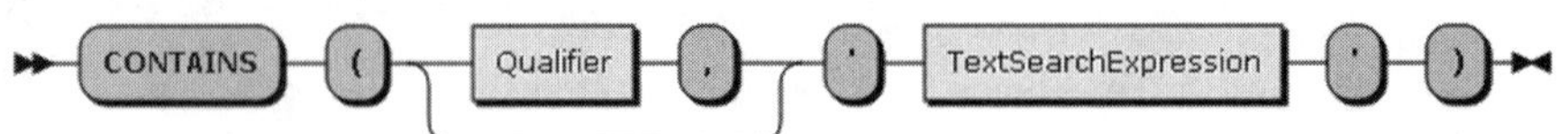


```
TextSearchPredicate
        ::= 'CONTAINS' '(' ( Qualifier ',' )? "'"
         TextSearchExpression "'" ')'
```

Referenced by

`BooleanTest`

FolderPredicate

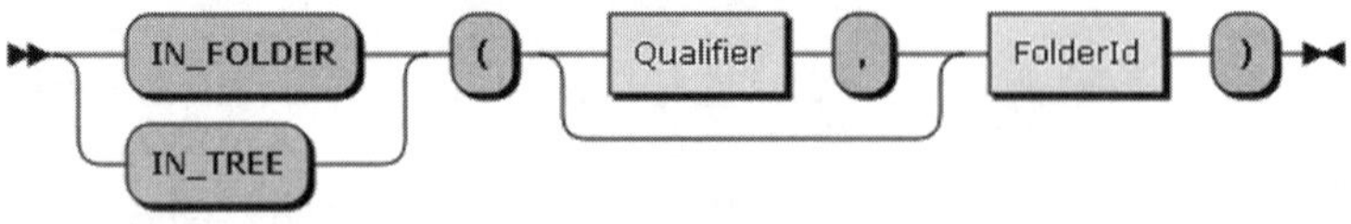


```
FolderPredicate
        ::= ( 'IN_FOLDER' | 'IN_TREE' ) '(' ( Qualifier ',' )?
         FolderId ')'
```

Referenced by

`BooleanTest`

SortSpecification

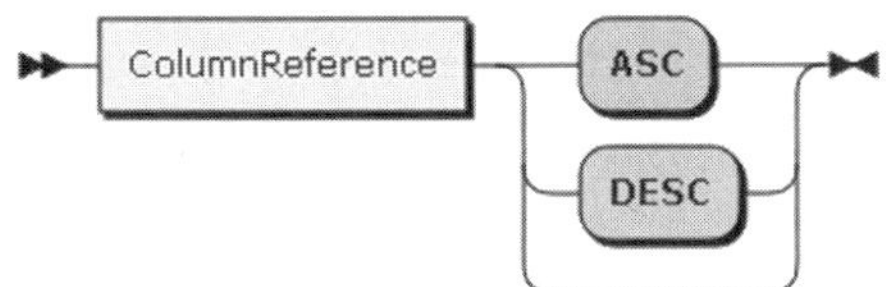


```
SortSpecification
        ::= ColumnReference ( 'ASC' | 'DESC' )?
```

Referenced by

CMIS11QueryStatement

CorrelationName

```
CorrelationName
        ::= Identifier
```

Referenced by

Qualifier
TableReference

TableName

```
TableName
        ::= Identifier
```

Referenced by

Qualifier
TableReference

SecondaryTypeTableName

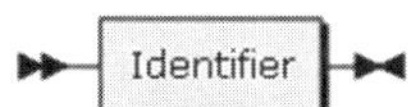


```
SecondaryTypeTableName
        ::= Identifier
```

Referenced by

ColumnReference
MultiValuedColumnReference

ColumnName

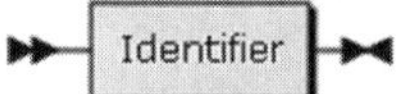


```
ColumnName
        ::= Identifier
```

Referenced by

```
ColumnReference
SelectSublist
```

SecondaryTypeColumnName

```
SecondaryTypeColumnName
        ::= Identifier
```

Referenced by

```
ColumnReference
```

MultiValuedColumnName

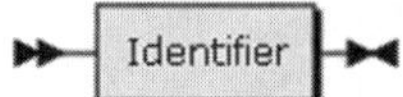


```
MultiValuedColumnName
        ::= Identifier
```

Referenced by

```
MultiValuedColumnReference
```

SecondaryTypeMultiValuedColumnName

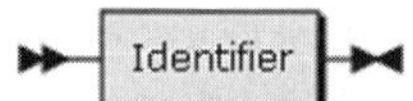


```
SecondaryTypeMultiValuedColumnName
        ::= Identifier
```

Referenced by

```
MultiValuedColumnReference
```

FolderId

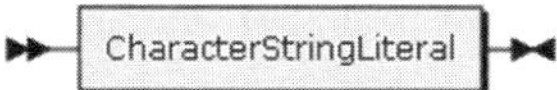


```
FolderId ::= CharacterStringLiteral
```

Referenced by

```
FolderPredicate
```

Identifier

```
Identifier
        ::= QueryName
```

Referenced by

```
ColumnName
CorrelationName
MultiValuedColumnName
SecondaryTypeColumnName
SecondaryTypeMultiValuedColumnName
SecondaryTypeTableName
TableName
```

SignedNumericLiteral

```
SignedNumericLiteral
        ::= SQLLiteral
```

Referenced by

```
Literal
```

CharacterStringLiteral

```
CharacterStringLiteral
        ::= SQLLiteral
```

Referenced by

```
FolderId
LikePredicate
Literal
```

TextSearchExpression

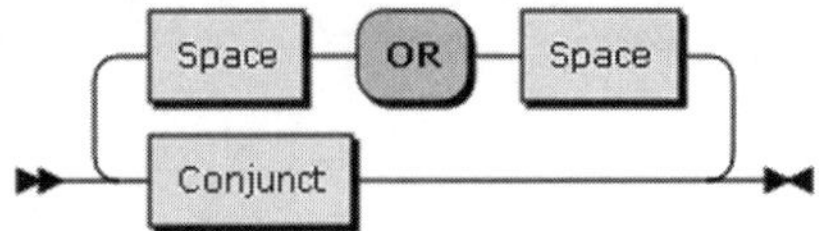


```
TextSearchExpression
         ::= Conjunct ( Space 'OR' Space Conjunct )*
```

Referenced by
    TextSearchPredicate

Conjunct

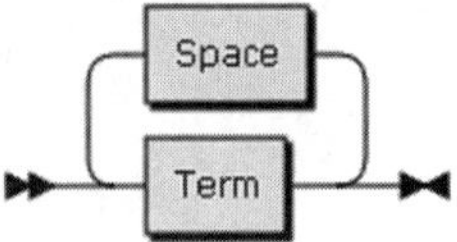


```
Conjunct ::= Term ( Space Term )*
```

Referenced by
    TextSearchExpression

Term

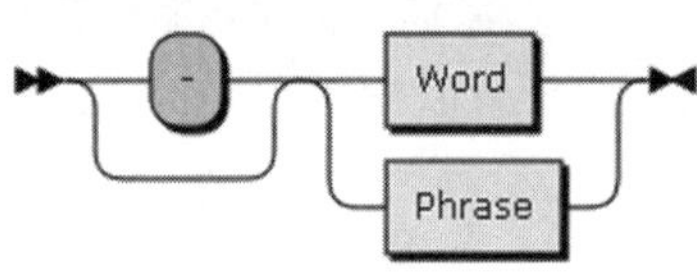


```
Term     ::= '-'? ( Word | Phrase )
```

Referenced by
    Conjunct

Word

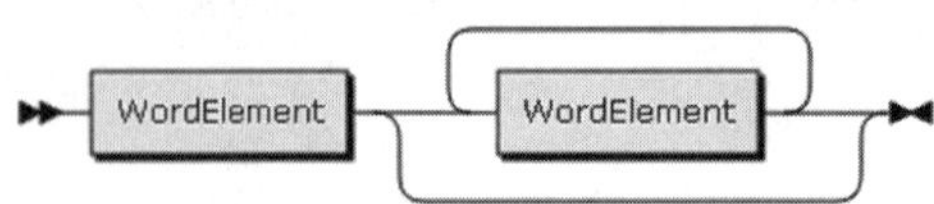


```
Word     ::= WordElement WordElement*
```

Referenced by
    Phrase
    Term

Phrase

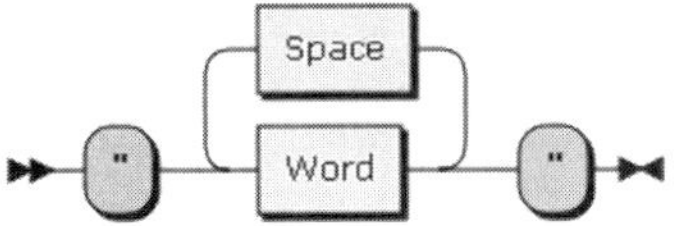


```
Phrase    ::= '"' Word ( Space Word )* '"'
```

Referenced by

```
Term
```

QuoteSymbol

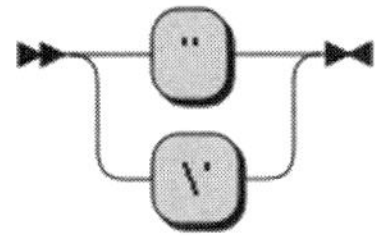

```
QuoteSymbol
          ::= "''"
            | "\'"
```

No references

WordElement

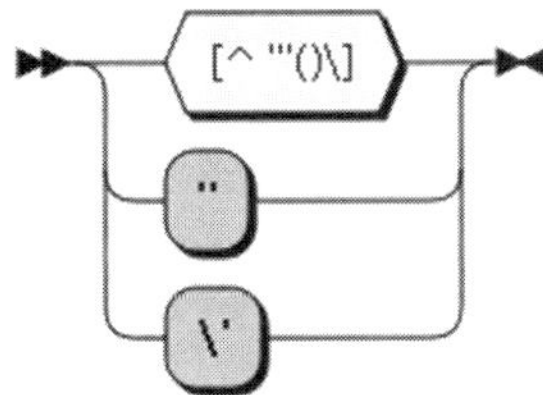

```
WordElement
          ::= [^(' ')("\")("'")('"')]
            | ( "''" | "\'" )
```

Referenced by

```
Word
```

Space

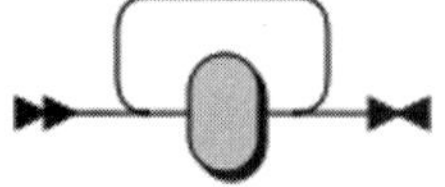

```
Space     ::= ' '+
```

Referenced by

```
Conjunct
Phrase
TextSearchExpression
```

Char

```
Char      ::= AnyCharacter
```

No references.

DatetimeLiteral

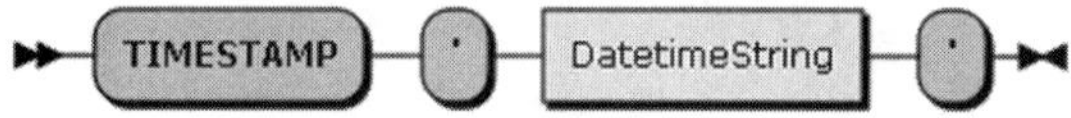


```
DatetimeLiteral
          ::= 'TIMESTAMP' "'" DatetimeString "'"
```

Referenced by

```
Literal
```

DatetimeString

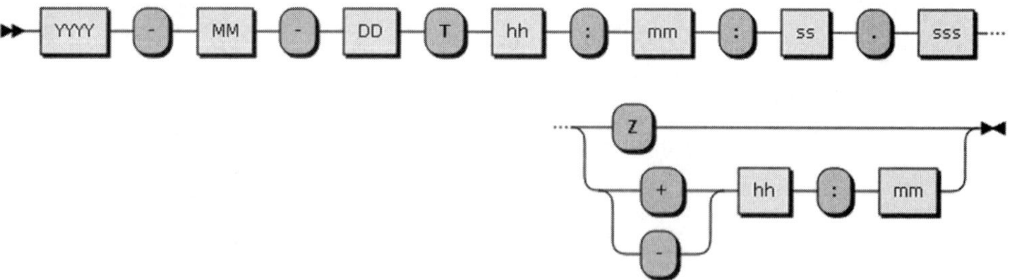


```
DatetimeString
          ::= YYYY '-' MM '-' DD 'T' hh ':' mm ':' ss '.' sss ( 'Z' | ( ➥
           '+' | '-' ) hh ':' mm )
```

Referenced by

```
DatetimeLiteral
```

BooleanLiteral

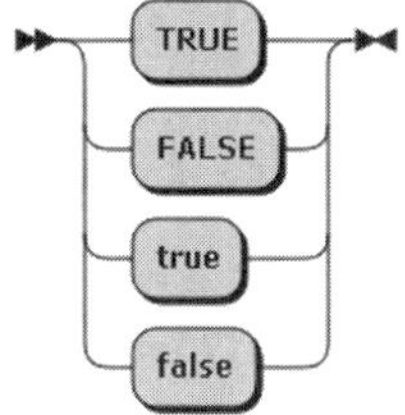


```
BooleanLiteral
         ::= 'TRUE'
           | 'FALSE'
           | 'true'
           | 'false'
```

Referenced by

`Literal`

appendix C CMIS cheat sheet

Legend (Abbreviations used in the following tables)

T	Types
O	All objects
D	Documents
F	Folders
R	Relationships
P	Policies
I	Items
1.1	New in CMIS 1.1

Services and operations

Repository service

	getRepositories
	getRepositoryInfo
T	getTypeChildren
T	getTypeDescendants
T	getTypeDefinition
T, 1.1	createType
T, 1.1	updateType
T, 1.1	deleteType

Navigation service

F	getChildren
F	getDescendants
F	getFolderTree
F	getFolderParent
D, P, I	getObjectParents

Object service

D	createDocument
D	createDocumentFromSource
F	createFolder
R	createRelationship
P	createPolicy
I, 1.1	createItem
O	getAllowableActions
O	getObject
O	getProperties
D, F, P, I	getObjectByPath
D	getContentStream
D, F	getRenditions
O	updateProperties
O, 1.1	bulkUpdateProperties
D, F, P, I	moveObject
O	deleteObject
F	deleteTree
D	setContentStream
D, 1.1	appendContentStream
D	deleteContentStream

Versioning service

D	checkOut
D	cancelCheckOut
D	checkIn
D	getObjectOfLatestVersion
D	getPropertiesOfLatestVersion
D	getAllVersions

Multifiling service

D, F, P, I	addObjectToFolder
D, F, P, I	removeObjectFromFolder

Discovery service

O	query
O	getContentChanges

Relationship service

O	getObjectRelationships

Policy service

O	applyPolicy
O	removePolicy
O	getAppliedPolicies

Policy service

O	getACL
O	applyACL

Properties

O	String	cmis:name	read-write
O, 1.1	String	cmis:description	read-write
O	ID	cmis:objectId	read-only
O	ID	cmis:baseTypeId	read-only
O	ID	cmis:objectTypeId	on-create
O	String	cmis:createdBy	read-only
O	DateTime	cmis:creationDate	read-only
O	String	cmis:lastModifiedBy	read-only
O	DateTime	cmis:lastModificationDate	read-only
O	String	cmis:changeToken	read-only
O, 1.1	ID (multi)	cmis:secondaryObjectTypeIds	read-write
D	Boolean	cmis:isImmutable	read-only
D	Boolean	cmis:isLatestVersion	read-only
D	Boolean	cmis:isMajorVersion	read-only

D	Boolean	cmis:isLatestMajorVersion	read-only
D	String	cmis:versionLabel	read-only
D	ID	cmis:versionSeriesId	read-only
D	Boolean	cmis:isVersionSeriesCheckedOut	read-only
D	String	cmis:versionSeriesCheckedOutBy	read-only
D	ID	cmis:versionSeriesCheckedOutId	read-only
D, 1.1	Boolean	cmis:isPrivateWorkingCopy	read-only
D	String	cmis:checkinComment	read-only
D	Integer	cmis:contentStreamLength	read-only
D	String	cmis:contentStreamMimeType	read-only
D	String	cmis:contentStreamFileName	read-only
D	ID	cmis:contentStreamId	read-only
F	ID	cmis:parentId	read-only
F	String	cmis:path	read-only
F	ID (multi)	cmis:allowedChildObjectTypeIds	read-only
R	ID	cmis:sourceId	on-create
R	ID	cmis:targetId	on-create
P	String	cmis:policyText	read-write

Allowable actions

F	canGetDescendants
F	canGetFolderTree
F	canGetChildren
F	canGetFolderParent
D, F, P, I	canGetObjectParents
F	canCreateDocument
F	canCreateFolder
F	canCreateRelationship
F, 1.1	canCreateItem
O	canGetProperties
D, F	canGetRenditions
D	canGetContentStream
O	canUpdateProperties
D, F, P, I	canMoveObject
O	canDeleteObject
D	canGetContentStream
D	canSetContentStream
D	canDeleteContentStream
F	canDeleteTree
D, P, I	canAddObjectToFolder
D, P, I	canRemoveObjectFromFolder
D	canCheckOut
D	canCancelCheckOut
D	canCheckIn
D	canGetAllVersions
O	canGetObjectRelationships
O	canApplyPolicy
O	canRemovePolicy
O	canGetAppliedPolicies
O	canGetACL
O	canApplyACL

Exceptions

invalidArgument
objectNotFound
notSupported
permissionDenied
runtime
constraint
contentAlreadyExists
filterNotValid
nameConstraintViolation
storage
streamNotSupported
updateConflict
versioning

Permissions

cmis:read
cmis:write
cmis:all

Renditions

ID	streamId
String	mimeType
Integer	length
String	title
String	kind
Integer	height
Integer	width

Rendition filter

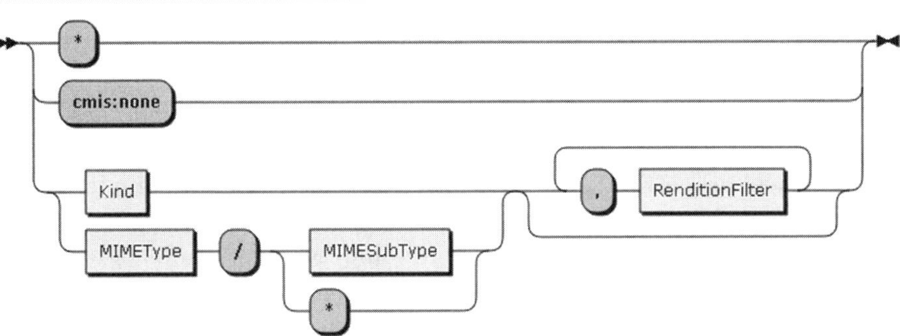

appendix D Building web applications with JavaScript

This appendix discusses how to use the new CMIS 1.1 Browser binding with JavaScript code, and provides hands-on examples to demonstrate some basic concepts. Hold on tight; the pace will be very fast. If we explained all the background along the way, this appendix could take an entire book on its own. For that reason, we're assuming you already know HTML, Ajax, and JavaScript for this high-speed survey of the subject.

D.1 JavaScript and CMIS background

Over the last few years, rich web applications have become more and more popular. Several factors are influencing this trend. The invention of the asynchronous JavaScript plus XML (Ajax) technologies in the late 1990s laid the foundation to overcome the traditional request-response scheme, where each action on a web page resulted in a new HTML page being delivered to the browser. Instead, now you can build web applications that behave more like desktop applications by changing only parts of a web page and manipulating the DOM tree on the fly. A second trend has been the enormous progress in JavaScript technology in web browsers over the last few years. The evolution from primitive language interpreters to highly optimized on-the-fly compilation has made it possible to build a new generation of browser applications that formerly were restricted to the desktop, such as in-browser games.

Powerful libraries have accompanied the evolution of the language. JQuery (http://jquery.com/) is among the most popular candidates in this space, taking much of the burden off the developer to deal with browser and platform differences. Other libraries have a more specific domain, such as UI widget elements, layout management, or Model-View-Controller frameworks helping with the modularization of complex web applications.

Another important factor is the enormous demand for mobile applications. Nearly all smartphones and tablets today have a powerful web browser with JavaScript support. HTML plus JavaScript makes it possible to build platform-independent mobile applications. This is a huge advantage, given the abundance of mobile platforms with their proprietary and/or incompatible programming languages and associated APIs. Dozens of frameworks and JavaScript libraries are focused on mobility.

Last but not least, HTML5 is in the final stage of standardization, closing even more gaps when compared to traditional desktop applications (for example, better support for rich media). Today many browsers support HTML5 or parts of it.

D.1.1 CMIS and web browsers using XML

How does CMIS fit into the world of browsers and web applications? When you first look at CMIS 1.0, you might be disappointed. As you'll recall from earlier chapters, CMIS 1.0 supports two protocols:

- SOAP (web services)
- AtomPub

Both are web protocols based on HTTP, but their support in JavaScript isn't the best match. SOAP is heavyweight, chatty, and nearly impossible to use without good library support. It isn't very browser friendly and therefore is almost never used in browser applications. For these reasons, SOAP loses momentum. Things look a bit better for AtomPub, but data is still transferred over the wire, which is an issue, especially for mobile applications. A JavaScript application has to do a lot of work to parse the large AtomPub responses.

D.1.2 Creation of the Browser binding

In early 2011, the CMIS TC recognized this situation, and a subcommittee was founded to specify another binding focusing on web browsers and JavaScript. This work resulted in the CMIS Browser binding. The Browser binding comes with CMIS 1.1 (targeted to be finalized around the time this book is published).

What makes the Browser binding better suited for web applications? First, the underlying data encoding isn't based on XML but on the JSON protocol (www.json.org). The JSON syntax is oriented closely to the syntax of JavaScript. In theory, a single statement in JavaScript can parse and process a JSON document. This makes parsing and generating JSON a natural and easy task in JavaScript.

Second, JSON is lightweight and far less verbose than XML. This makes it better suited for low-bandwidth connections and mobile applications while still being readable and text-based. The mapping between JSON and the CMIS domain model is direct and straightforward. There's no overhead from a predefined structure as in AtomPub, and there's a 1:1 mapping from the CMIS JSON protocol to its domain model. The Browser binding also defines a fixed URL syntax compared to the more flexible approach in AtomPub. From a CMIS consumer perspective, this makes life a lot easier. You don't have to deal with various possibilities like, for example, how a link is formed to get the content of a document. The URL always looks the same, and the client always uses the same form of URL no matter what repository is used as a back end. The CMIS Browser binding is restricted to the HTTP methods `GET` and `POST`. (All browsers on all platforms support `GET` and `POST`.)

D.1.3 OpenCMIS support for the Browser binding today

The OpenCMIS Java library already supports the CMIS Browser binding, even if it isn't yet an official standard. It's also supported in the Chemistry Workbench, and you may have noticed the additional option in the login dialog box where you select the binding, shown in figure D.1.

You just have to enable it in the configuration of whatever server you're using. Although a full tour of the Browser binding and JavaScript is out of scope for this book, we'll cover the most important aspects here.

The remainder of this appendix will guide you through the first steps to take for a CMIS application in JavaScript running entirely in a web browser. Before you begin, you should be familiar with the basics of HTML, Ajax, and JavaScript. You can find many tutorials on the web if you need more background on these things. To dig deeper, you definitely should look in the Browser binding section of the CMIS 1.1 specification.

For each method in each service of the CMIS domain model, you'll find the URL and the JSON syntax required. We'll start with plain vanilla JavaScript to provide an understanding of how things really work. Later we'll switch to the popular JQuery library to demonstrate how such a library can simplify your life. We'll restrict ourselves to a few select methods of the CMIS domain model to keep this section manageable. But once you get the basic concepts down, it should be easy to apply them to the remainder of the services not covered here. You can use your favorite IDE for

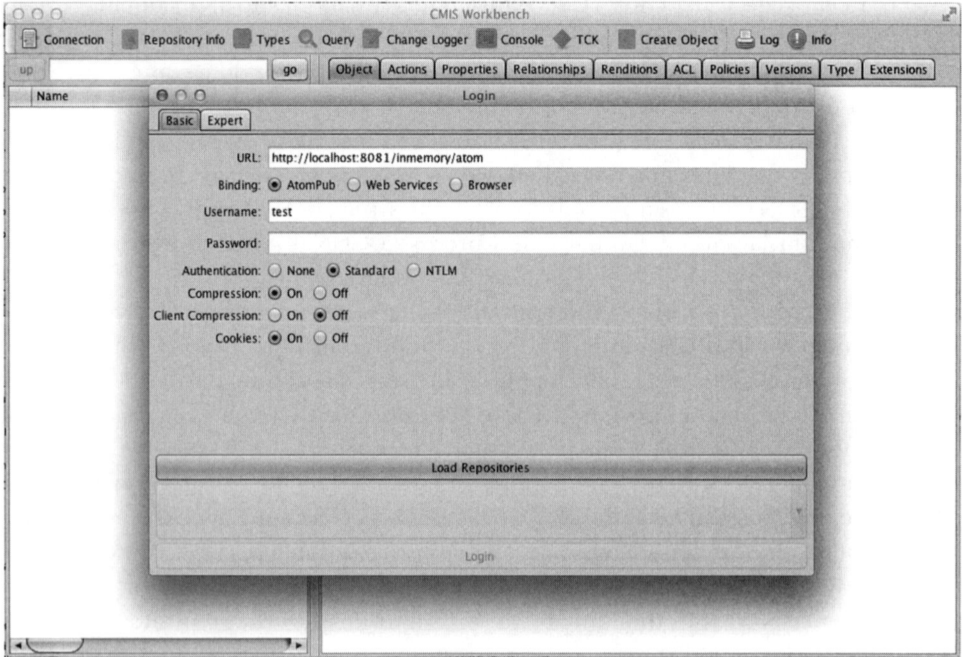

Figure D.1 The Chemistry Workbench supports the Browser binding today.

JavaScript; we don't require a specific one. A JavaScript debugger will be useful, though. Often these are simple browser add-ons (such as Firebug for Firefox). A simple text editor, a browser, and a JavaScript debugger are sufficient.

D.2 Try it—Hello Browser binding

Let's get started! We'll use the Apache InMemory Repository and the data model of the Blend application from elsewhere in the book. See chapter 1, section 1.2.2, for setup instructions for the Apache InMemory Repository. The first exercise is the simplest way to get access to a CMIS repository. Open a web browser and enter the following URL: http://localhost:8081/inmemory/browser.

You'll see a page containing a lot of cryptic-looking braces and colons. This is a JSON response. The URL calls the `getRepositories` method of the CMIS repository service. You can use a browser add-on that formats the output nicely to make the information much more readable. Figure D.2 shows an example from the JSON-View add-on for Firefox.

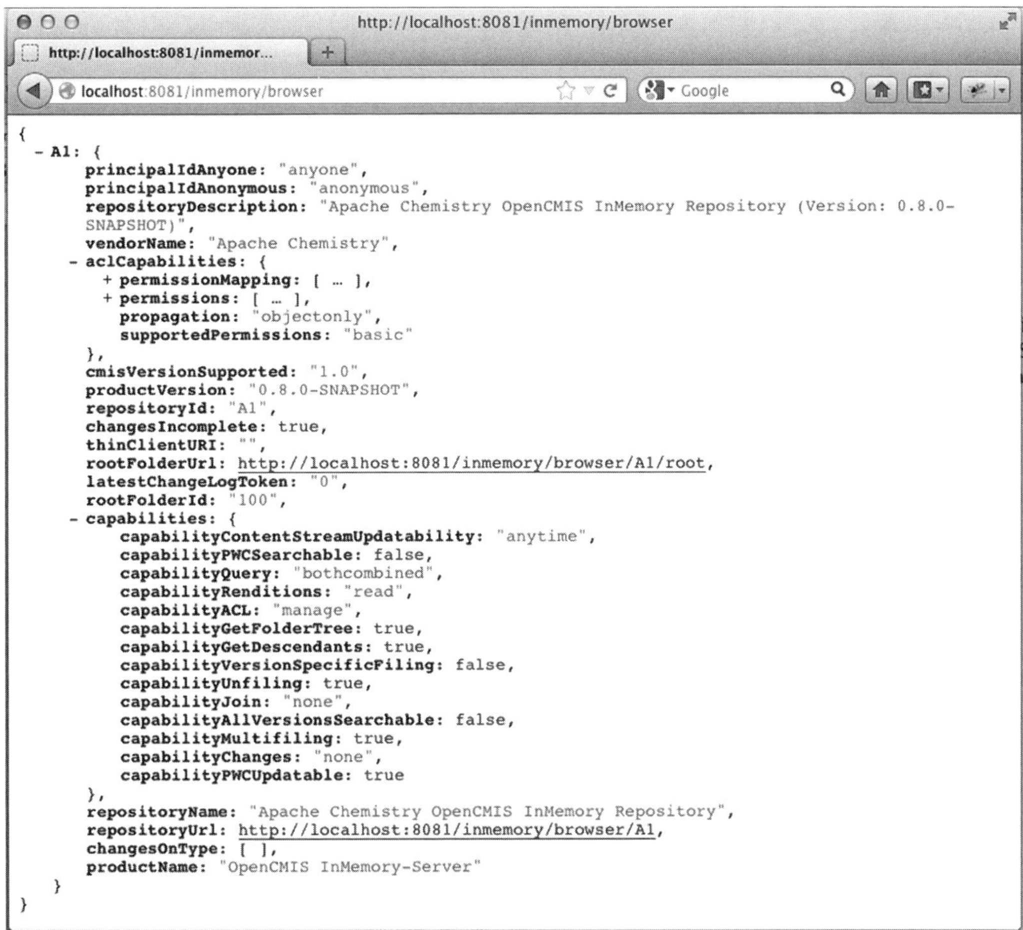

Figure D.2 JSON data response for the `getRepositories` call

D.2.1 *First steps*

Let's see how you can use the information from the Browser binding from a JavaScript application. First you need some infrastructure for a basic web application. Open a text editor and create a file called index.html with the following contents:

```
<!DOCTYPE html>
<head>
  <meta charset="UTF-8">
  <title>OpenCMIS Browser Binding</title>
  <meta http-equiv="Content-Type" content="text/html; charset=UTF-8">
  <link rel="stylesheet" type="text/css" href="../css/opencmis.css"/>
  <script src="cmis.js" type="text/javascript"></script>
</head>

<body>
  <h3>CMIS and JavaScript</h3>
    <p>Get repository info from Apache InMemory Repository: </p>
    <input type="button" value="Get RepositoryInfo"
                         onClick="doRepositoryInfo()">
    <div id="repositoryInfo"></div>
</body>
</html>
```

Save your file, and open a web browser with a URL like file:///<path-of-index.html>/ code-step01/index.html. Replace <path-of-index.html> with the path where you stored your file. Alternatively, you can drag the file to the browser's address bar. (You can find the full code for all the examples in this appendix in the JavaScript sample from the download accompanying this book.)

Now create a second file named cmis.js with the following contents:

```
function doRepositoryInfo() {
   alert("TODO: call repository info");
}
```

If all works well, you should see a page like the one shown in figure D.3.

When you click the Get RepositoryInfo button, you should see a pop-up window displaying "TODO: call repository info." You've created your first web application, consisting of an HTML page with a JavaScript method. The JavaScript is included from a separate file (you can also create JavaScript inline in the same HTML page if you prefer this style). What remains to be done is the real work calling the remote repository.

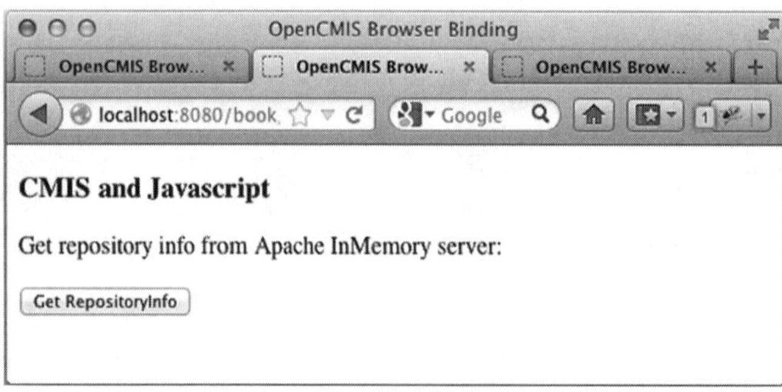

Figure D.3 First signs of JavaScript output on your new page

D.2.2 *Your first Browser binding call (getting the repository info)*

Ideally, what you'd like to do now is use a JavaScript method that calls the URL http://localhost:8081/inmemory/browser using the Ajax technique, parse the JSON response, and display the information from the response on your web page. Let's try it by adding the code from the following listing to the file cmis.js.

Listing D.1 Getting the repository info

```
function doRepositoryInfo() {
   callCmisRepository("http://localhost:8081/inmemory/browser",
     function (json_object) {
       printRepositoryInfos(json_object);
   });
}

function callCmisRepository(url, callback) {
  var json_object = {};
  var http_request = new XMLHttpRequest();
  http_request.open("GET", url, true);
  http_request.onreadystatechange = function() {
    if (http_request.readyState == 4 && http_request.status == 200) {
      json_object = JSON.parse(http_request.responseText);
        callback(json_object);
      }
  };
  http_request.send(null);
}

function printRepositoryInfos(infos) {
  for(repId in infos) {
    var ri = infos[repId];
    document.getElementById('repositoryInfo').innerHTML =
      '<h4>Repository "' + ri.repositoryName + '" ('
         + ri.repositoryId + ')</h4>' +
      '<table>' +
      '<tr><td>Id:</td><td>' + ri.repositoryId + '</td></tr>' +
      '<tr><td>Name:</td><td>' + ri.repositoryName + '</td></tr>' +
      '<tr><td>Description:</td><td>' + ri.repositoryDescription
         + '</td></tr>' + '<tr><td>Product:</td><td>'
         + ri.vendorName + ' ' + ri.productName + ' ' +
         ri.productVersion + '</td></tr>' +
      '<tr><td>Root folder id:</td><td>' + ri.rootFolderId
         + '</td></tr>' + '<tr><td>Repository URL:</td><td>'
         + ri.repositoryUrl + '</td></tr>' +
      '<tr><td>Root folder URL:</td><td>' + ri.rootFolderUrl
         + '</td></tr>' + '</table>';
  }
}
```

Make XMLHttpRequest, and hook up your callback handler

Callback handler where returned JSON is rendered

When the button is clicked, you call a JavaScript function called `doRepositoryInfo`. This calls the CMIS repository with a URL returning the available repositories using an Ajax request. Later, if the call succeeds, a callback method is fired. This callback parses the JSON response and dynamically adds an HTML table in your index.html page in the <div> tag, which you use as a placeholder.

Note that the JSON response from the CMIS server can be parsed in a single line of JavaScript code!

```
json_object = JSON.parse(http_request.responseText);
```

Also note how simple and straightforward processing the result can be when creating the HTML table. The elements in the `RepositoryInfo` are directly accessible as JavaScript elements, such as `ri.repositoryName`.

D.2.3 Complications: the same origin policy

Unfortunately, if you try the code and open the index.html page from your local file-system, the code doesn't work. The reason is a security mechanism in the browser called the *same origin policy*. Ajax calls are only processed if the server is in the same domain from which the originating page comes. Your page comes from the local file-system, and your server runs on localhost:8081. The browser doesn't process the call in this case. Add a web.xml file, and package your two files into a WAR package as a real web application first. Then deploy this on the same Tomcat server where the InMemory Repository runs. Now it will work, and you'll see the result shown in figure D.4.

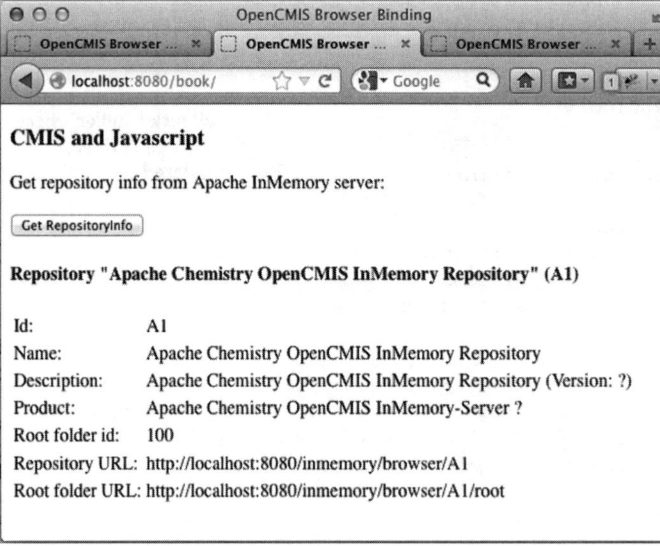

Figure D.4 Repository info displayed after you work around the same-origin issue

D.2.4 Using JSON-P

You may be thinking that things look pretty bleak. Requiring that the web application run on the same server as the repository is a severe restriction! What if you want to use the public Alfresco server at cmis.alfresco.com, for example?

For this reason, there's a common technique for web applications called JSON-P. We can't cover the details here, but the trick is to wrap the server response in a JavaScript method and dynamically add this method to your index.html page.

> **WANT TO KNOW MORE ABOUT JSON-P?** Check the following web pages for more details on JSON-P: http://www.json-p.org and http://en.wikipedia.org/wiki/JSONP.

The server must support JSON-P. So the CMIS specification adds an optional URL parameter, `callback=`. You can try opening a modified form of the previous URL: http://localhost:8081/inmemory/browser?callback=myFct. The result will be the same as before, but wrapped in a function call:

```
myFct(
{
 "A1": {
  "principalIdAnyone": "anyone",
  "principalIdAnonymous": "anonymous",
  "repositoryDescription":
     "Apache Chemistry OpenCMIS InMemory Repository (Version: ?)",
  "vendorName": "Apache Chemistry",
  "aclCapabilities": { … },
  "cmisVersionSupported": "1.0",
  "productVersion": "?",
  "repositoryId": "A1",
  "changesIncomplete": true,
  "thinClientURI": "",
  "rootFolderUrl": "http://localhost:8080/inmemory/browser/A1/root",
  "latestChangeLogToken": "0",
  "rootFolderId": "100",
  "capabilities": { … },
  "repositoryName": "Apache Chemistry OpenCMIS InMemory Repository",
  "repositoryUrl": "http://localhost:8080/inmemory/browser/A1",
  "changesOnType": [ ],
  "productName": "OpenCMIS InMemory-Server"
  }
 }
)
```

Now you have to add a `myFct`-like function to your script that's called from the server response. The code looks like this:

```
function doRepositoryInfo() {
  performJsonpRequest(
    "http://localhost:8080/inmemory/browser",
    "processGetRepositories");
}

function processGetRepositories(json_object) {
  printRepositoryInfos(json_object);
}

function performJsonpRequest(url, callback) {
  var callUrl = url;

  var paramChar = (url.indexOf('?') == -1) ? '?' : '&';
    callUrl = url + paramChar + 'callback=' + callback;

  var script = document.createElement('script');
  script.setAttribute('src', callUrl);
  script.setAttribute('type', 'text/javascript');
  document.body.appendChild(script);
}
```

Leave the function `printRepositories` as it was. `performJsonpRequest` dynamically adds a `script` tag to the web page fed from the server response. The InMemory Repository responds with a function call, `processGetRepositories`, and passes the JSON data as a parameter. `processGetRepositories` parses the result and displays the repository information as before.

For a real web application, things become more complicated because you may need more callback functions. Usually a unique ID is added to the generated script, which allows later removal. The ID must be modified on each JSON-P request. The article at http://mng.bz/G5Y2 gives more background about JSON-P. You can find the full code in the code download folder step2.

This is a lot of work for a simple function call. A JavaScript library can take most of the burden from these JSON-P requests and do the magic behind the scenes. It can then be as simple as setting a flag that specifies whether you want to use JSON-P.

D.2.5 Hello JQuery

JQuery is such a library, and it's very popular and widely used. It hides many browser differences and makes the JavaScript code more readable and compact. From now on we'll use JQuery for the examples.

One of the pitfalls with JSON-P is the error handling. In case of an error, the `script` tag isn't added, and there's no chance to get more information about the error (such as the HTTP status code). The CMIS specification for this reason adds an optional query parameter, `suppressResponseCode=true`. A client can add this parameter to a URL, and the server will always return the HTTP status code 200. The client can use the response body to get information about the kind of error (see the spec for error responses).

Also note that JSON-P processing in JavaScript opens the door for cross-site request forgery (XSRF) attacks. We don't cover the details here; you can find more information in chapter 11 and in the CMIS spec. OpenCMIS contains some example JavaScript code for how to use this. Let's do the same now using JQuery. First you have to add JQuery to your main page in index.html:

```
<head>
  …
  <meta charset="UTF-8">
  <script type="text/javascript"
    src="https://ajax.googleapis.com/ajax
          /libs/jquery/1.7.1/jquery.min.js">
  </script>
  <script src="cmis.js" type="text/javascript"></script>
</head>
```

The code now looks like this (the full code is in the step3 folder):

```
function doRepositoryInfo() {
  performRequest(
    "http://localhost:8080/inmemory/browser",
    null,
    "GET",
    printRepositoryInfos,
    true);
}

function errorHandler(event, jqXHR, settings, excep) {
  alert("Call was aborted:" + jqXHR);
}

function performRequest(url, params, method, cbFct,
     jsonp, username, password) {
    $.ajax( {
        url: url,
        data: params,
        dataType: (jsonp ? "jsonp" : "json"),
        type:  method,
        username: username,
        password: password,
        success: cbFct,
        error: errorHandler,
        timeout: 5000
    });
}

function printRepositoryInfos(infos) {
  for(repId in infos) {
    var ri = infos[repId];
    $('#repositoryInfo').html(
      '<h4>Repository "' + ri.repositoryName + '" ('
        + ri.repositoryId + ')</h4>' +
      '<table>' +
```

```
        '<tr><td>Id:</td><td>' + ri.repositoryId + '</td></tr>' +
        '<tr><td>Name:</td><td>' + ri.repositoryName + '</td></tr>' +
        '<tr><td>Description:</td><td>' + ri.repositoryDescription
          + '</td></tr>' +
        '<tr><td>Product:</td><td>' + ri.vendorName + ' '
          + ri.productName + ' ' + ri.productVersion + '</td></tr>' +
        '<tr><td>Root folder id:</td><td>' + ri.rootFolderId
          + '</td></tr>' + '<tr><td>Repository URL:</td><td>'
          + ri.repositoryUrl + '</td></tr>'
          + '<tr><td>Root folder URL:</td><td>' + ri.rootFolderUrl
          + '</td></tr>' +
        '</table>');
    }
}
```

You can see that the choice of whether to use JSON or JSON-P is a parameter to the `ajax` function. The code to generate the result is more compact because it uses the `$` syntax instead of `document.getElementById`. By adding a timeout value, you have the chance to catch an error even when using JSON-P. JQuery generates the necessary `script` tags and callback function on its own.

D.3 CMIS basic operations with the Browser binding and JQuery

With all those details out of the way, you're ready to perform some actual CMIS operations. The next few sections go over a few basic CMIS operations like getting the children of a folder, creating a document, and querying. First up are folder children.

D.3.1 Enumerating a folder's children

It's time to do something useful. You'll get the children of a folder and display the result on a web page (full code is in the step4 folder). Begin by adding a text box to your web page in which a folder ID can be entered:

```
<body>
  <h3>CMIS and JavaScript</h3>
    <h4> Get Children of folder: </h4>
    <form >
    <fieldset>
      <legend>Enter a folder id</legend>
      <input type="text" id="folderidfield" value="?"/>
    </fieldset>
  </form>
  <p></p>
    <button id="getchildren">Get children!</button>  <br/>
  <p></p>
    <div id="foldersection">
    </div>
    <div id="docsection">
    </div>
</body>
```

Then modify your JavaScript file:

```
$(document).ready(function() {
   $('#getchildren').click(function() {
      getChildren($('#folderidfield').val());
   });
   rootFolderId = "100";
   baseUrl = "http://localhost:8080/inmemory/browser/A1";
   $('#folderidfield').val(rootFolderId);
});
```

When the page is loaded, including the JQuery library `$(document).ready`, you add an event handler for the event when the user clicks the Get children! button. This function reads the text entered in the text box and performs a request to the server. You pass some additional parameters to indicate that you don't want all the information the server can return.

The `createChildrenTable` method parses the JSON response and creates two tables: one for the folder and one for the documents found in the response. For each result, a row is added to the table and the values for the returned properties are filled in the columns. You omit some technical properties so the table doesn't get too wide. Note that some value types (such as `DateTime`) need a conversion to `String`. The JSON result is an array of properties that once again can be directly parsed to JavaScript elements. For each folder, the name is translated to a hyperlink that again calls the function to get its children. You end up in a kind of mini browser for CMIS, even if you miss a possibility to navigate up the hierarchy. For each document, you add a link pointing to the content instead.

Probably the best way to understand the details is to use a JavaScript debugger to step through the code. Some debuggers can also display the HTTP communication between browser and repository. JQuery handles all the details nicely regardless of whether you want to use JSON or JSON-P.

In a real-world program, you wouldn't hardcode the URL and the ID of the root folder. Instead, you'd first do a `getRepositoryInfo` request and get the values from the response. But this example keeps things simple. The modification is a nice exercise for you. To add an Up link, you need to store the parent ID for each folder you enumerate and dynamically add a link navigating to the parent folder. Figure D.5 shows the finished page.

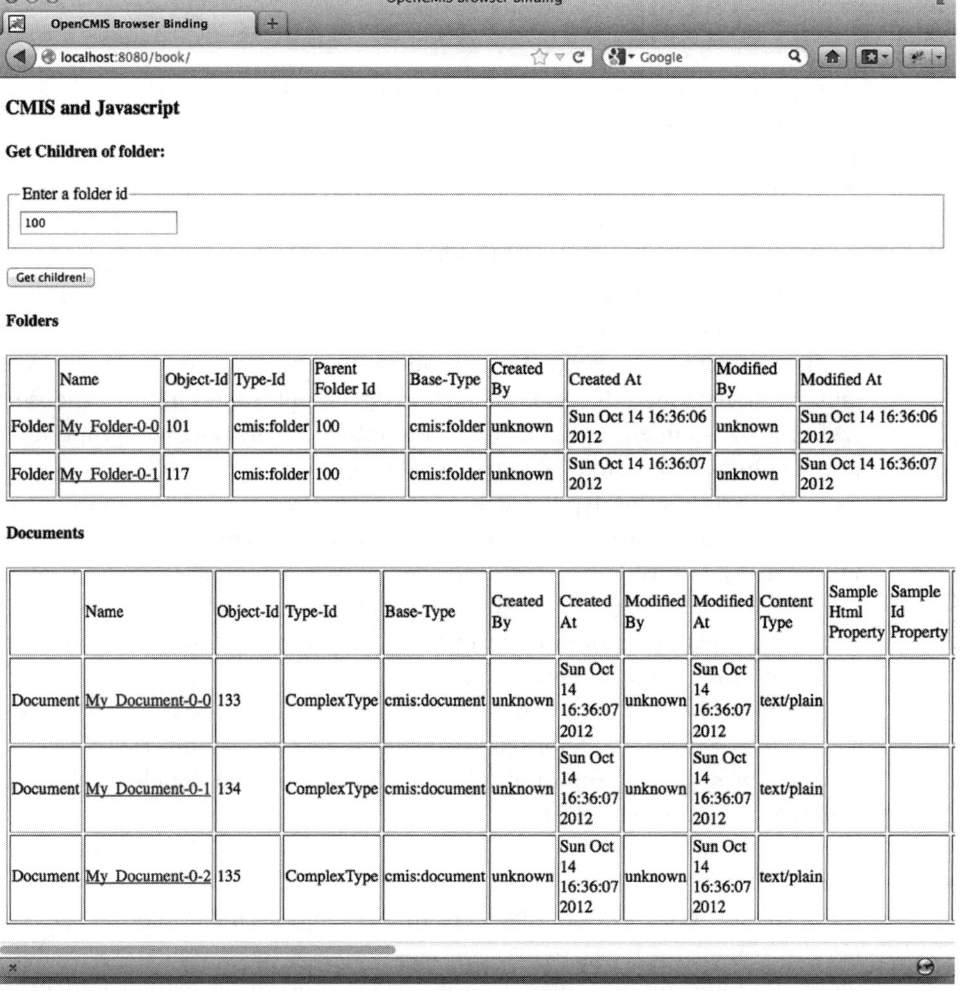

Figure D.5 Get Children of Folder page showing child folders and documents

D.3.2 *Integrating JavaScript components*

As mentioned earlier, one of the cool things about JavaScript is that tons of reusable components are available. Why not modify the example a bit and integrate it with a JavaScript media player? We'll use The Blend application from part 2 of the book; but instead of creating a table, you'll feed the media player the songs found in a folder. (The full code is in the step5 folder.)

Be sure to import the sample data into the application. To be able to listen to the music, you have to deploy the application to a web server. Opening index.html from the filesystem will give you the playlist but won't play the songs. Because entering a folder ID is a bit inconvenient, you modify the code to use the path instead of the ID. You extract the artist and title properties from the metadata and construct the proper URL for the content (the song) and feed that data to the player. The result looks like figure D.6.

Figure D.6 Using a JavaScript player component to listen to music from your repository

That looks much better, doesn't it? Now that you have components figured out, let's move on to adding data.

D.3.3 Uploading a document

The next step will be to upload a document. The CMIS spec for the Browser binding requires sending an HTTP `POST` request. Uploading a document mostly requires transferring content from the browser to the server. Uploading content in HTTP from a web form in a browser uses the `multipart/form-data` content type. The CMIS spec for the Browser binding follows this approach. This makes document creation easy and doesn't even require Ajax calls. In fact, uploading content with Ajax is difficult because you have to encode into `multipart/form-data` on your own. Doing this directly from a simple HTML form is much easier; Ajax doesn't offer an advantage here.

The tricky part is getting the return value from the server. You're interested in the object ID of your newly created document. But browsers aren't prepared to programmatically process a form response and will directly present the JSON result to the user. Usually, web applications respond with another HTML page from a form `POST`, but in this case you get a JSON response. The spec therefore suggests sending the response to an invisible IFrame. If your web application is on the same server as the CMIS repository, you can directly process the response from the IFrame.

If you're on a different server, you're once again in the trap of the same origin policy, and the browser won't give you the response. The CMIS spec in this case suggests doing another `GET` request, passing a token that identifies the former upload request. The token is an arbitrary string but must be unique. Passing properties along with the content can be done easily using HTML forms. In this example, you do the minimum with name, folder ID, and type ID, but these can quickly be extended to other properties. Here's the HTML code for the upload (the full code is in the step6 folder):

```
<form id="createdochtmlid" action="" target="createresultframe"
        enctype="multipart/form-data" onsubmit="prepareCreate()"
        method="post">
      <fieldset>
       <legend>Create document HTML</legend>
       <table>
         <tr>
           <td><label for="name">Name:</label></td>
           <td><input name="propertyValue[0]" type="text" id="name"
                value="My Document"/></td>
         </tr>
         <tr>
           <td><label for="typeId">Type-Id:</label></td>
           <td><input name="propertyValue[1]" type="text" id="typeId"
                value="cmis:document"/></td>
         </tr>
         <tr>
           <td><label for="folderId">Folder-Id:</label></td>
           <td><input type="text" id="folderId" name="objectId"
                value="100"/></td>
         </tr>
         <tr>
           <td><label for="contentId">Content:</label></td>
           <td><input id="contentId" name="Browse..." type="file"
                size="50"/></td>
         </tr>
         <tr>
         <td><input id="createdochtml" type="submit"
               value="Create Doc!"/></td>
         <td></td>
         </tr>
       </table>
      </fieldset>
      <input name="propertyId[0]" type="hidden"
           value="cmis:name" />
        <input name="propertyId[1]" type="hidden"
             value="cmis:objectTypeId" />
```

```
        <input name="cmisaction" type="hidden"
              value="createDocument" />
        <input id="transactionId" name="token"
              type="hidden" value="" />
   </form>
```

On submitting the form, you call a JavaScript `prepareCreate` function that dynamically generates a unique ID for the transaction as a token and adds the URL to post the request to `prepareCreate` as shown here:

```
function prepareCreate() {
    init = true;
    $("#transactionId").val(createRandomString());
    $("#createdochtmlid").attr("action", rootUrl);
    return true;
}
```

The global variable indicates that the user has started an upload and that when the IFrame is loaded the code should do something. The target of the request is this invisible IFrame:

```
<iframe id="createresultframe" name="createresultframe"
        style="width:0px;height:0px;visibility:hidden"
        onload="createDocumentDone()">
 </iframe>
```

Once it's loaded, the JavaScript method `createDocumentDone()` is called. It retrieves the object ID from a second call, using the token identifying the transaction:

```
function createDocumentDone() {

  if (init == null || !init)
    return;

  var transId = $("#transactionId").val();
  getObjectFromTransaction(transId, function(data) {
      var text = "Document successfully created with id: " +
                     data.objectId + " and transaction id: " + transId;
      $("#createdocsection").html(text);
  });
}
```

The `getObjectFromTransaction` method (shown next) gets the object ID by doing a `GET` request. It passes a callback function that parses the object ID from the response and handles the output on the HTML page:

```
function getObjectFromTransaction(transId, cbFct) {
    var params = {
        cmisselector: "lastResult",
        token: transId,
        suppressResponseCodes: true
    };
    $.ajax( {
        url: baseUrl,
        data: params,
        dataType: "jsonp",
```

```
        type:  "GET",
        success: cbFct
    });
}
```

If the CMIS repository is on the same server, you can avoid the second call and get the object ID directly:

```
function createDocumentDone() {
  try {
    cont = $('#createresultframe').contents().text();
    if (cont) {
      var json = jQuery.parseJSON(cont);
      if (!checkError(json, "#responsesection")) {
        $("#responsesection").html("Document successfully
        created with id: " + json.properties["cmis:objectId"].
        value + " and transaction id: " + transId);
      }
    }
  } catch (ex) {
      trace("Same origin policy for transaction: " + transId + ",
          exception: " + ex);
}
```

You can find the full code in the step6 folder. The final result is shown in figure D.7.

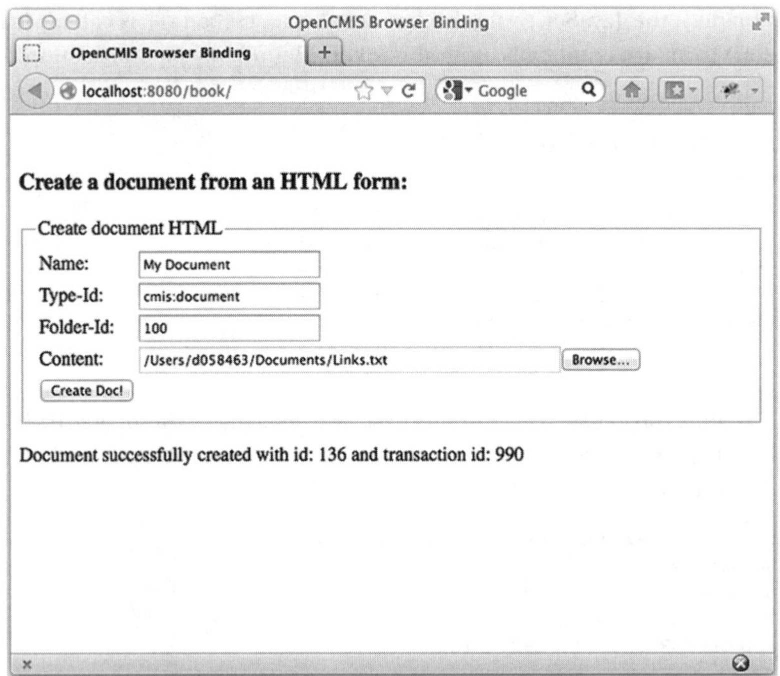

Figure D.7 Creating a document by posting an HTML form

D.3.4 Query

As a next step, you perform a CMIS query and display the result in your web page (the full code is in step05-cmisquery). First, add a text box to the web page in which the user can enter a query string:

```
<body>
  <h3>CMIS and JavaScript</h3>
    <h4> Make a Query: </h4>
    <form >
    <fieldset>
      <legend>Enter a query</legend>
      <textarea id="queryfield" cols="80" rows="5">
          SELECT * from cmis:document
      </textarea>
    </fieldset>
  </form>
<button id="doquery">Do query!</button>  <br/>
    <div id="queryresponsesection"></div>
</body>
```

Then modify the JavaScript file:

```
$(document).ready(function() {
   $('#doquery').click(function() {
      doQuery($('#queryfield').val());
   });
});

function doQuery(queryString) {
        $("#queryresponsesection").html(null);
        trace("doing query: " + queryString);
        var params = {
            cmisaction: "query",
            q: queryString,
            searchAllVersions: "false",
            includeAllowableAction: "false",
            includeRelationships: "none",
            suppressResponseCodes: "false"
        };

      performRequest("http://localhost:8080/inmemory/browser/A1",
         params, "POST", createQueryTable, true);
}
```

When the page is loaded, including the JQuery library `$(document).ready`, you add an event handler for the button-click event of the query button. This function reads the text entered in the text box and performs a request to the server. Note that this time you do an HTTP `POST` request instead of a `GET`, and you pass some additional parameters to filter out all versions, allowable actions, relationships, and renditions. The `createQueryTable` method parses the JSON response, adds a row to the table for each found object, and displays the values for some selected properties in the

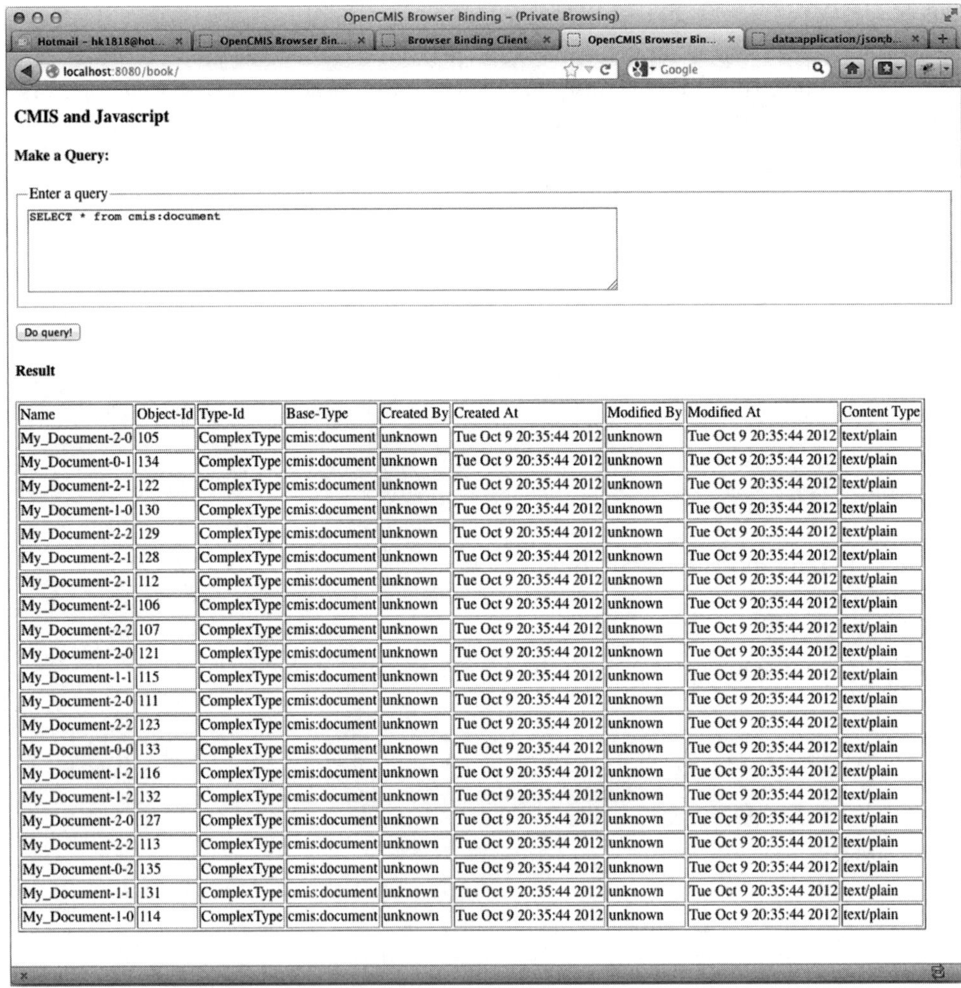

Name	Object-Id	Type-Id	Base-Type	Created By	Created At	Modified By	Modified At	Content Type
My_Document-2-0	105	ComplexType	cmis:document	unknown	Tue Oct 9 20:35:44 2012	unknown	Tue Oct 9 20:35:44 2012	text/plain
My_Document-0-1	134	ComplexType	cmis:document	unknown	Tue Oct 9 20:35:44 2012	unknown	Tue Oct 9 20:35:44 2012	text/plain
My_Document-2-1	122	ComplexType	cmis:document	unknown	Tue Oct 9 20:35:44 2012	unknown	Tue Oct 9 20:35:44 2012	text/plain
My_Document-1-0	130	ComplexType	cmis:document	unknown	Tue Oct 9 20:35:44 2012	unknown	Tue Oct 9 20:35:44 2012	text/plain
My_Document-2-2	129	ComplexType	cmis:document	unknown	Tue Oct 9 20:35:44 2012	unknown	Tue Oct 9 20:35:44 2012	text/plain
My_Document-2-1	128	ComplexType	cmis:document	unknown	Tue Oct 9 20:35:44 2012	unknown	Tue Oct 9 20:35:44 2012	text/plain
My_Document-2-1	112	ComplexType	cmis:document	unknown	Tue Oct 9 20:35:44 2012	unknown	Tue Oct 9 20:35:44 2012	text/plain
My_Document-2-1	106	ComplexType	cmis:document	unknown	Tue Oct 9 20:35:44 2012	unknown	Tue Oct 9 20:35:44 2012	text/plain
My_Document-2-2	107	ComplexType	cmis:document	unknown	Tue Oct 9 20:35:44 2012	unknown	Tue Oct 9 20:35:44 2012	text/plain
My_Document-2-0	121	ComplexType	cmis:document	unknown	Tue Oct 9 20:35:44 2012	unknown	Tue Oct 9 20:35:44 2012	text/plain
My_Document-1-1	115	ComplexType	cmis:document	unknown	Tue Oct 9 20:35:44 2012	unknown	Tue Oct 9 20:35:44 2012	text/plain
My_Document-2-0	111	ComplexType	cmis:document	unknown	Tue Oct 9 20:35:44 2012	unknown	Tue Oct 9 20:35:44 2012	text/plain
My_Document-2-2	123	ComplexType	cmis:document	unknown	Tue Oct 9 20:35:44 2012	unknown	Tue Oct 9 20:35:44 2012	text/plain
My_Document-0-0	133	ComplexType	cmis:document	unknown	Tue Oct 9 20:35:44 2012	unknown	Tue Oct 9 20:35:44 2012	text/plain
My_Document-1-2	116	ComplexType	cmis:document	unknown	Tue Oct 9 20:35:44 2012	unknown	Tue Oct 9 20:35:44 2012	text/plain
My_Document-1-2	132	ComplexType	cmis:document	unknown	Tue Oct 9 20:35:44 2012	unknown	Tue Oct 9 20:35:44 2012	text/plain
My_Document-2-0	127	ComplexType	cmis:document	unknown	Tue Oct 9 20:35:44 2012	unknown	Tue Oct 9 20:35:44 2012	text/plain
My_Document-2-2	113	ComplexType	cmis:document	unknown	Tue Oct 9 20:35:44 2012	unknown	Tue Oct 9 20:35:44 2012	text/plain
My_Document-0-2	135	ComplexType	cmis:document	unknown	Tue Oct 9 20:35:44 2012	unknown	Tue Oct 9 20:35:44 2012	text/plain
My_Document-1-1	131	ComplexType	cmis:document	unknown	Tue Oct 9 20:35:44 2012	unknown	Tue Oct 9 20:35:44 2012	text/plain
My_Document-1-0	114	ComplexType	cmis:document	unknown	Tue Oct 9 20:35:44 2012	unknown	Tue Oct 9 20:35:44 2012	text/plain

Figure D.8 Query results rendered in the browser

columns. Note that some value types need a conversion to `String`. The JSON result is an array of properties that once again can be directly parsed to JavaScript elements. The full code is in the step7 folder, and the resulting page is shown in figure D.8.

appendix E References and resources

E.1 Source code and listings

The source code used in this book is available from the Manning website. It also provides a forum to get in touch with the authors. Feel free to post questions there.

- *CMIS and Apache Chemistry in Action* website—www.manning.com/mueller
- *Source code package*—www.manning-source.com/books/mueller/CMIS_and_Apache_Chemistry_In_Action.zip
- *Authors Online forum*—www.manning-sandbox.com/forum.jspa?forumID=833

E.2 OASIS CMIS references

The OASIS CMIS Technical Committee (TC) is responsible for the CMIS specification. If you have any questions about the specification or the specification process, or if you want to join the TC, visit the TC's website or send a question or comment to the mailing list.

- *CMIS TC website*—https://www.oasis-open.org/committees/cmis
- *CMIS mailing list*—cmis-comment@lists.oasis-open.org

The CMIS specification documents are hosted on the official OASIS server. The CMIS 1.0 and CMIS 1.1 specification documents are available as a PDF document and as an HTML document. Both renditions contain exactly the same content. Each specification also provides schema files and examples.

- *CMIS 1.0 Specification*—http://docs.oasis-open.org/cmis/CMIS/v1.0/
- *CMIS 1.1 Specification*—http://docs.oasis-open.org/cmis/CMIS/v1.1/

E.3 Apache Chemistry–related resources

The Apache Chemistry website is the best source for the latest information on the project. It provides links to the subprojects, documentation, and download pages. If you have any question about Apache Chemistry, please send an email to the Apache Chemistry mailing list. If you found a bug or want to suggest an improvement, please open an ticket in the Apache Chemistry bug tracker.

- *Apache Chemistry website*—http://chemistry.apache.org
- *Apache Chemistry mailing list*—dev@chemistry.apache.org

- *Apache Chemistry mailing list archive*—http://mail-archives.apache.org/mod_mbox/chemistry-dev
- *Apache Chemistry bug tracker*—https://issues.apache.org/jira/browse/CMIS

The Apache Chemistry source code is managed on the Apache SVN servers. There you'll find the most current and unreleased source code as well as the source code of all released versions. Keep in mind that the unreleased source code is a work in progress and might not always work as expected.

- *Apache Chemistry source code (SVN repository)*—http://svn.apache.org/repos/asf/chemistry
- *Apache Chemistry source code (browsable)*—http://svn.apache.org/viewvc/chemistry

The OpenCMIS and DotCMIS session parameters are documented here.

- *OpenCMIS session parameters*—http://chemistry.apache.org/java/developing/dev-session-parameters.html
- *DotCMIS session parameters*—http://chemistry.apache.org/dotnet/session-parameters.html

E.4 Other libraries used in this book

The Blend makes use of a few other libraries besides OpenCMIS. Here are the links to project sites of these libraries.

- *Apache Tika*—http://tika.apache.org
- *Apache Commons FileUpload*—http://commons.apache.org/proper/commons-fileupload
- *The Open Web Application Security Project (OWASP) ESAPI (Enterprise Security API)* —https://www.owasp.org/index.php/Category:OWASP_Enterprise_Security_API

index

Symbols

A

C

D

H

I

J

K

L

M

P

Q

R